DRURY'S GUIDE
TO BEST PLAYS

Third Edition

by
JAMES M. SALEM

The Scarecrow Press, Inc.
Metuchen, N.J. & London
1978

PN
1655
.D78
1978

Library of Congress Cataloging in Publication Data

Drury, Francis Keese Wynkoop, 1878-1954.
    Drury's Guide to best plays.

    Includes indexes.
    1. Drama--Bibliography. 2. Drama--Indexes.
3. Drama--Stories, plots, etc. I. Salem,
James M. II. Title. III. Title: Guide to
best plays.
Z5781.D8 1978   [PN1655]   016.80882   77-18139
ISBN 0-8108-1097-2

Copyright © 1978 by James M. Salem

Manufactured in the United States of America

FOREWORD

If you were running a reference library on such a small budget that you could only buy one drama tool, you might do well to get Drury's Guide to Best Plays. For almost 25 years Drury has been the best all-purpose book in the field. Finding a library that doesn't have Drury on its ready-reference shelf is a little bit like finding an American who didn't see Roots.

"It is hoped that this Guide," Francis K. W. Drury wrote in the 1953 introduction, "will be of service to the groups for which it is intended: Play-Givers, Play-Goers, Play-Readers, and the Librarians which serve them." It was. Ten years later, as a Ph.D. student at Louisiana State University, I discovered that there were two things you needed to do research in drama: Drury's Guide to Best Plays and a complete set of Burns Mantle, et al., Best Plays of the Year.

At the time I was writing a dissertation called "Revolution in Manners and Morals: The Treatment of Adultery in American Drama Between the Wars." Drury helped me identify plays I needed to include in my investigation (and where I could find a copy) and helped me eliminate titles which did not treat my "theme" without reading them. The third edition of Drury, incidentally, is still good for this purpose. Some librarians, like Cary Fredrich of the University of Alabama, think that the Annotations/Synopses are the book's primary strength.

For others, like the late Ralph Shaw, the book's primary strength was in its "indispensability" as a tool for covering classical and national drama entries. My own opinion is that the book's strength derives from its utility and scope. Since Drury selectively covers all non-musical plays in English from all dramatic periods (Greece, Rome, Medieval, Renaissance, Restoration/18th Century, Victorian, Modern, Contemporary) and places (Britain, the Continent, Scandinavia, Central Europe, Russia, America)--from long ago to the newest On/Off Broadway hit (season of 1975-76)--it is the book to go to first for any play that isn't a musical.

WHAT THE THIRD EDITION IS GOOD FOR

Librarians: Annotations/synopses, author-title connections, dates of plays, names of main characters, reading editions, tracking down

iii

plays according to the following "subjects": Biographical, The Black Experience, Courtroom, Fantasy, Historical, Labor, Marriage, Mystery/Detective, Newspaper, Old-Fashioned Melodrama, Prison, Religious, School and College Life, Teenager, War, Western, and The Woman Experience.

Play-Readers and Goers: If you're stuck on trivia like the name of the crazy family in You Can't Take It with You, the title of Neil Simon's first hit play, what else the author of Equus has written, who wrote Dead End, what the new play Serenading Louie is all about, the date of Tea and Sympathy, Drury has the answers and a lot more information.

Play-Givers: The essential information about old and new plays is here. The indexes can help you track down a play about blacks, a play with a cast of 17, an all-female play, a new one with a court-room setting, a comedy being played in high school theaters all over the country, a play requiring no scenery, one which won a Pulitzer or a New York Drama Critics' Circle Award, the titles that play publishers consider their best, how much it costs to put on Jesse and the Bandit Queen, and who has the acting editions.

ACKNOWLEDGMENTS

In preparing this edition I owe a debt of gratitude to the following people: Mr. F. Andrew Leslie of Dramatists Play Service, Mr. M. Abbott Van Nostrand of Samuel French, Inc., Ms. Ann Smit of Dramatic Publishing Co., Ms. Virginia Butler of Performance Publishing Co., Ms. Anne Fendrich of Pioneer Drama Service, Mr. Thomas A. Barker, Editor of Dramatics Magazine, and Cary Fredrich and Louise Rich, Reference Librarians at the University of Alabama.

As usual, the Scarecrow Press gave me good ideas and advice, and my wife and older children did much of the hard work.

James M. Salem

University, Alabama
March 1977

TABLE OF CONTENTS

PLAYWRIGHTS AND THEIR PLAYS

ABBOTT, George. Broadway. See entry under Dunning, Philip H.

_____ and Ann P. Bridges. Coquette (1927). Samuel French.
Norma's father is a gentleman of the Old South and warns the young man, Michael, away, as socially impossible. On his return he is shot by her father, who pleads at the trial, defense of his daughter's honor. Since the little flirt is with child by Michael, she takes her own life to avoid a medical examination and save her father.
3 acts; 7 men, 4 women; 1 interior. Royalty: $25-20.

_____ and James Gleason. The Fall Guy (1925). French, 1928; abridged in Mantle 1924/25.
Dannie Walsh, out of a job, is tricked into a rather dubious one. But he helps capture and convict a "snow" peddler. His difficulties in keeping up the installment payments on his saxophone provide much amusement.
3 acts; 7 men, 2 women; 1 interior.

_____. Three Men on a Horse. See entry under Holm, John Cecil.

ABELL, Kjeld. Anna Sophie Hedvig (1939). Tr. by Larsen in Scandinavian Plays of the 20th Century, ser. 2, Princeton Univ. Pr., 1944 (SCA-2).
Anna Sophie, a middle-aged provincial school-teacher, defends her little school world against the appointment of evil-minded Fru Møller, who is about to be made Director of her school. Her act of defense is to kill Fru Møller. This is symbolic of protest and positive action against Nazi tyranny.
3 acts; 11 men, 10 women; 1 interior.

ABELMAN, Paul. Green Julia (1966). Dramatists Play Service.
Jake and Bob are college roommates, sharing an untidy "dig" in a university town in England. The most active communication between them is in the form of improvised gaming, in which they play topdog-underdog parts where Jake is always "Carruthers" and Bob is "Bradshaw." Jake is leaving school to work abroad, and most of the time spent while he waits for his taxi is used in trying to "leave" Bob his boozy mistress, "Green" Julia.
2 men; one interior. Royalty: $35-$25.

1

ACHARD, Marcel. A Shot in the Dark (1961). Adapted by Harry
     Kurnitz. Samuel French.
     A parlor maid who was found nude, unconscious, clutching
a gun, and lying beside her dead lover is brought before the magistrate on a murder charge. The judge is so impressed, though, with
her honest accounts of affairs with her lover (a chauffeur) and her
aristocratic employer that he decides she is not the guilty party.
The investigation is enlarged to include the employer and his wife
(carrying on an affair with her husband's best friend), and when the
judge does discover the murderer, the girl is so appreciative that
she offers herself as a present.
     5 men, 3 women; 1 interior. Royalty: $50-25.

ACKLAND, Rodney. The Old Ladies (1935). Samuel French.
     Three aged genteel folk in adjoining rooms live out their
lives in an imaginary past; one in the hope that her boy will return;
another, a spinster, has only tragic memories; the third is a sort
of evil genius which frightens the spinster almost to death.
     3 acts; 3 women; 1 interior. Royalty: $25-20.

AESCHYLUS. Agamemnon (458 B.C.). Many translations, among
     them: Smyth in Loeb Library, Blackie in Everyman's, Camp-
     bell in World's Classics, & Buckley in Bohn's; other recom-
     mended translations are: by Gilbert Murray, Oxford (also in
     CAR, TEN, TRE-1, -2 [v. 2]); TREA-1; by Morshead, Mac-
     millan (also in MAU); FIT; HAM; HARC-8; OAT.
     Agamemnon returns in triumph from the victory of the
Greeks at Troy, bringing with him Cassandra, a prophetess of woe,
who is fated to be never believed. He is welcomed by his wife
Clytemnestra, who leads him into the house but there kills him with
the help of her paramour Aegisthus. She gives as her reason his
immolation of their daughter Iphigenia.
     1 continuous act; 4 men, 2 women, chorus of old men; 1
     exterior (before palace of Argos).

_____. Prometheus Bound (ca 470 B.C.). Many translations,
     among them: Smyth in Loeb Library, Blackie in Everyman's,
     Campbell in World's Classics, & Buckley in Bohn's; other
     recommended translations are: by Gilbert Murray, Oxford; by
     Morshead, Macmillan, & CLF-1; GREN; HAM; SML; FIT; CLS;
     HARC v. 8.
     For his presumption in bringing fire to men, Prometheus
the Titan incurs the wrath of Zeus and is chained to a mountain
peak by Hephaestus. He is comforted by Io, beloved of Zeus but
hated by Hera. Hermes brings him a message from Zeus, asking
him to yield, but Prometheus defies the Olympian monarch, who
then sends his thunderous lightning bolts whereby an earthquake
causes the crag to sink with Prometheus to Hades.
     1 continuous act; 6 men, 1 woman, chorus of sea nymphs;
     1 exterior.

AESOP. See Paul Sills' Story Theatre.

AGEE, James. A Death in the Family. See Tad Mosel's All the Way Home.

AIDMAN, Charles. Spoon River Anthology (1966). Dramatic reading based on the poems of Edgar Lee Masters. Samuel French.
In a cemetery we are introduced to the ghosts of those who lived in Spoon River and to the secrets they carried to the grave. In the some sixty characterizations and vignettes there are young lovers, teachers, preachers, sordid stories, and humorous ones.
3 men, 2 women; bare stage; Royalty: $50-25.

AIKEN, George L. Uncle Tom's Cabin. See entry under Stowe, Harriet B.

AKINS, Zoë. The Old Maid. See entry under Wharton, Edith.

AKUTAGAWA. Rashomon. See entry under Kanin, Fay.

ALBEE, Edward. The Ballad of the Sad Café (1963). Adapted from Carson McCullers' novel. Dramatists Play Service.
The play treats the love and violence of its three main characters: the huge, mannish woman who runs the Sad Cafe; her moody, ex-convict husband; and her distant cousin, a hunch backed dwarf whose taunting brings on the violence between husband and wife. The love relationships are mostly grotesque among the threesome. The husband is in love with the wife, the wife with the dwarf, and the dwarf with the husband.
14 men, 6 women; unit set. Royalty: $55-30.

_____. A Delicate Balance (1966). Samuel French.
Into the loveless home of a man and wife comes their daughter, who has just left her fourth husband, and their two best friends, who have just made a shocking discovery. Already in the house is the wife's alcoholic sister. The visiting couple locks the door and forces the group to face the reality of the same terror: that they have lost love to the extent that they are at the delicate balance between sanity and insanity.
2 men, 4 women; 1 interior. Royalty: $50-25.

_____. Everything in the Garden (1967). Based on the play by Giles Cooper. Dramatists Play Service.
Jenny and Richard could be totally happy in their suburban home if it were not for the money problem they always have. A Mrs. Toothe shows Jenny how she can end their money troubles forever and have the expensive greenhouse that the couple currently cannot afford for their garden. Later, at a cocktail party Jenny and Richard are throwing for their country club friends, Richard realizes that Jenny is making the extra money with her body, that in fact all the wives assembled at his house are, and that their husbands know it, and condone it, too.
5 men, 1 boy, 5 women; one interior. Royalty: $50-25.

_____. Malcolm (1966). Based on the novel by James Purdy.

Dramatists Play Service.
A story about the destruction of a young adolescent boy named
Malcolm, who is taken under the wing of an elderly astrologer named
Cox. Cox sends Malcolm out on various visits ostensibly to inte-
grate him with the world. He meets a former prostitute and her
man (who claims to be 192 years old), a middle-aged couple in
which the wife has four lovers, an author and painter couple who
are hip, and a blonde pop singer who takes the boy on as a husband
and kills him with alcohol and sex. All of these people know one
another and meet to mourn at Malcolm's deathbed.
16 men (doubling possible), 7 women; multiple simple sets.
Royalty: $50-25

_____. Seascape (1975). Dramatists Play Service.
Nancy and Charlie, a middle-aged married couple, are
lounging on the beach, talking about their home and children and
lives. Nancy wants to do something exciting; Charlie believes he
deserves a rest. They are joined by a pair of humanoid lizards
named Leslie and Sarah, who are at an advanced stage of evolution
and have decided that maybe they should make the big break and begin to live on land. The lizards are frightened, though, about living
out of the water and are curious about what it's like. Nancy and
Charlie, bored by the kind of life that "living on land" entails, have
the answers to the lizards' questions.
2 men, 2 women; one exterior. Royalty: $50-35.

_____. Tiny Alice (1964). Dramatists Play Service.
The play begins with a hostile conversation between a lawyer
and a Roman Catholic Cardinal. The hatred between the two goes
back to boyhood days. Eventually the lawyer offers the Cardinal a
gift to the church of 100 million dollars a year for twenty years.
The benefactress is Miss Alice, the richest woman in the world.
When the Cardinal's secretary, Julian, goes to Miss Alice's castle
to complete the details of the gift, she tries to make him her lover.
As Norman Nadel observed, "The transmutation of his religious ecstacy into an orgasmic ecstacy is utterly candid, and terrifying."
4 men, 1 woman; 2 interiors; 1 simple exterior. Royalty:
$50-25.

_____. Who's Afraid of Virginia Woolf? (1962). Dramatists Play
Service.
George, a history professor at a small college, and Martha,
his wife who is the daughter of the college president, invite Nick
and Honey, a new young instructor and his wife over for a nightcap.
The night and the drinks never end. Until the dawn the couples
tear at one another, singly and in pairs. Nick is revealed as a
scholar on the make--figuratively and literally. Honey is found to
be so violently afraid of childbirth that she has aborted her pregnan-
cies. And George and Martha, who play "games" with one another,
have a kind of outrageous bitterness toward one another that has its
roots in great personal sadness. A powerful psychological study
with the intensity of O'Neill's Long Day's Journey into Night.
2 men, 2 women; 1 interior. Royalty: $50.

_____. The Zoo Story (1960). Dramatists Play Service.
    A young, neat, ordered, well-to-do, conventional man, read-
ing in the sunlight in Central Park, is confronted by his opposite:
a young, unkempt, undisciplined bum. The bum is tortured and
anxious to communicate with the other man, who is fearful of him.
Finally the bum brings the conventional man down to his level.
    2 men; simple set and props. Royalty: $25. (Presented
    professionally with Beckett's Krapp's Last Tape.)

ALEICHEM, Sholom. Tevya and His Daughter. See entry under
    Perl, Arnold.

ALENÇAR, José Marteniaño de. The Jesuit (1875). Tr. by de
    Britto, in Poet Lore, v. 30, 1919.
    The scene is laid in Rio de Janeiro in 1759. Dr. Samuel,
an Italian Jesuit, has a magnificent plan to populate and civilize
Brazil. He wants his adopted son, Estavao, to carry it on as a
Jesuit, but Estavao loves Constança and in the end marries her.
    4 acts; 9 men, 2 women; 3 interiors, 1 exterior; costumes
    of time and place.

ALEXANDER, Ronald. Time Out for Ginger (1953). Dramatists
    Play Service.
    Ginger is the tomboy daughter of a rather staid banker. Her
father has delivered a series of lectures at her school on the need
for self-fulfillment, and Ginger decides that her own true fulfillment
can best be realized by going out for the football team. Any number
of complications result: the father's job is jeopardized because the
bank president doesn't approve; Ginger's older sisters insist she has
ruined their social life; and worst of all, Ginger's boyfriend disap-
proves of her actions. After many other mishaps the play ends on
a happy note with the entire family going to see one of the other
sisters in the high school play, Ginger escorted by her reconciled
boyfriend.
    5 men (2 are teenagers), 5 women (3 are teenagers); 1 in-
    terior. Royalty: $50-25.

ALFIERI, Vittorio. Saul (1782). Tr. by Lloyd in his Tragedies,
    London, 1815, v. 3; Bohn, 1876, v. 2; tr. by Bowring in
    CLF-2.
    Before the battle at Gilboa, David comes to Jonathan and
Michal his wife and is reconciled to Saul. But overnight Saul's
mood changes and he wants to kill David and orders the death of
Ahimelech, priest of Nob. Deserted and defeated in the battle, Saul
falls on his sword.
    5 acts; 5 men, 1 woman; extras; 1 exterior (camp); costumes
    of the period.

ALFRED, William. Hogan's Goat (1965). Samuel French.
    The setting is turn-of-the-century Brooklyn. The mayor has
been caught with his hand in the till, and Hogan runs against him as
a reform candidate. The mayor learns, however, that Hogan is
really married to two women, one of them dying of drunkeness and

low living. Hogan not only loses the election, but causes the death of his wife. As he waits for the police to arrive he recognizes that he never really loved anyone but himself.
  10 men, 5 women, 5 extras; composite interior-exterior convertible unit. Royalty: $50-25.

ALGREN, Nelson. The Man with the Golden Arm. See entry under Kirkland, Jack.

ALLEN, Jay. Forty Carats (1969). Adapted from the French of Barillet and Gredy. Samuel French.
  A fortyish American divorcée traveling in Greece falls in love with a young man of 22. Back in New York after her trip, her life is complicated by her real estate business, her mother, her 17-year-old daughter, and a 45-year-old client who is courting her. A boy who comes to take her daughter out one night turns out to be the young man she had the affair with in Greece. The old attraction is as strong and mutual as ever, and she discovers that her middle-aged client is really interested in her daughter.
  5 men, 6 women; 3 interiors. Royalty: $50-35.

_____. The Prime of Miss Jean Brodie (1968) Adapted from the novel by Muriel Spark. Samuel French.
  Miss Brodie is a teacher in a girls' school in Edinburgh in the early 1930's. She is a formidable figure, and an interesting one, but she does not always practice what she preaches. Miss Brodie's girls write a letter in her name to her current lover (the music teacher, who has taken the place of her previous lover, the art teacher) which falls into the hands of the headmistress of the school. Miss Brodie saves herself from dismissal, but she is vulnerable to her students, who are growing too wise too fast.
  4 men, 15 women; platform set. Royalty: $50-25.

ALLEN, Woody. Don't Drink the Water (1966). Samuel French.
  An American tourist and his wife and daughter rush into the American Embassy in an Iron Curtain country. They are pursued by the secret police who insist they are spies who have photographed communist secrets. The embassy is not the best refuge, however, for the ambassador is absent and his son (who has been expelled from a dozen countries and all of Africa) is in charge. An escape plot is planned, and a romance is born.
  12 men, 4 women; 1 interior. Royalty: $50-25.

_____. Play It Again, Sam (1969). Samuel French.
  A homely man trying to make it in a world of beautiful people is rescued by his hero, Humphrey Bogart, who comes to him offering advice and urging him on. Bogart is so charming, in fact, that even the homely man's best friend's wife succumbs one night. A comedy in the Woody Allen manner.
  3 men, 8 women; one interior. Royalty: $50-35.

ALVAREZ, Quintero Serafín, and Joaquin Alvarez. Doña Clarines (1909). Tr. by Granville-Barker in their Four Comedies,

French, 1932; CHA.

The heroine, Doña Clarines, is a middle-aged lady who is reputed eccentric and even mad because of her absolute honesty of deed and speech. Marcela, her niece, fears to tell her of her love for Miguel because he is the son of the man who caused her aunt's hair to turn white and made a recluse of her when he left her years before. But she shows her generous spirit by bringing them together.

2 acts; 4 men, 5 women; 1 interior.

_____. The Lady from Alfáqueque (1914). Tr. by Granville-Barker in their Four Comedies, French, 1932.

Some small-town provincials come to Madrid where they mingle with their own kind of people and so remain provincials. Among them is a clever rascal who sponges on others, but his way of doing it is so perfect that no one can take offense.

2 acts; 5 men, 6 women; 1 interior.

_____. Malvaloca (1912). Tr. by Fassett. Doubleday, 1916; DIE.

Salvador and his brother Leonardo are remolding a cracked bell in the cloister. Salvador has seduced Malvaloca, but she has come to love Leonardo. When the casting is finished, Leonardo tells her that he will seek to remold her life in the fire of his love.

3 acts; 7 men, 11 women; 2 interiors; 1 exterior.

_____. Papá Juan; or, The Centenarian (1909). Tr. by Walsh in Poet Lore, v. 29, 1918; tr. by Granville-Barker as A Hundred Years Old in their Four Plays, Lond., Sidgwick, 1927.

Papá Juan celebrates his 100th birthday, for which he gathers his descendants together. They represent great differences, from the combativeness of Doña Filamena to the waywardness of Gabriela. He insists on still running things, and unites his favorite great-granddaughter Currita and his free-thinking jolly grandson Trino, who as a gay blade has been rather scorned by the rest.

3 acts; 6 men, 6 women; 1 interior.

_____. The Woman's Town (1912). Tr. by Turrell in TUR; tr. by Granville-Barker as The Women Have Their Way in their Four Plays, Lond., Sidgwick, 1927.

A young lawyer from the city, Adolpho, comes to a small town, and without in the least intending it, finds that because of women's gossip, he has become engaged to a young girl whom he has had no thought of marrying. Though at first he demurs, he finally falls in love with her, thereby becoming a victim of feminine cleverness and match-making.

2 acts; 6 men, 8 women; 1 interior.

ANDERSON, Maxwell. Anne of the Thousand Days (1948). Dramatists Play Service.

Depicts episodes in the courtship and marriage of Henry VIII and Anne Boleyn. He is the rugged vital king; she the tempestuous lady who demands recognition as queen. A memory play in which

the winds of passion blow on both.
    11 men, 5 women, extras; 1 unit setting. Royalty: $50-25.

_____. The Bad Seed (1954). Adapted from William March's
novel. Dramatists Play Service.
    Little Rhoda Penwork is ostensibly a sweet, lovable, good
natured child. Actually she is a diabolical beast. Her mother begins to suspect that something is awry when the boy who beat Rhoda
for the penmanship award is mysteriously drowned. Then others are
done away with and finally Mrs. Penwork herself. In the chilling
last scene Rhoda has her arms around her distraught father, promising to take care of him.
    7 men, 4 women, 1 small girl; 1 interior. Royalty: $50-25.

_____. Barefoot in Athens (1951). Dramatists Play Service.
    Depicts Socrates at home, abroad, at his trial, and in his
cell. Presents discussions with Pausanias concerning forms of
government in Sparta and Athens. At his trial he insists on free
inquiry and free discussion, but he is condemned on the charge of
undermining the safety of the State. In his cell he is ready to drink
the hemlock after his discussions with Pausanias, Crito, and Phaedo.
    16 men, 2 women, extras: 2 interiors, 2 exteriors. Royal-
ty: $50-25.

_____. Both Your Houses (1933). Samuel French.
    A young, idealistic Congressman is able to pad the appropri-
ations bill that is ridiculously dishonest and he expects it to be killed; but it is passed, and he is hailed as a political genius. One of
the best propaganda plays, satirizing political corruption and grafting
politicians.
    13 men, 3 women; 2 interiors. Royalty: $25-20.

_____. Elizabeth the Queen (1930). Samuel French.
    Presents the conflict between her love for Essex and her de-
sire to rule alone. Essex, the popular general, sent by craft to
Ireland, returns in power and considers his blood the equal of hers.
The ambitious, cruel, and crafty queen has him arrested, expecting
him to ask forgiveness and mercy. He will not plead and is condemned to die.
    16 men, 7 women, extras; 4 interiors, 1 exterior. Royalty:
$25-20.

_____. The Eve of St. Mark (1942). Dramatic Publishing Com-
pany.
    Young Quizz West in the army goes with his outfit to an is-
land in the Pacific, which is to be attacked in April 1942 on St.
Mark's Eve, the time when those who are about to die can talk to
their loved ones. In a mystical scene, the young soldier talks with
his girl at home.
    13 men, 8 women; 6 interiors, 2 exteriors. Royalty: $35.

_____. High Tor (1937). Dramatists Play Service.
    The Hudson river headland, High Tor, owned by Van Dorn,

is threatened with removal for trap rock by unimaginative realtors.
He doesn't wish to sell. In a storm he is visited there by Henry
Hudson's ghostly crew and the maid Lise. Van realizes next morning he will be forced to sell.
  3 acts; 14 men (& extras), 2 women; 1 exterior. Royalty:
$35-25.

     . Joan of Lorraine (1946). Dramatists Play Service.
  Using the dramatic pattern of a stock company rehearsing a
play so that various aspects are brought out, Joan of Arc is shown
at home, en route to the Dauphin, at Orleans, at the coronation, at
the dedication of her armor, and finally at her trial and in her cell.
The actress who plays Joan learns the lessons Joan taught the world.
  18 men, 5 women; bare stage. Royalty $50-25.

     . Key Largo (1939). Dramatists Play Service.
  King McCloud, American volunteer for Loyalists in Spain,
leaves the battle ground in time to save his life; the other seven in
his company are killed. To expiate his desertion, he visits each
family to tell how their son died, coming finally to the d'Alcala
family on an island in the Florida Keys, where a gangster is terror-
izing the inhabitants. At first he plays deserter again, but finally
he understands that sacrifice is necessary to uphold truth. He kills
the gangster and is himself killed.
  17 men, 7 women; 2 exteriors. Royalty on application.

     . Mary of Scotland (1933). Samuel French.
  Mary returns from France to be Queen of Scotland, wishing
only to live, love, rule, and worship as she pleases. Three great
forces are against her: Scottish oligarchy in her half-brother Murray; Scotch religious inflexibility in John Knox; and English jealousy
in Queen Elizabeth. The star-crossed lady wins our sympathy in
her 6-year, gallant, losing fight. She sees Elizabeth's hand in her
betrayal to the English, but she claims victory over her as a woman,
for she has lived and loved and born a child, while Elizabeth has
only schemed and hated and has no heir.
  3 acts; 22 men, 5 women; 4 interiors, 1 exterior. Royalty:
$25-20.

     . Saturday's Children (1927). Longmans, 1927; GASE;
  TUCD; abridged in Mantle 1926/27.
  Intimate study of two middle-class Americans who try to
prove that two can live as cheaply as one. When they quarrel over
money and a job for her, she leaves. But they become reconciled,
for their love is real and vital--more so than any materialistic considerations.
  3 men, 4 women; 3 interiors.

     . Valley Forge (1934). Anderson House, 1935; French,
  1937; in his Eleven Verse Plays, Harcourt, 1940; abridged in
  Mantle 1934/35.
  A very human Washington is depicted in the dark winter of
1777/78 as he suffers with his men, rebels against the supercilious

contempt of two fatuous Congressmen, and takes pride in the loyalty of his frontiersmen who will continue to fight for freedom.
3 acts; 32 men, 3 women, extras; 4 interiors.

_____. What Price Glory? with Laurence Stallings (1924). In his Three American Plays, Harcourt, 1926; CHA; GASE; TRE-1, 2, 3; TREA-3; abridged in Mantle 1924/25.
Captain Flagg and Sergeant Quirk, regular Army men, chafe under the hard unglamorous daily grind of war at the front. As rivals for the French girl Charmaine they come to hate each other, but respond immediately to the call of duty. The play is famous for its shocking language (at least to 1924 ears) and for its unromantic treatment of war.
26 men, 1 woman; 3 interiors.

_____. The Wingless Victory (1936). Dramatists Play Service.
Tragic story of the love of a Malay queen, Oparre, for the New England captain of the "Wingless Victory," Nathaniel McQueston. He marries her and brings her and their two children home with much wealth. His family and friends like his money but not his wife and children. McQueston tries to buy acceptance for his wife, but his brother blackmails him into sending her home. When she sees that her husband won't stand by her, she kills herself and her children.
8 men, 8 women; 2 interiors. Royalty: $25.

_____. Winterset (1935) Dramatists Play Service.
In the shadow of Brooklyn bridge, Mio seeks to clear his father's name. Here he meets and loves Miriamne, who however is loyal to her brother Garth, who could have testified for and cleared Mio's father's name. Over all hangs an atmosphere heavy with fate, introducing Trock, the leader of a murder gang, and Judge Gaunt, tortured in conscience as to the justice of his sentence. (A slightly fictionalized Sacco-Vanzetti case.)
16 men, 3 women, extras; 1 interior, 1 exterior. Royalty: $25.

ANDERSON, Robert. All Summer Long (1954). Adapted from Donald Wetzel's novel. Samuel French.
As the two boys (the oldest crippled from an accident) work together to make a retaining wall to save their home from the rising river, their father complains, criticizes, and accuses his sons of not having a sense of responsibility. The makeshift wall does not keep the water away, and the house crumbles. In addition, the daughter's vanity leads to her horrible death. Nothing can save this family, but during the summer the youngest came of age all by himself.
3 men, 2 women, 2 juveniles; composite interior-exterior. Royalty: $50-25.

_____. The Footsteps of Doves. See You Know I Can't Hear You....

_____. I Never Sang for My Father (1968). Dramatists Play
Service.
Gene is a widower with an elderly mother he loves and an
80-year-old father he doesn't. Just as he is about to remarry and
move to California his mother dies, and he is saddled with the
father he has never been able to "sing for," to love and understand
with the knowledge that the song will be accepted and appreciated.
Gene's sister, who married a Jew and was driven away by the father
years before, urges him not to throw his life away on a mean and
ungenerous man.
7 men (several are bits), 4 women; area staging. Royalty:
$50-25.

_____. I'll Be Home for Christmas. See You Know I Can't Hear
You....

_____. I'm Herbert. See You Know I Can't Hear You....

_____. The Shock of Recognition. See You Know I Can't Hear
You....

_____. Silent Night, Lonely Night (1959). Samuel French.
On Christmas Eve in a small New England town, two people
meet at an inn: an unhappily married man and an unhappily married
woman. They are alone except for a honeymooning couple. She
worries over her woman-chasing husband while she awaits the release of her son from the nearby school infirmary. He worries over
his wife, who has been in a mental institution since she learned,
five years ago, that he was seeing another woman. In his wife's
despair she let their child drown in a neighbor's pool. The two are
lonely, and they give in to each other. The next day she takes a
plane with her son to meet the repentant husband, and he learns that
his wife is in one of her "good" periods.
2 men, 3 women, 1 child; 1 interior. Royalty: $50-25.

_____. Tea and Sympathy (1953). Samuel French.
The sympathy and understanding of the headmaster's wife enables a sensitive youth at a boarding school to regain his confidence
in this successful Broadway drama. The boy has become the object
of rumors because he played girls' parts in amateur theatricals and
because of his sensitivity. The headmaster joins in this persecution,
and even the boy's father fails to understand him. Determined to
prove his masculinity, the boy visits a local prostitute but is sickened at the sight of her. Now the rumor and hazing turns to out-
right ostracism, and the boy faces expulsion. The beautiful and understanding master's wife visits him in his room and offers him the
kindness and tenderness he needs to regain his confidence in his
masculinity.
9 men, 2 women; composite interior. Royalty: $50-25.

_____. You Know I Can't Hear You When the Water's Running
(1967). Four short comedies ("The Shock of Recognition," "The
Footsteps of Doves," "I'll Be Home for Christmas," and "I'm

Herbert") under an omnibus title.   Dramatists Play Service.
    In "The Shock of Recognition" a young dramatist and his pro-
ducer are arguing about the opening of the dramatist's new play
(breakfasting in bed, a wife speaks to her husband who comes out
of the bathroom buck naked to say, "You know I can't hear you when
the water's running").   The conflict is one of taste.   An out-of-work
actor enters the argument, gets into the spirit of the play, and even
strips to show how he would handle the role, playing opposite the
producer's secretary.   (3 men, 1 woman; 1 interior.)   In "Footsteps
of Doves" a couple who have been married for 25 years come to a
store to pick out a new bed (or beds).   The salesman is not hetero-
sexual enough to care what kind of bed/beds the couple should buy,
but a young blonde who enters the discussion opts for the big bed,
since she is all alone.   (2 men, 2 women; 1 interior.)   In "I'll Be
Home for Christmas" a couple discusses the sex education of their
almost-adult children, who are establishing their independence from
the family.   (1 man, 2 women; 1 interior.)   In "I'm Herbert" two
old people rock their chairs and talk about their lives.   (1 man, 1
woman; 1 exterior.)   The title You Know I Can't Hear You When the
Water's Running can be used only when all four plays (individual
royalty of $25 each) are presented.
    Royalty: $50-35.

ANDREEV, Leonid N.   Anathema (1909).   Tr. by Bernstein.   Mac-
    millan, 1910.
    The Devil, in this play called Anathema, requesting a
glimpse of heaven, is denied entrance.   He returns to earth, de`er-
mined to get even with God.   Working on David Leizer, a pious Jew,
he strips him of wealth and gloats as a mob stones him to death.
Anathema returns to the gates to point out God's failure, only to be
told that the patient David has been admitted to Christ-like immortality and is even then seated at the right hand of the throne.   Anathema curses and returns to earth to begin another campaign.
    Prolog & 7 scenes; 12 men, 6 women; 2 exteriors.

_____.   The Black Maskers (1908).   Tr. by Meader & Scott in
    his Plays, Scribner, 1915.
    The human soul in its castle (the body) is invaded by the
black maskers--doubt, despair, and madness, who represent the
hero's involuntary thoughts of evil.   The soul of Duke Lorenzo struggles, is overwhelmed, but dies unyielding; he is master of his fate.
    5 acts; 5 men, 1 woman, extras; 3 interiors.

_____.   He Who Gets Slapped (1915).   Tr. by Zilboorg.   Dial
    Pub. Co., 1921; Brentano, 1922; DIE; MOSH; TUCG; TUCM;
    WATI; WATL-4; abridged in Mantle 1921/22.   (Acting ed.,
    French)
    To cover his personality, a lonely intellectual joins a circus
and becomes an absurd clown who amuses as a butt for blows, welcoming the slaps as preferable to suffering in the outside world.
He worships the lovely bareback rider, Consuelo.   When he thinks
she is being sacrificed by her money-seeking guardian through marriage to a degenerate baron, he saves her from a living death by

poisoning her, and then himself.
>   4 acts; 20 men, 13 women; 1 interior; some circus costumes.
>   (French royalty: $25-20.)

_____. The Life of Man (1906). Tr. by Seltzer. Little, 1914
& 1920; DIK-2; MOSQ; tr. by Meader & Scott, Scribner, 1915;
SML; tr. by Hogarth, Lond. , 1915.
>   Man is born in darkness; he lives and loves, but Inexorable
> Fate (the Being in Grey) is ever by his side; till in darkness he
> dies. Depicts the folly and futility of life, breathes despair and
> bitterness.
>   Prolog & 5 scenes; 5 men, 3 women, extras; 5 interiors.

_____. The Sabine Women (1912). Tr. by Meader & Scott in
his Plays, ser. 1, Scribner, 1915; tr. by Seltzer as The Pretty
Sabine Women in Drama, #13, Feb. , 1914.
>   A ludicrous skit on a bit of Roman history. The Romans
> carry off the scratching, screaming, kicking women and are ex-
> hausted by the struggle; they beg a truce. The women are intrigued
> by their new husbands but are disappointed that their old Sabine men
> refuse to come and re-abduct them. The play is really a burlesque
> satire on Russian politics of the time. The Romans represent daring
> and force (the reactionary government of the Czar), the Sabines rep-
> resent law, order, and reason (the Constitutional Democracy), the
> women are the spoils of the stronger (their liberties are taken away).
>   3 acts; 7 men, 7 women, many extras; 2 exteriors; costumes
>   of the period.

ANNUNZIO, Gabriele d'. The Daughter of Jorio (1904). Tr. by
Porter in Poet Lore v. 18, 1907; Little, 1907; MOSQ.
>   A young shepherd, Aligi, wins the love of Mila, the daughter
> of the noted sorcerer, Jorio, and they live happily together in pas-
> toral simplicity. Aligi's father, Lazaro, comes to their cave and
> attacks Mila; she calls for help; Aligi rushes in and strikes his
> father dead. When brought to trial for the patricide, Mila saves
> him by claiming she did it through some magic from her father
> Jorio. She is carried away to be burnt as a witch.
>   3 acts; 8 men, 11 women, extras; 1 interior, 2 exteriors;
>   costumes of the period (16th century in Italy).

_____. Francesca da Rimini (1901). Tr. by Symons, Stokes,
1902; DIK-1; TUCG; TUCM; WATL-3.
>   Strongly characterizes each one in the eternal triangle, es-
> pecially Francesca, who rather glories in her guilty intrigue since
> she believes she was trapped into marriage. D'Annunzio rather de-
> lights in depicting the more sensuous scenes and episodes; he writes
> in beautiful symbolic verse, ornate and colorful.
>   5 acts; 17 men, 8 women, extras; 2 interiors, 2 exteriors;
>   costumes of the period (13th century in Italy).

_____. Gioconda (1898). Tr. by Simons, Heinemann, 1901;
Russell, 1902; DID, SMI; abridged in Pierce & Matthews v. 2.
>   The sculptor Lucio finds his inspiration in his model Gioconda

and not in his devoted wife Sylvia, who sacrifices her hands to save
his masterpiece from breaking as it falls. He sacrifices her devotion; for art is a greater force than human passion.
        4 acts; 3 men, 4 women, 1 girl; 3 interiors.

ANOUILH, Jean. Antigone (1944). Translated and adapted by Lewis
        Galantiere. Based on Sophocles' play. Samuel French.
        Based on the play of Sophocles, but developed in present-day
situations, symbolic of the captive French nation nobly defiant of the
Nazi's despotic tyrannical rule. Follows the plot of Sophocles: Antigone rebels at the edict and covers her brother's body with earth.
Brought before the Regent Creon he orders her to be walled up alive.
She hangs herself, his son stabs himself beside her, and Creon's
wife also kills herself.
        1 continuous act in 6 scenes; 8 men, 4 women, the chorus is
        represented by one man; 1 exterior. Royalty: $25-20.

_____. Becket (1959). Translated by Lucienne Hill. Samuel
        French.
        Personal friendship and principle clash in this historical dra-
ma based on England's King Henry VIII's attempts to justify his divorce and remarriage. Since the church refused to allow it, Henry
decided to make himself head of the church of England. Because he
took this action he lost the friendship and support of his closest
friend, Becket. Although he loved Becket, Henry felt he had no
choice when faced with this affront to his authority; and through a
suggestion, he brought about the death of his former friend.
        15 men, 3 women; various interiors and exteriors. Royalty:
        $50-25.

_____. Dinner with the Family (1937). Translated by Edwin
        Owen Marsh. Samuel French.
        A charming young man finds he can no longer stand his rich,
hysterical wife and yearns for the simple joys of life with a quiet,
unsophisticated young girl. The young man, Georges Delachume,
not only has to endure his wife, Barbara, but also his parents and
his best friend Jacques, all of whom live with him. Then Georges
is swept off his feet by the sweet, uncomplicated Isabelle and describes for her the life he dreams of living. Isabelle, however,
forces Georges into some panicky preparations when she insists on
visiting this idyllic home. To preserve the illusion Georges hires
a house and actors to pose as his family, but his dinner for Isabelle
is suddenly interrupted by the appearance of his pistol-brandishing
wife and the rest of his real "family." Isabelle proves that she is
worthy of Georges' high estimation of her when she sticks by him
as he frees himself from the entanglements of his Paris life.
        6 men, 6 women; 2 interiors. Royalty: $35-25.

_____. The Fighting Cock (1959). Samuel French.
        A strict, by-the-numbers general finds that his rigid devo-
tion to moral absolutes is quite unworkable outside a military environment. Although he's now retired, he retains this attitude and
tries to impose it on his countrymen. He launches a campaign to

"rid the world of Maggots and teach the people honor." The general's posturings become more absured as the play progresses. He
fights a duel with a young man who jilts his daughter, and is humili-
ated. The final blow comes when Truth loses its appeal for him.
He learns that his wife will always be true to him, out of truth itself rather than love. His new awareness leads him to admit, finally: "Ideals are all very well, but life does have to be lived."
     9 men, 3 women, 2 children; 1 interior, 1 exterior. Royal-
ty: $50-25.

_____. The Lark (1953). Adapted by Lillian Hellman. Drama-
tists Play Service.
     The story of Joan of Arc, the country girl who heard voices
which told her to lead the French armies against the invading British.
In this version, an attempt has been made to divorce the drama
from the limitations of time, sequence, and space. There is no
scenery per se, merely platforms and lighting effects. Thus the
story can move backward and forward in story line without inter-
ruption.
     15 men, 5 women; movable platforms (no scenery). Royalty:
$50-25.

_____. Mademoiselle Colombe (1950). Adapted by Louis Kron-
enberger. Samuel French.
     A young man loses his sweetheart to the dazzling life of the
theater in this drama about the often capricious ways of romance.
A pretty girl delivering flowers to the home of a famous prima donna meets the opera heroine's son, and they immediately fall in love
and marry. Then the young man goes off to war and his mother
takes the girl to the theater, where she is enchanted by the glamour.
She forgets her husband and embraces the theater with all her love.
He returns to find her merrily pursuing her new career and their
romance ended.
     10 men, 5 women; 4 interiors. Royalty: $50-25.

_____. Poor Bitos (1965). Translated by Lucienne Hill. Sam-
uel French.
     A seemingly innocent dinner party recreates the terrors of
the age of Robespierre. A group of French patricians have gathered
for a party in an old chateau, and among the guests is an intransi-
gent prosecutor named Bitos, whom the rest of the guests fear and
detest. To them he is the reincarnation of Robespierre and sets off
a chain of associations in their minds of the age of Revolution and
repression. Their mental images are recreated for the audience as
the guests change to coats of the Revolutionary period. Through
this shift in time the point becomes clear that the inflexible blindness of the dedicated often leads to more destruction than good.
     10 men, 3 women; 1 interior. Royalty: $50-25.

_____. The Rehearsal (1950). English version by Pamela H.
Johnson and Kitty Black. Samuel French.
     A count has decided to present a performance of Marivaux'
Double Inconstancy, and has cast himself, his wife, his mistress,

and his wife's lover in the principal roles. As they don their costumes the actors drift into the cynicism of the period. The count falls in love with a young girl, the countess calls on a friend to seduce the girl, the friend is reminded of his first love and invites a duel and certain death. The rehearsal goes on.

5 men, 3 women; 1 interior, 1 inset. Royalty: $50-25.

_____. Ring Round the Moon (1948). Dramatists Play Service.

Twin brothers have very different temperaments: Hugo is a cynical young man, heartless and aggressive; Frederick is sentimental, sensitive, and shy. Hugo introduces a ballet-dancer, Isabelle, at a houseparty to show that a child of the slums might be the belle of the ball; also to break up Frederick's infatuation with the heiress, Diana, who really craves the wilder Hugo.

6 men, 7 women, extras; 1 exterior. Royalty: $50-25.

_____. Romeo and Jeannette (1945). Translated by Miriam John. Samuel French.

An upper class young man takes his mother to the lower class family of his fiancee. The family is mostly degenerate, but the young man falls in love with his fiancee's sister, Jeannette, a girl whose reputation is bad. The two run off to a cabin where Jeannette puts on a wedding dress and slashes her wrists to show her love for the youth. Just then word arrives that the abandoned sister has taken poison. Later, on the day that Jeannette is to wed her first lover, the two meet again and drown together embraced.

4 men, 3 women; 2 interiors. Royalty: $25-20.

_____. Thieves' Carnival (1938). Translated by Lucienne Hill. Samuel French.

An honest thief wants to continue thieving but is finally persuaded to give up his life of crime in this mystery farce. The setting is a palatial home where two attractive girls reside. Their happy life is soon rudely interrupted by the appearance of three thieves, and later, the most country of all country bumpkins. Then one of the girls falls in love with the youngest thief. Because he is so honest, however, he cannot accept her love. He refuses to let her marry a thief. But the girl soon outsmarts him and convinces him that he cannot be honest if he won't admit his love for her and give up his life of crime.

10 men, 3 women; 2 exteriors, 1 interior. Royalty: $35-25.

_____. Time Remembered (1939). Translated by Patricia Moyes. Samuel French.

A handsome prince aided by his aunt, the Duchess, struggles to keep the memory of his dead wife alive in this romantic comedy, but soon surrenders to the much stronger attraction of a living love. Amanda, a poor young milliner, has attracted the Duchess' interest because she so closely resembles the dear departed Leocadia. To make Amanda dependent on her, the Duchess causes Amanda's dismissal from her job and proposes that she try to impersonate Leocadia. As the Duchess is coaching Amanda, however, Prince Albert discovers them. But his initial anger soon turns to fascination

when he realizes how closely Amanda resembles Leocadia. Amanda's attempts to impersonate the bizarre Leocadia only anger Albert, but the Duchess realizes that there is real love between the two and manages to persuade both to give their love a chance.
    13 men, 2 women; 1 interior, 2 exteriors. Royalty: $50-25.

_____. Traveller Without Luggage (1936). Translated by John Whiting. Samuel French.
    A psychiatrist's attempts to discover the identity of an amnesia victim lead to the former soldier's total disillusionment with his family in this drama. For eighteen years Gaston has had no memory of his life before the war. Then his doctor arranges for him to visit a family which is probably Gaston's. The mother is certain that Gaston is her son, and his sister-in-law, with whom he once had an affair, is equally convinced. Gaston, however, soon realizes that his brother was a cruel, vicious, and immoral individual and refuses to admit that this could be his family even though his identification seems more and more certain. Then another claimant appears, an orphan boy with no family and no past vices, adding a new complication to the already entangled situation. The intrigues and eventual resolution of these questions of identity result in an interesting drama.
    8 men, 5 women; 2 interiors, 1 inset. Royalty: $50-25.

_____. The Waltz of the Toreadors (1951). Translated by Lucienne Hill. Samuel French.
    The toreador in this farce is a general who considers himself quite a "toreador" with the ladies. Interspersed with the many comic scenes, however, are revealing moments in which the bitterness and disgust of the general toward his shallow conquests are shown.
    4 men, 7 women; 1 interior. Royalty: $50-25.

ANSKY, S. The Dybbuk (1914). Tr. by Alsberg & Katzin, Boni, 1926; DIE; CEW; abridged in Mantle 1925/26.
    The Dybbuk is believed to be an evil spirit which enters into a person. As a Russian Jew sect is worshipping in a synagogue, Sender, a wealthy merchant announces that he has found a bridegroom for his daughter Leah. When Channon, who had been betrothed to Leah at birth, drops dead, Sender is held responsible. The Dybbuk is exorcised, but Leah hears the call of the soul of Channon and joins him in death.
    4 acts; 25 men, 7 women, extra children; 2 interiors, 1 exterior. Russian costumes.

ANSPACHER, Louis K. The Unchastened Woman (1915). Stokes, 1916; Harcourt, 1920; Dramatists Play Service, 1937 (in revised form); BAK, DIG; abridged in Mantle & Sherwood 1909-19.
    Vigorously draws a memorable though unpleasant and unscrupulous heroine who seeks to ensnare a young architect but is outwitted by his loyal clearsighted wife. Exciting story with strongly contrasted groups, compelling attention to the vital social significance of such a person.
    3 acts; 3 men, 5 women; 2 interiors.

ANTHONY, C. L.   See entries under pseud. of Dodie Smith.

ANZENGRUBER, Ludwig.   The Farmer Forsworn (1872).   Tr. by
    Busse, FRA v. 16.
        Matthias Ferner, a rather wicked farmer, swears that his
brother left no will and thus deprives the daughter Veroni and the
son Jacob of their inheritance.   His son Frank has seen him burn
the will; for 14 years this has been on their consciences.   Frank
returns to die and gives the family Bible to Veroni in which is an
unopened letter proving the will.   His father so worries that he
shoots at Frank but fails to kill him.
        3 acts; 11 men, 11 women, extras; 4 interiors, 2 exteriors;
    German costumes.

ARCHER, Daniel.   Mr. Barry's Etchings.   See entry under Bullock,
    Walter.

ARCHER, Jules.   Murder Is a Matter of Opinion.   See entry under
    Dawson, Ronald.

ARCHER, William.   The Green Goddess (1921).   Samuel French.
        Contrasts the natives, somewhere beyond the Himalayas, with
their fanaticism for their desecrated goddess, and the English party
stranded there from their disabled airplane, at the mercy of the
smooth but revengeful Raja of Rukh.
        7 men, 2 women, many extras; 3 interiors, 1 exterior.
    Royalty: $50.

ARCHIBALD, William.   The Innocents (1950).   Adapted from Henry
    James' story, "The Turn of the Screw."   Samuel French.
        "The Innocents" begins when a young governess arrives at an
English estate to take charge of two inhibited, orphaned children.
A motherly cook completes the household, but the four are haunted
by fears and ghosts.   Giant shadows and haunting faces terrify the
cook and the governess, but the two children, possessed by spirits,
welcome their presence with no fear.   The two adults learn that the
visiting spirits are those of the former caretaker and maid who had
previously corrupted the souls of the young innocents.   Finally, to
the governess' horror, the children and the spirits become insep-
arable.   There is nothing anyone can do to reclaim the children.
        1 man, 3 women, a boy and a girl aged 10 to 13; 1 interior.
    Royalty: $50-25.

ARDREY, Robert.   Thunder Rock (1939).   Dramatists Play Service.
        Charleston, a lighthouse keeper on Thunder Rock in Lake
Michigan, has fled the world as detestable, and is not persuaded by
his friend Streeter, who is returning to the world to do something
about it.   In the keeper's fancy, some shipwrecked people appear,
who have fled Europe and the 1948 revolution to seek sanctuary and
freedom.   Old Joshua, their captain, convinces the keeper to return
to useful work and to help create a new order out of the chaos of
the old.
        3 acts; 8 men, 3 women; 1 interior (inside the lighthouse).
    Royalty: $25.

ARIOSTO, Lodovico. Supposes (1509). Tr. by Gascoigne in his
   Works, Lond., 1584; Heath's Belles-Lettres ser., 1906; in
   Bond, R. W. ed. Early Plays from the Italian, Oxford, 1911.
      Erostrato, a student in Ferrara, in order to woo Polymnesta,
the daughter of Damone, dresses as his servant and gets his servant,
Dulipo, to dress as the master.   She is also wooed by the rich
Cleandro, who offers 2000 ducats as dowry.   Erostrato can't match
this, but Dulipo induces a Sienese traveler to pose as Erostrato's
father.   Complications develop when his real father arrives.
      5 acts; 14 men, 4 women; 1 exterior (a street); costumes of
the period.

ARISTOPHANES.   The Birds (414 B.C.).   Tr. by Rogers in Loeb
   Library; by Frere in Everyman's; by Hickie in Bohn's; by Way,
   Macmillan; by MacGregor in CLS; OAT.
      Two old men, weary of the corruption in Athens, decide to
leave the country and seek advice from the King of Birds.   They are
given permission to build Cloud-Cuckoo-Town, a walled city, anti-god
and pro-bird, where the birds shall be masters of all things.   Envoys
from Athens are summarily dismissed, but a peace offer from the
gods (who are in a sorry state since the founding of the city) is accepted, provided that the Birds be restored to all their former
rights and privileges.   An exuberant burlesque on Athenian hopes
of success in the expedition to Sicily.
      1 continuous act; 19 men, 0 women, chorus of birds; 1 ex-
terior.

_____.   The Clouds (423 B.C.).   Tr. by Rogers in Loeb Library;
   by Hickie in Bohn's; tr. by Way, Macmillan; BAT; CLF-1 (tr.
   by Mitchell); OAT.
      Attacks the absurdities of the Sophists, with Socrates as the
scapegoat.   Strepsiades, almost ruined by the extravagance of his
son, Pheidippides, asks Socrates how to cheat his creditors.   He
finds it is the Clouds which are the authors of things.   When Pheidippides at last comes to the Thought Shop, he is taught the difference between Just and Unjust Reason (or Valid and Specious Argument).   So well does he learn that he confounds both his creditors
and his father with his newly acquired logic.   He beats his father
under pretext that he is behaving reasonably.   Strepsiades sets fire
to the house and school of Socrates.
      1 continuous act; 10 men, 0 women, chorus of men; 1 ex-
terior.

_____.   The Frogs (405 B.C.).   Tr. by Rogers in Loeb Library;
   tr. by Hickie in Bohn's; Tr. by Gilbert Murray, Oxford; tr. by
   Way, Macmillan; tr. by Frere in MAU, SMR, TEN; HARC-8;
   OAT; TREA-1.
      Dionysus, the god of the theatre, is worried lest there be no
good plays left; he descends with his slave Xanthias to Hades to
bring back the recently deceased Euripides.   Here he finds Euripides
and Aeschylus quarreling as to which is the greater dramatic poet.
They parody each other's lines and place them on the scales.   Euripides has wit, subtility, and ability to anger by his sophistries;
Aeschylus has passion and tragedy.   Dionysus is appointed judge;

the public contest decides in favor of Aeschylus.   Dionysus leads
him back to Athens.
>   1 continuous act; 9 men, 3 women, chorus of frogs; 2 ex-
>   teriors.

_____. Lysistrata (411 B. C.).   Tr. by Rogers and Loeb Libra-
ry; tr. by Hickie in Bohn's; tr. by Way, Macmillan, 1928; tr.
& adapted by Drake from the French of Donnay, Knopf, 1929;
tr. anon. in WOR; also in OAT; tr. & adapted by Seldes, Farrar, 1930, & TRE-1, -2 (v. 2).
>   Lysistrata leads a revolt of Athenian women against war;
> they are to deny themselves to the men till peace with Sparta is
> made.   With the aid of Lampito, a Spartan woman, it is accom-
> plished.   Presents Kalonika as weakening and playing pathetic tricks
> to escape.   Shows also the anxieties of the men to get their wives
> back.
>   1 continuous act; 5 men, 4 women, extras; choruses of
>   women, men, and ambassadors; 1 exterior.

ARLISS, George.   Hamilton.   See entry under Hamlin, Mary P.

ARMONT, Paul and J. Manoussi.   The Purple Mask (1920).   Adapted
by Mrs. Louise J. Miln, Stokes, 1921; adapted by Matheson
Lang, French, 1923.
>   Armand, Comte de Trévierès, is the leader of the Royalists
> during the French Revolution.   He abducts Republicans and holds
> them for ransom.   He masquerades as the Chevalier of the Purple
> Mask, deceiving both friends and foes.   When his friends try to
> help with a spurious mask, he becomes his own decoy.   After many
> exciting adventures he escapes to England.
>   4 acts; 15 men, 9 women; 5 interiors; costumes of the period.

ARONSON, Alvin.   The Pocket Watch 1965).   Samuel French.
>   A tender Jewish domestic comedy about a family of three
> generations, led by Grandpa, who owns a small trucking business,
> and Grandma, who still believes that her husband has the golden
> pocket watch given to him on his wedding day (actually the watch
> was pawned years ago, when the family desperately needed the
> money).   Most of the action centers around a wise and caring grand-
> ma, who slips her grandson some hard-earned money as he is going
> off to college and who dies in a touching scene.
>   4 men, 3 women; composite interior-exterior set.   Royalty:
> $35-25.

ARTZYBASHEV, Mikhail P.   War (1914).   Tr. by Seltzer in Drama,
v. 6, 1916.
>   All is pleasant in the family until war is declared (World
> War I).   Then the men must go and tragedy strikes.   The son,
> Volodya, is killed, the son-in-law, Vladimir, is wounded, losing
> both his legs.   Life before and after is contrasted.
>   4 acts; 7 men, 4 women, 2 children, extras; 1 interior;
>   1 exterior; costumes of the period.

ASHTON, Herbert, Jr. <u>Brothers</u> (1928). Samuel French.
        Heredity or Environment, which influences more? Twin
boys are placed for adoption by three doctors; one (Bob) in a cultured family, the other (Eddie) in the slums of New York. The
sheltered West-side boy becomes a lawyer, also a dope fiend, a cad
and a rotter; the East-side boy, a piano player in a dive, is friendly and upright with ambitions and ideas. Bob the lawyer effects the
release of Eddie, accused of murder. Later Bob is put in a sani-
torium, and there dies. Eddie takes his place in the cultured family. The doctors are still arguing the posed question.
        3 acts; 14 men, 5 women, extras; 3 interiors. Royalty: $25.

ATKINSON, Eunice and Grant Atkinson. <u>The Perfect Idiot</u> (1949)
        Dramatic Publishing Company.
        Everyone in the high school hates Dan, the boy with the high
I. Q. and the abrasive personality. Dan has such a problem, in
fact, that his parents won't let him take the college entrance exams
until he improves in popularity. Then Puff, the star athlete, is
disqualified from athletic events, and someone has to tutor him.
Dan offers a trade: he'll tutor Puff if the gang will pretend to like
him. Reluctantly they agree. Linda is the most reluctant because
she is assigned the job of Dan's steady date. Before long, Dan has
invented a hypnotic box which helps Puff turn into an "A" student.
But then the applecart gets tipped.
        8 men, 7 women; 1 interior. Royalty: $25.

ATKINSON, Grant. <u>The Perfect Idiot</u>. See entry under Atkinson,
        Eunice.

ATLAS, Leopold. <u>Wednesday's Child</u> (1934). French, 1934;
        abridged in Mantle 1933/34.
        Shows the tragedy of the child of divorced parents, and its
social significance. When Bobby is ten years old his parents are
divorced and each marries again. Bobby doesn't like his step-
father; and his own father seems to have no time for him after he
remarries. The boy is indeed "full of woe" with no place for him
among his four parents. He is sent to a military academy.
        2 acts, in 9 scenes; 14 men, 4 women; 5 interiors, 2 ex-
teriors.

AUDEN, Wystan Hugh and Christopher Isherwood. <u>The Ascent of F. 6</u>
        (1936). Lond., Faber, 1936; Random House, 1937.
        Mountain peak F. 6 is considered sacred by the natives of
Ostnia, and if the peak be scaled, control would be theirs. The
British aim to beat the Ostnians and send idealistic Michael Ranson
and four others to reach the summit first. The climb is strenuous,
the four die en route, only Ranson reaches the top to die there.
He is found two days later by Blavek of Ostnia, is hailed as a hero,
and a monument is erected to him.
        9 scenes in 2 acts; 13 men, 3 women, extras; 4 interiors,
        5 exteriors.

AUGIER, Émile. <u>Giboyer's Son</u> (1862). Tr. by B. Papot, in

Drama, v. 1, 1911.

Maximilien is the unacknowledged son of Giboyer; he writes
and writes well under the name of Boyergi.   He loves Fernande,
but she treats him haughtily and becomes affianced to a Count.
Later she softens and comes to love Max.   In the background of the
plot are the factions of the clerical party, antagonistic to modern
democratic principles, so that the play might be termed "The cleri-
cals" who meddle in politics.

5 acts; 10 men, 3 women; 4 interiors; costumes of the
period.

_____.   The House of Fourchambault (1878).   Adapted by Magnus
& Bunner in the N.Y. Drama, v. 4 #42, 1878; tr. by B. H.
Clark in his Four Plays, Knopf, 1915; French, 1915.

Guided by his mother, M. Bernard, the illegitimate son of
M. Fourchambault, saves the house and fortune of the family without disclosing his identity.   He keeps Blanche from marrying a
baron's son, since there is no love there, and rescues Marie from
the false scandal of being mistress of Léopold.   He finally wins
Marie for himself.

5 acts; 4 men, 4 women; 3 interiors.   (French's edition
lists 4 acts; 4 interiors.)

_____.   The Marriage of Olympe (1855).   Tr. by B. H. Clark
in Drama, v. 5, 1915; in his Four Plays, Knopf, 1915.

Henri de Puygiron marries Pauline Morin, who is really
the famous courtesan Olympe, reputed to have died in California.
She finds life as a Countess very dull and decides on a separation
in order to join Baudel de Beausejour.   When it is disclosed that
Henri knows about her past and her intention, his uncle, the Marquis, shoots Olympe.   (Adapted in 1901 by Clyde Fitch as The Marriage Game.)

3 acts; 5 men, 4 women; 2 interiors; costumes of the period.

_____ and Jules Sandeau.   The Son-in-law of M. Poirier (1854).
Tr. by B. H. Clark in his Four Plays, Knopf, 1915; CLF-2;
MAU.

Developed from a novelette by Sandeau.   A penniless aristocrat, Gaston, the Marquis de Presles, marries Antoinette, the
daughter of a wealthy shopkeeper, M. Poirier.   The young husband
is shiftless and pretentious and has plainly married her for her
money.   M. Poirier wants him to give up being lazy and to be really
doing something.   His wife makes every effort to get him to love
her as much as she loves him.   She twice saves his honor.   As
her character develops, she takes the reins, until finally he is obliged to resort to work.

4 acts; 10 men, 1 woman; 1 interior; costumes of the period.

AULGER, Addison.   Adrift in New York (1961).   Dramatic Publishing Company.

A Gay Nineties melodrama which can be played with or without songs of the period.   Nell is enticed to leave the Old Homestead
by the villain for a music hall career in New York.   What he has

in mind, though, is more on the order of a Bowery honky-tonk, with
appropriate lifestyle. Nell endures it all and returns home with her
purity intact.
    9 men, 6 women, extras; 2 interiors. Royalty: $35.

AUSTEN, Jane. Pride and Prejudice (1935). Dramatized version
    of the novel (1796) by Mrs. Helen B. Jerome. Doubleday, 1935;
    French, 1936; FOUP; THH, abridged in Mantle 1935/36. (Sim-
    plified version by Jane Kendall, Dramatic Publishing Company.)
        Mrs. Bennet is determined to get her daughters married, for
to be a wife is to be a success. Elizabeth is not content with things
as they are; she actually refuses the pompous Rev. Mr. Collins. In
this her father backs her up. Darcy's pride is worn away and he is
acceptable to prejudiced Elizabeth after he proves himself a gentleman in bringing to a happy ending the elopement of Lydia, the dashing younger sister. Jane's beauty and sweetness overcome the
resistance of Bingley's sister.
        10 men, 16 women; 3 interiors. Royalty: $25-20. (Ken-
        dall version: 5 men, 11 women; 1 interior. Royalty: $25.)

AXELROD, George. Goodbye Charlie (1959). Samuel French.
        Charlie's contributions to the world were limited mostly to
his way with other men's wives. In fact, he died trying to escape
through a porthole of a cuckold's yacht. Now he has returned to
life reincarnated as a girl, and his big problem is to get rid of his
male attitudes, expressions, and gestures. Posing as his own wife,
Charlie meets many of his old mistresses and begins a collection
(at $5,000 apiece) for a memorial to himself. To complicate mat-
ters, his old friend begins to feel romantically about the female
Charley.
        4 men, 3 women; 1 interior. Royalty: $50-25.

_____. The Seven Year Itch (1952). Dramatists Play Service.
        A middle-aged man, whose wife is off to the country for the
summer, begins to believe that his life is passing him by. His
nervous stomach has forced him to stop smoking and drinking, he
has never been unfaithful to his wife (though he's had plenty of opportunities), and he is lonesome. So he lights a cigarette, pours
himself a scotch, and invites the girl upstairs down for a little
hanky-panky. Then his conscience gets to bothering him. He ima-
gines seducing the neighbor on the piano bench, his wife finding out
about it, shooting him through the heart, and refusing his dying
wish for a last cigarette.
        5 men, 1 boy, 5 women; 1 interior. Royalty: $50-25.

_____. Will Success Spoil Rock Hunter? (1955). Samuel French.
        An ineffectual young reporter comes to interview a motion
picture goddess. He meets a Hollywood agent who, for successive
ten percents of his soul, arranges for the goddess to fall in love
with him, writes him a successful screen play, and wins him an
Oscar. In the last act, however, Rock Hunter manages to get free
from both Hollywood and the goddess.
        6 men, 2 women; 2 interiors. Royalty: $50-25.

AYCKBOURN, Alan.   The Norman Conquests (1975).   (An omnibus
    title for three interlocking plays: Living Together, Round and
    Round the Garden, and Table Manners.)   Samuel French.
        Each play takes place on the same weekend, in three dif-
ferent parts of the same shabby Victorian house, peopled by the
same six characters.   The plays are interlocking in the sense that
though they can be produced independently and in any order, they
play best by being produced simultaneously--taking turns with each
other.   In Table Manners, for example, when Sarah learns that her
brother-in-law Norman is on the premises she rushes off the set.
In Round and Round the Garden she rushes on, to confront him.
The whole set deals effectively with a family of daughters and their
husbands/boyfriends, in which one blacksheep brother-in-law makes
everything of interest happen.
        3 men, 3 women; 2 interiors, 1 exterior.   Royalty on appli-
    cation.

BABE, Thomas.   Rebel Women (1976).   Dramatists Play Service.
        The play gives personal dimension to the historical General
William Tecumseh Sherman, who commandeers the Georgia home of
three Southern ladies on his "march to the sea."   Sherman is burned
out by the war--only his military pragmatism carries him from day
to day.   The Southern ladies are also burned out, simultaneously
repelled and attracted to the Yankee general, but one of them is
attracted enough to take Sherman to bed for the night.
        9 men, 4 women (one black); 1 interior.   Royalty: $35-25.

BACON, Frank.   Lightnin'.   See entry under Smith, Winchell.

BAGNOLD, Enid.   The Chalk Garden (1954).   Samuel French.
        An English woman lives with her granddaughter.   Her life is
simple, centered around the child and her garden.   She amuses herself by interviewing applicants for a companion to the child but never
hires one until one candidate shows up who is excellently qualified
and an excellent gardener to boot.   Between the child, who is curious about the companion's background, and a famous jurist who
comes to dinner, it is revealed that the lady was a convicted murderer.
        2 men, 7 women; 1 interior.   Royalty: $50-25.

_____.   The Chinese Prime Minister (1964).   Samuel French.
        An aging actress muses on the wisdom of age and the rever-
ence for age in the days of ancient China.   At a party her husband
appears, and it is revealed why he left her many years before.   We
also meet her two sons and their rowdy and unfaithful wives.   But
all three marriages are given a new breath of life.
        5 men, 3 women; 1 interior.   Royalty: $50-25.

_____.   National Velvet (1946).   Dramatists Play Service.
        A little girl who refuses to give up her dream of winning
England's famous Grand National horse race makes this a warm and
exciting play.   The girl, Velvet Brown, wins an apparently useless
horse in a lottery.   Yet she is determined to enter him in the Grand

National. Her mother shares her dreams since she too had tried
the "impossible" and succeeded. She had swum the English Channel
as a girl and knew that one should strive to achieve his goals even
if they are seemingly out of reach. With the help of her mother
and Mi Taylor, a friend, Velvet begins to transmute her dream to
reality. How she accomplishes this and the obstacles she overcomes make this a very enjoyable play.
    3 girls, 1 woman, 1 boy, 6 men; many male parts which
    can be doubled; unit set. Royalty: $35-25.

BAHR, Hermann. The Concert (1909). Tr. by Morgan in DID.
    Gustav Hein is a piano-teacher maestro and virtuoso; he is
also a philanderer, so that when he goes to give a "concert" it
means a three-day meeting with a lady at his cottage. This time
it will be with Delphina, wife of Frank Jura. Marie, Hein's wife,
agrees to have a liaison with Jura and they follow him to the cottage. Here the shallowness of Delphina is revealed to him, and he
is glad to give her up and return to Marie.
    3 acts; 3 men, 10 women; 2 interiors.

_____. The Master (1903). Tr. by & adapted by Glazer. Ni-
    cholas Brown, 1918.
    A strong superman from his heights of Reason and Sanity
tries to subdue every emotion and pours out contempt for mere mortals and their frailty. His forcefulness drives his all-too-human
wife away from his inhumanity to a less complex union. He pays
dearly for his faith.
    3 acts; 9 men, 3 women; 1 interior.

BAKER, Elizabeth. Chains (1909). Lond., Sidgwick, 1910; Boston,
    Luce, 1912; DIG; PLAP, v. 1.
    Intimate study of the humdrum, dull, numbing life of the
middleclass in London. The clerk thinks of going to Australia but
never does; the shop-girl thinks of marrying a middle-aged widower
but doesn't. They are irresistibly bound by the chains of convention.
    4 acts; 7 men, 5 women; 2 interiors.

BALDERSTON, J. L. and J. C. Squire. Berkeley Square (1926).
    Samuel French.
    Peter Standish of New York City inherits an ancestral mansion
in London. On visiting it, he exchanges places with Peter Standish
of 1784, but retains his 20th century viewpoint. He loves the art
and architecture and the girl of the 18th century (Helen), but not the
conditions of life at that time. When he returns to the 20th century
he is disillusioned, and breaks his engagement to the modern rich
girl.
    3 acts; 7 men, 8 women; 2 interiors. Royalty: $25-20.

_____. Dracula. See entry under Deane, Hamilton.

BALDWIN, James. The Amen Corner (1965). Samuel French.
    The Amen Corner is a store-front church in Harlem. The
preacher, a woman, is torn by the crumbling of the church world

she has created. Her son, the church organist, is determined to
follow in the footsteps of his father, a jazz musician, who finally
comes home to die.
    4 men, 10 women; composite interior. Royalty: $50-25.

_____. Blues for Mr. Charlie (1964). Samuel French.
    Described by the New York Times as having "Fires of fury
in its belly, tears of anguish in its eyes and a roar of protest in its
throat," this drama deals with the most disturbing theme of our
time. A cynical, caustic Negro, a former junkie who has kicked the
habit, returns from the North to his small southern hometown. With
his often bitter temperament, he infuriates almost everyone he meets.
In the eyes of an illiterate, poor white he goes too far, and the indignant Lyle kills him. Although at the trial the murderer is acquitted, the eulogy which has preceded it makes a violent, moving
appeal for compassion for both white and black.
    16 men, 7 women; bare stage. Royalty: $50-25.

BARASCH, Norman and Carroll Moore. Send Me No Flowers (1961).
    Samuel French.
    The antics of a hypochondriac who is convinced that he has a
terminal heart condition provide a wealth of humorous complications
for this comedy. George Kimball, the hypochondriac, had never
caused any problems with this fixation until he overheard his doctor
discussing another patient's heart trouble. Immediately assuming
that he is the patient in question, George prepares to meet his
death. He puts his affairs in order and writes a letter to his wife,
to be read after his death. He even suggests a man who will make
his wife a good second husband. His wife, however, realizes that
George is not really ill and stages a false "another man" scene.
Although threats of a divorce arise, the truth soon comes out and
George manages to feel healthy again.
    9 men, 3 women; 1 interior. Royalty: $50-25.

BARILLET, Pierre and Jean P. Gredy. The Cactus Flower. See
    entry under Burrows, Abe.

_____. Forty Carats. See entry under Allen, Jay.

BARKER, James N. Superstition (1824). HAL; QUIK; QUIL.
    The love of Charles for Mary, the daughter of the Puritan
clergyman, is opposed by her father because he believes that Charles' mother, Isabella, is a sorceress. Meantime the colony is
saved from an Indian attack by an Unknown, who really is the father
of Isabella and Charles' grandfather. Yet Charles is tried for sorcery and is executed; Mary dies. Impending doom hangs over the
pair, though they struggle against evil fate wrought by prejudice and
superstition.
    5 acts; 16 men, 4 women, extras (villagers & Indians); 2 in-
teriors, 5 exteriors; costumes of the period.

BARRETT, William E. Lilies of the Field. See entry under Les-
    lie, F. Andrew.

BARRIE, Sir James M.   The Admirable Crichton (1902).   Samuel
   French.
      Social positions are reversed in this fantasy as a group of
highborn ladies and gentlemen are shipwrecked on a desert island.
Crichton is the butler for the Earl of Loam and believes that in the
natural order of things there must always be a master and a servant.
Then a yachting cruise ends in disaster for the Earl, his three
daughters, their guests, Crichton, and Tweeny, the ladies' maid.
Through his resourcefulness Crichton gradually takes command of
the party.   In the process he wins the admiration of the women and
decides to marry one of the Earl's daughters, Lady Mary.   Then a
liner appears and Crichton decides to signal to it, although he knows
that in their rescue, all will revert to their former positions.
      13 men, 12 women; 2 interiors, 1 exterior. Royalty: $35-25.

_____ . Alice Sit-By-The Fire (1905).   Samuel French.
      In whimsical fashion presents Alice, a popular vivacious
mother, returning to her children from India, winning their love,
and pretending with keen insight to give place to her growing, romantic daughter, Amy, who knows all about life from going to plays.
Amy fears that a family friend is her mother's lover.   Alice fears
he is Amy's lover.   He is neither, and the mistake is ironed out.
      3 men, 6 women; 2 interiors. Royalty: $35-25.

_____ . The Boy David (1936).   Samuel French.
      A period in the boyhood of David is depicted in this play.
Although he's the butt of his brothers' jokes, David is the son of
Jesse whom Samuel anoints as the next king of Israel.   Then David
kills Goliath arousing the jealous wrath of King Saul.   While upset
by the King's anger, David finds comfort in his close friendship with
Jonathan.
      14 men, 2 women, extras; 1 interior, 4 exteriors. Royalty:
      $35-25.

_____ . Dear Brutus (1917).   Samuel French.
      An amiable visualization of what might happen if restless
mortals had the second chance, for which they crave, to reconstruct
their lives.   The members of a houseparty are sent into the magic
woods on Midsummer Eve and find their chance, only to learn that
it leaves them quite unchanged in spirit--"the fault, dear Brutus, is
not in our stars, but in ourselves."
      3 acts; 4 men, 6 women; 1 interior, 1 exterior (the woods).
      Royalty: $35-25.

_____ . A Kiss for Cinderella (1916).   Samuel French.
      An undernourished little serving maid in her delirium dreams
of a prince and attends a ball as Cinderella, where she meets him
and populates her world as she would have it.   On her return to
reality, she finds her prince in a friendly policeman.
      11 men, 10 women; 4 interiors. Royalty: $35-25.

_____ . Peter Pan; or, The Boy Who Would Not Grow Up (1904).
   Samuel French.

Care-free prankish Peter, the boy who would not grow up, visits the Darling home and teaches Wendy, John and Michael to fly as he does. They go with him to his fairy world in the Never-never land, where they are attacked by Captain Hook and his pirates, whom Peter subdues. Wendy promises to return each spring to do the annual cleaning of Peter's tree-top house.
14 men, 4 women, 8 boys, extras; 2 interiors, 3 exteriors. Royalty: $35-25.

_____. Quality Street (1901). Samuel French.
A delicate tale of two sisters who maintain a school to support themselves till the men return from the wars. Then the men succumb to the tantalizing Phoebe who dresses in lavendar and swoons effectively.
6 men, 9 women, extras; 2 interiors. Royalty: $35-25.

_____. What Every Woman Knows (1908). Samuel French.
Contrasts and pits the wisdom of a woman against the unawareness of a man. After Maggie Wylie became the wife of stolid John Shand, she kept herself in the background while supplying clever ideas to her husband. When he has an affair with Lady Sybil, Maggie gives her enough rope and wins John back. He still thinks it is his own intelligence and ingenuity which gets him into Parliament.
7 men, 4 women, extras; 4 interiors. Royalty: $35-25.

BARRINGTON, Eloise. Spring Dance. See entry under Barry, Philip.

BARRY, Philip. The Animal Kingdom (1932). Samuel French.
Tom has mistakenly married the wrong woman, for his wife Cecilia acts more like a "kept woman," while Daisy, his former sweetheart and mistress, is a truer spouse. He thinks marriage should be a union of spiritual and intellectual equals rather than just a physical relationship. He therefore casts off Cecilia and returns to Daisy through whom he seeks to recover his soul.
3 acts; 5 men, 4 women; 2 interiors. Royalty: $50-25.

_____. Cock Robin. See entry under Rice, Elmer.

_____. Here Come the Clowns (1938). Samuel French.
The play deals with illusion and truth, and the search for meaning in life. Clancy, an actor who has been absent for a year, turns up at Ma Speedy's Cafe, a hangout for theater people. Clancy is looking for God, and Pabst, who calls himself an illusionist, proceeds to tell the people gathered there some truths about themselves. Clancy, for example, discovers that when his wife left him she was pregnant with another man's child. One of the actors tries to shoot Pabst but kills Clancy instead.
10 men, 4 women; 1 interior. Royalty: $50.

_____. Holiday (1928). Samuel French.
Johnny Case doesn't want just to make money; life, he thinks, has something more worthwhile and he wants to enjoy it--more like a

holiday.   Such an attitude is denounced by his wealthy fiancée and
cannot be conceived of by his prospective father-in-law.   But Linda,
the second daughter, realizes that he has something there and that
the family may be wrong; she will marry him.
        3 acts; 7 men, 5 women; 2 interiors.   Royalty: $50-25.

_____. Hotel Universe (1930).   Samuel French.
        All the people at Ann Field's houseparty at her villa in
Southern France feel thwarted, unhappy, and worried.   They become
introspective, debating what life is, what death is, where they are
going and why--baffling problems that everyone faces.   Ann's father
helps each to go back in memory to some outstanding happenings in
the past, some illusions still being cherished.   These reminiscences
serve to clear their minds and bring them back to normal.
        2-hour play with no intermission indicated; 5 men, 4 women;
        1 exterior throughout.   Royalty: $50-25.

_____. In a Garden (1925).   Samuel French.
        Adrian Terry is a playwright who does not, his wife Lissa
claims, make the proper distinction between art and real life.   When
Adrian discovers that his wife's old flame, Norrie Bliss, is coming
to visit, he sets out to prove a thesis suggested for a new play:
that every woman is at heart another man's mistress.   Adrian knows
that Norrie and Lissa once spent a romantic evening in a garden,
and he sets out to prove that "romantic incidents don't bear repeating"
by constructing a stage garden and leaving the two alone together.
But everything backfires.   Lissa discovers that Norrie, long ago,
was following the plot of a novel he had read, and that Adrian was
putting her through paces as if she were a stage character.   She
will neither go off with Norrie nor stay on with Adrian.
        4 men, 2 women; 1 interior.   Royalty: $25-20.

_____. John (1929).   Samuel French.
        Successfully depicts the heart and mind of John the Baptist
through the more significant episodes of his life as he proclaims
the arrival of the Messiah, who hovers in the background as a domi-
nating influence.
        5 acts; 16 men, 2 women; 3 interiors.   Royalty: $50-25.

_____. The Joyous Season (1934).   Samuel French.
        A youthful Mother Superior finds her faith and serenity en-
able her to bring peace to her family in this comedy.   The Mother
Superior has inherited two houses, one in which her large family is
living.   She must choose one for the convent and one for the family.
Because of her confidence and faith she solves the dilemma and
demonstrates to all involved that her choice was the right one.
        6 men, 6 women; 1 interior.   Royalty: $50-25.

_____. Paris Bound (1927).   Samuel French.
        Jim and Mary have married for love and have agreed not to
be jealous; but when Jim goes to Paris and the Riviera, where he
spends months with Miss Noel Farley, Mary thinks of divorce.   But
Jim's father points out the difference between mere physical attraction

and real love. Mary learns this when she is tempted to have an affair with a young composer, so when Jim returns, happy to see her and the children, she decides not to mention Noel.
     5 men, 5 women; 2 interiors. Royalty: $50-25.

_____. The Philadelphia Story (1939). Samuel French.
     A society gossip weekly sends Mike Connor to report on the second marriage of Tracy Lord, a cold, unawakened, spoiled beauty, with George Kittredge, a successful young snob. Tracy gets interested in Mike, and after a pre-wedding party, takes a dip au naturel with him in the swimming pool. As he carries her back, they meet George and her ex-husband Dexter. Next morning she breaks her engagement with smug George. She will not marry Mike; she takes Dexter back again to the satisfaction of all.
     9 men, 6 women; 1 interior. Royalty: $50-25.

_____. Second Threshold (1951). Revised version by Robert E. Sherwood. Dramatists Play Service.
     For Josiah Bolton, after a brilliant career in public service, life has lost its savor; he has now no longer a wish to live; he feels he stands on that second threshold which separates life from death. His brilliant daughter, Miranda, is about to leave him for England to marry a man twice her age. If she goes, it will break his last tie. Dr. Toby Wells demonstrates by his love for Miranda the mistake both father and daughter are making; and when Miranda expresses her emotions of love and loyalty, Josiah discovers he does not wish to die.
     2 acts; 4 men, 2 women; 1 interior. Royalty: $50-25.

_____. Spring Dance (1936). Adapted from an original play by Eleanor Gallen and Eloise Barrington. Samuel French.
     Alex Benson is a New England college girl who finds it very difficult to attract men. She has set her heart on a Yale man, Sam Thatcher, who is interested only in cameras and going to Russia. However, Alex enlists the aid of her girl friends, and with this combination of feminine wiles arrayed against him, Sam has no chance. The antics of the girls in making Sam jealous and in making Alex the belle of the ball provide many amusing episodes in this comedy.
     6 men, 7 women; 2 interiors. Royalty: $25-20.

_____. Tomorrow and Tomorrow (1931). Samuel French.
     To a college town in the mid-West comes to lecture Dr. Nicholas Hay, distinguished and attractive psychologist. He falls in love with Eve Redman, who has had no child by her staid reliable husband. After Hay has left, she bears a boy, who some years later meets with an accident. She sends for Dr. Hay, who cures their son; but she will not go away with him, realizing what "tomorrow and tomorrow" would mean to her devoted husband. So she stays rather than hurt him, accepting responsibility and becoming a spiritually complete woman.
     3 acts; 5 men, 6 women; 1 interior. Royalty: $50.

_____. Without Love (1942). Samuel French.

Two people who have forsworn love rediscover it after they
have been married, in this deft and entertaining comedy. Jamie
Rowan is a rich young widow who has decided never to love again
because of the idealistic memory she holds of her deceased husband.
Patrick Jamieson, an Irish diplomat, shares Jamie's distaste for
love because the girl he loved suddenly married someone else.   When
Patrick appears at Jamie's party to return one of her intoxicated
guests, Jamie is intrigued by him. He insults her guests and then
starts in on Jamie, and no one is supposed to insult wealthy, attractive widows. They soon decide to marry, but with the agreement that each is free to live his own life. Although they both resist it as much as possible, love finds its way. After much feigned
indifference, they surrender to their feelings.
          7 men, 4 women; 1 interior. Royalty: $50-25.

_____. You and I (1923). Samuel French.
          An artist father had to forego his desire for painting because
the heel of expediency rested on the neck of inclination; his son is
in a like situation in regard to architecture; both had to go into
business. The father paints a picture which his wife arranges shall
be sold at auction. Four thousand dollars is bid, but to his chagrin
he discovers that his old boss has bought it for advertising purposes.
He recognizes his own limitations, and sacrifices his pride for
parental duty.
          4 men, 3 women; 2 interiors. Royalty: $25-20.

_____. The Youngest (1924). Samuel French.
          Downtrodden youngest son Richard is inspired by Nancy, a
charming busybody, to revolt against his family's selfishness. The
revolt almost fails, but he learns he has a right to the family fortune. He asserts himself and turns on his oppressors in a comic
way.
          4 men, 5 women; 1 interior, 1 exterior. Royalty: $25-20.

BATSON, George. Design for Murder (1960). Samuel French.
          The murder of her maid forces Celia Granger to face some
unpleasant realities in this mystery drama. Safely ensconsed in a
magnificent old mansion, Celia and her son David are far from the
troubles of everyday life. Then the maid is murdered and David
becomes a suspect. The climax finds Celia alone and the murderer
ready to strike again.
          4 men, 6 women; 1 interior. Royalty: $25-20.

_____. The House on the Cliff (1957). Adapted from the tele-
          vision play by George Batson and Donn Harmon. Samuel
          French.
          The house on the cliff is rumored to have been the last stop
on the Civil War Underground Railroad. Years ago an excursion
boat had been lost on the lake below the cliff, and there are stories
that the lake has since been haunted. In the house reside Ellen
Clayton, an heiress confined to a wheelchair; her stepmother, Karen;
an austere housekeeper, Jenny; and two guests: Nurse Pepper and a
substitute doctor, Corey Phillips, who sees no reason why Ellen

should not walk again. To begin the action there is a violent murder.
    2 men, 4 women; 1 interior. Royalty: $25-20.

BAUM, Vicki. Grand Hotel (Menschen im Hotel, 1927). Tr. by
    Creighton, Lond., Bles, 1930; Doubleday, 1931; CEW; abridged
    in Mantle 1930/31.
    Depicts the episodic events during one day in the lives of
several guests in such a hotel. An aging dancer, Grusinskaia,
finds new life in her love for Baron von Gaigern; she leaves not
knowing he has been killed. A stenographer, Flaemmchen, escapes
from Preysing, a manufacturer, and goes with Kringslein, a clerk,
who has heart trouble but is ready to spend his savings and enjoy
life while he may.
    18 scenes; 16 men, 5 women; 1 interior.

BEAUMARCHAIS. The Barber of Seville (1775). Tr. by Myrick,
    Dent, & Dutton, 1905; MAU; tr. by Taylor, Baker, 1922; CLF-2;
    tr. by Robb, French, 1939.
    The cunning scamp, Figaro the barber, a man of the people,
helps to thwart the plans of Bartolo to marry his ward, Rosine, for
she prefers Count Almavira. With Figaro's connivance the Count
comes to the house, first as a soldier, then as a music teacher, to
see Rosine. Bartolo is tricked into signing a marriage contract
which he thinks is his own, but turns out to be her marriage to Almavira. His rage is allayed by the Count's dowry.
    4 acts; 8 men, 2 women, extras; 1 interior, 1 exterior;
    costumes of the period.

_____. The Marriage of Figaro (1784). Tr. by T. Holcroft,
    Lond., 1785; tr. as "Follies of a Day" in Oxberry, v. 13; also
    in London Stage, v. 2, 1824.
    Sequel to The Barber of Seville. Figaro wishes to marry
Suzanne, both servants of Count and Countess Almavira. When the
Count demands as reward that Suzanne become his mistress, they
plan to deceive him by dressing Cherubin, a fellow servant, as Suzanne, but the Countess keeps the rendezvous. The Count then
wishes Figaro to marry Marceline, but she turns out to be his
mother. After a series of incidents of mistaken identity, Figaro
and Suzanne are married and the Count and Countess are reconciled.
    5 acts; 7 men, 3 women; interior and exterior scenes; costumes of the period.

BEAUMONT, Francis and John Fletcher. A King and No King (1611).
    In their Works, various editions; in Mermaid ser., Scribner,
    1887, v. 2; in Belles Lettres ser., Heath, 1910.
    Arbaces, King of Iberia, has not seen his sister Panthea for
years and now requires that Tigranes, conquered King of Armenia,
marry her. But when the three meet, an apparently incestuous passion for her is aroused in Arbaces, while Tigranes is in love with
an Armenian damsel, Spaconia. Gobrias, the ruling protector while
Arbaces has been at the wars, now reveals that Arbaces is really
his son, adopted by the former Queen; Panthea was born to her six

years later and is the rightful ruler of Iberia.   Now, no longer king
nor brother, Arbaces and Panthea are married and so are Tigranes
and Spaconia.
            5 acts; 13 men, 3 women, extras; 5 interiors, 4 exteriors;
         costumes of the Orient.

_____. The Knight of the Burning Pestle (1607).   In various edi-
     tions of their Works; BAS; BAT; HOW; NEI; OLH; OLI v. 2;
     SCI; SPE; WHE.
         A burlesque parody of some plays of the period, ridiculing
the taste of the citizens.   A grocer and his wife, in the audience,
insist on a play about a London merchant, instead of the romantic
play already prepared; they also nominate their apprentice to play
the lead.   He, as Grocer Errant, undertakes adventurous errands,
with a burning pestle as his shield.
            5 acts; 19 men, 4 women, extras; many indoor and outdoor
         scenes; costumes of the period.

_____. The Maid's Tragedy (1609).   In various editions of their
     Works; BAS; CLF v. 1; CLS; DUN; NEI; OLH; OLI v. 2; RUB;
     SCI; SPE.
         The maid Aspatia is beloved by Amintor, a courtier; but he
is commanded by the King to marry Evadne, who has been the King's
mistress.   He is smitten by Evadne's charm, but she remains true
to the King until her brother Melantius compels her to kill the King,
which she does.   Meantime the rejected Aspatia, disguised as a boy,
claims to be brother to Aspatia and challenges Amintor to fight;
they fight and he mortally wounds her.   Evadne now returns and urges Amintor to accept her as his true wife; he refuses and she kills
herself.   The dying Aspatia reveals herself to Amintor, who now has
no wish to live and kills himself.
            5 acts; 9 men, 5 women, extras; 8 interiors, 1 exterior;
         costumes.

_____. Philaster; or, Love Lies Bleeding (1608), printed 1620.
     In all editions of their Works; BAS; HARC v. 47; HOW; HUD;
     LIE; MAT; NEI; OLH; OLI v. 2; PAR; SCH; SCI; SPE; TAU;
     THA; WHE.
         Prince Philaster, rightful heir to the throne of Sicily, loves
and is beloved by Princess Arethusa of Spain.   Euphrasia so worships Philaster that she disguises herself as a page Bellario to be
with him, but she is given by him to wait on Arethusa.   After much
court intrigue Philaster and Arethusa are married.   Later the King,
on false testimony, orders them put to death, but an uprising of the
people saves them.
            5 acts; 7 men, 6 women, extras; 6 interiors, 4 exteriors;
         medieval costumes.

BECKETT, Samuel. Endgame (1957).   Samuel French.
         Hamm is blind, paralyzed, and tyrannical.   He is served by
Clov, his lame slave, and his parents Nagg and Nell, who live in
garbage cans.   Hamm unsuccessfully tries to find meaning in life
while Nagg and Nell sentimentalize their memories and finally

disintegrate.
        3 men, 1 woman; bare stage. Royalty: $35-25.

_____. Happy Days (1961). Samuel French.
        There are only two characters and two acts in this Beckett
play, but there is an abundance of ideas and comments on life. In
the first act Winnie is buried to her waist, yet she still has access
to such personal paraphernalia as a toothbrush, mirror and pistol.
In the second act she has sunk to her neck and has only her eyes
and mind to work with. With only these things Winnie still has
happy days.
        1 man, 1 woman; 1 interior. Royalty: $35-25.

_____. Krapp's Last Tape (1958). Samuel French.
        A vivid contrast between the vitality of a man's youth and
the shabby decay of his old age is shown in this comedy. The playwright affectionately portrays an aging man living out his life in a
lonely room. At the end of the year he takes a bottle of wine and
a banana and turns on his tape recorder. The voice is his, from
his more youthful days, and it recounts the hopes and glories of
those times.
        1 man. Royalty: $20-15.

_____. Waiting for Godot (1953). Dramatists Play Service.
        Not so much a story as a comment on man's endurance in
the face of little hope for the future. Two bums pass the time
waiting for Godot, who will explain their insignificance or put an
end to it. They bicker in the meantime, and depend upon one another. They observe a brutal man exploiting his slave, and the
same man, now blind, being led by his slave--their relationship unchanged. Every day a child comes to put off Godot's arrival until
the next day.
        4 men, 1 boy; simple stylized exterior. Royalty: $50-25.

BECQUE, Henri. The Vultures (1882). Tr. by Tilden, Kennerley,
        1913, later Little; MOSQ; WATL; tr. by Papot as The Crows in
Drama, v. 2 #5, 1912; abridged in Pierce & Matthews, v. 2; TRE-
3; TREA-2.
        The wealthy M. Vigneron dies suddenly. His widow and her
three children are immediately beset by three of his quondam friends
who turn from fawning to plotting how to fleece the family and pluck
them bare. Her husband's unscrupulous associates are depicted with
bitter irony and superior realism, especially Teissier, whom one of
the daughters, Marie, is forced to marry in order to turn off the
other vultures.
        4 acts; 11 men, 6 women; 2 interiors.

BEHAN, Brendan. Borstal Boy (1970). Adapted by Frank McMahon.
        Samuel French.
        A series of scenes dramatized from Brendan Behan's auto-
biography. At age 16 Behan is caught in England with a suitcase
full of dynamite (he was going to blow up some English ships for
the IRA). He is sent to a reformatory where he endures many

hardships, and shipped back to Ireland where he shies away from revolutions forever after.

    19 men, 4 women, 20 extras; multiple setting. Royalty: $50-35.

_____. The Hostage (1958). Samuel French.

    In this comedy the author attempts only to entertain. Filled with a series of improbable episodes, the plot concerns an innocent British soldier who is captured and held as hostage in a bawdy Irish bar by the IRA. Although he is supposedly an enemy, the barmaid finds him attractive, and they have a romance going soon after he arrives. The British have captured an IRA youth and plan to execute him. If they carry out this intention the IRA has promised to kill the soldier. The barmaid hates the thought of losing her new love so soon after she's found him, so she tries to arrange his escape. But he's shot when he makes his attempt. Nothing is as it seems in this play, however. Right in the middle of his own requiem the soldier rises to sing a final rousing song.

    11 men, 7 women; composite interior, exterior. Royalty: $50-25.

_____. The Quare Fellow (1957). Samuel French.

    A grim indictment of capital punishment is given in this controversial drama. The scene is a jail where prisoners are awaiting the hanging of one of their fellows. One by one, through their bitter speeches they profane everything, revealing at the same time the failure of capital punishment.

    22 men; 1 interior, 1 exterior. Royalty: $35-25.

BEHRMAN, S. N. Amphitryon 38. See entry under Giraudoux, Jean.

_____. Biography (1932). Samuel French.

    Unconventional liberal Marian is asked to paint the portrait of her former lover, the stiff, cautious, ambitious statesman, Bunny Nolan, and also to write her autobiography for the radical magazine of which ardent Dick Kurt is editor. Nolan fears any disclosures in the biography, and she is finally persuaded to burn the manuscript. Kurt raves, but she refuses him; she is left to pursue her casual career, for she seems quite unsuited to marry him or anyone.

    5 men, 3 women; 1 interior. Royalty: $35-25.

_____. Brief Moment (1931). Farrar, 1932; abridged in Mantle 1931/32.

    After six months of marriage to Rodney, Abby is aping high society and chasing celebrities. She cares little for Cass but encourages him. Rodney tells her to go to Cass, but she realizes she loves Rodney and he agrees on a fresh start, as he really loves her.

    3 acts; 6 men, 3 women; 1 interior.

_____. But for Whom Charlie (1964). Samuel French.

    The owner of a foundation which gives grants to writers is a book-wormish man who leaves the direction of affairs to an opportun-

istic man, formerly his college roommate. The two pressing problems of the foundation are an application by the drunken son of a
former Nobel Prize winner (and his daughter, who will go to any
lengths to help her brother) and Lilith, formerly the Nobel winner's
mistress, who magnetizes all of the men she meets, especially the
owner, the director, and the drunken son.
     5 men, 5 women; composite interior. Royalty: $50-25.

_____. The Cold Wind and the Warm (1959). Samuel French.
     In this drama, a youth filled with idealistic visions finds
them destroyed one by one and soon looks for solace in death. The
boy's first jarring encounter with reality results from his devotion
to a self-centered neighborhood girl. After she spurns his devotion,
he finds the love he seeks from another girl, but soon realizes he
is not satisfied. One by one his visions evaporate, and in a dramatic scene, he decides that only in death can he find the fulfillment
he seeks. His exaggeration of his situation and the final maturing
which results from it provide many touching and often humorous
episodes.
     8 men, 4 women; unit composite set. Royalty: $50-25.

_____. End of Summer (1936). Dramatists Play Service.
     Three generations react to present-day conditions and timely
problems. Grandma sees the old order ended; Leonie, her daughter,
finds her wealth cannot bring happiness; Paula, the granddaughter,
an energetic young woman, tries to adjust herself to the economic
inequalities, even to marrying a penniless writer. Dr. Rice, the
brilliant psychiatrist, makes love to both Leonie and Paula, and the
end of the summer comes for him as he is put out of the house.
     7 men, 3 women; 1 interior. Royalty: $35-25.

_____. I Know My Love (1949). Samuel French.
     Thomas and Emily Chanler are celebrating their fiftieth wed-
ding anniversary in 1939, surrounded by their children and grandchildren. Flashbacks show them becoming engaged in 1888, and
then through various crises in their lives. Thomas, a penniless
writer, marries a rich girl, Emily, despite her father's opposition.
Tom sacrifices his craft of writing to become a business man, and
in time assumes control of the family's textile mills. He expects
his son to do the same. In 1920 he might have strayed, but his
loyal wife holds him by her loving understanding.
     3 acts; 11 men, 10 women; 1 interior. Royalty: $50-25.

_____. Jacobowsky and the Colonel. See entry under Werfel,
Franz.

_____. Jane (1952). Based on a story by W. Somerset Maugham.
Samuel French.
     Jane is an unimpressive widow who marries an architect
twenty years her junior. Her new husband transforms her into an
attractive woman and a celebrity. When Jane tires of the social
whirl, she gives her young husband his freedom and reforms a
brash newspaper tycoon into a companion willing to live in peaceful

tranquility.
        5 men, 4 women; 1 interior.   Royalty: $50-25.

_____. Lord Pengo (1962). Samuel French.
        A fluent and persuasive art dealer gulls many uncultured
American millionaires in this comedy, but also brings some of the
world's greatest art treasures to America.   As Lord Pengo repeat-
edly tells his potential customers, "No matter what you pay for a
priceless picture, you are getting it cheap." As the nouveaux-
riches of America flock to buy from his collection of Rembrants,
Van Dycks and Giorgiones, many betray their avaricious devotion to
acquisition and the shallowness of their love for great art.   Like the
millionaire's passion for wealth, however, Pengo has made art his
principal passion; and his family relations suffer from his neglect.
        7 men, 4 women; 2 interiors.   Royalty: $50-25.

_____. No Time for Comedy (1939). Samuel French.
        Gaylord Easterbrook is a writer of comedy of manners plays
which his wife, Linda, stars in.   But he is dissatisfied with his
life, especially since he is Jewish and World War II seems hardly
the time to write such pleasant comedies.   He comes under the influence of Amanda Smith, wife of a dull businessman and dabbler in
the lives of artists, who encourages him to write serious tragedy.
He does--a terrible play about death and the Spanish Loyalists.
Linda plays it cool, and Amanda gives up when she discovers that
Gay will not elope with her.
        4 men, 3 women; 2 interiors.   Royalty: $35-25.

_____. Rain from Heaven (1934). Samuel French.
        At a houseparty the English hostess serves as mediator
among five diverse guests, a German-Jewish music critic, a Russian
pianist, a Russian scholar, an American millionaire, and his younger
brother, an aviator.   They express their opinions on many social and
political evils, such as Nazi inquisition and race prejudice, with
recommended cures.
        3 acts; 6 men, 4 women; 1 interior.   Royalty: $35-25.

_____. The Second Man (1927). Samuel French.
        Novelist Storey Clark has a dual character: one is irrespon-
sible, loving life and luxury; the other is calm, and observant, with
witty counsels of common sense.   The rich widow Mrs. Frayne wins
him, over the young girl Monica, because she is aware of both sides
of his nature.
        3 acts; 2 men, 2 women; 1 interior.   Royalty: $50-25.

BEIN, Albert. The Heavenly Express (1940). Samuel French.
        A Santa Fe train, lowered by the Almighty Vagabond, is
slated one wintry night to pick up all tramps for a trip to their hobo
paradise.   Highly imaginative, with rollicking ballads.
        3 acts; 17 men, 1 woman; 1 interior, 1 exterior.   Royalty:
        $25-20.

BELASCO, David and J. L. Long. The Darling of the Gods (1902).

In his Six Plays, Little, Brown, 1928; abridged in Mantle & Sherwood 1899-1909.

Lovely Yo-San conceals the outlaw Kara, but the merciless war minister, Zakkuri, has means of torment and tricks her into revealing the hiding place of Kara's followers.   Patriotism, heroism, and love are the fundamental themes.

5 acts; 35 men, 11 women, many extras; 3 interiors, 6 exteriors; Japanese costumes.

_____. The Girl of the Golden West (1905).   Samuel French, 1933; in his Six Plays, Little, Brown, 1928; MOSJ; MOSL.

Courageous, passionate heroine runs the Polka saloon and gambling parlor in the Western frontier.   She is loved by all, but especially by Jack Rance, the sheriff.   But she has met her man, Dick Johnson, a road-agent, who, pursued by the sheriff, and wounded, seeks shelter and is concealed in her loft.   She and the sheriff play a game of poker for her or her lover, till a drop of blood from the loft reveals the wounded man.   Touched by her great love, the miners let her and Johnson go to start a new life.   Made into an opera by Puccini in 1910.

4 acts; 21 men, 2 women; 3 interiors, 1 exterior; Western costumes.   (S. French Royalty: $25-20.)

_____. The Heart of Maryland (1895).   In his Heart of Maryland & other plays, Princeton Univ. pr., 1941 (Amer. Lost Plays, v. 18).

Laid in the old Calvert home in Maryland during the American Civil war, the heroine keeps the big bell silent by clinging to its iron tongue so that her sweetheart, a Northern prisoner, may escape from the Confederate sentries.

4 acts; 22 men, 1 boy, 4 women, extras; 3 interiors, 2 exteriors; costumes of 1860 and military.

_____. The Return of Peter Grimm (1911).   In his Six Plays, Little, Brown, 1928; French, 1933; BAK; MIL; MOSS-3; abridged in Pierce & Matthews v. 1.

Grandfather Peter returns after death to visit his beloved grandson.   He is the means of uniting lovers and of saving the family property from a scheming nephew.

3 acts; 8 men, 3 women, 2 extras (men offstage); 1 interior.

_____ and R. W. Tully. The Rose of the Rancho (1906).   French, 1936.

Lovely Juanita Castro, the rose of the rancho, attracts government agent Kearney when the United States takes over California from Mexico and the land claims are being adjusted.   The Castros, along with other native landowners, refuse to register.   Kearney tells Juanita that land jumpers will take her home.   She deceives her family and her lover, Don Luis, when she gives Kearney the papers for proper registration.   When the land jumpers appear and she sees Kearney with them, she is angry, but agrees to wait. After a night of trouble, troops from Monterey arrive, the rancho is given to its rightful owners, and the Rose finds happiness

with her Gringo.
>   3 acts; 22 men, 9 women, extras; 1 interior, 2 exteriors;
>   American & Mexican costumes of 1850.

BENAVENTE y MARTÍNEZ, Jacinto.   The Bonds of Interest (1907).
>   Tr. by Underhill in Drama, v. 5, 1915; in his Plays, ser. 1,
>   Scribner, 1917; DID; MOSQ.
>   A deft and facile satire on the duality of human nature, con-
> trasting the good and the bad, the generous and the sordid, when a
> penniless adventurer, Leandro, is imposed on elegant society by
> Crispin, who pretends to be his swaggering impudent servant.
> Crispin plans to marry him to an heiress, but Leandro falls in love
> with the fair Silvia--a happy union brought about by the material
> bonds of interest.
>   Prolog & 3 acts; 13 men, 6 women; 1 interior, 2 exteriors;
>   costumes of 17th century.

_____.   The Governor's Wife (1901).   Tr. by Underhill in Poet
>   Lore, v. 29, 1918; in his Plays, ser. 2, Scribner, 1919.
>   Josefina is a great influence and gets her husband, Gover-
> nor Don Santiago, to first forbid and then allow a theatrical produc-
> tion.   Shows how personalities underlie many actions.
>   3 acts; 18 men, 10 women, extras; 2 interiors, 1 exterior.

_____.   The Passion Flower (1908).   Tr. by Underhill in his
>   Plays, ser. 1, Scribner, 1917; TUCG; TUCM; WATL-3.
>   A young girl, Acacia, thinks she hates her step-father, the
> well-to-do farmer Estaban, who however has conceived a passion
> for his step-daughter.   He causes his servant to kill her betrothed,
> Faustino, and later, when her hate has changed to love, they arrange
> to elope.   Her mother (his wife), Raimunda, blocks their path and
> provokes Estaban to shoot her, believing that Acacia would never
> care to marry the man who had killed her mother.
>   3 acts; 7 men, 8 women; 2 interiors.

BENELLI, Sem.   The Jest (1909).   Tr. & adapted by E. Sheldon,
>   French, 1939; abridged in Mantle 1919/20.
>   The mild-mannered artist Giannetto is in love with Ginevra,
> the beautiful daughter of a fish monger.   He is rather the butt for
> cruel jests by his brothers Neri and Gabriello, so that, once es-
> caping death, he plans a cunning revenge: he causes Neri to enter
> Ginevra's house with intent to kill Gianetto, but he slays his brother
> Gabriello by mistake.   Then the madness attributed to Neri in jest
> becomes madness in reality.
>   4 acts; 13 men, 5 women, extras; 3 interiors; costumes of
>   the period.

BENET, Stephen Vincent.   "The Devil and Daniel Webster."   See
>   Archibald MacLeisch's Scratch.

BENNETT, Alan and Peter Cook, Jonathan Miller, and Dudley Moore.
>   Beyond the Fringe (Revue) (1963).   Samuel French.
>   A series of funny sketches.   One deals with a preacher who

gets carried away and strays so far from his text that he can't find
his way back.   Another is a spoof on Shakespeare.   Other scenes
find experts on nuclear war talking the subject to death; and two
philosophers arguing the importance of their profession to the real
world but using jargon that nobody can understand.
    Flexible cast; various sets.   Royalty: $50-25

BENNETT, E. Arnold.   The Great Adventure (1913).   Lond.,
    Methuen, 1913; Doran, 1913 & revised, 1927; carried by Baker;
    COT.
    Ilam Carve, famous artist, allows himself to be thought dead,
while his valet is buried with honors as himself at Westminster Ab-
bey.   Unfortunately an art expert recognizes him and it may all be
disclosed, but Lord Alcar remedies the situation.
    4 acts; 15 men, 3 women; 4 interiors.

_____. The Honeymoon (1911).   Lond., Methuen, 1911; Doran,
    1912.
    An aviator feels the urge of his flying when he hears what
his competitor has done; but his bride claims an equal right to
charm as he to work.   Shall business intrude on a honeymoon?
    3 acts; 7 men, 2 women; 2 interiors, 1 exterior.

_____ and Edward Knoblock.   Milestones (1912).   Lond., Methuen,
    & Doran, 1912; CEU; COD; DID; MAP; MOD; PEN; TUCJ.
    Illustrates the march of ideas from one generation to another,
especially how the point of view grows more conservative as one
grows older.
    3 acts; 9 men, 6 women; 1 interior, but with changes of
    furniture; costumes change from 1860 to 1885 to 1912.

_____. What the Public Wants (1909).   Lond., F. Palmer, 1910;
    Doran 1911.
    Sir Charles Morgan has made a success of publishing through
papers which appeal to every sort, giving them what the public wants.
Then he takes over a theatre, organizing it on a business basis and
giving them Shakespeare.   He asks the actress Emily to marry him,
more as a business proposition, but she feels she can't because of
their different points of view.
    4 acts; 10 men, 6 women; 2 interiors.

BENRIMO, J. H.   The Yellow Jacket.   See entry under Hazelton,
    George C.

BENSON, Sally.   Meet Me in St. Louis.   See entry under Sergel,
    Christopher.

BENTHAM, Josephine, with Herschel Williams.   Janie (1942).
    Samuel French.
    The Colburn household is crowded with overnight guests, in-
cluding Dick, Janie's boyfriend, and his mother, a Southern widow
who is not about to let go of her son.   When Janie, Dick and their
friends have a party that gets out of hand while the old folks are

having dinner at the country club, everything becomes complicated, partly as a result of Janie's seven year-old sister, who has an inventive mind and makes herself a terrible pain in the elbow.
13 men, 8 women; 1 interior.   Royalty: $35-25.

BENTLEY, Eric, with Maja Bentley.   The Caucasian Chalk Circle.
See entry under Brecht, Bertolt.

_____.   The Good Woman of Setzuan.   See entry under Brecht,
Bertolt.

_____.   Mother Courage and Her Children.   See entry under
Brecht, Bertolt.

_____.   The Private Life of the Master Race.   See entry under
Brecht, Bertolt.

_____.   La Ronde.   See entry under Schnitzler, Arthur.

BERG, Gertrude.   Dear Me, the Sky Is Falling.   See entry under
Spigelgass, Leonard.

_____.   Me and Molly (1948).   Dramatists Play Service.
Depicts the trials and tribulations of a hardworking, honest, loyal, Jewish family in the Bronx.   Jake asks Simon to be a partner in the dress-making business, but when Molly goes in for regularly-made half-sizes, Jake starts a successful business for himself. Uncle David provides a piano for Rosie, while Mollie and Jake plot a romance between her piano-teacher and Mr. Mendel.
3 acts; 12 men, 9 women; 1 interior.   Royalty: $35-25.

BERGER, Henning.   The Deluge (1908).   Tr. & adapted by Allen.
Samuel French.
Seven men and a girl are trapped in a basement when the river overflows.   Facing death, their natures change: a cheating broker will form a chain of brotherhood; a shyster lawyer preaches the claims of the soul; a self-seeking broker admits he married for money, telling the girl of the streets that she was the only girl he ever loved.   A half-hour after their release, they all revert to type and become as they were before: selfish, tricky, and human.
3 acts; 9 men, 1 woman; 1 interior.   Royalty: $25-20.

BERGSTRÖM, Hjalmar.   Karen Borneman (1907).   Tr. by Björkman
in his Two Plays, Kennerley, 1914.
A creature of passion, Karen has had two relations outside marriage; one a novelist who died; the other a sculptor in Paris. Back in Copenhagen she truly loves a doctor, but he withdraws when the sculptor appears.   Her father is shocked and embittered, but she claims that the contemporary emancipated woman can have affairs if she wants to; she is a modern adult and emotionally honest.
4 acts; 4 men, 6 women; 3 interiors.

_____.   Lynggaard & Co. (1905).   Tr. by Björkman in his Two

Plays, Kennerley, 1914.
Studies the social problem of labor and capital and presents, without indicating a preference, the viewpoints of the impractical socialist, the improvident philanthropist, the idle dilettante, and the scheming efficient manager.
4 acts; 6 men, 3 women; 1 interior.

BERLIN, Irving. Annie Get Your Gun. See entry under Fields, Dorothy.

BERNARD, Jean-Jacques. Invitation to a Voyage (1924). Tr. by Frith in his Five Plays, Lond., Cape, 1939; tr. by Boyd as Invitation to Travel, in DIK-2; tr. by Katzin as Glamour in KAT.
Marie Louise, wife of Oliver Mailly, a country-bred heroine, endows her husband's friend, Philippe, with glamor as he sails for the Argentine on business, and morbidly dreams she is in love with him. When he returns, she realizes how very business-like and prosaic he really is; she is brought down to earth and back to her husband.
3 acts; 3 men, 2 women, 1 boy; 1 interior.

_____. Martine (1922). Tr. by Katzin in Eight European Plays, Brentano, 1927; tr. by Frith, Baker, 1932; also in his Five Plays, Lond., Cape, 1939.
Martine is a peasant girl who romances about a city charmer, Julien. Though married to Alfred, her heart still throbs for the youth, casually met years before. Julien had abandoned her when his cultured fiancée, Jeanne appeared, leaving the country lass to her shattered dream.
5 scenes; 2 men, 3 women; 2 interiors, 1 exterior.

BERNEY, William. Dark of the Moon. See entry under Richardson, Howard.

BERNSTEIN, Elsa Porges. Twilight (1894). Tr. by Grummann in Poet Lore, v. 23, 1912; separately, Badger, 1912.
Delicate demure love of a highly educated woman, Sabine, an eye doctor, for a happy old man, Henry Ritter. The raging jealousy of his daughter, Isolde, who is going blind, requires their sacrifice--he to care for his daughter in her total blindness and she to lose Carl who was too young to marry her. She goes on to Berlin to study.
5 acts; 2 men, 4 women, 1 child; 1 interior.

BERNSTEIN, Henry. The Thief (1906). Tr. by Haughton, Doubleday, 1915; taken over by French; abridged in Pierce & Matthews, v. 2.
Because he has fallen in love with the wife of a guest, the son of the host in a chateau takes on himself the blame for the theft of certain funds which she has taken. When the husband discovers the truth, he forgives his wife; the son is sent away to recover from his infatuation. Cleverly throws the audience and reader off the track of the thief in Act I, thus increasing the surprise in Act II,

which is rather unique in utilizing only two characters.
　　3 acts; 5 men, 2 women; 3 interiors (can be played with only
　　2 interiors).

BERRIGAN, Daniel, with Saul Levitt.　The Trial of the Catonsville
　　Nine (1971).　Samuel French.
　　　　An edited and condensed transcript of the Berrigan brothers
and their seven confederates trial, where they were convicted of illegally removing and burning Selective Service System records in
protest against the Viet Nam War.　Though the verdict is well known,
the play is nevertheless compelling.
　　9 men, 2 women; courtroom setting.　Royalty: $50-35.

BESIER, Rudolf.　The Barretts of Wimpole Street (1930).　Drama-
　　tists Play Service.
　　　　A sentimentally moving recital of the romance of Elizabeth
Barrett and Robert Browning--the immortal lovers.　The invalid
Elizabeth is virtually a prisoner to her father, whose affection is
tyrannical.　Life for her is brightened by the liveliness of her sisters and brothers.　Her interest in poetry leads to correspondence
with Robert Browning, who at last comes to call on her and courts
her against her father's wish.　Forced to elope, they flee to Italy.
　　3 acts; 12 men, 5 women (plus Flush, the dog); 1 interior;
　　costumes of the period.　Royalty: $50-25.

BETTI, Ugo.　Corruption in the Palace of Justice (1949).　Samuel
　　French.
　　　　When one man gains justice someone else loses it in this
melodrama about the universal corruption of man's mind and spirit.
The suicide of a corruptor and a rumored bribery bring an investigation to discover which of the judges in the Palace of Justice is
dishonest.　As the investigation progresses, however, all are shown
to be stained by some venality, illustrating that the reason of all
men is corrupt.
　　9 men, 2 women; 1 interior.　Royalty: $35-25.

BEVAN, Donald and Edmund Trzcinski.　Stalag 17 (1951).　Dramatists
　　Play Service.
　　　　Some captured American airmen in a Nazi prison camp discuss with irrepressible humor the many subjects which interest them.
Since escape plots are revealed, they are sure that a German spy is
among them.　Which one is it?　They finally unmask the right one.
　　3 acts; 21 men, 0 women; 1 interior.　Royalty: $50-25.

BIBLE.　The Book of Job (ca 400 B.C.).　Tr. in King James ver-
　　sion in SML; tr. in American Revised version & adapted by
　　Kallen in TRE-1, -2 (v. 2).
　　　　Satan gets permission from God to try the faith of Job.　He
causes him to suffer pain and the loss of family and goods.　Job is
told by his comforting friends that he is being punished for sins committed.　Job does not think so, though he has racking doubts as to
the nature of divine justice.　His patience is rewarded by the Voice
of God cutting the tangled knot of human passion and doubt.　After

this test, Job's family and goods are restored to him.
Prolog, & 1 continuous act; 7 men, 0 women, chorus of
men; prolog in Heaven, 1 exterior; oriental costumes.

BIDDLE, Cordelia Drexel. My Philadelphia Father. See Kyle
Crichton's The Happiest Millionaire.

BIRD, Robert M. The Broker of Bogota (1834). QUIK; QUIL.
A merchant of the middle-class, true to the standards and
pride of his own caste, resents the oppression of the ruling noblemen in South America, though his daughter is to be the wife of one
of them.
5 acts; 9 men, 2 women, extras; 3 interiors, 3 exteriors;
costumes of the country and period.

_____. The Gladiator (1831). In Clement Foust's Life of Bird,
N.Y., 1919; HAL.
Spartacus leads the Roman gladiators in an insurrection after
he had been forced to fight his brother in the arena. Well represents the eternal struggle for freedom against tyranny, the rebellion
against a state of slavery.
5 acts; 12 men, 1 boy, 2 women, extras; 3 interiors, 7 exteriors; costumes of the period.

BIRO, Lajos. School for Slavery (1942). Tr. & ed. by Paxton in
his Plays, Lond., Faber, 1942.
A striking indictment of the German invasion of Poland,
1939-40, as the governor demonstrates the ruthlessness of the con-
querors. He takes over the house of the Pole, Dr. Jablonsky, and
forces him to take charge of the electric laboratory with another
Pole, Pawlik, and a wounded German, Richard, as his assistants.
He lets Richard keep Anna Jablonsky as his servant, and they fall
in love. Other Poles escape to an island in a marsh. Jablonsky
arranges to get the governor into his underground laboratory and
there practically tortures him till a fire and an explosion kill them
both.
4 acts; 9 men, 4 women, extras; 2 interiors, 1 exterior;
some German military costumes.

BJÖRNSON, Björnstjerne. The Bankrupt (1874). Tr. by Sharp in
his Three Dramas, Dutton (Everyman's), 1914.
A business man, Tjaelda has practiced dishonest dealings
in his commercial life where "white lies" are common. Through
his business failure he is regenerated and converted to integrity and
to the belief that the moral values must be the standards of action.
4 acts; 15 men, 3 women; 2 interiors, 1 exterior.

_____. Beyond Our Power (1883). Tr. by Björkman in his
Plays, Scribner, 1913; TUCG; abridged in Pierce & Matthews,
v. 2; tr. as Beyond Human Power by Hollander in DIC; tr. as
Pastor Sang by Wilson, Lond., Longmans, 1893.
Pastor Sang, who has been able to work miracles through
prayer in such as believe, fails when he wills to do more than he

can perform; he is a man, not a superman. A careful study of the
various degrees of faith and doubt, and their effect on the will.
2 acts; 10 men, 4 women; 2 interiors.

_____. A Gauntlet (1883). Tr. by Braekstad, Lond., 1890; tr.
by Edwards, Longmans, 1894; BAT v. 17; tr. as A Glove by
Sogard in Poet Lore v. 3, 1892; tr. by Björkman in his Plays,
Scribner, 1913; tr. by Sharp in his Three Dramas, Dutton, 1913
        Svava Riis throws her glove into Alfred's face when she
learns of his unchastity. She claims a woman has a right to demand
of her fiance the same purity that he demands of her; there should
be no different standards of morality.
        3 acts; 5 men, 4 women, extras (6 young girls); 1 interior.

_____. The Newly-Married Couple (1865). Tr. by Sharp in his
Three Dramas, Dutton (Everyman's), 1914.
        In this "lesson in marriage" a worthy young husband, Axel,
to preserve his self respect, takes his bride, Laura, to his own
house instead of going to live with her jealous protective parents.
Her parents are angry at first, and the young couple are estranged;
but later they are happily reconciled.
        2 acts; 2 men, 3 women; 2 interiors (1 is possible).

_____. When the New Wine Blooms (1909). Tr. by Hollander in
Poet Lore, v. 22, 1911.
        Mrs. Arvik, in rather neglecting her husband, sets an example
to her daughters of lack of respect for their father. When he turns
for comfort to a young girl and is supposed to have eloped with her,
his wife learns a lesson of regard for him.
        3 acts; 4 men, 8 women; 1 exterior (a veranda).

BLACK, Kitty. The Rehearsal. See entry under Anouilh, Jean.

BLOCH, Bertram. Dark Victory. See entry under Brewer,
        George E.

BOKER, George H. Francesca da Rimini (1855). In his Plays &
        Poems, Bost., 1856; in McDowell, T. ed. The Romantic Tri-
        umph, 1830-60, N.Y., 1933; HAL; MOSS-3; QUIK; QUIL.
        A sympathetic interpretation of Francesca, a woman much
alive and with great capacity for love, unintentionally deceived in
thinking Paolo, the younger brother, was her intended husband.
With a lofty conception of Lanciotto, a great soul imprisoned in a
misshapen body, depicts the pathos of the deformed husband. In
this play, Pepé, the jester, brings about the catastrophe.
        5 acts; 7 men, 2 women; 5 interiors, 4 exteriors; costumes
        of 13th century Italy.

BOLOGNA, Joseph. Lovers and Other Strangers. See entry under
        Taylor, Renee.

BOLT, Robert. Flowering Cherry (1958). Samuel French.
        Cherry is an insignificant insurance clerk who, through his

many misfortunes, is sustained by the dream that someday he will
return to the land and plant an apple orchard. Now he has lost his
job, is drinking, and resorts to stealing money from his wife's
purse. At this point his family recognizes him as a complete
failure. To salvage some respect, he attempts to bend an iron bar
in a show of determination. The attempt causes a heart attack,
from which he dies.

   4 men, 3 women; 1 interior. Royalty: $25-20.

_____. A Man for All Seasons (1960). Samuel French.
   This widely acclaimed tragedy portrays the conflict faced by
Sir Thomas More when his friend, Henry VIII, wants to declare
himself spiritual as well as secular master of England so he can
marry Anne Boleyn. Henry is already married to Catherine of Aragon, and the Pope refuses to grant him a divorce. To by-pass this
hindrance, the king contrives his Act of Supremacy which would give
him authority to grant divorces. More, the Lord Chancellor, cannot
agree to Henry's usurpation of spiritual authority and quietly follows
his own conscience. Faced with Sir Thomas' lack of support, Henry
accuses him of treason, but this still fails to make Sir Thomas compromise his convictions. This leads ultimately to his assassination,
but his life remains a monument to a man unswervingly devoted to
his integrity.

   11 men, 3 women; Unit set. Royalty: $50-25.

_____. Vivat! Vivat Regina! (1971). Samuel French.
   A modern version of the historical conflict between Mary
Stuart and Queen Elizabeth for the British throne. The play covers
the period from Mary's marriage to the French Dauphin to the edict
calling for her execution, and the death scene itself.

   27 men, 2 women, extras; area staging. Royalty: $50-35.

BOLTON, Guy. Adam and Eva (with George Middleton) (1919).
Samuel French.
   Unable to manage his extravagant selfish family, a wealthy
business man goes on a long trip and leaves his young manager,
Adam, in charge. Adam has his troubles, especially with Eva, the
young daughter; but by deluding them into thinking their father's
business is ruined, they pitch in to remedy the situation and meet
the emergency. It does them all good and brings out the best in
them.

   3 acts; 6 men, 4 women; 1 interior, 1 exterior. Royalty:
$25-20.

_____. Anastasia (1953). Adapted from the play by Marcelle
Maurette. Samuel French.
   An unscrupulous former Russian prince tries to use a forlorn,
amnesia stricken girl to gain control of the ten million pounds inheritance available to any surviving children of the Russian czar.
The former prince, Beunine, is now a Berlin taxi-driver, and while
working he met a girl who claimed to be Anastasia, the czar's
youngest daughter and the only survivor of the Red massacre. Without much effort Beunine persuades the confused girl to pursue her

inheritance and let him manage the recovery. Things proceed
smoothly until the final test. Anastasia must meet the Imperial
grandmother and have that lady declare that she actually is Anastasia. The two women meet and recognition slowly comes. With the
strength from a renewed assurance of identity and the love of a
grandmother, Anastasia disavows her shady associates and finds a
new life.
       8 men, 5 women; 1 interior. Royalty: $50-25.

_____. Chicken Feed (Wages for Wives) (1923). French, 1924;
    abridged in Mantle 1923/24.
       "Wages for wives"--should they have a proper share in the
family income instead of "chicken feed" doled out by the husband?
Organized by Nell Bailey, a group of women go on a strike to determine the rights of wives in the division of the family funds. A
debatable family problem, during which a husband learns his lesson.
       3 acts; 7 men, 4 women; 2 interiors (1 may be exterior).

_____. Nine Coaches Waiting (1966). Adapted from Mary
    Stewart's novel. Dramatic Publishing Company.
       In this mystery-thriller, Linda Martin takes on a job as
governess to Phillippe de Valmy, the young heir to a large estate.
Immediately she senses a tension between her charge and the older
relatives who control his affairs. At first she doesn't know whether
she must protect the boy or whether she is only imagining a danger
that does not exist. Even while she falls in love with Raoul de
Valmy she is not entirely sure she can trust him. Soon the threat
to Phillippe's life is extended to her own.
       5 men, 1 boy, 4 women; drapes. Royalty: $35.

_____. Wings of the Dove (1964). Adapted from Henry James'
    novel. Dramatic Publishing Company.
       Milly is an American girl in love with London and her new
English friends. She is totally unaware that she has a terminal
illness and almost unaware of her great wealth. However, Richard,
a handsome though poor young writer, and Kate, the girl who loves
him and would marry him if he had money, both are aware of Milly's situation. When Milly falls in love with Richard, it is decided
that he should marry Milly and, after her death has made him a
rich widower, later marry Kate. But as Richard begins to court
Milly the sudden happiness she feels begins to affect a cure.
Richard discovers, too, that he really does love the wealthy American. Before he can admit to her the whole truth, a well-meaning
friend reveals the plot to Milly.
       5 men, 6 women; 2 sets. Royalty: $35.

BOND, Nelson. Animal Farm (1964). A dramatic reading adapted
    from George Orwell's novel. Samuel French.
       For George Orwell, communism is an idealist's dream, con-
verted by realists into a nightmare. As the story opens the animals
are celebrating their emancipation from human owners. But the
celebration is short lived as they discover their new masters--the
pigs--are even more autocratic and ruthless.

5 men, 2 women; bare stage.   Royalty: $25-20.

BOOTHE, Clare (Mrs. H. R. Luce).   Kiss the Boys Good-Bye
    (1938).   Dramatists Play Service.
    Parodies the attempt to find a Scarlet O'Hara for the movie
Gone with the Wind.   A Southern belle, Cindy Lou, comes to a
houseparty in the North, hoping to get the role of Velvet in a movie,
based on a novel entitled "Kiss the boys good-bye."   Though a lamb
among Northern wolves, waking up, she lets loose her full innate
talent and tells them a few things.   Result: she may have what she
wants; and she is not slow in making her choice.
    3 acts; 10 men, 3 women; 3 interiors.   Royalty: $25.

_____.   Margin for Error (1939).   Dramatists Play Service.
    The Nazi German consul to the U.S. is killed--stabbed,
poisoned, or even shot--while guarded by the Jewish policeman
(Finkelstein).   Four suspects are in the room, any one of whom
might wish to kill him.   Though the Nazis admitted to margin for
error, the consul was certainly dead; the question was who did it.
    2 acts; 7 men, 2 women; 1 interior.   Royalty: $25.

_____.   The Women (1936).   Dramatists Play Service.
    A group of women play their respective roles in our modern
metropolitan world, entertainingly exposing some of the more common character weaknesses of the sex, especially the empty vicious
lives of the well-to-do idle rich.   The plot revolves around Mary
Haines, who divorces her husband so that he may marry beautiful
but shallow Crystal, a shop girl.   Two years later, when Mary
learns that Crystal is deceiving her ex-husband, Mary adopts Crystal's jungle technique and wins him back.
    35 women; 11 simple interiors.   Royalty: $25.

BORETZ, Allen.   Room Service.   See entry under Murray, John.

BOUCICAULT, Dion L.   London Assurance (1841).   Lond., Lacy,
    & N.Y., French, 186-; Dramatic Pub. Co., 1877; Yale Univ.
    Dramatic Assn., 1910; Baker, 1911; BAT; MAT; MOSO.
    Grace Harkaway is being forced by her father's will to marry
elderly Sir Harcourt Courtley or lose her inheritance.   His son, under an assumed name, goes to the country estate with Dazzle and
London assurance, outfaces his father, wins Grace, and all is forgiven.
    5 acts; 9 men, 3 women; 1 interior, 2 exteriors; costumes
of the period.

_____.   The Octoroon, or, Life in Louisiana (1859).   QUIK; QUIL.
    Zoe, the beautiful octoroon daughter of a plantation owner,
has been given her freedom by her father, but the villainous Jacob
McCloskey manages to buy her as a slave.   The taint of her blood
sacrifices her to be the property of one whom she hates.   The
nephew of her father and a benign overseer and an Indian save her
from the villain.
    5 acts; 14 men, 6 women, extras; 1 interior, 5 exteriors;
costumes of the time.

_____. Rip Van Winkle. See entry under Irving, Washington.

BOWEN, John. After the Rain (1967). Samuel French.
        The action of the play is based on the Bible: an ark, a flood,
and the sacrifice of the Godfigure. The time is 200 years after the
Rain of 1969. A young man and girl are introduced to the community on board the floating raft and learn the rituals of a religion begun
by the leader of the community, Arthur. Arthur believes he has
miraculous powers and thinks he is divine. He is later convinced,
however, that he is not God, only God's vicar, and must be sacrificed.
        9 men, 3 women; drop and wing set. Royalty: $50-25.

BOWSKILL, Derek. The Trojan War (1975). Adapted from Homer's
        The Iliad. Performance Publishing.
        This dramatization covers from the quarrel among the gods
on Mount Olympus to the wooden horse trick of Odysseus which
brings about the fall of Troy.
        3 men or more, 5 women or more; one representational set.
Royalty: $35.

BRACCO, Roberto. The Hidden Spring (1905). Tr. by St Cyr in
        Poet Lore, v. 18, 1907.
        The poet Sephen seeks inspiration and believes he finds it in
Meralda rather than in his wife Theresa. She stands as a sublime
figure before the vagaries of her husband who is finally made to
realize the large part she has played in his success as a poet.
        4 acts; 5 men, 2 women; 1 interior, 1 exterior.

_____. Phantasms (1906). Tr. by St Cyr in Poet Lore, v. 19,
        1908; TUCG.
        Professor Artunni made his wife Giulia promise that she
would not re-marry if he died, and particularly not to marry Lu-
ciano, his pupil. He was thus able to stifle the very existence of
the woman, for his masculine acquisitiveness held even after death.
She opens a home for widows and comes near to breaking her vow;
but she is haunted by her husband's presence and cannot be untrue
to it. She suffers inhibition which strangles her happiness.
        4 acts; 8 men, 9 women, extras; 2 interiors.

BRADFORD, Roark. "Ol' Man Adam an' His Chillun." See Marc
        Connelly's Green Pastures.

BRECHT, Bertolt. Brecht on Brecht (1962). Arranged and trans-
        lated by George Tabori. Samuel French.
        Readings and enactments from the works of Brecht. The
first half shows Brecht's philosophy on bookburning and ideology.
There is a piece of advice to actors, one on critics, and the ballad
of Marie Farrar. The second half consists of a song, a monologue,
and excerpts from the plays.
        4 men, 3 women (or any mixture from 2 to 8); bare stage.
Royalty: $50-25.

_____. The Caucasian Chalk Circle (1945). Translated by Eric and Maja Bentley.   Samuel French.

Although imbued with tragic elements, this play has essential-
ly a comic tone.   During a civil war the governor and his family
are scattered.   A woman named Grusha saves the governor's child
and flees with it to safety.   For her own protection and the child's
she marries a man whom she thinks will soon die.   He remains
quite alive, however, and when her fiance returns from the war he
is understandably shocked and angry.   Then the child's real mother
appears and wants him back.   A ludicrous self-appointed judge decides the case; and, in the only decision of his life, awards the
child to Grusha and her fiance.

39 men, 14 women, chorus, 4 children, extras; 6 interiors,
4 exteriors, 1 composite interior-exterior.   Royalty: $50-25.

_____. Galileo (1939).   Samuel French.

Deals with Galileo at the time of the emergence of the age
of reason from the middle ages.   When the play opens Galileo is
teaching his students that the earth moves around the sun and that
the moon and Jupiter only reflect the sun's light.   For these hereti-
cal statements Galileo is summoned to the Vatican, where he is imprisoned and where he recants, even though he continues his scientific writings surreptitiously.

27 men, 4 women, extras; cyclorama and platform set, 6
drops, set pieces.   Royalty: $50-25.

_____. The Good Woman of Setzuan (1940).   Translated by Eric
Bentley.   Samuel French.

The common human dilemma of kindness versus acquisitiveness is analyzed in this morality play.   Three gods searching in a
small village for one good woman find her in the prostitute Shen Te.
With her reward of 1,000 pieces of money Shen Te buys a tobacco
store and generously gives aid to the needy and parasitic alike.   Because of her generosity and kindness her business begins to fail.
Faced with this problem, Shen Te disguises herself as her cousin
and no longer offers free room and board.   Her business prospers,
but the authorities are suspicious about the disappearance of Shen
Te and arrest the "cousin" for kidnapping her.   At the trial the gods
appear and explain that while kindness pleases the gods, in the world
only the mercenary prosper.

18 men, 11 women, extras; 4 interiors, 3 exteriors.   Royalty: $50-25.

_____. Mother Courage and Her Children (1939).   Translated by
Eric Bentley.   Samuel French.

The idea that war, like love, is perpetual is explored in this
morality play.   Set in early seventeenth century Sweden, the plot
recounts the adventures of Mother Courage and her three children
as they follow the holy war through Poland, Finland, Bavaria, and
Italy.   Although not very bright, Mother Courage's oldest son is an
able soldier and greedy plunderer.   Her second son is honest, but
he soon dies, executed by a firing squad.   Accompanied by her third
child, a dumb daughter, Mother Courage follows the armies and her
plundering soldier son.   After a short-lived peace, the seemingly

neverending war resumes; and, in a final illustration of the futility of it all, the daughter, who has fallen in love and plans to get married, is shot instead.

    18 men, 5 women, extras; 1 interior, 5 exteriors. Royalty: $50-25.

_____ . The Private Life of the Master Race (1941). Translated by Eric Bentley. Samuel French.

    Through a myriad of characters and scenes this melodrama presents a vivid picture of Hitler's war machine. The worker who only mumbles his "Heil Hitlers" is marked for life by the Gestapo. The unjustly accused Jew receives justice from a judge, and the judge is tortured for his actions. A mother and father live in terror because they believe their son has informed on them. Two bakers meet in prison and learn that one was imprisoned for putting bran in the bread, while the other was jailed because he didn't. Through these and other episodes this play follows Hitler's armies across Europe, providing a bitter and incisive commentary on Nazism.

    Numerous characters and scenes. Royalty: $25-20.

BREIT, Harvey. The Disenchanted. See entry under Shulberg, Budd.

BREWER, George E., Jr., and Bertram Bloch. Dark Victory (1934). Dramatists Play Service.

    After performing a delicate brain operation on her, Dr. Steele asks Judith to marry him; but she thinks he does so from pity. Her return to her gay life doesn't satisfy her; she humbly goes to the doctor; they marry and achieve happiness. Some time later she feels the warning of a stroke that may carry her off in a few hours. She will not tell him, but sends him off joyously to perform another important operation. She has had her moment and won great happiness.

    3 acts; 7 men, 7 women, extras; 2 interiors. Royalty: $25.

BRIDGES, Ann P. Coquette. See entry under Abbott, George.

BRIDIE, James. The Anatomist (1930). Lond., Constable, 1931; in his Anatomist & Other Plays, R. R. Smith, 1931; French carried.

    Wed to the science of anatomy, Robert Knox wishes corpses for dissection; he uses them as furnishing till he discovers that they come not merely from body-snatching episodes but that murders are being committed to provide the corpses. His assistant, Anderson, is loyal to him till after the trial. The incidents are based on episodes in Scottish history.

    3 acts; 7 men, 5 women, extras; 3 interiors; costumes of 1828.

_____ . A Sleeping Clergyman (1933). Lond., Constable, 1934; Dodd, 1934; in his A Sleeping Clergyman & Other Plays; Constable, 1934 & 1942.

Two doctors talk shop in a Glasgow club and point out how unpredictable is heredity. They tell of Charles Cameron II, a famous physician, who was able to conquer a polio plague, for which he was knighted. Yet he was descended from a debauched medical student, whose daughter Wilhelmina also begat bastards. The doctors had the story of the three generations from the late Dr. Marshall.

2 acts; 13 men, 9 women; 8 interiors, 1 exterior.

_____. Susannah and the Elders (1937). In Susannah and the Elders and Other Plays, Constable, 1940.

Two elderly judges are inflamed by the beauty of Susannah, the wife of Joachim the Jew, and are jealous of young Dionysos the Greek, who also desires the fair lady. The elders invite her to enjoy their garden with its swimming pool while they are away on the king's business, but both return to spy on her. Daniel confutes their testimony and proves them liars.

10 scenes in 3 acts; 15 men, 4 women, extras; 3 interiors, 2 exteriors; 2 street scenes; Babylonian costumes.

_____. Tobias and the Angel (1930). Samuel French.

Tobias, son of Tobit, is sent by his father to get some money owed. Raphael, the archangel, accompanies him; he gets him to bring in fish, whose liver and gall later exorcises the demon Asmodeus and later restores his father's sight. Raphael also helps him to win Sara.

3 acts; 8 men, 8 women; 1 interior, 3 exteriors. Royalty: $25-20.

BRIEUX, Eugène. Blanchette (1892). Tr. by Eisemann in his Blanchette & The Escape, Luce, 1913.

Having qualified, Blanchette gets a certificate to teach in the schools of France but finds no opening. She helps her father, an innkeeper, and tries to get him to improve the place. She is driven away by her father, but returns and accepts marriage with Auguste, a peasant's son. The play is a criticism of social conditions which will not give young girls an opportunity of earning a living by teaching.

3 acts; 8 men, 4 women; 1 interior.

_____. Damaged Goods (Les Avariés, 1902). Tr. by Pollock in his Three Plays, Brentano, 1914; new tr. by Pollock, Lond., Cape, 1943.

Georges Dupont learns on the eve of his wedding that he has syphilis. He gets six months' treatment from a quack; then marries Henriette. His child inherits the affliction; his wife wants to divorce him, his father-in-law wants to shoot him. His physician intervenes and pleads for tolerance, holding out hope if the treatment is continued. A thesis play attacking society's secrecy about venereal diseases and pleading for compulsory premarital examination.

3 acts; 5 men, 6 women; 3 interiors.

_____. The Escape (1896). Tr. by Eisemann in his Blanchette
& The Escape, Luce, 1913.
Heredity is accepted as proved by Dr. Bertry. He proclaims
that Jean, his stepson, inherits melancholia and will kill himself because his father did, and that Lucienne, his brother's daughter, will
have loose morals because her mother was a courtesan; he therefore forbids their marriage. But Jean and Lucienne do marry; and
when the Doctor relaxes in his belief, they find their escape.
3 acts; 11 men, 5 women, extras; 2 interiors, 1 exterior.

_____. False Gods (1909). Tr. by Fagan, Brentano, 1916; TUGG.
Satni, a young priest in ancient Egypt, is convinced that the
gods of Egypt are false gods; he knows they are wood and stone.
But the High Priest appeals to his pity, because the people need
something to believe in; so he makes the stone figure of Isis bow
her head, though he knows he perpetuates a lie. Even his beloved
Yaouma is willing to sacrifice herself to the Nile.
5 acts; 13 men, 6 women, extras; 2 interiors, 1 exterior;
Egyptian costumes.

_____. The Red Robe (1900). Tr. by Reed in DIC; tr. by
Miall as The Letter of the Law in his The Woman on Her Own,
Lond., Jenkins, & Brentano, 1916; abridged in Pierce & Matthews, v. 2.
The lawyers Mouzon and Vagret falsely accuse an innocent
peasant, Etchepars, of murder so as to secure a conviction, thus
hoping to win popular approval and advance to the red robe of magistrate, since promotion is based on the number of convictions.
4 acts; 15 men, 6 women; 3 interiors.

_____. The Three Daughters of M. Dupont (1897). Tr. by Han-
kin in his Three Plays, Lond., Cape, & Brentano, 1911.
What shall a woman do? Attractive Julie claims for herself
an unhappy, loveless marriage is better than to remain unmarried,
than to seek the consolation of religion as Caroline did, or than to
live a life of license as Angèle does. Contains an amusing scene
marking the arrangements for the marriage settlement. A thesis
play demonstrating the evils of the French system of marriage.
4 acts; 6 men, 8 women; 2 interiors.

BRIGHOUSE, Harold. Hobson's Choice (1915). Samuel French.
A miserly father, who owns a bootshop, is so domineered by
his eldest daughter, Maggie, that he has no choice left save to place
his settlements on his daughters and retire. A diverting slice of
Lancastershire life.
3 acts; 7 men, 5 women; 2 interiors. Royalty: $25-20.

BRINNIN, John M. Dylan. See entry under Michaels, Sidney.

BROADHURST, George H. What Happened to Jones (1897). Samuel
French.
Jones is a traveling salesman, who sells hymnbooks when he
can and playing-cards when he can't. He escapes from a raided

prize fight to a professor's home, and disguises himself as a bishop
to put the police off the trail.   An escaped lunatic further compli-
cates matters.   A celebrated and successful farce.
    3 acts; 7 men, 6 women; 1 interior.   Royalty: $25-20.

BRONTË, Charlotte.   Jane Eyre (1938).   Dramatized from the novel
    (1847) by Mrs. Helen B. Jerome, Samuel French; by Marjorie
    Carleton, Baker's Plays; by Jane Kendall, Dramatic Publishing
    Company.
    Jane comes from a children's home as governess to Thorn-
field, Mr. Rochester's house.   He is unhappy because of an insane
wife.   He would like to marry Jane, but is prevented because of
his wife.   Jane leaves for a time.   Returning to Thornfield she finds
the lunatic wife has set fire to the house and perished in the flames.
Now Rochester is free to marry Jane.
    Jerome version: 10 men, 12 women; 2 interiors.   Royalty:
    $25-20.   Carleton version: 3 men, 5 women; 1 interior.
    Royalty: $15.   Kendall version: 4 men, 9 women; 1 interior.
    Royalty: $25.

BRONTË, Emily.   Wuthering Heights (1939).   Dramatized from the
    novel (1848) by Randolph Carter.   Samuel French.
    Catherine, a willful tempestuous girl is willed Wuthering
Heights, a bleak house on the moors.   Living with her besides the
servants is Heathcliff, a wild gypsy boy who has grown up with her
and loves her.   He leaves after a quarrel.   She marries Edgar Lin-
ton and goes to live there.   Heathcliffe returns and goes to live in
the closed Wuthering Heights.   He marries Edgar's sister, but more
to spite Catherine than because he loves Isabel.   After another violent quarrel Catherine dies.
    3 acts; 3 men, 3 women; 2 interiors; costumes of early 19th
    century.   Royalty: $25-20.

BROWNE, Porter E.   The Bad Man (1920).   French, 1926; abridged
    in Mantle 1920/21.
    Scene is laid on the Mexican border in the time of Villa
(died 1923), where the Mexican bandit turns the tables on a group
of Americans.   Satirically shows how the supposedly "bad man"
turns out better than some others.
    3 acts; 13 men, 2 women (or 12 men, 3 women; cook may
    be either sex); 1 interior; some Mexican costumes.

BROWNING, Robert.   A Blot in the 'Scutcheon (1843).   In various
    editions of his Poems and Plays; ASH; HARC; MOSO.
    The Earl of Mertoun wishes to marry Mildred at the adjoining
estate, but seduces her before asking permission of her brother, the
Earl of Tresham, whose boast is that no blot has ever stained their
'scutcheon.   Tresham consents, but when he learns from her confession of her lover, he is beside himself with fury and shame.   He
kills Mertoun and poisons himself.   Mildred dies of a broken heart.
    3 acts; 4 men, 2 women, extras; 4 interiors, 1 exterior;
    costumes of the 18th century.

BULLINS, Ed. The Taking of Miss Janie (1974). Samuel French.
     The play begins with young and black Monty just having sexu-
ally "taken" a young blonde white girl named Janie, or "Miss Janie"
as he prefers to call her. She claims he raped her, but as the
flashbacks subsequently show, rape is much too strong a word. In
an extended party scene with each of the players doing monologues
and dialogues (wasps, Jews, Muslims, racists, musicians) white-
black relations are shown to be as simple, and as complex, as they
really are.
     5 men (3 black), 4 women (2 black); one abstract interior.
     Royalty: $50-35.

BULLOCK, Walter and Daniel Archer. Mr. Barry's Etchings (1950).
     Dramatists Play Service.
     The accomplished engraver, Judson Barry, just to exercise
his skill, fabricates a passable $50 bill, even though he gave Gene-
ral Grant a bit of a smile. To help worthy causes, hospitals and
such, he donates these bills; but some real counterfeiters want to
horn in and help pass the bills. Then the T-men want him. He
realizes that what he has done is anti-social; he gets into and out
of so much trouble that he rather anticipates a short jail sentence
which might give him some peace and quiet.
     3 acts; 7 men, 6 women; 1 interior. Royalty: $25.

BURDICK, Eugene. The Ugly American. See entry under Lubar,
     Bernard.

BURROWS, Abe. The Cactus Flower (1966). Based on a play by
     Pierre Barillet and Jean P. Gredy. Samuel French.
     To keep himself single, a bachelor dentist tells his girl
friends that he has a wife and three children. It always works.
But it backfires when he finds a girl he'd like to marry, for she
demands to see the wife and children of the home she's been asked
to wreck. The dentist is forced to find someone to play the part
of his wife (he uses his nurse) and then to find a lover for the wife
to soothe his girl friend's conscience. Complications follow.
     7 men, 4 women; 4 sets. Royalty: $50-35.

BYRNE, Dolly. Enter Madame. See entry under Varesi, Gilda.

CALDERON, George. The Fountain (1909). Lond., Gowans &
     Gray, 1911; French, 1911; in his Three Plays and a Pantomime,
     Lond., Richards, 1922.
     Young Mrs. Wren doles out money to the poor in the slums,
who are paying her a high rent from the houses she owns there.
She is like a fountain which pours back into the basin the water
pumped into the horn of plenty.
     3 acts; 10 men, 7 women, extras; 1 interior.

CALDERON de la Barca, Pedro. Belshazzer's Feast (ca. 1625).
     Tr. by MacCarthy in BAT.
     Belshazzer has apparently taken Vanity and Idolatry as his
wives, but, as he boasts of his conquests at his feast, the hand of

Death writes on the wall: Mene, Mene, Tekel, Upharsin. Daniel, who has been joined by Thought, is called in and interprets that Death has stepped in and claimed the king.
20 scenes; 5 men, 2 women, extras; 1 exterior (a garden).

_____. Life Is a Dream (1636). Tr. by MacCarthy, Lond., Paul, 1853; HARC-26; MAU; tr. by Fitz-Gerald as Such Stuff as Dreams Are Made Of, Macmillan, 1906.
Segismundo, son of Basilio, King of Poland, is kept from birth in solitary confinement in a mountain cave, but instructed by Clotaldo, because of predictions that he would be a monster and a fatal enemy to his father and his country. Reaching the age of 21, he is brought in drugged sleep to the palace, and on awaking he is hailed as Prince. He shows violent wrath and his actions are so savage and arbitrary that he is returned to the cave. Here he comes to think that the day at court was all a dream, until Rosura, a Muscovite lady, brings help; they fight and defeat the king's men; he is really hailed as prince and king, with the expectation of marrying his cousin Estrella, who will be his queen.
5 acts; 4 men, 3 women, extras; 3 interiors, 2 exteriors; costumes of the period and place (Warsaw).

_____. The Mayor of Zalamea (1651). Tr. by Fitzgerald in his Six Dramas, Lond., Chatto, 1903; also in his Eight Dramas, Macmillan, 1906.
A farmer in Zalamea, Pedro Crespo, puts his daughter Isabel in the attic when a Captain is quartered in his house. By trickery the Captain abducts both Isabel and her father, and ravishes her. On his release, Crespo is advised by the citizens that he has been appointed Mayor; as such he imprisons the Captain. After King Philip II has heard the complaints, he appoints Crespo as perpetual mayor of the city.
3 acts; 8 men, 3 women, extras; 3 interiors, 9 exteriors; costumes of the period.

CALDWELL, Erskine. Tobacco Road (1933). Dramatized by Jack Kirkland. Samuel French.
The scene is laid in the cotton region of Georgia on the exhausted farm of lazy degenerate Jeeter Lester, who, though impoverished and starving, clings to his land. His 16-year-old son, Dude, marries Sister Bessie, a lustful woman preacher, in order to drive her auto. The youngest daughter, Pearl, married in her teens to Lov, runs away from him and Ellie May with a hare-lip and animal instincts take her place. Prof. Quinn writes: "shows the depths of degradation to which drama may descend."
3 acts; 6 men, 5 women; 1 exterior. Royalty: $50-25.

CALDWELL, Taylor. Dear and Glorious Physician. See entry under Fernand, Roland.

CAPEK, Karel and Josef Capek. Adam the Creator (1927). Tr. by Round, Lond., Allen & Unwin, & R. R. Smith, 1929; MOSH.
Adam destroys the world with his Cannon of Negation. Then

he tries to recreate it according to his plans.   He tries five, and
finds the godhead is difficult and discouraging, for there are always
shortcomings.   When done, the new earth is exactly like the old.
Adam favors the individual, his Alter Ego favors the masses; Oddly-
Come-Short represents the common man who would prevent Adam
from destroying the world, for, bad as things are, he prefers this
life to non-existence.   The play attacks priestcraft, militarism,
communism, capitalism, and skepticism.
    6 scenes & epilog; 21 men, 3 women, extras; 1 exterior with
background changes; fanciful costumes.

_____. The Makropoulos Secret (1922).   Adapted by Burrell.
Luce, 1925.
    Elena Makropoulos, a Greek living in 1585, by a precious
formula is rejuvenated every 30 years.   As a singer and idol of
men she lives 300 years, being at different times a German, a Russian, a Spaniard, a Scot, and a Czech.   In her final incarnation,
as Emilia Marty, the secret is offered to several people; each declines, and one, Kristina, destroys it.   Emilia now welcomes death.
Longevity is neither ideal nor desirable; eternal life would be terrible unless the key to eternal happiness were discovered.
    3 acts; 8 men, 4 women; 3 interiors.

_____. R.U.R. (Rossum's Universal Robots) (1922).   English
version by Paul Selver and Nigel Playfair.   Samuel French.
    The robots are manufactured men turned out by the thousand
to perform the labor of the world; but they lack souls.   They cannot
appreciate the higher things of life, and the real men do not know
how to, even with the leisure they have gained.   Modern mechanistic
civilization is satirized in terms of a weird and fantastic melodrama,
which points out that human values are more important than the
machinery of civilization created by modern science.
    13 men, 4 women; 2 interiors (1 set possible).   Royalty:
$25-20.

_____ and Josef Capek.   The World We Live In (The Insect
Comedy) (1921).   Adapted by Owen Davis.   Samuel French.
    Insects have affairs and problems strikingly like those of
humans.   The butterflies flutter and make violent love like philan-
derers, beetles hoard their wealth and live selfishly like avaricious
misers, parasites greedily devour what others have worked to save,
red ants and yellow ants wage war to see which has the right of
way over two blades of grass comparable to the strifes of industry
and war.   They struggle along with the same trivia of selfishness,
self-importance, and futility as humans do.
    21 men, 9 women, extras; 5 exteriors.   Royalty: $25-20.

CAPEK, Josef.   See entries under Capek, Karel.

CAPEK-CHOD, Karel M.   The Solstice (1912).   Tr. by Schonberger
in Poet Lore, v. 35, 1924.
    Hans Karvan returns home after several years of war service
and exile, including five years in America, to find that Anna has

married his cousin John; John has also taken over the business
when he craftily showed that Hans had probably died. Julia, Anna's
sister, is mistaken by Hans for Anna, as she so much resembles
her. She has a five-year-old boy, Jackie, by a doctor who has died
in an epidemic. John wants to get rid of Hans; Hans agrees to return to America, taking Julia and Jackie with him.
     3 acts; 9 men, 3 women, 2 boys; 1 exterior; costumes of the
period (1874).

CAPUS, Alfred. The Adventurer (1910). Tr. by Papot in Drama,
    v. 4, 1914.
     Etienne Ranson, who went to Australia and Africa and made
a fortune in 10 years, returns as a sort of prodigal now cleared of
an accusation. He finds himself falling in love with Genevieve, who
is engaged to André Vareze, who was his accuser. M. Gueroy at
60 and his son-in-law Jack have reached the end of their resources
in maintaining a factory and ask Ranson to come in with his money.
He refuses unless given sole authority. Gueroy refuses, but Jack
agrees. Genevieve realizes Ranson's position and offers to become
his wife, a situation which is confirmed when André backs out.
     4 acts; 9 men, 7 women; 2 interiors, 1 exterior.

_____. Brignol and His Daughter (1894). Tr. by Clark. French,
    1915.
     A jolly impecunious optimist, Brignol, is always in debt and
borrowing. He plans various marriages for his daughter, especially
to recoup his finances. She straightens out his affairs when she
marries the wealthy nephew of his chief creditor, with whom she
luckily falls in love.
     3 acts; 5 men, 4 women; 1 interior.

CAREY, Ernestine G. Cheaper by the Dozen. See entry under
    Sergel, Christopher.

CARLETON, Marjorie. Jane Eyre. See entry under Brontë, Char-
    lotte.

CARMICHAEL, Fred. Any Number Can Die (1965). Samuel French.
     An island mansion is the setting for four ingenious murders
and their solution by a pair of elderly detectives in this takeoff on
the mystery plays of the late Twenties. All the expected ingredients
are included: a raging storm, sliding panels, robed figures, unexpected guests, and a missing fortune. One character after another
comes under suspicion as the intricate plot moves quickly through a
series of intriguing and humorous situations. The unexpected twists
and turns of the plot lead eventually to the final surprising episode
when the murderer is discovered and the fortune regained.
     7 men, 5 women; 1 interior. Royalty: $25-20.

_____. Exit the Body (1962). Samuel French.
     Bodies appear and reappear in rapid succession in this farce.
A woman mystery writer rents a house which is supposed to be a
rendevous site for some stolen jewels. She soon discovers a body

in the closet which promptly disappears, only to be replaced by a
second corpse. Then at two a. m. four couples, all unknown to each
other, turn up to hunt for the jewels setting off a chain of hilarious
events which climax in the capture of the thieves.
5 men, 5 women; 1 interior. Royalty: $25-20.

CAROLE, Joseph and Alan Dinehart. Separate Rooms (1940). Samuel
French.
The columnist Jim threatens to retaliate on Pam the actress
for marrying his naive brother Don but failing to make him happy.
He will blackmail her in his column into making her a good wife.
His secretary pleads for a three months' armistice, after which he
himself is lured into matrimony by his Girl Friday.
3 acts; 5 men, 3 women; 1 interior. Royalty: $25-20.

CARPENTER, E. C. Whistling in the Dark. See entry under Gross,
Laurence.

CARROLL, Lewis. Alice in Wonderland. See entry under Le Galliene, Eva.

CARROLL, Paul Vincent. Shadow and Substance (1934). Dramatists
Play Service.
Contrasts three points of view in the Roman Catholic Church
in Ireland: the scholarly, orthodox Canon, Thomas Skerritt, who is
a bit cynical and worldly; the pugnacious, skeptical young schoolmaster, O'Flingsley; and the steadfast, unselfish Brigid, the maid
in the Canon's household, who has a childlike acceptance of faith
and who tries to reconcile these two and bring them together through
her patron saint.
4 acts; 6 men, 4 women; 1 interior. Royalty: $35-25.

_____. The White Steed (1938). Samuel French.
Presents a clash between two Roman Catholic priests, one a
skeptical humanist, Canon Matt Lavelle; the other a fanatic moralist,
Father Shaughnessy. The latter wants to enforce right living through
his Vigilance Committee. In the end the Canon must take hold of
the situation.
3 acts; 8 men, 5 women; 3 interiors. Royalty: $25.

CARSON, Murray. Rosemary. See entry under Parker, Louis N.

CARTER, Randolph. A Texas Steer (1894). In the original version
by C. H. Hoyt. French, 1940 in this modern version.
Hard-riding Texan cattle-king, Maverick Brander, is elected
to Congress, to the embarrassment of the Washingtonians because
of his crudeness. Two years later however they have been accepted
socially; yet when three gun-toting Texans arrive, pandemonium
breaks loose. Next morning, Maverick helps his daughter get the
man she loves, rebels against his sycophants, and spirits away his
three gun-shooting Texans.
3 acts; 13 men, 6 women; 1 interior, 1 exterior; some
Texan costumes.

_____. Wuthering Heights. See entry under Brontë,
Emily.

CASELLA, Alberto. Death Takes a Holiday (1929). American
   stage version by Walter Ferris. Samuel French.
      Wearied of defeat by Love, Death takes three days off to
visit the world as a human, trying to discover the reason. As
Prince Sirchi he visits an Italian family and falls in love with the
daughter, Grazia. When he must leave, she begs to go with him;
and Death takes her, for perfect love casts out fear.
      3 acts; 7 men, 6 women; 1 interior. Royalty: $50-25.

CASPARY, Vera and George Sklar. Laura (1948). Based on Vera
   Caspary's novel. Dramatists Play Service.
      Mark McPherson, a Special Investigator, comes to Laura's
apartment to try to solve her murder. He falls in love with the
dead woman from her portrait, her letters, her personal effects,
and the comments of the three men who loved her during her lifetime. But Laura turns up, alive, during a storm. Her girlfriend
becomes the murder victim. All the evidence points to Laura's
guilt. In spite of his love for her, Mark is about to pin the crime
on Laura. But the real murderer returns and attempts to repeat
the crime by killing the right girl. She is saved by Mark.
      5 men, 3 women; 1 interior. Royalty: $35-25.

THE CHALK CIRCLE. (13th century). Tr. by Ethel Van der Veer
   in CLF-1; many parts in BAT-3.
      Hai'tang becomes the second wife of Ma. His first wife has
a lover and plans to poison Ma and get the fortune through claiming
his five-year-old son as hers. When Ma returns he is told by Mrs.
Ma #1 that Hai'tang has a lover and has given her head-dress and
ornaments to him. She bribes all witnesses with silver; Hai'tang is
brought before the governor and supreme judge. He places the child
in the chalk circle to let the two women lead him out. Mrs. Ma
(wife #1) does it twice, but Hai'tang refuses to pull. The judge
awards the child to Hai-tang.
      Prolog & 4 acts; 5 men, 5 women, extras; 4 interiors;
      Chinese costumes.

CHAMBERS, C. Haddon. The Saving Grace (1917). Brentano, 1918;
   French carried.
      Buoyed through every crises by his sense of humor, Blinn
Corbett regains his place in the army through his wife.
      4 acts; 3 men, 4 women; 1 interior.

_____. The Tyranny of Tears (1899). Lond., Heinemann, &
   Bost., Baker, 1902; abridged in Pierce & Matthews, v. 1.
      With sly humor and pleasing freshness relates how Clement
Parbury is ruled by a loving but tearful wife, Mabel. He is inclined
to rebel at last, when his wife becomes jealous of his secretary,
Hyacinth and desires her dismissal. The question is solved when
her brother returns and marries Hyacinth.
      4 acts; 4 men, 3 women; 1 interior, 1 exterior.

CHAPIN, Harold. Art and Opportunity (1917). In his Comedies,
   Chatto, 1921; French, 1924.
      Presents the maneuvers of a fascinating widow, Pauline, dis-
playing her woman's art in using opportunity. She is pursued by
Lord Algernon, his father, and a duke, but she finally accepts the
secretary Henry Bently.
      3 acts; 5 men, 2 women; 2 interiors, 1 exterior (1 interior
      is possible).

_____. The New Morality (1920). French, 1924; MAP; in his
   Comedies, Chatto, 1921.
      From a houseboat on the Thames Mrs. Betty lets fly some
fierce public invectives at Mrs. Muriel on the next boat, caused by
her husband's trivial attentions. Muriel demands an apology which
Betty refuses to give. Betty's brother, a lawyer, advises about
libel and its consequences. Muriel's husband, after a few drinks,
boasts about the new morality of women, while Betty agrees to write
an apology.
      3 acts; 4 men, 3 women; 1 interior, 1 exterior.

CHASE, Mary Coyle. Harvey (1944). Dramatists Play Service.
      Pulitzer prize play 1945. An invisible white rabbit (Harvey)
always accompanies the amiable bibulous hero, Elwood. When he
is sent to a sanitarium for observation, his sister gets the treatment
by mistake.
      6 men, 6 women; 2 interiors. Royalty: $50-25.

_____. Mrs. McThing (1952). Dramatists Play Service.
      Rich Mrs. Larue and her small son Howay are hexed by the
witch, Mrs. McThing, because her girl Mimi may not play in the
guarded yard. Howay is replaced by a polite, obedient, but priggish
Stick, while he hobnobs delightedly with gangsters. Likewise his
mother is bewitched into a scrub-woman in the gangsters' lunch room.
Finally the mother appreciates her son the way he is, and adopts
Mimi in the bargain.
      8 men, 1 boy (doubles), 10 women; 2 interiors. Royalty:
      $50-25.

CHAUCER, Geoffrey. The Canterbury Pilgrims. See entry under
   MacKaye, Percy.

_____. The Canterbury Tales (1973). A new prose adaptation
   by Brainerd Duffield. Performance Publishing.
      Four of Chaucer's tales (Wife of Bath, Nun's Priest, Par-
doner's, and Friar's) set to traditional English folk songs ("Oh
Landlord Fill the Flowing Cup Until it Doth Run Over," "Summer
Is Icumin In," "Now Is the Month of May Time," etc. Can be performed without the music.
      Flexible cast; representational sets. Royalty: $60.

CHAYEFSKY, Paddy. Middle of the Night (1956). Samuel French.
      The question of the rights of an old man to claim the love
of a young girl is treated in this drama. A 53 year old widower

meets an unhappy girl nearly 30 years his junior, the victim of a
marriage with a fly-by-night musician. Although their families
strenuously object, the decision ultimately is theirs as to whether
to marry and bring the matter to a conclusion.
     3 men, 8 women; 1 interior. Royalty: $50-25.

_____. The Passion of Josef D. (1964). Samuel French.
     Lenin's intellectual Bolshevik zeal evolves to disillusionment
in this historical drama about Stalin's fanatical dedication to canoni-
zing Lenin. Stalin, a former seminarian, wants to make Lenin an
object of veneration for Russian people, and in his single minded
devotion to constructing the legend, reveals the inner soul of Lenin.
The New York Daily News commented: "And here, too, is Lenin,
surveying the years of the revolution, not with bitterness, but with
the realization that (it) has done nothing to change mankind. The
Soviets have done the same brutal things and give the same reasons
that other governments have through history. "
     20 men, 3 women; various sets. Royalty: $50-25.

_____. The Tenth Man (1959). Samuel French.
     An old meeting room used as a temple houses ten very inter-
esting characters and the beginning of a romance. It is a winter
day, and a group of Jewish men have gathered at their makeshift
temple for prayer. Some are not so devout, however. One is an
atheist who says he only comes to the temple to keep warm, and
another is a young agnostic lawyer who can find no contentment in
his cynicism and skepticism. Then the final worshippers arrive, an
elderly man, and his attractive granddaughter, who is in a trance
which some think is caused by a dybbuk, or evil spirit. At times
she is irrational, then in the trance, and sometimes she is very lu-
cid. During her saner moments she and the lawyer are strongly
attracted to each other, and this developing love brings hope to the
girl and a previously dormant capacity for love to the young agnostic.
     12 men, 1 woman; composite interior. Royalty: $50-25.

CHEKHOV, Anton P. The Cherry Orchard (1904). Tr. by Calderon
     in his Two Plays, Lond., Richards, 1912; same in DIC; in WATI
     & WATL-4; in HATS; tr. by West in his Plays, ser. 2, Scribner,
     $ Lond., Duckworth, 1916; & in his Five Famous Plays, Scribner,
     1939; tr. by Covan in MOS; tr. by Garnett, Lond., Chatto, 1923;
     same in his Plays, Modern Lib., 1930; & in TRE-1, 2, & 3;
     TREA-2; tr. by Butler, Lond., Deane, & Bost., Baker, 1934;
     tr. by Koteliansky in his Plays, Dutton (Everyman's) 1938); same,
     Penguin Bks, 1941; NOY; tr. by Young, French, 1947; in WOR.
     Acting edition: Samuel French.
     The aristocratic family, the Ranevskys, are forced to sell
their estate because of indifference towards business and money matters. The family orchard is bought by Lopakhin, the son of a serf
on their estate, and as they leave they hear the ring of the axes
chopping down the cherry trees. Supplies one reason for the passing
of the Old Russia before the New, depicting the' triumph of industrial
civilization over pastoral tradition. (From this play, in The Wisteria
Trees, Joshua Logan fashioned an American equivalent of the same

theme, laying the scene in the deep South).
    4 acts; 11 men, 4 women, extras; 3 interiors, 1 exterior
(1 set is possible). (S. French Royalty: $25-20.)

_____ ₀ A Country Scandal (1881). Adapted by Alex Szogyi.
Samuel French.
    Man's failures in times of crises are amusingly portrayed in
this comedy about a man who is irresistible to women. Women
find Misha almost unbearably attractive. His wife, a widow, and the
widow's daughter-in-law all pursue Misha, but this apparent good
fortune only makes trouble for him, as when the widow's son challenges Misha to a duel. Finally, succumbing to the pressures of
his scandalous life, Misha tries to commit suicide. But pointing up
the theme of the play, even this fails.
    11 men, 5 women; 2 interiors, 2 exteriors. Royalty: $35-25.

_____ . The Good Doctor. See entry under Simon, Neil.

_____ . The Sea Gull (1896). Tr. by Calderon in his Two Plays,
Lond., Richards, 1912; MOSQ; tr. by Fell in his Plays, ser. 1,
Scribner, 1912 & Lond., Duckworth, 1912; also in his Five Fa-
mous Plays, Scribner, 1939; tr. by Eisemann in Poet Lore, v.
24, 1913; tr. by West, Lond., Henderson, 1915; tr. by Garnett
in his Cherry Orchard, Lond., Chatto, 1923; & in his Plays,
Modern Lib., 1930; & in CEW; in CLS; tr. by Koteliansky in his
Plays & Stories, Dutton (Everyman's) 1938); & in his Three Plays,
Penguin Bks, 1941; tr. by Young, Scribner, 1939; French, 1950;
abridged in Pierce & Matthews, v. 2. Acting edition: Samuel
French.
    Irina, an actress, is adored by Constantine, a sensitive poet,
but she turns from his symbolic plays to a better-known playwright,
Trigorin. After a time she finds herself deserted by him, turned
out by her father, and reduced to a third-rate company, but she still
refuses Constantine's attentions, feeling she is destined to fly away
alone like a wounded sea gull. Constantine is embittered by his
failure and dies a slave to love.
    4 acts; 8 men, 5 women; 2 interiors, 2 exteriors. (S.
French Royalty: $25-20.)

_____ . The Three Sisters (1901). Tr. by West in his Plays,
ser. 2, Scribner, 1916 & in his Five Famous Plays, Scribner,
1939; tr. by Covan, Brentano, 1922; tr. by Garnett in his Cherry
Orchard, Chatto, 1923; in his Plays, Modern Lib., 1930; LEG;
MOS; tr. by Young, French, 1941; BLO. Acting edition: Samuel
French.
    The three sisters, Olga, Masha, and Irina, are stranded in
a small provincial town by their father's death, but are ever dreaming of returning to Moscow. Olga looks straight ahead, advancing
as a schoolteacher, but still weak. Masha looks down, for though
married to Kaligin, she falls in love with a visiting colonel. Irina
looks up, for she is still young and hopeful, though her lover is
killed in a duel. They lack the will to make their aspirations come
true.

4 acts; 9 men, 5 women; 2 interiors, 1 exterior; costumes
of the period (1900). (S. French Royalty: $25-20.)

_____. Uncle Vanya (1899). Tr. by Fell in his Plays, ser. 1,
Scribner, 1912; & in his Five Famous Plays, Scribner, 1939; tr.
by Saphro in Poet Lore, v. 33, 1922; tr. by Garnett in his Cher-
ry Orchard, Lond., Chatto, 1923; MIL; MOS; WATI; WATL-2.
Acting edition: Samuel French.
        Uncle Vanya is disillusioned at 47. He and his relatives
have slaved to educate Alexander, who turns out rather shallow.
Vanya makes a futile attempt to kill his infuriating brother-in-law
Prof. Serebriakov who tries to sell the estate, to build up which
Uncle Vanya has given his life. Sofia begs him to stick at his job.
Life settles down to distressing mediocrity. For people without a
purpose life becomes sad and futile; depicts the corroding effect of
frustration.
        4 acts; 5 men, 4 women; 3 interiors, 1 exterior. (S. French
Royalty: $25-20.)

CHLUMBERG, Hans. The Miracle at Verdun (1930). Tr. by Leigh,
Brentano, 1931; tr. by Crankshaw, Lond., Gollancz, 1932; CHA;
FAMC.
        In 1934, Heydner, a German soldier, visits the French ceme-
tery at Verdun. He visions the dead soldiers arising to go to resume life. But in Paris, London, and Berlin they find the world
getting along very well without them. In fact the diplomats become
alarmed, fearing an international crisis. So they return to their
graves.
        8 scenes; many characters & extras; many interior and ex-
terior scenes; costumes.

CHODOROV, Edward. Decision (1944). French, 1946; abridged in
Mantle 1943/44.
        A reactionary senator, who also owns the local newspaper,
dominates the city and stirs up racial feeling. A fearless high
school principal leads the better element in an effort to show the
senator up. He is arrested on a rape charge and hanged in the jail
to make him look guilty. The principal's soldier son on leave
reacts to his father's death to join the fight on the issues involved.
        3 acts; 12 men, 5 women; 1 interior.

_____. Kind Lady (1935). Samuel French.
        Dramatized from a story by Hugh Walpole. Clever crooks
surround the dignified and aristocratic Mary Herries and gradually
alienate the kind lady from her relatives and friends. They almost
convince her that she herself is insane. With some skill she gets
word to her banker and help is on the way.
        3 acts; 6 men, 8 women; 1 interior. Royalty: $25-20.

CHODOROV, Jerome, with Joseph Fields. Anniversary Waltz (1954).
Dramatists Play Service.
        Celebrating a 15th wedding anniversary with too much wine,
a husband makes the mistake of telling his wife's parents all that

went on between him and their daughter before the wedding ceremony. His in-laws are shocked and outraged, but his children are unimpressed. In fact, his 13-year-old daughter tells the whole world about it on television. Tempers rise, and the husband leaves home. He returns, but his irate wife leaves. Finally, they are brought back together by news from another front: they are going to have another baby.
    7 men, 5 women; 1 interior. Royalty: $50-25.

_____ with Joseph Fields. Junior-Miss (1941). Dramatists Play Service.
    Sub-deb Judy at 13 imitates her older sister Lois who is 16. With her confidante, Fluffy, she plots to fix things up in general, for father, mother, Uncle Willie, and all. This results in many highly amusing situations.
    21 men (some have no lines), 3 women, 3 girls; 1 interior. Royalty: $25.

_____ . My Sister Eileen. See entry under Fields, Joseph.

_____ . The Ponder Heart. See entry under Fields, Joseph.

CHRISTIE, Agatha. The Hollow (1952). Samuel French.
    The philandering of a wealthy society doctor leads to his murder in this tension-filled mystery drama. Three women are in love with Dr. John Cristow: a sculptress, Henrietta Angkatell, his present mistress; film star Veronica Craye, his former mistress; and Gerda, his wife. One weekend all four stay at a country home, and Veronica persuades John to spend the night at her cottage. Since John is not particularly secretive about his affairs, several people know of his indiscretion. The next morning John refuses to give up his wife, and Veronica threatens him. Within five minutes John has been fatally shot. The suspects are many: Gerda, Henrietta, Veronica, and even the household servants who were not overly fond of the doctor. The identity of the murderer remains unknown as the suspense builds to the final scene.
    6 men, 6 women; 1 interior. Royalty: $50-25.

_____ . The Mousetrap (1938). Samuel French.
    During a snow storm, a boarding house provides shelter for a group of strangers, one of whom is killed. The newly married couple who run the house, a spinster, an architect, a retired Army major, a man whose car has overturned in a snowdrift, and a woman jurist survive the murder. Then a policeman arrives on skis, and the jurist is suddenly murdered. The policeman probes the background of everyone in the house, but it is discovered that the man in the police uniform is the real culprit.
    5 men, 3 women; 1 interior. Royalty: $50-25.

_____ . Spider's Web (1940). Samuel French.
    A disorganized woman who is fascinated by the world of fancy she creates in the tales she tells to her daughter and her friends comes face to face with reality when a man is murdered in her living

room. Clarissa, Henry's second wife, even spins wild yarns to the
police as she tries to cover up for her daughter, Pippa, because she
thinks Pippa committed the murder. To add to the complications,
the victim is the man who was responsible for the failure of Henry's
first marriage. Clarissa's main worry is in getting the case solved
quickly, for Henry is expected shortly with a V.I.P., and a body
lying in the living room might create a bad impression. Luckily
for Clarissa the police are acute enough to unravel the truth from
her wild stories, and after some hair-raising experiences, manage
to unmask the murderer. When Henry returns the house is quiet,
but he is angry because no refreshments have been prepared for his
guest. For once Clarissa tells him the truth to explain her lack of
preparation. Henry, of course, cannot accept such an obvious fabri-
cation, but he loves her and with good-natured resignation forgives
her.

        8 men, 3 women; 1 interior. Royalty: $50-25.

_____. Ten Little Indians (1946). Samuel French.
      Although "The Ten Little Indians" refers only to a static
group of mantelpiece statuettes, these figures provide the background
for some very lively action in this mystery comedy. Eight guests
and two servants are assembled in a weird country house. At cocktails a voice from an unseen speaker accuses all of murder. Suddenly one Indian topples from the mantel and breaks, and immediately thereafter one of the guests falls dead, choking from a poisoned
drink. One by one the Indians fall and the guests die as the action
moves toward the suspenseful climax.

        8 men, 3 women; 1 interior. Royalty: $50-25.

_____ with Gerals Verner. Towards Zero (1957). Adapted
from Miss Christie's novel. Dramatists Play Service.
      Mystery, suspense, murder, and the twist at the end. Lady
Tressilian's house guests are Kay and Nevile Strange; Nevile's first
wife, Audrey; a man in love with Audrey; and Mary, the Lady's
companion secretary. Near-by is Ted, a friend of Kay's. When
Nevile tells Kay he wants to divorce her and remarry Audrey, his
wife says she'll see them both dead before she permits it. The
next morning Lady Tressilian is found murdered. At first it looks
like Nevile is the culprit, then that someone is framing him, then
that Audrey is the murderess. It takes the family lawyer and police
to solve the crime.

        7 men, 4 women; 1 interior. Royalty: $35-25.

_____. The Unexpected Guest (1960). Samuel French.
      A stranger walks into a house to find a woman standing with
a gun and her dead husband lying on the floor. The woman is dazed,
though she admits the killing. The stranger is not convinced and
decides to help her frame the murder on an intruder. The police,
however, find clues implicating a man who died two years earlier.
Then come the complications. Just as the murder seems solved
there is an unexpected twist.

        7 men, 3 women; 1 interior. Royalty: $50-25.

_____. Witness for the Prosecution (1954). Samuel French.
A young married man is accused of the murder of a rich
older woman he has been seeing. At his trial, his wife gives such
damaging testimony against him that it looks as if he will be convicted. Then a mysterious woman appears with letters which make
the wife's testimony suspect, and the man is freed. The mystery
woman turns out to be the wife herself, who felt this was the only
way she could get her husband off. When he goes off with another
woman (he was guilty of the murder all along), she kills him and
prepares for her own trial.
    17 men, 5 women, 8 extras; 2 interiors. Royalty: $50-25.

CHRISTOPHER, Jay. The Nut Factory (1974). Performance Pub-
    lishing.
    Christine and Karen McNutt run a "half-way house" for emo-
tionally disturbed adolescents. Their resident psychiatrist is missing, they are one patient under their minimum quota, and a state
inspector is due any minute. To save their license, Karen pretends
to be a patient and has her boyfriend pose as the psychiatrist. The
inspector turns out to be a handsome young man Karen has seen
often at the library and with whom she is gradually falling in love.
He believes she is suffering from a mild neurosis and seeks consultation with the phony psychiatrist.
    7 men, 8 women; 1 interior. Royalty: $35.

CLAUDEL, Paul. The Tidings Brought to Mary (1912). Tr. by
    Sill, Yale Univ. Pr., 1916; DIK-1; HAV; TUGC.
    The good Violaine is made leprous through a lover's kiss.
Exiled and suffering taunts and revilings, she yet restores to life
her sister Mara's child, thus preaching that supreme faith and hu-
mility may work miracles.
    Prolog & 4 acts; 5 men, 3 women, many extras; various ex-
    teriors; mediaeval costumes.

CLEMENTS, Colin C. See entry under Clements, Florence Ryer-
    son.

CLEMENTS, Florence Ryerson and Colin C. Clements. Harriet
    (1943). Samuel French.
    Depicts very simply some episodes in the life of Harriet
Beecher Stowe and how she came to write Uncle Tom's Cabin. She
saw the evils of slavery when she started her married life in Cin-
cinnati. When they transferred to Maine, circumstances brought
about the writing of the book. Brings in all the Beechers, including
Henry Ward Beecher. Reports her interview with Lincoln, from
whom she learned a philosophy of hope and courage.
    3 acts; 7 men, 10 women; 3 interiors (may be unit set or
    just curtains). Royalty: $50-25.

_____. Strange Bedfellows (1948). Samuel French.
    A militant suffragette, Clarissa Blynn, marries Matthew
Cromwell, the son of a conservative old-line senator and politician.
Her invasion in the 1890's of the Nob Hill home in San Francisco

is opposed by the fire-eating senator and his cronies, by the women of the household, and even by her husband. She fights for women's rights, and finally maneuvers first the women, then everybody else to her side of the political fence.

> 3 acts; 7 men, 11 women; 1 interior; costumes of 1896. Royalty: $50-25.

COCHRAN, Joseph. Murder Is a Matter of Opinion. See entry under Dawson, Ronald.

COHAN, George M. Seven Keys to Baldpate (1913). Samuel French.
> On a bet that he can write a play in a week, an author goes to a supposedly deserted house on Baldpate mountain. But the place has become a rendezvous for thieves and others, whose comings and goings rather upset the author's writing schedule. He wins the bet.
> 3 acts; 9 men, 4 women; 1 interior. Royalty: $25-20.

COLETTE Gigi. See entry under Loos, Anita.

COLMAN, George, Sr., and David Garrick. The Clandestine Marriage (1766). BAT; HAN; MCM; MOR; MOSE-2; INCH, v. 16; OXB, v. 5.
> Fanny Sterling has been secretly married to penniless Lovewell against her father's wishes. Meanwhile a couple of lords make love to her, as they want to get some of the merchant's money. The final act is considered a masterpiece, when Lovewell is caught in his wife's room.
> 5 acts; 10 men, 6 women; 6 interiors, 2 exteriors; costumes of the period.

COLTON, John R. with Clemence Randolph. Rain (1922). Adapted from a story by Somerset Maugham. Samuel French.
> Sadie Thompson, a woman of the streets of San Francisco, is detained with others for several days in Pago Pago on the island of Tutuila, where the incessant rain oppresses them. A zealous missionary believes he must save her soul, but in trying to do so, falls a victim to her physical attractiveness. Tortured by a sense of guilt, he kills himself. Instead of returning to San Francisco as persuaded by him, Sadie feels free and leaves with the handsome marine for Sidney for a fresh start.
> 3 acts; 10 men, 5 women; 1 interior. Royalty: $50-25.

_____. The Shanghai Gesture (1926). Boni, 1926.
> A Chinese princess was sold down the river to the junkmen by a Britisher with whom she eloped. Twenty years later, as Madame Goddam, she invites the same Britisher and his friends to dinner, and before their eyes she sells a white girl to the junkmen; then she informs him that she is his own daughter. The girl has become a dope fiend and degenerate; Mme. Goddam strangles her to death.
> 4 acts; 9 men, 8 women; 4 interiors; some Chinese costumes.

CONGREVE, William. <u>Love for Love</u> (1695). In Mermaid ser.,
Scribner; in World's classics, Oxford; CAR; MIL; STM; TWE;
BEL, v. 4; BRI, v. 2; DIB, v. 6; INCH, v. 13.
Angelica, who has not acknowledged her love, believes that
Valentine is in love with her, though he pretends to be insane and
unable to sign over his inheritance to pay his debts. She induces
her father to propose; she gets possession of the bond; but tears it
up when Valentine admits he is sane and ready to marry her. Many
characters are introduced, representing the affectations and foibles
of English society of that day, such as Tattle, Mrs. Frail, Prue,
and Ben Legend with his sea talk.
5 acts; 11 men, 6 women, extras; 2 interiors; costumes of
the period.

_____. <u>The Way of the World</u> (1700). Acting edn, Baker, 1928;
in his <u>Collected Works</u>; in Mermaid ser., Scribner; in World's
classics, Oxford; ASH; BEL v. 2; GOSA; LIE; MAT; MCM; MOR;
MOSE v. 1; NET; RUB; SMO; STM; TAU; TRE-1, & 2 (v. 2);
TREA-1; TUQ; TWE.
A philosophical gentleman, Mirabell, is in love with Millamant, but her aunt and guardian, Lady Wishfort, being angry at
Mirabell, threatens to deprive Millamant of her inheritance. Mirabell plots to have the stingy and tyrannical town coquette (Lady W.)
fall in love with Sir Rowland (really his servant in disguise); but he
also saves Lady Wishfort's fortune from the scheming Fainall. As
a comedy of manners, it is frequently revived.
5 acts; 6 men, 8 women; extras; 2 interiors, 1 exterior;
costumes of the period.

CONKLE, E. P. <u>Prologue to Glory</u> (1938). Samuel French.
Young Abe Lincoln at 22 is a rail-splitter who clerks in a
store at New Salem. He falls in love with Ann Rutledge and through
her influence becomes aware of his powers as he makes an election-
eering trip through Illinois.
8 scenes in 3 acts; 14 men, 7 women, extras; 1 interior,
5 exteriors. Royalty: $25-20.

_____. <u>Two Hundred Were Chosen</u> (1936). Samuel French.
To colonize Matanuska in Alaska, two hundred families were
located there in 1935 under the Army's direction. At first the living quarters were poor and fever broke out, but they are won over
to the government by Jim Conwell, a civil employee, and Jennie
Walters, a sane woman worker.
3 acts; 25 men, 7 women; 1 exterior (U. S. Govt. camp).
Royalty: $25.

CONNELLY, Marc. <u>Beggar on Horseback</u>. See entry under Kaufman, George S.

_____. <u>Dulcy</u>. See entry under Kaufman, George S.

_____. <u>The Green Pastures</u> (1930). Dramatists Play Service.
Pulitzer Prize play 1930. Effective expression of the Negro's

idea of creation, the flood, and the history of the world up to the
coming of Christ, adapted from material in "Ol' man Adam an' his
chillun" by Roark Bradford. The non-Biblical Hezdrel is a unique
conception, as well as the development of the idea of mercy and
forgiveness through suffering.
  18 scenes in 2 parts; 44 men, 10 women, children & extras;
5 interiors, 10 exteriors. Royalty: $25.

_____. Merton of the Movies. See entry under Kaufman, George
S.

_____. To the Ladies! see entry under Kaufman, George S.

_____. The Wisdom Tooth (1926). Samuel French.
  Bemis, an unsuccessful clerk of 30, has become a "yes-man"
and thinks of following each suggestion about his wisdom tooth. He
believes he is a failure and fears to ask for a raise which might
bring about his discharge. In his dreams he goes back to his grand-
parents and to his childhood successes. He awakens to make a
fresh start; he will go to his own dentist about his tooth. He is encouraged by Sally who now believes in him, which adds to his self-
respect.
  3 acts; 19 men, 10 women; 5 interiors. Royalty: $25-20.

CONNERS, Barry. Applesauce (1925). Samuel French.
  Small town folk show optimism and ability to tell others how
nice they are--it's applesauce. Hazel is really in love with Bill who
is hard up, but she has become engaged to Jenkins. But Bill
achieves success and also happiness as Hazel's future husband.
  3 acts; 4 men, 3 women; 2 interiors. Royalty: $25-20.

_____. The Patsy (1925). Samuel French.
  Blamed when anything goes wrong and playing second fiddle
to her older sister, Patricia is rescued from being the patsy by her
father, a traveling man who returns to find how things stand. She
wins the love of the man she wants--after studying a book on personality and being coached on how to do it.
  3 acts; 5 men, 4 women; 1 interior. Royalty: $25-20.

COPPEL, Alec. The Gazebo (1959). Based on a story by Alec and
  Myra Coppel. Dramatists Play Service.
  A television writer of mystery drama, a man always on the
lookout for "perfect crime" plots, has a wife who is being black-
mailed. Putting his story creation talents into direct action, he
murders the blackmailer and hides the body in a gazebo his wife is
having installed in the back yard. There are others, however, who
are interested in the gazebo. And soon the body gets stashed in the
middle of the living room. Things become further complicated when
the district attorney and detectives arrive and begin asking questions.
  9 men, 3 women; 1 interior. Royalty: $50-25.

COOK, Peter. Beyond the Fringe. See entry under Bennett, Alan.

COOPER, Giles. Everything in the Garden. See entry under Albee,
Edward.

CORMACK, Bartlett. The Racket (1927). French, 1928; abridged
in Mantle 1927/28.
A Chicago police captain, McQuigg, fights it out with the local gangster and powerful crook, Nick Scarsi. The play exposes
with all the fervor of a muckraker the vice of linking city politics
and crime.
3 acts; 19 men, 1 woman, 2 interiors.

CORMAN, Eugene. The Two Orphans. See entry under d'Ennery,
Adolphe P.

CORNEILLE, Pierre. The Cid (1636). Tr. by Landis & Henderson
in Six Plays by Corneille and Racine, Modern Lib., 1931; tr. by
Cooper in CLF-2; SMN; tr. by Lockert, Princeton Univ. Press,
1952.
The conqueror of the Moors, declared the Cid (Comander-in-
chief), is the lover of Chimène. He feels he must revenge an insult to his father and in the duel which follows he kills her father.
She is torn between loyalty to her father and her love for Rodrigo.
When he fights another duel with Don Sanche, who does so for
Chimène, he will not injure the champion of Chimène; and she shows
her love for him.
5 acts; 7 men, 4 women, 1 page; 1 interior; costumes of the
period.

_____. Cinna (1640). Tr. by Landis in Six Plays by Corneille
and Racine, Modern Lib., 1931; KRE; tr. by Lockert, Princeton
Univ. Press, 1952.
Cinna, the grandson of Pompey, plots with Maximus to kill
the Emperor Augustus if he may have Amelia as his reward. Augustus forgives them both and wins them to his side.
5 acts; 6 men, 3 women; scenes in Rome; costumes of the
period.

_____. Polyeucte (ca. 1641). Tr. by Nokes, Hachette, 1885;
tr. by Constable in HARC v. 26; STA; tr. by Lockert, Princeton
Univ. Press, 1952.
In Armenia, which the Romans had conquered in the days of
the Emperor Decius (250 A.D.), Polyeucte, a Christian general, has
married Pauline, the daughter of the Roman governor Felix. Polyeucte and Nearchus as Christians attack the idols of the Roman gods
and are condemned to death. They go as willing martyrs. This so
impresses Pauline that she becomes converted to Christianity and
wins others to that belief.
5 acts; 7 men, 2 women, extras; scenes in the palace; costumes of the period.

CORWIN, Norman. The Rivalry (1960). Dramatists Play Service.
A dramatized presentation of the great debates between Lincoln and Stephen Douglas when they were campaigning for the Illinois

Senatorship. These debates were held in seven Congressional districts during the campaign and attracted nationwide attention. The issues were not only partisan but also concerned basic questions of states rights vs. human rights. Douglas favored the right of separate states to make their own choice on the question of slavery. Although perhaps not quite the orator Douglas was, Lincoln's deep conviction that the nation could not endure half slave, half free added a tone of compelling sincerity to his arguments. In addition to the presentation of the political issues, this drama also shows the personal relationships and the changes of attitudes that developed during the debates.
  2 men, 1 woman, 3 bit parts; no scenery; series of platforms. Royalty: $50-25.

_____. The World of Carl Sandburg. See entry under Sandburg, Carl.

COWARD, Noel. Blithe Spirit (1941). Samuel French.
  Charles invites a medium to his home who summons back Elvira, his first wife of seven years ago. The wraith of Elvira torments him until Ruth, his second wife, is convinced that he is losing his mind. Elvira plots to get him to join her in the spirit world by a planned auto accident, which kills Ruth instead. Now he has two blithe spirits from whom to extricate himself.
  3 acts; 2 men, 5 women; 1 interior. Royalty: $50-25.

_____. Come into the Garden Maud. See Noel Coward in Two Keys.

_____. Design for Living (1933). Doubleday, 1933; in his Play Parade, Doubleday, 1933; abridged in Mantle 1932/33; SIXH.
  Three comrades in Paris, Gilda, Otto, and Leo, live a Bohemian life, taking outrageous liberties with established moral standards, until the two men leave on a freighter. An art connoisseur, Ernest, marries Gilda and they go to New York. The two wandering men reappear, cause Ernest to break with Gilda, and the three are left again to carry on their mad career.
  3 acts; 7 men, 4 women; 3 interiors.

_____. Fallen Angels (1925). Samuel French.
  A charming Frenchman asks to see two former mistresses together and provokes a chain of funny episodes in this sophisticated comedy. Julia and Jane are now both happily married, but Maurice's coming visit to London has them in a dither of excitement as they quarrel, make up, get high on champagne, and nervously await Maurice's arrival. He finally shows up, very late. Then the husbands return unexpectedly and the action becomes even more comic.
  3 men, 3 women; 1 interior. Royalty: $50-25.

_____. Hay Fever (1925). Samuel French.
  The Bliss family is ultra-Bohemian, headed by Judith, the mother and retired actress, who still plays many roles: neglected wife, sacrificing mother, sad but glamorous woman. Each of the

family invites a guest for a week-end; it proves wild indeed, and
all get mixed up in the free and easy life of the Bliss family. The
guests stand it as long as they can and then escape back to London.
3 acts; 4 men, 5 women; 1 interior. Royalty: $50-25.

_____. I'll Leave It to You (1920). Samuel French.
A rather destitute widow with five grown-up children turns to
her bachelor brother Daniel who has returned from South America,
reputedly wealthy. Uncle Daniel says his doctor has given him only
three years to live and that he will leave his money to the one who
has made good. The rivalry spurs each to work and to win success;
but his supposed riches are a myth. Nevertheless his plan has succeeded in rousing the family from its lethargy.
3 acts; 4 men, 6 women; 1 interior. Royalty: $25-20.

_____. Noel Coward in Two Keys (1966). Samuel French.
(Consists of two one-acts: "Come Into the Garden Maud" and
"A Song at Twilight," which have the same set and the same number
of actors.) In the first play, an awful American social-climbing
wife is left by her husband--rich but uninterested in high society--
when he decides to go away with a woman who has real class.
When he makes this decision, he and his wife are staying at a
fashionable private suite in a luxurious Swiss hotel. In the second
play, the occupants of the suite are another man and wife--a famous
author and his wife of convenience. One of his former loves arrives, ostensibly asking for his permission to publish the letters he
once wrote to her in her autobiography. He refuses, and then she
reveals that she has another set of love letters--the ones he wrote
to his homosexual lover. The writer's wife is able to take care of
the whole matter.
2 men, 2 women; 1 interior. Royalty: $25-25 for the first
play, $50-25 for the other.

_____. Nude with Violin (1956). Samuel French.
A great painter's death brings out a bizarre assortment of
avaricious friends and relatives all eager for a share of his glory
and his money. After they have all gathered, the painter's valet,
Sebastian, startles the entire group with some jolting revelations
about his former master. This leads to confession from other
characters, like an eccentric Russian princess and an ex-show girl.
When they are finished, reputations have been arranged and rear-
ranged and Sebastian ends up with a sizable nest egg for his old
age.
8 men, 6 women; 1 interior. Royalty: $50-25.

_____. Peace in Our Time (1947). Samuel French.
After the Nazis have conquered England and are in control,
assorted people are depicted: the weak surrender to the enticements
of the Nazis; the strong grow stubborn and rebellious. A resistance
movement develops. With ironic justice, Americans and British
Colonials storm onto England's shore to save the motherland and
establish peace.
22 men, 13 women; 4 exteriors. Royalty: $50.

_____. Present Laughter (1946). Samuel French.
A popular actor, Garry Essendine, is called on by a stage-
struck youngster, Daphne. While entertaining her, how is he to explain to his wife, his partners, his other admirers? He locks
Daphne in a room and flees with his wife.
3 acts; 5 men, 6 women; 1 interior. Royalty: $50-25.

_____. Private Lives (1931). Samuel French.
Elyot Chase, arriving with his bride Sybil at a hotel on the
Riviera, discovers his first wife Amanda (divorced five years before) as bride to Victor Prynne in the adjoining apartment and balcony. Elyot and Amanda suddenly realize they are still desperately
in love with each other; so they run away to her flat in Paris.
Here Victor and Sybil catch up with them, but they leave them for
a second time.
3 acts; 2 men, 3 women; 2 interiors. Royalty: $50-25.

_____. Relative Values (1951). Samuel French.
Miranda, an American movie actress, is going to marry an
English earl. But during a dinner party at the nobleman's home, a
visitor arrives, Don--an actor and former flame of Miranda's. She
tries to send Don away, but the Countess, who is not thrilled at the
thought of Miranda as a daughter-in-law, encourages Don and invites
him to stay over night. The engagement is broken soon after, when
the maid shows up Miranda's pretenses by revealing that they are
sisters. Don and Miranda go off together at the end.
5 men, 5 women; 1 interior. Royalty: $50-25.

_____. A Song at Twilight. See Noel Coward in Two Keys.

_____. This Happy Breed (1943). Samuel French.
Depicts incidents in the life of the Gibbons family (English
middle class) over the 20-year period from 1919 to 1939. They are
ordinary folk, loyal to each other and their country, with common
devotion and a sense of responsibility for the happiness of others,
and showing England quiet and firm in its moments of crisis. Three
generations are presented: the querulous grandmother, Frank Gibbons and his wife Ethel; his sister Sylvia, a hypochondriac nuisance
till she becomes fairly happy and smug with her new-found religion;
and the three children, each with their problems, especially Queenie,
who runs away but settles down to marry Billy next door.
6 men, 6 women; 1 interior. Royalty: $50-25.

_____. Waiting in the Wings (1960). Samuel French.
Jealousies arise in a home for retired actresses in this
comedy, but the tragedy of one of their number brings them to their
senses. With the construction of a new solarium, their life becomes
so pleasant that one of the actresses even chooses to spend the rest
of her days there rather than join her son and his family in Canada.
4 men, 14 women; 1 interior. Royalty: $50-25.

_____. The Young Idea (1923). Samuel French.
After fourteen years George Brent's son and daughter come

to visit their father in England, having been brought up in Italy by
his divorced wife Jennifer. They force a break by their antics between their father (who is restive and unhappy) and his not too happy
second wife Cicely; they irritate her so much that she elopes with a
co-respondent. They also cause a break between their mother and
an American to whom she has become engaged. Then they bring
their father and mother together again in Italy.
> 3 acts; 7 men, 7 women; 2 interiors. Royalty: $25-20.

COWEN, Lenore Coffee and William J. Cowen. Family Portrait
(1939). Samuel French.
> Introduces the family and friends of Jesus during His last
three years. He is misunderstood--by His brothers in Nazareth
who blame him for leaving at the height of the building season;--by
the promoters in Capernaeum who wish to capitalize on His popularity;--by the fickle crowd in Jerusalem who sing hosannas on Palm
Sunday but turn against Him later in the week. All His family save
His mother have feelings of delusion, failure, and disgrace; but Mary
knows that some of His followers are continuing His work.
> 3 acts; 12 men, 10 women; 1 interior, 3 exteriors; Biblical
costumes. Royalty: $25-20.

COWEN, William J. Family Portrait. See entry under Cowen,
Lenore Coffee.

CRAVEN, Frank. The First Year (1920). Samuel French.
> One of the longest-running plays in the history of Broadway,
this drama deals with the adjustments that Jommy and Grace have
to make during their first year of marriage and the social and domestic difficulties that result from their move from a small town to a
big city.
> 5 men, 4 women; 2 interiors. Royalty: $25.

CRAWFORD, "Texas Jack." Life On the Border (1876). Pioneer
Drama Service.
> Buffalo Bill is the expected "larger than life" hero in this
collector's edition of the 1876 play which starred Buffalo Bill. Along
with sidekick, Old Sloat, Bill rescues the heroine, and survives
numerous encounters with villains, bears and Indians.
> 16 men, 3 women; extensive doubling possible. No Royalty;
books $2 per copy.

CRICHTON, Kyle. The Happiest Millionaire (1957). Suggested by
Cordelia Drexel Biddle and Kyle Crichton's My Philadelphia Father. Dramatists Play Service.
> Anthony J. Drexel Biddle is a Philadelphia millionaire des-
cribed as having an enthusiasm for lunacy. Mr. Biddle collects al-
ligators and prizefighters and rules his family by blustery gruffness.
"You yelled, sir?" is the butler's standard response when Mr.
Biddle summons. He also tries to rule his daughter, Cordelia, but
when she falls in love with the multi-millionaire Southern boy, Angier
Duke, he meets defeat. Mr. Biddle, an ardent amateur boxer, has
no use for his prospective son-in-law because he knows nothing about

boxing. Angier, however, turns to ju-jitsu and throws a professional boxer as well as Mr. Biddle to the floor. This wins Biddle's
heart and he is resigned to losing his daughter.
     9 men, 6 women; 1 interior. Royalty: $50-25.

CROTHERS, Rachel. As Husbands Go (1931). Samuel French.
     Meeting two super-gigolos in Paris, two ladies from Dubuque
rediscover romance; Lucile, married to a rather dullish business
man, meets the Englishman, Ronald, who thinks mostly of himself;
Emmie, still an attractive widow, meets Hippolitus the Frenchman.
Returning to crude America with these two friends, the ladies per-
ceive the striking contrast between American and continental con-
cepts of marriage. Lucile stays with her husband, but Emmie marries Hippolitus.
     3 acts; 7 men, 5 women; 3 interiors. Royalty: $50-25.

_____. Expressing Willie (1924). Baker, 1925; in her Expres-
     sing Willie & other plays, Brentano, 1924; COT.
     The son of a successful toothpaste manufacturer, Willie in-
vites a group of faddists to a week-end party in the hope that they
will help him to express himself. Despite this cult of self-expres-
sion, through his mother's shrewdness and a girl's unselfish love,
Willie discovers Minnie and saves his money.
     3 acts; 6 men, 5 women; 2 interiors.

_____. He and She (1911). Revised form 1920. Baker, 1933;
     QUIK; QUIL.
     A story of woman's rights and responsibilities, centering
about one who is artist, wife, and mother. Rivalry and professional jealousy are conflicting interests. Her design wins over her
husband's, but she declines the commission.
     3 acts; 3 men, 5 women; 2 interiors (1 interior possible).

_____. Let Us Be Gay (1929). Samuel French.
     Although Bob declares their own love has been and is sincere
and untouched, Kitty divorces him when she discovers he has been
unfaithful. Three years later she is asked to rescue a girl from
what is thought to be mistaken love for a certain man. To Kitty's
surprise and chagrin he turns out to be her former husband, Bob.
After some confusion, they become reconciled, a more tolerant pair.
     3 acts; 7 men, 5 women; 2 interiors. Royalty: $50-25.

_____. A Little Journey (1918). French, 1923; in her Mary the
     Third, Brentano, 1923.
     Through a railroad accident to a sleeping car bound from
New York to the Pacific coast, a young woman, Julie, learns a lesson in human kindness and the joy of service; she also wins Jim as
a husband.
     3 acts; 8 men, 7 women; 1 interior, 1 exterior.

_____. Mary the Third (1923). Baker, 1925; in her Mary the
     Third and other plays, Brentano, 1923; DIG; TUCD; TUCJ; &
     TUCM; abridged in Mantle 1922/23.

Reveals the differences in points of view of three generations. Mary's grandmother mated by the lure of physical attraction; her mother married the most insistent of her lovers.   Mary the Third intends to determine her marriage by considerations of economics and eugenics (even by trial).   But she chooses her mate because she thinks he needs her; romantic love triumphs.

Prolog & 3 acts; 5 men, 5 women; 2 interiors.

_____.   Nice People (1920).   In her Expressing Willie & other plays, Brentano, 1924; MOSJ; MOSL; QUI; abridged in Mantle 1920/21.

Presents an unflinching picture of the idle rich in their mad search for pleasure, and of the flapper, her manners and morals and lack of restraint.   Teddy gets stranded with Scotty at the family's cottage in Westchester, into which Billy comes out of the storm.   Scandal seems about to land on Teddy, but a way out is shown by the clean-cut Billy to the girl who is better than her background though still of it.

3 acts; 6 men, 4 women; 2 interiors, 1 exterior.

_____.   "Old Lady 31" (1916).   French, 1923; in her Mary the Third & other plays, Brentano, 1923.

Abe and Angie, an aged couple, must leave their little house; she to go to the Old Ladies Home, he to the Poor Farm five miles away.   At the Home, Blossy proposes that she give up her big room and let the couple stay.   (Abe to be "Old Lady 31.")   It works out fairly well.   He encourages Blossy to marry Sam Darby after thirty years of courting.   In the end, his 20-year-old stock pays off, and they can go back to their old home.

Prolog & 3 acts; 4 men, 10 women; 1 interior, 2 exteriors.

_____.   Susan and God (1937).   Dramatists Play Service.

A flighty social butterfly, Susan, returns from Europe, enthusiastic over a new religious cult, which she has taken up as a sort of escape from an alcoholic husband.   But Barrie, the husband, is now contrite and wants to be included in this new way of salvation. So Susan must now put her religion into practice or admit insincerity. She makes a home for her husband and her neglected daughter, and in reclaiming her family she finds happiness and also her God.

3 acts; 5 men, 6 women; 3 interiors.   Royalty: $25.

_____.   39 East (1919).   Baker, 1925; in her Expressing Willie & other plays, Brentano, 1924.

In the boarding house at 39 East, romance comes to plucky Penelope Penn who has come to New York to sing and dance but can only get a job as a chorus girl.   She is determined to stick it out. Well-to-do Napoleon Gibbs stays on at the house just to be near her; then he proposes to her and assures the landlady that Penelope is really a good girl; so she takes her under her protection.   The gossipy boarders nearly wreck the romance.

3 acts; 6 men, 8 women; 2 interiors, 1 exterior.

_____.   When Ladies Meet (1932).   Samuel French.

A tolerant wife and a prospective mistress discuss an imaginary case of a philandering husband, without knowing their common interest in the same man. Rogers loses them both when the wife suspects and leaves him and the other no longer trusts him.
3 acts; 4 men, 3 women; 2 interiors. Royalty: $50-25.

CROUSE, Russel. Tall Story. See entry under Lindsay, Howard.

CROWLEY, Mart. The Boys in the Band (1968). Samuel French.
In this play a homosexual lifestyle is taken for granted. Michael invites some of his gay friends over for a birthday party in honor of one of them. (The present the birthday boy likes best, by the way, is a male hustler, prepaid for the entire evening.) The conflict comes by way of Michael's old college roommate, who is straight, and who comes to the party uninvited and beats up the most effeminate of the guests. Michael is sure that his old roommate is merely a homosexual who has never emerged from the closet, so he devises a game which will let him "come out." The game backfires, and Michael is left swimming in his own guilt.
9 men; 1 interior. Royalty: $50-35.

CUMBERLAND, Richard. The West Indian (1771). HAN; MCM; MIL; MOR; collections: BEL v. 18; BRI v. 2; DIB v. 12; INCH v. 18; OXB v. 1.
Brings Belcour from a plantation in the West Indies to London, where, as a child of nature, he has many adventures. The other hero is an Irishman, Major O'Flaherty. Presents an attack on dueling as a way of satisfying one's honor.
5 acts; 9 men, 6 women, extras; 6 interiors; costumes of the period.

CUREL, François de. A False Saint (1892). Tr. by Clark, Doubleday, 1916.
Julie tried to kill a rival who had won her sweetheart, after which she renounced the world and became a nun. Hearing that her former lover was dead, she comes out of the cloister, wishing to hear some message of tender sentiment from him. She meets Christine, the daughter of the woman she hated and the man she loved, and the old resentment flares up; she becomes a spiteful vixen and shows little that is saintly. But when she hears Christine repeat her father's dying message of love, she encourages Christine to find happiness in love. Julie returns to the convent content.
3 acts; 1 man, 5 women; 1 interior.

_____. The Fossils (1892). Tr. by Clark in Four Plays of the Free Theatre, Stewart & Kidd, 1914, Appleton, 1915; WATI-1.
An aristocratic Duke has retired with his wife, son, and daughter to a lonely castle in Northern France, where the family is in danger of becoming fossilized. The Duke has intrigues with Hélène the governess, but she falls in love with Robert, his son, by whom she has a child. Robert marries Hélène to give the boy the family name. Father and son quarrel over the boy's education; shall it be with the Duke or with Hélène? Certain to die soon of

tuberculosis, Robert commits the care of his wife and son to his sister Claire and goes from Nice to the castle in the north where he dies. They give up happiness and honor to save the family name.
    4 acts; 6 men, 4 women; 2 interiors.

DALE, Jim. Scapino. See entry under Dunlop, Frank.

DALY, Augustin. A Night Off (1885). Dick & Fitzgerald; French, c1897.
    An old staid college professor wants to have his play produced. The tragedian-manager of a wandering theatrical company undertakes to put it on. The professor's wife objects and tries to prevent this. It is produced, but its run is "For one night only."
    4 acts; 6 men, 5 women; 2 interiors.

DALZELL, William, with Anne Coulter Martens. Onions in the Stew (1956). Adapted from Betty MacDonald's novel. Dramatic Publishing Company.
    The experiences of a city family that moves to a remote home on an island in the Puget Sound provide many humorous complications for this comedy. Betty MacDonald has talked her husband and two attractive teen-age daughters into sinking every cent they have into this Puget Sound island home. They soon yearn for the city life they have left behind. The first day the tide comes in unexpectedly and washes half of their possessions out to sea. The girls are afraid they'll never have dates again because who wants to go out to an island to pick up a date? Betty is completely miserable at having brought this apparent disaster on them all. Yet, in the midst of the humorous difficulties, the family finds a special value in the life they are creating, giving this comedy a very satisfying conclusion.
    7 men, 11 women, extras optional; 1 interior. Royalty: $35.

DANE, Clemence. A Bill of Divorcement (1921). Lond., Heinemann, & Macmillan, 1921; French carried; COT; MAP; MOSO.
    Under the terms of an English marriage law (assumed to be in effect), a husband or wife adjudged hopelessly insane may be divorced. On the eve of her remarriage, her divorced husband appears, cured after 18 years. Their daughter, learning of insanity in her father's family, true to the teachings of eugenics, gives up her own idea of marriage and devotes herself to her father.
    3 acts; 5 men, 4 women; 1 interior.

_____. Will Shakespeare (1921). Lond., Heinemann, & Macmillan, 1922.
    Attempts to explain his literary power, his genius, and his rise to fame. Not founded on historical facts, for it depicts him as disillusioned with Anne Hathaway, as having ill-luck with Mary Fitton, the dark lady of the sonnets, and as the accidental slayer of Christopher Marlowe.
    4 acts; 6 men, 5 women, 2 boys, many extras; 6 interiors; costumes of the period.

DAVIDSON, William. Brother Goose (1942). Dramatic Publishing
    Company.
    Jeff Adams is an architect and sole supporter of his orphaned
brothers and sisters. He has been commissioned by Lenore Hudson
to build her a new house on the neighborhood football lot. Lenore
wants Jeff as a husband, but his brothers and sisters hate her for
ruining their football field. Jeff discovers that he really doesn't
want Lenore and her inherited million dollars. He's in love with
Peggy, a poor girl who turns up one day at the Adams house selling hosiery but stays on to care for the children as a maid.
    3 men, 9 women; 1 interior. Royalty: $35.

_____. The Many Loves of Dobie Gillis (1961). Adapted from
    Max Shulman's novel. Dramatic Publishing Company.
    Dobie Gillis is in love with Helen, who is, unfortunately,
going steady with Petey Bellows, the captain of the football team,
Student Council President, and editor of the paper. Dobie pursues
his dream girl (while at the same time being pursued by Bonnie)
for three acts. In the course of his chase he almost wrecks the
school lab, fails to get Helen elected Miss Echo, and hires Stella
Kowalski's Schottische Five instead of a name band for the school
dance.
    6 men, 12 women, bits; 1 interior. Royalty: $35.

_____. Room for One More (1951). Adapted from Anna Perrott
    Rose Wright's novel. Dramatic Publishing Company.
    Pappy and Mother Rose can never say "no" to a homeless
child. Consequently, their summer cottage is filled to the brim.
Yet they still accept two more charges: Janey, who is frightened
of everyone; and Jimmy John, who can walk only with the assistance
of braces. Then the family has a series of financial setbacks:
Pappy has a heart attack, Jimmy John's leg operations drain the
family treasury, and Mother's stack of rejection slips keeps increasing. All of the members of the family pitch in, and Joey, entering his first year of medical school, wishes to drop out to save
expenses. His mother won't permit it. Jimmy John, realizing that
the family is planning to sell the cottage to pay his medical bills,
runs away. At the end, these drastic steps are not necessary.
    4 men, 8 women; 1 interior. Royalty: $25.

DAVIES, Hubert Henry. Cousin Kate (1903). Lond., Heinemann,
    & Boston, Baker, 1910; in his Plays, Chatto, 1921, v. 1.
    Two days before her marriage with the artist Heath Desmond,
Amy quarrels with him and he leaves. Returning, he encounters on
the train her cousin Kate Curtis, who is unaware that he was Amy's
fiancé. When Kate finds that out and they quarrel, she tries to reunite them, engaging in a delightful sparring love match with Heath.
But Amy decides she is cut out more as a clergyman's wife than an
artist's, so Kate can accept Heath.
    3 acts; 3 men, 4 women, 2 interiors.

_____. The Mollusc (1907). Lond., Heinemann, 1907; Baker,
    1914; in his Plays, Chatto, 1921, v. 2; DIG.

Skillfully details the process of energizing the invertebrate
wife who spends all her ingenuity and even huge exertions to avoid
being disturbed--mollusk-like, in order to stick instead of to move.
She is reformed by her determined brother.
3 acts; 2 men, 2 women; 1 interior.

_____. A Single Man (1910).   Baker, 1914; in his Plays, Chatto,
1921, v. 2.
Robin, a bachelor in his forties and a writer, sees how happy his younger brother is with his wife and thinks he might also
marry.   He looks around and picks Maggie Cottrell, age 17.   His
secretary for five years, Miss Heseltine, has been devoted to him,
but he has accepted her as part of his business.   He becomes engaged to Maggie, but can't keep up with her youthful activities.
When Miss Heseltine brings back a typed article and is asked to
stay to supper, his eyes are opened to her good qualities.   He wants
to break his engagement, but Maggie does it for him; and all ends
happily.
4 acts; 3 men, 9 women; 2 interiors.

DAVIOT, Gordon. Richard of Bordeaux (1932).   Samuel French.
Richard II, King of England, was born in Bordeaux, France,
and was far more French in his tastes and sympathies than an English hero.   In his 19th year he rebelled against his guardian uncle,
John of Gaunt, dreaming of an England peaceful and rich and wishing
to avoid foreign wars, but he is beaten down by the nobles.   His
gentle wife, Anne of Bohemia, and his best friend, Robert de Vere,
side with him, till both die.   Then he overplays his luck, is forced
to abdicate, and dies in prison.
12 scenes in 2 parts; 23 men, 6 women, extras; 10 interiors,
1 exterior.   Royalty: $25-20.

DAVIS, Hallie Flanagan, assisted by Sylvia Gassel and Day Tuttle.
E=MC^2 (1947).   Samuel French.
Utilizing the "Living Newspaper" technique, this play shows
the past, present, and future of the atom bomb.   Through dramatic
scenes, music and movies, it explains the nature of atomic power,
its potential for constructive use, and closes with a reminder of our
responsibility to use it wisely.
6 men, 2 women, 20 or more extras.   Various sets.   Royalty: $25-20.

DAVIS, Ossie. Purlie Victorious (1961).   Samuel French.
Pokes fun at the popular cliches of the Old South and the
warm relationship between plantation owners and their slaves.   The
plot deals with Purlie Victorious's attempts to reacquire the local
church and ring the freedom bell.   Unfortunately, the plantation owner stands in the way of this plan, but by the end of the play he is
defeated.   As Purlie is about to beat the Southern colonel with the
white man's own whip, the advice he is given is (as a sample of the
play's dialogue):   "You can't do wrong just because it's right."
6 men, 3 women; exterior and 2 composites.   Royalty:
$50-25.

DAVIS, Owen. <u>The Detour</u> (1921). Samuel French.

Sincerely and realistically depicts the revolt of a strong-willed woman against the narrowness of her life in New England, and her determination to secure a fuller life for her daughter. When these hopes come to nothing, she looks forward to her dreams being realized in her grandchild.

5 men, 4 women; 1 interior, 1 exterior. Royalty: $25-20.

_____. <u>The Donovan Affair</u> (1926)   Samuel French.

Having boasted at a dinner party of the luminosity of his turquoise ring, Jack Donovan has the lights turned out so as to see it in the dark. When the lights come on, Donovan is sprawled on the table, dead, with the game knife in his ribs. Because of the ring's baleful influence, several present might have wished the ring done away with, as well as the owner.

3 acts; 11 men, 6 women; 1 interior. Royalty: $25-20.

_____. <u>Ethan Frome</u> (1936). Adapted from Edith Wharton's novel. Dramatists Play Service.

Ethan Frome is saddled with a mean and hypochondriachal wife, Zenobia, who makes his life miserable. Into the household comes a relative of Zenobia's, Mattie Silver, with whom Ethan falls in love. Instead of sending her away as Zenobia insists, Ethan takes Mattie on a romantic sled ride to their death. But death does not occur. Mattie is made an invalid by the accident and takes her turn at the Frome household--screaming at and complaining about her treatment at the hands of Ethan and Zenobia.

7 men, 4 women, extras; interiors and exteriors. Royalty: $25.

_____. <u>The Haunted House</u> (1924). Samuel French.

Jack and Emily arrive at Emily's father's cottage to spend their honeymoon. Queer sounds are heard in the house, and a murder is committed (Jack's ex-girlfriend). A neighbor, the local sheriff, and a New York detective try to solve the mystery. Several people are arrested, including the bride and her father. Finally everyone takes a truth potion to discover the real culprit.

8 men, 3 women; 1 interior. Royalty: $25-20.

_____. <u>Icebound</u> (1923). David McKay.

Pulitzer prize play 1923. The stern unemotional New England family of Jordans have greedy squabbles among themselves, nor do they welcome the return of Ben, the black sheep of the family. They are much put out to find the entire estate of Mother Jordan left to Cousin Jane, who has been caring for her. Jane gets Ben to stay and work on the farm; the drudge proves her mettle, rescues Ben from a life of crime, and makes a man of him. This is what Mother Jordan asked her to do; "to look after him till he is worthy of the money." When Jane announces she is ready to leave and will turn the farm over to Ben, he finds he loves her, and she marries him.

5 men, 6 women, 1 boy or girl; 1 interior. Royalty: $25.

_____. Mr. and Mrs. North (1941). Samuel French.
Pam and Gerald North live uneventful lives until a dead body
falls out of their closet. Lt. Weigand investigates, hindered rather
than helped by Pam, until she herself unmasks the murderer.
16 men, 4 women; 1 interior. Royalty: $35-25.

_____. The World We Live In. See entry under Capek, Karel.

DAWES, Rodney. Around the World in 80 Days (1957). Adapted
   from Jules Verne's novel. Dramatic Publishing Company.
Phileas Fogg and his pal, Passepartout, set out to win their
bet of going around the world in eighty days. The time is 1872.
When Fogg actually gets off, detectives around the world are looking
for him as the robber of the Bank of England. In Suez he is almost
arrested, in India he rescues a beautiful girl from burning to death,
in Calcutta he jumps bail, in Hong Kong he misses the boat, in the
West he fights Indians. Though Fogg seems to have ice water in
his veins, there is a chance he is in love with the beautiful Aouda.
(Musical version also available.)
   13 men, 11 women, (8 men and 8 women with doubling);
   simple props to suggest the various sets. Royalty: $25.

DAWSON, Ronald, with Joseph Cochran. Murder Is a Matter of
   Opinion (1973). Adapted from a story by Jules Archer. Performance Publishing.
A murder shatters the tranquility of a college campus, di-
viding community loyalties. Journalists and television reporters
cover every aspect of the murder, prejudging the guilt of the young
man who claims he was simply acting a part in a planned and harmless hoax.
   5 men, 5 women, extras; 1 set. Royalty: $35.

DAYTON, Katharine and G. S. Kaufman. First Lady (1935). Dramatists Play Service.
Skillfully pictures the interrelation of social and political life
in Washington. Irene has stolen Lucy's cook and the feud is on between these two Washington hostesses, each of whom thinks her husband should be in the White House.
   3 acts; 14 men, 11 women, extras; 2 interiors. Royalty:
   $25.

DAZEY, Charles T. In Old Kentucky (1892). Fine Book Circle of
   Birmingham, Mich., 1937; released through Dramatists Play
   Service.
A mountain girl, Madge, helps her unfortunate sweetheart
Frank out of financial difficulties by riding, disguised as a jockey,
his famous horse, Queen Bess, in the Ashland Oaks to victory.
This restores the family fortune, and of course they fall in love.
The race is viewed through a knothole as Col. Doolittle woos and
wins Aunt Lethe after twenty years of courtship. The underhanded
villainies of Horace Holton are successfully foiled.
   4 acts; 5 men, 3 women, extras; 2 interiors, 6 exteriors;
   costumes of 1870.

DEANE, Hamilton, with John L. Balderston. Dracula (1927). Based
on Bram Stoker's novel. Samuel French.
    Lucy Seward, daughter of a doctor in charge of an English
sanatorium, suffers from a mysterious illness. A specialist named
Dr. Van Helsing believes that the girl has been attacked by a vam-
pire--discovered to be Count Dracula, whose ghost is laid finally to
rest in what is touted as a striking and novel manner.
    6 men, 2 women; 3 interiors. Royalty: $25-20.

DEKKER, Thomas. Old Fortunatus; or, The Wishing Cap (1600).
In his Works, 1873; in his Best Plays, Fisher Unwin; in Mermaid
ser., Scribner; in Temple ser., Dutton; SCH.
    Lady Fortune offers to the beggar Fortunatus on the brink of
starvation his choice of wisdom, strength, long life, health, beauty,
or riches. He chooses riches and receives a purse which never
runs dry. So he starts on his travels with a wishing cap which will
transport him anywhere. Just as life becomes enjoyable, he dies;
and his son likewise dies miserably. The gift proves the ruin of
both.
    5 acts; 15 men, 7 women, extras; many scenes, simple or
    elaborate (out-of-doors production possible); costumes of the
    period.

_____. The Shoemakers' Holiday (1599). In his Works, 1873;
In his Best Plays, Fisher Unwin; in Mermaid ser., Scribner;
BAS; BLO; CLS; COF; DUN; HARC v. 47; HOW; MCI; NEI; PAR;
RUB; SCI; SCW; SPE; TAU; WHE.
    Rowland Lacy, a young nobleman in love with Rose Oateley,
daughter of Sir Roger, disguises himself as a Dutch shoemaker,
Hans, and works in a shop with Simon Eyre, having sent a friend
to France in his place. He wins Rose. Through Hans, Eyre gets
a fortune, becomes sheriff, and then Lord Mayor of London; as such
he declares a shoemakers' holiday, feasting all apprentices.
    5 acts; 17 men, 4 women, extras; 6 interiors, 8 exteriors;
    costumes of the period.

DE KRUIF, Paul. Yellow Jack. See entry under Howard, Sidney.

DELMAR, Anton. Outrageous Fortune (1973). Performance Publishing.
    Lefty is a tough 17-year-old girl living in a state orphanage.
She and her friends, none of them eligible for adoption, want out.
They launch a series of assaults on the peace of mind of the orphanage authorities which works too well and soon gets out of hand,
threatening the lives and careers of everyone. This play is a comedy with a remarkably flexible cast.
    1 to 4 men, up to 16 women; unit set. Royalty: $50.

DEMILLE, H. C. The Lost Paradise. See entry under Fulda, Ludwig.

DeMILLE, William C. Strongheart (1905). French, 1909; abridged
in Pierce & Matthews, v. 1.

Strongheart, the son of an Indian chief, after studying at
Carlisle, enters Columbia and stars as halfback. He is suspected
of divulging the signals; and his love for the captain's sister is opposed by her family. Just as they decide to be married anyway,
his tribe sends for him to become chief, succeeding his father.
Torn between love and duty, he finally returns to his people.
  4 acts; 17 men, 5 women; 3 interiors.

DENKER, Henry.   A Case of Libel (1963).   Based on Louis Nizer's
  My Life in Court.   Samuel French.
      A famous war correspondent sues a widely syndicated news-
paper columnist for libel in this successful Broadway melodrama.
The columnist, a dedicated defender of the extreme right, has made
repeated unjust attacks on the columnist's patriotism and his personal life.   The courtroom action centers around the prosecutor's attempts to expose the dangers of extremism and the defense attorney's spirited defense of justice and freedom of speech.   The lively
arguments and often heated cross-examinations keep a high interest
level throughout the play.
  11 men, 3 women, 3 extras; 1 interior/inset.   Royalty:
  $50-25.

d'ENNERY, Adolphe P. and Eugène Cormon.   The Two Orphans (1873).
  Adapted by N. H. Jackson.   Dramatists Play Service, 1939;
  CERC.
      Henriette and her blind sister Louise become separated as
they arrive in Paris from the country.   They are taken by abductors;
blind Louise is made to beg, Henriette is made the plaything for dissolute nobility.   Henriette is saved by Chevalier de Vaudrey who
falls in love with her.   The sisters search for each other and just
miss; they are united in a melodramatic climax.
  4 acts; 14 men, 10 women, extras; 4 interiors, 3 exteriors;
  costumes of the period (1785).

DENNIS, Patrick.   Auntie Mame.   See entry under Lawrence,
  Jerome.

DEVAL, Jacques.   Tovarich (1933).   Adapted by R. E. Sherwood.
  Samuel French.
      Prince Mikail and Grand Dutchess Tatiana, White Russians
of the Czar's court, are impoverished in Paris, but take service as
butler and maid in the home of Charles Dupont, a wealthy banker.
The son and daughter of the house are glad to know them, but when
their identity is revealed, they seem liable to lose their jobs.   The
Soviet Gorotchenko persuades Mikail to sign over the Czar's money
for the glory and preservation of Russia; and Dupont asks them to
stay on as servants.   They do not try to return to the aristocracy
but continue with the bourgeoisie with whom they happily mingle.
  8 men, 7 women; 4 interiors.   Royalty: $35-25.

DINEHART, Alan.   Separate Rooms.   See entry under Carole, Joseph.

DINELLI, Mel. The Man (1950). Dramatists Play Service.
Mrs. Gillis, a widow who has a rooming house, engages a
handy man in Howard Wilton. She takes a motherly interest in him,
and he wants to be loved and admired. He proves however to be a
psychopathic criminal, and he has lapses, as when he prevents her
from sending out any messages to her friends. She is imprisoned
by a maniac in her home. The telephone man manages to get a call
through to the police, but too late. (Play has an alternative ending,
supplied on request.)
2 acts; 5 men, 2 women; 1 interior. Royalty: $50-25.

_____. The Spiral Staircase. See entry under Leslie, F. An-
drew.

DODD, Lee Wilson. The Changelings (1923). Dutton, 1924; abridged
in Mantle 1923/24.
Two couples, after a quarrel, decide to exchange partners.
They are adult in their discussion of feminism and the new freedom,
being an editor, a novelist, a publisher, and a college instructor.
But they return to their former status.
3 acts & epilog; 6 men, 3 women; 2 interiors.

DONNAY, Maurice. Lovers (1895). Tr. by Clark in his Three
Plays, Kennerley, later Little, 1915; also in MOSQ; tr. by Steeves
in STE.
Two young people, Vetheuil and Claudine, are passionately
devoted to each other, but circumstances prevent them from marrying. Their love buds, blossoms, but it also withers, since life has
become as matter of fact as marriage. And so they part; he to
marry an heiress, she to retire to the country with a Count, after
he has been loosed from an uncongenial wife. The lovers do not allow defection to wreck their lives.
5 acts; 9 men, 6 women, 2 boys, 1 girl; 4 interiors, 1 exterior.

_____. The Other Danger (1902). Tr. by Charlotte T. David in
Drama, v. 3, 1913; also in Three Modern Plays from the French,
ed. by B. H. Clark, Holt, 1914.
An unhappily married mother, Claire Jadin, takes a lover,
Freydières, but for her daughter Madeleine's sake she gives her to
him for a husband, sacrificing her own love for him. Freydières
finds in the daughter who resembles her mother his first and early
love, so mother loses out to her daughter's youth. A thesis play
demonstrating that happiness is short-lived, therefore seize it when
it comes and accept with calmness its inevitable loss.
4 acts; 10 men, 8 women; 2 interiors, 1 exterior.

DOS PASSOS, John and Paul Shyre. U.S.A. (1960). Based on John
Passos' trilogy. Samuel French.
A panorama of America from 1900 to the stock market crash
of 1929. The story is of J. Ward Morehouse, who falls in love with
a beautiful girl and works himself up to the top. Interwoven are the
headlines and personalities of the period: Henry Ford, Valentino,

Debs, the Wright Brothers, Isadora Duncan, the Suffragettes, etc.
3 men, 3 women; cyclorama and platform.   Royalty: $50-25.

DOUGLAS, Lloyd C.   The Robe。   See entry under McGreevey, John.

DRINKWATER, John.   Abraham Lincoln (1918).   Samuel French.
Pictures the beauty and power of Lincoln's soul and his stu-
pendous coping with events as they occur, from accepting the nomination in Springfield, through the war years, pointing up Sumter, the
emancipation proclamation, Lee's surrender, and the assassination.
Flexible cast of 30 to 50; 5 interiors.   Royalty: $25-20.

_____.   Bird in the Hand (1927).   Samuel French.
Joan, daughter of the proprietor of the Bird in Hand Inn,
Thomas Greenleaf, falls in love with the Squire's son, Gerald.
Thomas thinks that Gerald is only intending to seduce Joan; she
thinks her father's fears ridiculous--she is a modern girl.   One
night Thomas drags Joan home and sits with three guests of the Inn
to straighten matters out and help Thomas to reach a decision.
Finally the Squire formally asks Joan to marry his Gerald.
3 acts; 6 men, 2 women; 2 interiors.   Royalty: $25-20.

_____.   A Man's House (1934).   Lond., Sidgwick, & French,
1935.
Using a modern psychological approach, shows the subtle
effect of the teachings of Jesus in a Jewish household in ancient
Jerusalem, where youth is open-minded to new ideas but their elders have a well-ordered reactionary philosophy.
3 acts; 12 men, 2 women, extras; 1 interior, costumes of
the period.

_____.   Mary Stuart (1921).   Samuel French.
The play opens with a prolog, that it is possible for some
wives to love loyally and devotedly more than one man.   The play
then fades into Mary Stuart's affair with Riccio, who was killed by
her husband Darnley, and points up her later interest in Bothwell.
She was not fickle, but had ideals too high for one person to attain:
she wanted strength, beauty, and passion--not to be found in one
man.
6 men, 2 women; 2 interiors.   Royalty: $25-20.

_____.   Oliver Cromwell (1921).   Lond., Sidgwick, & Houghton,
1921; French carried; in his Collected Plays, Sidgwick, 1925,
v. 2; DIG.
Presents the impressive figure of Cromwell through his military progress until he became Lord Protector of the Commonwealth;
when offered the crown, he refused it.   He was firm in his single
purpose, being heart and soul for the Puritan cause.
8 scenes; 18 men, 3 women; 7 interiors; costumes of the
period (English, 17th century).

_____.   Robert E. Lee (1923).   Lond., Sidgwick, & Houghton,
1923; French carried; in his Collected Plays, Sidgwick, 1925,

v. 2.
Episodes built around Lee's personality and his momentous
choice between command of the Northern or Southern forces.   Brings
out clearly the grounds on which the two sides rested their cause.
Follows Lee's heroic campaigns through to his surrender and farewell to his soldiers.
9 scenes; 18 men, 3 women; 4 interiors, 4 exteriors; some
military costumes of the Civil war.

DRURY, Allen.   Advise and Consent.   See entry under Mandell,
Loring.

DRYDEN, John.   All for Love; or, The World Well Lost (1677).
In various editions of his plays; BEL v. 13; BRI v. 2; DIB v. 1;
DOB; GOSA; HARC v. 18; INCH v. 6; LIE; MAT; MCM; MIL;
MOO; MOR; NET; SMN; STM; TAU; TUQ; TWE.
A fine adaptation of Shakespeare's Antony and Cleopatra.
Centers on the emotions of the royal lovers and their personal
reactions.   Brings in the efforts of Ventidius, Octavia, and others
to win Antony from Cleopatra.
5 acts; 8 men, 4 women; extras; 2 interiors; costumes of
the period.

DUBERMAN, Martin B.   In White America (1964).   Samuel French.
This is a series of enactments from the actual history of the
United States.   It traces the history of the Negro from slave times
to Little Rock.   The emotion filled scenes are as follows: The
heart of a runaway slave is bared to his master in a letter answer-
ing a plea to come home; John Brown, the war and the Emancipation Proclamation; a heart rending account of a molested, widowed
Negro woman and her crippled child and the Ku Klux Klan; a southern senator, in all his eloquence, delivers a moving speech justifying
a lynching that is the height of emotionalism; Booker T. Washington, DuBoise, Father Divine, and the Scottsboro Case are all suffi-
cient in themselves.
3 Negroes (2 men, 1 woman); 3 white (2 men, 1 woman);
platform stage.   Royalty: $35-25.

DUERRENMATT, Friedrich.   The Physicists (1961).   Samuel French.
Three nuclear physicists in an asylum become pawns in a bizarre spy plot with the world as the stake.   While they at first seem
harmless lunatics, we soon realize that perhaps one is using the
knowledge and disillusionment of the other two for his own selfish
ends.   In a final frightening episode the woman psychiatrist at the
head of the asylum must enact a contrived scene which reveals the
plotters.
16 men, 4 women; 1 interior.   Royalty: $50-25.

_____.   The Visit (1956).   Adapted by Maurice Valency.   Samuel
French.
An incredibly wealthy woman returns to her home town and
agrees to end its economic woes--for a price.   She wants the life
of a villager who had led to her expulsion from the town many years

earlier. At first the burgomaster refuses. Then everyone in town
gradually yields to the temptation of her money. The man is executed and the money passed over his coffin.
    25 men, 5 women, 2 children; drop--and wings. Royalty:
    $50-25.

DUFFIELD, Brainerd. The Canterbury Tales. See entry under
    Chaucer, Geoffrey.

DUKES, Ashley. The Man with a Load of Mischief (1924). Lond.,
    Benn, 1925; in his Five Plays, Lond., Benn, 1931; French in
    revised edn, 1933; MAP.
    To an English inn, called The Man with a Load of Mischief,
in Georgian days, come a nobleman with his servant Charles and a
lady with her maid. His lordship desires to humble the lady and
asks his valet to make love to her. Charles had heard her sing
years before and has adored her ever since. He woos and wins
her, and they find in each other the beauty of life together. The
play satirizes aristocratic arrogance and champions the common
man.
    3 acts; 3 men, 3 women; 1 interior; costumes of the period.

_____. Ulenspiegel (1926). In his Five Plays of Other Times,
    Lond., Benn, 1931; in Theatre Arts Monthly, v. 10, 1926.
    The son of Flemish parents is named Tyl Ulenspiegel, after
the legendary German prankish trickster Tyll Eulenspiegel. He
grows up to emulate his namesake by joyous heroic adventures with
his fat pal, Lamme Goedzak. He displays his charlatanism with
Lamme before a crowd in a market place; he is passed through the
Spanish lines with his bride Nele, and culminates his exploits in a
repulse of an attack by the soldiers of the Duke of Alva on a be-
leaguered ship caught in the ice. The episodes of the play are based
on a Flemish romance by Charles de Coster, published 1867.
    7 scenes; 12 men, 5 women, extras; 3 interiors (one a ship's
    deck), 1 exterior; costumes of the period (ca. 1575).

DUMAS, Alexandre, fils. Camille (1852). Tr. anon, Page, 1906;
    tr. & adapted by Mildred Aldrich, Baker, 1907; tr. by Metcalf,
    French, 1931.
    An intensely alive woman, Marguerite Gautier, is spending
the summer happily with Armand Duval until his father comes to
beg her to leave him. With a love that uplifts and redeems her,
she lets Armand believe that she has jilted him to become the mistress of another. Not until she is dying does he learn the truth,
when he comes to ask forgiveness; she dies in his arms.
    11 men, 6 women, extras; 3 interiors; costumes of the
    period. Royalty: $25-20.

_____. The Demi-Monde (1855). Tr. by Harper in CLF-2; tr.
    by Clark in MAU as The Outer Edge of Society; abridged in Pierce
    & Matthews v. 2.
    Suzanne, calling herself a Baroness, seeks to forget the past
and attain security through a respectable marriage. She is well on

her way in her design through marriage with a younger soldier, Raymond de Nanjac, until her shady past is revealed to him by a friend, a former lover of Suzanne.

5 acts; 7 men, 5 women; 3 interiors; costumes of the period.

DUNCAN, Ronald. The Trojan Women. See entry under Euripides.

DUNLAP, William. André (1798). Ogilvy of London, 1799; Dunlap Society, Pubn #4, 1887; HAL; MOSS-1; QUIK; QUIL.

Major André has been arrested and various efforts are being made to save him: by Mrs. Bland, by young Bland, and by Honora, who came from England to see him. Through it all André is shown dignified and courageous.

5 acts; 9 men, 2 women, 2 children, extras; 3 interiors, 3 exteriors; civilian & military costumes of the period.

DUNLOP, Frank, with Jim Dale and Molière. Scapino (1975). Dramatic Publishing Company.

A modern version of Molière's The Cheats of Scapin in which two men get into trouble with their fathers by falling in love with two girls of unknown family origin. Scapino comes to the rescue: "The good Lord has blessed me with quite a genius for clever ideas and inspired inventions which the less talented, in their jealousies, call deceits and trickery."

10 men, 4 women; 1 set. Royalty: $50.

DUNNING, Philip H. and George Abbott. Broadway (1926). Doran, 1927; French, 1929; CARC; GASE; abridged in Mantle 1926/27.

In a New York night club a hoofer, Roy, is in love with Billie, a cute member of the chorus; he wants her to form a "team" with him. Rival bootleggers are also present and their strife leads to murder and its detection.

3 acts; 11 men, 8 women; 1 interior. Royalty: $25-20.

DUNSANY, Edward Plunkett, Lord. The Gods of the Mountain (1914). In his Five Plays, Lond., Richards, & Kennerley, 1914; Little, 1917; separately, Lond., Putnam; MOSO.

Some Oriental beggars contrive to be taken for gods disguised as beggars, until the real gods leave their mountain thrones to punish and turn the beggars into the idols they represented.

3 acts (short); 10 men, 5 women, extras; 1 interior, 1 exterior; oriental costumes.

_____. If (1921). Putnam, 1922; French carries; HAU.

A prosaic London clerk misses the 8:10 train to work, and for years he worries over what he may have missed. Looking into a crystal globe he asks for another start, and finds himself in the wilds of Persia, the country's swashbuckling ruler, where he has adventure after adventure. His fortunes change and he returns to London; he wakes from his dream, cured of regrets, and contented to resume his placid humdrum existence.

4 acts; 14 men, 4 women; 4 interiors, 2 exteriors; some costumes of the Orient. Royalty: $50.

d'USSEAU, Arnaud and James Gow. Deep Are the Roots (1945).
   Dramatists Play Service.
   In a deeply moving human fashion presents striking aspects
of the race question in the deep South. A Negro war hero, Brett,
returns to the Langley family where he was raised with the white
children, especially the daughter Genevra. After Brett has been
accused of the theft of a watch and jailed, Genevra is willing to
marry him, but he wants to help the Negro in the South and plans
to do so. Senator Langley is still an unreconstructed Southerner
and opposes his daughter Alice marrying a Northerner.
   3 acts; 7 men, 4 women; 1 interior. Royalty: $50-25.

_____. Tomorrow the World. See entry under Gow, James.

DYER, Charles. Rattle of a Simple Man (1963). Samuel French.
   A trollop, using the aristocratic background that she borrowed from novels she reads, picks up a lonely man who has come
to London for a frolic. At her apartment the man's pretended
worldliness quickly loses its genuiness, and he is totally incapable
of the new situation. Neither is what he pretends; one by one they
strip away the masks that cover their loneliness.
   2 men, 1 woman; 1 interior. Royalty: $50-25.

_____. Staircase (1966). Samuel French.
   A play about the tormented relationship between two aging
homosexuals. The older one is awaiting the first visit of a daughter
he fathered 20 years before. The younger one, a middle-aged former juvenile actor, has been caught in a transvestite situation and
must go to court. As they wait for these events to take place the
two barber/hair-stylists enjoy their Sunday off, and give one another
trims, manicures, and the love of outcasts.
   2 men; 1 interior. Royalty: $50-25.

ECHEGARAY y EIZAGUIRRE, José. The Great Galeoto (1881). Tr.
   by Lynch, Lond., Lane, 1895; Doubleday, 1914; tr. by Fassett,
   Badger, 1914; tr. by Bontecou in CLDM; tr. & adapted by Nord-
   linger as The World and His Wife in MOSQ; abridged in Pierce
   & Matthews, v. 2.
   The false gossip of the neighbors links pure-minded Teodora
with her husband's protegé, Don Julian, until her husband, Ernesto,
comes to believe that she is unfaithful. Teodora, innocent up to
now, decides she may as well live up to the accusations and takes
Don Julian as her lover. Thus the tongue of gossip can do inestim-
able harm and ruin even the virtuous. The gossiping public tends
to make real whatever it assumes, and, though unseen, is really
the protagonist of the play.
   Prolog & 3 acts; 7 men, 2 women; 2 interiors.

_____. Madman or Saint (1877). Tr. by Lansing in Poet Lore,
   v. 24, 1913; tr. by Lynch as Folly and Saintliness, Lond., Lane,
   1895.
   Lorenzo's old nurse, Jane, was put in prison for stealing a
locket. She did so because it contained a letter from his mother

saying she was not his mother; but Jane the nurse insists she was. Lorenzo believes the letter, and this in his mind would prevent the marriage of his daughter to a Duke. The generous-minded, even saintly Lorenzo is willing to give up name, wealth, and position because of this taint; and he will offer the letter as proof. But Jane has burned the letter and substituted a blank paper in order that he might not forego everything. Without any real proof, all are convinced that he is really mad.

    3 acts; 7 men, 4 women; 1 interior.

EDWARDS, Maurice. <u>American Kaleidoscope</u>. See entry under
    Palmer, Winthrop.

EHRMANN, Max. <u>David and Bathsheba</u> (1917). In <u>Drama</u>, v. 7,
    1917.

    Follows the Bible story closely. From his roof David sees Bathsheba bathing and summons her to visit him. She yields. David's counselor, Hushai, advises that her husband Uriah be summoned from the battlefield. He comes, but sleeps in the guardhouse. Then Hushai advises a letter to Joab, to have Uriah placed in the forefront of the battle--so that he might be killed. Nathan the prophet accuses David: "Thou are the man" and foretells that the child shall die.

    3 acts; 4 men, 11 women (10 of them, wives of David); 1
    exterior (the roof); Biblical costumes.

ELIOT, T. S. <u>The Cocktail Party</u> (1949). Samuel French.

    Presents a group of urbane English people at a cocktail party given by a troubled husband, Edward, whose charming wife, Lavinia, seems to have left him to do the honors. They all have a neurotic sense of frustration, characteristic of contemporary society. The messiah-like doctor, with the aid of meddlesome Julia who gathers data for him, appears as an unorthodox psychiatrist--part mystic, part man-of-the-world. He treats his three patients according to their needs, telling them that illusions must be dropped and reality faced. He brings Edward and Lavinia together, relieving their feeling of loneliness. He gives Celia, the sensitive idealist, a release by which her selfishness turns into selflessness.

    3 acts; 5 men, 4 women; 2 interiors. Royalty: $50-25.

    _____. <u>The Confidential Clerk</u> (1953). Samuel French.

    Sir Claude Mulhammer, a British financier, believes himself to be the father of an illegitimate son and daughter. (His wife, Lady Elizabeth, thinks she has a son somewhere, too.) Both are partly right. Sir Claude's daughter is actually his, and the one he suspects as his illegitimate son--his new clerk, Colby, a frustrated organist--is really the child of his former love's sister. But other surprises follow.

    4 men, 3 women; 2 interiors. Royalty: $50-25.

    _____. <u>The Elder Statesman</u> (1958). Samuel French.

    A retired elder statesman goes to a retreat to rest from his labors and honors. Then his past begins to catch up with him. At

the same retreat he meets a former show girl, bought off long ago
by his father, and a rich South American, corrupted by the statesman. The lives of both acquaintances are stained with dishonor,
and they go to work on the statesman and his family.
  5 men, 3 women; 1 interior. Royalty: $50-25.

_____. The Family Reunion (1939). Samuel French.
  A family gathers for a supposedly happy reunion in this
morality play, but one son is haunted by the impression that he has
killed his wife. The New York Times calls this "... the finest
verse play since the Elizabethans. "
  7 men, 4 women; 1 interior. Royalty: $25-20.

_____. Murder in the Cathedral (1935). Samuel French.
  After a quarrel with Henry II and a six-year exile in France,
Thomas à Becket returns to England and his cathedral in Canterbury, is partially reconciled to Henry, but infuriates him by his
utter devotion to the church. He is murdered on the steps of the
cathedral by Henry's order--martyred with grace and spiritual satis-
faction. He is mourned by his flock, for his simple faith triumphs
over himself as well as his enemies, and gains for him martyrdom
and immortality.
  10 men, 9 women; 3 interiors. Royalty: $35-25.

EMERY, Gilbert. The Hero (1921). QUI; TUCD; abridged in Mantle
  1921/22.
  Two brothers are compared as types of moral and physical
courage. Andrew sacrifices himself to cover his brother's defalca-
tions; Oswald returns from the war in 1919 with a heroic record but
unchanged in his moral stamina. He steals again, but has the physical heroism to save his brother's child.
  3 acts; 3 men, 3 women; 2 interiors.

_____. Tarnish (1923). Brentano, 1924; abridged in Mantle
  1923/24.
  Pictures the plight of Letitia, a girl of good social background,
when no longer sheltered but forced to work in an office and earn her
living in business. Nettie the vamp gets Emmett to call, though he
has broken relations with her and asked Letitia to marry him. When
Letitia finds him at Nettie's house, she thinks he has doublecrossed
her. The shrewd Irish landlady tells Tishy to take him: "the men
are a poor lot ... but the thing is, darlin', to get one that cleans
easy. " So Letitia takes him for the love she has.
  3 acts; 2 men, 6 women; 2 interiors.

ENGLAND, Barry. Conduct Unbecoming (1971). Samuel French.
  Two new lieutenants arrive at a British regiment stationed in
19th-century India. One of them is accused of assaulting the widow
of a war hero, and the other serves as his defense counsel. In an
unofficial trial, the "honor" of the regiment begins to unravel, and
the investigation gets turned toward one of the senior officers, who
is sick in a kinky sort of way.
  14 men, 4 women, extras; one interior. Royalty: $50-35.

EPHRON, Henry. See entries under Ephron, Phoebe.

EPHRON, Phoebe and Henry Ephron. Take Her She's Mine (1962).
    Samuel French.
        The special relationship of parents and college age children
    is amusingly dramatized in this comedy about two typically American
    girls enroute to college. These girls enter college with a determined
    air of sophistication and independence. As their education progres-
    ses, they move on to a period of interest in causes and humani-
    tarianism. With their college days coming to an end, however, they
    start to think seriously of life and marriage. Such phases are en-
    tertaining--to everyone but the father--who lives through them and
    shares them with his daughters. He also suffers through their
    dating and their love life as this humorous portrayal of the agonies
    of parenthood comes to its finish.
        11 men, 6 women; various sets. Royalty: $50-25.

_____ and Henry Ephron. Three's a Family (1943). Samuel
    French.
        The small apartment starts with three in the family; but
    daughter Kitty and her baby move in when her husband goes to war.
    Then son Archie and his wife have their baby there because the hos-
    pitals are full. Thus there are eight, not counting the maids who
    come and go, nor the visits of the doctor.
        3 acts; 8 men, 8 women; 1 interior. Royalty: $50-25.

ERVINE, St. John G. The First Mrs. Fraser (1928). Macmillan,
    1930; Baker carried; abridged in Mantle 1929/30.
        After twenty years of marriage Janet Fraser lets her infatu-
    ated husband James get a divorce to marry Elsie, a hard-boiled
    self-seeking gold-digger. After a few years Elsie is seeking greener
    fields with Lord Larne who is wealthier. So James gets another di-
    vorce after Elsie has eloped with Lord Larne; and again courts the
    first Mrs. Fraser, who rather likes the idea.
        3 acts; 4 men, 4 women; 1 interior.

_____. Jane Clegg (1913). Lond., Sidgwick, 1914; imported
    first by Holt and later by Macmillan; PLAP, v. 1; abridged in
    Mantle 1919/20.
        In a sincere and engrossing way depicts the long-suffering
    wife, who remains the captain of her soul, the contemptible husband,
    who tries to steal her money and elope with another woman, and the
    way she finally dismisses him from her life. A credible transcript
    from life in London.
        3 acts; 3 men, 2 women, 2 children; 1 interior.

_____. John Ferguson (1915). Lond., Allen & Unwin, 1915;
    Macmillan, 1928 & 1935; CHAR; THF; TUCD; TUCM; DUR;
    abridged in Mantle & Sherwood, 1909-1919.
        The old farmer, John Ferguson, remains triumphant in the
    midst of adversity. When his daughter Hannah is seduced by his
    enemy, Witherow, Jim Caesar rushes out to kill him. Next morning
    he confesses he didn't have the nerve to do it; but Witherow is found

shot to death, and Caesar is arrested. Andrew, Ferguson's son,
confesses he shot him and that he can't allow Caesar to die for a
crime he didn't commit. As Andrew and Hannah go to confess,
Ferguson laments like David of old "Oh, Absalom, my son, my
son."
> 4 acts; 7 men, 2 women; 1 interior.

_____. The Lady of Belmont (1923). Lond., Allen, 1923.
Depicts the household of Portia exactly 10 years after Antonio's trial in the Merchant of Venice. Married life has not proved
easy going for the three couples: Bassanio is a philanderer, this
time intriguing with Jessica, and is despised by Portia; Lorenzo
and his wife Jessica deceive each other; Gratiano is the drunken
and faithless husband of Nerissa. To this disrupted household come
others; Antonio in his dotage, grieved that no one recalls his trial;
Dr. Bellario, Portia's lawyer cousin who deplores the way Portia
conducted the trial; and Shylock, who wants to see his grandchildren,
though no one wants to have him around. Portia alone is gracious
to him.
> 5 acts; 10 men, 1 boy, 3 women, extras; 3 interiors, 1 ex-
> terior; costumes of the period.

_____. Mary, Mary, Quite Contrary (1923). Lond., Allen &
Unwin, & Macmillan, 1923; Baker 1928.
Mary Westlake, a popular temperamental London actress,
journeys to the vicarage of a country town to hear read a play by
the young poet son. While there she disturbs the regularity of the
quiet English household and causes considerable stir by fascinating
the boy and also his uncle, a confirmed bachelor. After which, she
laughingly exits to London.
> 4 acts; 5 men, 5 women; 1 interior, 1 exterior (or can be
> played with 1 interior).

_____. Private Enterprise (1947). Lond., Allen & Unwin, 1948;
Macmillan, 1948.
Edmund Delaware, with his son Philip, owns a factory in
England and insists on managing it. The workmen likewise insist
on the rights of the Labour Union. This brings on a strike. Various angles of the question are presented by members of his family
and by the workmen's representatives. It appears that the Government will have to step in, though the play is a vigorous polemic
against nationalism and in favor of private enterprise.
> 3 acts; 9 men, 4 women; 1 interior.

_____. The Ship (1922). Lond., Allen & Unwin, & Macmillan,
1922.
Unfolds the eternal struggle between the old order and the
new, the conflicting ideals of father and son. The old man's heart
is in his shipyard, the son refuses to carry it on; to him it is the
epitome of modern materialism. Finally he does carry out his father's wishes by directing the initial voyage of a fast liner, which
meets a disaster similar to that of the Titanic.
> 3 acts; 4 men, 4 women; 2 interiors, 1 exterior.

EURIPIDES.   Alcestis (438 B. C.).   Tr, by Way in Loeb Library;
    tr. by Woodhull in Everyman's; tr. by Buckley in Bohn's; tr. by
    Gilbert Murray, Oxford, & in CLS; tr. by Fitts & Fitzgerald,
    Harcourt, 1947, & in FIT; tr. by Hadas & McLean, Dial, 1936;
    tr. by Potter in CLF-1; OAT.
        Admetus, King of Thessaly, threatened with death, was told
that he might live if some one would die in his stead.   He asks his
father, mother, and kinsmen; they all refuse; but his wife, Alcestis,
offers to go to Hades for him.   She dies, but Heracles brings her
back from the shades because Admetus had been kind to him.   As
the play opens, Alcestis is loyally facing her doom.   Admetus
promises the usual things; faithful devotion to her memory, etc.
His father sarcastically advises him "to woo many women so that
more may die for you. "
        1 continuous act; 7 men, 3 women, chorus of women; 1 ex-
    terior.

_____.   Hippolytus (429 B. C.).   Tr. by Way in Loeb Library;
    tr. by Buckley in Bohn's; tr. by Woodhull in Everyman's; tr. by
    Gilbert Murray, Longmans; GREN; HARC-8; MIL; OAT; FIT.
        Phaedra, wife of Theseus, pines for the love of her step-
son, Hippolytus, and falsely accuses him of making love to her.
As he is going into exile, he is killed when his horses run away.
On hearing this Phaedra commits suicide.   His father however is
assured of his son's innocence by Artemis, who appears in a cloud
and explains that he was the innocent victim of Aphrodite's jealousy,
because he worshipped only Artemis.
        1 continuous act; 4 men, 4 women, choruses of men and of
    women; 1 exterior.

_____.   Iphigenia in Tauris (414 B. C.).   Tr. by Way in Loeb
    Library; tr. by Buckley in Bohn's; tr. by Hades & McLean, Dial,
    1936; tr. by Gilbert Murray, Oxford; OAT; TEN.
        Iphigenia, dedicated as a priestess in the Temple of Diana,
has sworn to slay the first Greek who comes to Tauris.   When it
proves to be her brother Orestes, in a tense scene of recognition,
she breaks her vow, and by her influence and cunning saves him
and Pylades, and escapes with them.
        1 continuous act; 5 men, 2 women, chorus of women; 1 ex-
    terior.

_____.   Medea (431 B. C.).   Many translations, among them:
    Way in Loeb Library; Woodhull in Everyman's; Buckley in Bohn's;
    tr. by Gilbert Murray, Longmans; MAU; SMP; TEN; several
sinsince 1936; in OAT; & FIT; tr. by Jeffers, Random House, 1946,
    French, 1948, in Theatre Arts, Ag-S, 1948; GAS-3.
        Depicts an ill-mated pair: Jason, a self-seeking, self-delud-
ing husband, accepting the results of crimes committed by his wife;
Medea, the bloodiest of heroines.   Her love turns to hate when Jason deserts her for Glaucé, the daughter of the King of Corinth.   In
revenge she sends poisonous gifts to the bride, kills her two sons
by Jason, and flies away in her dragon chariot.
        1 continuous act; 4 men, 2 women, 2 children, chorus of
    women; 1 exterior.

_____. __Medea.__ See entry under Jeffers, Robinson.

_____. __The Trojan Women__ (Troades, 415 B. C.). Tr. by Way
in Loeb Library; tr. by Buckley in Bohn's; tr. by Potter in
Everyman's; tr. by Gilbert Murray, Longman's, (also in CAR;
TEN); tr. by Lattimore in FIT; HAM; OAT; STA; TREA-1.
　　　　Presents one long lament over the consequences of war by
those who suffer most--the women. After the fall and sacking of
Troy, they bemoan their fate: they are brought into bondage by lot.
Cassandra falls to Agamemnon (and prophecies his death); Andromache falls to Neoptolemus; her son, Astyanax, is cast from the
walls and his mangled body is brought to Hector's mother. Troy
is burned to the ground, its red flames lighting up the last of the
horrors.
　　　　1 continuous act; 3 men, 5 women, chorus of women; 1 ex-
　　　　terior. (For a modern acting version: Ronald Duncan's
　　　　English version of John-Paul Sartre's adaptation of Euripides'
　　　　play. Samuel French: 4 men, 6 women, extras. Royalty:
　　　　$50-25.

EVERYMAN, a Morality Play (15th century). Carried by French;
　　　ADA; ASH; BAT v. 4; CLF v. 1; COJ; KRE; LEV; LIE; MOO;
　　　PAR; RUB; SCW; SNL; STA; TAU; TRE-1, -2 (v. 2); TREA-1.
　　　　Everyman (symbol of Humanity) is summoned by Death to appear before God and give an account of his life. All his worldly
friends desert him: Fellowship, Riches, Kindred; others go with
him: Strength, Beauty, Discretion: Five-wits, until they approach
the grave when they likewise leave. Even Knowledge remains outside. Only Good Deeds will accompany him.
　　　　1 act in a succession of scenes; 11 men, 6 women (or all
　　　　male or female). No royalty.

EVREINOV, Nikolai N. __The Chief Thing__ (1919). Tr. by Bernstein
　　　& Randole. Doubleday, 1926.
　　　　Mr. Paraclete, as helper, advocate, and comforter, secures
the services of three actors--a lover, a dancer, and a comedian--
who, as suitor, slavey, and doctor, bring a feeling of happiness to
an unfavored stenographer, a depressed student, and a morose
school teacher. The chief thing is to "act" a part in life so as to
encourage others, by giving them at least an illusion of happiness
in life.
　　　　3 acts; 13 men, 11 women, extras; 3 interiors.

FAGAN, James Bernard. __"And So to Bed"__ (1926). Samuel French.
　　　　Samuel Pepys calls on attractive Mistress Knight to receive
her thanks for rescuing her. He is forced to hide in a closet when
his visit is interrupted, first by King Charles II who makes love to
the fascinating lady, and later by the jealous Mrs. Pepys, to whom
he is still later at some pains to explain his presence.
　　　　3 acts; 8 men, 8 women; 2 interiors; costumes of the period.
　　　　Royalty: $50.

FARQUHAR, George. __The Beaux' Stratagem__ (1707). In his __Best
Plays__, Fisher Unwin, Lond.; in Mermaid ser., Scribner; BAT

v. 22; BEL v. 7; BRI v. 1; CLF v. 1; DIB v. 1; GOSA; HUD;
INCH v. 8; MAT; MCM; BLO; MOR; MOSE v. 2; NET; OXB v.
7; STM; TAY; TUQ; TWE; UHL.

Aimwell and Archer, two London beaux, who have dissipated
their fortunes, go to the country as master and servant to win a
country heiress. Aimwell rescues Dorinda from three highwaymen
and later inherits from his brother. Archer protects Lady Bountiful and wins her after her separation from her brutal husband
Squire Sullen. The names of Boniface, the inn-keeper, and Lady
Bountiful have entered the language.

5 acts; 11 men, 5 women, extras; 6 interiors; costumes of
the period.

FAULKNER, William. Requiem for a Nun (1952). Adapted for the
stage by Ruth Ford. Samuel French.

Temple Drake (from Faulkner's novel Sanctuary) has married the college boy who first led her astray but wants to run away
with her latest "find." She even plans to take her six-month-old
baby with her. Her maid, Nancy, will not permit the baby to go,
and smothers the child to prevent it. We learn of this in Temple's
confession to the Governor, to whom she goes, unsuccessfully, to
plead clemency for Nancy.

5 men, 2 women; unit set. Royalty: $50-25.

FEIFFER, Jules. Feiffer's People (1973). Dramatists Play Service.

Social satire in the perceptive Feiffer manner, on the state
of America and modern existence. Instead of a completed script,
the play is made up of sketches, observations, and playlets which
can be arranged, formed, and organized as the producing group
wishes.

Flexible cast; simple and flexible staging. Royalty: $35-25.

_____. Knock Knock (1976). Samuel French.
Two fiftyish men, one overweight and one under, live together
in a cabin in the woods, where they quarrel all the time about their
notions of reality and fantasy. Then Joan of Arc shows up, her intention apparently being to stock a new kind of Noah's ark spaceship
for God. She is to bring two of everything, in this case two
Schlepps. The effect of the world of magic on old Abe and old Cohn
is hilarious.

3 men, 1 woman; composite interior. Royalty: $50-35.

_____. Little Murders (1967). Samuel French.
Deals with meaningless violence in American life. A Manhattan family made up of a domineering mother, a spineless father,
a "normal" daughter, and a latently homosexual son have a paranoid
fear of snipers, muggers, and other purveyors of violence. After
daughter is married (she and her young man find a radical priest who
will marry them without pronouncing the name of God) and after the
priest has blown everyone's cover on hidden dreams and desires, the
girl is killed by a sniper. Paranoia soon turns into aggression, and
the new son-in-law and the rest of the family begin to pick people off

the street with rifles from the security of their fortress/apartment.
6 men, 2 women; 1 interior. Royalty: $50-25.

_____. The White House Murder Case (1970). Samuel French.
A satire set in the future. The war this year is in Brazil,
and the President is worried about what to tell the American people
about the poison gas attack which backfired, or even how to explain
the existence of the gas in the U.S.'s "peace arsenal"--especially
since the truth will cost him the approaching election. While the
cabinet is concocting the cover story, the First Lady is murdered--
making more nasty business to report. (The murderer, by the way,
uses his deed as leverage to be appointed the next Secretary of
State.)
9 men, 1 woman; 1 interior and an interior inset. Royalty:
$50-25.

FERBER, Edna. Dinner at Eight. See entry under Kaufman,
George S.

_____. The Land Is Bright. See entry under Kaufman, George
S.

_____. Minick. See entry under Kaufman, George S.

_____. The Royal Family. See entry under Kaufman, George S.

FERNAND, Roland. Dear and Glorious Physician (1963). Adapted
from Taylor Caldwell's novel. Dramatic Publishing Company.
The story of the apostle Luke, who wanted above all to be a
healer, to alleviate pain and fight back the powers of death. As a
young man he is embittered when he fights for the life of Rubria,
the girl he loves, but who dies in spite of his efforts. His faith
shattered, he buries himself in his work. But Luke finally finds he
must rediscover his faith which he lost.
10 men, 13 women, extras (doubling possible); 1 set. Royalty: $25.

FERRIS, Walter. Death Takes a Holiday. See entry under Casella,
Alberto.

FEUCHTWANGER, Lion. Warren Hastings (1916). Tr. by Muir in
his Two Anglo-Saxon Plays. Viking, 1928.
As Governor-General of India, Hastings struggles against local prejudice and three representatives of the East India Company
who have come out to investigate his administration, led by Sir Philip
Francis, who will later bring up his impeachment in London. Hastings has built a road through the jungle to combat famine; he secured
the money from two wealthy women, rather than tax further the poor
of India. He will not take a bribe and his skirts are clean, but Lady
Marjory Hicks has accepted a rich jewel, which implicates him.
Chief Justice Impey justifies his execution of Rajah Nuncomar.
3 acts; 12 men, 1 woman, extras; 3 interiors, 1 exterior;
costumes of India in 1775.

FEYDEAU, George. A Flea in Her Ear (1968). Dramatic Publishing Company.
      A French farce in the classic sense. Madame Chandebise
opens a package addressed to her husband, sent from the Hotel Pus-
sy Cat. The package contains her husband's suspenders. She decides to trap her mate by sending him a perfumed letter suggesting
a rendevous at the Hotel. To disguise the handwriting, she enlists
the aid of her best friend, married to a jealous Spaniard. Then
come the confusions, complications, reversals, double roles, and
double meanings. Recommended for advanced groups only.
      9 men, 5 women; 2 sets. Royalty: $35.

FIELD, Salisbury. Wedding Bells (1919). Samuel French.
      The wedding bells are ringing for Reggie, when in pops a
lady to whom he was married briefly in Santa Barbara; after a dis-
pute she left, and he couldn't follow because he got the measles.
Now she appears, grabs Reggie from his bachelor dinner, tips off
the clergyman about Reggie's divorce, and finds a new groom for
the bride. It looks as if the bells would ring again for her and
Reggie.
      3 acts; 5 men, 4 women; 1 interior. Royalty: $25-20.

FIELDING, Henry. Tom Jones. Adapted by David Rogers (1964,
  Dramatic Publishing Company) and by Peter Walker (1974, Performance Publishing).
      Tom Jones is a foundling, the ward of Squire Allworthy. Al-
though he and Sophia Western are in love, Sophia's father has arranged for her to marry Blifil, Allworthy's underhanded nephew.
Tom is banished when his love is discovered, but Sophia sets out to
find him. She, in turn, is followed by her father, his sister,
Squire Allworthy and Blifil. They find madcap adventures and a host
of strange characters on the road to London. Tom, already in London, narrowly escapes marriage to an unscrupulous lady of fortune
and then is sentenced to hang for murder. In an amusing and unexpected ending, however, Tom and Sophia are united and Blifil's true
parentage is revealed.
      Rogers: 10 to 13 men, 8 to 11 women; drapes and simple
      props. Royalty: $35. Walker: 10 men, 10 women, doubling
      possible; representational set. Royalty: $35.

FIELDS, Dorothy and Herbert Fields. Annie Get Your Gun (1952).
  Based on the original musical by Dorothy Fields, Herbert Fields,
  and Irving Berlin. Dramatic Publishing Company.
      A non-musical play. Annie is a shy and awkward girl who
comes to town during a performance of Buffalo Bill's Wild West
Show. She accepts the shooting challenge of the show's sharpshooter,
Frank Butler, and promptly falls in love with him (and also out-
shoots him). Buffalo Bill hires Annie on the spot, but Frank is
jealous and insists she can only be his assistant. Annie is very
pleased with this arrangement, and soon Frank returns her love.
But when Buffalo Bill gives Annie a spectacular stunt to perform,
thus making her a star, Frank leaves the show and joins another.
Both are miserable at the separation. Finally friends bring them

together again, but the same argument begins: who is the best
shot? They decide to shoot it out for once and for all.
10 men, 9 women, extras; 1 exterior. Royalty: $35.

FIELDS, Herbert. See entry under Fields, Dorothy.

FIELDS, Joseph. Anniversary Waltz. See entry under Chodorov,
Jerome.

_____. The Doughgirls (1942). Dramatists Play Service.
An irreverent comedy about wartime Washington, designed to
reflect wartime conditions without bringing up wartime miseries.
Washington is so overcrowded with people who have come to help in
the war effort that four girls have to share a small hotel suite,
which they're lucky to get at all.
10 men (several bits), 6 women (several bits); 1 interior.
Royalty: $35-25.

_____. Junior-Miss. See entry under Chodorov, Jerome.

_____ and Jerome Chodorov. My Sister Eileen (1940). Dramatists Play Service.
Ruth, the ambitious writer, and Eileen, the pretty actress,
invade New York from Columbus, Ohio, in search of careers. They
suffer many Greenwich Village experiences in their basement apartment, fighting off a variety of pests, from the Greek landlord to the
six Brazilian navy officers, but emerge victorious over the many un-
believable hilarious incidents.
3 acts; 15 men (with 6 or more extras), 6 women; 1 interior.
Royalty: $25.

_____, with Jerome Chodorov. The Ponder Heart (1956).
Adapted from Eudora Welty's story. Samuel French.
This comedy tells the story of a daffy Southern gentleman so
naive that he doesn't even realize he's been accused of murder.
Uncle Daniel Ponder, getting on in years, decided one day to get
married. He picked an ignorant child-like young girl, who during
their one-month-trial marriage did nothing but order expensive ap-
pliances and play jacks with the maid. Because he loved the girl
so dearly and is himself so totally guileless, Uncle Daniel doesn't
know that he's being accused of murdering her. He buys ice cream
cones and invites everybody out to see the big trial. But at the
climax of the trial, the prosecutor makes it clear who the defendant
is, and the amiable Uncle Daniel really gets his dander up. With
his spirited, zany defense the play comes to a close.
20 men, 10 women, extras (some unessential children); 2 interiors, 1 exterior. Royalty: $50-25.

FINKLEHOFFE, Fred R. Brother Rat. See entry under Monks,
John Jr.

FISHER, Bob and Arthur Marx. The Impossible Years (1964). Samuel
French.

The story centers around a psychiatrist who is writing a
book about teen-agers.   Unfortunately, in the same household are
his two teen-age daughters.   The seventeen year-old has a court of
weird boyfriends: a Greenwich Village beatnik, the boy next door with
an overdeveloped itch, and an anemic Peace Corps reject.   One of the
boys, the psychiatrist learns, has just married his daughter, though
neither will say which one.   The younger daughter, meanwhile, is reading Fanny Hill and finding it tame.   Other weird people are also present.
        9 men, 5 women; 1 interior.   Royalty: $50-25.

FITCH, Clyde.   Barbara Frietchie, the Frederick Girl (1899).   Life
    pub. co., 1900; French 1900; in his Plays, Little, Brown, 1915,
    v. 2; abridged in Mantle & Sherwood 1899-1909.
        Barbara is a noble charming girl of Southern family in
Frederick, Md., during the Civil war.   She falls in love with a
Northern Captain and protects him when wounded.   The display of
the flag climaxes the drama.
        4 acts; 13 men, 6 women, extras; 3 interiors, 1 exterior;
    costumes of 1863, some military.

_____.   Beau Brummell (1890).   Lane, 1908; French, 1908; in
    his Plays, Little, Brown, 1915, v. 1; COH.
        Portrays the personality of the Georgian dandy and the arti-
ficial life during the Regency.   Brummell sacrifices himself to give
the girl he so hopelessly loves to the man of her choice.
        4 acts; 10 men, 7 women, extras; 2 interiors, 1 exterior;
    18th century costumes.

_____.   The City (1909).   Little, Brown, 1915; also in his Plays,
    Little, Brown, 1915, v. 4; MOSJ; MOSL.
        Father Rand had made a financial success in a small town
through shady deals.   After his death the family moves to a great
city, where they succumb to its life, for each tries to lie to it.
Young George in confessing the graft says: "The city brings out
what is strongest in us; it gives the man his opportunity; it's up to
him what he makes of it.   To the city he can't lie. "
        3 acts; 7 men, 5 women; 2 interiors.

_____.   The Climbers (1901).   Macmillan, 1906; French, 1906;
    in his Plays, Little, Brown, 1915, v. 2; COT; abridged in Man-
    tle & Sherwood 1899-1909.
        Satire on the foibles of New York society.   Each character
strives to attain his ambition, whether in love, happiness, finance,
or social recognition.
        4 acts; 12 men, 9 women; 3 interiors.

_____.   The Girl with the Green Eyes (1902).   Macmillan, 1905;
    in his Plays, Little, Brown, 1915, v. 3; QUIL.   Acting ed.,
    Samuel French.
        Possessed with the demon of jealousy, a hereditary fault,
Jinny would have been as happy in her married life as she was as
a bride.   But she is so suspicious when Ruth asks her husband's
help, that she tries to kill herself with gas.   Her husband discovers

her in time to save her and wins again her love by his understanding sympathy.
> 4 acts; 10 men, 14 women, extras; 3 interiors. Royalty: $25.

_____. Nathan Hale (1898). Russell, 1899; Baker, 1899; in his Plays, Little, Brown, 1915, v. 1.
Effectively presents stirring incidents in the life of the young patriot, culminating in the final scene in which he "regrets he has only one life to give for his country."
> 4 acts; 12 men, 4 women, extras (schoolboys, soldiers, and townsmen); 4 interiors, 2 exteriors; costumes of the period (1776).

_____. The Truth (1906). Macmillan, 1907; French, 1907; in his Plays, Little, Brown, 1915, v. 4; DIC; STA; abridged in Pierce & Matthews, v. 1.
Shows the hard lesson that Becky, who fibbed unnecessarily, had to learn in order to speak and live the truth. Her habitual falsehoods cause her husband to lose faith in her, and she almost loses him.
> 4 acts; 5 men, 4 women; 2 interiors.

FITZGIBBONS, Constantine. The Devil He Did (1972). Performance Publishing.
Originally produced at the Dublin Theater Festival, this play spoofs everything from the Adam and Eve creation story to religious warfare and air pollution. It is mostly a play about Good and Evil as discussed by Lucifer and the archangels, with the occasional presence of the Almighty (two converging shafts of light and a resonant voice).
> 8 or 9 men, 2 or 3 women, almost any combination; curtain setting. Royalty: $35.

FLANAGAN, Hallie. See entry under Davis, Hallie Flanagan.

FLAVIN, Martin. Broken Dishes (1929). Samuel French.
Henpecked husband Cyrus is constantly reminded by Jenny of the brilliant match she might have made with a perfect model. The wonderman turns up and turns out to be a crook and a penniless fugitive from justice. Elaine, the youngest daughter, rebels and in spite of her mother marries the man she loves, aided and abetted by her father.
> 3 acts; 6 men, 4 women; 1 interior. Royalty: $25.

_____. Children of the Moon (1923). Samuel French.
Moon-madness--the curse of dreaminess, a sort of insanity, affects the Atherton family; for the selfish mother wrecks the love affair of her daughter in order to keep her at home.
> 3 acts; 5 men, 3 women; 1 interior. Royalty: $25-20.

_____. The Criminal Code (1929). Liveright, 1929; French took over; abridged in Mantle 1929/30.

Robert Graham accidentally kills the son of the city's big
shot; Brady, the District Attorney, gets him a ten-year sentence.
Six years later Brady is appointed warden of the prison and has
Graham as the warden's chauffeur. This brightens his attitude, especially since the warden's daughter falls in love with him and he
with her. As chauffeur he is present and witnesses a murder in
the warden's office, but he adheres to the prisoners' criminal code
and refuses to divulge the murderer. He is put in the dungeon;
there he attacks Gleason, a prison official who has mistreated him,
with fatal results.
  3 acts; 20 men, 3 women; 9 interiors; prison costumes.

FLETCHER, John. A King and No King. See entry under Beaumont, Francis.

_____. The Knight of the Burning Pestle. See Beaumont.

_____. The Maid's Tragedy. See Beaumont.

_____. Philaster; or, Love Lies Bleeding. See Beaumont.

_____, with William Shakespeare. The Two Noble Kinsmen (1612).
  Harper, 1883 & 1898 ed. by Rolfe; in Temple dramatists ser.,
  Dutton; in PAR; THA.
    The story of Palamon and Arcite, based on The Knight's tale
by Chaucer. The two friends are captured and imprisoned in Athens.
From the prison they see Emilia and both fall in love with her.
Arcite is pardoned but exiled to Thebes, yet he remains in disguise.
Palamon is released by the gaoler's daughter. They meet in the
woods, but their fight over Emilia is interrupted by Theseus who
declares they must do it later. Arcite prays to Mars, Palamon to
Venus, Emilia to Diana. Arcite wins, but his horse kills him, so
Palamon is successful in winning Emilia.
  5 acts; 12 men, 7 women, extras; 5 interiors, 13 exteriors;
  Greek costumes of the period.

FLETCHER, Lucille. Night Watch (1972). Dramatists Play Service.
    A mystery thriller which begins with Elaine Wheeler pacing
the floor one sleepless night. Her husband tries to comfort her, but
when he steps away she sees a dead body in the window of an abandoned tenement across the way. She screams and calls the police,
but instead of a dead man they find only an empty chair. Next she
sees the body of a woman. The police are skeptical, the husband
claims she is having a nervous breakdown, and a lady psychiatrist
he calls agrees that Elaine should commit herself to a Swiss sanitarium for treatment. From this point on the plot thickens.
  5 men, 4 women; 1 interior. Royalty: $50-35.

FORBES, James. The Famous Mrs. Fair (1919). French, 1920;
  in his Famous Mrs. Fair & other plays, Doran, 1920; MOSJ;
  MOSL; abridged in Mantle 1919/20.
    Discusses the role of the married woman; can she combine
successfully the duties of wife and mother with a public career?

Mrs. Fair returns from war work, only to launch forth on a lecture
tour. The first absence is in the line of duty; but the second one
breeds disaster. She returns just in time to win back her husband
and her daughter.
    4 acts; 3 men, 10 women; 2 interiors.

_____. The Show Shop (1914). French, 1920; in his Famous
  Mrs. Fair & Other plays, Doran, 1920.
    Mrs. Dean, a stage mother, wants her daughter, Betty, to
be an actress and star on Broadway. Jerry, who wants to marry
Betty, is not so sure that she will succeed. Her first show "The
Wallop" is a failure; perhaps she will give up her theatrical career
if another fails. Rosenbaum guarantees to pick a failure; but, alas,
"Dora's Dilemma" is a great success. Nevertheless Jerry and Betty
steal away to be quietly married. Introduces several delightful
characters: the stage manager, older actors, the harassed author,
and the stage hands.
    4 acts; 14 men, 7 women; 3 interiors.

FORD, Ruth. Requiem for a Nun. See entry under Faulkner, William.

FORSYTH, James. Dear Wormwood (1961). Adapted from C. S.
  Lewis' The Screwtape Letters. Dramatic Publishing Company.
    Wormwood is a junior devil out to capture the soul of a young
architect. His method of operation, guided by advice from his Uncle
Screwtape, a minor official in Hell, is to corrupt his victim in
trifling ways and gradually get him in deeper and deeper. One of
the obstacles in Wormwood's way is Judy, a nice girl whom the architect loves. One of the advantages he has going for him, however,
is that England is at war, and the architect's emotions are aroused
and not very controlable. The victim thinks he is giving in to despair, but the audience knows it is the agent from below who uses
despair to fight faith and the joy in life that goes with it.
    9 men, 8 women; 1 set. Royalty: $35.

_____. If My Wings Heal (1968). Dramatic Publishing Company.
    A play about St. Francis of Assisi. When the play opens, the
Franciscan order is rehearsing a play honoring their founder, St.
Francis. As they make preparations, two monks arrive--St. Francis
and Pietro--who have returned to try to bring peace and understanding
between Christians and Saracens. St. Francis is repelled at the
stage portrayal of himself. He is also shocked to find the changes
that have taken place in the order--especially the laxity in the rules
of self-denial and poverty, and he enters into a great debate with the
contemporary Brother Elias.
    13 men, 8 women, extras, doubling possible; 1 set. Royalty:
  $35.

FRANCE, Anatole. The Man Who Married a Dumb Wife (ca. 1900).
  Tr. by Page, Lane, 1915, now carried by French; LEV; tr. by
  Jackson, in SMR.
    After his marriage, wishing to hear her speak, the man has

a surgeon operate.   Then the wife talks so volubly that her husband
seeks deafness to be at peace.
      2 acts; 7 men, 3 women, extras; 1 interior with exterior
      view; fanciful mediaeval costumes.   (French royalty: $25.)

FRANCIS, Sister Mary.   Smallest of All (1958).   Samuel French.
      The story of our Lady of Lourdes is presented in this religi-
ous drama.   A young girl, Bernadette Soubirous, sees a beautiful
lady in a vision.   Other visions follow and a townsman has his sight
restored.   Finally the simple, patient faith of Bernadette convinces
the church hierarchy and even a skeptical Chief of Police of the
truth of her vision.
      4 men, 4 women, extras; 1 interior, 1 exterior.   Royalty:
      $25-20.

FRANK, Anne.   Anne Frank: The Diary of a Young Girl.   See
      Frances Goodrich's Diary of Anne Frank.

FRANKEN, Rose.   Another Language (1932).   Samuel French.
      Mother Hallam rules her four married sons with an iron
hand.   They and their wives must spend each Tuesday evening with
her.   The wives mutter at an evening of chit-chat, but the sons
obey.   Stella, Victor's wife, alone rebels; she even encourages Jerry, Paul's son, to break away from the deadly Hallam uniformity and
pursue his artistic ambitions.
      6 men, 5 women; 2 interiors.   Royalty: $35-25.

_____.   Claudia (1941).   Samuel French.
      Though married to the promising young architect David,
Claudia is still attached to her mother's apron strings.   Suddenly in
24 hours she develops and achieves spiritual stature, because she
discovers she is going to have a baby and she learns that her mother
has only a short time to live.
      3 acts; 3 men, 5 women; 1 interior.   Royalty: $50-25.

_____.   Soldier's Wife (1944).   Samuel French.
      While John was in the war in the Pacific, his wife Kate
wrote him such excellent letters that, on his return, slightly
wounded, his pal's father insists that they be published.   They are
issued under the title "Soldier's Wife."   This brings much publicity
and even a Hollywood offer to the wife.   She is interviewed, and
asked to many meetings.   But Kate is satisfied to recapture and
keep John, even though she is receiving an income from royalties
which would give her financial independence.
      3 acts; 3 men, 2 women; 1 interior.   Royalty: $25-20.

FRECHTMAN, Bernard.   The Balcony.   See entry under Genet,
      Jean.

_____.   The Blacks.   See entry under Genet, Jean.

_____.   The Screens.   See entry under Genet, Jean.

FREDRO, Aleksander. <u>Ladies and Hussers</u> (1826). Tr. by Noyes,
French, 1925 (in World's best plays series).
    With amusing characterization presents scenes of military
life, intrigue, and love-making.
        3 acts; 6 men, 7 women; 1 interior; costumes and uniforms
    of the period.

FREEDMAN, Nancy and Benedict Freedman. <u>Mrs. Mike</u>. See entry under Roos, William.

FREEMAN, David. <u>Creeps</u> (1972). Samuel French.
    The setting is the men's toilet of a Canadian sheltered work-
shop for cerebral palsy victims. The men's room, it turns out, is
the only place that CP people can be themselves--where they can
retreat from the simple jobs they are given to do and deal with one
another as human beings. The five principals have CP, and by the
end of the play at least one of them will give up the security of the
sheltered workshop to face the world on his own, using his own
skills.
        5 men; 1 interior. Royalty: $50-35.

_____. <u>Jesse and the Bandit Queen</u> (1976). Samuel French.
    Jesse James and Belle Starr are the only characters in this
play, though each takes on other roles in dramatizing incidents from
their lives. We see them as young rebels in love, as old lovers
hurting one another, as train robbers in action. We see pulp writer
Richard Fox concocting his incredible story of Belle Starr for <u>The
Police Gazette</u> (he calls her a female Jesse James). At the end of
the play Jesse and Belle dramatize their deaths--he by cowardly
Bobby Ford's shot in the back, she by her son's knife.
        1 man, 1 woman; platform stage with cyclorama. Royalty:
    $50-35.

FREYTAG, Gustav. <u>The Journalists</u> (1853). Tr. by Henderson in
FRA, v. 12; tr. by House in <u>Drama</u>, v. 3, 1913.
    Depicts the part newspapers play in politics. Oldendorf,
editor of the Union, is to run for election, and is engaged to Ida
Berg, daughter of the retired Col. Berg. When Berg is persuaded
by a rival paper to run also, this rather breaks up the friendship
and threatens the engagement. Rich Adelaide Runeck buys up a
paper and enters the contest, putting Bolz, a real journalistic character, in charge. Bolz wins over the vote of Piepenbrink, a wine
merchant, in an amusing scene at a rival fete.
        4 acts; 18 men, 5 women, extras; 3 interiors; costumes of
    the period.

FRIEBUS, Florida. <u>Alice in Wonderland</u>. See entry under Le Galliene, Eva.

FRIEDMAN, Bruce Jay. <u>Scuba Duba</u> (1967). Dramatists Play Service.
    Harold Wonder has rented a chateau in the south of France

for him and the Mrs., but she has run off with a Negro skin-diver.
The American girl next door, who always wears a bikini, is willing
to help Harold and tell him pointless stories. He has a run-in with
a thief, but the French policeman takes the (French) thief's side
against him. Other visitors to the chateau include Harold's vacation-
ing psychiatrist and his floozie, Cheyenne, whose problem is too
many sexual climaxes (the good doctor is trying to "train her down"
to five a night). The group of characters presented has been
likened to a modern "You Can't Take It With You."
        7 men, 4 women; 1 interior. Royalty: $50-25.

_____. Steambath (1971). Samuel French.
        The steambath in this play is a kind of waiting room between
this world and the next, run by a Puerto Rican attendant who is God.
God, we learn, sends out his instructions to the world through a
television monitor--mixing up the good stuff with the bad, the serious with the insignificant. God also talks dirty and drinks six-foot
whiskey sours. Most people who die go immediately to the next
world, but the steambath is for neurotics, freaks, and people with
interesting stories to tell before they walk into the steamy haze and
forever disappear.
        12 men, 2 women; 1 interior. Royalty: $50-25.

FRIEL, Brian. Lovers (1968). Dramatic Publishing Company.
        A full-length play in two parts. In the first part, "Winners,"
two commentators are seated on either side of the stage, speaking
with emotion about a seventeen-year-old couple, Joe and Mag. Mag
bubbles with life and is very intense. She talks, teases, sulks, and
gets angry while Joe, more serious, tries to study for an examination. While the love scene develops, the commentators tell us that
the couple will soon be involved in a fatal accident. What we see,
then, is the lovers not only at the moment but for all time. They
are, as the title suggests, "Winners." The second part is called
"Weepers." It deals with a couple trapped by an invalid mother.
The mother, before their marriage, demands their immediate presence any time they stop talking in the parlor. After their marriage,
they are to come to her when they start talking.
        3 men, 5 women; 1 set. Royalty: $50.

_____. The Loves of Cass McGuire (1966). Samuel French.
        Cass returns home to Ireland after working fifty-two years
in America as a waitress. Her brother and family, to whom she
returns, promptly ship her off to an old people's home, and return
to her the five dollars a month she had sent them regularly. No
one needs her, nor was her money ever needed. At the rest haven
she begins to live off past memories.
        6 men, 4 women; unit set. Royalty: $50-25.

_____. Philadelphia, Here I Come! (1966). Samuel French.
        An Irishman looks over his rather hum-drum world the night
before he is to depart for Philadelphia. He sees little that is exciting and little that he will miss--except for the girl who is so
fond of him. But the image of Philadelphia is strong in his mind.

What the young man doesn't know, however, is that the aunt and
uncle he will be staying with are as unstylish as any he left behind.
All through the play the youth is saddled with a devilish alter-ego
who keeps putting irreverent thoughts in his head.

9 men, 4 women; composite interior. Royalty: $50-25.

_____. Weepers. See Lovers.

_____. Winners. See Lovers.

FRINGS, Ketti. Look Homeward Angel (1957). Adapted from
Thomas Wolfe's novel. Samuel French.

Through the characters of the hero, young Eugene Gant, and
his family, the familiar theme of a boy growing to manhood is portrayed. The mother, Eliza, seems remote to her son because of
her obsession with material things; W. O. Gant, the stonecutter
father, is imprisoned by his own failure; and Ben, the brother,
could never break away from the strangling grips of his family's
meaningless existence. Richard Watts of the New York Post, called
it "One of the finest plays in American dramatic literature."

10 men, 9 women; 2 exteriors and inset. Royalty: $50-25.

FRY, Christopher. Judith. See entry under Giraudoux, Jean.

_____. The Lady's Not for Burning (1949). Dramatists Play
Service.

A discharged soldier, Thomas Mendip, half swashbuckler and
half cynical misanthrope, wanders into the English market town of
Cool Clary to find it conducting a witch hunt. He announces that he
has committed murder and insists on being hanged. But when he
sees the alleged witch, a young and beguiling Jennet Jourdemayne,
he is willing to be cleared of the murder charge and of his misan-
thropy. His death wish is changed into a life urge. He does not
wish the lady to be burned.

8 men, 3 women; 1 interior. Royalty: $50-25.

_____. A Phoenix Too Frequent (1946). Dramatists Play Ser-
vice.

A satiric comedy which retells the story of the famous Matron
of Ephesus--the pious widow, and her maid, mourning the death of
her husband in front of his bier. The new widow has resolved to
withdraw from the world--until she sees a handsome guard. In no
time at all the widow is ready to return to a worldly and pleasant
life.

1 man, 2 women; 1 interior. Royalty: $25.

_____. Tiger at the Gates (1935). Adapted from a play by Jean
Giraudoux. Samuel French.

At the outset of the Trojan War, Hector comes to the Greek
hero, Ulysses, and convinces him and the populace of the insanity
of war. They agree that the war should not take place. Many selfish, special interest groups had not been considered, however. The
poets need the war for their odes and elegies; the kings, because

custom dictates, must lead their people in battle; and even the lawyer needs the war for his own personal honor. So in an incisive
commentary on the futility of war, logic and good will are tossed
aside, and the tiger of war once more roams freely.
        15 men, 7 women; 1 exterior. Royalty: $50-25.

_____. Venus Observed (1950). Dramatists Play Service.
        The star-gazing Duke of Altair has in mind to marry again。
He asks his son Edgar to help him choose one of three friends who
have been asked to his observatory. Edgar awards the apple to
Rosabel; but just then Perpetua arrives, the lovely daughter of the
Duke's clever but dishonest agent. This shifts the Duke's interest
to her and he becomes a rival with his son for Perpetua's attention.
While he and Perpetua are spending the evening in his observatory,
the jealous Rosabel sets the mansion on fire. The two are saved;
but Edgar wins Perpetua and the Duke will take Rosabel.
        7 men, 4 women; 1 interior, 1 exterior. Royalty: $35-25.

FUGARD, Athol. Boesman and Lena (1971). Samuel French。
        The simultaneously awful and tender story of a black couple
living in South Africa. They travel with the makings of a shack,
which they erect temporarily until a white man can knock it down.
Boesman's cruelty and physical violence is directed at his woman,
Lena, merely because she is the only object he can abuse and stay
clear of the white man's law. Their relationship becomes complicated by the arrival of an old and dying black African, and when
they set off to "walk" again it is with new awareness of who they
are.
        2 men, 1 woman; exterior set. Royalty: $50-25.

FULDA, Ludwig. The Blockhead (1907). Tr. by Bagdad in Poet
    Lore, v. 39, 1928.
        Grandfather Beck leaves his whole estate to the grandchild
to be voted the stupidest. Since none of the five gets a majority
vote, he gives all to Justus, a dreamer who thinks well of everyone. Ashamed of being the blockhead, he seeks to turn it over to
his cousins; each turns him down, and they ask a mental institution
doctor to pass on his being mad. The doctor finds he is physically
and mentally fit but too trusting to make his way in the world.
Doris, an American heiress, sees through the wiles of the cousins
and offers to take care of Justus by marrying him.
        5 acts; 9 men, 5 women; 3 interiors.

_____. The Lost Paradise (1890). Tr. & adapted by H. C.
    Demille, Goldmann, 1897; French, 1905.
        To take money for his daughter Margaret, Knowlton steals
an invention from Warner, who keeps silent because he loves Margaret. But the secret is discovered by her and all is rectified.
        3 acts; 10 men, 7 women; 2 interiors.

FULLER, Clark. A Canticle for Leibowitz (1967). Dramatic Pub-
    lishing Company.
        This play describes how the Church survived the nuclear

holocaust and prevented the loss of all knowledge in the dark ages that followed by preserving fragments of books either destroyed by the nuclear blasts or by the angry mobs who burned books and hanged scientists.   The Church hides some of the science of this civilization and a thousand years later must fear, all over again, the destructive use of this information.
    8 to 14 men, 5 to 12 women; 1 set. Royalty: $35.

GALANTIERE, Lewis. Antigone. See entry under Anouilh, Jean.

GALE, Zona. Miss Lulu Bett (1920). Appleton, 1921; CORF.
    Pulitzer Prize play 1921. A typical unmarried woman in a small town, Lulu sees no career ahead. Unexpectedly Ninian appears to make her starved life blossom. They marry and go on a month's wedding trip. Suddenly Ninian remembers he has had a wife somewhere, maybe in Seattle; perhaps he is a bigamist. Lulu returns home, definitely glad of her marital adventure. Her family exasperate her and she is about to leave them, when Ninian returns with proof of his first wife's death. Lulu is triumphant.
    3 acts; 4 men, 5 women; 2 interiors, 1 exterior.

_____ . Mr. Pitt (1924). Appleton, 1925.
    Mr. Pitt's fine qualities of generosity and goodheartedness are concealed under a lack of self-confidence and in oddities of manners and speech. He settles in a small mid-western town and marries Barbara. A year later Barbara has become so ashamed of him that she goes her own way (with a Mr. Maxwell), leaving a baby boy with Mr. Pitt. He places the baby in good care and goes to the Klondike. Twenty years later he returns to find his wife dead and his son in college. Alas, his son is as ashamed of him for a father, as Barbara had been of him for a husband. Yet he has overcome some of his deficiencies and his good qualities shine forth.
    3 acts; 5 men, 13 women; 5 interiors, 1 exterior.

GALLEN, Eleanor. Spring Dance. See entry under Barry, Philip.

GALSWORTHY, John. Escape (1926). Samuel French.
    Capt. Denant is conversing with a young woman in Hyde Park when a policeman arrests her. Denant sides with the woman, and in the argument, the policeman falls, strikes his head against an iron rail, and dies. Denant is sentenced to five years in Dartmoor. In his escape from the prison, some befriend, others want to turn him in. He finally reaches a church where the parson hides him, but Denant gives himself up to avoid incriminating the parson.
    Prolog & 9 episodes; 17 men, 9 women; 3 interiors, 7 exteriors. Royalty: $50.

_____ . Justice (1910). Samuel French.
    William Falder commits forgery to rescue Ruth from cruel treatment by her husband and suffers the penalties. Effectively and forcefully arraigns the English penal system; certain important reforms can be traced to this play. Dispassionately shows the inability of the law to cope intelligently with human problems and its

failure to assist the morally weak, as well as the failure of prison
authorities to meet individual needs.

> 4 acts; 17 men, 1 woman, many extras; 5 interiors.   Royal-
> ty: $25.

_____ . Loyalties (1922).   Samuel French.

A young society man, Capt. Dancy, is accused of stealing a
sum of money from a Jew at a country houseparty in England.   Immediately the various loyalties align themselves: the Jew for the
honor of his race, Dancy for the honor of an English gentleman,
loyalty to class, to race, to profession, even of wife to husband
who has deceived her.   The clan spirit is stronger than justice and
right.

> 3 acts (7 scenes); 17 men, 3 women; 5 interiors.   Royalty:
> $50.

_____ . Old English (1924).   In his Plays, Scribner, 1928.

Sylvanus Heythorp, "Old English" to his associates, is a
shrewd individualist, who though over 80, still wields power as
Chairman of the Island Navigation Co.   To insure financial security
for his two grandchildren by an illegitimate son, he gets his company to buy four ships for them, receiving a ten percent commission,
which he settles on their mother until the two are of age.   In order
to get the money, she wants to borrow on her expectations; if Heythorp refuses to cooperate, he will be exposed.   He dies of apoplexy
just before the scandal is to break.

> 3 acts; 17 men, 5 women; 3 interiors.

_____ . The Pigeon (1912).   Lond., Duckworth, & Scribner, 1912;
French carried; in his Plays, Scribner, 1924 & 1928.

Though the sentimental artist, the dupe or "pigeon" of the
social misfits, can accomplish little with his irresponsible philanthro-
py, yet his sympathetic human kindness in welcoming these few social outcasts enables them to understand a little better the lives they
are forced to live.   He seems to do more than the three specialists
in professional charity with their scientific theories.   It is the understanding spirit that counts; he is not discouraged by failures but remains a pigeon to be plucked.

> 3 acts; 12 men, 2 women, extras; 1 interior.

_____ . The Silver Box (1906).   Putnam, 1909; Lond., Duckworth,
1910; Scribner, 1916; in his Plays, Scribner, 1924 & 1928; CHAR;
MOSO; CLS.

A rich idler, Jack Barthwick, who has committed a theft, is
brought home drunk by Jones, the husband of a poor charwoman.
While in the house, Jones takes a silver cigarette box.   In the court,
the gilded fool lies, is protected by the law, and his father pays the
theft with a check; the poor laboring man tells the truth, cannot pay,
and is sent to jail.   Demonstrates the failure of the law to adminis-
ter justice to the poor.

> 3 acts; 11 men, 5 women, 2 children, extras; 3 interiors.

_____ . The Skin Game (1920).   Samuel French.

Pictures the bitter and costly feud in an English town between
the Hillcrists, of the old landed aristocracy, and the Hornblowers,
a newly rich family of manufacturers. The Hornblowers plan to
build a factory on Crescent hill which will decrease the value of the
Hillcrist property; the Hillcrists threaten to expose the scandal of
the wife of Hornblower's son. It is a deadlock; but the odds are in
favor of the Hornblowers who are in the stream of industrial progress.
        3 acts; 11 men, 4 women; 3 interiors. Royalty: $25.

_____. Strife (1909). Putnam, 1909; Lond., Duckworth, &
    Scribner, 1916, 1920; in his Plays, Scribner, 1916, 1924 &
    1928; DIC; MAP; WHI; WHK; DUR.
        The strike in the industrial plant in England is led by Roberts,
who represents labor and believes workmen should have some voice
in management; the capitalist employer Anthony thinks workmen are
too stupid for that. In the course of the play, strikes are discussed
fairly and justly, giving the motives, opinions, and points of view
held by capital, labor, labor-unions, and the public. Laments the
waste and even the futility of conflict; for when Roberts' wife dies
and the men desert him, and Anthony is forced to resign by his
company, the leaders are both in the same boat; and the strike is
settled by mutual concessions and a compromise--which is identical
with the agreement originally proposed before the strike was called.
        3 acts; 23 men, 7 women, extras; 3 interiors, 1 exterior.

GARCIA LORCA, Federico. Blood Wedding (1933). Tr. by Richard
    O'Connell and James Graham Leyan. Samuel French.
        A final tragedy strikes a Mother who has already lost all her
sons except one in this passionate allegorical tragedy. Except for
her youngest son, the Bridegroom, Mother has lost all her menfolk
in a feud with the Felix family. Now a wedding is arranged between
Bridegroom and the Bride, a girl loved by Leonardo, the son of the
Felix family. Immediately following the ceremony, the Bride runs
away with Leonardo. With the help of Death (a Beggar Woman)
Bridegroom overtakes the fleeing pair. He and Leonardo fight and
kill each other. Now the Mother is left alone in her empty house.
        9 men, 9 women, extras; 5 interiors, 2 exteriors. Royalty:
        $35-25.

_____. The Shoemaker's Prodigious Wife (1930). Tr. by O'Con-
    nell and Leyan. Samuel French.
        An elderly shoemaker, marrying late in life, finds he has a
shrew for a mate. She berates, he is not up to her ideal; she
creates a scandal by her constant revilings. Almost driven out, he
leaves; but returns disguised to find to his joy, that, whatever her
previous treatment she loves him truly.
        2 acts; 7 men, 9 women, extras; 1 interior. Royalty: $35.

GARDNER, Dorothy. Eastward in Eden (1947). Longmans, 1949;
    abridged in Mantle 1947/48.
        Presents the love story of Emily Dickinson. She would not
marry her youthful suitors; she was waiting for some one whom she

would know as her true love when she met him. She found him in
the Rev. Dr. Charles Wadsworth of Philadelphia, whom she met on
a visit there. They carried on an intimate correspondence; and it
was only later that she learned he was already married. After his
removal to California, she secluded herself in her home and garden,
but poured out her soul in unpublished poems. Some of the phrases
in her poems and letters are incorporated in the play.
    3 acts; 6 men, 8 women; 3 interiors; costumes of the period.

GARDNER, Herb. A Thousand Clowns (1962).   Samuel French.
    This is the story of a bachelor uncle who has been left a
nephew to rear. The uncle tires of writing cheap comedy and finds
himself unemployed. The unemployment, however, leaves him with
the time to roam the streets of New York and do all the things he
has always wanted to do. This is hardly the right upbringing for a
young boy, and a social service team soon comes to investigate.
Soon the uncle is solving problems for them. He is faced with the
problem of either going back to work or losing his nephew. Maybe
he could even marry the social worker and solve both problems.
What ever he does will be of a nonconforming nature.
    4 men, 1 woman, 1 12-year-old boy; 2 interiors. Royalty:
$50-25.

GARIS, Robert. The Stuck Pot (1963). Dramatic Publishing Com-
    pany.
    Every year Jason Boys School and the nearby Girls Academy
participate jointly in putting on a dance. Since some boy is always
stuck with a turkey of a date Jason students establish a consolation
prize, The Stuck Pot, which will be filled with money. The girls
find out about it and establish a Stuck Pot of their own, and soon
so much money has been collected for the Two Pots that everybody
wants to win one, even if it means going to a lot of trouble in order
to smell awful or look ugly.
    8 men, 15 women, extras; 1 interior. Royalty: $35.

GARRICK, David. The Clandestine Marriage. See entry under Col-
    man, George.

GASSEL, Sylvia. $E=MC^2$. See entry under Davis, Hallie Flanagan.

GAY, John. The Beggar's Opera (1728). In his Plays, Lond.,
    Chapman, 1928, v. 1; ASH; BEL v. 2; BRI v. 1; DIB v. 1; HAN;
    INCH v. 12; MCM; MOR; MOSE v. 2; NET; OXB v. 2; STM;
    TAY; TUG; TWE; UHL.
    A musical satire on thieving politicians and high-placed
rogues, with thieves and bandits the principal characters. The high-
wayman, Macheath, is secretly married to Polly Peachum who remains stedfast. He gets arrested, is reprieved, and acknowledges
her as his wife.
    3 acts; 14 men, 12 women; 5 interiors; costumes of the
    period. (Performance Publishing offers a modern acting
    edition in which the 18th century grammar is "unscrambled"
    and the street slang of the thieves is "clarified" for modern

audiences. 16 men, 12 women, extras; several representa-
tional settings. Non-royalty.)

GAZZO, Michael V. A Hatful of Rain (1955). Samuel French.
In a New York apartment live a husband, his wife, and his
brother. After the husband comes home from the hospital he is
strangely different--he can't hold a job and he stays away nights
without explanation. To make matters worse, he is visited by
strange people, and his brother is sexually attracted to the young
wife. We discover that during the hospital stay the husband has
been addicted to drugs, and his visitors are pushers who come to
collect. Though he vows to cure himself of the habit, it is not
certain that he will be successful. His wife will, however, see
him through his withdrawal.
7 men, 2 women; 1 interior. Royalty: $50-25.

GENET, Jean. The Balcony (1956). Translated by Bernard Frechtman. Samuel French.
The setting is a brothel in a place where revolution has
wiped out the entire power structure except for the Chief of Police.
He enlists the regular customers of the brothel to play out fantasy
roles. The man from the gas company becomes a bishop; a bank
clerk violates the Virgin Mary; one customer becomes a flagellant
judge; another is a victorious general. A mocking view of man and
society.
9 men, 4 women; various scenes. Royalty: $35-25.

_____. The Blacks (1957). Translated by Bernard Frechtman.
Samuel French.
A symbolic drama. A group of Negro players enacts before
a jury of white-masked Negroes (caricatures of a missionary, a
governor, a queen, and her dwarf lackey) the ritualistic murder of
a white; a murder they have been accused of. When they have
played out their crime, they turn on the judges and condemn them
to death.
9 men, 5 women; 1 interior. Royalty: $35-25.

_____. Deathwatch (1949). Samuel French.
Three young men wait in a prison cell: a murderer who will
soon be executed, a petty criminal who will soon be released, and
a younger criminal. In the prison world the most depraved criminals are the most glorified; therefore the murderer is in command.
The petty thief tries to build up his importance by borrowing from
the legends of other criminals, but he is jeered at by the third man
and finally strangles him. The murderer is not impressed. The
stigma of criminal glory is not something one chooses, he says, and
thus the petty thief has achieved nothing.
4 men; 1 interior. Royalty: $30-25.

_____. The Maids (1947). Samuel French.
Two servants, who are sisters, take turns pretending to be
the rich lady of the house. They put on her clothes and act out
their own vicious charades. It is the pretending that keeps them

alive and willing to endure the hardships they suffer. While they
are acting at being rich, Madame has gone for a rendezvous with
her lover, who is out of jail on bond.
>   3 women; 1 interior. Royalty: $35-25.

_____. The Screens (1962). English version by Bernard Frecht-
man. Samuel French.
>   Genet's vision of life and death set in Algeria at the time of
the war between the Arabs and the French colonials. The three
continuing characters are a young Arab thief named Said, his ugly
wife Leila, and his mother. Around these three the story of the
rebellion is told, and the relationships between the French military
and colonials and the natives. The screens of the title have to do
with the props used, which permit more than one scene to be played
at a time.
>   88 characters (can be played by 7 men & 8 women); platforms
and screens. Royalty: $50-35.

GERSHE, Leonard. Butterflies Are Free (1969). Samuel French.
>   Don is a young bachelor living in a cold-water flat, trying to
make it on his own as a song writer. The pretty actress next door
suggests that they remove the door connecting their two flats. The
actress (and the audience) learns that Don is blind, and that he is
trying to escape from an overprotective mother. Mother and actress
do not hit it off well together, and Don's mother succeeds in breaking
up the two. When mother decides that the girl was actually good for
her son, she helps them get together again.
>   2 men, 2 women; 1 interior. Royalty: $50-35.

_____. Miss Pell Is Missing (1963). Suggested by a story by
Saki. Samuel French.
>   Miss Pell has been missing for six weeks, and the police
have given up on the case for lack of evidence of wrong-doing.
Miss Pell's brother and niece hire a detective to find out what happened to her. Because Miss Pell was a stingy tyrant over the rest
of the family, nobody is really interested in finding her, and the detective hired is one who has had a string of failures. But he does,
much to everyone's consternation, find Miss Pell and restore her
memory--making her as unbearable as ever. Then her brother discovers a way to bring back her amnesia and turn her into a pleasant
house servant.
>   4 men, 3 women; 1 interior. Royalty: $35-25.

GIACOSA, Giuseppe. As the Leaves (1900). Tr. anon in Drama,
v. 1, 1911; tr. by Updegraff as Like Falling Leaves, Kennerley,
1913; same in his Three Plays, Little, 1913; MOSQ.
>   With sympathetic character development depicts how some go
up and others go down under the stress of a reversal of family fortune; the weak as leaves drifting into the path of least resistance.
Giovanni has many disappointments, as do his wife and children.
Cousin Massimo is healthy and lifts up the daughter Nennele by telling her of his love for her.
>   4 acts; 8 men, 7 women, extras; 2 interiors.

_____. The Stronger (1904). Tr. anon in Drama, v. 3, 1913;
tr. by Updegraff in his Three Plays, Kennerley, later Little,
1913.
     Depicts opposing views of honesty as represented by the
banker Cesare Nalli and his artist son, Silvio. The son feels his
father gets his money by ruining others; he is skillful but ruthless,
honest within the letter of the law but evading its spirit. Silvio
therefore will not accept such money; he leaves home to earn his
living by his art; he stands as the stronger of the two.
     3 acts; 9 men, 6 women, extras; 1 interior.

_____. Unhappy Love (1888). Tr. by Twombly in Poet Lore,
v. 27, 1916.
     Emma has an intrigue with a rather worthless dishonest fel-
low, Fabrizio, her husband's law assistant. Emma is a weak drift-
er; she longs for affection, which her husband Giulio fails to satisfy. She is willing to leave her home with Fabrizio, but as she is
going, she is so touched by the sight of her child's doll that she
cannot. Her husband does not forgive her indiscretion but is willing to have her remain--decency is thus preserved.
     3 acts; 4 men, 2 women, 1 child; 1 interior.

GIBBS, Wolcott. Season in the Sun (1950). Samuel French.
     A caustic magazine writer, George Crane, with his wife
Emily and their two children, seeks to get away from the city in
order to write his great novel in the idyllic environment of Fire Island. But his front porch becomes a sort of rendezvous of screw-
balls, dipsomaniacs and others, among them: forgetful Mrs. Jer-
myn, proprietor of the local boarding house and bungalows; Molly
Burden, the madame of a New York bordello; Deedy Barton, a predatory blonde; and finally his editor, Arthur Dodd (who can be none
other than Harold Ross of the New Yorker). They give up in despair and return to the city.
     3 acts; 9 men, 6 women; 1 exterior (the front porch).
     Royalty: $50-25.

GIBSON, William. The Miracle Worker (1959). Based on the life
     story of Helen Keller. Samuel French.
     This is a dramatization of the story of Helen Keller and her
relationship with her blind tutor Annie Sullivan. Little Helen, a
deaf mute, is bitter, violent, spoiled and at first, almost animal-
like. Annie, however, realizes that there is a good mind waiting
to be rescued from that dark tortured silence, and in some very
emotional scenes the process of drawing Helen out and teaching her
to speak and love is revealed to the audience.
     7 men, 7 women; unit set. Royalty: $50-25.

_____. Two for the Seesaw (1958). Samuel French.
     After escaping a life and career run by the well-to-do mid-
western family of his socialite wife, a lonesome lawyer comes to
New York. There he meets a plain Jewish girl from the Bronx.
He needs love, understanding, and commiseration, and she seems
to be a woman who lives to make others happy. Each fills the
other's needs until reality catches up with them. He is an educated,

prosperous gentile who can not forget his wife; she is a plain Jewish
girl, uncultured, with a heavy Bronx accent. The happiness they
have found together is not enough to make them compatible for society, and they each realize the affair must end.
    1 man, 1 woman; 1 interior. Royalty: $50-25.

GILBERT, Sir William S. The Gondoliers (1889). In his Original
    Plays, Chatto, 1903, ser. 3; in his Plays & Poems, Random,
    1932; in his Complete Plays, Modern Lib. Giant, 1936; in his
    Authentic Libretti, Crown, 1939.
    The romances of three couples. One of the gondoliers in
Venice is thought to be the son of the King of Barataria and married
in infancy to the daughter of the Duke of Plaza-Toro. But the Spanish nurse reveals her humble drummer boy is the king's son, whom
the Duke's daughter has loved all along. So he becomes King, and
the gondoliers as commoners can retain their brides.
    2 acts; 9 men, 8 women, extras; 1 interior, 1 exterior;
    costumes of about 1750.

_____. H. M. S. Pinafore (1878). In his Original Plays, Chatto,
    1902, ser. 2; in Modern Lib., 1925, Giants, 1936; in Modern
    readers ser., Macmillan, 1929; in his Plays & Poems, Random,
    1932; in his Authentic Libretti, Crown, 1939 MOSO. Samuel
    French (with band arrangements).
    Babies are changed in their cradles by Little Buttercup, so
that Ralph the patrician is an able seaman and Corcoran of common
birth is the Captain of the ship; Josephine, the Captain's daughter,
loves Ralph the sailor, but her father wishes her to marry Sir Joseph Porter. Of course all is straightened out in the end.
    2 acts; 7 men, 3 women, extras; 1 exterior (quarterdeck);
    naval costumes.

_____. The Mikado (1885). In his Original Plays, Chatto, 1903,
    ser. 3; in Modern Readers ser. Macmillan, 1929; in his Plays &
    Poems, Random, 1932; in Complete Plays, Modern Lib. Giant,
    1936; in his Authentic Libretti, Crown, 1939. Samuel French
    (with band arrangements).
    Nanki-Poo, son of the Mikado, disguised as a minstrel, runs
away from marrying elderly and rather ugly Katisha, falls in love
with Yum-Yum, ward of Ko-Ko, the Lord High Executioner, whom
he wishes to marry himself. An execution must take place within a
month; he will allow Nanki-Poo to marry Yum-Yum for a month, if
he consents to be beheaded then. But when it turns out that Nanki-
Poo is the Mikado's son, the beheading is indefinitely postponed.
Many well-known songs are featured in this operetta.
    2 acts; 5 men, 4 women, extras; 2 exteriors; Japanese cos-
    tumes.

_____. Patience (1881). In his Original Plays, Chatto, 1903,
    ser. 3; in Modern Lib. 1925 & Giants, 1936; in his Plays &
    Poems, Random 1932; in his Authentic Libretti, Crown, 1939;
    SMR.
    A delightful take-off on the esthetic extravagances of Oscar

Wilde. The pale fleshy poet Reginald Bunthorne loves the milkmaid
Patience, but she returns the love of an idyllic poet Archibald Gros-
venor. Being too near perfection, Archibald decides to become a
"commonplace young man" so he and Patience can be married. The
20 love-sick maidens all marry manly dragoons, and Bunthorne remains without a bride.
    2 acts; 6 men, 5 women, many extras; 2 exteriors.

_____. The Pirates of Penzance (1880). In his Original Plays,
Chatto, 1902, ser. 2; in Modern readers ser., Macmillan, 1929;
in his Plays & Poems, Random, 1932; in his Complete Plays,
Modern Lib. Giant, 1936; in his Authentic Libretti, Crown, 1939.
Samuel French (band arrangements).
    Frederic is raised by the pirate king instead of a pilot, be-
cause of the deafness of nurse Ruth. He falls in love with Mabel,
the daughter of "the very model of a modern major-general." A
slave to duty, Frederic feels obliged to help the police liquidate his
pirate friends, but the pirates all marry the General's daughters.
    2 acts; 5 men, 5 women, extras; 2 exteriors; costumes.

_____. Pygmalion and Galatea (1871). French carried as sepa-
rate; in his Original Plays, Chatto, & Scribner, 1902; ser. 1;
MAP; MAT.
    Pygmalion prays that his statue of Galatea come to life, and
to his surprise, it does. By her want of worldly knowledge she
causes considerable misunderstandings, even causing Cynisca his
wife to think Pygmalion unfaithful. Galatea reconciles them and returns to being a statue.
    3 acts; 5 men, 4 women; 1 interior (studio); Greek costumes.

GILBERT, Willie. Catch Me If You Can. See entry under Wein-
    stock, Jack.

GILBRETH, Frank Bunker. Cheaper by the Dozen. See entry un-
    der Sergel, Christopher.

GILLETTE, William H. Electricity (1910). In Drama v. 3, 1913;
    French, 1924.
    Emeline will have nothing to do with the money her father
gained through a corrupt corporation, nor will she look at Jim, who
loves her but has also inherited great wealth. So Jim swaps jobs
with Bill, the electrical repairman; and because Emeline thinks he
is Bill and an underdog and earning his way, she is won by Jim,
who now goes into the electrical business with Bill.
    3 acts; 7 men, 5 women; 2 interiors.

_____. Held by the Enemy (1886). Samuel French.
    Shows the old South occupied by the Northern army during the
Civil war, with thrilling episodes of love and war, and an effective
trial scene.
    5 acts; 13 men, 3 women, extras; 4 interiors; military cos-
    tumes. Royalty: $25.

_____. Secret Service (1895).   French, 1898; QUAK; QUAL;
abridged in Pierce & Matthews v. 1.
        Vivid and intense military drama of the Civil war (1864).
Pictures the cool and resourceful men of action who are in the
Secret Service.   Presents the heroic motives of both the North and
the South, showing patriotism, loyalty, and personal honor.
        4 acts; 14 men, 5 women, extras; 2 interiors; some military
costumes.

_____. Sherlock Holmes (1899).   London, 1922; Doubleday, 1935;
CARC.
        Skillfully plotted American melodrama; developed from Conan
Doyle's stories.   Introduces the famous detective, his foil, Dr. Wat-
son, and his enemy, Moriarty.   He shrewdly escapes from seemingly overwhelming dangers, as in the Stepney gas chamber.   Demonstrates his well-known methods of deduction.
        4 acts; 15 men, 5 women; 5 interiors.

GILROY, Frank D.   The Subject Was Roses (1962).   Samuel French.
        A pampered son comes back from the war his own man, and
the varying effects on the father and mother are disasterous.   The
family tries to love each other and rebuild the past, but the links of
communication between the trio have collapsed.   They have grown
irreparably apart and cannot sustain the dream and reality too.   The
mother and son dance together and are thrown into fits of laughter,
but this isn't the son she once knew.   The father breaks an important business appointment to take the boy to the ball game.   They
have a marvelous time, but the next morning an argument between
the husband and wife turns the father-son love sour.   They all want
to love each other, but they do not know how.
        2 men, 1 woman; 1 interior.   Royalty: $50-25.

GIRAUDOUX, Jean.   Amphitryon 38 (1929).   Adapted by S. N. Behrman.   Dramatists Play Service.
        Jupiter comes down from Olympus in search of unselfish love.
His early dalliance this time brings him to Alcmena while her husband is away at war.   He wins her as Amphitryon; Hercules is the
result.
        6 men, 5 women; 1 interior, 3 exteriors.   Royalty: $25.

_____. The Enchanted (1950).   Adapted by Maurice Valency.
Samuel French.
        A charming young lady obsessed with a belief in the super-
natural runs afoul of the law in this widely acclaimed comedy.   The
girl lives in a small town where the inhabitants know her and tole-
rate her obsession quite tranquilly.   The government inspector, however, regards her mystic dabblings as a threat to the order, security, and safety of the state.   With all the authority at his disposal he
tries to change the girl's preoccupation with spirits.   Nothing seems
to work until she falls in love.   Then she discovers the joys of the
real world and accomplishes in a split second what the inspector
could not do with all the forces of law and logic.
        9 men, 11 women; 1 interior, 1 exterior.   Royalty: $50-25.

_____. Judith (1931). Translated by Christopher Fry. Drama-
tists Play Service.
 This play treats the story of Judith and Holofernes. The
Judean city is about to surrender to Holofernes. Its army has de-
fected and its people are resigned to defeat. The prophets of the
city convince the beautiful virginal Judith that God has chosen her
to save her people, that only she can get an audience with Holofernes
and divert him with her charms--then kill him. Judith resolves to
go, refusing the offer of a prostitute, Susannah, who resembles her,
to go in her place. Holofernes, Judith finds, is not a barbarian,
but rather a man she can surrender to without restraint. The next
morning she kills him, but when her leaders celebrate her Godly
act she admits that the slaying was an act of love and that she also
wishes to be executed. An angel appears and convinces Judith that
she must preserve the lie that she murdered out of patriotism and
religious commitment. She agrees to play the role of a saint.
 26 men, 7 women (doubling possible in both); 2 interiors.
Royalty: $50-25.

_____. The Madwoman of Chaillot (1945). Translated by Mau-
rice Valency. Dramatists Play Service.
 At the suggestion of a prospector big businessmen are in-
duced to get at oil that underlies Paris. The madwoman overhears
and with practical goodness plans to exterminate the greedy ones
who make life unhappy. They are tried at a mad tea-party and pro-
nounced guilty; they are lured into a bottomless pit to see the oil.
After the wicked and selfish are thus disposed of, joy and justice
and love return to the world again, but "what a bore if humanity
had to be saved every afternoon."
 2 acts; 17 men, 8 women, extras; 1 interior, 1 exterior.
Royalty: $50-25.

_____. Ondine (1954). Adapted by Maurice Valency. Samuel
French.
 The disparity between things as they should be and the actual
situation leads to tragedy in this fantasy drama. An ideal love develops between a beautiful sea nymph and a handsome knight, and
they are married at court. The harsh realities of the world soon
intrude on their idyllic life, and their love is too ideal to survive
the shock. The handsome knight, his world crumbling around him,
dies from grief; the nymph, totally disillusioned, returns to the
calm, perpetual beauty of the sea.
 17 men, 11 women; 3 sets. Royalty: $50-25.

_____. Tiger at the Gates. See entry under Fry, Christopher.

GLASPELL, Susan. Alison's House (1930). Samuel French.
 Pulitzer Prize play 1931. A famous American poet, Alison
Stanhope (supposedly Emily Dickinson) left, at her death eighteen
years before, self-revealing poems of love. Agatha, symbolizing
the older generation, has guarded them and kept their secret from
the public. Agatha passes the poems on to young Elsa of the newer
generation, who like Alison has had an affair with a married man.

Elsa believes the family of a dead poet has no right to withhold such fine poems.
    3 acts; 5 men, 6 women; 2 interiors.   Royalty: $25-20.

GLEASON, James. Fall Guy. See entry under Abbott, George.

_____ and Richard Taber. Is Zat So? (1925).   Samuel French.
    A prize-fighter, Chick Cowan, and his trainer, Hap Hurley, go to work as footman and butler in a fashionable New York home, being brought in by Clint Blackburn to superintend his training as a boxer, so that he may whip his brother-in-law, suspected of being the family crook.   When the fight comes off, Clint is knocked out, but the blow clears his mind and he knows his brother-in-law for the crook he is.
    3 acts; 9 men, 5 women, extras; 2 interiors, 1 exterior. Royalty: $25-20.

_____ . The Shannons of Broadway (1927).   Samuel French.
    The owner of the hotel in a small New England town refuses to take in Emma and Mickey Shannon, small-time vaudevillers, even when they are stranded there and ask to get warm.   They buy the inn and become landlords themselves, help settle many local minor problems, present all kinds of farcical stunts, and then go back to the show business.
    3 acts; 18 men, 6 women; 1 interior.   Royalty: $25.

GODFREY, Thomas. The Prince of Parthia (1767).   Little, Brown,
    1917; in MOSS-1; QUIK; QUIL.
    First play written by an American to be produced in America by professional actors.   Arsaces returns in triumph from the war, to be welcomed by Evanthe with whom he is in love.   But envy and jealousy cause his imprisonment.   He is freed by his brother Gotarzes, and together they fight the attacking Arabians.   Arsaces is reported killed; Evanthe takes poison; the lovers meet to say good-bye; she dies and he kills himself; and Gotarzes reigns.
    5 acts; 8 men, 4 women, extras; 3 interiors, 1 exterior; costumes.

GOETHE, Johann Wolfgang von. Faust (1806).   Tr. by Taylor in
    his Dramatic Works, Bohn, 1892; Houghton, 1898; Macmillan,
    1930; Oxford, 1932; Grosset, 1936; in FRA v. 1; in HARC v. 19;
    BAT v. 11; TRE-1, & 2, (v. 2); TREA-1; WOR; tr. by Latham,
    Dutton, 1907; tr. by Andrews, Princeton, 1929; tr. by Raphael,
    Cape & Smith, 1930; tr. by MacNeice abridged, Oxford, 1952.
    Mephistopheles gains permission to try to ruin Faust's soul. The discontented Faust promises to forfeit his soul if the devil can give him one moment of perfect contentment.   He gains the sensual pleasure of Margaret, but gains no contentment.   In Part 2, he gains the world of public affairs; but he now desires to serve mankind and in it finds the only real satisfaction and gains contentment. Though he has lost his wager, his soul is taken to heaven.
    Various scenes; 13 men, 3 women, extras; various interior and exterior scenes; various costumes.

_____. Iphigenia in Tauris (1787). Tr. by Swanwick in his Dramatic Works, Bohn, 1892; FRA v. 1; BAT v. 11; tr. by Dowden, Dutton, 1906.

Iphigenia is priestess in the temple of Diana in Tauris where Thoas, King of the Taurians, seeks her as his bride; therefore he seeks to kill each stranger. Orestes and Pylades arrive. They are threatened with death until Iphigenia recognizes Orestes as her brother. Though she is a priestess, she is a living soul and is willing to leave with her brother and Pylades; they go with the blessing of Thoas.

5 acts; 4 men, 1 woman; 1 exterior; costumes of the period.

GOETZ, Augustus. The Heiress. See entry under Goetz, Ruth.

GOETZ, Ruth and Augustus Goetz. The Heiress (1947). Dramatists Play Service.

A rather shy girl, Catherine Sloper, falls in love with a young fortune-hunter, Morris Townsend. Her father sees through the money-seeking young man and forbids the marriage. She thinks Morris is in earnest in his love and proposes an elopement; but this would lose him the fortune and he will not do it. Two years later he again proposes, but she realizes he has grown greedier and locks the door against him.

3 acts; 3 men, 6 women; 1 interior; costumes of 1850.
Royalty: $50-25.

GOGOL, Nikolai V. The Inspector-General (1935). Tr. by Sykes, Lond., Scott, 1892; adapted by Anderson, French, 1931 & 1943; Tr. by Mandell, Yale Dram. Assn., 1908; tr. by Davies in BAT v. 18; tr. by Seltzer, Knopf, 1916; tr. by Garnett as The Government Inspector, Chatto, 1926, Knopf, 1927; tr. & adapted by Dolman & Rothberg, Baker, 1937; NOY; tr. by Seymour & Noyes in TREA-1.

An impoverished clerk, Ivan Khlastakov, finds himself stranded in a small Russian village where all the officials are grafters. Mistaking Ivan for an Inspector-general whom they are expecting and thinking he is incognito and to cover their guilt, the officials fete him handsomely and feed him generously. Ivan has a thoroughly good time and escapes from town just before the real Inspector-general arrives.

4 acts; 14 men, 9 women, extras; 2 interiors; costumes of the period.

GOLDEN, Harry. Only in America. See entry under Lawrence, Jerome.

GOLDING, William. The Brass Butterfly (1957). Dramatic Publishing Company.

The setting of this comedy is 300 A.D., in Caesar's summer home. Caesar has just sent Postumus off to war and is trying to cure his grandson of a bad case of boredom. Two Egyptians arrive: Phonocles, who has invented a steamboat and a cannon; and his sister, Euphrosyne, a secret Christian. A romance begins

between the sister and Caesar's grandson, while Phonocles works on
his inventions. By the time he finishes them, Postumus returns to
forcefully retire Caesar. Both the steamship and the cannon fall into the rebels' hands. At the crucial moment, Caesar invokes Jupiter, Euphrosyne prays to God, and Phonocles appeals to Reason.
Then the situation becomes better.
     8 men, 1 woman; 1 simple set. Royalty: $50.

GOLDMAN, James. The Lion in Winter (1964). Samuel French.
     King Henry of England and his queen are quarreling over a
matter of great significance: who will rule the kingdom after Henry's death. Of the three sons the royal pair have, Henry prefers
the youngest son. The queen favors the eldest. The middle son
hopes to play both ends against one another to finally win out. And
Henry, who understands the consequences for his kingdom if he does
not decide, gives up the idea of having another heir by his mistress
as just one more contender for his throne.
     5 men, 2 women; cyclorama, arches, wagons. Royalty:
$50-25.

GOLDONI, Carlo. The Beneficent Bear. Tr. by Clark. French,
    1915.
     Crabbed, old M. Géronte has a rough exterior but a kind
heart, sentimentally sympathetic. He saves his nephew Delancour
from financial ruin and his niece Angélique from an undesirable marriage.
     3 acts; 4 men, 3 women; 1 interior; costumes of 18th century
France.

_____. The Coffee-House (1750). Tr. by Fuller. French, 1925.
     The intrigues developed at the coffee-house give rise to much
infectious mirth. Among the characters reflecting contemporary
manners is an aristocratic scandalmonger, Don Marzio.
     3 acts; 8 men, 2 women; 1 exterior; costumes of the period.

_____. A Curious Mishap (1757). Tr. by Zimmern, McClurg,
    1892; Dramatic Pub. Co. carried; tr. by Hollister, Ann Arbor,
    G. Wahr, 1924.
     A French lieutenant, M. de la Coterie, a younger son with
no prospects, has been hospitalized for wounds in the home of Philibert, a rich Dutch merchant. He falls in love with the merchant's
only daughter, Giannina, who reciprocates; but both feel that her
father will not approve because of his having no money. So she
tells her father that Costanza, daughter of the broker Riccardo, is
in love with the lieutenant and he with her, but Riccardo will not
consent. Philibert gives the lieutenant 500 guineas and tells him to
go ahead and marry without the father's consent--which de la Cot-
terie and Giannina proceed to do.
     3 acts; 4 men, 3 women; 1 interior; costumes in character.

_____. The Fan (1765). Tr. by Zimmern, McClurg, 1892; tr.
    by McKenzie, Yale Univ. Press, 1911; tr. by Lloyd in Litera-
    ture of Italy, 1907, v. 8; tr. by Fuller, French, 1925; CLF-2.

Signora Candida breaks her fan. Her lover, Evaristo, buys her another, but, too bashful to present it to her direct, gives it to Giannina to deliver. This causes misunderstandings. The inanimate fan passes from hand to hand: Giannina's two lovers get it, then a count, then a baron; but finally the fan reaches Candida and Evaristo wins.

3 acts; 10 men, 4 women; 1 exterior; costumes of the period.

_____. The Mistress of the Inn (1753). Tr. by Pierson in MAU; tr. by Lady Gregory, Putnam, 1924; French, 1924; Longmans, 1927; tr. by Lohman in LEG.

Lively Mirandolina is the mistress. She forces the misanthropic misogynist Cavaliere di Ripafratta to succumb to her charm, and she benefits from the attentions of two noble lovers, a marquis and a count. But in the end she marries Fabrizio, her humble faithful servant.

3 acts (6 scenes); 6 men, 1 woman; 4 interiors; costumes of the period. (In Lady Gregory's adaptation, entitled "Mirandolina," 5 men, 1 woman; 3 interiors.)

_____. The Squabbles of Chioggia (1762). Tr. by Lemmi in Drama, v. 4, 1914.

Weaves a light comedy out of the sturdy folk in a small fishing village. They squabble, they gossip, but they take the consequences for the common good when matters become serious.

3 acts; 10 men, 5 women, extras; 2 interiors, 3 exteriors; costumes in character and of the period.

GOLDSMITH, Clifford. What a Life (1938). Dramatists Play Service.

Henry Aldrich, the somewhat frustrated son of a Phi Beta Kappa father, is in high school and is expected to make Princeton as his father did; but he can't even make the Spring Dance. He runs into manifold student and faculty problems of adjustment in the lives of boys and girls. An understanding Assistant Principal helps Henry to get straightened out.

3 acts; 8 men, 10 women, extras; 1 interior. Royalty: $25.

GOLDSMITH, Oliver. She Stoops to Conquer (1773). Many good editions; BEL v. 11; BRI v. 1; CLF v. 1; DIB v. 10; HARC v. 18; HUD; INCH v. 17; MAT; MCM; MOO; MOR; MOSE; v. 2; NET; OXB v. 4; RUB; SMO; STA; STM; TAU; TAY; TUQ; TWE; UHL.

Young Marlow, supposedly bashful and reserved, goes to visit the Hardcastles because his father has proposed a match with the daughter, Kate. Tony Lumpkin sends him to the house as an inn, where Marlow treats Hardcastle as a landlord and makes violent love to Kate as a maid servant. Kate continues the deception to win him. Excellent situations make for successful revivals of this famous play.

5 acts; 7 men, 4 women, extras; 2 interiors, 1 exterior; costumes of the period.

GOODMAN, Arthur. If Booth Had Missed (1932). Samuel French.
    What Lincoln might have faced in the Reconstruction era.
Thaddeus Stevens, Stanton, and Grant enter into a political conspiracy
and impeach "that pious humbug" (Lincoln) who would receive the
Secessionists back into the Union without punishment or political advantage. They are infuriated at his humaneness. He is tried in the
Senate and acquitted, but is shot down by an embittered newspaper
editor.
    3 acts; 17 men, 2 women, extras; 4 interiors. Royalty:
    $25-20.

GOODMAN, George. The Wheeler Dealers. See entry under Les-
    lie, F. Andrew.

GOODRICH, Frances and Albert Hackett. The Diary of Anne Frank
    (1956). Dramatized from Anne Frank: The Diary of a Young
    Girl. Dramatic Publishing Company.
    Winner of the Pulitzer Prize for 1956 and the New York Dra-
ma Critics' Circle Award. Popularized further by the screenplay.
No summary is needed for this touching story of a young Jewish girl
and her family and friends living in an attic hideaway to escape the
wrath of the Nazis. Their luck runs out at the end of the play.
    5 men, 5 women; 1 interior. Royalty: $50-25.

GORDON, Ruth. Over Twenty-One (1944). Dramatists Play Service.
    In a training camp for flyers in Florida during World War II,
are Max and his wife Polly, he a brilliant journalist and she a successful writer. Because he is a bit over age, Max is having dif-
ficulty with his army flying studies but Polly keeps encouraging him.
His boss in New York wants him back and urges him to keep on
writing--which Polly does for him. They long to get to a pleasant
camp, but Max is sent to the very worst one; Polly goes with him.
    3 acts; 6 men, 5 women; 1 interior; some military costumes.
    Royalty: $35-25.

_____. Years Ago (1946). Dramatists Play Service.
    Ruth at 16 wants to be an actress; she even gets an inter-
view with John Craig at his stock company theatre in Boston, but
he tells her to wait. Father thinks she might be an athletic instructor and insists that she graduate from high school. Friend
Fred wants her to go with him to Harvard Class Day exercises, but
instead she sets out for New York to make her own way. Father
relents enough to send her off with his old spy-glass which will be
good for $100 if she needs money.
    3 acts; 4 men, 5 women, 1 cat; 1 interior; costumes of
    1913. Royalty: $35-25.

GORDONE, Charles. No Place to Be Somebody (1969). Samuel
    French.
    The owner of a black neighborhood bar has big plans for the
time when his former mentor gets out of prison and rejoins him.
He discovers, however, that his friend is now pacified and against
carrying on the fight against white society. Next, in response to

Mafia pressure over his bar operation, the owner picks up a white liberal girl whose father is a judge and former Mafia lawyer, begins to live with her, and gets her to steal information from her father's files so that he can blackmail the mob. His black girlfriend commits suicide over the humiliation of losing him to a white girl, and in the finale the Mafia men, the bar owner, and his former mentor are all killed。
    11 men, 5 women; 1 interior.   Royalty: $50-35.

GORKI, Maxim.   The Lower Depths (1902).   Tr. by Hopkins,
    Four Seas, 1920; same in DID; SMP; TUCG; WATI; WATL v. 3;
    tr。 by Covan in CEW; DIK v. 2; HAV; MOS; TRE-1, 2, & 3;
    TREA-2; tr. by Chambers as In the Depths in BAT v. 18; tr.
    by Hopkins as A Night's Lodging in Poet Lore v. 16, 1905; tr.
    by Irving, Lond。, Unwin, 1912; tr. & adapted by Laurence as
    At the Bottom (the literal translation), French, 1930; tr. by
    Bakshy & Nathan, Yale Univ. Pr., 1945.
    The scene is a lodging house of outcasts, rather revolting in its setting, almost devoid of plot (it is more a series of pictures), with no humor or romance.   The grim biographies of the waifs are hinted at, and some of the derelicts are characterized.   Into the group of wretched creatures comes the pilgrim, Luka, who still has hope--that he who seeks will find.
    4 acts; 12 men, 5 women, extras; 1 interior, 1 exterior.

GOTTLIEB, Alex.   Dear Phoebe.   See entry under Taggart, Tom.

GOW, James.   Deep Are the Roots.   See entry under d'Usseau,
    Arnaud.

_____ and Arnaud d'Usseau.   Tomorrow the World (1943)。 Dramatic Publishing Company.
    Treats the post-war problem of the indoctrinated Nazi youth.   During World War II Emil Bruckner, a twelve-year old Nazi, is smuggled out of Germany, after his father has been murdered in a concentration camp because of his liberal ideas (which were unknown to Emil), and is brought to his uncle's home in a midwestern town.   Emil thinks himself a good spy in an enemy country, resists his Jewess teacher (whom his uncle is to marry), and even strikes down his cousin Patricia (10 years old) who tries to make his birthday pleasant.   He breaks down when he realizes that he really wants to have and give love.   There is hope for him.
    3 acts; 2 men, 4 boys, 3 women, 1 girl; 1 interior.   Royalty: $25-20.

GRANVILLE-BARKER, Harley.   The Madras House (1910).   Lond.,
    Sidgkick, 1910; Kennerley, 1911, later Little; DIC; MOSO.
    The drapery trade depends on women largely and the proprietors of the Madras house discuss woman's relation to society, showing many aspects: the woman in business, the emancipated woman, woman's dress and the lure of the manikin, the six anemic Huxtable daughters who have no hope of a husband (horrible examples of what our artificial civilization leads to), the woman who doesn't

care to have a husband, the flirtatious wife of a good but neglectful
male, and the nagging wife whose husband has such peculiar ideas
that he turns to Mohammedanism and its harem as his sane solution
of woman's place.
    4 acts; 8 men, 12 women, extras; 4 interiors.

_____. Marrying of Ann Leete (1901). French, 1901; in his
    Three Plays, Kennerley, 1911, later Little.
    George Leete, son of a decadent 18th century family, mar-
ries a farmer's daughter, much to the wrath of his relatives. His
sister Ann follows his example, renounces marriage with Lord John
Carp, and marries the gardener.
    4 acts; 14 men, 6 women; 1 interior.

_____. Prunella. See entry under Housman, Laurence.

_____. The Voysey Inheritance (1905). Lond., Sidgwick, &
    Brentano, 1909; in his Three Plays, Kennerley, 1911, later
    Little; DIG; PLAP v. 1; abridged in Pierce & Matthews, v. 1.
    Studies the effect of commercialism on a typical English
middleclass family. Edward Voysey, entering business with his
father, finds their wealth has come through speculations with funds
entrusted by clients, the spoils of which have come to his family.
This crooked business, his father says, his father did before him--
all for the good of the clients. Edward who inherits the business
will try to put it straight, yet he must still use the same tactics
as his father in doing so. A problem in practical ethics.
    5 acts; 10 men, 8 women; 2 interiors.

GRAY, Patricia. The Hobbit (1968). Based on J. R. R. Tolkein's
    fantasy novel. Dramatic Publishing Company.
    Bilbo, one of the most conservative of all Hobbits (Middle
Earth creatures) is prodded by the wise magician Gandalf to leave
his home and set off as chief robber in an attempt to recover an
important treasure. The Hobbit is the first story of Tolkien's Lord
of the Ring tales, all of which deal with the world of imagination,
magic, fairies, and elves.
    Large, variable cast (about 26); several playing areas.
    Royalty: $35-20.

GRAY, Simon. Butley (1971). Samuel French.
    A play about a university professor named Ben Butley and his
former prize student, Joey, now Ben's colleague. The two not only
share an office together but a flat as well. Butley's cynicism and
futility overpower everything in his life, and, in the day we see him
operate, his former wife cuts off their relationship to marry "the
most boring man in London" and Joey himself leaves Butley to live
with a homosexual lover.
    4 men, 3 women; 1 interior. Royalty: $50-35.

GREDY, Jean P. and Pierre Barillet. The Cactus Flower. See
    entry under Burrows, Abe.

_____. Forty Carats. See entry under Allen, Jay.

GREEN, Paul. The House of Connelly (1931). Samuel French.
Subtitle: "A play of the old and new South." The once proud
Southern family of Connelly is disintegrating on a plantation, while
in vivid contrast the tenant farmers show vigor. Patsy, the daughter
of the tenant, poor white trash but with brains, urges spineless Will
to brace up and be an active landlord; she will help him. She loves
the land, then she comes to love him, and they marry. The opposing members of the family leave, unwilling to accept Patsy as mistress of the house. Undaunted, Will and Patsy go ahead to bring
prosperity back to the House of Connelly.
    6 scenes in 2 acts; 4 men, 6 women, extras; 1 interior, 2
    exteriors. Royalty: $25-20.

_____. In Abraham's Bosom (1926). Samuel French.
    Pulitzer Prize play 1927. Pictures the struggles of Abe, the
mulatto son of a white man in a Southern community, to attain some
small share in a white man's world where Negroes are not allowed.
Abe's passionate nature has an intellectual groping for higher things;
he wants to teach himself and others; but he is handicapped by his
marriage to Goldie. He is a brave soul but not a leader of men;
he is defeated by his own limitations and by circumstances.
    7 scenes; 7 men, 2 women, 3 children; 3 interiors, 2 ex-
    teriors. Royalty: $25.

_____. Johnny Johnson (1936). Samuel French.
    Persuaded by his girl and Woodrow Wilson's assurance,
Johnny, a pacifist, enlists in the war to end all wars (World War I).
Many disillusionments come to him in the army. After being wounded, he comes out of the hospital with a tank of laughing gas, with
which he sprays the French High Command and gets them to decree
the end of the war. Before this order can be made, Johnny is committed to an asylum, though he is the only sane man there and is
only a common soldier seeking to reconcile the insanity of war with
the sanity of man. When the war is over, he is forced to sell toys
on the street.
    49 men, 6 women; 13 scenes. Royalty: $50.

GREENE, Graham. The Complaisant Lover (1959). Samuel French.
    At a dinner party a guest is propositioned by the daughter of
a visiting couple. He explains that he only has affairs with married women and politely declines the invitation. After she leaves,
the hostess appears and we learn that she is the guest's mistress.
When the husband enters, the pair are almost discovered as they
plan for a meeting abroad. Finally the husband does find out about
the alliance, and he meets with his wife's lover. Neither wishes to
lose her, so they plan to share her, becoming complaisant lovers.
    6 men, 3 women; 2 interiors. Royalty: $50-25.

_____. The Living Room (1952). Samuel French.
    Upon the death of her parents, a young girl moves in with
her two maiden aunts and her crippled uncle, a priest. She is in

love with an older married man, but she does not see this love as
sinful or indecent.   There is a blistering scene when the love affair is found out, and finally the man's wife visits the girl.   Although the girl struggles, she is overwhelmed by the descending
tragedy.
     2 men, 5 women; 1 interior.   Royalty: $50-25.

          .   The Potting Shed (1957).   Samuel French.
     A young man did something in the potting shed when he was
fourteen years old which makes him quite the pariah to his own
family in this melodrama.   Although his father is on his deathbed,
the mother will not allow her son to see him.   The boy's mind is
a blank, and his mother refuses to tell him what he did.   With the
help of his uncle, a pastor, the son finally pieces together the truth
about that dark event.
     6 men, 5 women; 3 interiors.   Royalty: $50-25.

GREENE, Patterson.   Papa Is All (1942).   Samuel French.
     Among the Mennonites in Pennsylvania Papa is a tyrant in his
home.   He won't let Mama go to the movies or have a telephone in
the house.   He won't let Emma his daughter have a surveyor as a
beau; but Emma steals away with him to a picture show and Papa
goes after them with a gun.   His car stalls on the railroad crossing.   Jake his son whacks him on the head with a wrench, and
leaving his body in an empty freight car, returns to report that Papa is all (i.e., dead).   There is much happiness until Papa turns up
again; but in the meantime the telephone is in and other innovations
have begun, and Papa is going to be powerless to stop these intro-
ductions of the mechanical age.
     3 acts; 3 men, 3 women; 1 interior.   Royalty: $35-25.

GREENE, Robert.   Friar Bacon and Friar Bungay (1589).   In Mer-
    maid ser., Scribner; ASH; BAS; GAY; HOW; MCI; MIO v. 2;
    NEI; PAR; OLH; OLI v. 1; SCI; SCW; SPE.
     Two English friars are conjurers and rivals in magical powers.
They make a head of brass which the Devil promises will speak in a
month.   It does, but after their servant and pupil Miles is carried
off by the Devil, the head falls and breaks.   A sub-plot concerns the
romance of Margaret, the game-keeper's daughter, who is wooed by
Lacy for Prince Edward, but she falls in love with Lacy and marries him.
     5 acts; 25 men, 4 women, extras; simple or elaborate scene-
    ry; costumes of the period.

GRESSIEKER, Hermann.   Royal Gambit (1956).   Translated and
    adapted by George White.   Samuel French.
     Deals with King Henry VIII of England and his relationships
with the six women in his life.   Beginning with the divorce of Katherine of Aragon, we see Henry's alliances with Anne Boleyn, Jane
Seymour, Anna of Cleves, Kathryn Howard, and Kate Parr.   The
women progress in dress right up to modern times, showing the
lasting effects of Henry's thoughts.   And Henry's thoughts progress
from those of a Renaissance man to a contemporary liberal, finally

concluding that the 20th century is the dead-end of humanism.
1 man, 6 women; platform set.   Royalty: $50-25.

GRIBOIEDOV, Aleksander S.   The Misfortune of Being Clever (1824).
Tr. by Pring, Lond., Nutt, 1914; tr. by Pares as The Mischief
of Being Clever, School of Slavonic Studies, Univ. of London,
1925; in NOY as Wit Works Woe.
A young intellectual, Chatski, returns to Moscow after three
years abroad, eager to see Sophie whom he loves and his fatherland
again.   He finds Sophie throwing herself at a worthless and sneaking
sycophant (her father's secretary); he finds Moscow still with the
same old prejudices.   He tells people what he thinks of them, and
they look on him as a dangerous dreamer, a crazy madman, who
has read too many books.   He rails against the follies of society
and leaves in disgust, bereft of Sophie.
4 acts; 11 men, 7 women, 6 girls, extras; 2 interiors; costumes of the period (early 19th century in Russia).

GRIEG, Nordahl.   The Defeat; a Play about the Paris Commune of
1871 (1936).   Tr. by Watkins in Scandinavian Plays of the 20th
Century, ser. 2, Princeton Univ. Pr., 1944; tr. by Arkwright,
Lond., Gollancz, 1944.
Depicts vivid scenes in the streets of Paris during the Commune of 1871.   Introduces some historical characters, but emphasizes the faith of the masses that a society of love and justice for
all will finally triumph.
4 acts; 30 men, 10 women, many extras; 4 interiors, 3 exteriors; costumes of the period.

GRILLPARZER, Franz.   Medea (1819).   Tr. by Miller in FRA v. 6.
Jason and Medea are banished from Iolcus and seek refuge
with Creon in Corinth.   She tries to become a Greek but in vain.
Banished from Corinth, she kills Creusa and her own two children.
Exiled, they flee separately.   The curse of the Golden Fleece is
over them.
5 acts; 4 men, 3 women, 2 children, extras; 1 interior, 2 exteriors; costumes of the period.

_____.   Sappho (1818).   Tr. by Frothingham, Roberts, 1876;
SMN.
Returning to Lesbos after receiving the crown for poetry in
Greece, Sappho is accompanied by Phaon, a young peasant, who deceives himself into believing that admiration is love.   He is unde-
ceived when a naive maiden, Melitta, awakens in him sentiments
which mean love.   The artistic temperament of Sappho is ill-suited
to the demands of practical life; thus she unfits herself to be high
priestess of poetry.   She forfeits her life by casting herself from
the cliff into the sea.
5 acts; 3 men, 3 women, extras; 1 exterior; Greek costumes.

GRIMM BROTHERS.   See Paul Sills' Story Theatre.

GROSS, Laurence and E. C. Carpenter.   Whistling in the Dark (1932).

Samuel French.
　　A writer of crime fiction, Wallace Porter, with his fiancée,
is looking for a house to rent up the Hudson. They find it, but it
is a hideout for gangsters. He boasts to them that he can concoct
a perfect crime, so they lock him up with his fiancée to think up a
murder plan against the Crime Commissioner. He plans a beautiful murder; and then concocts another plan to prevent it.
　　3 acts; 10 men, 2 women; 1 interior. Royalty: $35-25.

GUARE, John.　The House of Blue Leaves (1971).　Samuel French.
　　On the day that the Pope is visiting New York, a frustrated
song-writing middle-aged zoo attendant is persuaded by his mistress
to call an old school chum (now a big-time Hollywood producer) for
a job writing movie scores. Before the producer arrives the zoo
attendant's son does--AWOL from the Army and carrying a bomb to
blow up the Pope and all of Yankee Stadium. Then comes the producer's fiancée, who has broken her hearing aid. About the time
that the would-be songwriter calls for the men in white coats to
come and take away his wife (her name is Bananas), three sightsee-
ing nuns drop in and the son's bomb goes off prematurely. Finally,
the producer elopes to Australia with the songwriter's mistress, and
the poor soul is left with his nutty wife--whom he strangles.
　　4 men, 6 women; 1 interior. Royalty: $50-35.

GUIMERÁ, Angel.　Daniela (1902).　Tr. by Gillpatrick, Putnam,
　　1916 (Hispanic Society, Pubn #107); CLDM.
　　Daniela, an adopted daughter of Ramón and Antonia, left 14
years before as a young girl to go to Paris with a Frenchman. Now
suffering from heart attacks, she returns to them. Ramón doesn't
want her back, for his early love for her turned to hate when she
left; but on her return he falls in love again. Excitement caused by
Antonia's jealousy brings on a heart attack from which Daniela dies.
　　3 acts; 8 men, 7 women, 1 little girl; 1 interior.

　　　　　　.　Marta of the Lowlands (1896).　Tr. by Gillpatrick,
　　Doubleday, 1914.
　　With much human sympathy depicts the helpless and unfortunate exposed by society to the blows of chance, with the peasant
and laborer in conflict with the landlord. A wealthy farmer, Sebastian, foists his mistress, Marta, in marriage on his laborer, Mannelich; after which he seeks to resume his former intrigue with her.
Mannelich takes vengeance on him.
　　3 acts; 8 men, 3 women, 1 child; 1 interior.

GUITRY, Sacha.　Deburau (1918).　Tr. by Granville-Barker, Lond.,
　　Heinemann, & Putnam, 1920; abridged in Mantle 1920/21.
　　Delightfully fables the life of the famous French pantomimist
of the early 19th century, presenting his love affair with Camille,
his successes and failures, and his final retirement in favor of his
son.
　　Prolog & 4 acts; 12 men, 9 women, extras; 3 interiors, 1 exterior; costumes of the period.

_____ . Pasteur (1919). Tr. by Brown in DID.
Presents scenes in the life of the great savant, centering
especially on his researches in bacteria and inoculation. Dramatizes the event of the boy bitten by a mad dog.
5 acts; 9 men, 1 boy, 0 women, extras as students; 5 interiors, costumes of the period.

GUTZKOW, Karl Ferdinand. Sword and Queue (1944). Tr. by
Colbron in FRA v. 7.
Princess Wilhelmine, daughter of Frederick William I of
Prussia, is sought in marriage by the Prince of Bayreuth, as well
as by the English Prince of Wales and an Archduke of Austria.
The Prince wins as a proposed grenadier recruit with Queue and
Sword. One scene depicts an evening at the "Tobacco Parliament"
where the Prince feigns tipsiness and in a mocking funeral oration
tells the pseudo-deceased king some bitter truths.
5 acts; 10 men, 5 women, extras; 5 interiors; costumes of
the period (about 1710).

HACKETT, Albert. The Diary of Anne Frank. See entry under
Goodrich, Frances.

HAIGHT, George. Good-Bye Again. See entry under Scott, Allan.

HAINES, William W. Command Decision (1946). Dramatists Play
Service.
General Dennis is in charge of an airplane division in England during World War II. He must meet agonizing problems in
deciding to bomb certain European areas in order to get the most
effective results. Some government officials object, placing politics
above practical issues. After their interference Dennis is delighted
to be shifted to a B-29 command in the Pacific area.
3 acts; 18 men, 0 women; 1 interior. Royalty: $50-25.

HALBE, Max. Mother Earth (1897). Tr. by Grummann in FRA
v. 20.
Having quarrelled with his father, Paul went to Berlin 10
years before and married Hella; with her he edited for the intel-
lectuals a feminist magazine about the New Woman. When his father
dies, he returns to bury him. After the funeral he meets again his
old sweetheart, Antoinette, who had married rather out of spite;
Paul realizes how they have loved each other and that he has forfeited real happiness for a vague ideal. Two days later Antoinette
comes to him and they agree to die together at her old estate.
5 acts; 14 men, 7 women; 2 interiors.

_____ . Youth (1893). Tr. by Barrows. Doubleday, 1916.
In wronging Annaschka, Stephen pleads that youth calls to
youth in the spring when there is a sudden awakening. Her brother,
the imbecile Amandus, shoots at Stephen to kill him but hits his
sister instead, and the girl dies.
3 acts; 4 men, 2 women; 1 interior.

HALL, Wilton E., Jr. 1984. See entry under Owens, Robert.

HAMILTON, Patrick. Angel Street (Gaslight) (1938). Samuel
   French.
       The suave but sinister Mr. Manningham, under the guise of
kindliness, is torturing his gentle wife into insanity. Enter Rough,
amiable and paternal, from Scotland Yard, on the track of a murderer who committed the crime in this very house. Together he and
his wife build up the evidence to convict.
       3 men, 2 women, 2 extras as policemen; 1 interior. Royal-
ty: $50-25.

_____. Rope (Rope's End) (1929). Samuel French.
       Two rather degenerate undergraduates at Oxford, seeking a
thrill just for the fun of it, murder a classmate, crowd his body
into a chest in their room, and then serve tea from the top of it to
the victim's father and aunt. Watched relentlessly by the suspecting
lame poet Rupert Cadell, the two murderers break down under the
strain and confess their guilt.
       6 men, 2 women; 1 interior. Royalty: $25-20.

HAMLIN, Mary P. and George Arliss. Hamilton (1917). Baker,
   1918.
       Seizing on the moral courage of Hamilton as the central
theme, when he would not be intimidated by fear of personal scandal
in the Reynolds affair nor sacrifice his bill for the assumption of
State debts, vitalizes him and other builders of the Republic.
       4 acts; 11 men, 5 women, extras; 3 interiors; costumes of
the period (1790).

_____. The Rock (1921). Samuel French.
       Develops the character of Simon Peter from his self-asser-
tion and overweening confidence, through his desertion and utter
abasement, to his forgiveness and realization that he has finally
succeeded where he seemed to fail.
       3 acts; 5 men, 3 women, extras; 2 exteriors. Royalty: $10.

HAMPTON, Christopher. The Philanthropist (1971). Samuel French.
       A professor of philology, Philip, listens with another faculty
member to a student reading a play. Philip likes it. The other
finds it incredible--especially the suicide in it. The student playwright reenacts the scene for credibility's sake, and actually kills
himself. Later, at a party at Philip's house, the professor plays
"philanthropist" again: he lets a cynical novelist take his fiancée
home, while he sleeps with the hooker.
       4 men, 3 women; 1 interior. Royalty: $50-35.

HANKIN, St. John E. C. The Cassilis Engagement (1906). In his
   Three Plays with Happy Endings, Lond., French, 1907; also
   separately, French; in his Dramatic Works, Secker, 1912, v.
   2; in his Plays, Secker, 1923, v. 2; MOSO; DIG.
       A wise mother maneuvers the breaking of a mistaken engage-
ment of her son to a pretty girl much his inferior by showing what

his fiancée is really like when she visits his home.
4 acts; 6 men, 8 women; 2 interiors, 1 exterior.

_____. The Charity That Began at Home (1907). In his Three
Plays with Happy Endings, French, 1907; also separately,
French; in his Dramatic Works, Secker, 1912, v. 2; in his
Plays, Secker, 1923, v. 1.
An idealistic enthusiast, Margery, invites a miscellaneous
collection of outcasts to a houseparty. However, when Margery
goes so far in charity as to become engaged to the unworthy Hugh
Verreker, the liberal preacher Hylton and the cause of her enthusiasm, being in love with her himself, recants his principles and
contrives to have the engagement broken.
4 acts; 6 men, 6 women; 2 interiors.

_____. The Last of the DeMullins (1907). Lond., Fifield, 1909;
in his Dramatic Works, Secker, 1912, v. 3; in his Plays,
Secker, 1923, v. 2; CHA; CHAR.
Hugo DeMullins is conventional, genteel, and proud of his ancestry. He wants his name carried on. Janet, his daughter, emancipated and exiled because she ran away without marrying, returns
to her sick father with her eight year old son. She turns the merciless light of her experiences and reason on the absurdities and
perils of an obsolete feudalism; also challenges conventional morality
and demands as an individualist to live her own life.
3 acts; 5 men, 7 women, a boy of 8; 1 interior, 1 exterior.

_____. The Return of the Prodigal (1905). In his Three Plays
with Happy Endings, French, 1907; also separately, French; in
his Dramatic Works, Secker, 1912, v. 1; in his Plays, Secker,
1923, v. 1; MAP.
After various failures at home, Eustace has been sent to
Australia with £1000. He loses that in the far country and works
his way back to England. He fakes a faint on his father's front
lawn and is taken care of. When he "recovers," the problem again
arises, what to do with him. He is given an allowance to go to
London and live, without any scandal in his home town, where his
brother Henry is so successful, having become a partner in his
father's manufacturing firm.
4 acts; 7 men, 5 women; 2 interiors, 1 exterior.

_____. The Two Mr. Wetherbys (1903). French, 1907; Kenner-
ley, 1913; in his Dramatic Works, Secker, 1912, v. 1; in his
Plays, Secker, 1923 v. 1.
The good and bad brothers Wetherby are married to sisters,
both conventional and rather narrow-minded. One brother, Richard,
has emancipated himself by telling the truth and letting others ima-
gine the worst; the other brother, James, is still in bondage to his
wife's apron-strings, though continually deceiving her by consistent
lying. Aided and abetted by his "bad" brother Richard, James tries
to free himself and it looks as if he would secure a better domestic
life without Aunt Clara and Cousin Robert.
3 acts; 3 men, 4 women; 2 interiors (1 interior possible).

HANLEY, William. Slow Dance on the Killing Ground (1964). Dramatics Play Service.
    The play takes place in a dusty stationery store near the
Brooklyn Bridge. The owner of the store, an old man named Glas,
is a non-Jewish refugee from Nazi Germany who deserted his Jewish
wife and son during the bad times. In Act I Glas "dances" with a
black street dude named Randall who is being hunted by the police for
killing his mother. In Act II both "dance" with a black girl named
Rosie, who is lost in this section of town while searching for the
apartment of a doctor who will perform an abortion on her. The
"Killing Ground" is Randall's name for the outside world, the world
beyond the dirty windows of the store. The richness of the play
comes from the way in which these three characters come to relate
to, and care for, one another.
    2 men, 1 woman; 1 interior. Royalty: $50-25.

HANSBERRY, Lorraine. A Raisin in the Sun (1959). Samuel
French.
    A Negro family (a widow, her son, his wife, his sister, and
his son) live in a cramped flat in south side Chicago. The widow
is expecting a $10,000 insurance check on her late husband's life,
and the son, a chauffeur, begs her to give him the money to invest
in a liquor store. The widow, instead, puts a down payment on a
home for the family, one where there is sunlight and no roaches.
Reluctantly she gives her son the remaining $6,500, which he gives
to his liquor store partner who leaves town. Though that dream is
dead, the family will move to the new neighborhood--in spite of the
white representative who warns them against moving and offers to
reimburse them for the down payment.
    7 men, 3 women, 1 boy; 1 interior. Royalty: $50-25.

_____. The Sign in Sidney Brustein's Window (1964). Samuel
French.
    Sidney Brustein is a Jewish intellectual and editor, living in
Greenwich Village. His wife Iris is a striving actress. Their
circle of friends and relatives include crooked politicians, homosexuals, and prostitutes. The plot revolves around idealistic Sidney's attempts to get a reform politician elected, and to do so he
must fight the establishment. The issues the play deals with are
the fragility of love, morality, drugs, interracial relationships, conformity, and withdrawal from society.
    6 men, 3 women; 1 interior. Royalty: $50-25.

_____. To Be Young, Gifted, and Black (1969). Samuel French.
    A play based on the life and works of Lorraine Hansberry,
in her own words, adapted by her husband, Robert Nemiroff. Part
I deals with her childhood in Chicago. Part II draws on material
from her other plays, her novel, and other writings.
    3 men, 5 women; platform stage. Royalty: $50-25.

HARDT, Ernst. Tristram the Jester (1907). Tr. by Heard. Bost.,
Wagner, 1913; FRA v. 20; same in Poet Lore v. 43, 1937.
    Tristram is denied access to King Mark's court because of

his attachment for Isolt, the King's wife. She is condemned to the
lepers, whence she is saved by Tristram. He returns a second
time, disguised as a jester. Isolt does not recognize him but his
hound does, and then she knows.
     5 acts; 11 men, 3 women, extras; 2 interiors, 1 exterior;
medieval costumes.

HARDY, Thomas. The Dynast (1904-1908). Macmillan, 1904-1908,
    3 v.; in his Works, Macmillan, 1912-1913, v. 2-3; Macmillan,
    1 v., 1920 & 1931.
     Centers around the figure of Napoleon who represents Force
and Will that move the world. An episodic epic of the Napoleonic
wars, with impressive scenes, rich in historic lore and literacy
fancy. Though written in dramatic form, it is hardly a stage play,
but some scenes are powerfully dramatic and could be produced.
     In 3 parts, with 19 acts & 130 scenes.

HARMON, Donna. The House on the Cliff. See entry under Batson,
    George.

HART, Moss. Christopher Blake (1946). Dramatists Play Service.
     Presents the problem of the divorce orphan--to which parent
shall he go? Christopher is twelve years old; his parents have their
divorce complete, except as to the boy. He dreams fantasies which
might bring them together: he is a national hero, he is a famous
playwright, he is an abandoned school-boy at Christmas, his parents
are in the poor-house and he is a South American who spurns them.
In the court the parents present their sides; the boy chooses his
father.
     12 men, 2 women; various interiors and exteriors. Royalty:
$50-25.

_____. George Washington Slept Here. See entry under Kaufman,
    George S.

_____. Lady in the Dark (1941). Dramatists Play Service.
     The successful editor of a fashion magazine, Liza, feels lost
and seeks help from a psychoanalyst. There she sees (and acts)
her dreams and memories, and through their analyses she comes out
of the dark and back to her belief in herself and her sanity. The
dreams are musical fantasy interludes.
     2 acts; 9 men, 11 women; 2 interiors. Royalty: $50-25.

_____. Light Up the Sky (1948). Dramatists Play Service.
     An experimental play by Peter Sloan is to be tried out in
Boston. The tearful director, the temperamental leading lady, the
dynamic backer and his sardonic wife--all have great hopes for its
success. When they meet after the opening, they all believe they
have a flop; they blame everyone in sight, but especially the author,
who plans to escape by plane. The morning reviews however turn
out to be favorable, and all are happy again--all except the author
who now says he has graduated--and he lays down the law.
     3 acts; 9 men, 4 women; 1 interior. Royalty: $50-25.

_____. The Man Who Came to Dinner. See entry under Kaufman, George S.

_____, with George S. Kaufman. Once in a Lifetime (1930). Samuel French.
    Three down-and-out troupers go West to try their luck with the talkies, especially to teach them how to speak correctly. The most stupid of the three, George, blunders to the top of the industry because Glogauer, the big producer, mistakes his errors for marks of genius.
    3 acts; 24 men, 14 women; 5 interiors. Royalty: $50-25.

_____, with George S. Kaufman. You Can't Take It With You. (1936). Dramatists Play Service.
    The slightly mad Sycamore family, headed by Grandpa Vanderhof, follows each his hobby: fireworks being manufactured in the basement, printing press running in the living room, artists at work, dancing, typing--wealth for them does not compare with the joy of human affection and doing what really interests them. In contrast, the rich Kirbys are basically unhappy. Tony, their son, is in love with Alice, and gets his parents to the crazy household on the wrong night. They act very snobbishly, but are finally converted, especially after Mr. Kirby's interview with an ex-Grand Duchess who is earning her living as a waitress.
    3 acts; 9 men, 7 women, 3 extras; 1 interior. Royalty: $25.

HARTLEBEN, Otto Erich. Hanna Jagert (1893). Tr. by Holmes in Poet Lore v. 24, 1913.
    Depicts the rise of a poor working girl to be a baroness. Hanna is intelligent and self-reliant. She advances beyond her fiancé Conrad, through her teacher Alexander. She experiments with socialism and individualism; and marries Baron Bernhard as a means of securing greater freedom.
    3 acts; 6 men, 3 women, extras; 3 interiors; costumes of the period.

HARTOG, Jan de. The Fourposter (1951). Samuel French.
    Presents Agnes and Michael in a series of rather uneventful incidents in their married life, from their arrival as a bridal couple, through the birth and marriage of their children, to their departure to another residence.
    6 scenes in 3 acts; 1 man, 1 woman; 1 interior with furniture and costume changes, 1890 to 1925. Royalty: $50-25.

_____. Skipper Next to God (1949). Dramatists Play Service.
    Pious and idealistic Captain Kuiper has brought 156 Jewish refugees from Europe during World War II, but he is not allowed to land at any port in South or North America. He arrives with them off Sandy Hook. He is unwilling to return them to Europe and feels he must do with them as if he were God. He schemes to blow up the boat and have the Jews rescued by the Yachts in a regatta there; this will give his passengers a decent chance for a

safe home, for he feels the humans will be cared for through
public opinion.
> 3 acts; 15 men, 0 women, extras; 1 interior (the cabin).
> Royalty: $50-25.

HAUPTMANN, Gerhart. The Assumption of Hannele (1893). Tr.
by Archer, Heinemann, 1894; in BAT v. 12; in Drama v. 12,
1922; tr. by Meltzer, Doubleday, 1908; in his Dramatic Works,
Huebsch, v. 4, 1912; HAV; HUD; tr. by Bryan in Poet Lore
v. 20, 1909.
   A young girl, Hannele, ill-treated by her drunken step-father,
tries to follow her mother by drowning herself. In the sordid hospital she dreams glorious fantastic pictures based on the Bible. She
thinks she is in heaven, where she sees the nurse as her mother,
the school-ma'am who reprimands her step-father becomes the
Saviour Jesus. As the doctor hovers over her, we realize she has
died.
> 2 acts; 7 men, 4 women; 1 interior.

_____. The Sunken Bell (1896). Tr. by Meltzer, Russell, 1896;
Doubleday, 1899 & 1914; Heinemann, 1900 & 1907; in his Dramatic Works, Huebsch, & Lond., Secker, 1914, v. 4; FRA v.
18; MOSQ; WHK; tr. by Harned in Poet Lore v. 10, 1898.
   A pious bell-founder, Heinrich, is surprised by a goblin who
throws into the lake a bell meant for a chapel; he lures Heinrich
away to an amiable water nymph, an elf-maiden Rautendelein. He
sets about to construct a complete set of chimes, but becomes exhausted, and stricken with remorse, he returns home to die, as the
sunken bell tolls. Blends the natural with the supernatural, the physical with the spiritual, presenting the creative soul of the idealistic
artist in his struggles to reconcile his highest aspirations with every
day duties.
> 5 acts; 7 men, 2 women, 2 children, extras; 1 interior, 2
> exteriors; some fanciful costumes.

_____. The Weavers (1892). Tr. by Morison, Heinemann, 1899,
in his Dramatic Works, Huebsch, & Secker, 1912, v. 1; FRA
v. 18; CEW; DIC; DIK v. 1; SMP; TRE-1, 2, & 3; TREA-2;
WHI; abridged in Pierce & Matthews v. 2.
   Presents the suffering of the oppressed weavers during the
labor riots in Silesia in 1844: a sociological study of the conflict
between capital and labor. Moritz Jaeger, back from the army,
shows righteous indignation at the treatment of the weavers. When
an old weaver is killed by accident, the maddened weavers sack the
home of the capitalist Dreisigger. In the end the mill owners ac-
cede to their demands.
> 5 acts; 27 men, 13 women, extras; 5 interiors; costumes of
> the period.

_____. The White Saviour (1920). Tr. by Muir in KRE; in his
Dramatic Works, Huebsch, v. 8.
   In the conquest of Mexico Catholic Cortez overcomes the mys-
tic Montezuma who worships the white men as gods.

11 scenes; 26 men, 4 women, extras; 6 interiors, 2 exteriors; costumes of the period.

HAWTHORNE, Ruth. Mrs. Partridge Presents. See entry under
Kennedy, Mary.

HAYES, Joseph. The Desperate Hours (1955). Adapted from his
novel. Samuel French.
This polished melodrama portrays a helpless suburban family
held prisoner in their home by three escaped criminals. One morning the Hilliard family is preparing for the day's activities when
three armed and desperate criminals invade the home. Mr. Hilliard and 19-year old Cindy are allowed to go to work, while Mrs.
Hilliard and 10-year old Ralphie are held hostages. While the terror mounts within the home the police search is closing in on the
Hilliard house.
11 men, 3 women; unit set. Royalty: $50-25.

HAZELTON, George C., Jr. Mistress Nell (1900). Pub. in Phila.,
1900; in v. 16 of America's Lost Plays, Princeton Univ. Pr.,
1941.
An orange-girl, Nell Gwyn, is made an actress by Jack Hart
who loves her; the Duke of Buckingham courts her, and he in turn
must yield to the King. She goes to a ball masked and disguised as
the lad Beau Adair, where she is given papers signed by the King to
be delivered to France. She is chased back to her rooms, where
all follow to seek Adair. There she discloses what the King has
signed--and also herself as Adair.
4 acts; 11 men, 4 women, extras; 4 interiors; 1 exterior;
costumes of the time of Charles II.

_____ and J. H. Benrimo. The Yellow Jacket (1912). Bobbs-
Merrill, 1913; French, 1939; in DID.
With delicate touches which reach the emotions and with
whimsical and subtle art the story of Wu Hoo Git is unfolded, from
his birth until he attains the Yellow Jacket of Emperor. Tests and
develops the imagination of reader or listener. Furniture changes
are made in full view of the audience by a supposedly invisible
property man.
3 acts; 17 men, 12 women; 1 set: interior or stage of a
Chinese theatre; Chinese costumes. Royalty: $25-20.

HEBBEL, Friedrich. Agnes Bernauer (1855). Tr. by Pattee in
Poet Lore v. 20, 1909; in SMK.
Prince Albrecht, son of Ernest, Duke of Bavaria, marries
a barber's daughter, the beautiful Agnes Bernauer. He is disowned
by his father. After a few years of happy marriage, Agnes is condemned to death by a court, because she could not be recognized by
the nobility and is also thought of as a witch. Asked to give up Albrecht, she refuses and drowns herself, the victim of social convention. Albrecht's father upholds the State at the expense of his
own happiness and that of his son, who finally comes to recognize
his responsibility.

5 acts; 16 men, 3 women, extras; 7 interiors, 3 exteriors;
costumes of the period (about 1425).

_____. Judith (1841). Tr. by Van Doren in Poet Lore v. 25,
1914.
Bethulia in the mountains of Palestine is besieged by the As-
syrian general, Holofernes, sent by Nebuchadnezzar to subdue all
that land. Judith a beautiful Jewish widow, offers to go to Holofernes. There he insults her dignity. After he has disgraced her
and lies drunk, she cuts off his head and returns it to the people.
When they see the head they rush out after the fleeing invaders.
5 acts; 13 men, 3 women, extras; 2 interiors; costumes of
the period.

_____. Maria Magdalena (1944). Tr. by Thomas in FRA v. 9;
SMI; tr. by Green in Poet Lore v. 25, 1914; in Clark, W. S.;
tr. by Fairley in his Three Plays, Dutton, 1914; TRE-2 (v. 2);
TREA-1.
When Karl, the son of the family, is accused of theft, his
stern father, Anton, does not defend him. Later he is proved innocent. Meantime Leonhard deserts Clara, the daughter of the
family, when Karl is arrested. Through it all Clara is blamed by
her father; his strait-laced morality drives her to suicide; she jumps
down the well.
3 acts; 8 men, 3 women; 2 interiors; costumes of the period.

HECHT, Ben, with Charles MacArthur. The Front Page (1928).
Samuel French.
Authentically depicts the rushing atmosphere of a newspaper
office. Hildy Johnson, an old school reporter, on his way to be
married, reaches the newspaper office as the news comes that Earl
Williams, about to be executed for killing a policeman, has made a
jail break, just as the Governor has sent a reprieve. Williams
drops in through a window and is hidden in a desk. The reprieve
arrives and Hildy has saved an innocent man; he leaves for New
York with his bride, but his boss finds a way to get him back on
the job--as a single man.
17 men, 5 women; 1 interior. Royalty: $50-25.

HEDBERG, Tor. Johan Ulfstjerna (1907). Tr. by Colquist in Poet
Lore, v. 32, 1921.
Scene is laid in Finland, formerly a Swedish province. Johan's son Helge is pledged to kill the Governor of Finland, but the
father does it, so that his son may live and marry Agda. Johan
meets a martyr's death as a patriotic champion of an oppressed
people, offering himself for the benefit of his fellowmen.
5 acts; 5 men, 3 women; 2 interiors; costumes of the period.

HEGGEN, Thomas, with Joshua Logan. Mister Roberts (1948). Dramatists Play Service.
On board a drab Navy cargo ship in the Pacific during the
war with Japan, the martinet of a captain is hated by all. Lt. (j.g.)
Douglas Roberts is popular and shares the crew's dislike of their

captain. He secures shore leave for the entire crew from the captain by his own sacrifice. He finally gets his transfer to a combat
zone, whereupon the crew award him the "Order of the Palm for
action above and beyond the call of duty"--for casting overboard the
captain's pet palm tree.
   2 acts (with fade-outs); 19 men, 1 woman, extras; 1 set
   (deck with 3 interiors). Royalty: $50-25.

HEIBERG, Gunner. The Balcony (1894). Tr. by Vickner & Hughes
   in Poet Lore, v. 33, 1922.
   Presents different aspects of the nature of love: the conflict
between erotic passion and intellectual culture. Julie tires of her
sensuous husband Ressman and takes on two lovers: idealistic Abel
and healthy Antonio. She rejoices when her husband is killed by the
fall of the balcony, by which her lovers have entered. She then
marries Abel, but deceives him in turn, and when deserted by him,
she is left with Antonio.
   3 acts; 3 men, 1 woman, 1 servant; 1 interior.

_____. The Tragedy of Love (1904). Tr. by Björkman in DID.
   Presents the difference between masculine and feminine love.
Erling and Karen both experience the passion, but to her it is everything, to him it is subordinate to his work. When she finds existence meaningless, she ends her life.
   4 acts; 3 men, 4 women, 2 children, extras; 3 interiors.

HEIJERMANS, Herman, Jr. The Ghetto (1899). Tr. & adapted by
   Fernald. Lond., Heinemann, 1899 & 1910.
   In a sordid home in the Jewish quarter of Amsterdam old
Sachel, a rich but blind merchant, wishes to marry his son Rafael
to Rebecca, daughter of his neighbor Aaron, in order to secure a
rich dowry and annex the two houses. But Rafael, a musician who
is composing a symphony, has already married by civil ceremony
Rosa, a Christian servant whom Sachel and his sister Esther have
reared. Hounded by them and persuaded that Rafael has deserted
her (he having gone to London about his symphony and his letters
having been withheld), Rosa throws herself into the river. Just then
Rafael returns; Rosa is carried in and revives. Rafael denounces
his father and bears Rosa away to a happier world.
   4 acts; 7 men, 3 women, extras; 1 interior, 2 exteriors;
   costumes of time and place.

_____. The "Good Hope" (1900). Tr. by Higgins in Drama,
   v. 2, 1912; tr. by Saunders & Heijermans-Houwink; abridged
   in Pierce & Matthews, v. 2. Acting edition: Samuel French.
   A callous shipowner, Clemens Bos, allows a rotten schooner
"The Good Hope" to sail again, though he knows that all the crew
may be sacrificed. Chronicles the departure of the sailors, and reveals the agony of those left without a husband when the ship is lost.
The sea is victor in man's struggle to gain a living from it; man is
cruel to man in the eternal struggle for gold.
   4 acts; 11 men, 7 women; 2 interiors; Dutch costumes.
   Royalty: $25-20.

HELLMAN, Lillian. <u>Another Part of the Forest</u> (1946). Dramatists
  Play Service.
      Going back twenty years, shows how the Hubbards (see <u>Little
Foxes</u>, below) cut their eye teeth, the beginning of their dirty doings in the deep South. Father Marcus Hubbard is a self-made ego-
maniac and has a vicious influence over his children: Ben, a
Machiavellian son; Oscar, a whining ninny who joins up with the
KKK; Regina, diamond hard and already talking of going to Chicago
where she can get fine clothes. Ben is ordered out of the house,
but he discovers a way to blackmail his father and become the new
family tyrant.
      8 men, 5 women; 1 interior. Royalty: $50-25.

_____. The Autumn Garden (1951). Dramatists Play Service.
      Most of the guests at Constance Tuckerman's hotel are un-
happy. Sophie, Constance's niece, is engaged to a man whose mother will never permit the marriage to take place. General Grigg's
wife will not divorce him; she uses her heart condition to hold him.
Edward Crossman blames his alcoholism on Constance for marrying
another man. But when she, long since a widow, asks him to marry her, he realizes he never loved her. Nicholas Denery and his
wife are miserable together. All of the characters come to realize
that they cannot revolt from their own past.
      5 men, 7 women; 1 interior. Royalty: $50-25.

_____. The Children's Hour (1934). Dramatists Play Service.
      Demonstrates the havoc a lie can create. Two intelligent
high-principled women, Karen and Martha, run a girls' school. A
malicious lying youngster of 14, a rather intolerable child, starts
a scandal to defend herself which wrecks the school. The girl
claims that Karen and Martha have an "abnormal" relationship.
Later it is proved that the gossip was entirely wrong, but the damage had been done, and Martha has killed herself.
      2 men, 12 women; 2 interiors. Royalty: $35-25.

_____. The Lark. See entry under Anouilh, Jean.

_____. The Little Foxes (1939). Dramatists Play Service.
      Sordid selfishness rules the Hubbard family in the deep South
(see Another Part of the Forest, above). Scheming Ben is arranging
to build a bigger cotton mill but needs $75,000 more. Leo, Oscar's
son, "borrows" the bonds from Horace's safe deposit box. Horace,
with a bad heart, discovers this but before he can carry out his
will, dies on the stairs, going up after his medicine and unaided by
his wife Regina. Now she demands of her brothers 75 percent in
the mill instead of her third. But Ben rather suspects her, and her
daughter Alexandra's love for her mother turns to hate.
      6 men, 4 women; 1 interior. Royalty: $25.

_____. Montserrat. See entry under Robles, Emmanuel.

_____. My Mother, My Father and Me (1963). Dramatists Play
  Service.

An ironic study of a "modern" family, depicting its greed, stupidity, and lack of values. Though the Halpern family lives at a fancy Manhattan address, the various members are losers. Herman, the husband, is on the verge of bankruptcy; Bernie, the son, dabbles in everything in an effort to find himself; Rona, the mother, spends all of her time buying useless and expensive "bargains." Also present is Rona's mother, whom the family keeps in a broom closet before sending her off to a chamber-of-horrors rest home. Herman gets deeper in debt, Bernie turns to painting, and Rona continues to buy until the bankruptcy is complete. At the end the husband and wife have moved to Cleveland to begin the cycle again; and Bernie, now an "Indian" living in the Far West, is selling a huge order of hand-made jewelry to his mother.

14 men, 14 women (doubling possible in both roles); multiple sets. Royalty: $50-25.

_____. Toys in the Attic (1960). Samuel French.

Two sisters live together in a southern town. Though they dream of going to Europe someday, they continue to spend their money bailing their brother out of trouble. This time brother returns rich. He pays off the home mortgage, buys them new clothes and fur coats, sends letters of resignation to his sisters' employers, and has $150,000 in cash left. Instead of being pleased, the sisters are disappointed that their assistance is no longer needed, and the younger one makes sure the secret deal the brother is pulling off does not succeed.

4 men, 4 women, 3 extras; interior-exterior. Royalty: $50-25.

_____. Watch on the Rhine (1941). Dramatists Play Service.

An idealistic anti-Nazi German, Kurt, comes to America with his American wife and children, hoping for respite from his dangerous work in the underground in World War II. What he finds is Teck, a Nazi agent who blackmails him for the large amount of money Kurt has--money to be used to free captured anti-Nazis. Kurt kills Teck, then leaves his family and returns to Germany, to what may be his death.

6 men (2 of them boys), 5 women (1 a girl); 1 interior. Royalty: $25.

HERBERT, Frederick Hugh. For Love or Money (1947). Dramatists Play Service.

An unsophisticated girl is driven by an auto breakdown and a storm into the home of an aging matinee idol. He is pursued by women of his own age, but her innocence and enthusiasm conquer him. They decide to get married.

3 acts; 4 men, 4 women; 1 interior. Royalty: $50-25.

_____. Kiss and Tell (1943). Dramatists Play Service.

Corliss Archer at 16 wants to be grown up and acts the young lady when Private Earhart is entertained. She also must not reveal the secret that Mildred Pringle, her neighbor, and her brother Lennie are married, and even more--that Mildred is to have a baby.

Because Corliss goes with Mildred to the doctor's, the parents think
Corliss is to have the baby. Being sworn to secrecy, Corliss can
say nothing and does not until the end, when all is cleared up.
    3 acts; 9 men and boys, 6 women & girls; 1 interior.
    Royalty: $35-25.

_____. The Moon Is Blue (1951). Dramatists Play Service.
    Patty O'Neill and Donald Gresham meet on the observation
tower of the Empire State building. They agree to dine together,
but the rain houses them in his apartment, where she prepares dinner. While he is getting the groceries, David Slater, father of
Cynthia (Donald's fiancée), drops in and mixes things up. But once
in a blue moon affairs straighten themselves out on short notice.
    3 acts; 3 men, 1 woman; 1 interior, 1 exterior. Royalty:
    $50-25.

HERNE, James A. Hearts of Oak (1879). In his Shore Acres &
    Other Plays, French, 1928.
    Terry and Ned are pals; both love Chrystal. Terry marries
Chrystal who loves Ned. He finds this out and leaves for the Arc-
tic. He returns blind, blesses them, and dies.
    6 acts; 7 men, 4 women, extras; 3 interiors, 3 exteriors.

_____. Margaret Fleming (1890). QUIL.
    Amid scenes of domestic happiness, Margaret's sister Lena
has a child. Lena dies in childbirth, revealing to Margaret that her
husband Philip was her lover. She entrusts the child to Margaret.
At first she is horrified, but as she takes care of the illegitimate
baby she develops the maternal instinct. The shock of the revelation however has increased her blindness, and Philip attempts suicide; but they find they need each other.
    4 acts; 7 men, 5 women; 3 interiors.

_____. Shore Acres (1892). In his Shore Acres & Other Plays,
    French, 1928.
    The scene is laid at the Berry farm, Shore Acres, near Bar
Harbor, Me. The love of Helen for Dr. Sam is opposed by her
father; they flee in a sail boat with Captain Ben to the lighthouse.
Uncle Nat brings about her freedom, her marriage, and her reconciliation with her father.
    4 acts; 19 men, 11 women; 2 interiors, 2 exteriors; cos-
    tumes of 1890's.

HERSEY, John. The Child Buyer. See entry under Shyre, Paul.

HERVIEU, Paul E. In Chains (1895). Tr. by Asckenasy in Poet
    Lore, v. 20, 1909; also by him in Dramatist, v. 1, 1910, as
    Enchained; also spoken of as The Nippers.
    Divorce is refused, first by the husband when the wife asks
it, later by the wife when the husband wants it; so both are riveted
to the same ball and chain. She refuses because the child they now
have is an obligation; they can no longer think of themselves only.
    3 acts; 4 men, 3 women; 2 interiors.

_____. Know Thyself (1909). Tr. by Cerf in DIC.
Two triangles are precisely balanced: The General, his wife,
and his ward; his guest, his guest's wife, and his own son. The
General revises his advice as to honor when it concerns his wife
and his son. A thesis play, declaring against hasty judgments and
divorce, a theme which controls the action though it never obtrudes.
3 acts; 5 men, 2 women; 1 interior.

_____. The Trail of the Torch (1901). Tr. by Haughton, Dou-
bleday, 1915; abridged in Pierce & Matthews, v. 2, as The
Torch Race.
Depicts almost too perfectly maternal and filial love: The
instinctive self-sacrifice made by parents for their children who accept it as their right. Pictures the motives and actions of three
generations: Savine, the mother, steals money from her mother to
save her daughter, Marie-Jeanne; later she allows her mother to
die that Marie-Jeanne may be happy. A thesis play, demonstrating
one generation handing on to the next the torch of the joy of life.
4 acts; 7 men, 8 women; 2 interiors, 1 exterior.

HEYWARD, Dorothy and DuBose Heyward. Porgy (1927). Doubleday, 1927; Theatre Guild, 1928; GASE; THF; abridged in Mantle
1927/28.
Crippled Porgy has super-luck at shooting dice and has super-
power in his arms. He chokes to death gigantic stevadore Crown
when he returns seeking Bess. Porgy has freed Bess from Crown,
but she has left for the North with Sportin' Life. (Made into an
opera, 1935, as Porgy and Bess; music by George Gershwin.)
4 acts; 18 men, 6 women, extras; 2 exteriors.

HEYWARD, DuBose. Porgy. See entry under Heyward, Dorothy.

HEYWOOD, Thomas. A Woman Killed with Kindness (1603). In his
Works; in Mermaid ser., 1888; in many collections.
When her husband Frankford discovers the guilty love of his
wife Anne for his friend Wendoll, he sends her to his lovely manor
seven miles away, with every comfort but never to see him nor her
children. Loneliness and remorse break her spirit; at her deathbed there is a touching scene of forgiveness.
5 acts; 17 men, 3 women, extras; 11 interiors, 5 exteriors;
costumes of the period.

HILL, Lucienne. See entries under Anouilh, Jean.

HOCHHUTH, Rolf. The Deputy (1963). Adapted by Jerome Rothenberg. Samuel French.
The horrors of the World War II Nazi genocide are recalled
in this historical drama about the Pope's refusal to speak out against
the annihilation of the Jews. Sickened by his job, a German death
camp officer goes to the Papal legate in Berlin with positive evidence
that the Nazis are practicing genocide. His message is carried to
Pope Pius XII himself, but he continues to vacillate, and with

specious reasoning defends his refusal to get involved. In several documented scenes the bravery of the lower ranking church officials is shown as they hide as many Jews as possible in monasteries. One young priest is so intensely concerned that he pins the Star of David upon himself and joins the Jews in their march to the gas chambers.

  22 men, 2 women, extras; several X-ray sets. Royalty: $50-25.

HODGE, Merton. The Wind and the Rain (1933). Gollancz, 1934; French, 1934 & 1938; FAME.

  Charles Tritton arrives in Edinburgh to study for five years for his medical degree. He left Jill, his fiancée, in London; he is homesick for her and for his mother. In Edinburgh he meets Anne Hargreaves, who comes to stand in the place of his fiancée and his mother. At the end of the five years he finds he can't go on without Anne and he goes to London to tell Jill, and returns to Edinburgh.

  3 acts; 6 men, 3 women; 1 interior.

HODGINS, Eric. Mr. Blandings Builds His Dream House. See entry under Lawrence, Reginald.

HOLBERG, Ludvig. Erasmus Montanus; or, Rasmus Berg (1731). Tr. by Campbell & Schenck in MAU; also, American Scandinavian Foundation, 1914 (Comedies of Holberg).

  Rasmus Berg, son of a poor peasant, returns from the university as Erasmus Montanus, with all his newly acquired manners and information. He proves his mother is a stone, the deacon a cock; he argues with the bailiff, quarrels with his family and his prospective father-in-law; he is finally subdued by a lieutenant who threatens to draft him for the army. An effective satire on the Latin-crammed pedantry of the Danish students of the 18th century.

  5 acts; 8 men, 3 women; 1 interior, 1 exterior; costumes of the period.

    . Jeppe of the Hill (1722). Tr. by Campbell & Schenck, (Comedies of Holberg) Amer. Scandinavian Foundation, 1914; tr. by Jagendorf in CLF-2.

  A laughter-loving baron plays a joke on Jeppe. He takes him while drunk to his castle; the next morning he makes Jeppe think he is a lord and that his memories of poverty are but illusions. Later Jeppe reverts to being a peasant and remains the same drunkard. (Compare Calderon's Life Is a Dream, and Shakespeare's Christopher Sly in the Taming of the Shrew.)

  5 acts; 13 men, 2 women, extras; 2 interiors, 1 exterior; costumes of the period.

    . The Political Tinker (1722). Tr. by Campbell & Schenck, American Scandinavian Foundation (Comedies of Holberg), 1914.

  Satirizes Herman the tinker and a group of other artisans who sit and criticize the management of the city. It would appear that they know everything; in reality they know nothing. When two prac-

tical jokers declare Herman burgomaster, he is quite set up, being
bitten by a desire to shine in politics.   But when he has to make
some difficult decisions, he decides to remain a tinker without political aspirations.
    5 acts; 12 men, 6 women, extras; 1 interior, 1 exterior;
    costumes of the period.

HOLM, John Cecil.   Best Foot Forward (1941).   Dramatic Publishing
    Company.
    The boys at Winsocki Prep are preparing for the arrival of
girls to take to the annual prom.   Everyone is happy except Bud
Hooper.   Bud saw a movie the month before starring Gale Joy, the
wham girl.   He got so carried away that he wrote her an invitation
to the dance and she needed publicity so badly that she accepted.
Now Bud must write his regular date Helen that he will be ill until
after the dance.   Then he tries to pass Gale Joy off as his regular
girl Helen.   When Helen arrives, Bud gets into deeper and deeper
trouble.
    10 men, 7 women; 1 set.   Royalty: $35.

_____.   Gramercy Ghost (1951).   Dramatists Play Service.
    A young girl not only inherits an old house when her landlady
dies, but finds that she also owns the ghost of a handsome young
Revolutionary soldier in this zany, improbable comedy.   Nancy Wil-
lard, the heiress, is engaged to Parker Burnett.   She soon finds
herself the object of the affections of two additional suitors: Charley Stewart, an attractive young newspaperman and Nathaniel Coom-
bes, the ghost.   The situation really gets complicated when Nathaniel's girl friend and two of his soldier cronies return to earth in
order to get him into heaven.   George Washington has prevented
Nathaniel's leaving the earth because he forgot his duty when he fell
in love with the bar maid.   However, Nathaniel helps Nancy choose
the right man for a husband--which brings her happiness--and wins
Washington's approval and admittance to heaven.
    6 men, 6 women; 1 interior.   Royalty: $35-25.

_____, with George Abbott.   Three Men on a Horse (1935).   Dra-
    matists Play Service.
    As he rides to town on the bus, a timid greeting-card poet,
Erwin, dopes out the probable winners at the race track.   He gives
a trio his tips and they win.   They shanghai Erwin and set him
picking winners.   All goes well until he makes a bet of his own--and
the charm is gone.   He goes back to his greeting-card job.
    3 acts; 11 men, 4 women; 3 interiors.   Royalty: $25.

HOLMES, John Haynes and Reginald Lawrence.   If This Be Treason
    (1935).   Macmillan, 1935; French carried.
    Peace-minded John Gordon faces the problem of declaring war
on the very day of his inauguration as President of the United States.
He believes incitement to peace should be made as exciting as incitement to war.   The Japanese have attacked Manila.   Congress is certain to declare war; but he tells the Congressmen that as Commander-
in-Chief he will refuse to order the Army and Navy into action.   His

opponents call it treason and make plans to impeach him. He goes
on a mission of peace to Japan, where his proffers are refused.
But the Japanese people have heard of his offer of peace; they free
their leader Koyé, and the soldiers will not shoot down the populace.
He feels he has proved his conviction that the masses do not want
war.
  3 acts (7 scenes); 23 men, 3 women, extras; 5 interiors.

HOME, John. Douglas (1756). BAT; BEL v. 3; BRI v. 1; DIB v.
 4; INCH v. 16; MCM; MOR; MOSE; NET; OXB v. 12; STM
  Shortly after the Lady's secret marriage with Douglas, one
of the family's bitterest enemies, a son is born, who is lost to her
when Douglas goes to war and is killed. Years later, that son,
Norval, now grown, saves Lord Randolph, now her husband, and is
promised protection. By jewels she discovers that Norval is her
son. At a secret meeting-place, Glenalvin, the villain of the play
and in love with the Lady, stabs Norval, who however kills him before he dies. Lady Randolph in despair leaps off a cliff and Lord
Randolph goes to the wars.
  5 acts; 4 men, 2 women, extras; 2 exteriors; costumes of
 the 12th century in Scotland.

HOMER. The Iliad. See entry under Bowskill, Derek.

HOPKINS, John. Find Your Way Home (1971). Samuel French.
  A homosexual play about Julian Weston (called Julie) and his
lovers. Most of the action concerns a former lover who comes
back to Julie--Alan Harrison, who is pursued (this is Act Two) by
his wife. Julie and Mrs. Harrison attack and insult one another,
as do Alan and his wife, in an indictment against modern hetero-
sexual marriage and child-raising. In the end it is not exactly
clear what will happen to Julie and Alan, who will attempt to make
a go of it as a couple, nor how long their relationship is apt to
last. Julie, we learn, has considerable experience as a male hustler; Alan is experienced at running away.
  3 men, 1 woman; 1 interior. Royalty: $50-35.

HOPWOOD, Avery. The Bat. See entry under Rinehart, Mary
 Roberts.

HOUGHTON, W. Stanley. Hindle Wakes (1912). Sidgwick, 1912;
 Luce, 1913; French carried; in his Works, Constable, 1914,
 v. 2; DIG; PLAP v. 1; TUCD.
  From their various viewpoints both families argue that the
boy should be forced to marry the girl as a cure for sick honor,
after their holiday lark at the Hindle Wakes. But Fanny doesn't
respect him and declares she won't marry him; she insists on equal
freedom with the man, thus upsetting all their calculations and giving a new turn to the familiar situation.
  3 acts; 4 men, 5 women; 2 interiors.

_____. Independent Means (1909). French, 1911; in his Works,
 Constable, 1914, v. 1.

After his father, ruined financially, dies, his son Edgar, a rather hopeless weakling, can't get or hold any position--he was educated as a gentleman. His wife Sidney has independent ideas, takes the reins, and gets a position as a stenographer with their friend Ritchie, a motor car dealer. Later Edgar is engaged as a salesman there and develops out of his weakness, so that he and his wife are reunited.
4 acts; 3 men, 3 women; 2 interiors.

_____. The Younger Generation (1910). French, 1910; in his Works, Constable, 1914, v. 1.
Develops the idea that parents should alter their attitude and realize that the younger generation has ideas and rights of its own. The father and grandmother have been very strict with his three children. Their Uncle Tom helps them to gain release. He takes Arthur back with him to Hamburg, insists that Grace become engaged to Clifford (on a year's trial basis), and maybe Reggie can get to Canada, or Australia, or New Zealand.
3 acts; 7 men, 4 women; 1 interior.

HOUSMAN, Laurence. The Chinese Lantern (1908). Sidgwick, 1908; French carried in revised edition.
Depicts Chinese art student life. It is filled with the color, movement, joy, humor, and poetic atmosphere of China.
3 acts; 12 men, 2 women, extras; 1 interior; Chinese costumes. Can be produced with all-girl cast.

_____ and Harley Granville-Barker. Prunella (1906). Brentano, 1906; Lond., Bullen, 1907; Sidgwick & Jackson, 1914; Little, Brown, 1916; PLAP v. 2. Samuel French.
Sub-title: Love in a Dutch garden. Tells of the awakening of love in the heart of a young girl who lives in a little house guarded by her three aged aunts. As a fantastic allegory in felicitous style, gently satirizes false restraints in secluding a girl from life instead of preparing her for it.
3 acts; 11 men, 10 women; 1 exterior (a garden); fanciful costumes. Can be produced with all-girl cast. Royalty: $50.

_____. Victoria Regina (1934). Baker's Plays.
Presents selected scenes in the life of the beloved Royal Lady "Her Gracious Majesty" from her accession in 1837 to the Diamond Jubilee in 1897. Shows her selection of Albert as her Prince Consort, her marriage, and a bit of their loving if a bit tempestuous life together. A studied interpretation of her personality, vignettes of an astute yet bigoted woman. All based on the recorded word.
10 episodes in 3 acts; 20 men, 11 women, extras; 8 interiors. Costumes of the period. (May be produced as one-acts.) Royalty on application.

HOWARD, Bronson. The Henrietta (1887). French, 1901; HAL.
A satire on financial and social life with its rush and heart-

lessness. A grasping capitalist, Nicholas Van Alstyne, is opposed
by his elder son, Nick Jr., a thorough rogue, who tries to ruin his
father and get all the family wealth. The younger son, Bertie, the
Lamb, good-natured and unfitted for the ruthlessness of Wall Street,
has quiet and complete contempt for the feverish life of his father
and brother. Yet by a stroke of luck he achieves a financial coup
which gives his father everything and leaves Nick Jr. with nothing.
The deal is made in The Henrietta, the name of the mine in whose
stock they speculate. (Revised as The New Henrietta by Winchell
Smith & Victor Mapes & produced in 1913, pub. by French, 1913.)
          4 acts; 9 men, 4 women; 3 interiors.

_____. Shenandoah (1888). MOSS-v. 3; QUIK; QUIL; abridged
          in Pierce & Matthews, v. 1.
          Two West Point graduates are in Charleston when Fort Sum-
ter is fired on. Kerchival West from the North is in love with a
Southern girl, Gertrude Ellingham; her brother Robert, also from
the South, is in love with Kerchival's sister, Madeline West. These
lovers suffer, for they must take opposite sides in this Struggle between the States. All meet again at a farm house in the Shenandoah
Valley, the day when Sheridan's Ride is featured.
          4 acts; 15 men, 7 women; 2 interiors, 1 exterior; military
          & civilian costumes of the 1860's.

_____. Young Mrs. Winthrop (1882). French, 1899.
          When they lose their child Winthrop and wife drift apart, he
absorbed in his professional affairs, she taking refuge in the social
whirl. They think of divorce, but are brought together by the sentimental family lawyer who reminds them of their happy past. A Mrs.
Chetwyn demonstrates the power of rumor and provides much comedy.
          4 acts; 5 men, 4 women; 1 interior.

HOWARD, Sidney. Alien Corn (1933). Scribner, 1933; French,
          1934; FAMD; abridged in Mantle 1932/33.
          Hemmed in by the depressing surroundings of a woman's col-
lege in a small mid-Western town, Elsa Brandt, a piano teacher and
talented daughter of a German musician, feels frustrated because she
is denied the greater opportunities which have come to several less
talented persons. Her concert was cancelled, but she gave it anyway. A tragic love affair nearly wrecks her career.
          3 acts; 11 men, 3 women; 1 interior.

_____. Dodsworth (1934). Dramatists Play Service.
          A typical American industrialist, Sam Dodsworth, retires
from his auto company and goes to Europe with his wife Fran. She
becomes interested in Kurt von Obersdorf and wants a divorce so as
to marry him, but his mother points out the obstacles to that. During his wife's defection, he has come to appreciate the understanding
Mrs. Cortright, so he leaves his selfish and cheating wife on the
liner to go her own way.
          22 men, 14 women, doubling possible; 9 interiors (unit set
          possible). Royalty: $35-25.

_____. The Late Christopher Bean (1932). Samuel French.
        Satirically presents the Haggett family in a small New England town who had given refuge to the painter, Christopher Bean, but had deemed his paintings worthless. Abby, the housemaid, was the only one to appreciate him, so she kept what he had painted. Bean becomes famous after his death and his paintings are being sought by art dealers. The badgered Haggett family is shown up as hard, selfish, and ill-tempered; but they can't sell the paintings as they belong to Abby, who had also been Mrs. Christopher Bean.
        5 men, 4 women; 1 interior. Royalty: $25-20.

_____. Lute Song. See entry under Irwin, Will.

_____. Ned McCobb's Daughter (1926). Samuel French.
        Shrewd, honest, courageous Carrie proves her worth in preserving the tavern, in fighting for her children's future, in foiling the flashy bootlegger Babe Callahan, and in forgiving her worthless husband until he proves unfaithful. Her father, Captain McCobb, preserves his self-respect in raising the money stolen by Carrie's husband.
        3 acts; 8 men, 2 women; 2 interiors. Royalty: $25-20.

_____. The Silver Cord (1926). Samuel French.
        The Victorian-type mother loves her two sons too much; she is selfishly possessive, but with an air of preserving them from disaster. The young scientist, Christina, is more secure in her love and wins David her husband away; but Hester, Robert's fiancée, loses out--he remains tied to his mother's apron strings.
        3 acts; 2 men, 4 women; 2 interiors. Royalty: $25-20.

_____. They Knew What They Wanted (1924). Samuel French.
        Tony, a winegrower in California, gets a wife by mail by sending a picture of Joe, his hired hand. Amy is shocked to find out the fraud but marries Tony anyway. She needs the security of a home (and besides, Tony is in bed with two broken legs). On the wedding night Amy gives herself to Joe and becomes pregnant. By the time Tony finds out, Amy has begun to love Tony as a husband. After a very conventional reaction to the news of the pregnancy, Tony decides that what he wanted all along was children, what Amy wanted was a home, what Joe wanted was his freedom. They all got what they wanted.
        9 men, 4 women, extras; 1 interior. Royalty: $25-20.

_____, with Paul DeKruif. Yellow Jack (1934). Dramatists Play Service.
        Vivid dramatization of the fight against yellow fever. Walter Reed heads a commission in Cuba in 1900, trying to discover how yellow fever is caused. Dr. Carlos Finlay suggests his belief that it is a mosquito bearing the germs. The heroic members of the Commission and four brave volunteer soldiers are inoculated and prove this is true. Having learned how the disease is contracted, it became possible to prevent it. This is a bright page in the records of the medical profession and of the U.S. Army Medical corps.

1 continuous act; 26 men, 1 woman, extras; 1 unit set,
varied by lighting. Royalty: $25.

HOYT, Charles H. A Texas Steer (1894). MOSL.
      See entry of revised version (1940) above under Randolph
Carter.
      4 acts; 19 men, 4 women, extras; 3 interiors, 1 exterior;
some Western costumes.

HSIUNG, S. I. See Lady Precious Stream.

HUGHES, Hatcher. Hell-Bent Fer Heaven (1924). Samuel French.
      Pulitzer Prize play 1924. A half-crazed jealous fanatic who
has "got religion," Rufe Pryor, a pious rogue, hypocritically tries
to put his rival out of the way by reviving a slumbering feud; but
he himself suffers the consequences. Scenes are effective and the
native wit is skillfully introduced.
      3 acts; 5 men, 2 women; 1 interior. Royalty: $25.

HUGO, Victor. Hernani (1830). Tr. by Crosland in CAR; CLF-2;
      MAU.
      Donna Sol de Silva is betrothed to her guardian, the aged
Don Ruy; she is also besought by King Charles of Spain, but she is
in love with the outlaw Hernani. Her plan to elope with Hernani is
overheard by the King, who seizes her. Don Ruy and Hernani plan
to rescue her. After King Charles is made Emperor of Germany,
he pardons Hernani, who proves to be the noble Don Juan of Aragon.
Now again Hernani and Donna Sol can plan to marry, but on his wedding night Hernani hears the blast of Don Ruy's horn and, according
to his vow, he drinks the poison. His bride joins him in death.
      5 acts; 23 men, 2 women, extras; 3 interiors, 2 exteriors;
costumes of the period.

HULL, Raymond. The Drunkard (1967). Pioneer Drama Service.
      In this modern version of the most famous melodrama ever
written, love battles liquor for the life and soul of upstanding hero
Edward Middleton. Mary Wilson and her whiny mother stand on the
side of love. Lawyer Cribbs and his crony Stickler ply the liquor
with dastardly intent. At the end, of course, true love triumphs
over demon rum.
      3 men, 2 women; simple melodrama drops. Royalty: $25.

HUME, Cyril and Richard Maibaum. Ransom (1963). Samuel
      French.
      The father of a kidnapped boy makes a startling plea to the
kidnappers in this exciting mystery drama. He's supposed to signal
the kidnappers that the half-million dollar ransom will be paid
through a TV program his firm sponsors. Instead he appears on the
show himself, shows the money, and then announces that the ransom
will not be paid. If the kidnappers do not return the boy unharmed,
he will offer it as a reward for their capture. The father receives
universal condemnation; even his wife collapses in hysterics. Then
the tension ends in a shattering, harrowing climax.

11 men, 4 women, extras; 1 interior. Royalty: $25-20.

HUSSON, Albert. My Three Angels. See entry under Spewack,
Samuel.

HYMAN, Mac. No Time for Sergeants. See entry under Levin,
Ira.

HYMER, John B. East Is West. See entry under Shipman, Samuel.

IBSEN, Henrik. A Doll's House (1879). Tr. by Archer in his
Prose Dramas, v. 1, Lovell, 1890; in his Collected Works, v.
7, Scribner, & Heinemann, 1906-07; Baker, 1900; MAU; CLF-2;
COJ; tr. by Sharp, Dutton, 1910; tr. by Stratton, Ginn, 1931;
tr. not given, Macmillan (Mod. rdrs ser.) 1927; Nelson, 1941;
in his Eleven Plays, Modern Library giants, 1935; in his Works
in 1 vol., Blue Ribbon, 1932 & 1941; abridged in Pierce & Matthews, v. 2. Act. ed.: tr. by Ginsburg, French; tr. by Meyer, Dramatists Play Service.
Presents the right of a woman to self-development in a world
planned by and for men, and the falseness of marriage which does
not rest on true comradeship. Nora wants to help her husband,
Helmer, but in doing so by forging a check is brought face to face
with her position: her husband treats her like a doll and an orna-
ment to his house rather than as a thinking helpmeet. The slam of
the door as she leaves echoed around the world. (A valuable play
to study, with its unities of time, place, and action; with its unforced
exposition; with scarcely a superfluous word, all tending towards the
final scene.)
4 acts; 4 men, 4 women, 3 children; 1 interior. (Royalties:
Meyer, $25; Ginsburg, $15.)

_____. An Enemy of the People (1882). Tr. by Aveling as An
Enemy of Society in his The Pillars of Society, Lond., Scott,
1888; same in his Collected Works, v. 8, Scribner, & Heinemann, 1907; tr. by Archer in his Prose Dramas, v. 2, Lovell,
1891; same Baker, 1900; tr. by Sharp in his Ghosts, Dutton,
1911; tr. by Stratton, Ginn, 1931; tr. not given, Grosset, 1931;
in his 11 Plays, Modern Library Giants, 1935; in his Works in
1 v., Blue Ribbon, 1932 & 1941; DUR; adapted by Miller,
Dramatists Play Service, 1952; tr. by Meyer, Dramatists Play
Service.
Everywhere Dr. Stockmann, in his desire to remedy a shameful condition of the water supply, is met by the opposition of the
vested interests. No one will listen to him, and he is voted an enemy of the people. A scathing stinging satire on the shortcomings of
society.
5 acts; 7 men, 2 women, 2 boys, extras; 3 interiors. (Royalties: Miller, $25; Meyer, $25.)

_____. Ghosts (1881). Tr. by Archer in BAT; MIL, & Baker,
1900; tr. by Sharp, Dutton, 1911; tr. & adapted by Leverton,
French, 1937; tr. by Ginsbury, Baker, 1938, & Lond., French,

1938; tr. not given, Blue Ribbon, 1932 & 1941; in his 11 Plays,
Mod. Liby Giants, 1935; Nelson, 1941; tr. by LeGallienne in
BEN; TRE-3; TREA-2.   Tr. by Koefoed, French; tr. by Meyer,
Dramatists Play Service.

Oswald Alving has inherited syphilis from his degenerate father.   He returns home from his studies in Paris to be on hand for
the dedication of an orphanage, built in honor of his deceased father.
The orphanage, uninsured, is destroyed by fire.   Oswald learns that
the maid, with whom he desires an affair, is his half-sister.   When
he suffers a final attack from his dreadful disease, he begs his
mother to kill him.   Ibsen argues that Mrs. Alving should have left
her husband, before Oswald's birth, when she discovered that the
Captain was dissolute.   Some critics feel that the play is an answer
to the critics who objected to the ending of A Doll's House (above).

3 men, 2 women; 1 interior.   (Royalty: Leverton, no royalty; Koefoed, $15; Meyer, $25.)

_____. Hedda Gabler (1890).   Tr. by Gosse, U.S. Book Co.,
1891; Baker, 1900; tr. by Archer in his Prose Dramas, v. 3,
Lovell, 1891; tr. by Gosse & Archer in his Collected Works,
v. 10, Scribner, & Heinemann, 1907; CLS; tr. by LeGallienne
& Leyssac in LEG; tr. not given, Macmillan, 1927 (Mod. Read-
ers Ser.); 4 Plays, Grosset, 1931; Works in 1 v., Blue Ribbon,
1932 & 1941; 11 Plays, Modern Lib. Giants, 1935; abridged in
Pierce & Matthews, v. 2; BLO; HATS; TRE-1, 2, & 3; TREA-2.
Act. ed.: tr. by Meyer, Dramatists Play Service.   Also
French.

Realistic study of a woman who is out of harmony with her
surroundings but cannot rise above them, who, with selfish individu-
alism, wishes to test her will and influence, but fears to face the
consequences; who is ever a compromiser.   Like the pistols she
makes use of, she attracts and fascinates, but is cold, unscrupulous,
relentless, and passionless.

4 acts; 3 men, 4 women; 1 interior.   (Royalty: Meyer, $25.)

_____. John Gabriel Borkman (1894).   Tr. by Archer in his Col-
lected Works, v. 9, Scribner, & Heinemann, 1907; tr. not given,
in 11 Plays, Modern Lib. Giants, 1935.   Tr. by Meyer, Dramatists Play Service.

Borkman dreamed of the power which money could bring; for
it he sacrificed love, the love of Ella, marrying her hard sister
Gunhild because she could bring him more money.   Even after his
imprisonment for embezzlement he still tries for gain, but it is too
late.   All three have lost the power of real living; only the old clerk
Foldal had really lived.

4 acts; 3 men, 5 women; 2 interiors, 1 exterior.   (Royalty:
$25.)

_____. The Master Builder (1892).   Tr. by Gosse & Archer in
his Collected Works, v. 10, Scribner, & Heinemann, 1907;
Baker, 1900; in World's Great Plays, 1944; tr. by Stratton,
Ginn, 1931; tr. not given, Macmillan, 1927 (Mod. Readers ser.);
Works in 1 vol., Blue Ribbon, 1932 & 1941; 11 Plays, Mod.

Liby Giants, 1935; 4 Plays, Nelson, 1941; in WOR; tr. by Meyer, Dramatists Play Service.

Solness had won success as an architect at the expense of his wife and associates, but his conscience still bothers him. A fascinating girl, Hilda Wangel, encourages him to do great things still. He climbs to the top of a tower, becomes dizzy, and falls to his death.

3 acts; 4 men, 3 women; 2 interiors, 1 exterior. Royalty: $25.

_____. Peer Gynt (1867). Tr. by Archer, Lond., Scott, 1902; in his Collected Works, v. 4, Scribner, & Heinemann, 1907; acting version, Baker, 1900; tr. by Roberts, Lond., Secker, & Kennerley, 1913; tr. by Sharp, Dutton, 1922; tr. by Stratton, Ginn, 1931; tr. not given, Blue Ribbon, 1932 & 1941; Mod. Lib. Giants, 1935; Lippincott, 1936; Oxford, 1940 (World's classics). Tr. by Meyer, Dramatists Play Service; & Green, Samuel French.

Effective satire on human nature, developing the failure of one who is a compromiser by heredity, and who trims so many times that soon there is little distinctive left of him. He steals a bride at a wedding, he forsakes Solveig, the young girl who remains true to him to the end, he has many adventures but is always the selfish egoist, ever looking out for himself.

5 acts in 12 scenes; 31 men, 14 women, many extras; 2 interiors, several exteriors; variety of costumes. Royalties: Green, $35-25; Meyer, $25.

_____. The Pillars of Society (1877). Tr. by Aveling, Lond., Scott, 1888; tr. by Archer in his Prose Dramas, v. 2, Lovell, 1891; in his Collected Works, v. 6, Scribner, & Heinemann, 1907; tr. not given, Works, Blue Ribbon, 1932 & 1941; 11 Plays, Mod. Lib. Giants, 1935; abridged in Pierce & Matthews, v. 2; tr. Meyer, Dramatists Play Service; tr. by Leverton, French.

Bernick, the genial philanthropist and supposed model for the community, is in reality dishonest in thought, hypocritical in action, murderous in will. His deeper nature is so stirred by the discovery that his son would have been lost at sea if the unseaworthy vessel had sailed, that he confesses his sins. The only pillars of society are truth and freedom.

4 acts; 10 men, 9 women, extras; 1 interior. Royalties: Leverton, none; Meyer, $25.

_____. The Pretenders (1863). Tr. by Archer in his Collected Works, v. 2, Scribner, & Heinemann, 1907; SMK; tr. by Sharp, Dutton, 1913.

Out of the early Norse sagas the play develops the difference between Haakon, who believes in himself and his ideals, and Skule, who is cursed with self-doubt, a capable but not forceful regent. The fortunate Haakon becomes king of united Norway in 1247.

5 acts; 15 men, 5 women, extras; 6 interiors, 4 exteriors; costumes of the period (13th century, Norway).

_____. The Wild Duck (1884). Tr. by Archer, Baker, 1900; in
his Collected Works, Scribner, & Heinemann, 1907; LEV; MOSQ;
WHI; tr. not given in CEW; Plays, Macmillan, 1927 (Mod.
Readers ser.); Grosset, 1931; Blue Ribbon, 1932 & 1941; Mod.
Lib. Giants, 1935; Nelson, 1941. Tr. by Meyer, Dramatists
Play Service. Also French.

The Ekdal family is living happily, their dreamy illusions
symbolized by the crippled wild duck in the attic, adapting itself to
its environment. A young idealist, Gregers Werle, believing that
the truth should always be told and at all costs, brings tragedy to
the once-happy family. He talks to Hedvig, the young daughter,
about the joy of sacrifice, tells her she must kill her cherished pet,
the wild duck; instead she shoots herself.

5 acts; 9 men, 3 women, extras; 2 interiors. Royalty:
Meyer, $25.

INGE, William. Bus Stop (1955). Dramatists Play Service.

Several people are gathered at a bus stop restaurant in a
small Kansas town, but the main characters are a young cowboy,
Bo Decker, and a night club singer, Cherie. Bo has kidnapped
Cherie and insists she marry him and move to his Montana ranch.
She resists his blundering courtship procedures until it looks as if
Bo will have to sling her over his shoulder and carry a kicking,
reluctant bride all the way to Montana. But Bo learns something
about tenderness, and by the end of the play Cherie, too, desires
the marriage.

5 men, 3 women; 1 interior. Royalty: $50-25.

_____. Come Back, Little Sheba (1950). Samuel French.

Depicts two ordinary people, Doc and Lola his wife, living
rather drab lives because ambition is gone and dreams replace effective living. When their baby died, Doc took to drink, but for a
year has been a member of Alcoholics Anonymous. Lola still
dreams of a good life and the return of her pet dog Sheba. Doc
goes off the deep end until two A.A.'s take him away to recover.
When he returns a week later, he and Lola are ready to begin anew.
Lola has a new contentment and new dreams, but little Sheba is gone
for good.

8 men, 3 women; 1 interior. Royalty: $50-25.

_____. The Dark at the Top of the Stairs (1957). Dramatists
Play Service.

It is dark at the top of everyone's stairs, especially for those
in the Flood family. Ruben, the father, sells harnesses on the road,
and is insecure over his job which is becoming rapidly obsolete.
Sonny, the ten-year-old son, is bullied by his schoolmaster and feels
secure only while playing with his movie star pictures. Reenie, the
teen-age daughter, is shy and introverted. The climax of the play
comes over a Country Club dance. Ruben quarrels with his wife
over a dress purchased for Reenie. When he is accused of being
unfaithful he strikes his wife and storms out. Reenie's date, a
Jewish boy, is insulted at the dance and commits suicide, while she
hides in the restroom. At the end, both children break out of their

shells, and Ruben returns home as a machinery salesman with great
hope for the future.

13 men, 2 women, 3 boys, 2 girls; 1 interior. Royalty:
$50-25.

_____ . A Loss of Roses (1959). Dramatists Play Service.
The widow Miss Field and her twenty-one-year-old son live
in a small town near Kansas City. The time is 1933, but both have
jobs: she as a nurse and he as a gas station attendant. The mother
wishes her son was the kind of man his father was. Into the house
moves an old friend, an actress, and soon the son is having an affair with her. He proposes marriage, changes his mind the following day, and sets out on his own.

4 men, 4 women; 1 interior. Royalty: $50-25.

_____ . Natural Affection (1963). Dramatists Play Service.
Sue Barker has had a hard life. Her husband deserted her
before their son Donnie was born, and Donnie grew up in orphan
homes and penal farms. Presently Sue has a good job, a nice
apartment, and a lover, Bernie Slovenk, who is not interested in
marrying her. Sue is satisfied with this arrangement, but finds it
threatened when her son arrives for a Christmas visit and announces
that he will not have to return to the penal farm if his mother will
provide a home for him. The showdown comes on Christmas Eve
with a drinking party attended by the couple next door. The husband
soon passes out, and the wife throws herself at Bernie (who turns
out to be accustomed to it) and Donnie. The husband regains consciousness and goes out on the town. Sue and Bernie quarrel, and
he storms out to spend the night next door. The next morning Donnie begs his mother to let him make up for the loss of her lover,
but she runs off after Bernie. Donnie, who must now return to the
penal farm, takes out his anger by savagely attacking a woman in the
building.

7 men, 5 women; 1 interior. Royalty: $50-25.

_____ . Picnic (1953). Dramatists Play Service.
Deals with the effect that Hal Carter, young man of great
animal vitality, has on the lives of a feminine household in a small
Kansas town. The Owens' house includes a woman who has been
deserted by her husband, two maturing daughters, and a spinster
school teacher who is a boarder. Hal seriously upsets all of their
lives. Madge Owens, the oldest daughter, is willing to give up her
chance for a wealthy marriage to spend the annual picnic evening
making love to Hal. Millie, the younger daughter, sees herself as
something other than a tomboy because of Hal's charm. And the
school teacher feels compelled to beg her boyfriend of long standing
to marry her. At the end of the play Hal must flee from the town
to escape a car stealing charge.

4 men, 7 women; unit set. Royalty: $50-25.

_____ . Splendor in the Grass (1966). Adapted from Inge's
screenplay by F. Andrew Leslie. Dramatists Play Service.
The play is set in the midwest of the 1920's. Bud Stamper,

son of the town's richest man, is the star athlete at the local high
school; Deanie Loomis is his girl friend. The two young people
have powerful feelings about one another, but are restrained by the
bad example set by Bud's older sister. Though Bud wants to marry
Deanie and go on to agricultural school, his father insists that he
attend Yale and prepare to join the family oil business. The father
wins, and Bud convinces Deanie they should see less of one another
in preparation for his traveling East. Deanie reacts with an emotional crack-up which leads her to a mental institution. By the
time she is released, the stock market crash has forced Bud to
leave school and to take up farming with his wife, a former waitress. Deanie is engaged to a fellow patient, a former doctor. A
brief meeting enables the former sweethearts to break the old ties.
    10 men, 9 women; unit set. Royalty: $35-25.

IONESCO, Eugene. The Killer (1959). Translated by Donald Wat-
    son. Samuel French.
    This macabre morality comedy presents the author's obser-
vation on planned society, the welfare state, and regimentation.
Hiram Sherman is an average young man who leaves his dingy apartment one day and, after taking a wrong bus, ends up at a futuristic
housing development. Here everything is always perfect. As the
architect explains, "Nothing is left to chance." At first Hiram is
eager to buy a house; then, however, he notices how totally artificial, how dehumanized the development is. And the terrible truth,
as Hiram discovers, is that every day a killer disposes of 2 or 3
people in the beautiful lake which the development surrounds. Hiram
finds the killer's timetable and list of victims but can interest no
one, not even the police, in the bizarre situation. Then, at the end
of the play, Hiram meets the killer, alone.
    10 men, 2 women; cyclorama, collage, inset. Royalty:
    $35-25.

_____. Rhinoceros (1960). Translated by Derek Prouse. Sam-
    uel French.
    Man's hypocrisy and self delusion receive a savagely satiric
treatment in this play. One normal Sunday morning a roaring rhinoceros appears in a small town, precipitating a pointless argument
over whether it is an Asian or an African rhino. Then one by one
all the citizens change to rhinoceroses; they have no integrity, no
identity as true humans. Finally only Berenger, the publishing
clerk, is left as a human, unable to join the others because he refuses to compromise his integrity.
    11 men, 6 women, extras; 1 exterior, 2 interiors. Royal-
ty: $50-25.

IRVING, Washington. Charles the Second. See entry under Payne,
    John Howard.

_____. Rip Van Winkle. In his Sketch-Book, 1819.
    Rip escapes a shrewish wife, wanders up the mountain, meets
the Henry Hudson crew, and after drinking their liquor, sleeps twenty years. Returning to his village he identifies himself with difficul-

ty. In 1850 Charles Burke dramatized the tale in 2 acts; 11 men,
3 women, 1 child, simple scenery, costumes of the period. It was
published by French, 1857, in Bates, The Drama, v. 19; in MOSS-3.
In 1865 and thereafter Joseph Jefferson made the play famous in a
version by Dion Boucicault. It is in 4 acts; 7 men, 3 women, extras; 3 interiors, 3 exteriors; costumes of the period. It was published by Dodd, 1903; carried by Baker; LAW; CERC; QUIK; QUIL.
In 1937 G. H. Leverton revised an early dramatization by Walter
Kerr, pub. by French, 1937; has 3 acts; 25 men, 6 women; 3 exteriors; costumes of the period.
     Royalty: $15.

IRWIN, Will and Sidney Howard. Lute Song (1954). From the Chi-
    nese of Kao-Tong-Kia (circa. 1404). Dramatic Publishing Com-
    pany.
     A young scholar, under urging from his father, reluctantly
leaves his bride and goes to Pekin to become a success. He is
given a high office in the Imperial Court, but is forbidden to return
home or communicate with his family. His parents lose hope that
he will return, but his wife doesn't. She gives her own food to the
in-laws during a famine, but they die in spite of her efforts. She
travels alone to Pekin and finds her husband living in luxury. A
marvelous confrontation and climax follow. (A musical version is
also available.)
     9 men, 6 women, extras; simple props for "suggested" sets.
    Royalty: $35.

ISHERWOOD, Christopher. The Ascent of F. 6. See entry under
    Auden, Wystan Hugh.

JACKSON, Frederick. The Bishop Misbehaves (1935). Samuel
    French.
     An elderly and saintly Bishop and his equally elderly and
saintly sister stop by accident at a pub where a robbery has just
taken place. The Bishop, an avid reader of detective stories, is in
his glory; and before he leaves the pub he has gathered all available
clues and has the stolen jewels in his pocket. He takes them home,
hides them in a humidor, and waits for his expected company: several crooks, a masked hero, and a heroine. The odds change hands
several times until the hero has won out.
     7 men, 3 women; 2 interiors. Royalty: $25-20.

JACKSON, N. H. The Two Orphans. See entry under d'Ennery,
    Adolphe P.

JACKSON, Shirley. The Haunting of Hill House. See entry under
    Leslie, F. Andrew.

JAMES, Henry. The Aspern Papers. See entry under Redgrave,
    Michael.

_____. "The Turn of the Screw. " See William Archibald's The
    Innocents.

_____. Wings of the Dove. See entry under Bolton, Guy.

JEFFERS, Robinson. Medea (1946). Freely adapted from Euripides' Medea. Samuel French.
    In this version, the ambitious Jason gives up Medea, his foreign wife, to take a new bride more politically helpful. Medea, living in a strange land, thinks of possible ways of revenge. On the day she is to be banished she brings death to the new bride and horror to Jason.
    5 men, 5 women, extras; 1 exterior. Royalty: $50-25.

JELLICOE, Ann. The Knack (1964). Samuel French.
    The play deals with three young men and their relationships with one young girl, who got lost one day on her way to the YWCA. Tom paints the walls of his room various colors and hangs chairs on them (so they won't clutter up the floor). Colin is trying to learn all about sex second-hand by listening to, and questioning, his friends. Tolen is a real masher and lady-killer, who scores just about any time he wants to. The girl becomes distracted by having to deal with these three and begins to imagine the extent of her involvement with each of them.
    3 men, 1 woman; 1 interior. Royalty: $50-25.

JEROME, Helen B. Charlotte Corday (1936). Lond., H. Hamilton, 1937; FIP.
    Charlotte has made up her mind to kill Marat to rid France of him. She goes to Paris, on an excuse to help her friend recover her estates. She gets an appointment with Marat for 7:30, gets in, and stabs him in his bath. She is arraigned and tried. The final scene is in her cell.
    3 acts; 17 men, 7 women, extras; 5 interiors; costumes.

_____. Jane Eyre. See entry under Brontë, Charlotte.

_____. Pride and Prejudice. See entry under Austen, Jane.

JEROME, Jerome K. The Passing of the Third Floor Back (1908). Lond., Hurst, 1910, Dodd, 1908 & 1921; French carries.
    The failures and foibles of the boarders are presented with humour: the landlady who cheats her lodgers, the little slavey, the major who drinks and bullies his wife, a retired book-maker, and others. The mysterious passer-by who takes the Third Floor Back awakens in each by the right sympathetic touch and desire to develop a "better self." A parable which emphasizes the spirit of brotherly love.
    3 acts; 6 men, 6 women; 1 interior. Royalty: $25-20.

JIRÁSEK, Alois. The Lantern (Lucerna, 1905). Tr. by Buben & Noyes in Poet Lore, v. 36, 1925.
    The miller Libor has Hanicka, a waif, as a ward. He refuses to greet the Princess or allow Hanicka to go as a maid, though summoned by the bailiff and magistrate. But he has the duty of bearing the lantern before the nobility. This makes the Princess

curious and she gets the miller to bear the lantern to the old castle
from the ancestral linden tree. Then she gives him rights, and he
may marry his ward.
     4 acts; 17 men, 5 women, extras; 2 interiors, 3 exteriors;
costumes of the period.

JOB, Thomas. Therese (1947). Based on Emile Zola's novel.
    Samuel French.
     Therese Raquin is married to Camille, a dull, complaining
milliner who is not nearly as interesting as their boarder, an artist. So Therese and the artist take Camille out on a Sunday and
drown him. His mother accepts the story of an accident, and after
a year is pleased when Therese and the artist marry. But the
death of Camille comes between the two murderers, and they quarrel
continually. The mother overhears a conversation and is shocked
into paralysis. She is able, however, to communicate the incriminating information to the Inspector of Police--through the medium of
dominoes.
     4 men, 4 women; 1 interior. Royalty: $50-25.

_____. Uncle Harry (1942). Samuel French.
     Kindly, lovable Uncle Harry manages to do away with two
very unpleasant sisters, but ironically can not convince anyone that
he's guilty. Constantly bullied by the possessive spinsters, Harry
can stand it no longer. He murders one and frames the second for
the crime. Then his conscience begins to torment him and he decides to confess. However, no one can believe that such a likeable
fellow could commit murder. He loses all his friends and his
sweetheart; people avoid the brother of a condemned prisoner. Finally he begs his imprisoned sister for help. Strangely enough, she
refuses, realizing that for Harry the torture of his conscience and
being shunned by his former friends is the worst punishment he
could possibly face.
     9 men, 6 women; 3 interiors. Royalty: $50-25.

JOHNSON, Bertha. John and Abigail Adams, Family of Destiny
    (1976). Pioneer Drama Service.
     The story centers on John and Abigail Adams, their family,
their role in American history, and their identities, inner struggles,
and personal longings. Costumes and staging are simple, with one
permanent set and as simple or imaginative lighting as desired.
     5 men, 6 women; 1 interior. Royalty: $25.

JOHNSON, Bill. Dirty Work at the Crossroads (1942). Samuel
    French.
     Innocent Nellie Lovelace faces a series of evil assaults on
her virtue in this Gay Nineties melodrama. Nellie's mother has
been poisoned, and she is torn from the arms of the dying lady by
the very man who poisoned her, the villainous Munro. He is already married to Ida Rhinegold, the belle of the New Haven Music
Hall, but that does not prevent his pursuing poor Nellie. In spite
of his many evil deeds--which include blackmail and bewithment--love
and virtue triumph in the end, and Munro receives his just punish-

ment.
    3 men, 7 women; 1 interior. Royalty: $10.

JOHNSON, Pamela H. The Rehearsal. See entry under Anouilh,
    Jean.

JOHNSTON, Gregory. Curtain Going Up (1952). Samuel French.
    The production of a high school play provides the basis for
the humorous romantic complications in this comedy. Pretty young
Miss Burgess is the faculty director for the play, her first one,
and it seems every problem which could possibly arise, does. The
janitor who is supposed to help with the props is grouchy. Then the
playbooks disappear on the first day of practice. In addition to the
student romances which lead to all sorts of difficulties, Miss Burgess has the further problem of unwanted advice from a college
"actor" and a flamboyant professional actress. Difficult as they
seem, a solution to these problems is found, and in the process,
Miss Burgess discovers a romantic interest herself.
    7 men, 10 women, extras; no scenery. Royalty: $25-20.

JONES, Henry Arthur. The Case of Rebellious Susan (1894). Mac-
    millan, 1894; French, 1901; in his Representative Plays, Little,
    Brown, 1925, v. 2.
    Trying to retaliate on her disloyal husband, Lady Susan at-
tempts a romance which is checked by her wise uncle. Socially,
sauce for the gander is not for the goose.
    3 acts; 10 men, 4 women; 3 interiors.

_____. Dolly Reforming Herself (1908). French, 1910; in his
    Representative Plays, Little, 1925, v. 4; CHA.
    Making New Year's resolutions, extravagant Dolly decides to
economize and shake off her bad habits, her husband promises to
stop using profanity, and her friend Renie determines to end her
flirtation with Dolly's cousin. At the end, all three have failed to
live up to their New Year resolutions.
    4 acts; 6 men, 3 women; 1 interior.

_____. The Liars (1897). Macmillan, 1901; French, 1909; in
    his Representative Plays, Little, 1925, v. 3; DUR; MAP; MAT;
    abridged in Pierce & Matthews, v. 1.
    Lady Jessica, flirting with Edward Falkner and making her
husband furiously jealous, has a dinner engagement with Falkner.
Around this is fashioned a whole tissue of lies. With clever technique the follies and foibles of English society are satirized, em-
phasizing honesty as the best policy. A masterly climax at the end
of the 3d act.
    4 acts; 10 men, 6 women; 3 interiors, 1 exterior.

_____. The Lie (1914). Doran, 1915.
    Self-sacrificing Elinor gives up to her selfish younger sister
Lucy, helps her when she has a baby by a deceased lover, and by
wrong information (the lie) loses Gerald to Lucy with a Judas kiss.
Noll Dibdin offers a chance which Elinor will probably take.
    4 acts; 4 men, 5 women, 1 boy of 5; 2 interiors.

_____. Mary Goes First (1913).   Doubleday, 1914; taken over by
French; in his Representative Plays, Little, 1925, v. 4.
    Amusingly pictures social rivalry between two ambitious la-
dies in a small community in England.   Their social climbing is
complicated with a political campaign by their husbands.   In the end
the deposed social queen regains her place.
    3 acts & epilog; 8 men, 4 women; 1 interior.

_____. Michael and His Lost Angel (1895).   Macmillan, 1895;
in his Representative Plays, Little, 1925, v. 3; DIC; abridged
in Pierce & Matthews, v. 1.
    The clergyman Michael, living under a vow of celibacy,
makes a young girl Rose confess her sin before the congregation.
Later he commits a similar sin when left on an island with the insincere, frivolous fascinator Mrs. Lesden.   He publicly confesses
as he made Rose do.   Feelingly pictures the struggle between religion and love, code morality and nature.
    5 acts; 6 men, 4 women, many extras; 4 interiors.

_____. Mrs. Dane's Defence (1900).   Macmillan, 1905; French,
1909; in his Representative Plays, Little, 1925, v. 3; COT.
    Mrs. Dane hopes to make amends for her past sins by mar-
rying Lionel, a generous youth who loves her devotedly and who is
only too willing to believe her innocent.   But his step-father, Sir
Daniel, in his effective cross-examination, crumbles her defences
and assures Lionel he would always mistrust her.   They give each
other up; and the moralities of society are upheld.
    4 acts; 8 men, 4 women; 2 interiors.

_____. The Silver King (1882).   French, 1907; in his Represent-
ative Plays, Little, 1925, v. 1.
    Following Geoffrey Ware to his house, Will Denver is chloro-
formed by a group of thieves who shoot Ware with Denver's revolver.
He is accused of the crime but escapes to Nevada, where he strikes
it rich and becomes the Silver King.   Returning to England, his old
servant Jaikes restores the old house for his wife Nelly and the
children; his name is cleared, for Spider Skinner, the real murderer
is arrested.
    5 acts; 21 men, 5 women, 2 children, extras; 11 interiors,
    4 exteriors; costumes of the period.

_____. Whitewashing Julia (1903).   Macmillan, 1905; French,
1909.
    When Mrs. Julia Wren returns to the English village she is
snubbed by her family and friends because of stories about her conduct, her puff-box, and her reported morganatic marriage with a
titled continental.   She comes to the rescue of Eddie Pinkney and
helps Lady Pinkney in many ways, so that when Lady Pinkney's
brother, William Stillingfleet, proposes and burns some incriminating
confession, she is finally accepted socially and her reputation is
whitewashed.
    3 acts & epilog; 8 men, 10 women; 2 interiors, 1 exterior
    (a tent).

JONES, LeRoi. Dutchman (1964). Samuel French.
     A sexy white blonde, riding in a subway car, tries every
way she can think of to seduce a young Negro youth sitting beside
her. When even vulgarity does not work, she humiliates him until
he descends to her level to exchange insults. When he shouts that
the murder of whites by blacks would make everyone sane, she
stabs him. The other whites dispose of his body while she primps
for her next Negro victim.
     2 men, 1 woman, extras; 1 interior. Royalty: $35-30.

_____. The Slave (1964). Samuel French.
     Negroes have revolted and are burning and bombing the civi-
lization of white America. One Negro bursts into the home of a
professor, married to his former wife. His intention is to kill the
professor and his wife and take the children, two mulatto girls of
which he is the father, with him. He only partly succeeds. The
wife and children die in the collapsing house.
     2 men, 1 woman; 1 interior. Royalty: $35-20.

JONSON, Ben. The Alchemist (1610). In his Collected editions;
     ASH; BAS; BEL v. 4; GAY v. 2; HOW; LIE; NEI v. 2; OLH;
     OLI v. 2; SPE; TAU; THA; new ed. by Bentley, Crofts, 1947.
     Lovewit leaves his London house in charge of Face, his
housekeeper. Subtle, the quack alchemist, with Face and Dol, his
consort, use it as a place to cheat people, for they expect all men
to be rascally and avaricious, all women to be vain and libertine.
All who come are duped through avarice in the hope of getting gold
from metal through the pseudo-science of alchemy. The scheme is
ended when Lovewit returns unexpectedly.
     5 acts; 11 men, 1 woman, extras; 1 interior; costumes of
     the period.

_____. Epicene; or, The Silent Woman (1609). In his Collected
     editions; CLS; GAY v. 2; STA.
     Morose, a miserly bachelor, with an aversion to noise, would
disinherit his nephew, Sir Dauphine, to marry a Silent Woman--if
he can find one. Sir Dauphine brings in Epicene who does not speak
and the marriage takes place. Immediately after the ceremony she
recovers the use of her tongue. This is intolerable, and he accepts
Sir Dauphine's offer to rid him of her for one-third of his income,
whereupon Sir Dauphine pulls off Epicene's disguise and reveals that
"she" is a boy trained for the part.
     5 acts; 11 men, 5 women, 1 boy, extras; 5 interiors, 1 ex-
     terior; costumes of the period.

_____. Every Man in his Humour (1598). In his Collected
     works; BAS; BAT; BEL v. 8; BRI v. 2; CLF v. 1; GAY v. 2;
     INCH v. 5; MAT; NEI; OXB v. 16; PAR; SCI; SCW; SPE.
     Each character represents a peculiarity of temperament, cari-
caturing their follies and foibles: Kitely, jealous of his wife; Dame
Kitely, jealous of her husband (they are brought together where each
thinks the other is frequenting for an immoral purpose); their servant Brainworm who devises tricks to cure them; Capt. Bobadil, a

cowardly braggart, thrashed by Downright; stupid Stephen, suspicious Kno'well; kindly Justice Clement; and many others.

    5 acts; 14 men, 3 women, extras; 8 interiors, 4 exteriors; costumes of the period.

_____. Volpone; or The Fox (1605).   In his Collected works; BAS; DUN; HUD; KRE; NEI; PAR; OLH; OLI v. 1; SCH; SCI; SPE; TRE-1, & -2 (v. 2); TREA-1.

    Volpone, a rich Venetian nobleman but a miserly money-lender, gives out that he is at the point of death in order to draw gifts from his would-be heirs.   They flock to him like birds of prey. Mosca, his knavish parasite, persuades each that he is named as heir and thus extracts a costly gift.   Haled into court, Volpone is betrayed by Mosca, his property is forfeited, and his sentence is to lie in the worst hospital in all Venice.   The rest all receive just punishment.

    5 acts; 14 men, 2 women, extras; 4 interiors, 2 exteriors; Venetian costumes of the period.

JOUDRY, Patricia.   Teach Me How to Cry (1955).   Dramatists Play Service.

    Two young people who feel somewhat outside society discover each other, and in the process, discover many of the vital steps to maturity in this play.   The girl feels somehow different because her not-quite-bright mother was never married.   The boy, despite his ambitious, pushy parents, thinks of himself as "more the writer type."   After they meet the young couple find that they share many of the same attitudes; that they both feel like outcasts in a world of proms, sock hops, and the intrigues of high school dating.   Their first affectionate understanding soon develops into love.   Then the parents intervene.   The boy's mother and father refuse to allow him to continue seeing a girl whose mother is unmarried.   The girl's mother also finds their pretentiousness repulsive.   Thus, although the young couple are separated, through their love for each other they have come to feel individually worthwhile.   With such a new awareness they are now equipped to deal with the society they had previously found so alien.

    3 men, 7 women, extras; 1 interior.   Royalty: $35-25.

KAISER, Georg.   From Morn to Midnight (1916).   Tr. by Dukes in Poet Lore, v. 31, 1920; Brentano, 1922; in DIE; in MOSH.

    A petty bank clerk steals 60,000 marks, and to break his deadly routine goes on a prolonged debauch, ending up in a Salvation Army meeting.   After testing humanity in a series of symbolical groups, thoroughly disillusioned, he shoots himself.

    7 scenes; 15 men, 11 women, extras; 5 interiors, 2 exteriors.

KALISADA.   Sakuntala (ca. 500 A.D.).   Tr. by Monier-Williams, Dodd, 1885; also in CLF-1; & TRE-1, -2 (v. 2); TREA-1; tr. by Ryder in Everyman's, 1913; tr. by Edgren, Holt, 1894; in Eliot, Little Theatre Classics, Little, 1922, v. 4.

    King Dushyanta marries the maiden Sakuntala and gives her

a royal ring. She loses the ring in a pond, and without it the king does not recognize her. A fisherman finds the ring in a fish; it is brought to the king, who now remembers and claims Sakuntala again as his wife.

> 7 acts; 15 men, 13 women, extras; 1 interior, 1 exterior; oriental costumes.

KANIN, Fay. Goodbye, My Fancy (1948). Samuel French.

Twenty years after she hastily left Good Hope College, Agatha Reed, now a Congresswoman, returns for Commencement and to receive an honorary degree. She thinks she may be still in love with Jim Merrill, now its President; but she finds he is an irresolute compromiser whom she cannot trust. She turns back to Matt Cole, a Life photographer, who has filed a standing offer with her for six years. She meets many characteristic campus folk: the students, some of her old professors, and the prominent trustee whose gifts cause his opinions to carry weight.

> 3 acts; 8 men, 12 women; 1 interior. Royalty: $50-25.

_____ and Michael Kanin. Rashomon (1959). Adapted from the stories of Akutagawa. Samuel French.

The basic story is this: a Samurai warrior has been killed and his wife assaulted by a bandit. The bandit is brought to trial, where three versions (which have little in common) are told: by the bandit, the wife, and (through the use of a medium) the warrior. Then a fourth version is told by a peasant, who witnessed the crimes.

> 6 men, 3 women; 1 exterior. Royalty: $50-25.

KANIN, Garson. Born Yesterday (1946). Dramatists Play Service.

A domineering but ignorant egocentric, Harry Brock, who has made a fortune by buying up junk, goes to Washington to get permission from Congress to secure post-war junk. With him is Billie, a beautiful but uneducated chorus girl with good instincts, who has signed for many years as silent partner to Harry's grafting schemes. A newspaper man, Paul, is asked to instruct Billie, which he does so successfully, that Harry and his gang (including Senator Hedges) are in danger of indictment.

> 12 men, 4 women; 1 interior. Royalty: $50-25.

KANIN, Michael. Rashomon. See entry under Kanin, Fay.

KAO-TONG-KIA. Lute Song. See entry under Irwin, Will.

KATAEV, Valentine P. Squaring the Circle (1928). Samuel French.

Two couples must share a single room in Communist Russia. The wife of one is an earnest Communist, and her side of the room is Spartan-like, hard and bare; the wife of the other is bourgeoise, and she has pictures, cushions, and comforts. The husbands hanker after the atmosphere of the other half. After discussion of Soviet notions, etc., they exchange wives.

> 3 acts; 7 men, 5 women; 1 interior. Royalty: $25-20.

KAUFMAN, Bel. Up the Down Staircase (1969). Adapted by Christopher Sergel. Dramatic Publishing Company.
    Sylvia Barrett's first day of teaching is a disaster. The
high school students are rude and difficult, the school administration
uncaring and impossible. Sylvia becomes involved in the problems
of her students, in a battle with the administration, in the start of
a romance, and in the defense of a hostile student named Joe Ferone
who is about to drop out of school.
        12 men, 18 women (doubling possible); 1 interior. Royalty:
        $50.

KAUFMAN, George S. The American Way (1939). Dramatists Play
Service.
    The saga of a German immigrant to America, Martin Gunther,
who welcomes his wife in 1896. By his honesty and skill he attains
peace and happiness in their family group. He loses a son in the
First World War, lives through the depression of 1933 when he sacrifices all for his benefactor. In 1939 when his grandson is about
to join a fascist group, Martin interferes and is killed by the mob,
fighting still for freedom.
        2 acts; 27 men, 7 boys, 17 women, 3 girls, extras; 4 in-
        teriors, 13 exteriors (pageant effect possible with curtains).
        Royalty: $25.

_____, with Marc Connelly. Beggar on Horseback (1924). Samu-
el French.
    A cheerfully distorted fantasy of modern materialism, big
business, and life among the idle rich. A young composer, Neil
McRae, is about to sell himself to a rich wife, which would enable
him to take a rest and study music. He falls asleep and dreams
what the marriage would mean: bride's bouquet consists of bank
notes; his life spent in manufacturing widgets; shut in a cell and
ordered to produce masterpieces. Aroused by the awfulness of his
dream, he gladly turns back to Cynthia across the hall.
        2 acts; 16 men, 5 women, with 6 men, 2 women in the pan-
        tomime; 1 interior and an interior inset. Royalty: $50-25.

_____. The Butter-and-Egg Man (1925). Samuel French.
    A seemingly simple country boy comes to New York and is
inveigled into the play-producing game. He is instrumental in turn-
ing a "flop" into a "wow" after a highly satirical scene with the
cast and the backers.
        8 men, 5 women; 2 interiors. Royalty: $50-25.

_____. The Dark Tower. See entry under Woollcott, Alexander.

_____, with Edna Ferber. Dinner at Eight (1932). Samuel
French.
    A social climber, Millicent Jordan, invites various people to
dine "a week from Friday" and meet the Ferncliffes of the British
nobility. This event is more important to her than the fatal illness
of her husband or her daughter's infatuation with an actor at his
rope's end. Those invited are shown as they prepare to go to din-

ner, depicting love, jealousy, greed, ruin. In the culminating episode, the Ferncliffes couldn't come.
    3 acts; 14 men, 11 women; 6 interiors. Royalty: $50-25.

_____, with Marc Connelly. Dulcy (1921). Samuel French.
    Dulcy, the original blundering wife, invites a curiously as-
sorted group for the weekend: a scenario writer (an escaped lunatic), a businessman and his wife and daughter, a rich young man,
and an ex-convict. Dulcy nearly ruins her husband's business merger, but a final blunder brings success.
    8 men, 3 women; 1 interior. Royalty: $25-20.

_____. First Lady. See entry under Dayton, Katherine.

_____, with Moss Hart. George Washington Slept Here (1940).
Dramatists Play Service.
    Newton Fuller wants a little place in the country. He comes
with his wife and daughter, and they run into various troubles in
making the place habitable. First the search for water, then a
quarrelsome neighbor; his daughter tries to elope, and the usual
week-end guests arrive. In the end their dream house isn't a failure.
    3 acts; 9 men, 8 women; 1 interior. Royalty: $25.

_____. I'd Rather Be Right (1937). Random House, 1937.
    Phil Barker can't get a raise nor get married until the Presi-
dent of the U.S.A. balances the budget. In trying to do this, the
President gets into difficulties with the Supreme Court and a variety
of other fantastic complications. Finally he decides to balance the
budget and it becomes his platform for re-election.
    2 acts; 22 men, 4 women, extras; 1 exterior (Central Park).

_____. June Moon. See entry under Lardner, Ring W.

_____, with Edna Ferber. The Land Is Bright (1941). Drama-
tists Play Service.
    Gives a panoramic view of a rich family, showing outstanding
episodes in its social history. Lacy Kincaid amassed a fortune as
a robber baron and moved to New York in the '90s, one of the
gilded age dynasties. Three generations are depicted; the second
ran with the hounds and hunted with the rats; but the third generation,
sobered by the events leading up to the Second World War, were on
their way to demonstrate American idealism and love of democracy.
    3 acts; 19 men, 12 women; 1 interior. Royalty: $25.

_____, with Moss Hart. The Man Who Came to Dinner (1939).
Dramatists Play Service.
    An irascible individualist, Sheridan Whiteside, falls on the
ice and breaks his hip as he is leaving after dinner and is marooned
for six weeks with the Stanleys, a conventional middle-class family.
From his wheel chair he plots wondrous events for all who come.
He doesn't want to lose his secretary, Maggie, who wants to marry
the local editor Bert Jefferson, so he brings glamorous Lorraine into

the picture to lure Bert away from Maggie. He receives marvelous gifts, penguins and such. His plots culminate in shipping off Lorraine in a mummy case. As he finally takes his leave, he slips on the ice and breaks his hip again.

    3 acts; 15 men, 9 women, extras; 1 interior. Royalty: $25.

_____, with Marc Connelly. Merton of the Movies (1922). Samuel French.

A green country boy, Merton, comes to Hollywood to elevate the movies. He thinks of himself as a sincere emotional actor, but his crudeness makes a comedy of his performance. His ideals are shattered, but he decides to carry on as a comedian.

    4 acts; 7 men, 5 women, extras; 3 interiors, 2 exteriors (all simple). Royalty: $25-20.

_____, with Edna Ferber. Minick (1924). Samuel French.

Old man Minick comes to live with his son and daughter-in-law. After comic and pathetic complications ensue, he concludes that contentment can be found only among his friends in an Old Man's Home.

    3 acts; 6 men, 9 women; 1 interior. Royalty: $25-20.

_____, with Morrie Ryskind. Of Thee I Sing (1931). Samuel French.

Pulitzer Prize play 1932. "Put love in the White House" is the slogan of Wintergreen's campaign. He shall marry the winner of the beauty contest, who turns out to be Diana of Louisiana. Meantime he falls in love with Mary Turner "who bakes the best corn muffins." This brings on complications with France; and the buffoonery shrewdly satirizes the non-recognition of Throttlebottom the Vice-president, the nine old men of the Supreme Court, and other political material.

    2 acts in 11 scenes; 14 men, 5 women, extras; 6 interiors, 4 exteriors (all simple). Royalty on application.

_____. Once in a Lifetime. See entry under Hart, Moss.

_____, with Edna Ferber. The Royal Family (1927). Samuel French.

Demonstrates the lure of the theatre for the Cavendish family through three generations (supposedly reflecting the Barrymores). Fanny in her 70's still rules; Julie, at the height of her career, tirades against the theatre but always returns to it; Tony, the movie idol, is wild and uncontrolled; Gwen, in her 20's, is a promising ingenue, but forsakes the stage and marries Perry Stewart; but a year later presents a 4th generation Cavendish to the theatre.

    3 acts; 11 men, 6 women; 1 interior. Royalty: $35-25.

_____. The Solid Gold Cadillac. See entry under Teichmann, Howard.

_____. Stage Door (1936). Dramatists Play Service.

A capable young actress, Terry Randall, determines to stick

to the legitimate stage and not be lured into the easier and more profitable career in motion pictures. Many fellow aspirants are depicted: one gives up in despair; another marries; one goes to Hollywood before she has learned to act; all are struggling debutantes of the theatre--eager, earnest, and brave. Terry is helped to overcome hardships and discouragements by idealistic David Kingsley.
    3 acts; 11 men, 21 women; 2 interiors (1 set possible).
Royalty: $25.

_____, with Marc Connelly. To the Ladies! (1922). Samuel French.
    As many wives are responsible for the success of their husbands (without their knowing it--"as every woman knows!"), so the clever young wife, Elsie, from down in Mobile, saves the day for Leonard, her rather conceited and not very able husband, when she makes his after dinner speech for him--after the previous speaker had rather stolen it from him.
    3 acts; 11 men, 3 women; 3 interiors. Royalty: $25-20.

_____. You Can't Take It With You. See entry under Hart, Moss.

KELLER, Helen. See William Gibson's The Miracle Worker.

KELLOGG, Marjorie. Tell Me That You Love Me Junie Moon (1972). Adapted by David Rogers. Dramatic Publishing Company.
    Junie Moon, Arthur, and Warren meet in a hospital. Each has been tragically handicapped, but all three have strength, humor, and the will to lead fulfilling lives. They decide to pool their resources and face the world together. Their adventures are not always happy or successfully concluded, but the three are gallant in facing adversity while preserving their sense of humor and compassion.
    6 men, 6 women; 1 interior, 2 exteriors. Royalty: $35.

KELLY, George. Craig's Wife (1925). Samuel French.
    Pulitzer Prize play 1926. Incisive full-length portrait of a woman who attempts to dominate her entire household--her husband, his friends, and her relatives. Foiled by her selfishness, they leave her to an empty future life. She wanted a house, but she couldn't make a home.
    3 acts; 5 men, 6 women; 1 interior. Royalty: $50-25.

_____. Daisy Mayme (1926). Samuel French.
    A forty year old spinster teaches a bachelor of about the same age how to handle his self-seeking relatives in the comedy. In addition, she proves to him that there is a lot of fun to be got out of life, and then marries him.
    3 men, 5 women; 1 interior. Royalty: $50-25.

_____. The Deep Mrs. Sykes (1945). Samuel French.
    This drama by the Pulitzer Prize winning playwright presents

a searching analysis of an emotionally frustrated woman. Mrs.
Sykes has convinced herself that she can always read other people's
minds. She begins to detect what she considers infidelity on the
part of her husband. Although her conception of the situation is
totally erroneous, she stubbornly refuses to admit that her intuitions
could be wrong and brings dissension and tragedy to her family life.
        6 men, 8 women; 2 interiors.   Royalty: $50-25.

_____. The Fatal Weakness (1946).   Samuel French.
        Romantic Olivia simply can't resist a wedding. She learns
of her husband's infidelity, tracking it down with another feminine
detective, and gives him his freedom. Of course she has some injured pride, but curiosity takes her to witness her ex-husband's
marriage to another woman.
        3 acts; 2 men, 4 women; 1 interior.   Royalty: $50-25.

_____. The Show-Off (1924).   Samuel French.
        Veracious character study of a braggart, Aubrey Piper, with
a million-dollar imagination and an irritating personality. He nevertheless secures our sympathy despite his obnoxious traits through a
subconscious appeal to our own desire to reach the unattainable.
Presents also the serious problem of marriage for a young couple
on a meagre salary.
        3 acts; 6 men, 3 women; 1 interior.   Royalty: $50-25.

_____. The Torch-Bearers (1922).   Samuel French.
        The leader in local amateur theatricals, Mrs. Pampinelli,
calls on Mrs. Fred Ritter to take a part in a play. Rehearsals
follow, and the final production is seen backstage, with the many
trials of amateur production. Fred is so greatly irritated that he
insists that his wife stop this nonsense and take care of her home.
        3 acts; 6 men, 6 women; 2 interiors.   Royalty: $50-25.

KELLY, Tim. Lizzie Borden of Fall River (1976).   Pioneer Drama
        Service.
        Did Lizzie Borden really kill her father and stepmother with
an axe or was she the innocent victim of circumstance? This play
is designed to keep the audience guessing until the final scene. The
principal roles are Lizzie and her sister Emma, though we meet
friends, enemies, and visiting aunts with strong motives for murder.
        6 men, 9 women; 1 interior.   Royalty: $35.

_____. M*A*S*H (1973).   Based on the book by Richard
        Hooker.   Dramatic Publishing Company.
        Hawkeye and Duke, two of the best chest surgeons in South
Korea, decide to wage a campaign to send a Korean boy to school
in the United States. Other characters include a woman psychiatrist,
Radar Reilly, a rip-off sergeant, and the baby-talking Bonwit sisters (the worst tap-dancing act in the U.S.O. circuit).
        15 men, 15 women (doubling possible); 2 interiors.   Royalty:
        $50.

_____. Merry Murders at Montmarie (1972).   Performance Publishing.

Charlie, a young American, inherits a girls' school in Switzerland. He becomes romantically involved with a teacher named
Lily, who runs the school, and is fouled up by his young sister
Helen and her friends, who may be mixed up in something sinister.
Some of the parents who have visited the school, for example,
haven't been heard from since. There is mystery, and humor, and
light-hearted entertainment designed for younger members of high
schools.

7 men, 17 women; 1 interior. Royalty: $25.

KENDALL, Jane. Jane Eyre. See entry under Brontë, Charlotte.

_____ . Pride and Prejudice. See entry under Austen, Jane.

KENNEDY, Charles Rann. The Servant in the House (1907). Harper, 1908; French carries; in his Repertory of Plays ... for 7
Players, Chicago, 1930; in Golden Book, v. 2, p. 795.

As the new butler, Manson comes into the troubled household
of his clergyman brother and applies the teaching of Jesus Christ to
the life of today. He teaches the spirit of service and brotherhood,
indicating that brotherly love is greater than wealth or social position; that forms are nothing, humanity is everything.

5 acts (but playable in 3); 5 men, 2 women; 1 interior.
(Continuous action, embodying the 3 unities of time, place,
and action.) French royalty: $25-20.

KENNEDY, Mary and Ruth Hawthorne. Mrs. Partridge Presents
(1925). Samuel French.

With great success Mrs. Partridge manages her business,
her husband, her daughter, and her son. She has tremendous energy and wants to give her children the chances she missed. But the
children revolt against her well-meant management: she wanted
Philip to be an artist, he chooses to be an engineer; she wanted Delight to be an actress, she prefers to be married.

3 acts; 6 men, 6 women; 2 interiors. Royalty: $25-20.

KENYON, Charles. Kindling (1911). Doubleday, 1914; taken over
by French; DIG.

Strongly indicts conditions in New York tenements. For the
sake of her baby the young wife is driven to steal, hoping to provide an escape from the squalid surroundings by going to Wyoming.
A tense moving story relieved by the humor of the Irish washerwoman.

3 acts; 6 men, 4 women; 1 interior.

KERR, Jean. Finishing Touches (1973). Dramatists Play Service.

The Cooper family lives in a comfortable suburban home with
two sons (the third son is a Harvard senior, living away). Husband
Jeff is in line for a full professorship in English, but since the passion has gone out of his marriage a good bit of his energy is going
into an attractive student who has captured his attention. Wife Katy,
for similar reasons, is attracted to a bachelor professor who rents

the Cooper's garage apartment. Then the college son comes home
with a young actress who is his mistress, and the parents, who are
after all pretty conventional people, are shocked and put through a
series of resolved crises.
    3 men, 2 boys, 3 women; 1 interior. Royalty: $50-35.

_____. Jenny Kissed Me (1948). Dramatists Play Service.
    Amiable Father Moynihan takes into his rectory an ugly duck-
ling in Jenny, the 18-year old niece of his housekeeper. He tries
to improve the mousy pathetic orphan with clothes and a hair-do,
seeking such information from the beauty columns of a woman's magazine. He wants to make her attractive to the boys, and he tries
to pick a husband for her in Owen, a neighborhood boy; but she
picks her own--the harried but noble inspector of parochial schools,
Michael Saunders.
    3 acts; 4 men, 10 women; 1 interior. Royalty: $25.

_____. Mary, Mary (1961). Dramatists Play Service.
    Mary is witty and clever, a condition which caused her mar-
riage with Bob to fail. When she returns to Bob's apartment at the
request of his attorney, to help her former husband with his income
tax problems, her sense of humor has not waned. Bob is on the
verge of marrying Tiffany Richards, a rich, beautiful health fiend.
When Dirk Winston, a movie idol, offers Mary love, passion, and a
weekend together in Florida, Bob realizes his need for Mary and
locks her in the bathroom so that she can't make the Florida trip.
After a disgruntled Dirk Winston leaves alone, we discover that Mary
had her bathroom key all along. She attempts to stifle her sense of
humor long enough for another wedding with Bob.
    3 men, 2 women; 1 interior. Royalty: $50-25.

_____. Our Hearts Were Young and Gay (1946). Based on the
    book by Cornelia Otis Skinner and Emily Kimbrough. Dramatic
Publishing Company.
    The escapades of two young girls determined to prove how
mature and cosmopolitan they are as they take a trip to Europe make
this an entertaining comedy. Cornelia and Emily are in a frenzy of
excitement as they prepare to sail for Europe. But they try hard to
appear bored and casual. Then Cornelia's mother calls her "Baby"
as Cornelia prepares to leave and embarrasses her in front of everyone. After the ship has sailed the two girls have a series of adventures, including Emily's stocking all the lifeboats with cookies, and
Cornelia's bout with the measles. In Paris the girls encounter an
exploding gas meter, sleep in a bed Cardinal Richelieu once used,
and try to convince a great French actor to give them acting lessons.
The girls experience other entertaining adventures.
    8 men, 9 women; unit set. Royalty: $35.

_____. Poor Richard (1964). Samuel French.
    A belligerent but gifted poet on the order of Dylan Thomas
or Brendan Behan comes to America to see his publisher and to attend the dedication of a hospital to the memory of his late wife. He
is loaned a secretary from his publisher, a girl who has been se-

cretly in love with him since she was fifteen.   Soon she announces
plans to marry the poet.   The publisher also loves the girl, but he
is destined to lose both.   Beneath all the poet's charm, however,
he is terribly unsure of himself.   His public image is of one who
wrote beautiful haunting verses on the death of his wife and then
turned to drink for comfort.   What really troubles him is that he
did not love his wife at all and that he is a complete fraud.   The
biggest trial comes when he refuses to go to the dedication.   This
brings truth, and from reading his wife's diary comes peace.
     3 men, 2 women; 1 interior.   Royalty: $50-25.

_____, with Walter Kerr.   The Songs of Bernadette (1946).
     Adapted from Franz Werfel's novel.   Dramatic Publishing Com-
pany.
     Bernadette is a day-dreamer, always in trouble with her
teacher, Sister Vauzous, and her parents.   When she has a beautiful vision one day, no one believes her.   Her parents punish her,
and the Mayor and Chief of Police try to force her to deny the
visions.   She is rescued from the civil authorities who want to shut
her up in an asylum by Dean Peyramale, who offers her a choice.
She can either enter the sisterhood or deny the visions and lead a
simple village life.   Bernadette chooses the religious order where
she is under the strict discipline of her former teacher, who still
finds the girl insincere.   But then Sister Vauzous finally must admit
to the reality of the visions.
     7 men, 11 women, extras; interior and exteriors or curtains.
Royalty: $25.

KERR, Walter.   Rip Van Winkle.   See entry under Irving, Washing-
    ton.

_____.   The Songs of Bernadette.   See entry under Kerr, Jean.

_____.   Stardust (1946).   Dramatic Publishing Company.
     Students at the Academy of Dramatic and Allied Arts are ex-
pecting a famous actress to guest-star in one of their productions.
The director of the group once studied under Stanislavasky, and he
reminds his students of this fact so often that they are all a bit too
"arty" about their parts.   In one scene, for example, the director
has them represent such objects as a sliced orange, a mousetrap,
and three yards of muslin.   Phil, a young artist, begs his girlfriend
Jane to give up her part and her plans for a career and marry him.
She refuses.   When the great actress arrives, she is discovered to
be a normal, hard working girl with a distaste for overarty stunts.
Her personal problems are like those of Phil and Jane.   The personal problems are solved, and the young actors learn that there is
no substitute for hard work and good sense.
     7 men, 11 women; 1 interior.   Royalty: $25.

KESEY, Ken.   One Flew Over the Cuckoo's Nest.   See entry under
    Wasserman, Dale.

KESSELRING, Joseph.   Arsenic and Old Lace (1931).   Dramatists

Play Service.

Two mentally unbalanced old ladies with the aid of their grandfather's arsenic in elderberry wine help lonely old men escape from life and populate their cellar with 12 acceptable roomers. Their brother Teddy, who thinks he is Teddy Roosevelt, inters them in the "Panama Canal." Their brother Jonathan, equally unbalanced, wants to equal his sisters' record and plans to do so with his brother Mortimer. He is fortunately prevented. It turns out that Mortimer is only a step-brother and not affected with the family taint and can safely marry Elaine.

3 acts; 11 men, 3 women; 1 interior. Royalty: $35-25.

KESTER, Paul. Sweet Nell of Old Drury (1923). Samuel French.

After she becomes the mistress of Charles II, the ever-fascinating Nell Gwyn attempts to aid the escape of Sir Roger Fairfax, and in doing so, proves the Lord Chief Justice is the villain of the Cabinet.

4 acts; 15 men, 5 women; 3 interiors, 1 exterior; costumes of the Restoration. Royalty: $25.

KEYES, Daniel. Flowers for Algernon. See entry under Rogers, David.

KIELLAND, Alexander L. Three Couples (Tre par, 1886). Tr. by Lindanger in Drama, v. 7, 1917.

Two married couples, the Sandbergs and the Friedmans, plus a bachelor, Mr. Waage, and a secretary, Miss Svendsen, get interested in each other. Mr. Sandberg is almost willing to divorce his wife for Miss Svendsen; Mr. Friedman enjoys talking to Mrs. Sandberg; Mr. Waage exchanges pleasantries with Mrs. Friedman. The discussion ends when Mr. Waage becomes engaged to Miss Svendsen.

3 acts; 3 men, 4 women; 1 interior, 1 exterior.

KIMBROUGH, Emily. Our Hearts Were Young and Gay. See entry under Kerr, Jean.

KING, Philip. See How They Run (1949). Samuel French.

The characters move through the fast-paced action of this farce like sprinters in a footrace. Galloping in and out of the four doors of an English vicarage are an American actor and actress, a cockney maid, an old maid who has her first taste of alcohol, and four clergymen, only one is an escaped prisoner disguised as a clergyman. At the center of all this turmoil is a sedate Bishop who is aghast at all the goings on and the trumped-up stories that he's told.

6 men, 3 women; 1 interior. Royalty: $25-20.

KINGSLEY, Sidney. Darkness at Noon (1951). Adapted from Arthur Koestler's novel. Samuel French.

Rubashov, an old-guard Russian revolutionary, is imprisoned by younger sadistic Soviets, such as Gletkin. His former associate, Ivanoff, now head of the prison, can help him if he will "confess" to treason. Rubashov realizes his great dream, his whole philosophy of life, has been a delusion; he is the victim of misguided and false idealism: the destructive means used by him and the leaders have become an end in themselves. He remembers his past activities and especially his romance with his secretary Luba. A brilliant indictment of Communism.

18 men, 3 women; 1 interior. Royalty: $50-25.

_____. Dead End (1935). Dramatists Play Service.
On one side of a dead end street on Manhattan's East Side is a tenement. On the other side, a sharp contrast, is a posh apartment building. The young residents of the tenement belong to a street gang, joining together to protect themselves and to learn the tricks of the trade which permitted Baby Face Martin (from the neighborhood) to achieve success. Grimpty, an architecture student whose legs have been deformed by rickets, tries to dissuade them from a life of crime but realizes that the slum environment works against him. When Baby Face Martin returns to his old neighborhood, he finds that his former girl friend is now a prostitute and that his mother hates him for what he is. Grimpty reports Martin to the F.B.I., who kill the notorious criminal. Grimpty cannot persuade the girl he loves to leave her rich lover, so he will use the reward money to get a good lawyer for the leader of the street gang, arrested for knifing a wealthy resident of the posh apartment building. A harsh indictment of slum environment.

22 men (several bits), 6 women, extras; 1 exterior. Royalty: $35-25.

_____. Detective Story (1949). Dramatists Play Service.
Into the squad-room and office of a New York police station come all types of people in all sorts of trouble. One case stands out, however. A young man has been arrested for stealing money from his boss. Though the woman who loves him comes to his aid and his boss recovers all of the money, McLeod, a hard-working detective, refuses to let the young man off easily. McLeod has been hardened by his years on the force, and only severe punishment of law breakers ever satisfies him. He is about to complete his case against an abortioner when the man's attorney forces McLeod's wife to admit she once made use of the abortioner's services. The detective's whole world of good-guys-and-bad-guys collapses, and he seeks death in stopping a prisoner from escaping from the station.

24 men (doubling possible), 8 women, several nonspeaking extras; 1 interior. Royalty: $50-25.

_____. Men in White (1933). Samuel French.
Pulitzer Prize play 1934. As an intern in a great hospital Dr. George Ferguson is encouraged by Dr. Hochberg when he is forced to choose between marriage to Laura with a comfortable practice and five years of further study abroad as a surgeon. The death of a young nurse who has comforted him brings him closer to humanity. He leaves for Vienna without Laura.

18 men, 9 women; 7 interiors. Royalty: $25.

_____. Night Life (1962). Dramatists Play Service.

The play is set in the early morning hours at a New York
night club. Gathered there are a corrupt labor leader, a girl singer
in love with the union boss, an idealistic young attorney tortured by
the memory of the man he bayoneted in the war, a movie sex queen
with lesbian tendencies, and a tired old liberal and his wife--both
alcoholic. In the climax of the play the old liberal sacrifices his
life by saving the young attorney from the labor leader's knife.
17 men, 7 women, extras; 1 interior. Royalty: $50-25.

_____. The Patriots (1943). Dramatists Play Service.
Deals with Thomas Jefferson in the early days of the Republic. There are two main struggles in the play: Jefferson's personal
one to retire to private life, and the historical one between Jefferson
and Alexander Hamilton. These two statesmen have a falling out
when Jefferson learns that the economy measure he helped through
the Congress had worked only for the benefit of Hamilton and his
friends. At the end of the play, Jefferson's election to the presidency is being held up by Congress. Hamilton wants to make a
deal but Jefferson refuses. The two men understand that their goals
for America are similar, and Hamilton persuades Congress to elect
his rival.
18 men, 5 women, extras; 1 exterior, 6 interiors. Royalty:
$25.

KIPPHARDT, Heinar. In the Matter of J. Robert Oppenheimer
(1968). Samuel French.
A documentary drama based on the actual transcripts of the
government security clearance trial of Dr. Robert Oppenheimer, the
prime mover in getting the atomic bomb for the United States and
the one who hesitated over proceeding with the hydrogen bomb. A
government search reveals an affiliation with communists (the scientist's wife and brother-in-law) and other unsavory people. The
trial, in which other scientists like Dr. Albert Teller testify, also
reveals the dangers in invasions of privacy and the stagnation of
creativity inherent in governmental conformity.
14 men; 1 interior. Royalty: $50-35.

KIRKLAND, Jack. The Man With the Golden Arm (1956). Based
on the novel by Nelson Algren. Dramatists Play Service.
Because of painful wounds suffered in the war, Frankie Machine, a dealer in a Chicago gambling joint, becomes a dope addict.
The play treats his unsuccessful attempts to shake the habit and
finally his own destruction.
16 men, 5 women; unit set. Royalty: $35-25.

_____. Tobacco Road. See entry under Caldwell, Erskine.

KLEIN, Charles. The Lion and the Mouse (1905). French, 1917.
Develops the struggle of wits between a plucky girl who
beards the lion: an unscrupulous money king who is a wealthy male-
factor though a respected man. An effective story with interesting
characters.
4 acts; 10 men, 8 women; 3 interiors.

_____. The Music Master (1904). Samuel French.
      The piano-player in a dime museum in New York, Herr von
Barwig, demonstrates his fine character in a number of ways.
When asked uptown to teach music to a girl of 18, he becomes assured that she must be his daughter whom his wife took with her
when she ran away from Germany with a rich American. In the
house he confronts the man and is made sure; but he goes away
with his secret still kept. He sees her happily married--but she
learns from her false father that the music teacher is her real father, and she carries him off to happiness.
      3 acts; 14 men, 6 women; 3 interiors. Royalty: $25-20.

KLEIST, Heinrich von. The Prince of Homburg (written 1811, prod.
   1821). Tr. by Hagedorn in FRA v. 4; SMK.
      The Prince, a lover and a dreamer, doesn't realize the mili-
tary order is not to advance against the Swedes, but he does advance and wins a great victory. However, for disobedience the
Elector and the Court condemn him to death; he begs for his life
and even will forego his loved Natalie. Told he must judge himself,
if the verdict is unjust, he admits his guilt--and is pardoned.
      5 acts; 8 men, 2 women, extras; 6 interiors, 3 exteriors;
      costumes of the period (1675).

KNOBLOCK, Edward. Milestones. See entry under Bennett, E.
   Arnold.

KNOTT, Frederick. Dial "M" for Murder (1952). Dramatists Play
   Service.
      A mercenary man who tries to have his wife killed for her
money has his plans confounded by his wife's courage in this melodrama. After arranging a perfect alibi for himself, the husband
blackmails a scoundrel into strangling his wife. However, the murderer gets murdered and the victim survives. Then the husband
tries to have his wife convicted for the hireling's death. But through
the efforts of a Scotland Yard inspector and a young man who loves
his wife, the truth is revealed. In a suspense-filled climax they
trap the husband into revealing his guilt, thus freeing the wife.
      5 men, 1 woman; 1 interior. Royalty: $50-25.

_____. Wait Until Dark (1965). Dramatists Play Service.
      Three underworld figures attempt to recover a heroin-filled
doll, innocently brought across the Canadian border by a young
commercial photographer. When the photographer goes off on assignment, the three thugs descend upon his blind wife who, alone in
their Greenwich Village apartment, is terrorized by men who will
murder to achieve their goals. There are frightening moments and
shocks in the final acts. An example of "the school of chilling
menace," as Richard Watts, Jr. observed.
      6 men, 1 woman, 1 girl; 1 interior. Royalty: $50-25.

KNOWLES, James Sheridan. The Hunchback (1832). In his Dramatic Works, Routledge, 1841, v. 1; in New York Drama, v. 4,
   #47, 1878.

Master Walter, the hunchback, has raised Julia in the country; he has posed as representing her father and carrying out his
wishes. He plans to have her marry Sir Thomas Clifford, but he
loses his money, so Julia goes to the city with Cousin Helen. There
Julia is dazzled by the wealth of crude Master Wilford who becomes
Earl of Rochdale, but Walter manages to expose his falseness. He
brings about the marriage of Julia to Clifford and of Helen to Mo-
dus; and acknowledges that he is Julia's father.
     5 acts; 14 men, 2 women, extras; 7 interiors, 3 exteriors;
     costumes of the period.

_____. The Love-Chase (1837).   In his Dramatic Works, Rout-
    ledge, 1841, v. 2.
Three ladies are courted: Lydia the maid is wooed by Waller; the vivacious Constance quarrels with Wildrake, until both find
they love each other; the widow Green sets her cap for Waller but
takes Sir William.
     5 acts; 10 men, 7 women; 7 interiors; costumes of the
     period (Charles II).

_____. Virginius (1820).   In his Dramatic Works, Routledge,
    1841, v. 1; in Brown, C. S.; Later English Drama, Barnes,
    1898; MOSO.
A famous Roman story is dramatically unfolded. The father
Virginius slays his daughter Virginia to save her from the lust and
tyranny of Appius, whom he later also kills.
     5 acts; 18 men, 3 women, extras; 5 interiors, 4 exteriors;
     Roman costumes.

KOBER, Arthur. "Having Wonderful Time" (1937). Dramatists
    Play Service.
Up in a summer camp for two weeks, Teddy a stenographer
meets Chick, a young lawyer waiting on table to cover expenses.
They are attracted to each other but must overcome some obstacles
before marriage--which they do; she will support him until he gets
a position as a lawyer.
     3 acts; 17 men, 14 women (some doubling possible); 3 in-
     teriors, 2 exteriors (possible in 2 sets). Royalty: $25.

KOESTLER, Arthur. Darkness at Noon. See entry under Kingsley,
    Sidney.

KOPIT, Arthur. Indians (1969). Samuel French.
This apology for the treatment and exploitation of the American Indian is set in the form of Buffalo Bill's Wild West Show. The
hero is Buffalo Bill himself, the man whose love of Indian culture is
always undermined by his greater love for money. He is instrumental in destroying the buffalo herds on which the Indians depend, and
later he helps destroy the Indians themselves--and himself. (A
special effects music tape is available for producing this play.)
     22 men; special effects tape available. Royalty: $50-35.

_____. Oh, Dad, Poor Dad, Mama's Hung You in the Closet and

I'm Feeling So Sad (1961).   Samuel French.
        A widow and her young son arrive at a hotel with enough bag-
gage for an army of bellhops. The luggage includes the valuable
stamp collection of the son; some tall, wild plants; a fish bowl con-
taining a flesh eating piranha; and a coffin. Even though the widow
has decided to replace all the bellhops the next day, they are still
tipped with priceless coins worth thousands of dollars. Living at the
hotel is a babysitter who sits for children whose parents never come
home. The mother returns, however, accuses the sitter of harlotry,
and kicks her out. A yachtsman with a tremendous yacht throws himself at the widow's feet, offering himself and his fortune to her.
She accepts the money but refuses him. Similar incidents continue
to happen until the sitter attempts to seduce the son. At this point
poor Dad falls out of the closet.
        4 men, 2 women; 2 interiors. Royalty: $50-25.

KRAMM, Joseph.   The Shrike (1952).   Random House, 1952; abridged
    in Chapman 1951/52.
        Pulitzer prize play 1952. Ann Downs wants to control her
husband Jim, even if he has left her and is interested in another.
In his belief that he is a failure as a theatre director and as a husband, he attempts suicide. Acting as a shrike (a predatory bird),
Ann gets Jim into a mental hospital. There she continues to perse-
cute him subtly by keeping him a tormented prisoner in a psychopathic ward, where he is led by the psychiatrists to think he is an
imbecile. Realizing that he is trapped, he becomes a hypocritical
liar, and feigns sanity and goodwill, but is released only through
Ann's consent and into her custody.
        10 scenes in 2 acts; 17 men, 5 women; 1 interior with furni-
    ture changes.

KRASNA, Norman.   Dear Ruth (1944).   Dramatists Play Service.
        Romantic 16-year-old Miriam has been writing letters filled
with poetry to Bill Seawright, who had received the first in "Bundles
to Britain" and had responded. But Miriam had been signing the
letters with the name of her sister Ruth. Bill returns from the war
unexpectedly. Ruth, though already engaged to staid Albert, is willing to give him two days of enjoyment. She ends up by marrying
him.
        2 acts; 5 men, 5 women; 1 interior. Royalty: $25.

_____.   John Loves Mary (1947).   Dramatists Play Service.
        John brings Lily from England for Fred as his wife; but in
the meantime Fred has married and a baby is expected. To clear
the matrimonial tangle, since John wants to marry Mary, he plans
to go to Reno for 6 weeks to get a divorce from Lily. But Mary's
father, Senator McKinley, insists on a marriage at once. When
Lt. O'Leary is brought in to order John to Nevada, Lily reveals she
has been married to O'Leary in England and thought he was dead.
        3 acts; 7 men, 3 women; 1 interior. Royalty: $35-25.

_____.   Who Was That Lady I Saw You With? (1958).   Dramatists
    Play Service.

Play Service.

A chemistry professor gets involved with innocent pastimes, like making liquor. His wife threatens to leave him, however, when she discovers him engaged in another harmless pastime, kissing a pretty co-ed. A friend convinces the professor to tell his wife that he is an F. B. I. agent and the girl a foreign spy, and that he had to kiss her to get some vital information for the United States. The comic episodes multiply when a real secret agent becomes involved followed by a group of genuine F. B. I. agents. Finally it's all straightened out in a fast and hilarious finish, and the professor finds that he's a hero to his government, but, more importantly, a hero to his wife.

15 men, 6 women; interiors, exteriors. Royalty: $50-25.

KRONENBERGER, Louis. Mademoiselle Colombe. See entry under Anouilh, Jean.

KUMMER, Clare. Good Gracious Annabelle (1916). French, 1922; abridged in Mantle & Sherwood 1909/1919.

Always using the expression "Good gracious," Annabelle engineers herself and four temporarily impecunious friends as servants at the Wimbledon country estate. Then John Rawson arrives, a Montana mining millionaire, who has rented it while Wimbledon is supposedly away--and to be near Annabelle. Considerable complications ensue, until Rawson reveals himself as the Hermit (with beard) Annabelle had married out West six years before.

3 acts; 10 men, 4 women; 2 interiors, 1 exterior.

_____. Her Master's Voice (1933). Samuel French.

When Ned loses his job, rich Aunt Min, who has never seen him, comes to their little home in New Jersey and takes Queenie, Nat's wife, away so she can forget her worthless husband. In doing so, Aunt Min mistakes Ned for the house servant and employs him on her estate. Here he does well and she grows fond of him; so, when she finds he is the husband of her niece, she still thinks him pretty good, especially as he now has a place on a radio program.

3 men, 4 women; 1 interior, 1 exterior. Royalty: $25-20.

KURNITZ, Harry. A Shot in the Dark. See entry under Achard, Marcel.

KYD, Thomas. The Spanish Tragedy (1592). In his Works, Oxford; & Temple Dramatists, Dutton; BAS; HOW; MAT; MCJ; MIO v. 1; NEI; OLH; OLI v. 1; PAR; RUB; SCI; SCW; SPE.

A famous drama of revenge, rather reveling in stage massacres (10 of them). Horatio, son of Hieronimo, is beloved by Bel-Imperia of Spain. Found together, he is caught and hanged. His father vows vengeance: he gets Balthazar her suitor and Lorenzo her brother to act in a play, during the action of which they are both killed. Later both he and Bel-Imperia kill themselves.

4 acts; 25 men (12 of them important), 3 women, extras; 14 scenes (interior and exterior); costumes of the period.

LABICHE, Eugene H. and Michel Marc. A Leghorn Hat (1851).
   Tr. by Chesley in Poet Lore, v. 28, 1917; also separately,
   Badger, 1917.
     Fadinard's horse has eaten a hat that hung on a tree which
must be replaced by him before he can be married to Anais. He
can't find one like it at Clara's (an old flame), but she says she
sold one to the Baroness de Champigney. There he finds that the
hat has been given to her goddaughter Anais--which is the very hat
eaten by the horse. But a hat has been brought from Florence
which finally reaches Anais.
     5 acts; 9 men, 5 women, extras; 4 interiors, 1 exterior;
costumes of the period.

LADY PRECIOUS STREAM (Wang Pao Chuan, produced 1934 in NYC).
   Tr. and adapted by S. I. Hsiung. Samuel French.
     A naive fantasy of love and fidelity, introducing charming
Chinese conventions. Depicts the devotion of a wife, Lady Precious
Stream, to her adventurous husband. Presents his prowess as a
warrior, and his ultimate return after 18 years as King of the West-
ern Regions.
     5 men, 5 women, extras; 1 Chinese set. Royalty: $25-20.

LAGERKVIST, Pär Fabian. The Man Without a Soul (1936). Tr. by
   Kökeritz in Scandinavian Plays of the 20th Century, ser. 1,
   Princeton Univ. Press, 1944.
     "The man" has committed a political murder and comes by
accident to fall in love with "the woman" who bears a child of the
murdered man. He develops from a callous instrument of political
doctrine to see the humanitarianism of brotherly love and sacrifice.
His longing for peace symbolizes man's search for truth through the
ages.
     5 acts; 6 men, 6 women, extras; 4 interiors, 1 exterior.

LANGER, Frantisek. Camel Through the Needle's Eye (1929). Tr.
   & adapted by Moeller, Brentano, 1929; French, 1932.
     Susi, illegitimate daughter of a Prague beggar meets Alik,
the not-too-bright son of a rich father, and goes to live with him and
makes a man of him. His father tries to buy her off, but together
they open a model dairy lunch. It is a success; he marries her and
acknowledges her child.
     3 acts; 6 men, 4 women, extras; 3 interiors.

LANGLEY, Noel. Edward, My Son. See entry under Morley, Robert.

LARDNER, Ring W. and G. S. Kaufman. June Moon (1929). Samuel
   French.
     A young would-be songwriter, Fred, comes to New York.
From the song hit "June Moon" he spends all he makes on industri-
ous little gold-digger, Eileen, but he finds his love in faithful little
Edna. A devastating satire on tune factories.
     7 men, 5 women; 3 interiors. Royalty: $50-25.

LAURENTS, Arthur.   A Clearing in the Woods (1957).   Dramatists
    Play Service.
        Virginia, a mature woman, seeks a clearing in the woods--
some peace in her life.   She is tormented by her past, by her inability to find perfection, and by her belief that no one has ever
really loved her.   But phantoms from the past appear on stage, including Virginia at three stages of life and the men she has been involved with: father, first love, ex-husband, and a former fiance
whom she dumped.   At the end she arrives at an acceptance of her
own nature.
        5 men, 4 women, 1 small girl; unit set.   Royalty: $50-25.

_____.   Home of the Brave (1945).   Dramatists Play Service.
        Among U.S. soldiers on a Pacific island in World War II,
Coney, a Jew, feels he failed in his duty toward a dying buddy.   His
guilt complex is overcome by a sympathetic doctor through whom he
regains courage and confidence.
        6 men, 2 interiors, 2 exteriors.   Royalty: $35-25.

_____.   Time of the Cuckoo (1952).   Samuel French.
        A middleaged, unmarried American secretary is vacationing
in Europe, where she falls in love with a middleaged shopkeeper
from Venice.   The newly discovered love completely fulfills her until she finds that the man has a wife and children.   The shopkeeper
freely admits these facts and finds nothing especially wrong about
their relationship.   The American learns something of the difference
between European and American morality, and must choose between
having a short-term love affair or none at all.
        5 men, 5 women; 1 exterior.   Royalty: $50-25.

LAVEDAN, Henri.   The Prince d'Aurec (1892).   Tr. by Clark, in
    Three Modern Plays from the French, ed. by Clark, Holt, 1914;
    abridged in Pierce & Matthews, v. 2.
        The Prince, a suave but impoverished aristocrat, borrows
money from the bourgeoise banker, the Jew DeHorn, to pay his
gambling debts, but he feels no obligation to pay it back.   His mother
saves him and secures a promise of amendment from her volatile son.
        3 acts; 15 men, 8 women; 2 interiors.

LAVERY, Emmet G.   The Gentleman from Athens (1947).   Samuel
    French.
        A West Coast roughneck gets into Congress.   His secretary
tries to smooth out some of his rough edges.   To attract attention,
he introduces a bill calling for World Government, which will stave
off atomic warfare.   Using his gangster methods he gets it passed,
and he even comes to believe in it himself.   It finishes him as a
Congressman, but makes a man of him.
        3 acts; 10 men, 3 women; 1 interior.   Royalty: $35-25.

_____.   The Magnificent Yankee (1946).   Samuel French.
        Episodes in the life of Justice Oliver Wendell Holmes, giving
snapshots of his family life with an understanding wife, and introducing some of the young men from the Harvard Law school who each

served a year as his secretary.
   3 acts; 15 men, 2 women; 1 interior.   Royalty: $50-25.

LAWLER, Ray.   Summer of the Seventeenth Doll (1957).   Samuel
   French.
   Every year for the past sixteen years, Barney and Roo, two
itinerant cane-cutters, have been spending the summer with two bar
maids in a small southern Australian city.   And every summer Roo
has presented Olive with a doll, a symbol of their unusual but tender
relationship   This seventeenth summer is different, however.
Change has taken place, and the characters must face for the first
time some unpleasant truths about themselves.
   3 men, 4 women; 1 interior.   Royalty: $50-25.

LAWRENCE, Jerome and Robert E. Lee.   Auntie Mame (1956).
   Adapted from the novel by Patrick Dennis.   Dramatists Play
   Service.
   A hilarious play about Auntie Mame, a scatterbrained, energetic, warm lady who is completely devoted to her young nephew.
Her fortunes and marriages rise and fall.   The scrapes she gets
herself into mostly rise.   So does the laughter.
   25 men, 12 women, 3 boys (doubling possible); interiors and
   exteriors.   Royalty: $50-25.

_____.   The Gang's All Here (1959).   Samuel French.
   A compromise candidate allows, even encourages, political
corruption after his election as president.   Griffith P. Hastings is
a likeable sort of fellow, and when his party's nominating convention
cannot agree between the two more deserving candidates, it nomi-
nates him.   After his victory he brings all his poker-loving cronies
along with him to the White House where they promptly begin arranging scandalous deals.   The corruption spreads quickly until a
senator finds convincing evidence of the shady dealings.   When he
confronts Hastings with this material, the President finds a new
source of inner courage and exposes and fires all his crooked friends.
Then he himself dies, a disillusioned man.   The New York Times
describes this play as "Effective drama with a conscience.... "
   15 men, 4 women; 4 interiors.   Royalty: $50-25.

_____.   Inherit the Wind (1955).   Dramatists Play Service.
   The famous Scopes trial provides the plot for this widely acclaimed drama.   Atkinson of the N.Y. Times wrote, "The portrait
it draws of an explosive episode in American culture ... remains as
fresh as it ever was.   One of the most stirring plays in recent
years retains its folk flavor and spiritual awareness. "   The play
dramatizes not only the eloquent and heated courtroom battle of
Clarence Darrow and William Jennings Bryan, but manages to convey also the deep convictions of the others involved (including the
cynicism of H. L. Mencken) and the furor which this "monkey" trial
aroused throughout the nation.
   21 men, 6 women, 1 girl, 2 boys (doubling possible); unit
   set.   Royalty: $50-25.

_____. The Night Thoreau Spent in Jail (1970).   Samuel French.
The play begins with Henry David Thoreau in jail and ends
with his release.   In between we see the famous visit from Ralph
Waldo Emerson, Thoreau's refusal to pay taxes to a government
conducting an unjust war against Mexico, his transcendental school
which was too revolutionary for the student's parents, his friendship with an illiterate cellmate, his job as a handyman around the
Emerson household.
    11 men, 5 women, extras; platform stage.   Royalty: $50-35.

_____. Only in America (1959).   Adapted from Harry Golden's
    book.   Samuel French.
    This comedy is an account of an eastside New York Jew who
sets up a humorous journal in North Carolina, "The Carolina Is-
raelite."   His publication, filled with witty aphorisms and homespun
humor, soon becomes a success, and Harry becomes an accepted
member of the community.   Then Harry is asked to serve on the
local school board, and in declining, is forced to explain that a short
Depression prison term bars him from any political office.   But the
city's love for him does not lessen.   Even when an anonymous letter
to a New York paper reopens the old case, the people rally to his
support.   One telegram summed up the people's attitude.   "Harry,
we need you in Charlotte.   You may be the best Christian we got."
    17 men, 5 women, 3 extras; 1 interior-exterior, inset.
    Royalty: $50-25.

LAWRENCE, Reginald. If This Be Treason. See entry under
    Holmes, John Haynes.

_____. Mr. Blandings Builds His Dream House (1960).   Adapted
    from Eric Hodgins' novel.   Dramatic Publishing Company.
    Mr. Blandings takes his wife and female daughters to the
country, where he is building a home.   Everything seems to go
wrong.   The girls rebel, the well has to be blasted through granite,
the factory sends the wrong windows, Mrs. Blandings changes plans
in mid-housebuilding, and the bank turns him down on the mortgage.
Even the women of the local historical society attack him for destroying an historic monument (an old barn).   Finally Mr. Blandings
will lose his job if he doesn't come up with a new baby food slogan.
He does, and everything is saved.
    7 men, 10 women; 1 interior.   Royalty: $25.

_____. The Thread That Runs So True (1958).   Adapted from
    Jesse Stuart's novel.   Dramatic Publishing Company.
    Jesse is in his teens when he takes on the job of teacher in
Lonesome Valley School.   Many of his students are older than he,
and the school bully is bigger and tougher, too.   The bully, like
his friends, attends school during the season when work on the farm
is slack and gets his greatest fun in baiting the teacher.   Some of
the students do respond to the young teacher's enthusiasm, but those
who do have parents who resent book learning.   Soon Jesse finds
stiff opposition in the community (led by the school bully), and he
has to fight to keep his job.   The fact that the bully and the teacher

are both after the same girl, Naomi, does not help either.   Finally
Jesse is victorious.
    12 men, 16 women; 1 interior.   Royalty: $35.

LEDERER, William J.   The Ugly American.   See entry under Lubar,
    Bernard.

LEE, Harper.   To Kill a Mockingbird (1970).   Adapted by Christo-
    pher Sergel.   Dramatic Publishing Company.
    A young girl named Scout lives in a small southern town.
The time is 1935, and she doesn't understand why the black community has such a special feeling about her father, Atticus, a lawyer.
She also doesn't understand why some of her white friends are hostile.   Her father explains that he is defending a black man wrongfully accused of a serious crime and that even though he is fighting
their friends they are still "friends."   There are good roles for
black actors in this racially mixed cast.
    12 men, 17 women, extras; 2 sets.   Royalty: $35.

LEE, Robert E.   See entries under Lawrence, Jerome.

LE GALLIENE, Eva, with Florida Friebus.   Alice in Wonderland
    (1932).   Based on Lewis Carroll's classic book.   Samuel French.
    The fantasy world of the Lewis Carrol classic comes to life
in this dramatization.   The setting treated here is a world of illusion, fantastic shapes, and unreal perspectives.   The adventures of
Alice are traced from the moment she finds herself in an enormous
arm chair until she meets the Duchess whose baby turns into a pig.
The other familiar events which Alice experiences are presented also in this ingenious play in which nonsense begins to seem logical.
    More than 50 characters, extras; several exteriors and in-
teriors.   Royalty: $25-20.

LEGOUVE, Ernest.   The Ladies' Battle.   See entry under Scribe,
    A. Eugene.

Le MAÎTRE, Jules.   The Pardon (1895).   Tr. by Clark, in Three
    Modern Plays from the French, ed. by Clark, Holt, 1914; tr.
    by Fay, in Poet Lore, v. 24, 1913, as Forgiveness.
    Suzanne has been unfaithful to her husband Georges and is
told by him to leave.   When Therese brings them together again
after a few months' separation, Georges thinks he is in love with
Therese; now Suzanne is ready to leave, but he asks her to stay;
it was his vanity that erred.   They are both equally guilty; accounts
are balanced.   They forgive each other's unfaithfulness and will
start to live all over again.
    3 acts; 1 man, 2 women; 1 interior.

LENORMAND, Henri-René.   The Dream Doctor (1922).   Tr. by
    Orna, in his Three Plays, Lond., Gollancz, 1928; MOSH.
    Dr. Luke, a Freudian disciple, interprets the dream of
Fearon to show that she is a happy thief.   He interprets the dream
of Jeannine, who envisioned that she has killed her mother.   When

she finds that she practically did, she kills herself, urged on by
jealousy of Fearon, who now claims Dr. Luke.
Prolog & 9 scenes; 4 men, 5 women; 6 interiors, 2 exteriors.

_____. Time Is a Dream (1919). Tr. by Katzin, Knopf, 1923;
DIE; HAV.
A young man broods over his complex and torturing desire
and the unreality of time and space. His fiancée tells him of her
dream of a young man drowning. This gives him the idea, and he
does it.
6 scenes; 3 men, 2 women; 1 interior.

LESLIE, F. Andrew. The Haunting of Hill House (1964). Adapted
from Shirley Jackson's novel. Dramatists Play Service.
This is a chilling suspense drama about four people who
gather for a study of supernatural phenomena in a sinister mid-Vic-
torian mansion. Hill House, the old mansion, allegedly has mysterious powers, and none of the local inhabitants will approach it
except for its caretaker, Mrs. Dudley, and she refuses to stay after
nightfall. The organizer of the investigating team, Dr. Montague,
enlists three others, all unacquainted, to join him in his venture:
Eleanor Vance and Theodora, two girls in their twenties; and Luke
Sanderson, nephew of the present owner of Hill House. The terror
begins the first night when some powerful but unseen force races
through the house, trying to break into the girls' room. As their
fears mount so does the anger of the spirits, leading to the death
of one of the party before Dr. Montague and the rest of his group
decide to leave.
3 men, 4 women; 1 interior. Royalty: $35-25.

_____. Lilies of the Field (1967). Adapted from William E.
Barrett's novel. Dramatists Play Service.
Popularly known by the movie version starring Sidney Poitier.
Homer Smith, an ex-G.I., is bumming around the country on his way
West, stopping to do odd jobs to finance his trip. When he stops to
repair a leaky roof for a group of German nuns, the Mother Superior
believes that Homer has been sent to her by God. Despite his strong
Baptist background and his urge to move on, Homer is drawn into
the life of the nuns until he too shares their dream of building a
chapel. Overcoming seemingly impossible obstacles, Homer and the
local farmers build an adobe chapel. The play is a touching testimony of human goodness and the power of faith. (Note: in this
version Homer Smith may be played either by a Negro or white actor.)
4 men, 5 women; open stage with movable props. Royalty:
$35-25.

_____. Mr. Hobbs' Vacation (1963). Adapted from Edward
Streeter's novel. Dramatists Play Service.
Mr. Hobbs comes to Rock Harbor for "rest and relaxation"
over his objections. His wife, daughter, and aunt have all joined
forces to pressure him to travel from Cleveland to an island off the
coast of New England. Mr. Hobbs' objections are sustained. Their

vacation house is a monstrosity, complete with a temperamental hot water tank. One comic crisis follows another until the exhausted Mr. Hobbs heads back home. In the rush, however, he has forgotten his boat tickets and will undoubtedly be back for more wild vacation adventures.

    8 men (4 can be doubled), 7 women; 1 interior. Royalty: $35-25.

_____. The Spiral Staircase (1962). Adapted from the story by Mel Dinelli. Dramatists Play Service.

    A series of apparently insoluble murders of young girls with some noticeable deformity has produced terror in the household of Helen, a girl who has lost her voice. Helen is the companion of the bed-ridden Mrs. Warren and lives there with Mrs. Oates, the housekeeper, and Professor Warren, the invalid lady's stepson. One stormy night the Constable arrives with the news that another girl has been murdered. After warning the Warren household that the murderer is still at large, the Constable leaves. Then one by one the other members of the household apparently depart, leaving Helen alone, or so she thinks. Her terror intensifies and finally reaches a climax when Helen realizes that the murderer is in the house with her. She is saved, however, in a surprising and exciting finish to this suspense-filled play.

    4 men, 4 women; 1 interior. Royalty: $35-25.

_____. Splendor in the Grass. See entry under Inge, William.

_____. The Wheeler Dealers (1966). Adapted from George Goodman's novel. Dramatists Play Service.

    Henry Tyroon, the wheeler dealer, arrives in New York from Texas to find potential investors. Instead, he finds Molly Thatcher, a young Wall Street security analyst. She is pushing shares of Universal Widget, an obscure company she has been ordered to dispose of. In wheeling and dealing for Molly, Henry also provokes great interest in Universal Widget, and soon all of Wall Street is buying stock in the company. Finally the Justice Department investigates the mysterious corporation, Henry is revealed as a Bostonian, and Henry loses and then wins Molly.

    9-16 men, 4-6 women; open stage with movable props. Royalty: $35-25.

LESSING, Gotthold Ephraim. Minna von Barnhelm (1765). Tr. by Bell, Bohn, 1900; BAT v. 10; HARC v. 26; MAU.

    Tellheim, a discharged army officer, who loses his fortune through a false charge of embezzlement, refuses to marry Minna because now he is poor and she is wealthy. He recovers his fortune, and to punish him a bit for his pride, she tells him that she now is penniless, and therefore she refuses to marry him. But she tells him the truth and they are married.

    5 acts; 7 men, 3 women; 2 interiors; costumes of the period.

_____. Nathan the Wise (1779). Tr. by Taylor, Lpz, 1868; Bohn Lib.; in his Dramatic Works, Lond., 1900; tr. by Maxwell,

Bloch, 1939.
The scene is laid in Jerusalem during the third Crusade.
Recha, the supposed daughter of Nathan, a Jew, is a baptized
Christian. She is saved from a burning building by a Knight Temp-
lar, and they fall in love. Because Nathan has concealed the facts
about Recha, he is brought before the Mohammedan Sultan Saladin.
The three faiths thus come into close contact as Recha pleads for
Nathan's life. This shames the Templar into a broader tolerance
and permits the joining of the lovers.
    2 acts (8 scenes); 7 men, 2 women; 3 interiors, 1 exterior;
costumes of the period.

LEVERTON, G. H. Rip Van Winkle. See entry under Irving,
    Washington.

LEVIN, Ira. No Time for Sergeants (1955). Adapted from Mac
    Hyman's novel. Dramatists Play Service.
    The story concerns a simple and lovable, innocent young lad
who enlists in the Air Force with all its pompous earnestness of
military discipline and bureaucracy. The youth, a husky and good-
natured hillbilly, wants to be in the infantry. His determined efforts create chaos among generals, as well as sergeants. One of
the comic highlights occurs when he goes on a flight in an airplane
manned by some weary, hungover flying officers who get lost and
unknowingly fly straight for an atomic explosion in Yucca Flats.
    34 men (some parts can be doubled), 3 women; unit set.
Royalty: $50-25.

LEVITT, Saul. The Andersonville Trial (1959). Dramatists Play
    Service.
    A courtroom drama about the trial of Henry Wirz, command-
er of the notorious Civil War prison at Andersonville. Wirz, a
Swiss immigrant doctor who had been wounded in battle, insists he
was just acting under orders but admits that a hundred Union soldiers died a day in his camp. The play raises the question of when
individual responsibility transcends the power of authority.
    28 men (doubling possible); 1 interior. Royalty: $50-25.

_____. The Trial of the Catonsville Nine. See entry under Ber-
    rigan, Daniel.

LEVY, Benn W. Clutterbuck (1946). Dramatists Play Service.
    On a tropical cruise two couples meet. The ladies, Deborah
Pomfret and Jane Pugh, are old friends but haven't met for five
years. The men meet for the first time: Arthur Pomfret, an aci-
dulous rubber planter, and Julian Pugh, a pompous novelist. A
third couple are also on board, Mr. & Mrs. Clutterbuck, with each
of whom the other four have had experiences before being married:
the ladies with Clutterbuck in Venice, the men with Melissa in London. The light feathery comedy depicts the mild ups and downs of
married life as the past comes back to their memories.
    3 acts; 4 men, 3 women; 1 interior (the deck), 1 exterior
(on shore). Royalty: $35-25.

_____. Mrs. Moonlight (1929). Samuel French.
        Mrs. Moonlight gets her magic wish never to grow older nor
less beautiful, so that at 28 she still looks 18. She runs away, to
return later unknown to her family as her own niece. She guides
their destinies, helps her daughter to avoid an unhappy marriage,
then disappears again, to return at 70. When her husband dies, she
follows him into the shadows.
        3 acts; 4 men, 4 women; 1 interior. Royalty: $50-25.

_____. The Rape of the Belt (1957). Adapted from the legend
     of Hercules. Samuel French.
        Heracles, for his ninth labor, must take away the jeweled
belt worn by Antiope, queen of the Amazons. He sets out with
Theseus, his companion, knowing how to fight any enemy in battle
but uncertain as to how to attack two charming women like Antiope
and Hippolyte, her sister. Two spectators from heaven, Zeus and
Hera, comment on the action as Heracles wins the belt as a man
from a woman, not as a soldier from an enemy, and Theseus takes
a willing Hippolyte back to Greece as a trophy of war.
        3 men, 7 women; 1 exterior. Royalty: $50-25.

_____. Springtime for Henry (1931). Samuel French.
        A blundering Englishman, Henry Dewlip, a wealthy bachelor
even after having many secretaries, leads a life of ease until he is
taken in hand by his apparently innocent, prim, young secretary,
Miss Smith, who tries to persuade him to forego all his pleasant
vices. He is quite disillusioned when he learns the story of her
life: she has been married, has a small son, and shot her husband.
He turns her over to his best friend Jelliwell, receiving in exchange
Mrs. Jelliwell.
        3 acts; 2 men, 2 women; 1 interior. Royalty: $50-25.

LEWIS, C. S. The Screwtape Letters. See James Forsyth's Dear
     Wormwood.

LINDSAY, Howard. Life With Father (1939). Dramatists Play Ser-
     vice.
        Father Clare may have been the head of the family, but Vin-
nie, his wife, knew how to get her way. Depicts many laughable incidents, as family, relatives, and friends help Vinnie to get father
properly baptized.
        8 men (some boys), 8 women; 1 interior. Royalty: $50-25.

_____. Life With Mother (1948). Dramatists Play Service.
        The Day family is older and Mother wishes to provide an en-
gagement ring for one of the boys. She never had one herself.
When she learns that Father had given one to Bessie Fuller, now
Mrs. Logan, who wouldn't give it back when the engagement was
broken, and who now comes to visit, she demands that Father get
it back. It takes some maneuvering but Bessie finally relents.
        3 acts; 8 men, 8 women; 2 interiors. Royalty: $50-25.

_____. She Loves Me (1933). Samuel French.

Curley Flagg, a Philadelphia night club dancer, is witness to a murder and flees with only a cloak over her dancing costume. She rides as far as her money will take her on the bus, which happens to be Princeton, N.J. She crawls in the dormitory window of Buzz Lawton and asks for help. He and 3 other seniors gallantly agree, give her pajamas, cut her hair, and introduce her as a younger brother. Because of these and further efforts to help her they are almost expelled.

18 men, 7 women; 5 interiors. Royalty: $25-20.

_____. State of the Union (1945). Dramatists Play Service.
Pulitzer Prize play 1946. A party leader gets Grant Matthews to consider running for the Presidency of the U.S. if his wife will agree. So he makes a cross-country trip to inspect his plants and make speeches en route. Some of his addresses are too radical for the politicians so that at the final meeting at his house he gives up the idea, and he and his wife are again agreed.

3 acts; 11 men, 6 women, extras; 4 interiors (can be reduced to 3). Royalty: $50-25.

_____, with Russel Crouse. Tall Story (1959). Adapted from Howard Nemerov's The Homecoming Game. Dramatists Play Service.
Small Custer College has suddenly gained national prominence because of its basketball team. Not only does the college now make the newspapers, but alumni contributions have tripled, buildings are going up all around, and academic standards have risen. The cause of it all is star center Ray Blent, a science major who has worked out a formula for perfect basket shooting. In fact Ray can do about everything except marry June Ryder, and he would do that if he could afford it. Before the big game with Ashmore College, Ray receives a phone call asking him to throw the game. He does not accept, but he receives $1,500 and a promise of $2,500 after his team is defeated. Ray solves his problem by deliberately flunking two exams and becoming ineligible to play. The real fun comes when professors, students, alumni, and administration become involved in the resulting furor.

21 men, 8 women, 1 boy; interiors. Royalty: $50-25.

_____, with Bertrand Robinson. Tommy (1927). Samuel French.
As a paragon of virtue Tommy becomes rather dull in the eyes of Marie, the girl he loves. His uncle detects the danger and persuades Tommy to fake bad behavior. He does this so successfully that Marie rushes to defend him and discovers she loves him.

3 acts; 5 men, 3 women; 1 interior. Royalty: $25-20.

_____, with Bertrand Robinson. Your Uncle Dudley (1929). Samuel French.
A civic-minded bachelor becomes the most popular person in town in this comedy, but his mother runs a close second. Uncle Dudley is the one who helps with time and money on all the community projects. And the town glorifies him as its leading citizen. Dudley's mother, an active 78-year-old, adds comedy with her attempts

to be a debutante.
4 men, 4 women; 1 interior. Royalty: $50-25.

LOGAN, Joshua. Mister Roberts. See entry under Heggen, Thomas.

_____. The Wisteria Trees (1950). Dramatists Play Service.
On a run-down plantation in Louisiana where the oak trees
have been killed by the wisteria vines, Lucy Andrée Ramsdall of the
dreamy, wasteful, ineffectual aristocrats is at last forced to realize
that her lovely old family estate must be sold. It is bought at auction by capable, farsighted Yancy Loper, who has risen from shop-
boy to business success. He offers to keep it in the family, but
she refuses. So the trees are being cut down to make way for truck
farms and strawberry beds.
3 acts; 8 men, 6 women; 1 interior. Royalty: $50-25.

LONG, Arthur Summer. Never Too Late (1957). Samuel French.
A married man in his fifties suddenly learns that he is to
become a father again. He is not exactly overjoyed, since his other
child, now 24, still lives at home with her husband, a man who
plays solitaire all the time. To make matters worse, the mother-to-
be asserts herself and demands a nursery, a new bathroom, and her
own checking account. A delightful farce.
6 men, 3 women; 1 interior. Royalty: $50-25.

LONG, J. L. The Darling of the Gods. See entry under Belasco,
David.

LONSDALE, Frederick. Aren't We All? (1923). Brentano, 1924;
French. 1925.
Margot returns from Egypt to surprise her husband Willie
kissing Kitty Lake. She is inclined to be astonished and to protest,
but her father-in-law confronts her with her affair with John Wil-
locks, the romantic element in her Egyptian trip, so she subsides.
A sympathetic presentation of the natural foibles of a very human
set of people.
3 acts; 8 men, 4 women; 2 interiors.

_____. The High Road (1927). Lond., Collins, 1927; French,
1928.
The serenity of the home of Lord Carlyle is quite upset at
his son John's engagement to an actress, Elsie Hilary. They ask
her down for a month. She turns the house upside down, getting
staid members to do frivolous things. She proves herself worthy,
but then refuses to marry John, Lord Tylesmore, being more in
love with his cousin, the Duke of Worrington. In the end she returns to the stage, her first love.
3 acts; 8 men, 4 women; 1 interior.

_____. The Last of Mrs. Cheyney (1925). Lond., Collins,
1926; French, 1929; abridged in Mantle 1925/26.
In order to secure luxury, Mrs. Cheyney joins an accomplice,
Charles, to rob Mrs. Ebley of her pearls, in a house where he is

acting as butler.   Lord Dilling, falling in love with her at the
house-party, traps her.   She rouses the house and tells the truth.
The other guests prove to be quite a disreputable set, rather worse
than she.   She bargains to reveal nothing about them for £10,000.
Upon receiving the check, she destroys it, rehabilitates herself, and
agrees to marry Lord Dilling.
     3 acts; 8 men, 4 women; 3 interiors, 1 exterior.

_____.   On Approval (1926).   Samuel French.
     Mrs. Wislack, thinking about a second romance, this time
with Richard Halton, proposes they try each other out for a month
at her house in Scotland without marital intimacies.   They are followed there by the impecunious Duke of Bristol who wishes to sell
his title to Helen Hayle, the daughter of a pickle millionaire.
Thrown daily into contact, life becomes increasingly unbearable.
Richard and Helen discover they love each other and sneak away,
leaving the irascible Duke and the catty Mrs. Wislake to hate each
other and discover how disagreeable they really are.
     3 acts; 2 men, 2 women; 2 interiors.   Royalty: $25-20.

_____.   Once Is Enough (1938).   French, 1938.
     Really in love with her husband, Nancy, Duchess of Hamp-
shire, is threatened with the loss of him when he thinks he is desperately in love with the wily Liz Pleydell.   Liz would like to be a
Duchess, but she and the Duke are no match for Nancy, and she
withdraws when she discovers that Nancy has no intention of divorc-
ing the Duke; so there is no elopement.
     3 acts; 9 men, 5 women; 1 interior.

_____.   Spring Cleaning (1923).   Lond., Gollancz, 1925; French
     carried.
     Richard is distressed because his beautiful wife Margaret in-
sists on running with a terrible set of social degenerates.   As
heroic treatment, he brings a painted lady off the streets to the
dinner.   When the guests resent the insult, he pretends great surprise that amateurs should feel so about a professional.   The shock
sends his wife into the arms of the man with whom she has been
flirting--but it wasn't marriage he had in mind.   Discovering her
philanderer's true character, Margaret is thankful to be taken back
by her husband.
     3 acts; 6 men, 5 women; 2 interiors.

LOOS, Anita.   Gentlemen Prefer Blondes (1926).   Dramatic Pub-
     lishing Company.
     Lorelei and her friend Dorothy are going to spend the sum-
mer in Europe with Lorelei's father.   He is unable to get away
from work, but they convince him to let them go alone.   Lorelei,
a blonde, begins posing as a woman of the world.   She plays the
role so well that she loses the affection of a young man she meets
and likes and has to use her brain to get him back.
     7 men, 10 women, extras; 2 interiors.   Royalty: $35.

_____.   Gigi (1951).   Adapted from the novel by Colette.

Samuel French.

Gigi, a young French girl, has been brought up by her mother, grandmother and aunt to be a stylish cocotte. The dissipated man they have picked out for her visits the home often, bringing candy and letting Gigi cheat him at cards. When Gigi turns sixteen she is expected to become the man's mistress, but she doesn't think she'd like such an arrangement. So, much to the consternation of the ladies, she maneuvers the roué into a proposition of marriage.

2 men, 5 women; 2 interiors. Royalty: $50-25.

_____. Happy Birthday (1946). Samuel French.

Addie Bemis is a rather shy little librarian in Newark. She follows Paul, a young bank clerk, into a cocktail bar, ostensibly to discuss her savings account. She experiments with "pink ladies" and a double Scotch; then quite fantastic things begin to happen. In the end she wins Paul away from a contriving hussy, and learns a lot about life and alcohol.

3 acts; 11 men, 10 women; 1 interior. Royalty: $50-25.

LUBAR, Bernard. The Ugly American (1961). Adapted from Eugene Burdick and William J. Lederer's novel. Dramatic Publishing Company.

The setting is the Southeastern Asian country of Sarkhan, a country in the middle of the cold war. The American Ambassador there stays busy entertaining Congressional V. I. P.'s and performing insignificant social duties. In the meantime, his interpreter deliberately misquotes him, and bags of American rice are relabeled as gifts from the Soviet Union. Homer Atkins is also on the staff. He not only speaks the language, but has friends among the Sarkhan leaders. Homer and his wife both work on projects designed to help the people of the country. The conflict is that the Ambassador wants Homer replaced.

8 men, 7 women; 2 simple sets. Royalty: $35.

LUCE, Clare Boothe. See entries under Boothe, Clare.

LUKE, Peter. Hadrian the Seventh (1968). Samuel French.

Based on the life and works of Frederick William Rolfe, the play depicts the failed life of Fr. Rolfe, who lives in a drab London flat and bemoans his expulsion from seminary many years before. In a kind of dream excursion, a delegation of contrite priests arrives, bestows Holy Orders on him, and the new priest accompanies his bishop to Rome to elect a new Pope. In desperation, the conclave elects this new, unattached priest (Fr. Rolfe), who chooses the name Hadrian VII. As Pope, Hadrian sells all the Vatican art treasures to feed the world's poor, smokes on the throne, and entertains old friends. Finally, he is killed by an Irish assassin. In the last scene we are back at Fr. Rolfe's drab London flat, where the only visitors are a delegation of bailiffs, who have come to take possession of Rolfe's property--including the manuscript of the book he is writing.

26 men, 2 women; drop and wing set, with wagons. Royalty: $50-35.

LYNDON, Barré. The Amazing Doctor Clitterhouse (1937). Ran-
    dom House, 1937; French, 1938; THH; FOUP.
    As part of his laboratory research work, Dr. Clitterhouse
takes up crime in order to study the reactions of criminals at the
moment of committing crime and how their nerves respond to their
misdeeds. He joins a gang and helps further their illegal doings in
a huge fur robbery during which a murder occurs. When he leaves
to write up his material, he is trailed by Benny Keller who tries
to blackmail him; but the Doctor outwits him, for he is first of all
a gentleman.
    3 acts; 10 men, 2 women; 3 interiors, 1 exterior. Royal-
    ty: $25-20.

_____. The Man in Half-Moon Street (1939). Lond., H. Hamil-
    ton, 1939; SIXL.
    A chemist, John Thackeray, by experimenting on himself,
has lengthened his life by the transfer of adrenal glands, so that,
though 90 years old, he appears to be 40. He needs another trans-
fusion, as the present glands are weakening; also he needs money.
So he arranges a transfer from Catty Sims and a bank robbery with
Mr. Budd. Both go wrong, so that he fades away at 90 as he is
arrested, and Mr. Budd is dissolved in a chemist's bath.
    3 acts; 13 men, 1 woman; 4 interiors, 1 exterior.

LYTTON, Edward Bulwer-Lytton. The Lady of Lyons (1838). Both
    Baker and French carried; STA; TAU.
    A snobbish provincial society girl, Pauline in Lyons, falls in
love with Claude Melnotte, of humble birth, but who has been set up
as a prince by some Parisians. She marries him despite her father's objections, who secures a separation, after which Melnotte
leaves. Pauline is about to marry a wealthy suitor when Claude returns from the wars, an officer and a rich man.
    5 acts; 10 men, 5 women, extras; 2 interiors, 3 exteriors;
    costumes of the period of the French Revolution.

_____. Money (1840). DeWitt, 1874; French carried; in BAT
    v. 16.
    Well-written, to show how money, or the lack of it, affects
people. Alfred Evelyn, as indigent secretary to Sir John Vesey, is
rejected as a suitor by Clara Douglas, because she can't face a life
of struggling poverty. After Alfred has been left the estate of a
rich uncle, he pretends to have lost it all in order to show up those
who toady to money.
    5 acts; 17 men, 3 women, extras; 5 interiors; costumes of
    the period.

_____. Richelieu; or The Conspiracy (1839). In his Complete
    Works, Little; in his Dramatic Works, Dutton; Baker carried in
    Wm. Warren edition; French & Dramatic Publishing Co. carried;
    in Brown, C. S., Later English Drama, Barnes, 1898; in Win-
    ter, Wm., ed., Plays of Edwin Booth, Penn, 1899, v. 3; DUR;
    MAT; MOSO.
    The astute Cardinal is plotted against and is in danger of

losing his position at the French court. But he outwits King Louis
XIII (and his henchman Baradis), regains the King's favor, and reunited his ward with the man of her choice.
>   5 acts; 16 men, 2 women, extras; 3 interiors, 1 exterior;
>   costumes of the period. (A shortened version in 4 acts as
>   used by Walter Hampden was pub. by Appleton, 1929.)

MACARTHUR, Charles. The Front Page. See entry under Hecht,
>   Ben.

McCARTHY, Justin H. If I Were King (1902). Russell, 1901;
>   Heinemann, 1921; French, 1922, abridged in Mantle & Sherwood,
>   1899-1901.

François Villon, poet, duellist, brawler, vagabond, and lover,
becomes marshall of France with kingly power on the appalling condition, stipulated by the spider-king, Louis XI, that he forfeit his
life at the end of the week. He wins the love of Katherine de Vau-
celles and leads the French troops to victory. They save his life
from the scaffold, and he and Katherine go into exile.
>   4 acts; 18 men, 9 women, extras; 1 interior, 2 exteriors;
>   costumes of the period.

McCLEERY, William. Good Morning, Miss Dove (1963). Adapted
>   from Frances G. Patton's novel. Samuel French.

Concerns a greatly beloved schoolteacher who suddenly faces
charges of undue severity with the son of the community's wealthiest
family. The elderly Miss Dove has become an institution in the town.
Former graduates constantly return to her for advice, and she never
fails them. Then, after recovering from an illness, Miss Dove is
unjustly accused of being unnecessarily harsh with a student, the son
of the richest parents in town. The ensuing School Board confrontation reveals not only Miss Dove's honesty and courage, but also that
she richly deserves the love and respect which the townspeople have
for her.
>   12 men, 10 women, extras; 6 insets. Royalty: $35-25.

_____. Parlor Story (1947). Samuel French.
Having quit the newspaper game to become Professor of
Journalism in the state university, Burnett now wishes to be made
president--a political appointment. To block this the Governor
brings state troopers and a press tycoon into the professor's parlor.
He is called upon to expel a student in love with his daughter for
writing an editorial in the college paper. Burnett becomes a strong
man, a fighting man, a champion of liberalism in politics. The
discussion brings in progressive ideas on academic freedom, freedom of the press, and political chicanery.
>   3 acts; 6 men, 4 women; 1 interior. Royalty: $35-25.

McCULLERS, Carson. The Ballad of the Sad Cafe. See entry un-
>   der Albee, Edward.

_____. The Member of the Wedding (1949). Dramatists Play
>   Service.

A sensitive character sketch of Frankie, a lonely, twelve-year-old girl in Georgia. Her mother is dead, her father busy, and the older children neglectful of her, she spends most of the time bored with the cook and her younger cousin. When her brother marries, Frankie sees a way out of her rut: she will accompany the couple on their honeymoon. She is heartbroken when this plan does not materialize. A few months later she is Frances, not Frankie, and she is very interested in a boy next door.
        6 men, 7 women; unit set. Royalty: $50-25.

_____. The Square Root of Wonderful (1957). Samuel French.
        A charming southern lady has been married twice to the same man--a tormented intellectual who has made her miserable. She is trying to break away finally so that she can marry a young architect who both understands her and loves her. But her former husband and his domineering mother block the way. The play deals with the resolution of her problem.
        2 men, 3 women, 1 boy; 1 interior. Royalty: $50-25.

MACDONALD, Betty. The Egg and I. See entry under Martens, Anne Coulter.

_____. Onions in the Stew. See entry under Dalzell, William.

McENROE, Robert E. The Silver Whistle (1948). Dramatists Play Service.
        A romantically-minded tramp finds the birth certificate of Oliver Erwenter, showing him to be 77. He decides to impersonate Erwenter and as such enters a home for the aged. To help along the happiness of the inmates he promotes a bazaar for the church next door. He is exposed by his tramp companion, Emmett, but the bazaar takes place, furbished with many items appropriated by the two tramps. He persuades the bishop and the victims that the bazaar is worthwhile; they even make presents of the things the men have stolen. The call of the road takes them away, but not before the romance is achieved between the Rev. Mr. Watson and the attractive Miss Tripp.
        3 acts; 10 men, 5 women; 1 interior. Royalty: $50-25.

McGREEVEY, John. A Man Called Peter (1955). Adapted from Catherine Marshall's novel. Dramatic Publishing Company.
        Peter Marshall is a minister to whom life is a service. He always overtaxes his strength in behalf of others, and he continually evades his wife's efforts to get him to slow down. He is often opposed by conservative members of the church, and he crusades against a distinguished senator who is determined to jail a boy Peter thinks has reformed. In spite of his wife's poor health, and his own, he takes on a new and important job that is too much for him.
        7 men, 8 women; 1 interior. Royalty: $35.

_____. The Robe (1952). Adapted from Lloyd C. Douglas' novel. Dramatic Publishing Company.
        Marcellus, a young Roman officer, is ordered to crucify a

Galilean. Though he believes the man is innocent, he does as he
is told and then wins the executed man's Robe by throwing dice.
His slave behaves strangely after touching the Robe, and when Mar-
cellus finally puts it on, he becomes desperately troubled, restless,
and obsessed with thoughts of the Galilean and the persecuted Christians. He fights off the urge to accept Him, until at last he accepts
death for himself and his young wife rather than renounce his new
faith.
    13 men, 9 women, extras; curtains or more elaborate sets.
Royalty: $25.

MACINNES, Helen. Home Is the Hunter (1964). Samuel French.
    This comic dramatization of Ulysses' homecoming includes a
highly original twist to Homer's epic. Ulysses' return, his defeat
of the pirate-suitors, and reunion with his wife Penelope are all
here. In addition to these expected events, we find Homer included
as a character, and one so exhausted that he sleeps through all the
important events. Thus Homer's version is quite glamorized.
    7 men, 4 women, extras; 2 interiors. Royalty: $35-25.

MACKAYE, Percy. The Canterbury Pilgrims (1903). Macmillan,
    1903; in his Plays, Macmillan, 1916.
    The many travelers are introduced; they talk and act in har-
mony with their characters as sketched by Chaucer, forming a brilliant spectacle. Depicts the rivalry between the shy gentle Prioress
and the Wife of Bath for the attentions of Chaucer. The Wife wins
by trickery, but King Richard rules she must marry the Miller.
    4 acts; 45 men, 7 women; 2 interiors, 2 exteriors (but may
be set simply); costumes of the period.

_____. Jeanne d'Arc (1906). Macmillan, 1906; in his Plays,
    Macmillan, 1916; French, 1916.
    The simple peasant girl, Jeanne, becomes a leader; she is
the symbol of the faith that could arm a people to a supreme effort.
Gives a fine representation of her character and career, her life
and martyrdom.
    5 acts; 40 men, 7 women, extras; 4 exteriors; costumes of
the period.

_____. Mater (1908). Macmillan, 1908; in his Plays, Macmil-
    lan, 1916.
    The interest centers around the Mother who dominates the
play, helping her son to win his election, and bringing her daughter's
love affair to a satisfactory conclusion. Mater has unconquerable
youth; her children are solemn with the grim responsibility of growing up.
    3 acts; 3 men, 2 women; 1 interior.

_____. The Scarecrow (1908, produced 1910). Macmillan,
    1908; in his Plays, Macmillan, 1916; DIC; MOSJ; MOSL; QUIK;
    QUIL; abridged in Pierce & Matthews, v. 1.
    In the days of New England witchcraft, Goody Bess, with the
help of Dickon (a Yankee Mephistopheles), makes a scarecrow which

comes to life but is animated only when puffing a pipe. She sends
it as Lord Ravensbane to court Justice Merton's niece, with some
success, until he sees himself in the Mirror of Truth as he really
is, with his heart a red beet.
    4 acts; 10 men, 6 women; 2 interiors; colonial costumes.

_____. A Thousand Years Ago (1913). Doubleday, 1914; French,
    1914.
    Strolling Italian players come to China. Their leader, Capo-
comico, rules for a day and finds her lover for the Princess; then
they wander. on again.
    4 acts; 9 men, 2 women, extras; 3 interiors, 1 exterior;
    Chinese and fantastic costumes.

MACKAYE, Steele. Hazel Kirke (1880). French, 1899; QUIL in
    revised form.
    Hazel is driven from her home by her stubborn father who
objects to her marriage to a young man whom she had rescued and
nursed. She elopes with him. He turns out to be an English nobleman in disguise. When the marriage is thought to be illegal, Hazel
returns to her home and attempts suicide in the mill-race. She is
rescued by her husband, who proves that the marriage was legal
after all.
    4 acts; 9 men, 5 women; 2 interiors, 1 exterior.

_____. Paul Kauver; or Anarchy (1887). MOSS-3.
    When accusations of noblemen were being sought, Paul Kauver,
President of the revolutionary section, gives a blank to Gouroc, who
fills in the name of the Duke de Beaumont, Diane's father. His plan
is to save the Duke and thus gain Diane. He gets Kauver to take
the Duke's place, but the priest helps Kauver to escape. They all
meet again in the Vendee where Gouroc's villainy is unmasked, especially with the help of Jean Litais, a peasant and former servant
of the Duke.
    5 acts; 15 men, 4 women, extras; 3 interiors; costumes of
    France, 1794.

MACLEISH, Archibald. J.B. (1958). Samuel French.
    The necessity and efficacy of man's reconciling himself to
the apparent injustices of God are compellingly presented in this
Pulitzer Prize winning verse drama. Using two circus peddlers who
pretend they are God and Satan as a backdrop, the story of J.B., a
wealthy, happy business man unfolds. One by one his blessings are
capriciously taken away. Even his beloved wife is reported dead.
In spite of these humbling tragedies J.B., like his Biblical counter-
part Job, refuses to curse God. Then J.B. is reunited with his
wife, and with an unswerving devotion to God they begin life again.
    12 men, 9 women; 1 interior. Royalty: $50-25.

_____. Scratch (1971). Suggested by Stephen Vincent Benet's
    "The Devil and Daniel Webster." Dramatic Publishing Com-
    pany.
    Daniel Webster has voted for the Fugitive Slave Act in order

to preserve the union. A desperate, debt-ridden farmer, Jabez
Stone, appeals to Webster to save him from a disastrous deal with
"Scratch" (the devil) in which he sold his soul for seven years of
prosperity. Daniel Webster fights for the imperfect Jabez in an old
barn at night before a jury of American traitors and murderers
summoned by Scratch from Hell.
    4 principal men, and 13 small parts; 1 interior, 2 exteriors.
Royalty: $50.

McLELLAN, C. M. S. Leah Kleschna (1904). Samuel French,
    1920; abridged in Mantle & Sherwood 1899-1909.
    Brought up by her father, a famous thief in Vienna, to help
him in his robberies, Leah is also to help do it in Paris. She is
discovered at the safe by Paul Sylvaine, an amateur criminologist.
He believes she can be redeemed and succeeds in having her leave
her father and the evil life.
    5 acts; 11 men, 6 women; 2 interiors, 1 exterior. Royal-
ty: $25.

McMAHON, Frank. Borstal Boy. See entry under Behan, Brend-
    han.

McMAHON, Luella and Christopher Sergel. State Fair (1953).
    Adapted from Phil Strong's novel. Dramatic Publishing Com-
    pany.
    Everyone in the Frake family is involved in the excitement of
the State Fair. Dad has entered his prize hog Blue Boy, and Mom
her pickles. But the real tension at the fair revolves around the
romances of the son and daughter.
    6 men, 5 women; 1 exterior. Royalty: $25.

McNALLY, Terrence. Bad Habits (1974). Dramatists Play Service.
    Two one-act plays requiring the same number of actors. The
first, "Ravenswood," is about an expensive sanitarium for the unhappily married, run by Dr. Pepper--confined to an electric wheelchair with a built-in martini holder. Dr. Pepper's technique in
handling unsatisfactory marriages is to permit each partner unabashed
indulgence in the traditional bad habits of smoking, drinking, and
sexual promiscuity. The second play, "Dunelawn," is about a different kind of sanitarium, this one run by a Dr. Toynbee. Dr.
Toynbee's technique is to put his patients in straitjackets and to
shoot them up with tranquilizers so that they cannot indulge themselves in their bad habits: alcohol, transvestism, and sadomaso-
chism.
    6 men, 2 women; 2 simple exteriors. Royalty: $50-35.

_____. "Dunelawn." See Bad Habits.

_____. "Ravenswood." See Bad Habits.

_____. Next. See Elaine May's Adaptation/Next.

_____. The Ritz (1975). Samuel French.

Proclo, who is fat, straight, square, and married to the
daughter of a Mafia boss, is on the run. The mob is trying to kill
him, and in desperation he hides out in a gay bathhouse called The
Ritz. Inside the Ritz it is bedlam. Proclo is pursued by homosexual "chubby chasers," an awful Puerto Rican version of Bette
Midler who thinks he is a Broadway producer (he thinks she's in
drag), a private detective, hired by his Mafia brother-in-law to
track him down (who thinks Proclo is his brother-in-law), and Proclo's own wife, who saves the zany day.
14 men, 3 women; composite interior and 2 drops. Royalty: $50-35.

_____. Where Has Tommy Flowers Gone? (1972). Dramatists
Play Service.
In a series of skits and incidents, the protagonist Tommy
Flowers is revealed to be a disillusioned rebel against society.
Along the way he acquires a destitute old actor, a sheep dog, and
a lovely girl music student--none of whom can compensate for Tom-
my's unsatisfactory home life. His bright red shopping bag accumu-
lates many things he has not paid for, but in the end its main use
is to carry the bomb that Tommy uses to blow himself up as his
final gesture of alienation.
Flexible cast with a minimum of 3 men, 3 women; unit set.
Royalty: $50-25.

MAETERLINCK, Maurice. The Blue Bird (1908). Tr. by Teixeira
de Mattos, Lond., Methuen, & Dodd, 1911.
Two peasant children Tyltyl and Mytyl, search everywhere
for the blue bird of happiness. Accompanied by their Cat and Dog,
Bread, Sugar, Milk, et al., they visit in vain the Land of Memory,
the Realm of Night, and even the Kingdom of the Future. Finally
it is found right at home in an act of unselfishness. No sooner is
it found than it flies away, and the search must begin again.
6 acts in 12 scenes; 9 men, 13 women, 2 or more children,
many extras; 1 interior, 9 exteriors; fanciful costumes.

_____. Monna Vanna (1902). Tr. by Coleman, Harper, 1903;
tr. by Porter, in Poet Lore, v. 15, 1904; tr. by Sutro, in his
Joyzelle & Monna Vanna, Dodd, 1907; MOSQ; abridged in Pierce
& Matthews, v. 2.
To save the starving city of Pisa in the 15th century, Monna
Vanna heroically persuades her husband, Guido Colonna, the commander of the Pisan forces, to let her meet the opposing general's
demand that she go to his tent for the night. Prinzivalle, the head
of the Florentine besieging army, who has adored her for years,
gallantly refuses her harm and escorts her back to Pisa. Her husband, madly jealous, refuses to believe that she has not been seduced, and by his lack of faith drives her into her lover's arms,
with whom she will escape.
3 acts; 7 men, 1 woman, many extras; 2 interiors; costumes
of the period.

_____. Pelléas and Mélisande (1892). Tr. by Porter & Clark,

in Poet Lore, v. 6, 1894; tr. by Hovey, in his Plays, ser. 2,
Stone, 1896; Dodd, 1911; also in DIC; DIK, v. 1; HAV; SMN;
TUCG; TUCM; WATI; WATL, v. 2; WATR; WHI; tr. by Alma-
Tadema, Lond., Scott, later Allen, 1895; tr. by Winslow,
Crowell, 1894 & 1908; abridged in Pierce & Matthews, v. 2.

Beautiful Mélisande is found in the forest by Golaud, who
takes her to his castle and marries her. Her sadness and charm
appeal to Golaud's younger brother Pelléas and they fall in love.
She loses her wedding ring in the pool, which makes Golaud suspicious. Later when he comes upon them as they are bidding each
other a last farewell, the jealous husband kills his brother. Mélisande dies in childbirth. Features the mystic and romantic in atmosphere and setting and the poetic in dialog.

5 acts in 19 scenes; 6 men, 2 women, extras; scenes laid
in castle, garden, & forest; costumes of an undated period.

MAIBAUM, Richard. Ransom. See entry under Hume, Cyril.

MANDELL, Loring. Advise and Consent (1961). Adapted from
Allen Drury's novel. Samuel French.

Deals with the pressures and intrigues of government decision
making at its highest levels. The President has nominated an old
friend and apparently capable man for Secretary of State. What was
expected to be little more than a routine confirmation suddenly develops into a political donnybrook when a witness appears who testifies that the nominee was once a Communist. Then the credibility
of the witness is attacked, but no one can be sure if he were lying
previously or not. The nomination is withdrawn when an unscrupulous Senator attempts to blackmail the investigation committee's
chairman into supporting the nomination, forcing the chairman to
commit suicide to save his family from scandal. As the play ends
the entire Senate resolves to restore dignity and honor to that body.

18 men, 4 women, 12 extras; cyclorama, wings, wagon in-
sets. Royalty: $50-25.

MANHOFF, Bill. The Owl and the Pussycat (1965). Samuel French.

A curious author with a pair of binoculars gets into trouble
when he spies a prostitute plying her trade in a distant apartment
window. After he complains to her landlord, the prostitute is
evicted, and the author finds he has more trouble than he can handle.
Having been dispossessed, the lady reasons the writer owes her a
place to stay. The resulting situation provides high comedy and
eventually romance. She is practically illiterate and begins to increase her vocabulary only to have trouble finding sentences in which
to use her increased word power. He finds himself becoming softer
and more understanding about human nature. Eventually they fall in
love, an impossible situation that can only be resolved one of two
ways: suicide or drastic change for both of them. After failing in
a bumbling attempt to end it all, he gets a job clerking in a book
store and she becomes a receptionist.

1 man, 1 woman; 1 interior. Royalty: $50-25.

MANN, R. J. Our Miss Brooks. See entry under Sergel, Christopher.

MANNERS, J. Hartley. Peg O' My Heart (1912). Samuel French.
      Peg O'Connell, a poor Irish girl in New York, becomes an
heiress through the death of an uncle. She goes to England to be
reared for her new role in the household of her aunt, who is exces-
sively aristocratic, conservative, and stern, even to her own son
and daughter. Peg feels like a duck out of water, but she wins her
way by her wit and goodness of heart. She saves her snobbish
cousin Ethel from scandal, and also wins the love of a promising
young Englishman, Sir Gerald.
      3 acts; 5 men, 4 women; 1 interior. Royalty: $25-20.

MANOUSSI, J. The Purple Mask. See entry under Armont, Paul.

MAPES, Victor. The Boomerang. See entry under Smith, Winchell.

MARASCO, Robert. Child's Play (1970). Samuel French.
      A thriller which takes place at a Catholic boys boarding
school, where the students are becoming surly, sinister, violent,
and unmanageable. The boys begin to beat up one another in a
savage manner and to torture members of the class. Someone sends
obscene photographs to the dying mother of the classics teacher, who
later jumps to his death. At the end of the play the boys surround
the teacher who has always thought of the school as his and who has
never been afraid of any "of his boys."
      6 men, 9 boys; composite interior, interior wagon. Royal-
ty: $50-35.

MARC, Michel. A Leghorn Hat. See entry under Labiche, Eugene
      H.

MARCH, William. The Bad Seed. See entry under Anderson, Max-
      well.

MARCUS, Frank. The Killing of Sister George (1965). Samuel
      French.
      Sister George is a character in a BBC soap opera, a nurse
who rides around on her cycle singing hymns, doing good deeds, and
making everyone happy. But the radio show is slipping in ratings,
partly because of rumors about Sister George's private life. BBC
decides to write her out of the series by having her be killed by a
truck. The woman who comes to break the news to Sister George
finds her smoking cigars, drinking gin, cursing, and living with a
female lover. The radio executive promptly steals the lover from
Sister George.
      4 women; 1 interior. Royalty: $50-25.

MARLOWE, Christopher. Dr. Faustus (1588). In his Best Plays,
      Mermaid ser., Scribner, 1903; in his Three Plays, Nelson's
      classics, 1940; Oxford, 1950; BAS; CLF v. 1; COF; COH; DUN;
      HARC v. 19; HOW; HUD; LIE; MIL; MOO; NEI; OLH; OLI v. 1;
      PAR; RUB; SCH; SCI; SCW; SML; SPE; STA; TREA-1.
      Selling his soul to the devil, Faust revels for 24 years in
luxury and splendor, but when the bond is due he regrets his for-

feited life. Shows the tragical futile progress of a man attempting
to appropriate all beauty, power, and knowledge, to end only in
damnation.
> 4 acts; 16 men, 2 women, 2 angels, 7 deadly sins, many
> extras; 4 interiors, 5 exteriors; costumes.

_____. Edward the Second (1592). In his Best Plays, Mermaid
ser., Scribner, 1903; in his Three Plays, Nelson's classics,
1940; ASH; BAS; BAT; CLS; HARC v. 19; MAT; NEI; OLH; OLI
v. 1; PAR; RUB; SCH; SCI; SPE; TAU.
Covers the years of Edward's reign, 1307-1327. Chronicles
his fatal infatuation for Gaveston as his favorite. Later, Mortimer,
acting as chief of the nobles with Isabella, deposed him and put him
to death.
> 5 acts; 26 men, 2 women, extras; 9 interiors, 8 exteriors;
> costumes of the period.

_____. Tamburlaine the Great (1587). In his Best Plays, Mer-
maid ser., Scribner, 1903; in his Three Plays, Nelson's classics, 1940; BAS; HOW; KRE; NEI; RYL; SCI; SCW; SPE.
Depicts the rise and fall of the Oriental conqueror--the ruthless advancement of a peasant lad to mighty power, conquering,
slaying, and overriding the ordinary moral code to fulfill his ambition.
> In 2 parts, 5 acts each. Part 1: 5 acts; 20 men, 4 women,
> extras; many scenes; costumes.

MARQUAND, John P. Point of No Return. See entry under Osborn,
Paul.

MARQUIS, Don. The Dark Hours (1924). Doubleday, 1924.
Presents events of the last hours of the life of Jesus, from
Thursday evening to Friday afternoon. Jesus does not appear in
person, but His voice from off-stage uses the words of the New Tes-
tament. First Caiaphas and Annas secure witnesses and get the
services of mentally confused Judas. Then comes the arrest in
Gethsemane, followed by the trial before the Sanhedrin and Peter's
denials. Then Jesus is tried before Pilate, after Herod has sent
Him back. Pilate orders the scourging and is not dissuaded by his
wife from ordering the crucifixion. Finally the scene at Golgotha
is presented.
> 5 scenes; 8 men, 2 women, extras, & a Voice from Beyond;
> 2 interiors, 2 exteriors; costumes of the period.

_____. The Old Soak (1922). Doubleday, 1922; French, 1926;
abridged in Mantle 1922/23.
A genial alcoholic, "with a feelin' for liquor," a domestic
derelict with a weakness but a good heart, quite redeems himself
when the crisis comes. His wife has put away some bonds, their
son steals them because of a chorus girl; the Old Soak then takes
the blame, but all is cleared up.
> 3 acts; 5 men, 4 women; 2 interiors.

MARSHALL, Catherine. A Man Called Peter. See entry under
   McGreevey, John.

MARTENS, Anne Coulter. The Egg and I (1958). Adapted from
   Betty MacDonald's novel. Dramatic Publishing Company.
   Don MacDonald, much to the consternation of his wife and
two teen-age daughters, buys a little chicken farm in the mountains.
The women in the family soon tire of 4:00 A. M. risings and of
working all day for hundreds of peeping chickens. The girls don't
have time to find boyfriends, and the family is plagued by unwel-
come visitors, like skunks and surly Indians. The final blows
come, however, when Don chooses to buy a new chicken brooder
house instead of the indoor plumbing which the farm house needs,
and when Joan entertains a boy under an umbrella in the leaky
house, and Anne's new boyfriend would rather talk egg production
than romance. Finally, after too much work and too many financial
difficulties, the female members of the family decide to leave. But
in the last scene they reconsider.
   9 men, 13 women; 1 set. Royalty: $35.

_____. Onions in the Stew. See entry under Dalzell, William.

MARTIN, Elliot. More Stately Mansions. See entry under O'Neill,
   Eugene.

MARTINEZ-SIERRA, Gregorio and Maria Martinez-Sierra. The
   Cradle Song (1911). Tr. by John Garrett Underhill, Dutton,
   1923; in Poet Lore, v. 28, 1917; French carries; CEW; HAV;
   abridged in Mantle 1926/27.
   Teresa was left as a foundling at a convent of Dominican
nuns where she was reared by the gardener's wife, the nuns lavish-
ing on her all their tenderness. When 18, she falls in love with
Antonio and leaves to marry him mid fond farewells. A sensitive,
devoutly pious play, told with Spanish grace and tender touch.
   2 acts; 4 men, 10 women, extras; 2 interiors; nun's costumes. Royalty: $50-25.

_____. The Kingdom of God (1916). Tr. by Granville-Barker in
   his Plays, v. 2, Dutton, 1923; carried by French; abridged in
   Mantle 1928/29.
   Sister Gracia appears first as a young girl of 19 just taking
her vows and serving in an asylum for poor old men. Next she is
serving at 29 in a maternity house where she represses her very
human love for a young doctor. In the 3d act she is an elderly
woman of 70 serving in an orphanage where she stops a revolt, commanding by her wisdom unruly and half-starved orphans whom she
tells to work and pray for the Kingdom of God.
   3 acts; 14 men, 17 women, extras; 2 interiors, 1 exterior;
   nun's costumes.

_____. Madame Pepita (1912). Tr. by Underhill & May Broun
   in his Cradle Song & other plays, Dutton, 1923 & 1929.
   Depicts events in the life of Pepita, who was a dressmaker

and had been brought up in the house of Don Luis Condé; she had married a Russian nobleman in Paris who deserted her, but by whom she had a daughter, Catalina, who is now 16 years old. Don Guillermo, a roomer above, looks on Catalina as a daughter and instructs her; he also persuades Pepita to marry him. Fortunately she inherits some wealth from the Russian husband, so Catalina can go to Rome with Alberto, a rising young artist who has won a prize. Pepita and her husband remain to comfort each other.
    3 acts; 5 men, 6 women; 1 interior, 1 exterior.

_____. The Romantic Young Lady (1918). Tr. by Granville-Barker in Kingdom of God & other plays, Dutton, 1922; also in his Plays, v. 2, Dutton, 1923; French carried.
    A romantic girl, who regrets that she can't have adventures like a man, becomes interested in a strange young man whose hat blows into her room during a storm. Seeking his hat, he writes a letter of recommendation to be presented the next day. She applies for the job at the office of a famous popular novelist who turns out to be the young man. She is a bit disappointed, but his romantic self, like his novels, proves irresistible.
    3 acts; 5 men, 6 women; 2 interiors.

_____. The Two Shepherds (1913). Tr. by Granville-Barker in his Kingdom of God & Other plays, Dutton, 1922; also in his Plays, v. 2, Dutton, 1923; LEV.
    In a small Spanish village two men are forced to give up their posts: a priest, Don Antonio, for having too much faith, and Don Francisco, a doctor, for having too little. They cannot pass the necessary examinations in theology and science, chiefly because of age, but they are true shepherds who understand human nature and can give proper guidance to the souls and bodies of the country people of their rural area.
    2 acts; 10 men, 9 women, extras; 1 exterior (a garden).

MARX, Arthur. The Impossible Years. See entry under Fisher, Bob.

MASEFIELD, John. The Tragedy of Nan (1908). Lond., Richards, 1909; Kennerley, 1909; in his Poems & Plays, Macmillan, 1918; separately, Macmillan, 1921; in his Prose Plays, Macmillan, 1925.
    In the house of her uncle, Nan an orphan is a drudge; she is outcast because her father was hanged. Her lover deserts her. Tormented on every hand, she is driven to kill her jilting lover and to drown herself in the rising tide. Grimly but beautifully presents a vision of the heart of life.
    3 acts; 8 men, 5 women; 1 interior; costumes of 1810 in England.

_____. The Trial of Jesus (1925). Macmillan, 1925.
    Follows through the trial before Annas and Caiaphas who convicts Him of blasphemy. Introduces Peter's denial and Judas' return of the money. Then depicts the trial before Pilate, who would

only scourge Him, but on further accusation by Annas, sentences
Him to be crucified.   That evening the cynical Herod visits Pilate
and his wife, Procula.   Longinus the centurion testifies to his belief that "that was the Son of God, if one may say that. "
        Prolog & 3 acts; 18 men, 6 women, extras as a Chorus;
        1 curtain set: 2 levels, with a balcony; costumes of the
        period.

MASSEY, Edward.   Plots and Playwrights (1917).   Little, 1917;
        French, 1929; BAK.
        A satire on pot-boiling writers.   A playwright must com-
plete a play in a month but says he has no material.   A short-
story writer says there is material right in their boarding house
and proves it by writing three episodes from the lives of the tenants.
        Prolog & 2 acts; 10 men, 6 women; 2 interiors, 1 exterior.

MASSINGER, Philip.   A New Way to Pay Old Debts (1633).   In
        Mermaid ser. , Scribner; BAS; BAT v. 13; in BRI v. 1; HARC
        v. 47; HOW; INCH; v. 6; KRE; MAT; NEI; OLH; OLI v. 2;
        OXB v. 1; PAR; RUB; SCH; SCI; SMO; SPE; WHE.
        The avaricious usurer, Sir Giles Overreach, takes over all
the property of his nephew Frank Wellborn and, in order to get
more money, plans to marry his daughter Margaret to Lord Lovell.
Lady Allworth, a wealthy widow, has a stepson Tom, who is in love
with Margaret.   Aided by Lord Lovell, she deceives Sir Giles into
thinking Frank will marry her and Lord Lovell will marry Margaret.
Thus Frank gets his money from his uncle and can pay his debts,
Tom marries Margaret, and Lord Lovell marries Lady Allworth.
The greedy Sir Giles has overreached himself and becomes insane
at the deceit.
        5 acts; 12 men, 5 women, extras; 3 interiors, 3 exteriors;
        costumes of the period.

MASTERS, Edgar Lee.   Spoon River Anthology.   See entry under
        Aidman, Charles.

MAUGHAM, W. Somerset.   The Breadwinner (1930).   Doubleday,
        1931; in his Plays, Heinemann, 1932, v. 4; in his Six Comedies,
        Doubleday, 1937 & Star books, 1939; CHA; CHAR.
        Bored by his fatuous wife Margery and two unbearably bright
children, Judy and Pat (aged 18), Charles Battle decides to quit
working and let them fend for themselves with the £15,000 he will
leave them.   He no longer will be the breadwinner for the family,
thus shaking off domestic chains and meaningless drudgery.   A satire
on the annoying self-assurance of modern youth.
        3 acts; 4 men, 4 women; 1 interior.

_____.   The Circle (1921).   Heinemann, & Doran, 1921; Baker
        carried; in his Plays, Heinemann, 1932, v. 4; in his Six Com-
        edies, Doubleday, 1937, & Star books, 1939; CEU; COT; DIG;
        DUR; MAP; MCD; MOSH; MYD; TRE-3; TREA-3; TUCD; TUCM;
        WATF, v. 2; WATI; WATO; abridged in Mantle 1921/22.
        Cleverly insists that the young never profit by the experience

of the old. Thirty years ago Lady Kitty had run away from her
rather stuffy husband; she now returns and finds her son's wife about
to do the same thing. Example, warning, advice, even permission
fail to stop the romantic Elizabeth.
   3 acts; 4 men, 3 women; 1 interior.

_____. The Constant Wife (1926). Samuel French.
   Constance knows her husband is having an affair with her best
friend. She takes a partnership in Barbara's shop and earns enough
to pay back her board and lodging; then she plans to go off for six
weeks with Bernard; after which she will return to home and husband.
She claims, if her husband is not faithful to her and if she supports
herself, she is entitled to lead her own life in her own way. The
play is a protest against a double standard of morality in marriage:
what is sauce for the gander should be sauce for the goose.
   3 acts; 4 men, 5 women; 1 interior. Royalty: $50-25.

_____. Jane. See entry under Behrman, S. N.

_____. Lady Frederick (1907). Heinemann, 1912; in his Plays,
   Heinemann, 1931, v. 1.
   Young Charles Mereston is devoted to Lady Frederick, a
widow of uncertain years, so his mother calls in her brother Paradine to aid her in curing her son's infatuation. They reveal to him
Lady Frederick's shady past, but this only drives Charles to declare
his love. When however Lady Frederick reveals her real age to
Charles, he is sufficiently shocked. She now also refuses the hand
of Captain Montgomerie, who has helped her when in financial
straits, but does accept her former suitor Paradine.
   3 acts; 8 men, 5 women; 2 interiors.

_____. Our Betters (1917). Heinemann, 1923; in his Plays,
   Heinemann, 1932, v. 3; in his Six Comedies, Doubleday, 1937,
& Star books, 1939; DID; MOSO; SMO; WHI.
   An American girl marries a titled Englishman and becomes
Lady Grayson; then she tries to get her sister Elizabeth an English
husband. But the scandalous lives of her sister's set are too much
for her, so Elizabeth goes back to New York to marry Fleming
Harvey. The play is a cynical exposé of American title hunters in
London.
   3 acts; 7 men, 4 women; 2 interiors.

_____. Rain. See entry under Colton, John R.

_____. Smith (1909). Heinemann, 1913; Dramatic Pub. Co.,
   1913; in his Plays, Heinemann, 1931, v. 2.
   Tom Freeman returns from his Rhodesia farm to visit his
sister Rose in London and if possible to find a wife. A former
flame, Emily, gets him to propose again but balks at the prospect
in South Africa. All of his sister's friends are the idle rich of
London high society; he finds them objectionable, but he finds the
house-maid Smith the kind he wants for a wife.
   4 acts; 4 men, 4 women; 2 interiors (can be played in 1).

MAURETTE, Marcelle. Anastasia. See entry under Bolton, Guy.

MAY, Elaine, with Terrence McNally. Adaptation/Next (1969).
    Dramatists Play Service.
        A long running off-Broadway show made up of two one-acts:
May's "Adaptation" and McNally's "Next." In the first play life is
a television game show, and a Narrator and his two assistants play
all the other roles except that of Phil Benson, the contestant. Benson plays the game fully, searching futilely for the square on the
gameboard labeled The Security Square. What he doesn't know, the
Narrator tells us before the contestant is brought out, is that "he,
himself, may label any space on the Board the Security Square and
declare himself the winner any time it occurs to him to do so."
Of course it never does. McNally's "Next" deals with a reluctant
draftee reporting for his physical. (He is Marion Cheever, a fat,
late 40's, twice divorced, assistant manager of a Fine Arts Theater
who knows there's been some mistake.) The person in charge is a
hefty WAC named Sergeant Thech who finally rejects Marion, as
everyone else in his life has, and causes him to freak out.
        "Adaptation": 3 men, 1 woman; open stage, with lectern.
Royalty: $25. "Next": 1 man, 1 woman; simplified in-
terior. Royalty: $25.

MAYER, Edwin J. The Firebrand (1924). Samuel French.
        The eager, glamorous, impetuous youth, Cellini, is contin-
ually in hot water, from killing men to courting women. He con-
tracts to secure Angela from her mother, only to lose her to the
Duke when his eyes light upon her, while Cellini is being pursued
by the Duchess.
        3 acts; 8 men, 4 women, extras; 1 interior, 1 exterior;
costumes of the period. Royalty: $25-20.

MEDCRAFT, Russell G. and Norma Mitchell. Cradle Snatchers
    (1925). Samuel French.
        Three wives grow tired of sitting at home while their husbands
are enjoying themselves elsewhere, perhaps with flappers, so they
hire college boys to make love to them. The husbands return from
their "duck-shooting" to find a hilarious party with the hired cake-
eaters. A compromise may be expected by which the husbands will
be only too glad to act as escorts and attentive admirers.
        3 acts; 8 men, 7 women; 2 interiors. Royalty: $25-20.

MEDOFF, Mark. The Wager (1975). Dramatists Play Service.
        In this peculiar comedy a bright graduate student, Leeds, re-
luctantly bets his roommate, super-jock Ward, that he can't seduce a
faculty wife in the next 48 hours. Ward accomplishes it with Honor
Stevens and has 47 left to spare. Her husband Ron hangs around
the graduate students' apartment and whines, once coming back with
a machine gun to kill somebody, but he can't pull the trigger. (He
later decides to shoot up his car, but the gun doesn't work so he
washes the car.) Through all of this it is Leeds who is pulling
everyone's strings out of his fear of feeling anything for anybody.
At the end of the play Honor Stevens and Leeds are alone, and it is

certain that she will seduce him. But first they make a wager.
3 men, 1 woman; 1 interior. Royalty: $50-35.

_____. When You Comin' Back, Red Ryder? (1974). Dramatists
    Play Service.
    Stephen (Red) Ryder is about to turn over his night attendant
duties at the 24-hour diner in a small southwestern town to the day-
time attendant, Angel. Her friend Lyle, who runs the motel/filling
station across the road, comes in for breakfast, followed by two
couples. One pair is bound for New Orleans; the other is driving
a carload of marijuana to California. The male with the dope begins to taunt and bully all of the other diner occupants, tearing away
at them verbally and exposing their innermost secrets and fears.
    5 men, 3 women; 1 interior. Royalty: $50-35.

MELVILLE, Herman. See Orson Welles's Moby Dick--Rehearsed.

MICHAELS, Sidney. Dylan (1964). Based on the memoirs of Caitlin
    Thomas and John M. Brinnin. Samuel French.
    The life of one of the great twentieth century poets is depicted
in this biographical drama. Feelings for the Irish poet, Dylan Thomas, were as diverse and extreme as his life. The play begins as
he says goodbye to his wife before leaving on a poetry reading tour
of the United States and follows him through colleges, lecture halls,
bars and bedrooms, and finally to the hold of the ship that carried
his body back home to Ireland. He died at the age of thirty-nine,
but in his life he had exemplified the lines of his most famous poem,
"Do not go gentle into that good night. "
    15 men, 13 women; various sets. Royalty: $50-25.

MIDDLETON, George. Adam and Eva. See entry under Bolton, Guy.

MILES, William A. 1984. See entry under Owens, Robert.

MILLAY, Edna St. Vincent. The King's Henchman (1927). Harper,
    1927; Baker carried; TUCD.
    King Eadgar of 10th-century England sends his foster brother
AEthelwold to woo AElfrida for him. She finds him asleep in the
forest of Devon; they fall in love and marry. He sends back word
that she is unworthy of the King's love. When the King comes,
AEthelwold asks her to dress as a hag, but she appears in beautiful
garments. Because of her self-love and his mistake AEthelwold
kills himself; the King denounces her as indeed unworthy.
    3 acts; 13 men, 8 women, extras; 2 interiors, 1 exterior;
costumes of the period.

MILLER, Arthur. After the Fall (1964). Dramatists Play Service.
    At the beginning of the play Quentin seats himself at the edge
of the stage and starts to talk to the audience as one would to a
friend. Behind him the key figures in his life move in and out of
narrative, revealing and illuminating Quentin's past. Some of the
characters and incidents suggest Mr. Miller's personal past--es-
pecially Maggie, the sexy, popular entertainer who destroys herself

(Marilyn Monroe) and the preoccupation with naming names of Communists (Miller's troubles with Senator Joseph McCarthy). A brilliant play.

12 men, 11 women, several non-speaking roles; unit set.
Royalty: $50-25.

_____ . All My Sons (1947). Dramatists Play Service.

Exposes war-time cheaters. Joe, the father, wants his son Chris in the business with him, but Chris won't go in because he knows that cracked cylinders had been sent out of his father's factory and installed in a military aircraft. The other son, Larry, was killed by a dropping plane, in a suicidal gesture prompted by his awareness of his father's corruption. Joe even framed his partner to serve the sentence for the defective parts. Chris refuses to believe that Joe had the family's interest at heart and convinces his father that a man is responsible to the world, too, that all men are his sons. Rather than go to prison, Joe shoots himself.

6 men, 4 women; 1 exterior. Royalty: $35-25.

_____ . The Creation of the World and Other Business (1972,
1973). Dramatists Play Service.

Deals with the struggle between God and Lucifer, with Adam, Eve, Cain, and Abel as their pawns. The three acts of the play cover the creation of Eve (from Adam's observation that everything seems to come in pairs) and the eating of the forbidden fruit and the subsequent expulsion from Paradise to the murder of Abel by Cain. Each act poses a question on the human dilemma: 1) Since God made everything and God is good--why did He make Lucifer? 2) Is there something in the way we are born which makes us want the world to be good? 3) When every man wants justice, why does he go on creating injustice?

8 men, 1 woman; unit set. Royalty: $50-35.

_____ . The Crucible (1953). Dramatists Play Service.

Though the scene is Salem, Massachusetts in 1692 (the year of the famous witch trials) there are a number of parallels with America of the 1950's and the McCarthy "witch hunts." The play deals with lies and how they cause mass hysteria in the community. To keep from being punished severely, Abigail and her friends make up a story of witchcraft. They even name individuals who are in communion with the devil. One of those named is Elizabeth Proctor, wife of John Proctor whom Abigail loves. When John persuades his serving girl, Mary Warren, to admit the fraud in the charges, the rest of the girls pretend to faint and become stricken with Mary's evil spirit. She soon changes her story and accuses John of witchcraft. Both of the Proctors, and other townspeople, are imprisoned. John is offered his life for a confession of witchcraft, but he finally refuses and goes to his death.

10 men, 10 women; unit set. Royalty: $50-25.

_____ . Death of a Salesman (1949). Dramatists Play Service.

Pulitzer prize play 1948/49. After 40 years as a travelling salesman, Willy Loman finds the hollowness of just good-fellowship

as a means of selling. He is told he must work on a commission
basis instead of a salary. He comes to realize he has become a
failure as a salesman, and also an ineffectual father to his two sons
who have developed as good fellows but without good purpose. Willy
recalls some of his past experiences and successes which show how
he deceived himself with little lies which have led to gradual disintegration. He represents Everyman in a tragedy of mediocrity as he
comes to the end of his rope.
        8 men, 5 women; combination interior-exterior set. Royalty:
$50-25.

_____. An Enemy of the People. See entry under Ibsen, Henrik.

_____. Incident at Vichy (1964). Dramatists Play Service.
        Eight men have been picked up by the Nazis and are waiting
in the detention room of a Vichy police station. The time is 1942.
The men hope that their identification papers are merely to be
checked, but we discover that all of them are real or suspected
Jews. They will all be examined to see if they have been circum-
cized; those who have been will be shipped in freight cars to Polish
death camps. Of special interest to the playwright are three characters: a German guard who hates his present job and ironically is
himself circumcised; a former French officer who wants to escape
and aid in the underground movement; and an Austrian nobleman who
hates the Nazis only because they are crude, vulgar, and tasteless.
Finally the nobleman, who would undoubtedly have been released,
sacrifices his life so that the French Jewish officer can escape.
        21 men; 1 interior. Royalty: $50-25.

_____. The Price (1968). Dramatists Play Service.
        Two brothers meet after a 16-year estrangement to dispose
of their deceased father's belongings. One brother is a policeman,
who sacrificed his education and dreams of becoming a scientist to
care for his invalid father. The other is an eminent surgeon, who
walked out on the family to concentrate on his medical education.
The background is filled in with a conversation between the policeman and his wife. The philosophy is articulated by a Jewish dealer
of furniture who will not immediately set a price for the father's
possessions. The conflict and drama are provided by the meeting of
the sons after a long and bitter separation.
        3 men, 1 woman; 1 interior. Royalty: $50.

_____. A View from the Bridge (1955). Dramatists Play Ser-
vice.
        This long one-act play is told by a wise and sympathetic
neighborhood lawyer in the Italian section of Brooklyn. The story
concerns Eddie Carbone, a longshoreman, who helps two of his
wife's relatives enter the country illegally from Sicily. Eddie makes
room for Marco and Rodolopho in his home. He changes his attitude
about the men when Rodolopho (whom Eddie believes is homosexual)
falls in love with Catherine, Eddie's niece. Though Eddie believes
he thinks of Catherine as a daughter, it is obvious that his affection
is more physical. To prevent the two young people from marrying,

Eddie informs the Immigration Authorities, and the two are arrested.
When they are released on bail, Marco kills Eddie.
> 12 men, 3 women; 1 interior. Royalty: $50-25.

MILLER, J. P. Days of Wine and Roses (1973). Dramatists Play
> Service.
> This story was first a television play and then a major motion
picture. It deals with Joe Clay, an up-and-coming Madison Avenue
type who has a drinking problem. So does the woman he marries,
but both pretend that drinking is merely something they choose to do.
The failure to recognize alcoholism leads the couple right down the
drain: their marriage breaks up, Joe's career is in shambles,
friends and family find them hopelessly lost, and their child is victimized by the effects of booze.
> 10-15 men, 5-10 women, 1 girl; unit set. Royalty: $50-25.

MILLER, Jason. That Championship Season (1971). Dramatists
> Play Service.
> Five men meet for their annual reunion. Four of the men
were members of a hot-shot basketball team which won the state
high school championship twenty years ago. The other man is their
coach, now retired. The reunion is light-hearted at first, but the
desperation which characterizes everybody's present life begins to
emerge. The former players are now inept mayors, high school
principals, "successful" businessmen, despairing alcoholics; each
suffers from moral bankruptcy. At the end they are brought together again by feelings of self-preservation by the unconscious
cynicism and bigotry of their coach.
> 5 men; 1 interior. Royalty: $50-35.

MILLER, Jonathan. Beyond the Fringe. See entry under Bennett,
> Alan.

MILN, Louise J. The Purple Mask. See entry under Armont,
> Paul.

MILNE, A. A. Belinda (1918). Samuel French.
> A supposed widow, presenting her daughter as her niece,
keeps two suitors dangling; one a long-haired poet, the other a
prosaic gentleman. After 19 years the husband returns, unrecognized without his beard, and she falls in love again, just because
he is an attractive man and she a charming woman.
> 3 acts; 3 men, 3 women; 1 interior, 1 exterior (may be
> played with 1 exterior throughout). Royalty: $25-20.

_____. The Dover Road (1921). Samuel French.
> As a delightful bit of polite farce it depicts the amiable if
eccentric Mr. Latimer detaining by gentle force eloping couples who
are taking the Dover road to France. A double pair are thus
brought to see each other under the strain of a fresh cold at the
breakfast table, and are given a chance to change their minds.
> 3 acts; 6 men, 4 women; 1 interior. Royalty: $50-25.

_____. The Ivory Door (1927). Samuel French.
        On the point of marrying lovely Princess Lilia, King Pervale decides to walk through the ivory door, in spite of the tradition that no one who has walked through it has ever returned. He does so, but on his return no one knows him except the Princess, who also walks through it. Since no one recognizes either, another King is chosen, while the real King and his Princess have discovered truth and happiness.
        Prolog & 3 acts; 11 men, 4 women; 1 interior, 1 exterior; fantastic costumes. Royalty: $50-25.

_____. Michael and Mary (1929). Lond., Chatto, 1930; French, 1932; abridged in Mantle 1929/30.
        Though knowing that despondent Mary has been deserted by her husband, Michael marries her, despite no divorce. This adds spice and even danger to their venture. Fourteen happy years later, the first husband appears and proceeds to blackmail them, but in a scuffle he drops dead of heart failure. They fabricate an explanation which satisfies the police, though there is still a possibility of danger and adventure.
        3 acts; 10 men, 6 women; 3 interiors.

_____. Mr. Pim Passes By (1919). Samuel French.
        Mr. Pim, an absent-minded old gentleman, nearly wrecks the happiness of a charming couple on whom he chances to call by announcing that the lady's former husband, thought dead, is alive. All is due to Mr. Pim's trouble with names, and he remembers the right name in time to avoid disaster.
        3 men, 4 women; 1 interior. Royalty: $50-25.

_____. The Perfect Alibi (1928). Samuel French.
        Two of his guests murder Judge Arthur Ludgrove (in full view of the audience) and plant evidence of suicide. His niece, Susan, a young sleuth-hound, becomes suspicious and brings about the apprehension of the two; they were vindictive because the Judge had sentenced them years before as diamond thieves in South Africa.
        7 men, 3 women; 1 interior. Royalty: $50-25.

_____. The Red House Mystery. See entry under Sergel, Ruth.

_____. The Romantic Age (1920). Samuel French.
        Romantic Melisande, meeting a medieval knight in the woods, thinks he is her knight coming to rescue her; but he is only a stockbroker en route to a fancy-dress ball. She dreams of her knight, to meet him again the next morning. He comes for her that afternoon and she is quite disillusioned; she suffers agonies, but he succeeds in reconciling her. Romance can exist even on the Exchange.
        5 men, 4 women; 1 interior, 1 exterior. Royalty: $50-25.

_____. The Truth about Blayds (1921). Samuel French.
        The famous poet Blayds, who has dominated literature and his household, confesses on his death-bed that his whole career has

been a lie--that he appropriated the poems of another and had published them as his own.   What shall the family do about it?   Isobel
won't touch the royalty money and insists that the truth be told.
The rest do not agree.   Why does it seem best to keep silent?
They do, but Marian's husband may mention the scandal in his
memoirs.
     4 men, 4 women; 1 interior.   Royalty: $25.

MILTON, John.   Comus, a Masque (1634).   In editions of his Works
    or Poems; HARC; OLI v. 2; PAR; adapted by Lucy Chater, pub.
    by Baker.
     Comus, as the son of Bacchus and Circe, tempts travelers
to drink a magic liquor which would change their faces into those of
wild beasts.   A lady is left in the woods by her two brothers who
go to find a cooling fruit for her.   She falls into the hands of Comus,
and just as the god is offering her his magic potion, the brothers
come to her rescue.
     3 scenes; 6 men, 3 women, extras; 1 interior, 2 exteriors
(can be produced with 1 exterior); fanciful costumes.

MITCHELL, Adrian.   Marat/Sade.   See entry under Weiss, Peter.

MITCHELL, Langdon.   The New York Idea (1906).   Baker, 1908;
    MOSS-3; QUIL; WATC-1; HAL; abridged in Pierce & Matthews,
    v. 1.
     An incisive satire on social conditions caused by easy di-
vorce.   The Englishman, Sir Wilfred, is much confused by meeting
so many divorcees, but he catches Vida Phillimore on the rebound.
Cynthia balks at Philip and takes up again with her first husband,
who reports that the divorce was invalid anyway.
     4 acts; 9 men, 6 women; 3 interiors.

MITCHELL, Loften.   A Land Beyond the River (1964).   Pioneer
    Drama Service.
     The stories behind the integration headlines are humorously
and strikingly portrayed in this play about one of the first of the
desegregation cases.   According to Brooks Atkinson of the New York
Times, it is "... not a propaganda play.   Mr. Mitchell has concen-
trated on the character of the people, ... people who can laugh when
life gets ludicrous."
     2 male whites, 9 male Negroes (2 boys); 5 Negro women;
1 multiple set.   Royalty: $25.

MITCHELL, Norma.   Cradle Snatchers.   See entry under Medcraft,
    Russell G.

MOELLER, Philip.   Madame Sand (1917).   Knopf, 1917; HAL; TUCD.
     Vitalizes the many friends of George Sand, even her husband
Baron Dudevant.   She is the central figure in each act, first with
Alfred de Musset, then with Pietro Pagello, and finally with Frédé-
ric Chopin.   Pictures her as a writer who turns out just so many
pages a day, as she records clever ideas and scenes for future
use.

3 acts; 8 men, 7 women, extras; 3 interiors; costumes of
the period.

_____. Molière (1919).   Knopf, 1919.
        Gives a charming picture of the great French playwright in
the last year of his life, as he continues to act and also to write
(his last play: The Imaginary Invalid).   Shows his break with Louis
XIV and Mme. de Montespan.   In the final death scene, his wife
Armande returns in time, but the king is too late.
        3 acts; 13 men, 7 women, extras; 2 interiors; costumes of
1673.

_____. Sophie (1919).   Knopf, 1919.
        Presents an evening in the life of the capricious tempera-
mental opera singer Sophie Arnauld in the Paris of Louis XV.   She
secures from Gluck the role of Iphigenia in Aulis, rids herself of
the aged Austrian Ambassador in order that her lover Dorval may
come at midnight, and avoids arrest by sponsoring the marriage of
Vivienne, the daughter of the Chief of Police.
        3 acts; 9 men, 5 women, extras; 1 interior; costumes of the
period.

MOLIÈRE.   Le Bourgeois Gentilhomme (1670).   In all complete
    editions of his translated works (for list see note under his
    Tartuffe); Van Laun translates title as The Citizen Who Apes
    the Nobleman; Page as The Tradesman Turned Gentleman;
    Baker & Miller as The Citizen Turned Gentleman; also in
    CLF-2; tr. by Margaret Baker as The Merchant Gentleman,
    French, 1915; tr. and adapted by Fernand as The Would-be
    Gentleman, in 3 acts (4 men, 4 women, extras), Lond., Secker,
    & Dramatic Pub. Co., 1926.
        A retired middle-class shop-keeper who has made a fortune,
M. Jourdain, resolves to be a gentleman and cut a figure in Society.
He studies dancing, fencing, music, and philosophy, and tries to
have an affair with a marquise.   He is hoodwinked by all, especially
when made a mamamouchi.   He unknowingly marries his daughter
Lucile to a commoner, Cleonte, who poses as the Grand Turk's son.
        5 acts; 9 to 12 men, 5 women, extras; 1 interior; costumes
of the period.

_____. The Cheats of Scapin.   See Frank Dunlop's Scapino.

_____. The Doctor in Spite of Himself (1666).   In all complete
    editions of his translated works (for list see note under his main
    entry for Tartuffe); the Wall translation also in SMR; tr. by Baker &
    Miller as The Mock Doctor; tr. by Clark, Modern Lib., 1924;
    same, French, 1925; LEV; tr. and adapted (with 2m, 3w) by
    Hewitt, pub. by Row, Peterson, 1941.   Acting ed.: Samuel
    French.
        Sganarelle, a poor wood-cutter, is forced to act as a physi-
cian.   Once in, he rather likes the trade and works miraculous
cures.   He is called in by Géronte to cure Lucinde, who pretends
she is dumb because her father will not allow her to marry her lover,

Leandre.   A sharp satire on the medical profession.
    3 acts; 6 men, 3 women; 1 interior, 1 exterior; costumes of
    the period.   No royalty.

_____.   The Imaginary Invalid (1673).   In all complete editions
    of his translated works (for list see note under his main entry
    for Tartuffe); tr. by Baker & Miller as The Hypochondriak; tr.
    by Clark, French, 1925; tr. by Stone, French, 1939; tr. and
    adapted by Turner, Dramatic Pub. Co., 1939; tr. by Malleson,
    French.
    A hopeless hypochondriac, Argan, who imagines he has every
complaint, wishes his daughter Angélique to marry a dull physician
so as to have a doctor handy.   However she loves handsome Cléante,
and is saved by her maid Toinette, who disguised as a physician
works a permanent cure and also shows up Beline, Argan's shrewish
wife, who wishes Angélique to become a nun so she may inherit.
Argan plays dead to discover his wife's devotion.   She says, "Good
riddance," but Angélique is sincerely grieved.   Argan springs to
life to be the head of the house and to permit his daughter to marry
Cléante.   A satire on the medical profession.
    3 acts (or 5 in the original); 8 men, 5 women; 1 interior;
    costumes of the period.   Royalties: Stone, none; Turner,
    none; Malleson, $25-20.

_____.   The Learned Ladies (1672).   In all complete editions of
    his translated works (for list, see note under his main entry
    for Tartuffe).
    Philaminte, wife of Chrysale, her sister Belise (who sides
with her sister), and her daughter Armande (who advocates free or
platonic love) affect pretentious learning--a vogue popular at court.
The younger daughter, Henriette, with more common sense, has
little sympathy with these lofty flights and finds a sweetheart in Clit-
andre instead of Trissotin, whom her mother wishes her to marry.
When Chrysale's brother announces that their money is all lost,
Trissotin backs out, and old Chrysale finally musters up his courage
to brave his wife's anger and to champion Henriette's marriage.
Thus they escape from affectation.
    5 acts; 8 men, 5 women; 1 interior.

_____.   The Misanthrope (1666).   In all complete editions of his
    translated works (for list, see note below under Tartuffe); Van
    Laun translation in CAR & TRE-1, -2 (v. 2); TREA-1; Page in
    KRE; Baker & Miller translate as The Man Hater; tr. by Clark,
    Modern Lib., 1924; tr. by Giese, Houghton, 1928; tr. by Bent-
    ley in MIL; tr. Richard Wilbur, Dramatists Play Service.
    The hypochondriac Alceste is depicted as hating all mankind,
for all are dishonest, flatterers, cheats, and thieves.   Contrasted
with him is Philinte, a sensible fellow, who believes in moderation
and is prepared to accept the world as it is.   When the posturing
poet Oronte reads a very bad sonnet, Alceste frankly declares it
terrible; Philinte is more kindly.   Alceste perversely falls in love
with a gay, frivolous coquette, Célimène--just the wrong kind of
person for him.   Becoming disgusted, he prepares to retire from

the world. Philinte tries to persuade him to reconsider.
    5 acts; 8 men, 3 women; 1 interior; costumes of the period.
Royalty: Wilbur, $35-25.

          . The Miser (1668). In all complete editions of his trans-
lated works (for list see note under his main entry for Tartuffe); Wall translation in CLS; tr. by Clark in Modern Lib.,
1924; tr. & adapted by Kerr, Dramatic Pub. Co., 1942; tr.
anon. in STA & THO; tr. by Parks in BEN and French; tr.
Malleson, French.
    An old miser, Harpagon, and his son, Cléante, both wish to
marry Mariane. When Cléante gets hold of his father's casket of
gold, he gives him the choice between the girl and the treasure, as
the miser prefers the money, Cléante marries the lady. Next, Har-
pagon proposes to give his daughter Elise in marriage to an old man
because no dowry will be required. In the end the miser is left
with only his cash box.
    5 acts; 10 men, 4 women, extras; 1 interior; costumes of
    the period. Royalties: Kerr, none; Parks, $25; Malleson,
    $25-30.

          . The School for Wives (1662). Adapted by Miles Malle-
son. Samuel French.
    Arnolphe is a rich man, a bachelor of 50 years, who has
never married for fear of being cuckolded. He has, however, care-
fully educated his ward in convents, and now he plans to marry her.
But Agnes is so innocent that she curtsies to men who tip their hats
to her, and soon she falls in love with Horace. Horace tells Arnolphe how he has pulled the wool over the eyes of Agnes' guardian,
and Arnolphe tries to stop the romance. At the end Agnes' father,
thought dead, returns and awards his daughter's hand to Horace.
He thanks Arnolphe for his care in educating Agnes.
    6 men, 2 women; 1 interior-exterior. Royalty: $25-20.

          . Tartuffe (1664). In all complete editions of his trans-
lated works (see note below); Page translation in HARC, v. 26;
HUD; MAU; tr. by Clark, Modern Lib., 1924; tr. by Andley,
Oxford, 1933; tr. anon., in SMO; tr. Malleson, French; tr.
Wilbur, Dramatists Play Service.
    Credulous Orgon is thoroughly deceived by the hypocritical
cant of the self-seeking imposter, Tartuffe, who uses his religion as
a means of getting money and position. Orgon gives Tartuffe the
run of the house, promises his daughter to him in marriage, and
even signs over the estate to him. When finally convinced of Tartuffe's dishonesty, through the innate honesty of his wife, he is reminded that Tartuffe now owns the house. In court, Tartuffe is unmasked and recognized as a criminal. Orgon's house is restored
to him, and his daughter is free to marry the man she loves.
    5 acts; 7 men, 5 women; 1 interior; costumes of the period.
Royalties: Malleson, $25-20; Wilbur, $35-25.

          , pseud. of Jean Baptiste Poquelin. Various complete edi-
tions of his translated works: Tr. by Wall, Bohn edition,

1875-76, 3v. reprinted 1897-1900. Tr. by Van Laun, Peterson,
Edinburgh, 1875-76, 6v. Tr. by Wormley, Roberts, 1894-97,
6v.; later by Little, Brown, 1912, 6v. Tr. by Waller, Grant,
Edinburgh, 1907. Tr. by Page, in verse, Putnam, 1908, 2v.
Tr. by Baker & Miller, Everyman's Lib., Dent, & Dutton,
1929, 2v.

MOLNÁR, Ferenc. The Devil (1907). Tr. & adapted by Herford.
Kennerley, 1908.
    As a glib bland man of the world the devil brings about a
love affair between an artist, Karl, and a married woman, Olga.
Neither of them knows that he is destroying them for his own amusement.
    3 acts; 7 men, 7 women; 2 interiors.

_____. Fashions for Men (1915). Tr. by Glazer, Boni, 1922;
    also in his Plays, Vanguard, 1929, & Garden City, 1937.
    Depicts how a simple noble hero, Peter Juhasz, by his very
naiveté and generosity wins out over his more scheming rivals.
Paula, a poor pure-hearted girl, is menaced by a man of wealth
who is somewhat of a rake. Her problem is that she wants to quit
poverty but is in love with Peter. When he gets his job back he
gets his girl.
    3 acts; 13 men, 8 women; 2 interiors.

_____. The Guardsman (1910). Samuel French.
    Growing suspicious of his actress-wife's fidelity, and to test
her, an actor-husband writes her mash notes and sends her flowers
in the name of a Russian guardsman. When she appoints a rendezvous, he impersonates the guardsman, and when she seems about to
yield, he reveals himself. She insists that she knew him all the
time--but did she?
    3 acts; 4 men, 3 women; 1 interior; costume of the guards-
    man. Royalty: $25-20.

_____. Liliom (1909). Tr. by Glazer, Boni, 1921; in his Plays,
    Vanguard, 1929, & Garden City, 1937; French, 1944; CEW; DIE;
    HAV; LEV; MOSH; STE; THF; TRE-1, 2 & 3; TREA-2; TUCG;
    TUCM; WHI; abridged in Mantle 1920/21; acting ed. Samuel
    French.
    Depicts the young and graceless tough, and rough-neck carni-
val barker, Liliom, as moving through a world compounded of nature and imagination, with love and mistreatment for Julie, with
mock heroics on his own tragic death. In heaven he attains a soul,
and is given a chance to return to Julie for one day and to do a good
deed. His "good deed" is to steal a star from heaven and present
it to his daughter. The play runs through a gamut of emotions:
pert humor, wistful devotion, masculine harshness, and feminine
tenderness.
    17 men, 5 women, extras; 1 interior, 4 exteriors. Royal-
    ty: $25.

_____. The Play's the Thing (1925). Samuel French.

Albert is engaged to the actress Ilona. He with his playwright friend Turai arrives earlier than expected at her castle, and
having adjoining rooms they overhear a very compromising conversation between Ilona and her ex-lover, an actor named Almady.
While Albert is shattered by it, Turai writes a one-act play incor-
porating the lines they overheard. When Albert hears the rehearsal,
he feels relieved, Turai feels philanthrophic. Almady is grateful,
and Ilona is more affectionate than ever.
　　　3 acts; 8 men, 1 woman; 1 interior. Royalty: $50-25.

_____. The Swan (1914). Tr. by Glazer in his Fashions for
　Men & The Swan, Boni, 1922; in his Plays, Vanguard, 1929, &
Garden City, 1937; in CHA; arranged by Swartout, Longmans,
1929; abridged in Mantle 1923/24. Acting ed. tr. by Baker,
David McKay.
　　　With subtle satire on the ways of royalty, divertingly ana-
lyzes the varied emotions aroused when the haughtily-reserved swan-
like princess in sympathy kisses the tutor to the alarm of all. The
aristocratic patrician would lose her dignity if she married out of
her rank, so she sacrifices herself for the exaltation of her house.
　　　3 acts; 9 men, 8 women, extras; 3 interiors; court costumes.
Royalty: $25.

_____. The Tale of the Wolf (1912). Tr. by Baker in his Plays,
　Vanguard, 1929, & Garden City, 1937.
　　　Vilma dreams of Georg, a sweetheart of seven years ago,
who swore to return, famous and distinguished, and asked her to
wait. But she married Dr. Eugen and has a son, to whom her husband is telling the tale of the wolf; and while he is telling it, she
dreams of the return of Georg. On awaking and recognizing him,
he turns out to be a failure; so the "wolf" goes away.
　　　3 acts; 15 men, 8 women, extras; 3 interiors.

MONKHOUSE, Allan N. The Education of Mr. Surrage (1912).
　Lond. , Sidgwick, 1913; French, 1913.
　　　At the age of 50 Mr. Surrage has retired, rich enough to live
on his income. His son and two daughters, holding rather advanced
social views, invite for the weekend some questionable persons in
the artistic and theatrical world. How will their conventional father
receive them? They find him very adaptable, and he takes to the
new social environment so readily that he remains master of the
situation.
　　　4 acts; 6 men, 3 women; 2 interiors.

_____. Mary Broome (1911). Lond., Sidgwick, 1912; PLAP
　v. 2.
　　　The maid, Mary Broome, in an English household is seduced
by the son, Leonard, but marries him. The play depicts how she
is treated by his family and her own; reveals why she sticks to him
then, but later leaves him.
　　　4 acts; 5 men, 8 women; 2 interiors.

MONKS, John, Jr. and Fred R. Finklehoffe. Brother Rat (1936).

Dramatists Play Service.
Pictures life at VMI where a cadet in good standing is Brother
Rat. Bing, the star pitcher, is no student but hopes to win out as
best athlete. But he has secretly married Kate, and the day before
the crucial game she tells him he is to be a father. This and the
fear of expulsion so unnerve him that he loses the game. He finally
gets his diploma, and $300 for the first baby in the graduating class.
      3 acts; 14 men (mostly boys), 5 women & extra girls; 1 in-
      terior, 2 exteriors; military uniforms. Royalty: $25.

MONTGOMERY, James. Nothing But the Truth (1916). Samuel
      French.
      Bob bets it can be done--to tell the truth, the absolute truth,
for 24 hours. He accomplishes the feat, winning over difficulties
with his partner, his friends, and his fiancée.
      3 acts; 5 men, 6 women; 2 interiors. Royalty: $25-20.

MOODY, William Vaughan. The Faith Healer (1909). Houghton,
      1909; Macmillan, 1910; in his Plays (Works v. 2), Houghton,
      1912; QUIK, QUIL.
      In moving and effective fashion shows the effects of faith and
disillusion. When discouraged, the power of Michaelis the faith
healer ebbs away, but Rhoda's faith brings back the self-doubter's
strength and exalts it. The potency of love makes love potent to
regenerate faith.
      3 acts; 6 men, 5 women, extras; 1 interior.

_____. The Great Divide (1906). Macmillan, 1909; in his Plays
      (Works v. 2), Houghton, 1912; French, 1938; DIC; abridged in
      Mantle & Sherwood 1899-1909; abridged in Pierce & Matthews
      v. 1.
      Left alone in her brother's cabin in Arizona, Ruth Jordan
from New England is attacked by three vagrants; she gets protection
from Steve Ghent by promising to marry him, after he buys the
others off. She is not content and returns to Massachusetts with her
brother. Steve follows, and they are reconciled, despite the conflict
between the rigid morality of Puritanic New England and the freer
more human standards of the West.
      3 acts; 11 men, 3 women; 2 interiors, 1 exterior.

MOORE, Carroll. Send Me No Flowers. See entry under Barasch,
      Norman.

MOORE, Dudley. Beyond the Fringe. See entry under Bennett,
      Alan.

MOORE, Edward J. The Sea Horse (1969). Samuel French.
      Harry Bales arrives at The Sea Horse Bar, run by 200-pound
Gertrude Blum, just as he always does when he gets shore leave
from his job as a seaman. She is unsentimental and tough; he has
returned from this voyage with a dream of getting married, having
a baby, and buying his own boat. Gertrude, who makes part of her
living upstairs after she closes the bar, will first have nothing to do

with Harry's scheme. She can't even have children, she claims.
But he has brought back a lace wedding dress as a present for her,
and after fighting and making up several times it appears that the
two will get together permanently and compromise by running the
Sea Horse as a team.
    1 man, 1 woman; 1 interior. Royalty: $50-35.

MORATIN, José. Fanny's Consent (ca. 1925). Tr. by Bagstad in
    Poet Lore, v. 40, 1929.
        Don Diego, aged 60, is in love with and plans to marry Don-
na Francisca (Fanny), a young girl who has been in a convent but
who has met and loved Don Carlos, nephew of Don Diego. The wedding is planned, but through a note which comes into the hands of
Don Diego, the love of Fanny and Don Carlos is uncovered and
blessed.
    3 acts; 3 men, 4 women; 1 interior.

MOREAU, Emile. Madame Sans-Gene. See entry under Sardou,
    Victorien.

MORLEY, Robert and Noel Langley. Edward, My Son (1947). Dra-
    matists Play Service.
        An ambitious but unscrupulous man, Arnold Holt, rises spec-
tacularly, motivated by his devotion to his only son, Edward. The
play depicts episodes in the life of Edward: a problem child of 12,
kept in the school through his father; a playboy in his teens, dishonest and drinking, but defended by his father; a war hero, killed
as a plane pilot; leaving a son by Phyllis his wife, who is not willing that the grandson be brought up under the influence of Edward's
father. Arnold goes alone to Palm Beach.
    3 acts; 10 men, 4 women; 6 interiors; costumes of the vari-
    ous periods. Royalty: $25.

MORRIS, Leslie. The Damask Cheek. See entry under van Druten,
    John.

MOSEL, Tad. All the Way Home (1960). Adapted from James
    Agee's A Death in the Family. Samuel French.
        The inspiration for this drama is a typical family's encounter
with death. The family consists of a husband, expectant wife, and
young son. The husband also has a brother, an undertaker, who
fears that he carries the smell of formaldehyde with him constantly.
The husband's father is very ill, and he goes alone to visit the old
man. He never returns from his trip. Somewhere along the way
he was killed. The news of his death stuns and shocks his family.
The young wife had always depended greatly on her husband, and
while the son is still quite young, he has reached an age in which
he most needs a father. Their reactions and their necessary adjustment make this an interesting play.
    6 men, 7 women, 1 child, extras; composite interior, ex-
    terior. Royalty: $50-25.

MOWATT, Anna C. (Ogden). Fashion (1845). Lond., 1850; Bost.,

1855; French; Baker, 1935; in Halline; MOSS-2; QUIK; QUIL.
Acting ed., Samuel French.

Socially ambitious Mrs. Tiffany tries to be a New York lady
of fashion, being coached by her French maid. She is anxious for
her daughter Seraphina to marry a French count, but the match is
broken off by the governess Gertrude; also the maid discloses that
the Count is really a continental crook whom she knew in France.
In the shallow world of fashion Gertrude stands out as the one upright person; she is found by Adam Trueman to be his long-lost
granddaughter and an heiress.

5 acts; 8 men, 5 women; 5 interiors; costumes of the period.
No royalty.

MUNK, Kaj. Niels Ebbesen (1942). Tr. by Larsen in Scandinavian
Plays of the 20th Century, ser. 2, Princeton Univ. Pr., 1944;
SCA-2.

Presents a 14th century German oppressor of the Danish
peasantry in Holstein, a brutal officer, Vitighofen, representing
Count Gerhard. Niels won't resist until he finds that he must meet
violence with violence; so he slays the Count as an absolute necessity. The play is a thinly veiled attack on the Nazi oppressors in
World War II and expresses Munk's scorn for German aggression
and all it stood for.

5 acts; 12 men, 2 women; 2 interiors, 3 exteriors; costumes
of the period.

MUNRO, C. K. At Mrs. Beam's (1921). Knopf, 1936; French
carried; MAP; MOSO; PLAP v. 3.

When Mr. Dermott and Laura Pasquale register as guests
at Mrs. Beam's boarding house, they are supposed by Miss Shore
(who has a vivid imagination) of being the notorious French Blue-
beard and his next victim. But they turn out to be a pair of thieves
temporarily in hiding, and when they leave, they strip the place of
everything that attracts them; they are an unscrupulous and romping
pair of crooks.

3 acts; 3 men, 7 women; 2 interiors.

MURDOCH, Iris and J. B. Priestley. A Severed Head (1964).
Samuel French.

Described as "fun with Freud," this comedy portrays a married man, with a mistress, who thinks he is fooling everybody.
Then he learns that his wife has taken her psychiatrist as her lover
and that his brother is the one who has the real good thing going.
A satire on upper class sexuality.

3 men, 4 women; composite interior. Royalty: $50-25.

MURRAY, John and Allen Boretz. Room Service (1937). Dramatists Play Service.

A nimble-witted producer, Gordon Miller, desperately needs
a play. While staving off eviction from a hotel, he finds an angel
with $15,000, and he has the author in the room. The angel wishes
to withdraw, but they play hide-and-seek with him and with their
creditors. Meantime the author plays sick to hold the room; then

they have him fake a suicide, are obliged to announce his death and hold services over him. Finally the play is produced, but over many unexpected obstacles.
3 acts; 12 men, 2 women; 1 interior. Royalty: $25.

MURRAY, Thomas C. Autumn Fire (1924). Lond., Allen & Unwin, 1924; Houghton, 1926.
A widower at 55, Owen Keegan is still passionate and marries a young wife, Nance. His son Michael also loves her; the situation makes his daughter Ellen very bitter. Owen becomes enfeebled after being thrown from a horse; his brother Morgan hints at "youth to youth" which quite embitters Owen so that he sends his son away. There will be no solution of the situation until he dies.
3 acts; 4 men, 4 women; 2 interiors.

NASH, N. Richard. The Rainmaker (1954). Samuel French.
During a severe drought, one family has two serious problems: how to keep their cattle from dying and how to marry off their plain daughter/sister. Her father and brothers try every possible scheme to find a husband for her without success. Nor is there any relief in sight for the drought. Then a character arrives who will take care of both problems. He is, he says, a rainmaker, and promises to bring rain for $100. He also convinces the daughter that she is beautiful. Everyone believes in him, and rain and love follow.
6 men, 1 woman; composite interior. Royalty: $50-25.

_____. The Young and the Fair (1948). Dramatists Play Service.
Frances Merritt returns after ten years as teacher and personnel director at a girls' finishing school. Her younger sister, a student there, is falsely accused of stealing. The spoiled daughters of prominent trustees are involved but protected. Frances and her sister are glad to leave.
3 acts; 0 men, 21 women; 1 set in 3 sections. Royalty: $35-25.

NEMEROV, Howard. The Homecoming Game. See Howard Lindsay's Tall Story.

NICHOLS, Anne. Abie's Irish Rose (1922). Samuel French.
Struck a note of universal appeal with 2,327 consecutive performances, representing every form of love: boy-girl; parents-children; etc. Abraham Levy brings home as his bride Rosemary Murphy, to the resentment of both families. To appease them, they are married three times: by the Methodist minister, by the Jewish rabbi, and by the Catholic priest.
3 acts; 6 men, 2 women; 2 interiors. Royalty: $25-20.

NICHOLS, Peter. A Day in the Death of Joe Egg (1967). Samuel French.
A teacher and his wife have a child named Josephine, who is 10 years old, spastic, and dependent upon her parents for everything.

The wife believes that Josephine is a punishment to them from God for their premarital indiscretions. The husband sees it as black comedy. The two are visited one night by another couple who seem to have solutions to their problem. The woman visitor, who hates lameness in people, doesn't exactly believe in gas chambers but thinks the state ought to do something in these situations. The man visitor has a more direct plan for dealing with Josephine. The teacher plays along with the game of murder, but then discovers he can't laugh off his affliction, nor live with it either, so he runs away.

      2 men, 3 women, 1 child; 1 interior. Royalty: $50-25.

_____ . The National Health (1970). Samuel French.
      A kind of documentary of a men's ward in a British hospital. People come and go, live and die, hold up to the reality of their lives or don't. Through it all are discussions about socialism, about old values lost, about the quality of medical care. While we are watching the men on the ward, they are often watching a television program, in which the hospital staff become the romanticized characters of a TV hospital drama (where white Dr. Neil Boyd longs to marry black staff nurse Norton in spite of his family's objection).
      16 men, 7 women; 1 interior. Royalty: $50-35.

NICHOLS, Robert. Wings Over Europe (1928). Samuel French.
      To the English cabinet at #10 Downing street Francis Lightfoot, a scientist, offers his secret--the control of the atom bomb. But through pettiness and cowardice they vote to destroy the information. He refuses and gives them a limited time in which to reconsider or suffer the consequences with a timed bomb. But he is killed before it goes off; he leaves behind him a powerful plea for peace on earth. His main thought was to release energy from the atom and thereby free man from labor.
      3 acts; 20 men, 0 women; 1 interior. Royalty: $25-20.

NIZER, Louis. My Life in Court. See Henry Denker's A Case of Libel.

NOBLE, Dennis. Millie Goes a Miss (1974). Performance Publishing.
      Millie is scheduled to marry Harvey until she finds herself saddled with her two teenage brothers--one raised with total permissiveness and the other with strict discipline. Harvey objects to taking the brothers along on their honeymoon, so Millie orders him out of her life forever. Finally, she is able to hide the brothers and get Harvey back.
      5 men, 8 women; 1 setting. Royalty: $35.

NOYES, Alfred. Sherwood (1911). Stokes, 1911, also acting edition 1921; in his Collected Poems, Stokes, 1913.
      Subtitle: "Robinhood and the Three Kings." A fine poetic interpretation of the ballads and legends about the famous outlaw. Fanciful in thought and feeling, with good dramatic situations.
      5 acts; 16 men, 6 women, many extras; 3 interiors, 4 ex-

teriors (all can be played as exteriors); costumes of the
period (12th century in England).

NUGENT, Elliott. Kempy. See entry under Nugent, J. C.

_____. The Male Animal. See entry under Thurber, James.

NUGENT, J. C., with Elliott Nugent. Kempy (1922). Samuel
French.
Kempy, a young architect-plumber, is called to fix a pipe at
a house in a small Jersey town, just as Katharine quarrels with her
fiancé. Kempy has read her books, thinks he understands her, and
has sworn to marry her. She drags him to a Justice of the Peace.
That night he sleeps on the sofa with the dog. Next morning they
find they have acted hastily; a way out is found, as he discovers it
was the other sister who loved him.
4 men, 4 women; 1 interior. Royalty: $25-20.

_____. The Poor Nut (1925). Samuel French.
A shy freshman with an inferiority complex, John falls in
love with a charming co-ed, rises above himself, wins a track meet,
and becomes a leader on the campus.
3 acts; 11 men, 5 women, 3 interiors, 1 exterior. Royalty:
$25-20.

OBEY, André. Lucrece (1931). Adapted by Thornton Wilder.
Houghton, 1933.
Lucrece, the wife of Collatine, proves herself to be a virtuous Roman matron. Tarquin gains hospitality but commits rape.
She sends for her husband, tells him how Tarquin has violated her,
and stabs herself. Then follows an edict of banishment for all Tarquins.
4 acts; 5 men, 6 women, extras; 2 interiors, 2 exteriors;
Roman costumes.

_____. Noah (1931). Tr. & adapted by Arthur Wilmurt. Samu-
el French.
The voyage of the ark starts well, with Noah, his wife, three
sons and their wives, in the hope of a brave new world. When the
rain is over, they dance on the deck with joy; but the canker of the
old world has crept on board. Ham is the sore spot; he doubts, he
taunts, he asks his father skeptical questions. Noah grows lonely;
he is a simple old man with doubts; he is deserted by the young
folks; he asks: "God, are you satisfied?" The answer is the rain-
bow.
3 acts; 5 men, 4 women, extras; 3 exteriors; Biblical costumes. Royalty: $25-20.

O'BRIEN, Justin. The Condemned of Altona. See entry under Sartre, Jean-Paul.

O'CASEY, Sean. Juno and the Paycock (1924). Samuel French.
Juno's husband, Capt. Jack Boyle, struts but never does any-

thing; she calls him a "paycock. " When he believes he has inherited
a fortune, he plunges the family into debt by buying things; but there
is no fortune.   He goes back to his pal Joxer and his liquor; his son
is shot as an informer in the Irish Civil War; and Juno, the magnificent mother, takes the daughter Mary away to build a new life on
the ashes of the old.   An unforgettable tale with quick shifts, from
uproarious laughter to bitter despair and anguish.
          14 men, 5 women; 1 interior. Royalty: $25.

_____. Pictures in the Hallway. See entry under Shyre, Paul.

_____. The Plough and the Stars (1926). Samuel French.
          A vivid picture of people in Dublin tenements during the Easter
riots of 1916 and the abortive revolution.   Jack Clitheroe is killed in
the attack.   Nora his wife is driven insane.
          10 men, 5 women; 3 interiors, 1 exterior. Royalty: $25-20.

_____. Red Roses for Me (1942). Dramatists Play Service.
          Ayamonn Breydon sees hope for a new world in the shilling
per week the railwaymen are striking for--the strike that led to the
bloody Easter Week Rising of 1916.   But the emphasis is on man's
love, devotion, and hope in the future.
          21 men, 9 women; 1 interior, exteriors. Royalty: $35-25.

_____. The Shadow of a Gunman (1923). Samuel French.
          Donald Davoren and Seumas Shields are roommates in a Dublin
tenement.   Although he is merely a dreaming poet, the other residents consider Donald a gunman in the service of the Irish Republican
Party.   Donald, in fact, rather enjoys their speculation and says
nothing to correct their mistaken impression.   Then one of the Re-
publicans visits the supposed sympathizers and leaves a bag of bombs
with the young men.   They are in danger of arrest when the house is
raided by the authorities, but a friend, Minnie Powell, takes the
bombs to her room, assuming that she would not be investigated.
The bombs are discovered, however, and Minnie, vainly trying to
escape, is killed by the authorities for resisting arrest.
          8 men, 3 women; 1 interior. Royalty: $25-20.

ODETS, Clifford. Awake and Sing (1935). Covici, 1935; also in his
          Three Plays, Covici, 1935; in his Six Plays, Random House,
          1939; CER; HAT; MOSL; TRE-2; FAMI; abridged in Mantle
          1934/35.
          The saga of the Berger family, a lower middle-class Jewish
group in the Bronx, convincingly characterized, with their many
frustrations and thwartings.   Not until grandfather Jacob has jumped
off the roof does son Ralph follow his advice to awake and sing.
          3 acts; 7 men, 2 women; 1 interior.

_____. The Country Girl (1950). Dramatists Play Service.
          Georgie Elgin is a lovable, faithful, and forgiving wife to her
husband Frank, an alcoholic, has-been actor.   Through the years
she has bolstered up his morale, reassured him of his talent, and
tried to help him leave the bottle alone.   When director Bernie Dodd

picks Frank for the lead in his new play, Frank questions whether
he can get himself ready for the role. He tells Bernie that Georgie
is responsible for his career troubles, and the director subsequently
comes to hate Frank's wife. Later Bernie finds out just what she
is--a magnificent person--and loves her himself. But Georgie will
stick with her husband.
    6 men, 2 women; 5 simple interiors. Royalty: $50-25.

_____. Golden Boy (1937). Dramatists Play Service.
    A young Italian boy, Joe Bonaparte, cannot avoid compromise.
He might have been a great violinist, but to gain money he becomes
a prizefighter; he is torn between love for his art and gain. He becomes more brutish, breaks his hands, and can never play again.
His spirit breaks after he has killed an opponent. He drives his
auto madly through the night, ending in an accident which kills himself and Lorna, his girl.
    3 acts; 17 men, 2 women; 4 interiors, 2 exteriors. Royalty:
$25.

_____. Rocket to the Moon (1938). Dramatists Play Service.
    Sympathetic Cleo seeks a man who can give her love, but
she finds none in those about her; she has sense enough to refuse
those who offer. The characters grope, but are victims of time
and circumstance.
    6 men, 2 women; 1 interior. Royalty: $35-25.

_____. Waiting for Lefty (1935). In his Three Plays, Covici,
    1935; in his Six Plays, Random House, 1940; CET; DUR; HIL;
    in Kozlenko, Best Short Plays of the Social Theatre, Random
    House, 1939.
    The leader of the taxi drivers in New York, Lefty, is ex-
pected at a meeting called to decide whether to strike or not. In
flashbacks, the poverty and exploitation of the drivers is revealed.
When word comes that Lefty has been killed by the strong-arm men
of the company, the drivers decide to strike.
    6 episodes; 14 men, 3 women, extras; black-out sets.

OEHLENSCHLÄGER, Adam G. Hakon Jarl (1807). Tr. anon.,
    Lond., Hookham, 1840; tr. by Chapman, Lond., 1857; tr. by
    Lindberg, Univ. of Nebraska Studies, v. 5, 1905.
    A mighty man in Norway for 18 years in the 10th century,
Hakon, an Earl, wishes to be king and proposes to kill Olaf by
treachery and thus void his kingly descent. Because he wishes to
seize Gudrun, bride of a peasant, the peasants rise up against him
and he loses his battle with Olaf. Though protected in a cave by
his mistress Thora, his thrall Karker kills him. Olaf became King
of Norway in 995.
    5 acts; 16 men, 4 women, extras; 4 interiors, 5 exteriors,
    costumes of the period.

O'NEILL, Eugene. Ah, Wilderness! (1933). Samuel French.
    Set in a small Connecticut town in 1906, this comedy portrays
an average American family faced with average problems. Soon,

however, one of their average problems becomes somewhat extraordinary, at least in the eyes of the mother and father. That problem is their rebellious teenage son, Richard, an incipient, capital
hating anarchist who reads Swinburne, Shaw, and Wilde, and has a
passionate love for the girl next door. Trouble really starts brewing
when Richard begins to send her scraps of Swinburne love poetry.
Her father intervenes and forces the girl to break with Richard. To
spite her, Richard gets drunk with a strange woman. Now his parents are sure that the world has come to an end. But the neighbor's daughter proves her devotion to Richard at a moonlight beach
rendezvous, and Richard forgets his wild, rebellious ways.
    9 men, 6 women; 3 interiors, 1 exterior. Royalty: $50-25.

_____. Anna Christie (1921). Dramatists Play Service.
    Pulitzer prize play, 1922. With intense emotion and inspired
realism unfolds the tragic story of the poor bewildered Swedish waif
Anna, who, in the clutch of relentless fate, is dragged by circumstances through a sordid life as a prostitute, but is redeemed by the
very sea her father Chris hates and by the love of the Irish sailor
lad Matt. Presents a veritable slice of waterside life.
    8 men, 2 women, 3 extras; 2 interiors, 1 exterior. Royal-
    ty: $35-25.

_____. Beyond the Horizon (1920). Dramatists Play Service.
    The Mayo brothers are as different in temperament as brothers
can be. Robert is sensitive and a poet; he yearns for the adventure
and romance of the sea. Andrew wishes only to run the family farm.
But both brothers are in love with Ruth, and when she chooses to
marry the poet, Robert, the brother interested in farming goes off
to sea. After three years, Ruth is convinced that she married the
wrong man; Robert has failed to make a go of the farm. Andrew returns from his adventurous exploits, bored with his life. Happiness
is impossible for any of the characters.
    6 men, 4 women; 1 interior, 2 exteriors. Royalty: $35-25.

_____. Desire under the Elms (1924). Dramatists Play Service.
    The New England Farmer Ephraim Cabot, at 70, marries
Abbie, age 35. His 32-year-old son Eben is jealous of his step-
mother, for he feels the farm should be his. Abbie seduces Eben
and has a child by him. Eben believes that he has been tricked and
that he is now completely disinherited. But Abbie strangles the baby
to prove her love is greater than her greed for the farm.
    3 acts; 4 men, 1 woman, extras; 1 interior: a cross-section,
    showing 4 rooms and an exterior. Royalty: $35-25.

_____. The Emperor Jones (1920). Dramatists Play Service.
    Haunted by the ghosts and voodooism of his Congo forebearers,
an ex-Pullman porter, risen to be Emperor on a West Indian island,
is conquered by the very superstition he has flouted. Depicts his
struggle against fear and fate, as he relives his personal and racial
past.
    3 men, 1 woman, extras; 1 interior, 5 exteriors. Royalty:
    $35-25.

_____. The Great God Brown (1926). Dramatists Play Service.
The various characters wear masks which represent the
faces they present to the world. Their true faces are presented only
to those who understand them or when they are soliloquizing. A
subtle play of character, its symbolism carried over into their names
(as, Margaret is Marguerite of Faust--the eternal girl-woman).
Shows the conflicts in the soul of man. Brown represents the success of materialism which is doomed to frustration.
   9 men, 5 women; 5 interiors, 1 exterior. Royalty: $35-25.

_____. The Hairy Ape (1922). Dramatists Play Service.
Yank Smith, who is as elemental as a human being can be,
works in the stokehole of a steam ship. He thinks that he "belongs"
to steel, that it is he who makes everything move. When Mildred
Douglas, a rich social do-gooder, faints at the sight of this ape of
a man in his natural habitat, Yank's sense of belonging vanishes.
On shore he is rejected by all levels of society, from the radical
Wobblies to the wealthy people of Fifth Avenue. Finally he goes to
the zoo and steps inside the cage of an ape, where he is crushed to
death.
   6 men, 2 women; extras; 5 interiors, 2 exteriors. Royalty:
   $35-25.

_____. The Iceman Cometh (1946). Dramatists Play Service.
Ten down-and-out drunks await the arrival of Hickey, who
always sets them up. Hickey comes; but he has sworn off drink
and wants each to stop and do the things he always intended to do,
but always put off. The next day they all start out, but drift back
to the old routine. Hickey confesses he has killed his wife, and
gives himself up to the police.
   4 acts; 16 men, 3 women; 1 interior. Royalty: $50-25.

_____. Long Day's Journey Into Night (1940). Dramatists Play
Service.
The play is set in the living room of the Tyrone family's
summer house, in 1912. We learn that the father, James, is a
wealthy matinee idol who is somewhat of a miser. The mother,
Mary, is a drug addict. The elder son, Jamie, is a drunk. Edmund, the younger son just home from sea, has tuberculosis. Then
we learn the reasons. James has never gotten over his impoverished
youth to spend money reasonably; Mary's drug addiction has its roots
in medicine prescribed by a second-rate physician attending Edmund's
birth; Jamie's alcoholism is a result of disillusionment in following
his father into the theater; Edmund's consumption is being treated
by the cheapest local doctor, and his father plans to send him to the
state sanatorium. All of this is almost embarrassingly biographical
of the famous O'Neill family.
   3 men, 2 women; 1 interior. Royalty: $50.

_____. A Moon for the Misbegotten (1943). Samuel French.
The last of O'Neill's plays to deal with one of the "four haunted
Tyrones"; it follows his earlier play Long Day's Journey into Night.
This play concerns only James Tyrone, Jr. (the O'Neill older brother

figure). Tyrone is a hard-drinking, self-destructive Broadway playboy attempting, unsuccessfully, to blot out a haunting memory. Tyrone, staying at the home of his tenant farmer, Mike Hogan, encounters once again Hogan's daughter, Josie, a wonder-woman able
to do the work of three men. The climax comes when James
Jr. passes out on the farm porch and Josie is able to hold Tyrone
and claim him for her own. But when dawn comes James is gone,
and Josie is left with the challenge of bringing him back.
        3 men, 1 woman; 1 exterior. Royalty: $50-25.

             . More Stately Mansions (1964). An unfinished play edited
and abridged by Elliot Martin. Dramatic Publishing Company.
        O'Neill's last play--a contest between idealism and the drive
for material success. The central conflict is between two women,
Sara Harford and her mother-in-law, who alternately hate, love, and
misunderstand each other in their battle to dominate Simon, the husband and son. He desires to be dominated by them, but is cruel to
the two women--even suggesting that they murder one another.
While seeking domination by the women, Simon also seeks to dominate as a businessman. He can never reconcile the poet in himself
with the industrialist.
        7 men, 3 women; 1 set. Royalty: $50.

             . Mourning Becomes Electra (1931). Liveright, 1931; in
his Plays, Wilderness edn, Scribner, v. 2; in his Plays, Random house, 1940, v. 2; abridged in Mantle 1931/32.
        Reinterprets the Greek tragedy in terms of modern life in
New England; the characters are hounded by their consciences instead of the Greek Fates. Lavinia loves her father as immoderately
as she hates her mother; she brings tragedy to all and determines
to live alone with the dead in the family's house, a prey to the
ghosts which will haunt her. She has guarded the family honor
through a mistaken but lofty sense of duty.
        Trilogy in 13 acts; 13 men, 7 women; 4 interiors, 2 ex-
        teriors.

             . Strange Interlude (1928). Dramatists Play Service.
        Pulitzer prize play, 1928. A rather selfish woman, Nina
Leeds, seeks to overcome her love frustration and searches for
fulfillment with three men: Sam Evans, whom she marries; Dr.
Darnell, by whom she has a son; and finally dear old Charley (who
has had a mother complex) but with whom she finds peace after various interludes.
        9 acts; 5 men, 3 women; 5 interiors, 1 exterior. Royalty:
$35-25.

             . A Touch of the Poet (1947). Dramatists Play Service.
        Con Melody, a proud and profane Irishman, owns a tavern
near Boston. He is forever boasting of his wealthy background, of
his commission in the Duke of Wellington's army, and his contributions to the Duke's victory at Talavera--the date of which he always
celebrates, in uniform, riding about on his blooded mare. His arrogance gets to the Yankees who surround him, and they beat him

up. Finally he realizes who and where he is, and he shoots his
mare--a symbol of the past and his pretensions.
      7 men, 3 women; 1 interior. Royalty: $50-25.

ORTON, Joe. What the Butler Saw (1969). Samuel French.
      First of all, there is no butler in this zany farce. There
are, however, the Prentices. Dr. Prentice seduces his employees
(he is a psychiatrist with his own hospital); Mrs. Prentice is a nym-
phomaniac. He has a young thing he is trying to hide from her,
while she has a hotel bellhop she is trying to hide from him. At
the same time, the state inspector is visiting the hospital, making
it necessary for disguises, disappearances, and discoveries.
      4 men, 2 women; 1 interior. Royalty: $50-25.

ORWELL, George. Animal Farm. See entry under Bond, Nelson.

_____. 1984. See entry under Owens, Robert.

OSBORN, Paul. A Bell for Adano (1944). Dramatists Play Service.
      Major Joppolo, an Italian from New York, comes to the little
town in Sicily just after its liberation in World War II, restores order, and inspires the natives with a feeling of confidence and affection. Most of all they want a bell, and he secures one from the
Navy. He is set back by the General, but not before he hears the
bell ring.
      22 men (doubling possible), 5 women; 1 interior. Royalty:
$35-25.

_____. Morning's At Seven (1939). Samuel French.
      All the Gibbs family live near each other and are content to
live on past middle age. To Ida's house comes Myrtle, for almost
15 years engaged to son Homer, who can't break away from home.
Myrtle finally gets him to agree to marry and move into the house
prepared five years before.
      4 men, 5 women; 1 exterior. Royalty: $25-20.

_____. On Borrowed Time (1938). Dramatists Play Service.
      Gramps is idolized by Pud, his grandson, who models his
speech, behavior, and actions on the old man. Aunt Demetria,
strait-laced and Puritan, does not approve. The action of the play
consists of two conflicts: Aunt Demetria tries to take Pud away,
and Gramps fights her. Death, in the person of Mr. Brink, tries
to take Gramps away, and Gramps fights him, knowing that if he
submits Pud will go to Demetria automatically. Finally Gramps
gets Death to climb the apple tree, where he holds him with some
strange power. Only when Pud dies accidentally does the old man
let Death down from the tree so that he can die and rejoin his
grandson.
      11 men, 3 women; 1 set. Royalty: $35-25.

_____. Point of No Return (1951). Adapted from John P. Mar-
quand's novel. Samuel French.
      While bank executive Charles Grey wants an available promo-

tion, he refuses to engage in the back-slapping apple-polishing tactics
of his rival. To find out how he got in this business world to begin
with, Charlie recalls his life, trying to decide at which point he
made a decision which irretrievably committed him to his present
occupation. As he engages in this reminiscing, a witty portrait of
modern life unfolds. Through a series of humorous characterizations, Charlie recaptures his past, until he can finally come to a
satisfactory conclusion about his present situation.

14 men, 7 women, 2 children; 3 interiors, 1 interior inset.
Royalty: $50-25.

_____. The Vinegar Tree (1930). Samuel French.
Laura is restless because she realizes she is 40 with a husband still older. She relives an imaginative past when she spent an
afternoon with a handsome young artist, Max Lawrence, who is
coming to spend a weekend with the family. She maps out her stra-
tegy, but is distressed when her daughter seems to take Max away
from her, but becomes reasonably content when she discovers it was
Lawrence Mack, a pianist, and not Max Lawrence, the painter, with
whom she spent the romantic afternoon.

4 men, 3 women; 1 interior. Royalty: $25-20.

OSBORNE, John. The Entertainer (1956). Dramatic Publishing
    Company.
Archie Rice is part of a family of English music-hall enter-
tainers. He is glib, cheap, vulgar, and quarrelsome. He is insulting to his grandfather, Billy, and to his second wife, Phoebe. He
plans to dump Phoebe soon and marry a girl the age of his daughter,
Jean. He even reveals his plans to his daughter. His plot is slowed
down when his son is killed overseas. After the funeral Archie tries
to go on as before, but Billy informs the parents of the new bride-to-
be of Archie's status as a husband and father. The old man dies,
but Archie goes on singing.

5 men, 2 women; exterior and interior sets. Royalty: $50.

_____. Epitaph for George Dillon (1958). Dramatic Publishing
    Company.
George Dillon recites his own epitaph, and it is filled with
self-contempt. He has sold whatever artistic talent he may have
had in exchange for material and commercial success. He has lived
off, and despised, his middle-class family, and his comments about
his life are agonizing and bitterly ironic.

5 men, 4 women; 1 set. Royalty: $50.

_____. Inadmissible Evidence (1965). Dramatic Publishing Com-
    pany.
The play opens in a courtroom which could be the conscience
of Bill Maitland-English, an attorney, and a man tortured by a sense
of failure and guilt. Then we see Bill at his office, where during
the next two days he permanently alienates his wife, his mistress,
his clerks, the staff, his daughter, and himself. He performs the
role of inquisitor, confessor, torturer, executioner, and finally
beholder.

3 men, 5 women; 1 interior. Royalty: $35.

_____. Look Back in Anger (1956). Dramatic Publishing Company.

Jimmy Porter is an "angry young man" who cannot find himself in a British society that is heavily stratified socially. His boiling resentment emerges by making life impossible for those he loves most. He is hardest on his wife, Allison, whose father is from the older, imperialistic Britain. Cliff Lewis also lives with Porters in their one-room flat, and Jimmy abuses Cliff too. An actress, Helena Charles, comes to live with them while she is in town and starts a quarrel between Jimmy and Allison which results in the wife leaving, apparently for good. Several months later Helena is playing the wife, and being treated exactly like Jimmy treated Allison. When Allison returns after a miscarriage, Helena leaves, and Jimmy and Allison, who need one another, are reunited. A powerful and often brutal play.

3 men, 2 women; 1 interior. Royalty: $50.

_____. Luther (1961). Dramatic Publishing Company.

Deals with the reformation hero Martin Luther--his self-doubts, his bodily ailments, and his brilliant intellectual achievements. The play opens as Luther takes his final vows as a monk and leads up to the trial at which Luther cannot recant for his "heresies."

13 men, 1 woman, extras; 8 sets. Royalty: $50.

OSTROVSKII, Aleksandr N. Easy Money (1870). Tr. by Magarshack in his Easy Money & other plays, Lond., Allen, 1944; tr. by Daniels & Noyes as Fairy Gold in Poet Lore, v. 40, 1929.

Several men promise money to Lydia, who needs instruction in the spending of it, for she looks on it as fairy gold. Telyatev is a man-about-town, who owes much and therefore can never lend; he nearly gets engaged to Lydia; Kuchumov promises much but never delivers; Glumov always has hopes; he also views money as fairy gold, but realizes to be real it must be earned. Vasilkov earns money and marries Lydia; she leaves him but asks to come back. He will take her back if she will learn to be a good housekeeper.

5 acts; 9 men, 3 women, extras; 3 interiors, 1 exterior; Russian costumes.

_____. Even a Wise Man Stumbles (1868). Tr. by Magarshack in Easy Money & other plays, Lond., Allen & Unwin, 1944; tr. as Enough Silliness in Every Wise Man in MOSA.

A trickster, George Glumov, aims to advance himself and wishes to marry the daughter of a rich widow, but he plays around with the wife of Mamayev, a distant relative. He keeps a diary in which he writes his real opinions of acquaintances; the jealous Mamayeva steals it and confronts him with the evidence in it. He loses their friendship, but they agree that after due punishment he must be restored to favor, for they need such a "man of parts."

5 acts; 9 men, 7 women; 4 interiors, 1 exterior; Russian costumes of the period.

_____. The Forest (1871). Tr. by Winlow and Noyes, French,

1926.

Two actors, Neschastlivtsev the luckless one and Arkushka the lucky one, meet in the dark forest and go out to the former's aunt, Raisa Pavlovna, who is a hard miserly country gentlewoman. Neschastlivtsev saves a maiden, Aksyusha, the ward of his aunt, from drowning herself and gives her a dowry, forced from his aunt, to marry "play-actors" but they answer proudly that they have done a good deed, and go off back to the forest, prefering that to life with his relations.

5 acts; 9 men, 3 women; 1 interior, 3 exteriors; Russian costumes of 1870.

_____. Poverty Is No Crime (1854). Tr. by Noyes in his Plays, Scribner, 1917.

Gordey Tortsov, a rich merchant, has a brother, Lyubim, who is a sad rogue, a drunkard, albeit lovable. He reveals the pettiness and meaness of his merchant-brother's household and serves to bring about the marriage of Lyubov, daughter of Gordey, and the poor but honest clerk, Mitya, instead of her marrying an older man as her father wishes.

3 acts; 6 men, 1 boy, 6 women, extras; 3 interiors.

_____. The Storm (1860). Tr. by Garnett, Lond., Duckworth, 1898; same, Sergel (Dramatic Pub. Co.) 1899; same, Luce, 1907; tr. by Whyte and Noyes as The Thunderstorm, French, 1927; CLF-2.

A dreamy young girl, Katia, finds her husband is still dominated by his mother who makes life miserable for her and causes her husband to neglect her. He is glad to go away for a couple of weeks to escape from his domineering mother. Katia meets a dashing young man, Boris, by whom she is seduced during her husband's absence. When this is discovered by the husband and because Boris has to leave for three years, Katia jumps into the Volga. Her husband is left to face his mother.

5 acts; 7 men, 5 women; 1 interior, 4 exteriors; Russian costumes of the period (16th century).

_____. Wolves and Sheep (1875). Tr. by Colby and Noyes in Poet Lore, v. 37, 1926; tr. by Magarshack in his Easy Money & 2 other plays, Lond., Allen & Unwin, 1944.

Meropia wants to manage everything, and through her lawyer plans to entrap a rich widow, Evlampia, for her nephew, Apollonius, a sporting man. These predatory wolves are outwitted by Berkulov, who comes to Moscow and succeeds in saving Evlampia from their clutches, and wins her.

5 acts; 13 men, 4 women, extras; 3 interiors, 1 exterior.

OTWAY, Thomas. Venice Preserved; or, A Plot Discovered (1682). In all editions of his Collected works; in several series, as Mermaid, Temple; BEL v. 2; BRI v. 1; DOB; GOSA; INCH v. 12; MAT; MCM; MOR; MOSE v. 1; NET; OXB v. 4; RUB; STM; TAU; TUQ; TWE.

A conspiracy against Venice is betrayed by Jaffeir who is in

love with Belvidera, daughter of Priuli, a senator.   The plot is
varied and intense.
>   5 acts; 8 men, 2 women, many extras; 4 interiors, 4 ex-
>   teriors; costumes of the period.

OWENS, Robert, Wilton E. Hall, Jr., and William A. Miles, Jr.
>   1984 (1963).   Adapted from the novel by George Orwell.   Dra-
>   matic Publishing Company.
>   Winston Smith lives in London in 1984, in a totalitarian so-
ciety where Big Brother is always watching, where everything that
is not prohibited is compulsory, where war is peace, freedom is
slavery, and ignorance is strength.   His job is in the Ministry of
Truth, where he rewrites or "corrects" history to conform to the
party line.   Two people, however, change his life: O'Brien and
Julia, a girl who loves him even though love is forbidden (it is not
in the best interest of the State).   Winston is betrayed by one and
ultimately betrays the other.
>   14 characters (2 men, 2 women, others interchangeable with
>   doubling possible); 1 set or in curtains.   Royalty: $35.

PAILLERON, Édouard.   The Art of Being Bored (1881).   Tr. by
>   Clark, French, 1914; abridged in Pierce & Matthews, v. 2, as
>   The Cult of Boredom.
>   At a houseparty the guests affect the bored mien of the
pseudo-intellectual, which is the accepted manners of society.   But
when they escape to the conservatory, they behave more naturally.
The old Duchess de Reville overhears some of their talk and rights
the wrongs of this artificial society; she unites the well-suited and
gets political advancement for the deserving.
>   3 acts; 11 men, 9 women; 2 interiors.

PALMER, Winthrop, with Maurice Edwards and Jean Reavey.   Amer-
>   ican Kaleidoscope (1963).   Based on authentic source material.
>   Dramatic Publishing Company.
>   American history seen from authentic and unusual viewpoints:
Columbus in the Spanish court, the journals of John Winthrop, the
witchcraft trial of Anne Hutchinson, a ladies of the French court
version of De La Salle's latest expedition, a Southern belle's complaint that the Civil War is ruining the Atlanta social season.
>   Cast of 7 (expansion possible); simple set with several playing
>   areas.   Royalty: $50.

PARKER, Louis N.   The Aristocrat (1917).   Lane, 1917.
>   During the Reign of Terror, Duke Louis of Carcassone re-
fuses to recognize the Republic.   He invites some old aristocratic
friends to celebrate mass on New Year's eve, excluding however
Gautier Lalance, beloved of his daughter Louise.   An agent of the
Republic arrests them all; they are tried and condemned to the guillotine, but it is the night of Robespierre's death, and Louise, her
father, and some others are saved.   Ten years later the old Duke
is reconciled to Louise and Gautier, though this time he despises
Napoleon.
>   3 acts; 13 men, 5 women, extras; 3 interiors; costumes of
>   the period.

_____. Disraeli (1911).   Lane, 1911; Dodd, 1932; Baker car-
ried; abridged in Pierce & Matthews, v. 1; abridged in Mantle
& Sherwood 1909-1919.
        Deals ingeniously with an episode in the career of the Prime
Minister when he is negotiating for the purchase of the Suez Canal.
He is shown fighting racial, social, and political prejudice.   The
wit and epigram seem natural; the character sketching is subtle.
        4 acts; 14 men, 6 women, many extras; 4 interiors; costumes
        of the period (1876 in England).

_____. Joseph and His Brethren (1913).   Lane, 1913.
        Joseph the dreamer is sold to Zuleika, who in Egypt becomes
Potiphar's wife.   Resisting her blandishments, Joseph is put in prison with the Chief Butler and Chief Baker.   Brought out, he interprets Pharaoh's dream and is promoted.   His brothers come, and
his dreams come true.   Follows the Biblical narrative in events and
language.
        4 acts; in Canaan: 17 men, 5 women; in Egypt: 20 men,
        12 women, extras; 5 interiors, 6 exteriors; costumes of the
        period.

_____. Pomander Walk (1910).   Lane, 1911; French, 1915.
        A delightful, graceful, old-fashioned romance, embroidered
with clever lines, pathos, and sentiment, based on whosesome situations.   A young and an elderly pair of lovers are united after a
series of mishaps.
        3 acts; 10 men, 8 women; 1 exterior (a street facing a house
        with practical doors and windows); costumes of the period
        (1805) in England.

_____. and Murray Carson.   Rosemary (1896).   French, 1924 (as
revised by Parker).
        Noble and gentle Sir Jasper at 40 falls in love with Dorothy,
a young and excitable girl, who writes enthusiastically in her diary
about Sir Jasper, much to the annoyance of her devoted admirer,
William.   Sir Jasper helps William secure Dorothy from her stern
parent, and is persuaded by his friend Prof. Jogram to forego his
belated love.   Dorothy gives him rosemary--that's for remembrance.
        4 acts; 6 men, 4 women; 2 interiors, 1 exterior.

PARTRIDGE, Bellamy.   January Thaw.   See entry under Roos, Wil-
        liam.

[PATHELIN].   The Farce of Master Pierre Patélin (1469).   Tr. by
        Holbrook, Houghton, 1905; Baker, 1914; THO; tr. & adapted by
        Brueys as Master Patelin, Solicitor, French, 1915; tr. by Re-
        londe as Pierre Pathelin the Lawyer, in Poet Lore, v. 28,
        1917, also separately, Badger, 1917; tr. by Jagendorf, Appleton,
        1925; CAR; CLF-1; tr. & adapted into 1 act by Stone, French,
        1939.
        Pathelin gets cloth from a draper on credit and by acting
crazy gets out of paying.   He later instructs a thieving shepherd how
to avoid paying his debts.   His seemingly stupid pupil learns the

trick so well that he refuses to pay him his lawyer's fee.
     3 acts; 7 men, 3 women, extras; 1 interior, 1 exterior;
costumes of the period.

PATRICK, John. The Curious Savage (1950). Dramatists Play Ser-
    vice.
     The efforts of an old lady to use her inheritance for a good
cause and the attempts of her greedy stepchildren to get the money
for themselves provide this comedy with many humorous episodes.
Hoping to force Mrs. Savage to give up her inheritance, the scheming
stepchildren commit her to a sanatorium. In the sanatorium she
meets many social misfits who cannot adjust themselves to life. In
getting to know them she realizes that she can find happiness in
helping these people and decides not to return to the harsh, outside
world where people will do anything for money. The stepchildren
are driven to distraction by their vain attempts to get her money.
Mrs. Savage, however, remains calm and leads them on a merry
chase with all sorts of ridiculous mishaps for the completely frustrated relatives. After outwitting the stepchildren, Mrs. Savage is
persuaded to leave the sanatorium and manage her inheritance as a
trust fund for such unfortunates as she met there.
     5 men, 6 women; 1 interior. Royalty: $35-25.

_____. Everybody Loves Opal (1961). Dramatists Play Service.
     The bumbling attempts of three would-be assassins to murder
a kindly, scatterbrained lady provide many humorous episodes for
this comedy. Opal Kronkie, a middle-aged recluse, lives in a tumble-
down mansion at the edge of the city dump. Her house, like her
life, is totally disorganized since she has filled it with stacks of junk
collected while meandering through the dump. No matter how she is
treated by others, Opal always responds with kindness. Into this
rather bizarre existence come three equally bizarre characters:
Gloria, Bradford, and Solomon, con artists on the run from the law.
They decide what Opal needs is plenty of life insurance, a rapid de-
mise, and three beneficiaries named Gloria, Bradford, and Solomon.
No matter how sinister their schemes, however, they all go away
when faced with the disorganized jumble of Opal's life. Through it
all Opal radiates kindness, and one by one the plotters are won over,
realizing that friends are worth more than money. Then to their
shame and consternation they find that there was plenty of money
around all the time--bags full of it. In fact, any friend of Opal's is
welcome to as much as he wants.
     4 men, 2 women; 1 interior. Royalty: $50-25.

_____. The Hasty Heart (1945). Dramatists Play Service.
     A wounded Scotch soldier in a convalescent ward of a hospital
in the Orient is very independent and suspicious, and this nearly
wrecks the good intentions of those who want to make him happy.
He learns (after falling in love with the nurse) the great lesson of
love for one's neighbor and not to be indignant at offers of friendship.
     3 acts; 8 men, 1 woman; 1 interior. Royalty: $50-25.

_____. The Story of Mary Surratt (1947). Dramatists Play Service.

The boarders at Mary Surratt's are shown, with Mary innocent of the plot to kill Lincoln, although her son was in it with
money from Booth.   Later that evening, after the shooting of Lincoln, officers come for her son John and arrest Mary.   Reverdy
Johnson, an old sweetheart, now in Congress, offers to be her attorney.   The conviction at the trial was on slim evidence.
    35 men, 2 women; 3 interiors.   Royalty: $35-25.

_____. Teahouse of the August Moon (1953).   Dramatists Play
    Service.
The efforts of an Army of occupation officers to teach democracy to natives on Okinawa result in many humorous situations in
this familiar comedy.   To complicate his job, the young officer's
commander is a Colonel who demands the strictest enforcement of
the Manual of Occupation.   The charms of the village people, however, take all sterness out of the young officer's attitude.   Within
a few days he owns a Geisha girl, has built a Teahouse with mate-
rials sent for a school, and has begun selling the village's principal
product, potato brandy, to all the surrounding Officer's Clubs.
Then the Colonel arrives and threatens a court martial.   Just as
things seem the worst word arrives that Congress considers this the
most progressive village on the island and sends its congratulations
to all involved.
    18 men, 8 women, 3 children; 1 goat; interiors and exteriors.
Royalty: $50-25.

PATTON, Frances G. Good Morning, Miss Dove.   See entry under
    McCleery, William.

PAYNE, John Howard.   Brutus; or, The Fall of Tarquin (1818).   In
    O'Connor's Great Plays, Appleton, 1904; in Winter's Plays of
    Edwin Booth, Penn Pub. Co. , 1899, v. 3; MOSS-2.
Episodes in the life of Brutus, a great Roman patriot who
fought against the lust and tyranny of the Tarquins.   Includes the
rape of Lucrece by Sextus and the vengeance taken by Brutus and
Collatinus, her husband.   Pictures the establishment of the Republic
about 510 B. C. and the election of Brutus and Valerius as consuls.
His son, Titus, commits treason through love for Tarquina and is
condemned to death by his own father.
    5 acts; 15 men, 6 women, extras; 5 interiors, 6 exteriors;
costumes of the period.

_____ and Washington Irving.   Charles the Second (1824).   QUIK;
    QUIL.
Disguised as sailors, the merry monarch, Charles II, and
the Earl of Rochester visit Copp's tavern at night; the King is left
to pay the bill, and leaves his watch as earnest.   After various intrigues the King rather improbably promises to reform.
    3 acts; 4 men, 2 women, extras; 2 interiors, 1 exterior.

PEABODY, Josephine P.   The Piper (1910).   Houghton, 1909; in her
    Collected Plays, Houghton, 1927; French carried; DID; MOSJ;
    MOSL.

Emphasizes love as a compelling force--love in the home, in
the city, in religion. The Piper brings back crippled Jan to Veroni-
ca, his mother, because of Christ's love for little children. Has
imaginative quality and literary distinction.

> 4 acts; 13 men, 6 women, 5 children, many extras; 3 ex-
> teriors; medieval costumes.

PELLICO, Silvio. Francesca da Rimini (1818). Tr. by Bingham,
Lond., Francis, 1856; Unwin, 1915; Frowde, 1905; Cambridge,
Mass., Seaver, 1897.

Francesca had met Paolo some years before and loved him,
but because he had killed her brother and to conceal her real feeling
toward him from her husband, she pretends to hate him. The husband however suspects the mutual passion, quickly changes to a revengeful spouse, and kills them both.

> 5 acts; 4 men, 1 woman, extras; 1 interior.

PÉREZ GALDÓS, Benito. The Duchess of San Quentin (1894). Tr.
by Hayden in CLDM.

Rosario, the Duchess of San Quentin, a young widow, comes
to visit Don José. His son, Don César, a rather conventional nobleman, pays suit to her, but she becomes interested in his apparently
illegitimate son, Victor, who has been educated well and has ideals.
When it turns out that Victor is not his son but is of unknown parentage, Victor is to be turned out of the house. Then it is, to the
surprise and horror of all the family, that Rosario declares she will
go with him to America.

> 3 acts; 5 men, 4 women, extras; 1 interior, 1 exterior (1
> interior possible).

_____. Electra (1900). Tr. anon. in Drama, v. 1 #2, 1911; tr.
by Turrell in TUR; TUCG.

A young girl of 18, Electra, full of life and spirits, has an
affection for Maximo Yuste, an electrical engineer. Don Pantoja, a
religious fanatic, wishes to educate her for the convent. He plants
the idea that she and Maximo are brother and sister. He learns in
time from her mother's spirit that this is not so; so she joins Maximo, having discovered in time that she was not suited for convent
life. The play was interpreted as symbolic of the conflict in Spain
between the Church and the modern scientific spirit.

> 5 acts; 10 men, 6 women; 4 interiors, 1 exterior.

_____. The Grandfather (1904). Tr. by Wallace in Poet Lore,
v. 21, 1910.

An aging nobleman is informed that one of his two grand-
daughters is not the child of his son. Henceforth his ruling passion
is to ascertain which is the legitimate grandchild and to disown the
other, thus wiping out the blot on the family name. The problem
drives him almost insane until he realizes that honor is rather "pure
living, neighborly love, and wishing no evil." At last he understands
that love, and not honor is supreme. He finds perfect love in the illegitimate child and great affection in the other, and gains peace of
spirit.

5 acts; 7 men, 4 women; 1 interior, 2 exteriors.

PERL, Arnold. Tevya and His Daughter (1958). Based on the
   stories of Sholom Aleichem. Dramatists Play Service.
   The desires of a Jewish couple to see their daughters happily
married are presented in this amusing and warm-hearted play. Tevya is a poor drayman with seven daughters. He and his wife, Golde,
are attempting to arrange advantageous matches for the two eldest
girls, but in each instance their well-intentioned plans are foiled
when the girls fall in love with someone else. Tzeitl has attracted
the interest of a prosperous butcher, Lazar Wolf, which pleases
Golde immensely. The girl, however, falls in love with and marries
a poor tailor. Then Hodel falls in love with a poor student. To
compound their already difficult situation the new groom is exiled to
Siberia. Tevya, however, finds consolation in the fact that the five
remaining daughters are "too young to be problems; but they'll grow
into it. "
   6 men, 6 women; bare stage with some furniture. Royalty:
   $35-25.

PERRY, Eleanor. David and Lisa. See entry under Reach, James.

PHILLIPS, Stephen. Herod (1900). Lane, 1901; later, Dodd;
   abridged in Pierce & Matthews v. 1.
   In stately and beautiful blank verse develops the conflict between Herod's love for his queen and his self-love, his lust for
power, and his overmastering ambition. He puts to death the younger brother of his queen, for fear a new king will supplant him; and
when the queen spurns him, he thinks she will poison him and so
sanctions her death.
   3 acts; 12 men, 6 women; 1 interior; oriental costumes.

_____. Paolo and Francesca (1899). Lane, 1900; later, Dodd;
   DIG; SMN.
   Unfolds the story of a jealous husband. Though married to
the older brother, Francesca cannot control her love for Paolo nor
his for her. Youth goes toward youth, and unhappiness and death
come apace, caused by love which cannot be returned. Fine verse
with a touch of pageantry.
   4 acts; 7 men, 7 women, extras; 4 interiors, 3 exteriors;
   costumes of the period in Italy.

_____. Ulysses (1902). Macmillan, 1902; in his Collected Plays,
   Macmillan, 1921; in Cohen, H. L. ed., Junior Play Book, Harcourt, 1923.
   Gives pictures of his adventures from his departure from
Calypso's Isle and his descent into Hades to the vigorous combat
with the suitors in his palace in Ithaca. The verse flows freely;
real drama emerges in the final act.
   Prolog & 3 acts; 21 men, 8 women, many extras; 1 interior,
   6 exteriors; Greek costumes.

PINERO, Arthur Wing. The Amazons (1893). Lond., Heinemann,

& Baker, 1895.

The young daughters wear boys' clothes at home, but when lovers appear--the eternal feminine reappears. Whimsical farce comedy on the tendency to educate girls in masculine pursuits.

3 acts; 7 men, 5 women; 1 interior, 1 exterior.

_____. Dandy Dick (1887). U.S. Book Co., 1893; French carried; Baker, 1912.

Dandy Dick is a horse, owned by Georgianna, sporty sister of the Rev. Augustus Judd, who places a bet on him. He administers a stimulating bolus to help him win, but Blore, his butler, who has a bet against the nag, secretly inserts a poisonous dose. The Dean is caught and is in a mess.

3 acts; 7 men, 5 women; 2 interiors.

_____. The Enchanted Cottage (1922). Baker's Plays.

A war invalid, Oliver, and a plain girl, Laura, marry and move into a country cottage. They come to think they have changed, Oliver becoming strong and Laura lovely, for the enchanted cottage through love makes them see each other differently, as handsome and beautiful.

3 acts; 5 men, 4 women, extras; 1 interior, 1 exterior.

Royalty: $25-20.

_____. The Gay Lord Quex (1899). Heinemann, & Baker, 1901; Russell, 1900; in his Social Plays, Dutton, 1918, v. 2; MOSO; SMO.

Lord Quex resolves to reform and settle down in order to marry the charming Muriel, but he must first lay several ghosts of his gay past. He does succeed however in convincing the sisters that he is sincere. The play is a triumph of technique, a play for playwrights, in which Pinero essayed a hard task and fulfilled it. The third act is an accomplished orgy of dexterity with climax and suspense and surprise and surprise again.

4 acts; 4 men, 10 women, extras; 2 interiors, 1 exterior.

_____. The Magistrate (1885). Lond., Heinemann; U.S. Book Co., 1892; Baker, 1912; French, 1936; SMR.

A police court magistrate, Mr. Posket, marries a widow with a precocious son, who persuades his step-father to visit a sporty restaurant. Mrs. Posket also goes there, in search of her boy's godfather just returned from India. When the place is raided by the police, all the family must appear as criminals in her husband's own court.

3 acts; 12 men, 4 women; 3 interiors.

_____. Mid-Channel (1909). Lond., Heinemann, & Bost., Baker, 1910; French carried; in his Social Plays, Dutton, 1922, v. 4; HAU; SMI; WATF-1; WATI; WHI.

Married life is compared to crossing the English channel with its shoal halfway over. Theodore and Zoe, after 13 years, fail to weather the perils of mid-channel through selfishness, especially in not encumbering themselves with children. They seek

to find amusement elsewhere and both have outside liaisons. Weary
of sowing wild oats, they are ready to be reconciled, but it is too
late.
    4 acts; 8 men, 5 women; 3 interiors.

_____. The Second Mrs. Tanqueray (1893). Lond., Heinemann,
    & Bost., Baker, 1894; French carried; in his Social Plays, Dut-
ton, 1917, v. 1; DUR; FULT; COF; CEU; DIC; HUD; MAT; STE;
TAU.
    Study of a woman with a past, Paula, marrying a bit out of
her station so that she is not cordially accepted by her husband's
friends nor by her 19-year-old daughter Ellean. When Ellean becomes engaged to Captain Ardale, to whom Paula had been mistress,
she feels she must advise Ellean against the match, after which she
lacks the courage to face further consequences. An epoch-making
play, with the climax seized and the story built out of results rather
than causes.
    4 acts; 7 men, 4 women; 2 interiors.

_____. Sweet Lavender (1888). Hurst, 1893, Baker, 1893;
    French carried.
    The banker Wedderburn is rather upset when his adopted son
Clement falls in love with Lavender, the daughter of his housekeeper
Ruth Holt. He becomes reconciled however when Lavender proves
to be his own daughter through an early association with Ruth. The
play idealizes sordid human nature.
    3 acts; 7 men, 4 women; 1 interior.

_____. The Thunderbolt (1908). Lond., Heinemann, & Baker,
    1909; in his Social Plays, Dutton, 1922, v. 4; CHAR; TUCD;
TUCM; abridged in Pierce & Matthews, v. 1.
    On the death of Edward Mortimer, a bachelor brewer, his
brothers expect to inherit his money, although they have had nothing
to do with him for years. Since no will is found, they begin to
plan on spending the inheritance, showing the hypocritical conduct
to which this craving for money will lead professedly respectable and
pious persons. They become much discomfitted when they find that
Phyllis, the wife of Thaddeus (a poor professor), destroyed the will
when she found that all was left to Helen Thornhill, Edward's daughter by a secret marriage.
    4 acts; 9 men, 5 women, 2 children (14 & 15 years old),
    extras; 3 interiors.

_____. Trelawney of the "Wells" (1898). DeWitt, & Dramatic
    Pub. Co., 1898; Russell, 1899; French, 1936; MAP.
    Rose Trelawney, a beautiful actress from the Wells Theatre,
becomes engaged to aristocratic Arthur Gower. His uncle and aunt
oppose the match; ultimately their disapproval is overcome, and so
they are married. But she is a born trouper; she can't go to bed
at reasonable hours, she can't conform to his family's life; she returns to the theatre, her first love.
    4 acts; 14 men, 9 women; 3 interiors; costumes of 1860.

PINERO, Miguel. Short Eyes (1972). Samuel French.
    "Short Eyes" is prison slang for a child molester and the
name given to Clark Davis, a white man just brought into the day-
room of this house of detention where most of the inmates are black
or Puerto Rican. Everyone hates a Short Eyes, from the straights
to the homosexuals to the prison guards. First the new prisoner is
beaten up, then brought to consciousness by being soaked in a toilet
filled with urine; finally he is murdered by having his throat slit.
At the end of the play the prisoners learn that Clark Davis has been
the victim of mistaken identity, that he was not, in fact, a Short
Eyes. An investigation into the killing reveals that he committed
suicide.
        14 men; 1 interior. Royalty: $50-35.

PINSKI, David. The Treasure (1906). Tr. by Lewisohn, Huebsch,
    1915.
        As Judka buries his dog, he finds ten gold imperials. His
sister Tille gets half and dresses herself to catch a husband. When
word gets out about the treasure, many want a share in it. They
even dig up the graves of their ancestors in the hope of finding supposed treasure. Search for money makes men sordid, hard, and
ugly.
        4 acts; 12 men, 2 women, extras; 1 interior, 1 exterior.

PINTER, Harold. The Collection. See The Dumb Waiter and the
    Collection.

_____. The Dumb Waiter and The Collection (1962). Dramatists
    Play Service.
        An off-Broadway long-running show made up of two Pinter
short plays. In "The Dumb Waiter," two professional killers, Ben
and Gus, wait, argue, and worry in the windowless basement of an
abandoned restaurant for their next assignment. In "The Collection,"
the set is divided in two. On one side an older man named Harry
and a young dress designer named Bill live together. On the other,
a husband and wife, James and Stella, own a flat. Stella, a model,
confesses that she had a one-night affair with Bill. James wants to
see what this other man looks like, so he visits Bill (they are attracted and repulsed by each other). Harry casts doubt as to whether
the Bill-Stella affair ever took place.
        "Dumb Waiter": 2 men; 1 interior. Royalty: $25-15.
        "Collection": 3 men, 1 woman; divided interior. Royalty:
    $25-15.

_____. The Homecoming (1965). Samuel French.
        Four men live alone in a London home: a widower, who is a
retired butcher; his brother, who is a chauffeur; and two sons, one
a boxer and the other a pimp. The third son arrives home from
America, where he is a philosophy professor. He brings with him
his wife, a woman he was ashamed of in the past but now is the
mother of his three sons. The four Englishmen feel they need someone like her around the house, and as her husband is leaving soon
for the states, she agrees to stay in London and serve as cook, mis-

tress, and part-time prostitute to earn her keep.
5 men, 1 woman; 1 interior. Royalty: $50-25.

_____. Old Times (1971). Dramatists Play Service.
In a converted farmhouse near the English coast a movie-
maker named Deeley and his wife, Kate, prepare to entertain a
former friend and roommate of Kate's whom she hasn't seen in 20
years. The friend, Anna, is on stage when the curtain opens (she
is present in space but not in time), and the husband and wife talk
about her as if she isn't there. Later, the time frame shifts from
present to past, and we are never quite sure what people did, or
did not do, years before. Finally, Deeley and Anna enter into some
kind of struggle for Kate's soul, often acting as if she is not, in
fact, in the same room with the two of them.
1 man, 2 women; 1 interior. Royalty: $50-35.

PIRANDELLO, Luigi. As You Desire Me (1930). Samuel French.
Bruno Pieri thinks he has found his long-lost wife Lucia who
has been missing for ten years, captured by the enemy in World
War I; she is suffering from amnesia so that she cannot recover her
past. Now she must be as they desire her to be, though the audience
is not quite sure that she is the lost wife. When another woman appears who may be Bruno's wife, Lucia loses her newfound security
and leaves them for the open road, still the Unknown One. By the
time she departs, the audience is more convinced than ever that she
is the one Bruno seeks.
9 men, 7 women; 2 interiors. Royalty: $50-25.

_____. Each in His Own Way (1918). Tr. by Livingston, Dutton,
1923; CHA; in Naked Masks, Everyman's Lib., Dutton, 1952.
For the sake of Rocca, a young woman, Delia, deceives a
man and he commits suicide. Two men, Doro and Francesco, discuss the event, the former indulgently, the latter slanderously.
They quarrel, change their opinions, quarrel again and plan a duel.
Delia, ignorant of their change of sides, thanks Doro, who now returns to his indulgent position. The spectators of the play meet in
the story, connecting it with a real scandal in the supposed audience.
When Rocca reappears, he and Delia decide to run away together.
2 acts & 2 interludes; 8 men, 2 women, many extras; 2 interiors in one set.

_____. Henry IV (1922). Tr. by Storer in his Three Plays,
Dutton, 1922; WATI; WATL-4.
A young Italian marquis is injured by a fall from a horse
while portraying Henry IV in a pageant. Henceforth he believes
himself to be the real Henry, has a throne room built and courtiers
in costumes of the 11th century. Matilda, his old sweetheart, likewise appropriately disguises herself. After becoming apparently
sane, he must maintain the role of madness and continue in his
world of illusion to secure his self protection. When the madness
returns he stabs Baron Belcredi who caused his accident.
3 acts; 11 men, 2 women; 2 interiors; costumes of the
periods.

_____. Naked (1922). Tr. by Livingston in his Plays, Dutton, 1923; CLS; DIE.

In the drab life of Ersilia, a governess, had occurred a pas-sing flirtation by Franco, a young naval officer who had deserted her, and an affair with the consul. Because of the death of the con-sul's child by falling off a roof (for which her negligence was blamed), in a fit of despair she takes poison, from which she re-covers. Deprived of creating a new life for herself, she takes poison a second time, for death seemed the only solution for her muddled existence. All her life she had felt naked--unable to ob-tain a respectable position.

3 acts; 4 men, 3 women; 1 interior.

_____. No One Knows How (1935). Translated by Marta Abba. Samuel French.

Conscience and guilt, will and impulse are pondered in this morality play. Tormented by his conscience, Romeo goes mad. He has committed two impulsive crimes, murder and the seduction of his best friend's wife. Then the cuckold husband yields to im-pulse and kills Romeo.

3 men, 2 women; 2 interiors. Royalty: $50-25.

_____. Right You Are! (If You Think So) (1916). Tr. by Living-ston in his Three Plays, Dutton, 1922; MOSH; in Naked Masks, Everyman's Lib., Dutton, 1952.

Ponza's wife died four years ago; he marries again. Signora Frola, mother of the first wife, believes the second wife to be her lost daughter, all evidence being lost in an earthquake. They refuse to disillusion the mother. She thinks he is crazy; he thinks she is. He keeps his second wife and the mother apart. He laughs at his neighbors who try to learn the truth.

3 acts; 7 men, 7 women, extras; 2 interiors (1 possible).

_____. Six Characters in Search of an Author (1921). Tr. by Storer in his Three Plays, Dutton, 1922; DIK-2; CEW; TRE-1, 2, 3; TREA-2; WHI; in his Naked Masks, Everyman's Lib., Dutton, 1952.

Six characters are abandoned by Piradello because they won't behave as he has planned; they insist on acting a play he doesn't wish to write. So they drift into a theatre and demand that the di-rector let them act. They put on a play in which the husband per-mits his wife to elope with his secretary; then he lives to behold the outcome 20 years later, when his wife's offspring suffers disgrace and death. The director finds their play is terrible and shoos them out of the theatre; "Bring on," he says, " 'The Bride's Revenge'--that's what the people want. "

2 acts; 10 men, 10 women; 1 interior.

_____. Tonight We Improvise (1930). Translated by Marta Abba. Samuel French.

This play encompasses many of the dramatic techniques ori-ginated by Pirandello: direct address, improvisations, and in-and-out-of-character speeches. The play within the improvisation con-

cerns the wooing of a wife by a man who finds her bizarre family
quite a revelation.   The players actually live their parts, as the
drama, which includes narration, interludes, mime, film, and song
unfolds.
    Approximately 50 characters; 1 interior, 1 exterior.   Royal-
ty: $50-25.

PLAUTUS, Titus Maccius.   The Braggart Soldier (205 B. C.).   Trans-
    lated by Erich Segal.   Samuel French.
    A vain braggart of a soldier receives a fitting punishment in
this comedy.   He has kidnapped a beautiful girl, but her lover
manages a rescue.   Then they bamboozle the lecherous braggart into thinking that the girl next door is madly in love with him.   The
girl, a prostitute hired for the job, instead rejects him completely.
    6 men, 3 women; 1 interior.   Royalty: $25-20.

_____.   The Captives (ca. 190 B. C.).   Tr. by Nixon in Loeb Li-
    brary; tr. by Riley in Bohn's; tr. by Sugden, Sonnenschein,
    1873; CIF-1; MAU; DUC.
    Hegio had two sons.   The elder, Tyndarus, was stolen when
4 years old by a slave, Stalagmus, sold in Elis, where he grew up
as a slave to Philocrates.   During a war, both were captured.   The
younger son, Philopolemus, during the same war, was captured by
the Eleans and held by the father of Philocrates.   Hegio buys the
two war captives in the hope of ransoming his son.   Philocrates and
Tyndarus exchange places in the hope that the slave might escape.
Hegio ransoms his son and sends the supposed slave (really Philocrates) to negotiate the exchange, meantime in anger sending Tyndarus to the quarries.   Philocrates returns with Stalagmus who identifies the real Tyndarus, who is now welcomed as Hegio's long-lost
son.
    1 continuous act; 8 men, 1 boy, 0 women; 1 exterior.

_____.   The Pot of Gold (ca. 200 B. C.).   Tr. by Nixon in Loeb
    Library; tr. by Riley in Bohn's; tr. by Rogers as The Crock of
    Gold in his Three Plays, Routledge, & Dutton, 1925; tr. by Sug-
    den, Sonnenschein, 1873; tr. by Bennett in CLS; DUC; STA.
    An aged miser, Euclio, finds a pot of gold buried by his
grandfather.   He becomes so fearful lest he be robbed of it that he
re-buries it deeper and keeps a worried watch over it.   His elderly
neighbor is promised to his daughter Phaedra and a wedding feast is
under way.   But Phaedra is in love with young Lyconides, whose
slave Strobilus finds the pot of gold.   With this in hand, he forces
Euclio to give both his daughter and the gold to him, much to Euclio's relief.
    5 acts; 8 men, 3 women, extras; 1 exterior.

_____.   The Twins (ca. 200 B. C.).   Tr. by Nixon in Loeb Li-
    brary; HUD; tr. by Riley in Bohn's; tr. by Clark, French; tr.
    by Thornton & Warner in SMR; tr. anon. in TRE-2 (v. 2);
    TREA-1; DUC.
    One of twin boys, Menaechmus (I), had been stolen as a lad.
The other, originally Sosicles, had been given his name (Menaech-

mus (II) and lives with his wife in Epidamnus. When Menaechmus I arrives, he is mistaken for Menaechmus II, offered hospitality by his brother's mistress, reprimanded by his brother's wife, and chided by his brother's parasite. He feigns madness to get rid of them, a doctor intervenes, but the brothers finally meet and find they are the long-separated twins.

>1 continuous act, or in 5 scenes; 7 men, 2 women; 1 exterior (a street).

PLAYFAIR, Nigel. R. U. R. See entry under Capek, Karel.

POLLOCK, Channing. The Enemy (1925). Brentano, 1926; Longmans, 1927; abridged in Mantle 1925/26.

>Carl Behrend, the son of a war profiteer, is drafted into the Austrian army in World War I, leaving his bride of a month, Pauli, with her father, a pacifist university professor. On the eve of his homecoming Carl is killed. Hate is the real enemy of man; banish hatred, and greed and wars would cease.

>4 acts; 7 men, 3 women; 1 interior.

_____. The Fool (1922). Samuel French.

>Daniel Gilchrist, a young idealistic minister in a wealthy parish, attempts to answer the question: What would happen if anybody really tried to live like Christ? He forfeits his church, his friends, and the girl he loves; even the poor he tries to serve betray and desert him, but he finds happiness and contentment in service. Presents many striking evils in the world today in sincere and dramatic situations, and depicts a fine ideal of living.

>4 acts; 13 men, 8 women, extras; 2 interiors. Royalty: $25-20.

PORTO-RICHE, Georges de. A Loving Wife (1891). Tr. by Crawford in DID.

>A middle-aged writer, Etienne, wearies of the passionate displays of affection by his younger wife, Germaine. He rather throws her into the arms of his artist friend, Pascal. Even though he knows of her infidelity, he cannot resist her physical attraction and asks that she stay with him. They must endure each other, though unhappy.

>3 acts; 2 men, 5 women; 1 interior.

PRIDEAUX, James. The Last of Mrs. Lincoln (1972). Dramatists Play Service.

>Deals with the unhappy life of Mary Todd Lincoln following her husband's assassination. Rumors persist that as a southerner she hampered the Union cause. She is unable to obtain a pension from Congress to meet her financial needs. Her favorite son (Tad) dies, and for a time she is institutionalized by her sole surviving son (Robert). Nevertheless, she is courageous, understanding and compassionate.

>9 men, 2 boys, 5 women; unit set. Royalty: $50-35.

PRIESTLEY, J. B. Dangerous Corner (1932). Samuel French.

After a dinner party, one of the guests chances to remark
that she had seen the musical cigarette box in the home of Martin
Chatfield, Mrs. Chatfield's brother-in-law, who had been murdered.
That was impossible, says Mrs. Chatfield; and out of this chance
remark most of the group are exposed as the rotters they are. If
this chance remark had passed unnoticed, the dangerous corner
would have been passed. So, by returning to the first scene in the
play, it is shown that, had these sleeping dogs of suspicion been
permitted to lie, there would have been no unpleasantness--nor any
play!

3 acts; 3 men, 4 women; 1 interior. Royalty: $25-20.

_____. An Inspector Calls (1947). Dramatists Play Service.
In an English city the Birling family is celebrating the engagement of the daughter, Sheila, to Gerald Croft when an inspector
calls. Gradually by pointed questions he relates each member of
comfortable group to the suicide of Eva Smith, though it had appeared
they had nothing to do with it. But the father had fired the girl,
Sheila was responsible for her dismissal from a store, Gerald had
toyed with her as Daisy Renton, Eric had gone home with her and
stolen money on account of an expected baby, and the mother
wouldn't let a Board help her. Just as they think they have been
fooled by a fake inspector, they learn that Eva Smith has really died
on her way to a hospital and a real inspector is on the way.

4 men, 3 women; 1 interior. Royalty: $50-25.

_____. Laburnum Grove (1933). Samuel French.
Living among the lower middleclass English suburbanites,
George Radfern frightens off prospective borrowers by admitting that
he was making his money by counterfeiting. Though they think he is
spoofing, he really was providing the paper for the banknotes, and
he deceives for a time even the Inspector from Scotland Yard.

6 men, 3 women; 1 interior. Royalty: $25-20.

_____. The Linden Tree (1947). Samuel French.
When a college professor reaches retirement age, everyone
urges him to leave his gloomy academic surroundings and go off to
live comfortably. Not only do his wife and children want him to
leave; so does the university administration, which dislikes his edu-
cational views. He fights all of them; and even when most of his
work is taken away, he plans to stay on and teach those students
who continue to come to him.

4 men, 6 women; 1 interior. Royalty: $50-25.

_____. A Severed Head. See entry under Murdoch, Iris.

_____. Time and the Conways (1937). Samuel French.
During a family party to celebrate her 21st birthday and
while charades are being acted, Kay Conway dreams what will happen to the other five members of her family. In Act 2 she sees
them 20 years hence, each a failure: petty, mean, with unfulfilled
ambitions and a bitter outlook. This vision depresses her, but her
calm brother Alan assures her that time is purely relative and that

there is something fine and worthwhile beyond.
    3 acts; 4 men, 6 women; 1 interior. Royalty: $25-20.

_____. When We Are Married (1938). Samuel French.
        A young church organist, faced with a father's objections to
the attention he is paying his daughter, reverses the situation with
a surprising revelation in this comedy. Gerald, the organist, is
courting Nancy, Alderman Helliwell's daughter, and the Alderman
doesn't think much of Gerald's mixing romance and music. When
he comes to tell Gerald to stick to the organ, however, Gerald
shocks the Alderman with the news that the parson is not qualified
to perform marriages. This means that three of the most respected
families in the village are not really married. With this information
Gerald forces the villagers out of their smug, condescending attitude
and gains permission to marry Nancy.
        7 men, 7 women; 1 interior. Royalty: $25-20.

PURDY, James. Malcolm. See entry under Albee, Edward.

PUSHKIN, Alexandr S. Boris Godunov (1825). Tr. by Hayes,
    Lond., Kegan Paul, & Dutton, 1918.
        After Godunov became Czar (1598-1605) he lived in terror
that some usurper would take it from him. The grim Boris treats
his children with kindness but the common people in quite a different
key. He is suspected of having murdered Czarevitch Dimitri, son
of Ivan the Terrible. A young monk, Gregory, pretends he is Dimitri, heads up an uprising, is acclaimed by the people, and leads
an attack on Boris. Before the contest is decided, Godunov dies,
half insane.
        24 scenes (acts not indicated); 24 men, 5 women, extras;
        interior & exterior scenes; costumes of the period.

RABE, David. Sticks and Bones (1969, 1972). Samuel French.
        The setting is an American middleclass home in 1968. Oz-
zie, the father, is a hypocrite and a failure. Harriet, the mother,
is religious, racist, and willing to push anyone into her image of
how she wants people to be. The sons are coincidentally named
Rick and David--the latter home from the Viet Nam War, newly
blind, but perceptive to middleclass ways and values. Finally, Oz-
zie, Harriet, and Rick get together to help David commit suicide.
        5 men, 2 women; 1 interior. Royalty: $50-35.

_____. Streamers (1976). Samuel French.
        Three soldiers share a barracks room on a Virginia military
base: Billy, a straight middle American; Roger, a black; and
Richie, a homosexual. The three suffer from personal stresses, but
can get along peacefully together. With the addition of an angry
black street dude named Carlyle, everything falls apart. Carlyle is
strung so tight that when he turns loose in the final scene he kills
Billy and a sergeant with his knife.
        11 men (2 blacks); 1 interior. Royalty: $50-35.

RACINE, Jean. Andromaque (1667). Tr. by Boswell in his Dra-

matic Works, Bell (Bohn edn.), 1889, v. 1; also in Clark, W.
S.; tr. by Henderson in Six Plays by Corneille & Racine,
Modern Lib., 1931; tr. by Lockert, Princeton, 1936.

Pyrrhus (also called Neoptolemus), the son of Achilles, falls
in love with Andromache, who is now his captive after the fall of
Troy. Andromache is still devoted to her dead Hector and her living son Astyanax. Pyrrhus neglects Hermione, his affianced bride,
and threatens to kill Astyanax if Andromache does not marry him;
so she promises, intending to kill herself after the ceremony.
Orestes comes to love Hermione; and she, tortured by love and hate,
says she will marry him if he kills the faithless Pyrrhus. After he
does so, Hermione kills herself on Pyrrhus' dead body, and Orestes
goes insane.
    5 acts; 4 men, 4 women, extras; 1 interior (hall in Pyrrhus'
    palace); Greek costumes.

_____. Athalie (1691). Tr. by Boswell in his Dramatic Works,
    Bell (Bohn edn.), 1890, v. 2; KRE; tr. by Henderson & Landis,
    Modern Lib., 1931; tr. by Lockert, Princeton, 1936.

Athaliah, daughter of Jezebel and like her, and a follower of
Baal, dreams she will be killed by a child, whom she later identifies
as Joash. She believes she has killed all the sons of her son Aha-
ziah. But Jehosheba, the wife of the High Priest Jehoiada, has saved
and guarded Joash for six years. At the age of seven he is crowned
King of Judah. Athalia tries to get him out of the way or to kill
him, but he is protected by the Levites, and Athaliah is killed as she
leaves the temple.
    5 acts; 11 men, 4 women, extras; 1 exterior (court of the
    temple); costumes of the period.

_____. Bérénice (1670). Tr. by Boswell in his Dramatic Works,
    Bell (Bohn edn.), 1889; CLF-2; STA; adapted by Masefield in
    Esther and Bérénice. Lond., Heinemann, & Macmillan, 1922.

The beautiful but sensuous daughter of Agrippa has become
the mistress of the Emperor Titus, but the people of Rome demand
that he renounce his passion for her. In the conflict of love and
honor, duty to the State triumphs. He sends Antiochus to command
her to leave the city; he also comes under her spell. She leaves
them both.
    5 acts; 5 men, 2 women; 1 interior; costumes of the period.

_____. Esther (1689). Tr. by Boswell in his Dramatic Works,
    Bell (Bohn edn) 1890, v. 2; adapted by Masefield in Esther and
    Bérénice, Lond., Heinemann, & Macmillan, 1922.

King Ahasuerus, urged on by Haman, orders the slaughter of
all the Jews, not knowing that his queen Esther is a Jewess. Esther
saves her people and discloses the treachery of Haman. Mordecai,
her uncle, is put in Haman's place. Brings in the episode of honoring Mordecai with Haman leading him through the city.
    3 acts; 5 men, 4 women, extras; 2 interiors, 1 exterior;
    costumes of the period. (An all-girl cast is possible.)

_____. Iphigénie (1674). Tr. by Boswell in his Dramatic Works,

Bell (Bohn edn.), 1890, v. 2.

Iphigenia, the frail lovely daughter of Agamemnon, affianced to Achilles, must be sacrificed at Aulis so that the Greek forces may sail. Her father tries to avoid the sacrifice by warning her not to come, but it is too late. She arrives at the camp with Eriphyle, who also wishes to have Achilles. Instead of a wedding, the sacrifice is to be offered. When Eriphyle kills herself, she is accepted by the seer, Calchas, as the victim demanded by the gods, because her name is also Iphigenia.

5 acts; 5 men, 5 women, extras; scenes in and before the tent; costumes of the period.

_____. Mithridate (1673). Tr. by Boswell in his Dramatic Works, Bell (Bohn edn.) 1890, v. 2; tr. by Spoerl, Tufts College, 1926.

When Mithridates, King of Pontus, sworn enemy of Rome, has not returned from an expedition, his two sons, untrustworthy Pharnaces and gallant Xiphares, aim to seize the throne. Both become attached to Monima, the King's betrothed. After his return, Mithridates plans to march against Rome; Pharnaces opposes the plan, Xiphares favors it. Mithridates is defeated and fatally wounded; before his death he sanctions the union of Xiphares to Monima.

5 acts; 5 men, 2 women, extras; various scenes in the palace; costumes of the period.

_____. Phèdre (1677). Tr. by Boswell in his Dramatic Works, Bell (Bohn edn.), 1890, v. 2; CAR; HARC-26; MAU; MIL; SMP; tr. by Henderson in Six Plays by Corneille & Racine, Modern Lib., 1931; same in TRE-1, & 2 (v. 2); TREA-1; tr. by Lockert, Princeton, 1936. Acting edition: Samuel French. Tr. in alexandrine couplets by William Packard.

Phaedra, wife of Theseus, confesses to her old nurse, Oenone, her love for her stepson, Hippolytus, which he does not return, since he is in love with Aricia. Theseus, falsely reported dead, returning, is told by the nurse that Hippolytus had made advances to Phaedra. Hippolytus decides to flee into exile with Aricia, but is dragged to death by his horses. Oenone drowns herself, and Phaedra takes poison after exonerating Hippolytus.

5 acts; 3 men, 5 women, extras; 1 interior; costumes of the Greeks. (S. French Royalty: $35-25.)

RAND, Ayn. Night of January Sixteenth (1935). David McKay.

Karen Andre is being tried for the murder of Bjorn Faulkner, for whom she was secretary before his marriage to Nancy Lee Whitfield. A body of a man, after being shot, has fallen or been pushed from a penthouse parapet. The prosecution calls it murder, the defense claims it was suicide; but Larry Regan testifies the body was not Faulkner's, that he escaped but later crashed in an airplane, that Karen was party to this escape and was to join him in South America. The jury in the play is impanelled from the audience and is asked to bring in a verdict: if guilty, she will get a new trial; if not guilty, she goes free.

3 acts; 11 men, 10 women; 1 interior (the courtroom).
Royalty: $25.

RANDALL, Bob. 6 Rms Riv Vu (1970). Samuel French.
     A man and a woman who have never met before find that
they are locked in the vacant apartment with a river view they have
been inspecting as prospective tenants. Both are happily married,
young and attractive, and find one another interesting.
     4 men, 4 women; 1 interior. Royalty: $50-35.

RANDOLPH, Clemence. Rain. See entry under Colton, John R.

RAPHAELSON, Samson. Accent on Youth (1934). Samuel French.
     A middle-aged playwright, Stephen, works harmoniously with
his young secretary, Linda. He stands aside for Dickie and even
helps him with his courting. But Linda wearies of the strenuous
youth; she returns to Stephen and marries him.
     3 acts; 6 men, 3 women; 1 interior. Royalty: $35-25.

_____. Jason (1942). Dramatists Play Service.
     A conservative dramatic critic, Jason is upset when Mike
Ambler comes into his life to make him enjoy it more. Mike is
also attracted to Jason's wife, but she comes to realize Jason's
worth. Called on to review Mike's new play, shall Jason praise it,
or damn it? He finds he can realize what is good and detect what
is immature, and thus his spiritual education is complete.
     3 acts; 7 men, 4 women; 1 interior. Royalty: $35-25.

_____. The Jazz-Singer (1925). Samuel French.
     Rather than follow his father as cantor, Jakie Rabinowitz
runs away at 15 to sing jazz. As Jack Robin he returns to New
York to make his successful debut in a big revue, greeted by his
mother with love, by his father with suspicion. During the dress
rehearsal he learns that his father is too ill to sing at the Day of
Atonement--a date not missed in five generations. Torn by conflicting emotions, he finally hearkens to the call of race and quits
the show to sing as cantor.
     3 acts; 14 men, 3 women, extras; 2 interiors. Royalty on
application.

_____. Skylark (1939). Dramatists Play Service.
     Too absorbed in his advertising business, Tony even puts it
ahead of a proper celebration of his tenth wedding anniversary. His
wife Lydia, the skylark, rebels and walks out on him, threatening
divorce. His friends advise meeting the situation by starting all
over again, giving up his job, and selling the house. A wonderful
week of enjoyment follows. Then Tony is offered a splendid position,
which he now pretends he doesn't want. Lydia realizes how he has
worked to deceive her and joins him as he goes to accept the new
position.
     3 acts; 6 men, 4 women; 1 interior. Royalty: $25.

RASPANTI, Celeste. I Never Saw Another Butterfly (1971). Dramatic Publishing Company.

This play deals with a real place: Terezin, a castle outside of Prague which was used by the Nazis as a concentration camp for Jewish children of Prague before they were shipped to the gas chambers of Auschwitz. Of the 15,000 Jewish children who passed through Terezin, only about a hundred were still alive when the castle was liberated by the allies. One of the survivors, Raja, is the central character. She taught the children of Terezin when there was nothing to teach with, gave them hope at a time when there was little reason to hope, created a world for them of laughter, flowers, and butterflies--their symbol of life and defiance.

4 men, 7 women; simple set. Royalty: $35.

RATTIGAN, Terence. Deep Blue Sea (1952). Samuel French.

Described by the Herald-Tribune as "Probing, literate, and meticulously written," this drama tells the story of a woman determined to face up to what she has done. She had left her upright husband and nice home to live with her charming, but incorrigible lover. When the lover leaves her, she tries to escape by committing suicide. A neighbor saves her, however. Then her husband entreats her to come home, but she must face up to decisions, so she rejects his offer and goes to find her lover.

5 men, 3 women; 1 interior. Royalty: $50-25.

_____. French Without Tears (1936). Samuel French.

Several young Englishmen are studying French in the south of France. A fellow-student is frivolous Diana Lake, sexy and flirtatious, who plays with each in turn only to turn the last one over to any newcomer. The victims conspire to teach Diana a lesson by individually ditching her. She is hurt, but immediately lays plans to subjugate Lord Heybook who is on his way. On his arrival he is discovered to be a sturdy lad of 11 years.

7 men, 3 women; 1 interior. Royalty: $25-20.

_____. Man and Boy (1963). Samuel French.

An international financier finds that his empire is crumbling around him. His big merger with an American oil company has hit a snag following a financial investigation. At the time his indictment is announced he is arranging a meeting with the president of the other company, and he plans to sacrifice his son's reputation to save himself. His scheme backfires, however, and when his colleague and wife desert him he decides to kill himself.

5 men, 2 women; 1 interior. Royalty: $50-25.

_____. O Mistress Mine (1946). Samuel French.

Michael's mother, Olivia, is living in a house donated by Sir John Fletcher, a cabinet minister, who waits to be divorced from his wife until the war is over to avoid any embarrassment to the government. Michael is a young radical who objects to the arrangement and wants to save his mother. So he gets her to return to her own apartment; but he becomes reconciled when they propose going to a fancy restaurant so as to impress his snobbish flame, Sylvia.

2 men, 5 women; 2 interiors. Royalty: $50-25.

_____. Separate Tables (1954). Samuel French.
        Except for the two leading roles, the characters are the
same in this successful combination of two plays, "Tables by the
Window," and "Table Number Seven." Each play is set in the
lounge and dining area of a shabbily genteel hotel, and each tells
the story of a couple whose love is threatened. In each case, however, Miss Cooper, the hotel Manageress, comes to the rescue and
leads the couples in regaining their love.
        3 men, 8 women; 2 sets. Royalty: $50-25.

_____. The Winslow Boy (1946). Dramatists Play Service.
        Innocent Ronnie Winslow is expelled from an English school
for an alleged theft. His father challenges the right of the Royal
Naval Academy to do this without a trial; and the case is carried
up to the House of Commons. Sir Robert Morton defends Ronnie;
the Admiralty withdraws the case and Ronnie is exonerated. Right
is done, but during the process the family is faced with social ostracism and economic ruin.
        2 acts; 7 men, 4 women; 1 interior. Royalty: $50-25.

RAY, Nicholas. Rebel Without a Cause. See entry under Sergel,
    Clark F.

REACH, James. David and Lisa (1967). Adapted from the book by
    Theodore Isaac Rubin and the screenplay by Eleanor Perry.
    Samuel French.
        Tells the story of David and Lisa, two mentally disturbed
teen-agers. David, the only son of wealthy parents, has a mania
against being touched. Lisa, who has never known parental love,
has a split personality: one Lisa only speaks in childish rhymes
and insists upon being spoken to in the same manner. The play
follows them, and others, through their progress with psychiatrists
at Berkley School, and through their retrogressions.
        11 men, 11 women; drapes and representational props.
        Royalty: $35-25.

_____. Dear Phoebe. See entry under Taggart, Tom.

_____. For the Defense (1967). Samuel French.
        In this courtroom drama, the audience as a whole becomes
the jury at the end of the play and determines the guilt or innocence
of the defendant. The defendant in this case is Lucky Sam Luckey,
boss racketeer, who has been accused of shooting Marvin Stump.
The prosecuting attorney has only skimpy evidence to work with, but
he is confident of obtaining a conviction on the basis of Luckey's
shady reputation. The defense attorney, flamboyant Russell Holloway,
does his best to keep the trial focused on the present charge. A
final witness turns the case topsy-turvy.
        8 men, 7 women; 1 interior. Royalty: $25-20.

REAVEY, Jean. American Kaleidoscope. See entry under Palmer,
    Winthrop.

REDGRAVE, Michael. The Aspern Papers (1959). Adapted from
    Henry James' story. Samuel French.
        This intellectual mystery begins with a 90-year-old woman
and her niece living in seclusion in a once-palacial home in Venice.
Because they are poor, an American publisher convinces them to
lease some rooms to him. His apparent purpose is to write in their
garden, but his real purpose is to dig out the mystery of a brilliant
writer who once loved the aunt but who has been dead for years.
The renter is convinced that the writer will one day rise from ob-
scurity to fame, and he is in search of more of his letters, writings
and biography. The old aunt, however, rejects all inquiries into the
past. One night the young writer finds a trunk and is pilfering in it
when the old woman discovers him. She throws herself upon the
trunk, suffers a stroke and dies. After the funeral the young writer
returns to find the niece all alone. Pathetically she proposes to him.
He asks for the papers, but she says she has burned them. He rejects her. Then, truly alone, she locks the house and burns the
papers in the trunk one by one.
        2 men, 1 woman; 1 interior. Royalty: $50-25.

REED, Mark. Petticoat Fever (1935). Samuel French.
        A wireless operator in Labrador, Dascome Dinsmore, has
had no contact with people for months, and he is bored. Down drops
Sir James and his fiancee Ethel, en route to Montreal but forced to
land. While awaiting rescue, Dascome tries to entertain and makes
feverish advances to Ethel. Then his discarded sweetheart arrives,
and in the end Dascome wins Ethel and Sir James gets Clara.
        6 men, 4 women; 1 interior. Royalty: $25-20.

_____. Yes, My Darling Daughter (1937). Samuel French.
        Ellen's mother had campaigned for women's rights twenty-five
years before in Greenwich Village. Now Ellen, just out of college,
quotes her mother's writings to justify a farewell weekend trip with
Douglas, who is leaving for two years. After a farewell fling she
agrees to marry the young man.
        3 men, 4 women; 2 interiors (1 possible). Royalty: $35-25.

REGAN, Sylvia. The Fifth Season (1953). Samuel French.
        The plush office of partners in the clothing business is all
show. There are beautiful models, beautiful furnishings, but no
business. Bankruptcy is always just around the corner, but the two
will hock anything to put up a good front for a buyer. Finally it is
the models, and not the clothes, that pull the partners out of the
hole, and the fast life that comes with being successful nearly wrecks
the younger of the two.
        6 men, 7 women; 1 interior. Royalty: $50-25.

REINER, Carl. Enter Laughing. See entry under Stein, Joseph.

RESNIK, Muriel. Any Wednesday (1964). Dramatists Play Service.
        A young businessman is looking for the millionaire corporation
president that he sold his factory to (the millionaire has ordered the
factory closed to take advantage of a tax benefit for himself). A
new secretary directs the young man to the executive suite, but all

he finds there is the wealthy man's mistress (this is Wednesday,
and she's waiting for her sugar-daddy). Next comes the president's
wife, looking for her husband and believing merely that the young
man and woman are a married couple. Then the millionaire arrives,
who doesn't know what's going on.
    2 men, 2 women; 1 interior. Royalty: $50-25.

RICE, Elmer. The Adding Machine (1923). Samuel French.
    A powerful satire on the modern mechanistic world. Mr.
Zero, an overworked, underpaid bookkeeper, kills his boss in a
rage because he is being fired after 25 years to be replaced by an
adding machine. After his trial and execution he goes to the Elysian
Fields, where he is joined by his co-worker Dorthea, who committed
suicide after Zero's death. Zero vows to leave the Fields when he
discovers that he and Dorthea, who are in love, could live together
without being married. He remains hopelessly insignificant even in
heaven, and his servile soul is sent back to earth to become an even
greater mechanical slave.
    14 men, 9 women; 5 interiors, 2 exteriors. Royalty: $50-25.

_____, with Philip Barry. Cock Robin (1928). Samuel French.
    During rehearsals at the local Little Theatre, Hancock Robin-
son becomes disliked; in the duel scene at the performance he is
shot with the stage pistol which actually kills him. At the same moment he is stabbed in the back. The murder is solved and justified
because of Robinson's insulting treatment of a young lady in the cast.
    3 acts; 8 men, 4 women; 2 interiors (1 possible). Royalty:
$50-25.

_____. Counsellor-At-Law (1931). Samuel French.
    An East-side New York Jewish boy, George Simon, rises to
a commanding position as a criminal lawyer. A breach of ethics
during his climb catches up with him, and he is on the verge of dis-
barment. He is ready to commit suicide, but is thwarted by his
ever faithful Jewish secretary, in whom he finds real love and understanding in contrast to his Gentile wife.
    3 acts; 19 men, 9 women; 2 interiors. Royalty: $50-25.

_____. Cue for Passion (1958). Dramatists Play Service.
    Transposes the Hamlet legend to contemporary California.
A wealthy widow has recently remarried. Her new husband is the
only witness to the fatal accident which took the life of her former
husband. Her son, a college senior, returns home from a trip to
the Far East, and is determined to investigate closely his father's
death and his mother's hasty marriage. Like Hamlet, he disturbs
his mother's household and brings despair to his sweetheart and best
friend. His wild convictions are reported to those nearest him, but
their full implications are not revealed until the end of the play.
    4 men, 3 women; 1 interior. Royalty: $50-25.

_____. Dream Girl (1945). Dramatists Play Service.
    The imaginative Georgina, who runs a bookstore, has roman-
tic daydreams involving a series of men and women: a doctor, a

book reviewer, her sister, and others.
        25 men (some doubling possible), 7 women; 3 interiors, 1 ex-
terior (all suggestive rather than realistic). Royalty: $50-
25.

_____. Flight to the West (1940). Dramatists Play Service.
        On a plane flight from Lisbon to Bermuda during World War
II the passengers present a cross-section of the warring elements in
Europe and America, showing the antagonisms and convictions, the
problems of spying, appeasement, and persecution, and ending with
the discovery and detainment of a Nazi spy.
        3 acts; 16 men, 5 women; 1 interior. Royalty: $35-25.

_____. The Grand Tour (1951). Dramatists Play Service.
        Nell Valentine, a middle-aged schoolteacher, for the first
time in her life falls desperately in love during the course of a summer tour through Europe. Then the man she is in love with tells
her he is already married and that he is a fugitive from justice.
Nell is still willing to marry him, but his wife appears on the scene.
In parting, the schoolteacher offers to help both of them in any way
she can. In the last scene Nell is showing slides of her trip to her
students. Her superficial comments on her travels have undertones
of pathetic personal experiences. She is not bitter, however; rather
she is more mature and understanding.
        6 men, 3 women; various interiors and exteriors suggested
by backdrops. Royalty: $50-25.

_____. The Iron Cross (1915). Dramatists Play Service.
        One of the earliest plays about World War I, dealing with the
brutality and stupidity of war. The Dreiers, William and Margaret,
have a small farm in East Prussia. Brother Paul has already died
a hero, and now William and his friend Karl are called into the army. Soon Karl returns, blind, and Margaret carries on valiantly by
caring for the sick, the injured, and those dispossessed by war. By
the time her husband returns, wounded and ragged, Margaret has become the unwilling mother of a Cossack officer's child. William
leaves to seek restitution from his government but returns, empty
handed, realizing that Margaret struggled to preserve life while he
attempted to destroy it.
        6 men, 1 boy, 5 women, 1 girl; 1 interior. Royalty: $25.

_____. Not for Children (1935). Samuel French.
        The author's philosophy of the theater is explained by a group
described as expert lecturers in this comedy. They illustrate their
discussions with blackouts and vaudeville skits. In the process they
take tongue-in-cheek pokes at playwrights, producers, actors,
critics, backers and audiences.
        7 men, 5 women; bare stage. Royalty: $50-25.

_____. On Trial (1914). In his Seven Plays, Viking, 1950;
    CARC; abridged in Mantle & Sherwood, 1909-19.
        As incidents are uncovered by the testimony at the trial, they
are presented in acted form, similar to cut-backs in motion pictures.

In this way the events work backward until the mystery is cleared up.

> 4 acts with 11 scenes; 15 men, 4 women, and a jury of 12 men; 5 interiors.

_____. Street Scene (1929). Samuel French.

Pulitzer prize play, 1929. A panorama of the comedy and tragedy of daily life in front of a New York tenement. The wife of a theatrical scene-shifter has a sordid affair with the milkman. Her husband returns and kills them both. This crystalizes the viewpoint and shows the very human reactions of the entire neighborhood, as it touches every tenant indirectly.

> 3 acts; 16 men, 11 women, extras; 1 exterior. Royalty: $50-25.

_____. Two on an Island (1940). Dramatists Play Service.

Two young people, John from Iowa, Mary from New Hampshire, arrive in New York on the same day and seek a place in the world of the great city. Their paths cross several times, and when John is about to depart, discouraged, they decide to stick it out together. Presents many vignettes of life in Manhattan--the Bagdad on Hudson of O. Henry.

> 11 scenes; 38 speaking parts, only a few long ones; several stylized scenes; Royalty: $35-25.

_____. We the People (1933). Coward, 1933.

The depression has had tragic effect on the Davis family: it loses its home; William, the father, a foreman, loses his job and is shot during a strike; the daughter, Helen, a school teacher, hasn't been paid for months and can't marry her fiancé; the son, Allan, who was to go to college, is arrested for stealing coal, becomes a radical pacifist, and is convicted on a trumped-up charge of murdering a policeman. By contrast, some capitalists are pictured: the wealthy banker, the pompous university president, the unctuous Senator--many who talk much about suppressing agitators and such.

> 21 scenes; 33 men, 11 women; 12 interiors, 3 exteriors.

RICHARDSON, Howard and William Berney. Dark of the Moon (1945). Samuel French.

A mountain witch-boy sees the beautiful Barbara Allen and promptly falls in love with her. However, he is allowed to assume human form and marry her only if she remains faithful. After the marriage Barbara gives birth to a witch child. In the frenzy of a religious revival Barbara is led to betray her husband, resulting in her death and his return to the world of the mountain witches.

> 28 roles; various scenes. Royalty: $50-35.

RICHMAN, Arthur. Ambush (1921). Duffield, 1922; abridged in Mantle 1921/22.

A clerk, Walter, tries to live within his moderate income. His daughter, Margaret, wants pretty clothes and accepts gifts from richer men but deceives her father and mother about them. Walter

loses out on his investments and his job.   He confesses himself
beaten and accepts money to pay the rent from his daughter's current lover.   Circumstances of life lie in ambush to prevent him
from living an upright decent life.
    3 acts; 7 men, 3 women; 1 interior.

RIGGS, Lynn.   Green Grow the Lilacs (1930).   Samuel French.
    A Western pioneer play later developed into the musical
comedy "Oklahoma!" by Oscar Hammerstein II.   Laurey loves Curley the cowhand and is afraid of the dark-minded ranch hand Jeeter,
with whom she goes to the dance.   In the course of the shivaree
following her marriage with Curley, Jeeter is killed.
    6 scenes; 10 men, 4 women, extras; 6 exteriors; costumes
    of the Southwest.

_____. Roadside (1930).   Samuel French.
    In the Indian Territory before it became Oklahoma, Hannie,
a strapping hearty girl and her father (a tumbleweed) stop in their
covered wagon and make camp by the side of the road.   Along
comes Buzzie, her divorced husband, to plead with her to come
back.   But Texas, a tall-talking big man, has fallen for Hannie;
meantime the Law wants Texas for disorderliness; he staves them
off--the road is between--and the covered wagon plunges away.
Pictures the conflict between free spirits and law and order.
    3 acts; 8 men, 2 women; 1 interior, 1 exterior; costumes of
    the period there (1905).   Royalty: $25-20.

_____. Russet Mantle (1936).   Samuel French.
    On a ranch near Santa Fé, Kay is restless, unhappy, and
headstrong.   Along comes John Galt, a young poet on a tramp.   He
is given work and they are attracted; they are disgusted with the
failures of the older generation and express their freedom with the
usual biological result.   But John Brings Kay around to reality, and
helps others in the family to readjust their disappointed lives.
    3 acts; 6 men, 5 women; 1 interior, 1 exterior.   Royalty:
    $35.

_____. Sump'n Like Wings (pub. 1928).   Samuel French.
    Rebelling against the too strict bringing-up by her mother,
Willie Baker runs away and into adventures as she struggles to find
the meaning of her own life.   She returns home in disgrace; but is
inspired by her uncle to face life fighting.
    4 acts; 8 men, 6 women; 4 interiors.   Royalty: $25.

RILEY, Lawrence.   Personal Appearance (1934).   Samuel French,
    1934.
    The motion picture star, Carole Arden, with her manager, is
making personal appearances to promote her play.   She flirts with
the good-looking youth at the filling station and guest house where
they are stalled, and even suggests that he go with her to Hollywood.
But the manager (who is with her to keep her out of mischief) nips
this plan as they leave for her next appearance.
    3 acts; 4 men, 6 women; 3 interiors.   Royalty: $35-25.

RINEHART, Mary Roberts and Avery Hopwood. The Bat (1920). Samuel French.

Four people are after the money, missing from a dead banker's bank, which may be hidden in a secret chamber in his house. Cornelia Van Gorder, a determined lady of 60, has rented the house for the summer and despite threats and mysterious happenings refuses to move.

3 acts; 7 men, 3 women; 2 interiors. Royalty: $25-20.

ROBERTSON, Thomas W. Caste (1867). Roorbach, 1890; French #380; Baker, 1913; in Heath's Belles Lettres ser., 1905; in his Principal Dramatic Works, Lond., Low, 1889, v. 1; COD; COT; DUR; MAP; MAT; MOSO; TAU.

A ballet girl, Esther Eccles, marries the Hon. George D'Alroy, to the great annoyance of his rather arrogant mother, who will scarcely admit the existence of Esther's father and Sam Gerridge. George is reported killed in battle, but returns to rescue his wife and child from poverty and social snobbery.

3 acts; 4 men, 3 women; 2 interiors; costumes of 1860's.

_____. David Garrick (1864). Penn Pub. Co., 1903; French & Dramatic Pub. Co. carried; in his Principal Dramatic Works, Lond., Low, 1889, v. 1.

David Garrick has promised Ada's father to cure her of her infatuation for him, although he finds that she is the girl in his audience who has inspired him. He keeps his word by acting like a drunken boor at dinner in order to disgust her, but the scheme is disclosed and they are married with the father's blessing--hat in hand.

3 acts; 8 men, 3 women; 2 interiors; costumes of the period.

_____. Society (1865). Lond., Lacy, 18--; in his Principal Dramatic Works, Lond., Low, 1889, v. 2; BAT v. 16; RUB.

A poor but honest gentleman, Sidney Daryl, wins the love of Maud Hetherington and a seat in Parliament over his wealthy rival, John Chodd, Jr. whose father thinks money can buy anything, even a place in society. Before Sidney inherits his brother's estate he has a chance to compare his impecunious artistic friend with the men encountered at clubs and dinners.

3 acts; 16 men, 4 women; 4 interiors, 2 exteriors; costumes of the period.

ROBINSON, Bertrand. Tommy. See entry under Lindsay, Howard.

_____. Your Uncle Dudley. See entry under Lindsay, Howard.

ROBINSON, Lennox. The Far-Off Hills (1928). Samuel French.

Sober-minded Marian plans to become a nun after she gets her blind father settled and her two sisters educated and matched off. A melancholy man, Harold, with an insane wife, persistently woos her. When at last she is free, she loses her interest in the convent and in Harold, and marries another.

3 acts; 5 men, 5 women; 2 interiors. Royalty: $25-20.

_____. Is Life Worth Living? (1933). Samuel French.
A certain type of modern drama is amusingly satirized in
this play described by its author as an "exaggeration." Modern,
introspective drama often seems to present a rather hopeless view
of man's existence. The reactions of an unsophisticated audience
who takes plays of that type in all seriousness provide an interesting and amusing commentary.
8 men, 5 women; 1 interior. Royalty: $25-20.

_____. The White-Headed Boy (1916). Samuel French.
A doting mother and family have tried to make a genius out
of Denis, the youngest boy, their pet, but the hope of the family
turns out not to be "so different" after all. He fails in his medical
examination, he squanders his brother's money, he is self-satisfied
and irresponsible; they seem to have sacrificed themselves needless-
ly. Then Duffy demands payment for Denis' trifling with his daughter's affections, but when he finds that she is already married to
Denis, he gives them the money as a wedding present.
3 acts; 5 men, 7 women; 1 interior. Royalty: $50-25.

ROBLES, Emmanuel. Montserrat (1949). Adapted by Lillian Hellman. Dramatists Play Service.
During the revolution in Venezuela in 1812 led by the great
patriot Bolivar, the Spanish commander Izquiardo arrests Montserrat, a young Spanish officer who knows where Bolivar is hiding.
He tortures him mentally and spiritually by ordering six passersby
to be shot if he doesn't reveal the hiding place. They plead in vain
for their lives, but one of them realizes the ideals of freedom from
tyranny that Bolivar and Montserrat have. As word comes that
Bolivar has escaped, Montserrat goes willingly to his death.
2 acts; 15 men, 2 women; 1 interior. Royalty: $50-25.

ROGERS, David. F. L. I. P. P. E. D. (1971). Dramatic Publishing
Company.
This high school comedy takes on the women's liberation
movement (F. L. I. P. P. E. D. stands for Female Liberation Idealists'
Party for Permanent Equality and Democracy). Niki Pendleton has
joined F. L. I. P. P. E. D., and her mother is afraid her temperamental
father will find out. She sends Niki's older sisters to get Niki to
resign, but Niki talks them into joining. Finally mother joins herself, they all get arrested, and the resolution comes at a hearing
at Night Court.
17 men, 24 women (10m, 17w with doubling); simple set
pieces and props. Royalty: $35.

_____. Flowers for Algernon (1969). Based on the novel by
Daniel Keyes. Dramatic Publishing Company.
Experimental surgery on Algernon the mouse has increased
the creature's intelligence fourfold, so the technique is tried on
Charlie, a mentally retarded adult who rapidly changes from a
moron to a genius. At the peak of his brilliance Charlie is far
more intelligent than his teacher, with whom he is in love, and a
good deal smarter than the doctors who created the operating tech-

nique. Then Algernon shows signs of regression, and Charlie begins racing with time.
> 10 men, 17 women (8m and 9w with doubling); drapes with
> set pieces. Royalty: $50.

_____. Here and Now (1973). Dramatic Publishing Company.
A group of actors begins rehearsing a play based on an encounter group session made up of students, parents, and teachers.
The audience watches them rehearse and perform the play and sees
how their identification with the characters becomes stronger and
how the actors' own personal hangups begin to emerge until no one
knows for sure which is "play" and which is "reality." Neither
adults, teachers, nor students have a monopoly on contemporary
pressures and confusions.
> 6 men, 7 women, 3 parts for either; bare stage. Royalty:
> $35.

_____. If a Man Answers (1962). Based on the novel by Wini-
fred Wolfe. Dramatic Publishing Company.
Nineteen-year-old Chantal has a "proper" father from Boston
and an eccentric mother from Paris. When her father discovers
that she is engaged to three young Bostonians at the same time,
he moves the family to New York. There Chantal meets and marries a successful fashion photographer and follows her mother's
secret recipe for making a husband happy: Treat him like a dog.
She is doing fine until she shares the secret with Tina, an old Boston girlfriend, who promptly tells Chantal's husband and her father
about the dog manual method of training men. The men revolt, and
mama has to come up with some new tricks.
> 4 men, 9 women; 3 interiors. Royalty: $35.

_____. Rally 'Round the Flag, Boys! (1965). Adapted from Max
Shulman's novel. Dramatic Publishing Company.
Everyone objects when the U. S. Army decides to put a missile base in small town Putnam's Landing. Lt. Guido DiMaggio, a
home town boy, is appointed public relations officer to keep peace
between the military and civilians, but he can't even make peace
with Angela, his fiancée, a second-grade teacher in the local school.
To complicate matters, committee woman Grace Bannerman is determined to produce a pageant commemorating a Revolutionary War
battle. She forces the resentful town boys to play the Americans
and persuades the soldiers to play the British. The simulated battle, staged on July fourth, becomes a full-scale rumble, and in the
middle of the fireworks display a missile accidentally goes off.
> 20 characters or more; 1 set. Royalty: $35.

_____. Tell Me That You Love Me Junie Moon. See entry under
Kellogg, Helen.

_____. Tom Jones. See entry under Fielding, Henry.

ROLLAND, Romain. Danton (1900). Fourteenth of July (1902). Tr.
by Clark in his Fourteenth of July, & Danton, Holt, 1918.

Two French Revolution plays.

<u>Danton</u>: 3 acts; 13 men, 3 women, extras; 3 interiors; period costumes.

<u>14th of July</u>: 3 acts; 10 men, 4 women, extras; 3 exteriors; period costumes.

_____. <u>The Game of Love and Death</u> (1925). Tr. by Brooks, Holt, 1926.

A level-headed Girondist, Jerome, discovers that his young wife Sophie is harboring Claude Vallee, a fugitive, with whom she seems to be in love. Jerome secures passports for them, which he turns over to his wife and lover, and prepares to meet death. Sophie, inspired, sends Claude to freedom and remains to share her husband's fate.

3 acts; 8 men, 2 women, extras; 1 interior; costumes of the period.

_____. <u>The Wolves</u> (1898). Tr. by Clark, in <u>Drama</u>, v. 8, 1918; same, Random House, 1937. Acting ed., Dramatists Play Service.

Like a pack of wolves, the officers in the French Revolutionary army in Mayence are beset by personal quarrels, hates, jealousies, and suspicions. D'Oyron, an aristocrat, is accused by a spy's letter of being in the service of the enemy. He alleges a conspiracy, is defended by Teulier, but the generals refuse to listen and send him to the guillotine.

3 acts; 13 men, 0 women, extras; 1 interior; costumes of the period. Royalty: $25.

ROMAINS, Jules. <u>Doctor Knock</u> (1923). Tr. by Granville-Barker, Lond., 1925; French carried.

Depicts how an unlicensed doctor takes the place of old Doctor Parpalaid. The quack Dr. Knock builds up a lucrative practice by persuading the people that they are ill. Thus by creating unanimity of feeling that every healthy man is a potential patient, he bluffs his way.

3 acts; 8 men, 6 women; 2 interiors, 1 exterior.

ROMAN, Lawrence. <u>Under the Yum Yum Tree</u> (1961). Dramatists Play Service.

Hogan is ostensibly a good-hearted landlord. He rents one of his apartments at very reasonable rates to beautiful women. There are advantages to the arrangement: it gives Hogan the opportunity to lie, eavesdrop, peek through keyholes, use his passkey, and invent a mirror device with which to look in windows from a position on top of the roof. He becomes more than usually frustrated, however, when a beautiful Berkeley student moves in, and he discovers that she has invited her boyfriend to live with her (platonically, of course) in a kind of trial marriage. Though complications ensue, everything remains above board.

3 men, 2 women; 1 interior. Royalty: $50-25.

ROOS, William. <u>January Thaw</u> (1946). Adapted from Bellamy

Partridge's novel.   Dramatic Publishing Company.
The Gage family moves to an old farmhouse so that Mr.
Gage can have the peace he needs to write a "best seller." The
peace is short lived.   Jonathan Rockwood and his family, who according to an old deed have the right to live in the house, move in
too.   Neither family is able to turn the other out, and finally a
blizzard isolates them, all together, in the old house.   The electric
lines fail, the oil-burner and range refuse to work, and the Gages
breakfast on old cereal and olives.   From the old-fashioned Rock-
woods' rooms come the smell of coffee and ham and the warmth of
an old woodburner.   When the aroma of fresh biscuits reaches the
Gages, everyone deserts Mr. Gage.   It even looks like Barbara
Gage has eloped with the Rockwood boy.   But finally everything is
happily ended.
        7 men, 6 women; 1 interior.   Royalty: $35.

_____. Mrs. Mike (1972).   Adapted from the book by Nancy and
        Benedict Freedman.   Performance Publishing.
        A young Boston Irish girl named Kathy visits her uncle in
the north of Canada, falls in love and marries Mike, a Royal Canadian Mounted Policeman, and moves to his post in the frozen wilderness.   There she becomes involved with an Indian couple who
are in trouble with the law, loses her baby in a diphtheria epidemic,
and struggles to discover whether she can cope with the harsh realities of the cold land at Hudson's Hope.
        7 men, 8 women; 1 interior.   Royalty: $35.

ROSE, Reginald.   The Death and Life of Larry Benson (1960).
        Adapted by Kristin Sergel.   Dramatic Publishing Company.
        Larry Benson, reported missing in action three years ago,
is due home any moment, and his family and the town prepare to
give him a hero's welcome.   There are some problems to face,
however.   Larry's father had deserted his family but now insists
upon being home to receive his son.   Grace, Larry's sweetheart,
is now engaged to someone else.   When the car arrives, the soldier
who gets out is not Larry.   The soldier calls himself Larry and
recognizes the members of the family, Grace, and his first grade
teacher.   He even knows small, personal moments in the lives of
the family: he remembers the bad grade the teacher once gave
him, and he reminds Grace that he had to bend his class ring to
make it fit her finger.   Everyone waits for him to trip up on some
detail, but he never does.   Finally we understand who he is.
        5 men, 8 women; 1 interior.   Royalty: $25.

_____. Dino (1956).   Adapted by Kristin Sergel.   Dramatic
        Publishing Company.
        At the age of seventeen, Dino has already spent four years
behind bars.   He has just returned home from Reform School, and
his parents are totally inadequate to deal with him.   Dino's parole
officer, though, competent, but kind, takes the young man to a psy-
chotherapist for treatment.   Dino rejects the help, and his father
tells him not to go back because there aren't any "crazy people" in
the family.   Finally a sixteen-year-old girl is able to help him, but

when she discovers his background it appears she may reject him
too, and he almost joins a new gang. A serious play about the very
real problem of rehabilitating juvenile delinquents.
   7 men, 11 women, extras; 1 set. Royalty: $35.

_____. No Crime in the Streets (1966). Dramatic Publishing
 Company.
   Frank has dropped out of school. His intention was to earn
some quick money and make a good impression on the girl he cares
for. What he is able to achieve, though, is a low-paying part-time
job and too much time on his hands. Moreover, this girl friend's
father, a social worker, will be difficult to impress. When Frank
gets a chance at a good job, his part-time employer writes an un-
fair recommendation, and his last hope is smashed. Frank decides
to beat the man up for the damage he inflicted. Frank's girl tells
her father, who confronts the young man on the evening of the
planned attack. Here Frank makes the most important decision of
his young life.
   8 men, 8 women; 1 set. Royalty: $35.

_____. The Remarkable Incident at Carson Corners (1955).
 Adapted by Kristin Sergel. Dramatic Publishing Company.
   A play in which a group of students hold a mock trial to
determine who is responsible for a student's death. In this play
the actors come up from the audience to hold what looks to be a
humorous mock trial. But it isn't. The purpose of the hearing is
to fix responsibility for the death of the boy who fell from the
school fire escape. One revelation forces the next until the whole
town is implicated: the druggist who should have known better than
to move the boy and thereby aggravate the injury, the doctor who
didn't think the emergency call serious, and the politician who
thought the school appropriations could wait. Several attempts are
made to stop the trial, but it goes on, and the tension builds.
   13 men, 13 women; bare stage (chairs). Royalty: $25.

_____. Twelve Angry Men (or Twelve Angry Women or Twelve
 Angry Jurors) (1955). Adapted by Sherman L. Sergel. Dramatic Publishing Company.
   One foreign-born juror reminds his fellow jurors about some
basic truths in the American judicial system in this drama about
the deliberations of a jury in a murder trial. A nineteen-year-old
boy has just stood trial for the fatal stabbing of his father. Apparently the jury plans to return a verdict of guilty. As each juror
begins to speak, however, one juror reminds them that they must
be sure "beyond a reasonable doubt." As they continue to discuss
the testimonies, tempers get short, arguments grow heated, and the
jurors become twelve angry men. Before they reach the verdict a
new murder threat develops among their own number, giving an unexpected ending to this absorbing drama.
   Cast can be all men, all women, or any combination giving
 a total of 15; 1 interior. Royalty: $50.

ROSENBERG, James L. The Death and Life of Sneaky Fitch (1968).

Dramatists Play Service.

A Western spoof about a no-good, drunken, brawling nuisance named Sneaky Fitch, whom everyone in Gopher Gulch hates. The town is relieved when Sneaky dies, but then he rises from the coffin and takes over--without opposition--the positions of sheriff, mayor, and banker. He even faces down the man who is the fastest gun in the West. When Doc Burch returns to town (it was his medicine that "killed" Sneaky in the first place) the truth comes out and Sneaky is done for good.

    10 men, 3 women, extras; 1 exterior. Royalty: $35-25.

ROSTAND, Edmond. L'Aiglon (1900). Tr. by Parker, Russell, 1900; tr. by Norman as The Eaglet in his Plays, Macmillan, & Lond., Palmer, 1921, v. 2; tr. by Davenport, Yale, 1927.

    Recounts the tragic story of Napoleon's son, the little King of Rome, called The Eaglet by Victor Hugo, who has neither the strength of will nor of body to recapture his father's empire. He is held captive in Vienna among his enemies who are determined to tame his spirit. Covers the years 1830-32.

    6 acts; 33 men, 7 women, 2 boys, 1 girl, many extras; 3 interiors, 2 exteriors; costumes of the period.

_____. Chanticleer (1910). Tr. by Hall, Duffield, 1910; tr. by Newberry, Duffield, 1911; tr. by Norman, in his Plays, Macmillan, & Lond., Palmer, 1921, v. 2.

    Dressed out in the garb of the barn-yard animals, men and women are laughed at, especially the egotist in the rooster who believes his crowing evokes the sunrise.

    4 acts; 32 men, 14 women, many extras; 4 exteriors; fanciful costumes.

_____. Cyrano de Bergerac (1897). Tr. by Kingsbury, Bost., Lamson, 1898; LEV; same adapted by Kruckemeyer, French, 1934; tr. by Hall, Doubleday, 1898; DID; MOSQ; tr. by Dole, Crowell, 1899; same carried by Baker; & World Book Co., 1942; tr. by Norman in his Plays, Macmillan & Lond., Palmer, 1921, v. 1; tr. by Hooker, Holt, 1923; same Modern Lib., 1929; abridged in Pierce & Matthews, v. 2; tr. by Wolfe in BEN; BLO; TRE-1, 2, 3; tr. by Whitehall in WOR; tr. by Hooker, Dramatists Play Service; tr. by Forsyth, Dramatic Publishing Company.

    Cyrano is courageous and witty, but his proud spirit is hampered by his ridiculous nose. In love with Roxane, he nevertheless aids young Christian to win her. She doesn't realize his devotion until he is dying. Has high literary value and dramatic power, realizing perfectly the spirit of romance.

    5 acts; 12 leading men, 3 leading women, many extras; 2 interiors, 3 exteriors; costumes of the period. (Kruckmeyer: 30 men, 16 women. Royalty: $0-2.50. Hooker: 10 men, 5 women, extras. Royalty: $25. Forsyth: 5 men, 2 women, extras. Royalty: $35.)

_____. The Last Night of Don Juan (1921). Tr. by Riggs,

Yellow Springs, O., Kahoe, 1929; KRE.

The immortal lover, Don Juan, reviews his past just before his death and discovers that, though he may have conquered, he still possesses nothing. Stripped of pride and vanity, he is turned into a squeaking doll in the devil's puppet show.

Prolog & 2 acts; 5 men, many women as ghosts; 1 interior; fanciful costumes and puppet dresses.

_____. The Princess Far-Away (1895). Tr. by Renault, Stokes, 1899; tr. by Bagstad, Badger, 1921; tr. by Norman in his Plays, Macmillan, & Lond., Palmer, 1921, v. 1; tr. by Heard as The Far Princess, Holt, 1925.

The troubadour Rudel is dominated by his hopeless quest for his distant princess, Melissinde. He finally comes to her court only as he is dying in the ecstasy of his bliss. She in reality is a very human woman, and though weak and selfish, she becomes strong through his idealization.

4 acts; 21 men, 2 women; 2 interiors; costumes of the medieval period.

_____. The Romancers (Les Romanesques, 1894). Tr. by Hendee, Doubleday, 1899; same, Baker, 1906; tr. by Fleming as The Fantasticks, Lond., Heinemann, & Russell, 1900; tr. by Clark, French, 1915; tr. by Bagstad in Poet Lore, v. 32, 1921; tr. by Norman in his Plays, Macmillan, & Lond., Palmer, 1921, v. 1.

An amusing, dainty, and charming piece in which the lovers carry on their romance over a wall between their gardens to the pretended disapproval but secret delight of their fathers.

3 acts; 5 men, 1 woman, extras; 1 exterior (an excellent out-of-doors play). No royalty.

ROSTEN, Norman. Come Slowly, Eden (1966). Dramatists Play Service.

Treats the story of Emily Dickinson. The play opens shortly after the poetess' death with Lavinia Dickinson's discovery of her sister's poems and letters. With the help of T. W. Higginson, the literary critic, an attempt is made to discover which Emily Dickinson is the real one--the proper, protected Emily whom everyone knew, or the passionate, love-starved woman who wrote the poems. Tension develops in what Lavinia voluntarily offers about her sister and what she attempts to hide.

5 men, 2 women. Royalty: $35-25.

ROTHENBERG, Jerome. The Deputy. See entry under Hochhuth, Rolf.

ROTTER, Fritz and Allen Vincent. Letters to Lucerne (1941). Samuel French.

The girls in a boarding school in Lucerne, Switzerland, read aloud the letters from their families. Erna, a sensitive German girl, suffers because of the anti-German feeling. Her brother is in the German air force and is beloved by a Polish girl in the school,

270

who has heard that Warsaw has been bombed and her parents killed;
Erna too has a letter from her family, telling of her brother's death:
he chose to destroy himself and his plane rather than to drop bombs
on Warsaw.

    3 acts; 4 men, 9 women; 2 interiors (1 possible). Royalty:
    $35-25.

ROWE, Nicholas. Jane Shore, A Tragedy (1714). In his Works,
    Lond., 1728, v. 3; Belles Lettres ser., Heath, 1907; BEL v. 8;
    BRI v. 1; DIB v. 6; HAN; INCH v. 10; MOSE-2; NET; OXB v.
    8; STM; TUQ (1934 edn.).
    Jane Shore left her husband to become the mistress of Ed-
ward IV. After his death, Richard III drives her into the streets
where she drifts, half-starved for several days, deeply penitent.
Her husband tries to rescue her but in vain; he is caught by Richard's men and Jane dies.

    5 acts; 7 men, 2 women, extras; 3 interiors, 1 exterior;
    costumes of the period.

ROYLE, Edwin M. The Squaw Man (1905, pub. 1906). Abridged
    in Mantle & Sherwood 1899-1909.
    Jim leaves England for the American West to protect Diana's
husband, assuming the blame for his embezzlement. In the West
Jim becomes Carston and has a loyal group of cowboys. When Cash
Hawkins is shot in a saloon, an Indian woman, Nat-u-ritch, saves
Jim's life. He marries her and is called a Squaw man; they have
a son, Hal. Jim inherits an English estate and is to send Hal
abroad. His mother can't stand the separation and shoots herself,
thus leaving Jim free to go to England with Hal and Diana.

    4 acts; 23 men, 7 women; 1 interior, 2 exteriors; costumes.

RUBIN, Theodore Isaac. David and Lisa. See entry under Reach,
    James.

RYER, George W. The Old Homestead. See entry under Thompson,
    Denman.

RYERSON, Florence. See entries under Clements, Florence Ryer-
    son.

RYSKIND, Morrie. Of Thee I Sing. See entry under Kaufman,
    George S.

SACKLER, Howard. The Great White Hope (1968). Samuel French.
    Based on the life and career of Jack Johnson, the first black
heavyweight boxing champion of the world. Johnson, the symbol of
black aspiration, wins the championship from Frank Brady in a Reno,
Nevada fight (white man's country where large numbers of Negroes
will not be spectators) but loses it to another "Great White Hope" a
few years later.

    8 men, 3 women, many extras; representational sets.
    Royalty: $50-35.

SAKI. See Leonard Gershe's Miss Pell Is Missing.

SANDBURG, Carl. The World of Carl Sandburg. Adapted by Norman Corwin. (Reading) (1960). Samuel French.
Presents a selection of the best of Sandburg's verse and
prose including readings from Lincoln's biography and American
folk songs.
2 men, 1 woman. Royalty: $50-25.

SANDEAU, Jules. The Son-in-Law of M. Poirner. See entry under Augier, Émile.

SARDOU, Victorien. The Black Pearl (1862). Tr. by Clark.
French, 1915.
During a thunderstorm a pearl in a cabinet in a house has
disappeared. Christine is accused of the theft. All doubt her except her betrothed, Cornelius, who tracks down the real thief--a
bolt of lightning which has melted the medallion.
3 acts; 7 men, 3 women; 1 interior; Dutch costumes of 1825
may be used, or modern costumes.

_____ and Émile Moreau. Madame Sans-Gêne (1893). Tr. by
Reed, Street, & Smith, 1900; French, 1901.
Catherine Hubscher, a spirited French washerwoman, called
Madame Sans-Gêne, became the Duchess of Danzig in Napoleon's
court when she married Marshall Lefebvre. She retains her blunt
crudities which amuse the court, until she is ordered by Napoleon
to retire. She reminds him of his days of struggle 19 years before,
in which she shared, and also of his unpaid laundry bill of that
time. The Emperor relents and reinstates her.
Prolog & 3 acts; 21 men, 13 women; 3 interiors; costumes
of the period.

_____. Patrie! (1860). Tr. by Clark. Doubleday, 1915; LEV.
The fatherland is the Netherlands in the time of the Duke of
Alva (1568). The Count de Rysor has three loves: his country,
his wife, and his friend Karloo. He plots to capture Brussels and
kill Alva and the Spaniards. The plot is betrayed by his wife Dolores, who is also carrying on a liaison with Karloo. To avoid revealing the plot under torture, the Count stabs himself. Karloo discovers it was Dolores who betrayed them; he stabs her and gives
himself up to die with the others.
5 acts; 31 men, 6 women, extras; 4 interiors, 3 exteriors;
costumes of the period.

_____. A Scrap of Paper (1860). Tr. & adapted by Simpson.
Carried by Baker, Dramatic Pub. Co., & French; abridged in
Pierce & Matthews, v. 2.
Centers around an insignificant but mischievous bit of paper
until it is destroyed. It was written by Louise prior to her marriage, and now she fears her husband will find it. Her cousin Suzanne helps her hunt; they find it only to lose it. The excitement
continues until the paper is again found and this time done away with.

3 acts; 6 men, 6 women; 3 interiors.

SAROYAN, William. The Beautiful People (1941). Samuel French.
The belief that love is the only thing of consequence in the
world comes through in this comedy peopled with innocent characters
who engage in some of the most impractical activities possible.
One, a fifteen-year-old boy writes one-word novels, while the father
supports his family by cashing the pension checks of a complete
stranger, dead for seven years.
7 men, 2 women; 1 interior. Royalty: $25-20.

_____. The Cave Dwellers (1957). Samuel French.
An abandoned theater provides a temporary home for a group
of penniless nomads in this comedy about performers who have seen
much better times. Although the building is cold and the food is
scarce, the main problem these people face is that the theater is
soon to be torn down for a housing project. Their difficulties hardly
dampen their spirits, however, and they spend their time amusing
themselves, as well as the audience, with memories of former days
of glory. Among the characters is the Queen, a former actress;
the King, who used to be a famous clown; and the Duke, a former
prizefight champion. Their adventures together and the stories they
tell of earlier adventures results in an innocently humorous comic
improvisation.
9 men, 5 women; bare stage. Royalty: $50-25.

_____. A Decent Birth, A Happy Funeral (1949). Samuel French.
Death is predicted by the cards of the gypsy girl for Ernest
as he goes to war; August is to have a child by the burlesque woman he married. Word comes of Ernest's death and August occu-
pies the coffin for a happy funeral as his wife gives birth to his son.
3 acts; 11 men, 5 women; 3 interiors. Royalty: $35-25.

_____. Get Away Old Man (1943). Samuel French.
An infinitely wealthy and somewhat degenerate Hollywood producer finds that his money cannot corrupt a young pure-in-heart
writer in this comedy about young love and movie making. Although
the producer can usually buy and despoil any youthful movie aspirant
he wants, he runs into firm resistance from the writer who refuses
to compromise his talents for the promise of wealth. The young
writer's strength bolsters his girlfriend's will to resist, for she too
was the object of the producer's talent-grabbing guest. In the end
the bullheaded producer persists in thinking one can buy the talents
and loyalties of others and exploit them. The writer and his beloved,
however, disavow this carnivorous Hollywood existence and find real
happiness with each other.
8 men, 3 women; 1 interior. Royalty: $35-25.

_____. Love's Old Sweet Song (1940). Samuel French.
Out in California Ann Hamilton, unmarried at 44, receives a
fake telegram from Barnaby Gaul, so that when Jim Doherty, a
pitchman for a patent medicine, appears whistling "Love's old sweet
song" she claims him and he pretends he is Barnaby. The Yearling

family (Pa, Ma, and 14 children) appear from Oklahoma and take possession of her house, even burn it to the ground, but Georgie Americanos, the telegraph messenger, and his father rescue her and reunite Ann and Jim.

20 men, 10 women; 1 interior, 1 exterior. Royalty: $25-20.

_____ . My Heart's In the Highlands (1939). Samuel French.
To the family of a fantastically improvident poet comes old Jasper McGregor, playing so sweetly on his bugle that the neighbors bring food as a tribute. But Jasper is a runaway from an Old People's Home, and the guards take him back. Some months later he returns, just as the family is being evicted for non-payment of rent. His bugle reverberates the Scottish song as he dies. The young son of the family is wistful, ingenious, and inquiring, asking about the meaning of life.

No act divisions; 13 men, 2 women, extras; 1 interior, divided to show 2 rooms. Royalty: $25-20.

_____ . Sam Ego's House (1949). Samuel French.
Sam Ego is America's dream, and his house is the American nation. He is successful and builds a fine house, but many events spoil the dream and almost shatter the house. It is moved from its fine location to a junk yard in the slums. Ironic fun is made of many things, from Boy Scouts to church pastors.

3 acts (in 7 scenes); 20 men, 4 women, extras; 4 exteriors. Royalty: $35-25.

_____ . The Time of Your Life (1939). Samuel French.
Pulitzer prize play, 1940. Kindly Joe, drinking and dreaming, searches for happiness and the answers to the enigma of life in Nick's waterfront saloon in San Francisco. Many characters pass in and out. His errand boy Tom, huge and simple, falls in love with Kitty, a fragile prostitute. Joe almost shoots a vice raider who threatens Kitty, but Kit Carson, a character out of the Old West, takes care of that. The play seems a hymn to the joy of life and is suffused with nostalgic melancholy.

3 acts; 18 men, 7 women; 2 interiors. Royalty: $35-25.

SARTRE, Jean-Paul. The Condemned of Altona (1959). English version of Justin O'Brien. Samuel French.
The head of a German family dynasty, before he dies, forces his second son, his daughter-in-law, and his daughter to swear that they will carry on the family tradition. The son and his wife resent their promise because it places them in the bondage of guilt of the elder son, certified dead, but actually living in the attic. This son struts about in his Nazi uniform, mumbles into a tape recorder, and relives his inhuman acts of World War II. The two women convince him that what he thought of as a demolished Germany has now been resurrected, and he drives off into the night to die.

7 men, 2 women; 2 interiors. Royalty: $35-25.

_____ . Dirty Hands (Red Gloves) (1948). Tr. by Abel in his Three Plays, Knopf, 1949; adapted & produced in 1948 by Taradash as <u>Red Gloves</u>.

A young intellectual and political fanatic, Hugo, joins the communist revolution in Illyria in 1940 and is commissioned to kill the party leader, Hoederer. He becomes his secretary, but cannot bring himself to kill him until he sees his wife Jessica kissing Hoederer's hand. Then he shoots. Hoederer exonerates him by saying it was only a "crime passionel." When Hugo is released from prison after two years, he is bitter and disillusioned, for he finds the Party is following the very program he sought to prevent.

Prolog, 3 acts, & epilog; 9 men, 2 women; 3 interiors.

_____. <u>The Flies</u> (1943). Samuel French.

The flies represent the little avenging Furies (Eumenides) which afflict all in Argos with a sense of guilt and self-condemnation because of the murder of Agamemnon fifteen years before, and for which they seek to be condoned. Orestes returns, and, to secure freedom, plots with Electra to kill Aegisthus and Clytemnestra in revenge for killing Agamemnon. Introduces Zeus as the supreme god in which all have some belief and as much allegiance as faith justifies.

3 acts; 8 men, 6 women, extras; 2 interiors, 2 exteriors. Royalty: $25-20.

_____. <u>No Exit</u> (1946). Samuel French.

Two women and one man are locked up together for an eternity in one horrible room in hell. The windows are sealed, there are no mirrors, no exit, and the lights can never be turned off. This is not a hell of fire but of the humiliation of a soul stripped of all pretenses. Even the blackest deeds are mercilessly exposed to the fierce light of hell, an eternal hell. And the various sexual preferences of the trio make physical love impossible.

2 men, 2 women; 1 interior. Royalty: $25-20.

_____. <u>The Trojan Women</u>. See entry under Euripides.

SAWN, David. <u>Victims of the Devil's Triangle</u> (1975). Pioneer Drama Service.

A group of passengers has embarked on a holiday aboard a ship cruising through the notorious Devil's Triangle off the Florida coast. One by one the passengers begin to disappear. The climax comes during a fierce storm.

Flexible cast of 15 or more; 1 interior. Royalty: $25.

SCHARY, Dore. <u>Sunrise at Campobello</u> (1958). Dramatists Play Service.

A personal, rather than political, portrait of the pre-White House days of Franklin D. Roosevelt. The play covers Roosevelt from 1921, when he was stricken with infantile paralysis at his Canadian summer home, to 1924, when he was able to stand up at Madison Square Garden and nominate Al Smith for President.

19 men, 5 women (a few parts can be doubled); interiors. Royalty: $50-25.

SCHAUFFLER, Mrs. Elsie T. Parnell (1935). French, 1936;
    FAMJ.
        The leader of the Irish party, Charles S. Parnell, falls des-
perately in love with Mrs. Katharine O'Shea, whose husband is
rather a blackguard, as he uses her merely as a source of money.
She promotes Parnell politically and lives with him for nine years.
At the peak of Parnell's success in forcing Gladstone's support of
Home Rule for Ireland, Capt. O'Shea brings suit for divorce, naming
him as co-respondent, thus raising such a scandal that Gladstone
withdraws his support. Parnell is driven from the Irish party; he
dies shortly after.
        3 acts; 13 men, 5 women; 3 interiors; costumes of the
period.

SCHILLER, Johann Christoph Friedrich von. The Death of Wallen-
    stein (1800). Tr. by Coleridge in his Works, Bohn, 1903; FRA
    v. 3; KRE.
        Wallenstein was capable but a bit unscrupulous; he commanded
the armies of Germany in the 30 Years' War and repelled the invasion of the Swedes under Gustavus Adolphus. To protect himself
from enemies in the Emperor's Court who were jealous of him he
opened negotiations with the Swedes. When discovered, he was relieved of his command, which was transferred to Octavio Piccolo-
mini. His assassination was arranged and executed by an Irish
commander named Butler.
        5 acts; 21 men, 4 women, extras; 8 interiors; costumes of
the period.

_____. Maria Stuart (1800). Tr. by Mellish in his Works, Bohn,
    1901; & in the Weimar ed.; separately, Baker.
        Imprisoned by an English court and pronounced guilty, Mary
awaits Queen Elizabeth's death sentence. They meet in the park;
Elizabeth fears her too much to free her. Mortimer plans an escape, but when the plan is frustrated, he commits suicide. Double-
dealing Leicester fails to win either lady as his wife. Mary goes
with dignity to her death, having abased Elizabeth in an outburst.
        5 acts; 13 men, 4 women, extras; 4 interiors, 1 exterior;
costumes of the period.

_____. Wilhelm Tell (1804) Tr. by Martin in his Dramatic
    Works, Bohn, 1903; CLF-2; FRA v. 3; HARC v. 26; MAU;
    STA.
        The famous Swiss archer, Tell, is ordered by the cold-
blooded tyrant Gessler to shoot an apple off his son's head. He
does so, remarking that the next arrow was meant for Gessler.
Tell is imprisoned but escapes and kills Gessler. This was a signal for revolt; the Austrian tyranny was destroyed, and the Swiss
became independent. Wilhelm Tell is the strong self-reliant man
who rises and frees himself from oppressors.
        5 acts; 20 men, 7 women, 2 boys, extras; 4 interiors, 10
exteriors; costumes of the period (1307).

SCHISGAL, Murray. All Over Town (1975). Dramatists Play Service.

In this zany comedy, Dr. Lionel Morris, a psychiatrist who
is contemplating becoming a Buddhist, takes on as a special patient
in his home a man named Louie Lucas, who has fathered nine
children by different welfare mothers. The trouble is that everyone
believes that a black delivery man named Lewis is Louie. Lewis
plays along, since all he is after is front money which will let him
establish a tapdancing school in the ghetto. Finally this mad house
is filled with this threesome plus the doctor's wife and the military
colonel she's having an affair with, the colonel's wheel-chaired
wife, the doctor's daughter and her social worker boyfriend, servants, hard-of-seeing burglars, and gay business managers.

12 men, 6 women; 1 interior. Royalty: $50-35.

_____. Luv (1963). Dramatists Play Service.

As Howard Taubman points out, the fun in this play "is lar-
gely in misery." The play opens as Harry Berlin, looking like
something the cat wouldn't drag in, prepares to jump off a bridge
and end his ruined life. Milt Manville, an old friend who is the
picture of prosperity, intervenes. But Milt has his own problems--
his wife won't divorce him so that he can marry the woman he
loves. Ellen, Milt's wife, isn't the happiest of women either.
Milt's plan for ending everybody's frustration is to spruce Ellen up,
palm her off on Harry, and marry the girl of his dreams. Problems
ensue, the more the funnier.

2 men, 1 woman; 1 interior. Royalty: $50-25.

SCHNITZLER, Arthur. Anatol (1893). Samuel French.

A series of seven different scenes, centering on a melancholy philanderer, Anatol, who has a different woman in each scene.
He thinks to find happiness by flying from one to another, but he
remains unhappy; his experiences puzzle and worry him.

7 scenes; 4 men, 7 women; 7 interiors. Royalty: $50.

_____. Light O' Love (1896). Tr. by Morgan in Drama v. 2,
1912; DIK-1; TUCG; TUCM; WATI; WATL-1; tr. by Shand,
Lond., Gey & Hancock, 1914.

A girl of the people learns her lover, a young man of the
upper classes, has fought a duel for another woman. Realizing she
was but a plaything to him, she kills herself at his grave. Treats
a commonplace theme so artistically as to make a play full of delicate charm and soft melancholy atmosphere.

3 acts; 4 men, 3 women, 1 girl; 2 interiors.

_____. The Lonely Way (1904). Tr. by Björkman, Kennerley,
1915; Little, 1922; MOSQ; tr. by Leigh in WHI.

Julian is spurned by Gabrielle and his son by her because
he thought only of himself. His sister, Johanna, is in love with
von Sala, who is likewise selfish. She drowns herself and he commits suicide. The lonely way is the way of the selfish.

5 acts; 7 men, 4 women; 2 interiors, 2 exteriors.

_____. La Ronde (1900). English version by Eric Bentley.

Samuel French.
A rondelay of love in ten interlocking scenes, each scene
consisting of two characters. In the first, a soldier and a prostitute; then the soldier and a parlor maid; next the parlor maid and
her wealthy employer. The scenes which follow are: the wealthy
man and his mistress, a married woman; the married woman and
her husband; the husband and a girl of the streets; the girl and her
poet; the poet and an actress; the actress and the count; and, finally
the count and the prostitute of scene one.
5 men, 5 women; several scenes. Royalty: $25-20.

SCHULBERG, Budd, with Harvey Breit. The Disenchanted (1958).
Based on the novel by Budd Shulberg. Samuel French.
Depicts the decline of a famous novelist's (F. Scott Fitzgerald's) powers and marriage. Manley Halliday, the novelist, and
his beautiful wife, Jere, find their gay, whirlwind existence disintegrating. Once the most famous writer of his generation, Manley is
so beset by problems that his productivity has practically ceased.
He drinks constantly and tries to write while his wife is in New York
under psychiatric care. Since his financial situation is so bad, Manley agrees to write for a very commercial motion picture which he
considers contemptible. Subjected to unceasing pressures from his
wife and his producer, Manley begins to realize that men delude
themselves when they think they have a second chance. "A first
chance, that's all we have," but by then the realization can do him
no good.
10 men, 4 women, extras; 3 interiors. Royalty: $50-25.

SCHULMAN, Arnold. A Hole in the Head (1957). Samuel French.
This play centers around the attempts of a widower to hold
on to his shoddy Florida hotel and the affections of his twelve year
old son. Sidney, the widower, needs money and telephones his
wealthy brother in New York for help. The brother and his wife
decide to fly to Florida to straighten Sidney out and to rescue the
boy from what they consider an unsuitable environment. When they
arrive they try to get Sidney to marry a rich widow so he will
have the needed money for his hotel and so the boy will have a
mother. This falls through and in the process brings an end to a
love affair between Sidney and an attractive blonde. Now the brother
is really anxious to take Sidney's son back to New York and a decent home life, but with a newly discovered strength of purpose Sidney manages to hold his home together and rescue his hotel.
8 men, 5 women; 1 interior. Royalty: $50-25.

SCOTT, Allan and George Haight. Good-Bye Again (1932). Samuel
French.
A popular novelist and lecturer, Kenneth Bixby, with his
secretary, Anne Rogers, arrives in a Midwestern city where he is
greeted by Mrs. Julia Wilson. She claims undying love though now
married to Mr. Wilson. Kenneth gets into a mess in trying to say
good-bye again to Julia. It might result in his losing Anne, but the
lecture tour goes on.
3 acts; 8 men, 4 women; 1 interior. Royalty: $25.

_____ . Joy to the World (1948). Samuel French.
An executive in the production of Hollywood films, Alexander
Soren, broadcasts such a liberal speech that he is fired. The
speech had been prepared for him by Ann in the research department,
and it attacked censorship and Hollywood's concern with matters of
little moment. He is at once hired by an independent idealistic producer and wins Ann. They believe that films should not only purvey
joy, but also present serious matters to the world.
    3 acts; 15 men, 5 women, extras; 1 interior. Royalty: $50.

SCRIBE, A. Eugène and Ernest Legouvé. The Ladies' Battle (1851).
    Tr. by Coale, DeWitt, 1883, carried later by Dramatic Pub.
    Co.; also carried by French.
    Two ladies, the Countess and Leonie, fall in love with Henri,
a spy whom they have saved from capture and are employing as a
domestic servant disguised as Charles. As they fight this duel of
love, the Baron comes to arrest him. Gustav de Grignon appears
in Henri's place, but honorably returns to clear the man who has
been arrested in his place. An amnesty saves Henri, the Baron is
defeated, and Henri wins Leonie.
    3 acts; 7 men, 2 women, extras; 1 interior; costumes of
    the period.

SEAY, James L. Happy Haunting (1973). Performance Publishing.
    A microbus load of high school cheerleaders breaks down
near a deserted mansion. The cheerleaders are accompanied by a
Latin teacher and one boyfriend. The deserted mansion is populated
with bumbling crooks who have robbed a novelty store instead of the
currency exchange they intended to hit. The crooks hide behind a
secret panel in full sight of the audience.
    9 men, 12 women; representational set. Royalty: $35.

SELVER, Paul. R.U.R. See entry under Capek, Karel.

SERGEL, Christopher. Ask Any Girl (1960). Adapted from Wini-
    fred Wolfe's novel. Dramatic Publishing Company.
    Meg Wheeler comes to New York as a fresh college graduate
and a current husband hunter. She moves into a Manhattan boarding
house that is occupied by girls with the same goals as hers. She
finds a likely subject, Evan Doughton, girl-chasing, lazy younger
brother of Miles Doughton, the head of an advertising firm. Miles
is tired of his brother's work habits and decides to help Meg snare
Evan. Together they use the latest advertising techniques, including
motivation research. What happens is that while they can't get Evan
to propose, they fall in love with each other.
    5 men, 12 women, extras; 1 set. Royalty: $35.

_____ . Cheaper by the Dozen (1950). Adapted from the novel
    by Frank Bunker Gilbreth and Ernestine G. Carey. Dramatic
    Publishing Company.
    This is an amusing play about a father's attempts to turn his
family of teenage daughters into an efficient, smoothly functioning
organization. Despite his daughters' interest in boys and dates, Dad

pushes ahead with better organization for his family. He puts up a
chart for the young people to initial after completing each household
task, instructs them in taking an "efficient" bath, and levies fines
on wasters of electricity. Although the girls don't understand his
emphasis on running things smoothly Dad has an imperative reason
for it. He has a terminal heart condition and wants them to be
able to care for themselves. The play has many humorous as well
as some rather moving scenes as the girls and their father move
toward a new understanding.
 9 men, 7 women; 1 interior. Royalty: $35.

_____. Meet Me in St. Louis (1948). Based on Sally Benson's
 novel. Dramatic Publishing Company.
 This comedy concerns the efforts of 5 children to force their
father to remain in St. Louis instead of moving to New York to accept a better job. Four of the children are attractive girls, and
they are afraid they will lose their boyfriends if they move to New
York. Also the World's Fair is to open in St. Louis in a few days
and the girls, along with their only brother, hate to think of missing
that. Father refuses to yield to their pleas, forcing the girls to
unite for action. Their schemes, however, almost land the entire
family in jail. But as the fireworks signalling the start of the
World's Fair go off, they win through to a solution which gets
Father that better job there in St. Louis and also straightens out
their romantic complications.
 7 men, 9 women; 1 interior. Royalty: $35.

_____. Our Miss Brooks (1950). Adapted from the original
 material of R. J. Mann. Dramatic Publishing Company.
 Miss Brooks is the high school English teacher with so many
troubles that she dreams about her vacation coming up. She has
collected travel folders which she discusses with the basketball
coach, a sailing enthusiast, who seems to her to be "the man" for
her. But then the directorship of the school play is thrust upon
her, and she and the coach argue over who gets to practice in the
gym. Then his star athlete quits the team to take the male lead in
the play. And to top things off, the daughter of the school board
president is so bad as the girl lead that Miss Brooks replaces her
with a talented nobody. Because of this change the principal becomes involved, and soon Miss Brooks' personal and professional
problems are hopelessly intertangled until the final curtain. (A
musical version is also available.)
 5 men, 12 women; 1 interior. Royalty: $25.

_____. Pillow Talk (1963). Based on the motion picture. Dra-
 matic Publishing Company.
 Because most of her work is done out of her New York
apartment, attractive interior decorator Jan Morrow is quite upset
when new construction forces her to share a party line with playboy
Brad Allen. She complains to the phone company, but they send an
impressionable female inspector to talk to Brad. She is no match
for his charm, though, and sends in a report blaming Jan. Through
a friend and Jan's maid, Brad finally meets his neighbor, but he

passes himself off as a naive Texan, Rex Stetson. Jan learns to
love the gentle and trustworthy Rex in spite of the continuous stream
of cynical comments she hears from Brad. The play ends happily
for both, however, when Brad realizes that he is in love with Jan
and drops his masquerade.
> 6 men, 15 women, extras optional; 1 interior. Royalty:
> $35.

_____. State Fair. See entry under McMahon, Luella.

_____. To Kill a Mockingbird. See entry under Lee, Harper.

_____. Up the Down Staircase. See entry under Kaufman, Bel.

_____. Welcome to the Monkey House. See entry under Vonne-
gut, Kurt.

_____. You Were Born on a Rotten Day (1971). Dramatic Pub-
lishing Company.
> The play is a spoof on astrology, beginning with an astrologer
in direct communication with the audience. He urges Capricorns to
fight their primary weakness (delusions of adequacy), advises Aries
that "You are probably lonely--and with your personality it's no
surprise, " and explains how to identify a Leo ("A person who is
sucking his thumb and telling everyone how poor he is"). The performing roles are said to be those to which young people can relate.
> 8 men, 18 women (doubling possible); 1 set. Royalty: $35.

SERGEL, Clark F. Rebel Without a Cause (1958). Based on a
story by Nicholas Ray, screenplay by Stewart Stern, adaptation
by Irving Shulman. Dramatic Publishing Company.
> Jim has been warned to stay away from Judy, the girlfriend
of Buzz, who leads a gang of high school toughs. Jim tries to stay
out of trouble, but when his friend Plato is beaten up and Jim is
called "chicken, " he agrees to participate in a test of courage with
Buzz. During the test, Buzz is the victim of a tragic accident.
The rest of the gang pursues Jim while he and Judy hide together
and begin to discover in each other the things in life they seek.
When Plato is involved in tragedy, Jim's parents think he is involved,
but the two people, having discovered each other, see the end of the
futility of their lives and are finally able to understand their parents.
> 13 men, 10 women; bare stage (representational props).
> Royalty: $35.

SERGEL, Kristin. See entries under Rose, Reginald.

SERGEL, Ruth. Love Is Eternal (1955). Adapted from Irving Stone's
novel. Dramatic Publishing Company.
> Deals with the controversial Mary Todd Lincoln, from her
early abolitionist feelings as she watched the slave trade from her
Kentucky house, to her meeting with the "impossible" Abraham Lincoln and the stormy courtship and marriage that followed. The
story follows the Lincoln family into the White House and suggests

the problems, political and personal, the couple faced there.
14 men, 16 women, doubling possible; 1 interior or curtains.
Royalty: $25.

_____.   The Red House Mystery (1956).   Adapted from A. A.
Milne's work.   Dramatic Publishing Company.
In the middle of a summer house party, a warning of death
is brought.   Mark is greatly disturbed over this, even when the
threat is revealed as a prank by one of the guests.   The next day
Mark quarrels with his brother; his brother is shot, and Mark disappears.   To the police, the matter is simple manslaughter; but to
one of the guests, especially after an attempt is made on his own
life, it is a matter of premeditated murder.   The case is complicated by the number of guests who would have benefited from the
death.   Only at the end is the identity of the killer known.
7 men, 8 women; 1 interior.   Royalty: $25.

SERGEL, Sherman L.   See entry under Rose, Reginald.

SHAFFER, Anthony.   Sleuth (1970).   Samuel French.
The five roles in this suspense thriller are played by the
two male principals.   The setting in the English country home of a
famous mystery writer, Andrew Wyke.   The play begins with a
conversation between the writer and Milo Tindle, who is in love
with Andrew's wife.   The two engage in a phony robbery at the
writer's house, where Milo is killed.   But Milo returns in the
second act pretending he is a police inspector investigating his own
death.   By the end of the play he has been murdered all over again.
2 men; 1 interior.   Royalty: $50-35.

SHAFFER, Peter.   Black Comedy (1965).   Samuel French.
An uproarious farce which begins in total darkness (light to
the characters).   Then a fuse blows and the stage lights come on
(darkness to the characters) and the fun begins.   What we see is a
young sculptor preparing to entertain a wealthy art patron and a
prospective father-in-law.   To impress both, he moves the expensive
furniture from his neighbor's apartment into his own.   But when the
neighbor returns unexpectedly, he tries to move the furniture back
under the cover of darkness and much to the dismay of the gathered
guests.   During all of this, he must endure the escapades of a
former girl friend, hiding in the bedroom.
5 men, 3 women; 1 interior.   Royalty: $50-25.

_____.   Equus (1974).   Samuel French.
A psychiatrist in a psychiatric hospital is urged to take on
one more case: that of a 17-year-old boy who has just blinded six
horses with a metal spike.   Dr. Martin Dysart begins to work on
Alan Strang, to try to unravel the mysterious connection between
horses and religion and the boy's sudden violent outburst against
creatures he obviously loves.   This puzzle is more than the doctor
bargained for, and pretty soon Alan's problem is all mixed up in the
lack of meaning the doctor finds in his own life.   This is a powerful
play.   The setting is a simple wooden one in which all the charac-

ters are present throughout the play.

    5 men, 4 women, 6 actors as horses; basic setting. Royalty: $50-35.

_____. Five Finger Exercise (1958). Samuel French.

    A German orphan comes to England to tutor the daughter of a nouveau riche family. He comes hoping to be adopted by both the new country and the new family. The family, however, is not capable of love, but only of selfish passions. The immigrant sets them free from restraint. The audience is able to watch, knowingly, as the innocent tutor slowly comes to know that the pretended family love is a farce.

    3 men, 2 women; 1 interior. Royalty: $50-25.

_____. The Private Ear and the Public Eye (1962). Samuel French.

    A pair of comedies presented together. The first is a romance in which a boy makes a date with a girl he meets at a concert and receives coaching for the occasion from a worldly friend. Neither the coaching nor the girl meets the boy's expectations. The second features a snappy, eccentric private detective who dresses garishly and maintains a diet of yogurt and grapefruit. He has been hired to tail an accountant's wife, but he gives himself away at every turn.

    Each play: 2 men, 1 woman; 1 interior. Royalty for both together: $50-25.

_____. The Royal Hunt of the Sun (1966). Samuel French.

    Deals with the Spanish expedition under Pizzaro to the land of the Incas. The play shows the crossing of the sea, the climbing of the mountains, and the meeting of the Inca god. The Inca god wants to meet the Spanish God and is confused when that God cannot be seen. There is a slaughter of 3,000 unarmed natives and finally the murder of the Inca god.

    22 men, 2 women, extras; cyclorama, drops, inset. Royalty: $50-25.

_____. White Liars (1967). Samuel French.

    A young man comes to a fortune teller, dragging along his friend. He doesn't want his fortune told, but he wants to bribe the fortune teller to frighten his friend so that he will give up his girl friend to him. The friend sees through the scheme, and both he and the fortune teller make a discovery about love.

    2 men, 1 woman; 1 interior. Royalty: $50-25.

SHAIRP, Mordaunt. The Green Bay Tree (1932). Baker's Plays.

    A revealing drama of social decadence, depicting degenerate exquisites, spiritually bankrupt dilettantes, flourishing like a green bay tree. Julian at 8 is adopted by Mr. Dulcimer, rich but utterly selfish. They live in exquisite luxury. When Julian falls in love with Leonora, his allowance is cut off. His father kills Mr. Dulcimer, but his influence extends after his death, for Julian returns to live as Mr. Dulcimer did, without Leonora.

    3 acts; 4 men, 1 woman; 2 interiors. Royalty: $25.

SHAKESPEARE, William. Antony and Cleopatra; adapted as All for
Love by John Dryden.

_____. As You Like It (ca. 1600). Acting editions readily avail-
able; many reading editions, OLI; OXB v. 6; INCH v. 3.
   In the lovely Forest of Arden Rosalind's father, the rightful
duke, deposed by Celia's father, Frederick, lives in contentment
with his followers, among them the melancholy Jaques. There Rosalind goes, when banished from the court, disguised as the boy Ganymede, accompanied by Celia as a rustic maiden and by the witty
clown Touchstone. There Orlando has also fled from his cruel
brother Oliver, and meeting with the girls, talks ceaselessly to
Ganymede about his love for Rosalind, until she finally discloses
her identity. Meantime Oliver has had a change of heart toward
his brother, falls in love with Celia, and a double wedding takes
place, with word also coming that Duke Frederick has restored the
kingdom to the rightful duke.
   5 acts; 17 men, 4 women, extras; simple exterior scenes;
costumes of the period.

_____. A Comedy of Errors; based on The Twins by Plautus.

_____. Hamlet (1602). Acting versions readily available; many
reading editions; HARC v. 46; OLI; STA; INCH v. 1; in OXB
v. 3; TRE-1, 2 (v. 2); TREA-1.
   After he learns that his uncle Claudius has killed his father
to become king and marry his mother Gertrude, Hamlet broods and
wonders what to do. He hesitates to take action; his calculating
consideration exhausts his power of action. Although in love with
Ophelia, he pretends madness until she too gets worried, goes mad,
and drowns herself. Her brother, Laertes, blames Hamlet and
challenges him to a duel. The King has poisoned the tip of one of
the foils and also a cup of wine. Both the young men die of the
poisoned tip, the mother takes the poisoned cup (intended for Hamlet), and just before he dies, Hamlet stabs and kills the usurping
King.
   5 acts; 20 men, 2 women, extras; simple interior & exterior
scenes; costumes of the period.

_____. Henry the Fifth (1599). Acting editions readily available;
many reading editions; INCH v. 2; OXB v. 18.
   When Prince Hal becomes king as Henry V, he lays aside
the riotous tavern life and the wildness of his youth with Falstaff
and his pals (as developed in Henry the Fourth, parts 1 and 2). He
proves his virtues, winning the brilliant victory over the French at
Agincourt.
   5 acts; about 30 men, 4 women, extras; simple interior and
exterior settings; costumes of the period.

_____. Julius Caesar (ca. 1601). Acting editions readily avail-
able; many reading editions; INCH v. 4; OLI v. 1; in OXB v. 16.
   Cassius persuades Brutus to join the conspirators in the plot
against his friend Caesar. This culminates in Caesar's assassination

in the Senate on the Ides of March. Mark Antony's funeral oration
discredits the assassins, who are defeated at the battle of Philippi
by Caesar's friends.

    5 acts; 31 men, 2 women, extras; simple interior and ex-
terior settings; costumes of the period.

_____. King Lear (1605). Acting editions readily available;
many reading editions; HARC v. 46; INCH v. 4; OLI v. 1; OXB
v. 10.

At the age of 80, Lear, King of Britain, turns his realm
over to his two flattering daughters, Goneril and Regan, disinheriting
the youngest, Cordelia, since she says she loves him only as becomes a daughter to love her father. Cordelia goes to France,
where she marries the King. Meanwhile Lear is being so ill-treated
by his two ungrateful daughters that he goes out into the stormy
night, attended only by his faithful fool and the Earl of Kent. Cordelia returns from France to try to solace her father, but he has
gone mad and dies of grief. Cordelia is defeated and dies in prison;
Goneril poisons her sister Regan and takes her own life. Her husband, the Duke of Albany, who has never approved her actions, becomes King.

    5 acts; 17 men, 3 women, extras; simple interior and ex-
terior scenes; costumes of the period.

_____. Macbeth (1606). Acting editions readily available; many
reading editions; HARC v. 46; INCH v. 4; OLI v. 2; OXB v.
14.

Macbeth is hailed by three witches as a future King of Scotland, though he is only a thane. Urged on by his unscrupulous
wife, he murders King Duncan, and the prophecy is fulfilled. More
violence follows as the new King attempts to clear the field of all
who might supplant him. The murders torment the conscience of
Lady Macbeth until she commits suicide. Macbeth is killed by
Macduff in further fulfillment of the witches' prophecy.

    5 acts; 20 men, 6 women, extras; simple interiors and ex-
teriors; costumes of the period.

_____. The Merchant of Venice (ca. 1595). Acting versions
readily available; many reading editions; INCH v. 2; OLI v. 1;
OXB v. 10.

In order to aid his friend Bassanio to woo Portia at Belmont,
the merchant Antonio borrows 3,000 ducats from Shylock and pledges
a pound of his flesh. Bassanio is successful at Belmont through his
choice of a leaden casket, but Antonio's ships fail to return as expected and his bond is forfeited. On hearing this, Portia, disguised
as a young doctor of law, conducts his defense and saves Antonio's
life by insisting on the exact terms of the bond--only flesh, but no
blood, and neither more nor less than an exact pound.

    5 acts; 17 men, 3 women, extras; simple interior and ex-
terior scenes; costumes of the period.

_____. A Midsummer Night's Dream (ca. 1595). Acting ver-
sions readily available; many reading editions; OLI v. 1.

Written doubtless to celebrate a wedding, strange mixups occur in a forest near Athens during a midsummer night.   Puck, the
spritely servant of the fairy king, Oberon, secures a love juice
which shifts the loves of two pairs of Athenians and causes Titania
to fall in love with Bottom the weaver while he wears an ass' head.
Later at the Duke's wedding feast, three weddings are celebrated,
during which the tradesmen present as an interlude a burlesque version of the play Pyramus and Thisbe.

  5 acts; 13 men, 8 women, extras; simple scenes, mostly
  exterior; costumes of the period.

    . Much Ado about Nothing (1599). Acting versions readily
 available; many reading editions; INCH v. 2; OXB v. 18.

  The best remembered plot of the two in this play concerns
Beatrice and Benedick who carry on with each other a merry war
of words and wit, both having foresworn love and matrimony.   Their
friends cleverly trick them into becoming lovers, each being told
that the other is pining away of unrequited affection.   The other plot
involves Hero, engaged to Claudio, who rejects her at the altar because of a false impression of her unfaithfulness.   Hero faints, and
it is given out that she is dead.   Through the local constabulary,
Dogberry and Verges, the ruse is discovered, and Claudio agrees
to marry Hero's cousin to atone for Hero's death.   At the altar this
time the "cousin" turns out to be Hero herself.

  5 acts; 14 men, 4 women, extras; simple scenes, mostly exterior; costumes of the period.

    . Othello (1604). Acting editions readily available; many
 reading editions; SMP; in OLI; in OXB v. 5; INCH v. 5; BEB;
 BLO.

  The Moor of Venice, Othello, wins Desdemona as his wife,
and as Commander after a signal victory promotes Cassio as his
chief lieutenant.   This arouses the jealousy of Iago who plots revenge.   He fosters suspicion in Othello to disgrace Cassio, involving
Desdemona through a handkerchief which his wife Emilia steals and
which he places in Cassio's room.   The tortured Othello, believing
her false to him, strangles Desdemona, but when he learns how he
has been duped, he kills himself.   When Emilia reveals the villainy
of Iago, he stabs her and is led away to torture and to death.

  5 acts; 10 men, 3 women, extras; simple interior and exterior scenes; costumes of the period.

    . Richard the Third (1592). Acting editions available;
 many reading editions; INCH v. 1; OXB v. 3.

  The hero and villain of this tragedy, Richard, marches on
to be king.   He murders Henry VI and his brother the Duke of
Clarence, and after the death of Edward IV, he has the two young
princes (one, Edward V) killed in the Tower, thus gaining the throne
as Richard III.   Ambitious and ruthless, he executes those who oppose him but he is defeated and slain by the Earl of Richmond at the
battle of Bosworth Field.

  5 acts; 30 men, 3 boys, 4 women, 1 girl, extras; simple
  interior and exterior settings; costumes of the period.

_____. Romeo and Juliet (1591). Acting editions readily avail-
able; many reading editions; OLI; SMN; THO; OXB v. 6; INCH
v. 1.
       A Montague, Romeo, goes to a ball at the Capulets and there
sees Juliet. They fall in love. Because of the feud between the two
houses, they are secretly married by Friar Lawrence. Returning
from the ceremony, Romeo against his will mixes in a street brawl
and kills Tybalt, who had previously slain Romeo's great friend
Mercutio. For this Romeo is banished from Verona. To avoid a
marriage with Paris, which is being forced on her, Juliet takes a
sleeping potion given her by Friar Lawrence, which brings on a
semblance of death, and she is placed in the Capulet tomb. Romeo,
not having received the word about the magic potion, arrives at the
tomb and there takes poison and dies. Juliet awakes, finds Romeo
dead, and stabs herself. The double tragedy reconciles the two
houses.
       5 acts; 16 men, 4 women, extras; simple interior and ex-
terior scenes; costumes of the period.

_____. The Taming of the Shrew (1596). Acting versions read-
ily available; many reading editions; SMR.
       Baptista of Padua says his younger daughter, the lovable
Bianca, cannot marry until her older sister, the shrewish Katherina,
is married. Petruchio of Verona becomes a willing suitor of the
willful temperamental young woman. He appears for the wedding in
uncouth garments, behaves outrageously, and carries Katherine off
to Verona. There he refuses to let her eat, sleep, or dress re-
spectably (all done in reverent care of her), until he has "tamed"
her. His high-handedness makes her a more submissive wife, winning a bet with two other men on a test of their wives' obedience.
Bianca is won by Lucentio by becoming her tutor in disguise.
       5 acts; 11 men, 3 women, extras; simple interior & exterior
scenes; costumes of the period.

_____. The Tempest (1611). Acting versions readily available;
many reading editions; HARC v. 46; INCH v. 5; OXB v. 17.
       Prospero, the rightful Duke of Milan, lives with his daughter
Miranda on a desert isle, where he has drifted, and where through
his books he has developed magical powers. He is served by Ariel,
a spirit of the air, and by Caliban, a misshapen monster, son of
Sycorax, who had been an enchantress there. Prospero by his magic
arts raises a tempest which wrecks on the island a ship bearing his
usurping brother and others. Ferdinand, son of the King of Naples,
falls in love with Miranda, and after hard trials is accepted as son-
in-law by Prospero. He and Ariel foil plots, after teasing the conspirators with visionary banquets. Antonio asks his brother's forgiveness, Prospero is restored to his dukedom, and all sail with
favoring winds under Ariel's guidance back to Italy.
       5 acts; 13 men, 1 woman, 1 youth as Ariel, extras; exterior
scenes; costumes of the period.

_____. Twelfth Night (1600). Acting versions readily available;
many reading editions; MIL; OLI v. 1; INCH v. 5; OXB v. 12;

BEN.

The twin sister of Sebastian, Viola, is shipwrecked, disguises herself as a boy, and becomes page to Duke Orsino, with whom she falls in love. But Orsino is wooing the Countess Olivia and sends his page (Viola) to convey his love; Olivia, however, is attracted to the page. When Sebastian arrives, Viola's identity is revealed, Olivia transfers her affections to Sebastian, and the Duke transfers his to Viola, so both couples are married. The subplot attracts as much interest through the famous comic characters: boisterous Sir Toby Belch, brainless Sir Andrew Aguecheek, and joyous Maria, who arrange a duel between Sir Andrew and the supposed page Viola, which neither of them desire. They also plan the humiliation of the self-important steward Malvolio by making him think Olivia is deeply in love with him and who ask him to dress in an outlandish fashion.

5 acts; 11 men, 3 women, extras; simple interior and exterior scenes; costumes of the period.

_____. The Two Noble Kinsmen. See entry under Fletcher, John.

SHAW, George Bernard. Androcles and the Lion (1912). Lond., Constable, & Brentano, 1916; in his Nine Plays, Dodd, 1935; in his Complete Plays, Constable, 1931. Acting ed., French or Baker.

In the Roman arena the lion remembers the friend who removed the thorn from his foot. Androcles wins the respect of Caesar, who pardons all the martyrs.

Prolog & 2 acts; 10 men, 5 women; 1 interior, 2 exteriors; Roman costumes. Royalty: $25.

_____. The Apple Cart (1929). Samuel French.

In a future time the King of England does almost upset the proverbial apple cart. The King, tired of being simply a yes man for the Cabinet decisions, attempts to gain some real authority. Faced with the antagonism of his Prime Minister, the King threatens to abdicate and run for a seat in the House of Commons. Then comes the news that the United States desires to forget its Declaration of Independence and rejoin the British Empire. Such a move could only increase his problems, so the King, to prevent its occurrence, forgets his demands and resumes his position.

10 men, 5 women; 2 interiors, 1 exterior. Royalty: $25.

_____. Arms and the Man (1894). In his Plays, Pleasant, Brentano, 1913; in his Complete Plays, Constable, 1931; in his Nine Plays, Dodd, 1935. Acting ed., French or Baker.

With whimsical satire shows the romantic Sergius and "the chocolate soldier" Bruntschi as without illusions concerning the nature of war. Bruntschi wins Raina; Sergius finds consolation in marrying the maid.

3 acts; 4 men, 3 women; 2 interiors, 1 exterior; some military costumes. Royalty: $0-2.50.)

_____. Back to Methuselah (1922). Condensed version by Arnold

Moss. Samuel French.

The play begins in the Garden of Eden and ranges through time up to the future of 30,000 years from now. Mr. Moss compressed the original five play cycle into one of conventional length.

17 characters; various sets. Royalty: $35-25.

_____. Caesar and Cleopatra (Pub. 1899). Brentano, 1899 & 1913; in his Three Plays for Puritans, Brentano, 1906; in his Complete Plays, Constable, 1931; in his Nine Plays, Dodd, 1935; abridged in Pierce & Matthews, v. 1; in Theatre Arts for Sep., 1950. Act. ed., French or Baker.

Caesar, weary of war, finds Cleopatra in Egypt. She is a petulant charmer. He undertakes to establish her on the throne of Egypt. Her brother's adherents attack, he fights them off, scolds Cleopatra, and in leaving promises to send Mark Antony. Shaw has endeavored to make Caesar more human than history has recorded him.

5 acts; 18 men, 4 women, extras; 2 interiors, 3 exteriors; costumes of the period. Royalty: $25.

_____. Candida (1898). In his Plays, Pleasant, Lond., Richards, & Stone, Chicago, 1898 (later Brentano); Lond., Constable, & Brentano, 1905; 1919; Brentano, 1913; in his Complete Plays, Constable, 1931; in his Nine Plays, Dodd, 1935; TRE-1, 2, 3; TREA-3. Act. ed., French or Baker.

A satire on marriage, offering a sane solution of the eternal triangle. Candida with tact and intelligence will help her ministerial husband, the Rev. James Morell, to success--for he is the one who needs her love more than the visionary young poet Marchbanks.

3 acts; 4 men, 2 women; 1 interior. No royalty.

_____. Captain Brassbound's Conversion (1900). In his Three Plays for Puritans, Brentano, 1906; in his Complete Plays, Constable, 1931; in his Six Plays, Dodd, 1941. Act. ed., Samuel French.

Captain Brassbound, a sort of freebooter in Morocco, is asked by Lady Cicely and her brother-in-law, Judge Hallam, to escort them through Algeria. Brassbound is glad to get a chance for revenge on the judge, who is his uncle, and plans to sell him into captivity. But he falls victim to Lady Cicely's charm and graciousness and seems completely converted from his piratical ways when she secures his acquittal. He is saved from proposing marriage to her by being summoned back to his ship. She murmurs: "What an escape."

3 acts; 12 men, 1 woman, extras; 2 interiors, 1 exterior.

_____. The Devil's Disciple (1899). Brentano, 1899 & 1913; in his Three Plays for Puritans, Brentano, 1906; in his Complete Plays, Constable, 1931; in his Nine Plays, Dodd, 1935. Act. ed., French or Baker.

During the American Revolution the British have captured a New Hampshire town and decide to hang the most prominent citizen, the Rev. Mr. Anderson, as a lesson to the rebels. They mistake

for the parson a godless scamp, Dick Dudgeon, who calls himself
the devil's disciple as a protest against the bogus piety of his Puritan mother.   Dick insists on carrying out the imposture but, with
the noose around his neck, expecting to die nobly, is delivered by
the parson.   Shaw writes calculated insults to Americans and heavy
potshots at Puritanism.
   3 acts; 10 men, 3 women, extras; 4 interiors, 1 exterior;
   costumes of the period.   No royalty.

     . Fanny's First Play (1911).   In his Misalliance, etc.,
  Brentano, 1914; Lond., Constable, 1915; Brentano, 1917; in his
  Complete Plays, Constable, 1931; in his Nine Plays, Dodd, 1935.
  Act. ed., Samuel French.
   A play within a play.   Unknown Fanny has written a play to
the production of which all the well-known (English) critics are invited.   After the performance, the critics all agree they can't say
whether it is good or not until they know who wrote it--thus Shaw
ridicules his critics.   The plot of Fanny's play concerns the son of
the Lilley family who is thrown into jail after a brawl.   Margaret,
his fiancée, is also there for hitting a policeman.   While the families feel disgraced, the young people are drawn together still further.
   Prolog & 3 acts & epilog; 12 men, 5 women; 3 interiors.

     . Heartbreak House (written 1914; produced 1919).   Bren-
  tano, 1919; in his Complete Plays, Constable, 1931; in his Six
  Plays, Dodd, 1941.   Act. ed., Samuel French.
   At Heartbreak House a group of social parasites are assembled, among them Boss Mangan, a business executive.   They discuss social and political affairs which might lead to war, as they
did in 1914.   A burglar intrudes and passes the hat.   Bombs fall;
Mangan and the burglar are the only ones killed.
   3 acts; 6 men, 4 women; 1 interior, 1 exterior; costumes of
  the period.   Royalty: $25.

     . Major Barbara (1907).   In his John Bull's Other Island,
  Brentano, 1907; in his Complete Plays, Constable, 1931; in his
  Six Plays, Dodd, 1941.   Act. ed., French or Baker.
   Barbara Undershaft, daughter of a munitions maker, renounces high society to become a Salvation Army major.   To her
dismay she learns that the Army and other charitable organizations
accept money even from the capitalists--income from any source is
desirable, even if tainted.   Finally she is ready to accept her
father's dictum that poverty alone is shameful; she marries a man
in the munitions factory.
   3 acts; 9 men, 6 women; 1 interior, 2 exteriors.   Royalty:
  $25.

     . Man and Superman (1905).   Lond., Constable, & Bren-
  tano, 1905; Brentano, 1913; in his Complete Plays, Constable,
  1931; in his Nine Plays, Dodd, 1935.   Act. ed., French or
  Baker.
   Jack Tanner, appointed Ann Whitefield's guardian, discovers
she is interested in him romantically; in fact, she has decided to

marry him.   He objects to the idea, and warned by his chauffeur,
he flies from her in his motor car.   But she aggressively pursues
him and captures him in the mountains of Spain, for she is Every-
woman, the Life Force, which cannot be denied.

       4 acts (but Act 3 is usually omitted in production, showing
Don Juan in hell); 12 men, 5 women, extras; 1 interior, 3
exteriors.   No royalty.

           . Pygmalion (1913).   In Everybody's 31:577, Nov. 1914; in
Androcles, Overrules, & Pygmalion, Constable, & Brentano,
1916; Constable, Sep. 1920; in his Complete Plays, Constable,
1931; in his Six Plays, Dodd, 1941; Penguin books, 1942.   Act.
ed., French or Baker.

       A guttersnipe cockney flowergirl, Eliza Doolittle, is made
over in her speech into a duchess by a Professor of Phonetics, Henry Higgins.   She has the sensitivity of the respectable poor; he is
fanatically absorbed in his work and is insensitive to the feelings of
others.   He does not face the question: What are you going to do
with me now?   The satire on middle-class morality, lifting the un-
deserving poor into respectability, as developed by Eliza's father,
the dustman, is highly amusing.

       5 acts; 4 men, 7 women, extras; 2 interiors, 1 exterior.
Royalty: $25.

           . Saint Joan (1923).   Brentano, & Macmillan, 1924; in his
Nine Plays, Dodd, 1935; Penguin books, 1942; THF.   Act. ed.,
French or Baker.

       Pictures the Maid of Orleans in successive episodes of her
life of faith and disillusionment: before Baudrecourt, at the Dauphin's court, her victory at Orleans, the crowning at Rheims, her
trial before judges who have fanatic faith in their system.   Twenty-
five years later her sentence is reversed by Charles VII.   The epilog takes place in 1920 when she is canonized.

       6 acts & epilog; 22 men, 2 women, extras; 6 interiors, 1 ex-
terior; costumes of the period.   Royalty: $25.

           . You Never Can Tell (1898).   In his Plays, Pleasant,
Lond., Richards, & Stone, Chicago, 1898 (later Brentano);
Lond., Constable, & Brentano, 1905, & 1919; sep. Brentano,
1913; in his Complete Plays, Constable, 1931; abridged in
Pierce & Matthews, v. 1.   Act. ed., Samuel French.

       Satirizes many social conventions, making heroes of wise
William the waiter with a pompous lawyer-son and of a struggling
young dentist, Mr. Valentine, who falls impetuously in love with
Gloria.   Unmasks the woman's rights' advocate, Mrs. Clandon, who
has failed to make her daughter Gloria impervious to the advances
of men, or to control the twins, Dolly and Phil.   Mrs. Clandon has
brought up her three children in Madeira, away from their father
and has taken her maiden name; so they demand to know who their
father is.   He turns out to be Valentine's landlord, Fergus Crampton.

       4 acts; 6 men, 5 women; 2 interiors, 1 exterior.

SHAW, Irwin.   Children from Their Games (1963).   Samuel French.

A modern misanthrope has a thousand grievances with the
world, and he takes great pleasure in playing back to it, on his recorder, the awful sounds of the city.   He wants to end it all but
has theological reasons against suicide.   He tries to persuade an
army buddy to kill him, but the friend has married money and
doesn't wish to throw it all away on a murder rap.   And people
keep getting in the way of his hoped-for death: a quack doctor, a
daughter-in-law, a pro football player, and a widow who bribes him
with 1,000 phonograph records and the knowledge of a bar that sells
sixty-five cent martinis.   For every step toward destruction he takes
he meets frustration.
   5 men, 2 women; 1 interior.   Royalty: $50-25.

_____. The Gentle People (1939).   Dramatists Play Service.
   A Brooklyn fairy tale in which the meek seem justly to
triumph.   Two old pals, Jonah and Philip fish off Steeplechase
pier; they are saving up for a boat to travel South to the Gulf.
Harold Goff, a Brooklyn racketeer gangster, makes them pay $5 a
week for protection; makes passes at Stella, Jonah's daughter; and
learning they have saved up $190 toward the boat, he takes that
too.   Though they appeal to the law, a crooked judge dismisses the
case.   Outraged, the pair plan a way to be rid of Goff.   They take
him for a boatride, knock him off, and toss him overboard.   They
recover their savings and a bit more, and dream again of their
cruise to the tropics.   Their crime is never discovered.
   10 men, 3 women; 3 interiors, 2 exteriors.   Royalty: $25.

_____. The Survivors.   See entry under Viertel, Peter.

SHAW, Robert.   The Man in the Glass Booth (1968).   Samuel
   French.
   A rich New York real estate operator boasts of his German
Jewishness and carries a handgun for his protection.   But when Is-
raeli agents track him down to take him home to stand trial for war
crimes as a Nazi killer of Jews he surrenders meekly to them.   In
his glass booth he confesses to being a Nazi killer and guilty of all
counts, but this mask is ripped off him by a Jewish woman who remembers him--not as a Nazi, but as a Jew like herself.
   18 men, 3 women; 3 interiors.   Royalty: $50-35.

SHELDON, Edward.   The Boss (1911).   QUIK; QUIL.
   Courageous boss Regan, devoted to his standards, attracts
Emily, his wife, through his strength of character, getting first
pity, then sympathy, and finally love.
   4 acts; 13 men, 4 women; 3 interiors.

_____. The Jest.   See entry under Benelli, Sem.

_____. The Nigger (1909).   Macmillan, 1910.
   One of the first plays to deal with the social problem of the
Negro.   Portrays the tragic discovery by a Southern Governor that
he is the grandson of a Negress.   Introduces as issues connected
with the Negro question, lynch law, prohibition, and political dis-

franchisement.
    3 acts; 11 men, 3 women, extras; 2 interiors, 1 exterior.

_____ . Romance (1913).   French, 1914; Macmillan, 1924; BAK;
    abridged in Mantle & Sherwood 1909/19.   Baker's Plays.
    Pictures the love of a young rector in New York for an
Italian opera singer and its purifying effect upon her.   Unites realism harmoniously with romantic passion.
    Prolog, 3 acts, & epilog; 12 men, 9 women; 4 interiors;
    costumes of 1860.   Royalty: $25.

SHERIDAN, Richard Brinsley.   The Rivals (1775).   Acting editions
    readily available; BRI v. 1; DIB v. 9; INCH v. 19; MOR; NET;
    OXB v. 1; STM; TUQ; TWE; UHL.
    A country squire, Bob Acres, is a willing rival to Capt.
Jack Absolute for the hand of a romantic young lady, Lydia Languish.
She wants to elope with Ensign Beverley, the lower rank which Capt.
Jack assumes to win her.   A duel is arranged, but when Acres
finds that Beverley is his friend Capt. Jack, he calls the match off
and relinquishes all claims to Lydia.   Her aunt, Mrs. Malaprop,
has become famous for her blunders in the use of words.
    5 acts; 9 men, 5 women; 5 interiors, 4 exteriors (reducible
    to 2 interiors, 2 exteriors); costumes of the period.

_____ .   The School for Scandal (1777).   Acting editions readily
    available; BRI v. 2; CLA; CLF v. 1; COF; COH; HARC v. 18;
    HUD; LIE; MAT; MOO; MOSE v. 2; NET; RUB; SMO; STA;
    STM; TAU; THO; TREA-1; TUQ; TWE; UHL.
    Young Lady Teazle, married to older Sir Peter but quarreling
with him, joins the scandal-mongers: Sir Benjamon Backbite, Lady
Sneerwell, and Mrs. Candour in their discussions of London high
society.   The two brothers, Joseph and Charles Surface, are contrasted: Joseph is hypocritical and making advances to Lady Teazle;
Charles is goodnatured but extravagant.   When their uncle Sir Oliver
returns from India and poses as needing help, Joseph refuses, alleging the stinginess of his rich uncle; Charles is willing to help by
selling the family portraits--all save the one of his uncle.   In the
famous screen scene, Joseph is completely exposed as a villain, and
Sir Peter and Lady Teazle are reconciled.
    5 acts; 13 men, 4 women, extras; 7 interiors; costumes of
    the period.

SHERRIFF, R. C.   Home at Seven (1950).   Samuel French.
    The Prestons are happily, respectably, and dully married.
The husband, David, works in the city but always returns from the
office at 7 o'clock.   Mrs. Preston always has his tea ready at that
time.   But one day David stays away for twenty-four hours.   His
wife fears an "interest" somewhere, but it turns out that David lost
his memory momentarily.   He does, however, try to hide the fact
that he stopped for some sherry at a hotel on his way home.   But
complications arise: the club's money is missing, the club steward
murdered, and the crimes committed during David's lapse and disappearance.
    5 men, 2 women; 1 interior.   Royalty: $35-25.

_____ . Journey's End (1928).   Samuel French.
Pictures the effect of war on a group of young English officers in a dug-out in World War I.   Young Raleigh is bewildered by
the metamorphosis of Capt. Stanhope, his school hero, into a hardened drinker and ruthless soldier.   Stanhope's pose is abandoned
when Raleigh is wounded, for it was his way of enduring the war.
Stanhope comforts Raleigh before he dies.
        10 men; 1 interior.   Royalty: $50-25.

_____ . A Shred of Evidence (1960).   Samuel French.
A hit-and-run accident threatens to destroy Richard Medway's
recently won business success in this mystery.   Although he can re-
call no accidents, Richard's car is dented and a man attempts to
blackmail him, claiming he can prove Richard was the driver.
Finally Richard confesses and faces imprisonment, but a last minute
discovery of a shred of evidence changes the course of the play.
        6 men, 3 women; 1 interior.   Royalty: $35-25.

_____ . St. Helena (1936).   Lond., Gollancz, 1934; Stokes, 1935;
        abridged in Mantle 1936/37; FAMI.
Covering the last seven years of Napoleon's exile, depicts
various episodes as revealing the character of the military genius,
now an aged warrior.   He insists on being addressed as Emperor,
he sees pitiful quarreling among his friends, and he suffers minor
persecutions by the British government.
        3 acts; 20 men, 4 women; 4 interiors, 2 exteriors; costumes
        of the period.

SHERWOOD, Robert E.   Abe Lincoln in Illinois (1938).   Dramatists
        Play Service.
Pulitzer prize play, 1939.   Episodes in his life from New
Salem days up to his departure for Washington in 1861.   Shows a
maturing and apprehensive young man slowly realizing the great
destiny before him.   Presents Mary Todd's persistent pursuit and
capture of a coming great man; his anti-slavery debates with
Douglas; his desperate hope that he would not be elected; his de-
jected departure for Washington; his growing conviction that the
ideals of liberty and equality are not decadent nor doomed.
        12 scenes; 25 men, 7 women; 7 interiors, 3 exteriors; cos-
        tumes of 1830 through 1861.   Royalty: $25.   (Almost any
        scene can be done as a one-act with a fee of $10.)

_____ . Idiot's Delight (1936).   Dramatists Play Service.
Pulitzer Prize play, 1936.   A group of guests--an English
couple, a German scientist, a French Communist, a munitions mag-
nate, vulgar but lovable Harry Van and his troupe of chorus girls--
are at a small winter resort in the Alps, where an air raid threatens
and finally comes.   Exposes the idiocy of war; an ironic picture of
man who brings about wholesale destruction by war and can make
only a futile gesture against the forces he has set in motion.
        3 acts; 17 men, 10 women, extras; 1 interior.   Royalty:
        $25.

_____. The Petrified Forest (1935). Dramatists Play Service.
      On his way to the Petrified Forest, where he anticipates
death and burial in a defunct world, Alan Squire, a disillusioned intellectual, stops at a lunch room in Arizona where Gabby is the
waitress. Duke Mantee and his gangsters come to hide out there.
Alan Finds Gabby a worthwhile dreamer and signs over his life insurance to her before he welcomes being shot by Mantee.
      2 acts; 18 men (several bit parts), 3 women; 1 interior.
Royalty: $25.

_____. The Queen's Husband (1928). David McKay.
      A courageous king is ruler of all the people of the land ex-
cept one--his wife--in this romantic comedy. Princess Anne loves
her father's secretary, Granton, but her mother insists she marry
a strange prince. But her father, King Eric VIII, helps her elope
with Granton, and then goes bravely to face his wife's displeasure.
      11 men, 4 women; extras optional; 1 interior. Royalty: $25.

_____. Reunion in Vienna (1931). Dramatists Play Service.
      Reassembles, after ten years, a group of exiled Austrian
royalists. Former mistress Elena of the wild Hapsburgian crown
prince Rudolph, now the wife of an eminent psychiatrist Dr. Krug,
is advised by her husband to cure her old infatuation with Rudolf by
renewing contact with its inspiration. She succumbs, but only for
one night. Morning brings reality; she returns to her husband; Rudolf returns to his taxicab in Nice.
      3 acts; 23 men, 7 women; 2 interiors. Royalty: $25.

_____. The Road to Rome (1927). Samuel French.
      Amytis, the flighty, beautiful wife of Fabius the Dictator, de-
cides to see Hannibal, whose troops have surrounded Rome, rather
than to flee to her mother in Ostia. He falls for her instead of killing her. Amusing satire on the stolid Roman senators, giving as
good a reason as any why Hannibal failed to capture the city.
      3 acts; 22 men, 3 women; 1 interior, 1 exterior. Royalty:
$35-25.

_____. Second Threshold. See entry under Barry, Philip.

_____. Small War on Murray Hill (1959). Dramatists Play Ser-
vice.
      A comedy about the American Revolution. Sherwood hypothe-
sizes on why British General Sir William Howe tarried at the home
of Mrs. Robert Murray instead of driving a wedge between the armies of Generals Isaac Putnam and George Washington, and thereby
defeating the American patriots. Sherwood suggests that the delaying
tactics of Mrs. Murray consisted of unique cocktails, an excellent
creole lunch, bright conversation, good brandy, a steamed clam
dinner, and her own beauty.
      10 men, 3 women, 8 non-speaking men, 5 non-speaking
women; unit set. Royalty: $50-25.

_____. There Shall Be No Night (1940). Dramatists Play Service.

Deals with the Nazi invasion of Finland. Pulitzer Prize,
1941. Eric, the son of a patriotic Finnish scientist with an American wife, marries Kaatri. He is killed in the Russian invasion of
Finland. Kaatri goes to America to carry on. Uncle Waldemar
philosophizes on the struggle of man for freedom versus war with
its ignorance and bestiality; he emphasizes faith and courage of free
men everywhere and the essential soundness of democracy. Rich
in wisdom and pity, fired with the flame of indignation.
    13 men (2 bits), 4 women (2 bits); 3 interiors. Royalty:
    $35-25.

_____. Tovarich. See entry under Deval, Jacques.

SHIPMAN, Samuel and John B. Hymer. East Is West (1918).
    French, 1924.
    Billy Benson persuades a Chinese merchant from San Fran-
cisco at the auction in China, to buy Ming Toy instead of letting her
go to Charlie Yong, a trafficker in maids. So she is taken to San
Francisco and becomes a maid in the Benson household. Billy declares his love for Ming Toy, but the family objects. When Charlie
Yong comes with three tong men, Hop Toy, her supposed father,
reveals that Ming is not his daughter but was stolen as a babe from
some American people in China.
    Prolog & 3 acts; 13 men, 5 women, extras; 2 interiors, 1
    exterior; some Chinese costumes.

SHULMAN, Irving. Rebel Without a Cause. See entry under Sergel,
    Clark F.

SHULMAN, Max. The Many Loves of Dobie Gillis. See entry under
    Davidson, William.

_____. Rally 'Round the Flag, Boys! See entry under Rogers,
    David.

SHYRE, Paul. The Child Buyer (1962). Adapted from John Her-
    sey's novel. Samuel French.
    How a joint government and giant corporation scheme to "buy"
child prodigies and give them special training is analyzed in this
science fiction drama. The corporation has a fifty-year defense
contract and needs some super-intelligent specially educated children.
Their plan is to buy young prodigies, wipe out their memories, and
retrain them electronically, teaching nothing but science. The process, however, atrophies their senses, making them nothing but
human-like computers. At first citizens are horrified, but the child
buyer has unlimited amounts of purchase money and teachers. Finally one boy does submit, but only because he believes he can beat
the system.
    10 men, 4 women, 1 child; 1 interior. Royalty: $35-25.

_____. Pictures in the Hallway (Dramatic Reading) (1956).
    Adapted from the autobiography of Sean O'Casey. Samuel
    French.

In this section of O'Casey's early autobiography we find him in his first confrontation with women; in the episodes and skirmishes of the Irish Rebellion; in his first disastrous job at a book store; and in his first acquaintance with a family death. O'Casey makes a momentous decision here to move into the thick of life and mold his own impression on history.

4 men, 2 women; no scenery. Royalty: $50-25.

_____. U.S.A. See entry under Don Passo, John.

_____. A Whitman Portrait (Stage Reading) (1967). Dramatists Play Service.

A sketch of Walt Whitman, the poet and the man, from his early days in Brooklyn, through the Civil War, to his death. Both prose and poetry are included which emphasize Whitman's faith in man, his great humanitarianism, and his buoyant optimism. Brooks Atkinson wrote: "It is a portrait of not only a stirring American poet but of an exultant American nation."

3 men, 1 woman; unit set; incidental music included. Royalty: $35-25.

SIGURJÓNSSON, Jóhann. Eyvind of the Hills (1911). Tr. by Schanche in Modern Icelandic Plays, American-Scandinavian Foundation, 1916.

Halla loves the real character of the heroic Eyvind and elects to share with him the enforced outlaw life and hardships of a bleak wilderness. An intense inner life is revealed with poetic vision which creates actual flesh and blood, exalted with noble passion.

4 acts; 7 men, 5 women, 2 children, extras; 2 interiors, 2 exteriors, old Icelandic costumes.

_____. The Hraun Farm (1908). Tr. by Schanche in Modern Icelandic Plays, American-Scandinavian Foundation, 1916; in Smith, Short Plays.

Sveinung, a patriarch, the owner of the farm with a lava field on it, is torn between his love for the homestead and his daughter. He wants her to marry his neighbor's son who would keep up the estate. The tearful pleading of his wife wins his consent to the daughter's marriage to the man she loves, Sølvi, a geologist.

3 acts; 6 men, 6 women, 2 children; 3 exteriors.

_____. Loft's Wish (1915). Tr. by Johnson in Poet Lore, v. 46, 1940.

As an Icelandic Faust, Loft sells his soul to the Devil. He employs black magic to destroy Steinunn in order to marry Disa. Steinunn commits suicide, which drives Loft mad and on to his death. He fails because of his selfishness.

2 acts; 5 men, 4 women, 1 girl, extras; 1 interior; costumes of early 18th century in Iceland.

SILLS, Paul. Story Theatre (1970). Based on fables from Aesop and the Brothers Grimm. Samuel French.

Adult theater which dramatizes the stories of Henny Penny,
The Golden Goose, Venus and the Cat, the Fisherman and his Wife,
the Robber Baron, the Bremen Town Musicians, and others.
  5 men, 3 women; stage projections. Royalty: $50-35.

SIMON, Neil. Barefoot in the Park (1963). Samuel French.
  After a six-day honeymoon, a new lawyer, who has just won
his first case (six cents in damages), and his young wife, who is
as pretty and befuddled as can be, move into a new high-rent apartment that she has chosen. They find as many problems, however,
for in order to get to the apartment one has to climb six steep
flights of stairs. Once in the apartment there are more troubles:
the paint job is atrocious, there is no furniture, the skylight leaks
snow, and there is no room for a double bed. There is also an un-
believeable gourmet who lives in a loft on the roof and uses the
window ledge and the apartment as his only access to his perch.
The situation breaks the heart of the young lawyer. His wife kicks
him out when he refuses to walk barefoot in the snow in the park.
He returns, not for reconciliation, but because he thinks that since
he pays the rent she should be the one to go.
  4 men, 2 women; 1 interior. Royalty: $50-35.

_____. Come Blow Your Horn (1961). Samuel French.
  Harry Baker, owner of a large artificial fruit business, has
two sons. Alan, a thirty-three year old playboy, works two days
and plays five--usually accompanied by beautiful girls. Buddy,
twenty-one, has been up to now an obedient son. But he asserts
himself too, leaving a rebellious letter for his father and moving
into his older brother's bachelor pad. Comic complications follow.
  3 men, 4 women; 1 interior. Royalty: $50-25.

_____. The Gingerbread Lady (1971). Samuel French.
  Evy Meara is a pop singer, gone to pot from too much alcohol and sex. When the play opens, she is nearing the end of a
ten-week "drying out" period. A lady friend, a homosexual actor,
a daughter, and a former lover all try to help her adjust to her new
sober life, but they leave her worse off than before, and by the end
of the play Evy Meara is definitely off the wagon.
  3 men, 3 women; 1 interior. Royalty: $50-35.

_____. The Good Doctor (1974). Samuel French.
  A play made up of vignettes from the short stories of Anton
Chekhov: a scolding woman who berates a bank manager for his
gout and lack of money, a father who takes his son to a place where
he can be initiated into the mysteries of sex but then loses his
nerve and abandons his son there, a man who offers to drown himself for three rubles. The principal role is that of Writer--a composite of Checkhov and Neil Simon himself.
  2 men, 3 women; various settings. Royalty: $50-35.

_____. Last of the Red Hot Lovers (1970). Samuel French.
  Barney Cashman is forty-seven years old and has been faithful to his wife for 23 years. He decides to join the Sexual Revolu-

tion before it's too late for him, but it turns out that he is just too
gentle, or too inexperienced, to pull it off. His first attempt at
adultery (with a sex-pot) fails when he takes her to his mother's
apartment. His second (with an actress) and third (with his wife's
best friend) are also unsuccessful.

    1 man, 3 women; 1 interior. Royalty: $50-35.

_____ . The Odd Couple (1965). Samuel French.
    The boys are gathered in the messy apartment of one of the
group, recently divorced. They are waiting for another member who
is late. When they discover that his wife has just left him, they
fear he might commit suicide, and so they lock all of the windows
and take other precautions. When he does arrive, he decides to
stay and live with the resident of the messy apartment. Then the
patterns of their former marriages begin to reappear. One man is
too meticulous--the other too much a slob. They even quarrel over
the necessity to telephone if one will be late for dinner. A hilarious
comedy.

    6 men, 2 women; 1 interior. Royalty: $50-35.

_____ . Plaza Suite (1968). Samuel French.
    Three playlets about marriage, all taking place in the same
suite at the Plaza Hotel. In the first, a couple discovers that the
suite they have taken while their house is being painted is the same
one they honeymooned in 23 or 24 years ago. Their anniversary is
today, according to one, and yesterday according to the other. In
the second play a thrice-married Hollywood producer arranges a
meeting with a childhood sweetheart (now a suburban housewife) for
a little sexual diversion. She turns out to be more than he bargained for. In the last play a mother and father try to get their
daughter out of the locked bathroom and down to the ballroom for
her wedding.

    7 men, 5 women; 1 interior. Royalty: $50-35.

_____ . The Prisoner of Second Avenue (1972). Samuel French.
    Sympathetic humor over the plight of a well-paid executive
named Mel. He loses his job in a company rift. His wife takes a
job to tide them over, but she loses hers too. Pollution is killing
everything that grows outside on the terrace, the paper-thin walls
of the high-rise they live in reveal everything they never wanted to
know about the lives of the German stewardesses next door, burglars hit their apartment, and Mel's psychiatrist dies with $23,000
of his money. Mel does the only thing left to do--he has a nervous
breakdown. Then he recovers from it, getting stronger and surviving
in spite of his troubles.

    2 men, 4 women; 1 interior. Royalty: $50-35.

_____ . The Star-Spangled Girl (1966). Dramatists Play Service.
    Andy Hobart and Norman Cornell struggle to put out a pro-
test magazine in their combination office-apartment in San Francisco.
The two endure near-starvation, threatening calls from their unpaid
printer, and (to keep Mrs. Mackininee, the landlady, from asking
for the rent) dates with a middle-age woman who wants to go motor-

cycling, surfing, and sky-diving. Into the lives of the two young
radicals comes Sophie Rauschmeyer, a Deep South Olympic swimmer
and all-American girl, who moves into the apartment next door.
Sophie becomes convinced that the pair are editing a dangerously sub-
versive magazine, but when the right member of the pair becomes
romantically interested in her, she finds that some political accom-
modation is possible.
          2 men, 1 woman; 1 interior. Royalty: $50-25.

          . The Sunshine Boys (1973). Samuel French.
          Willie Clark used to be half of a dynamite vaudeville team
with Al Lewis. Now in their seventies, the two haven't seen one
another for 11 years and haven't spoken for 12. Willie's nephew Ben
aranges for the two to get together once more for a CBS television
salute to comedy (they'll earn $10,000). Willie doesn't want to, be-
cause Al is always sticking his finger into his chest and accidentally
spitting in his face. He finally relents, however, only to walk off
the rehearsal stage when Al pokes him in the chest and accidentally
spits in his face. At the end of the play, while Willie recovers
from a heart attack, the two old friends/foes look forward to spending
the rest of their lives together at a New Jersey old actor's home--
insulting one another.
          5 men, 2 women; 2 interiors. Royalty: $50-35.

SIMPSON, N. F. One Way Pendulum (1960). Samuel French.
          Based on a rather unique premise of a man's dedicated at-
tempts to make penny scales sing the chorus of Handel's "Messiah, "
this farcical comedy presents a host of bizarre and zany characters.
The man who wants the scales to sing "Messiah" also has a cash
register, which he bought in case he should ever want a typewriter
and need a trade-in.   Then his aunt arrives, after getting on the
wrong train, and constantly harrasses him to buy her a tricycle.
In a desperate attempt to establish some sort of order in his life,
the man reconstructs the Old Baily courthouse right in his own living
room and begins dispensing "justice" to all the characters who appear
until the man finally resolves his problems.
          10 men, 4 women; composite interior. Royalty: $35-25.

SKELTON, Geoffrey. Marat/Sade. See entry under Weiss, Peter.

SKINNER, Cornelia Otis. Our Hearts Were Young and Gay. See
     entry under Kerr, Jean.

SKLAR, George. Laura. See entry under Caspary, Vera.

SLADE, Bernard. Same Time, Next Year (1975). Samuel French.
          George is a C.P.A. and Doris a housewife. Each is happily
married with three children, but the two strangers get together one
night in February of 1951. George has flown to northern California
to do somebody's books; Doris is there on a religious retreat. They
carry on their affair by meeting at the same country inn every February. We track them as they meet all the way up to 1975, during
which time George has been neurotic and uptight, stuffy and rich,

into analysis, a with-it encounter groupie, a late blooming hippie,
and finally back into the establishment. Doris, meanwhile, has
moved from awkward young wife to restless, to back to college, to
overaged flower child, to successful businesswoman, to what is finally a mature woman. The transitions of the two are always revealing, but never are they in synch with one another.
    1 man, 1 woman; 1 interior. Royalty on application.

SMITH, Dodie (pseud. of C. L. Anthony). Autumn Crocus (1932).
    Samuel French.
    Two English school ma'ams are on holiday at an inn in the
Austrian Tyrol, Edith and Fanny. Fanny yearns for romance and
thinks she finds it with André, the young and handsome innkeeper,
amid the mountains and fields of autumn crocus. She wants to stay
on, even when she discovers he is married and has a little girl; but
Edith persuades her with hints of what might happen. She takes the
bus with Edith and goes back home to drudgery; but she has a
memory.
    3 acts; 4 men, 8 women; 1 interior, 2 exteriors. Royalty:
$25-20.

    _____. Call It a Day (1936). Samuel French.
    Crowds into the 16 hours of the first day of Spring the ups
and downs of the Hilton family: Roger, in and out with an actress;
Dorothy, touched by the loneliness of a rubber planter; Cathy, falling
for a philandering painter with a watchful wife; Ann, achieving a
Rossetti drawing; Martin, experiencing love at first sight; while below stairs, the cook and Vera and the daily help are living with
equal zest.
    3 acts; 5 men, 11 women; 2 interiors, 1 exterior. Royalty:
$25-20.

    _____. Dear Octopus (1938). Samuel French.
    Four generations of the Randolph family assemble for the
golden wedding of Charles and Dora--the family is the octopus which
holds them together, and from which none wishes to escape. Each
member of the family is distinctively sketched. A love plot revolves
around bachelor Nicholas (35) and Fenny (29), Dora's companion for
ten years.
    3 acts; 4 men, 10 women, 1 boy of 10, 2 girls of 9 & 12;
3 interiors. Royalty: $25-20.

SMITH, Harry James. Mrs. Bumpstead-Leigh (1910). French 1917;
    MOSJ; MOSL; abridged in Mantle & Sherwood 1909-1919.
    Richly characterizes the social climber who endeavors to land
herself and family as from England where hyphenated names are
popular. Her advance becomes complicated when she is recognized
by a unique fellow townsman from Ohio who is now agent for tomb-
stones--a monumentalist, as he calls himself.
    3 acts; 6 men, 6 women; 1 interior.

SMITH, Winchell and Victor Mapes. The Boomerang (1915).
    French, 1915.

The young doctor is so anxious to have a case that he undertakes to cure Bud of the disease of love.   However he develops the
same symptoms himself and succumbs to the nurse, Virginia.
3 acts; 6 men, 5 women; 2 interiors.

_____ and Frank Bacon. Lightnin' (1918).   French, 1918; CERC.
Lovable ne'er-do-well Lightnin' Bill Jones has a hotel on the
Nevada-California border, so that the Nevada sheriff can't arrest the
men who step over into California.   Lightnin' refuses to sell the hotel to two fake promoters who are trying to swindle his wife.   He
pleads his own case in court with striking success.
Prolog & 3 acts; 12 men, 12 women; 3 interiors.

SOMMER, Edith.   A Roomful of Roses (1956).   Dramatists Play
Service.
The fears of a 15-year-old girl whose parents are divorced
are effectively dramatized in this moving, yet often funny play.
Bridget's mother had left her family eight years earlier.   The little
girl has lived with her bitter, unloving father since then.   Now,
however, he's thinking of remarrying and sends Bridget to stay with
her mother.   Bridget arrives, lonely and scared, yet arrogantly refusing to admit that she needs and wants love.   For a while she insists on remaining aloof, but she can't resist the sincere affection
of her mother and her new husband, and Dick, the boy who lives
next door.   Just as she's preparing to go to a dance with Dick, however, his old girl friend appears and Bridget is left without a date.
Although this apparent rebuff forces her back into her shell, it's
only temporary.   With their obvious love, her mother and Dick convince her she is really wanted, and Bridget is at last part of a real
family.
5 women (2 teens), 3 men (1 teen), 1 small boy; 1 interior.
Royalty: $50-25.

SOPHOCLES.   Antigone (441 B.C.).   Many translations, among
    them: Storr in Loeb Library; Young in Everyman's; Campbell
    in World's Classics; Coleridge in Bohn's; tr. by Jebb, Mac-
    millan; HUD; TRE-1, -2, (v. 2); THO; tr. by Gilbert Murray,
    Oxford; tr. by Way, Macmillan; adapted & carried by Baker;
    BLO; tr. by Plumptre, Heath; tr. by Fitts & Fitzgerald, Har-
    court; FIT; OAT; TEN; tr. by Wildman, adapted by Cocteau in
    BEN; see also Anouilh's Antigone.
Antigone rebels against Creon's edict that the body of her
brother Polynices remain unburied.   She covers his body with dirt.
Brought before Creon, she is punished by being buried alive.
Creon rescinds the decree too late, for not only has she died, but
his son, Haemon, her betrothed, has stabbed himself beside her,
and his wife Eurydice has also killed herself.   The shattered Creon
is left alone to long for death.
1 continuous act; 6 men, 3 women, chorus of Elders; 1 exterior.

_____ .   Electra (ca. 420 B.C.).   Many translations, among
    them: Storr in Loeb Library; Young in Everyman's; Campbell

in World's Classics; Coleridge in Bohn's; other recommended
translations: by Way, Macmillan; by Jebb, Macmillan; by
Plumptre, Heath; by Ferguson, W. R. Scott; FIT; by Percy,
French; OAT; Plumptre tr. in CLS.   Compare treatment by
Euripides, tr. by Murray in TRE-1 & 2 (v. 2).

     After the murder of her father, Agamemnon, Electra has re-
mained in the household, enduring insult and humiliation for many
years.   She had sent her young brother orestes away for safe keeping.   Grown to manhood, Orestes returns with his friend Pylades.
He reveals himself to Electra, and, spurred on by her, murders
both Clytemnestra and Aegisthus.   She marries Pylades.
     1 continuous act; 4 men, 3 women, extras, chorus of women;
     1 exterior.

_____.   Oedipus Tyrannus (ca. 431 B. C.).   Many translations,
     among them: Storr in Loeb Library; Young in Everyman's;
Campbell in World's Classics; Coleridge in Bohn's; other recom-
mended translations: Jebb, Macmillan; MAU; by Gilbert Murray,
Oxford; CAR; COJ; MIL; by Way, Macmillan; Plumptre, Heath;
(also in SMP); Fitts & Fitzgerald, Harcourt, as Oedipus Rex;
Yeats as Oedipus the King, Macmillan; FIT; GREN; HARC-8;
OAT; TEN; TREA-1.

     The citizens of Thebes appeal for relief from the plague which
the oracle has said was caused by the presence of the murderer of
King Laius.   Oedipus the King vows he will find out who he is.   Ti-
resias the seer accuses him of being the man.   Slowly he realizes
that it is indeed himself who has fulfilled the prophecy, having killed
his father and married his mother.   In this hopeless struggle against
fate, he blinds himself, to live out his life in misery.
     1 continuous act; 7 men, 1 woman, 2 girls, extras; chorus of
     Theban men; 1 exterior.

_____.   Philoctetes (409 B. C.).   Tr. by Storr in Loeb Library;
     by Young in Everyman's; by Campbell in World's Classics; by
Coleridge in Bohn's; by Plumptre, Heath; by Way, Macmillan;
by Jebb, Macmillan; in OAT.

     On the way to the Trojan war, Philoctetes, a renowned ar-
cher, is left on the desolate isle of Lemnos because of a wound.
He has become naturally embittered by 9 years' neglect, but his nature has been chastened by suffering.   Because of a prediction that
the Trojan war could be won only through the bow of Heracles (entrusted to Philoctetes), Odysseus the unscrupulous and the young
Neoptolemus, the generous-hearted son of Achilles, undertake to
secure it.   Odysseus plans to get it by conscienceless intrigue.
Neoptolemus wants no part in the deception.   Philoctetes defies Odysseus, when Heracles appears in divine effulgence and promises re-
nown and healing of his wound; whereupon he follows them to Troy.
     1 continuous act; 5 men, chorus of sailors; 1 exterior.

SOWERBY, Githa.   Rutherford & Son (1912).   Lond., Sidgwick, &
     Doran, 1912; DIG; PLAP v. 2.
     Old John Rutherford is masterful and obstinate; he regards
his work as his religion and he sacrifices all for business.   He tries

to get a trade secret from his son, John Jr., who leaves because
of this, and he turns his daughter Janet out of the house because
she married Martin, a foreman in his glass factory. Industrialism
is the villain of the play; old Rutherford is its victim.
   3 acts; 4 men, 4 women; 1 interior.

SPARK, Muriel. The Prime of Miss Jean Brodie. See entry under
   Allen, Jay.

SPEWACK, Bella. See entries under Spewack, Samuel.

SPEWACK, Samuel, with Bella Spewack. Boy Meets Girl (1935).
   Dramatists Play Service.
      An extravagant lampoon on Hollywood and the cinema industry.
   To develop a story for Larry Toms, the cowboy film hero, the energetic writing team, Law & Benson, devise the starring of Susie-the-
   waitress' baby, who shall be called Happy. He steals the scenes
   from Larry, much to the producer's distress; then he gets the
   measles! They pose Rodney as the father, and after Susie marries
   him, he turns out to be a lord's son. So they must find another
   baby to succeed Happy as a star.
      3 acts; 14 men, 5 women; 2 interiors. Royalty: $25.

_____, with Bella Spewack. My Three Angels (1953). Based on
   Albert Husson's book. Dramatists Play Service.
      Three convicts (two murderers and a swindler) play Robin
   Hood to a family besieged by conniving relatives. The convicts take
   on the intruders, and by their warm hearts, sunny natures, and
   expertise of crime they make possible a Merry Christmas where,
   Time pointed out, it is easier "to bump Scrooge off than convert
   him."
      7 men, 3 women; 1 interior. Royalty: $50-25.

_____. Two Blind Mice (1949). Dramatists Play Service.
      Two nice elderly ladies, Mrs. Letitia Turnbull and Crystal
   Hower, still maintain the Office of Medical Herbs in Washington
   though it was abolished four years before, since no steps have been
   taken to close it out. A newspaper reporter, Tommy Thurston,
   takes them over and staffs their hideaway with people from other
   Departments, alleging security reasons. Thus he mystifies literal-
   minded government employees. A caustic satire on governmental
   bureaucracy, stupidity, and red tape.
      3 acts; 14 men, 4 women; 1 interior. Royalty: $50-25.

_____. Under the Sycamore Tree (1952). Dramatists Play Ser-
   vice.
      The reaction of ants who can speak, love, and hate to the
   present state of the world is presented in this farcical fable. The
   ant colony which we see has just achieved superiority over their
   enemies, the brown ants. In addition, they have radios and telephones. Then a scientist discovers the secret ingredient that makes
   man's world go around--love. He teaches it to a boy and girl ant
   and the queen, bringing contentment and happiness to their world.

They even discover how to wage a nondeadly war, and being unselfish ants, try to pass this information on to the President of the United States. Although the scientists' attempts to talk to the President are unsuccessful, he and his queen are happy with their discoveries, concluding that now, they have really lived.

> 5 men, 2 women, plus the nonspeaking roles for 3 men, 1 woman; 1 interior. Royalty: $50-25.

SPIGELGASS, Leonard. Dear Me, The Sky Is Falling (1963). Adapted from a story by Gertrude Berg and James Yaffe. Samuel French.

This comedy recounts the madcap escapades of a know-it-all, yet lovable, mother. This stern lady has ruled her husband and daughter completely and tries to take on the rest of the world, too. Finally the husband and unmarried daughter make some decisions on their own, decisions which are contrary to Mother's opinions. Faced with this rebellion, Mother calls for her psychiatrist, and after a humorous consultation with that Freudian expert, Mother emerges again with all the right answers. And surprisingly enough, the answers suit all the others as well.

> 5 men, 7 women; 1 interior and inset. Royalty: $50-25.

_____. A Majority of One (1959). Samuel French.

A Jewish widow from Brooklyn establishes a warm friendship with a Japanese gentleman and unwittingly almost wrecks some very delicate commercial treaty negotiations. The widow's son-in-law is a diplomat engaged in the negotiations which are of paramount importance to both the U.S. and Japan. He takes his wife and mother-in-law along when he has to go to Japan, and en route the widow meets a Japanese gentleman with whom she soon becomes close friends. The son-in-law, making some mistaken assumptions about the relationship, demands that it be broken off. This insult to the Japanese almost causes negotiations to be halted, but with a display of wisdom and tolerance, the elderly couple rescue the deal and demonstrate that nations as well as individuals need understanding in dealing with each other.

> 6 men, 8 women; 4 interiors. Royalty: $50-25.

SQUIRE, J. C. Berkeley Square. See entry under Balderston, J. L.

STALLINGS, Laurence. What Price Glory? See entry under Anderson, Maxwell.

STEELE, Richard. The Conscious Lovers (1722). In his Plays, Mermaid edn., Scribner; BEL v. 9; INCH v. 12; MCM; MOR; MOSE v. 1; NET; STM; TAU; TAY; TUQ.

Young Bevil is to marry wealthy Lucinda Sealand, old Sealand's daughter by his second wife, but he really loves Indiana, a poor orphan. When Indiana turns out to be the long-lost daughter of Sealand by his first wife, Bevil can marry her, while Lucinda can be won by his friend Myrtle. In the course of the play, the young man avoids a duel but remains a fine gentleman.

> 5 acts; 8 men, 5 women; 4 interiors, 2 exteriors; costumes of the period.

STEIN, Joseph. Enter Laughing (1963). Adapted from Carl
    Reiner's novel. Samuel French.
    The hilarious account of a delivery boy in a sewing machine
factory who yearns to be an actor. Though his parents want the
boy to be a druggist, as soon as he saves up enough money he buys
his way into a semi-professional company, directed by a man who
will put anybody on stage for the right price. The boy is a terrible
actor, and we see him flub his way through romantic scenes with
the director's daughter, with another man's date, and finally with an
office girl who was meant for him.
    7 men, 4 women; stage, wagons, insets. Royalty: $50-25.

STEINBECK, John. Of Mice and Men (1937). Dramatists Play
    Service.
    A character study of two roving farm hands. One of them,
Lennie, is a powerful giant of a man who has the intelligence of a
child. When he is teased by the young wife of the foreman, Lennie
kills her, though that is not his intention. He in turn is killed by
his friend, who cannot bear to see him arrested, tried, and imprisoned.
    9 men, 1 woman; 2 interiors, 1 exterior. Royalty: $25.

STERN, Stewart. Rebel Without a Cause. See entry under Sergel,
    Clark F.

STERNHEIM, Karl. A Place in the World (1913). Tr. by Katzin
    in KAT.
    Having advanced financially to be President of the Corporation,
Christian Maske sacrifices his former sweetheart Sybil who has
helped him develop social graces, also his father and mother, ad-
vising Count Palen that they are dead. He asks the Count for the
hand of his daughter, Countess Marianne. He is accepted; and he
even creates fictitious ancestry and implies that he is the bastard
son of a Vicomte, hence with blue blood in his veins.
    3 acts; 4 men, 4 women; 2 interiors.

STEVENS, Leslie. The Marriage-Go-Round (1959). Samuel French.
    A Professor of Cultural Anthropology at a suburban New York
college and his wife, the Dean of Women at the same school, stage
another battle in the war of the sexes. This happily married couple
had met the daughter of a Swedish colleague ten years ago when she
was a skinny kid. They are somewhat astounded when she shows up
as a houseguest, having grown up into a buxom amazon--an amazon
with brains. For genetic reasons the siren decides she must mate
with the professor. From this point the complications of the household blossom.
    2 men, 2 women; 1 interior. Royalty: $50-25.

STEVENS, Thomas Wood. Joan of Arc (1918). Samuel French.
    Episodes in the life of Joan of Arc are presented, from her
successful interview with Baudricourt through her identification of the
Dauphin, the winning of Orleans, and her trial, where her replies
are taken from the written testimony.
    32 men, 5 women; 6 interiors, 4 exteriors. Royalty: $15.

STEVENSON, William. Gammer Gurton's Needle (1560). ADA;
BAS; BOA; GAY-1; LEV; also in Manly, Pre-Shakespearean
Drama, Ginn, 1897, v. 2.
        While mending the breeches of her man, Hodge, Gammer
Gurton loses her valuable needle. Complications in the small village society follow and the whole parish is set by the ears, from
the curate down to the village ne'er-do-well, when Diccon tells her
the needle has been stolen by her neighbor, Dame Chat. However
the needle is discovered in Hodge's leg when he changes his
breeches. (Long attributed to John Still.)
        1 continuous act of about an hour; 6 men, 4 women; 1 ex-
terior; costumes of the period.

STEWART, Donald Ogden. Rebound (1930). Samuel French.
        Bill and Sara get married, after Bill has been given the air
by Evie, and Johnnie has failed to propose to Sara. Although Evie
is now married to Lyman, she still makes up to Bill. Disruption
is threatened for Bill and Sara, but the situation is intelligently exposed and sanely adjusted.
        3 acts; 7 men, 5 women; 2 interiors. Royalty: $25-20.

STEWART, Mary. Nine Coaches Waiting. See entry under Bolton,
Guy.

STITT, Milan. The Runner Stumbles (1976). Dramatists Play Service.
        Father Rivard, priest of the remote Solon, Michigan parish,
is in jail on charges of murdering a nun. The action of the play is
part interrogation, part courtroom, and part personal memory of
Father Rivard's relationship with Sister Rita--an extraordinary woman
who sees no conflict between the love of God and the love of life. At
the end it is revealed that Sister Rita was actually murdered by Father Rivard's housekeeper, who saw the lively nun as a threat to de-
cency, the church, and the priest's reputation.
        5 men, 4 women; unit set. Royalty: $50-35.

STOKER, Bram. Dracula. See entry under Deane, Hamilton.

_____. Count Dracula. See entry under Tiller, Ted.

STONE, Irving. Love Is Eternal. See entry under Sergel, Ruth.

STOPPARD, Tom. Jumpers (1972). Samuel French.
        Professor George Moore is getting ready to debate with a
logician the existence of a moral absolute, of metaphysical reality,
of God (his field is moral philosophy), when the logician is killed in
George's living room while performing gymnastics (the close association between gymnastics and philosophy is unique to George's university). Thumper, George's pet rabbit, is also killed, and later
eaten by George's wife Dotty (former musical comedy star) and one
of her boyfriends. A wild and absurd comedy.
        4 men, 2 women, 8 extras; basic set with three playing
areas. Royalty: $50-35.

_____. The Real Inspector Hound (1972). Samuel French.
        A farce with a play-within-a-play framework. Two critics
show up to review a play. One critic is substituting for a missing
regular reviewer, and the other is a lustful man. They watch the
action on stage performed by the four principal characters: a
countess, a girlfriend guest, a roué the countess has met through
the girlfriend, and the crippled brother of the countess's dead
brother. The roué is shot, and Inspector Hound arrives (though nobody ever called him) to inspect the body, which turns out to be
that of the missing first-string critic. The phone begins to ring on
stage and is finally answered by the lustful critic who leaves his
theater box just to shut it up. (The call is from his wife, whom
he berates for bothering him at work.) Then he begins to repeat
the lines of the roué shot in the beginning of the play, and the same
things start to happen all over. The substitute critic takes the
place of the Inspector this time, and the original roué and Inspector
take the places of the critics in the box. The former Inspector, in
fact, turns out to be the countess's long-lost (but not dead) husband.
        6 men, 3 women; 1 interior. Royalty: $50-35.

_____. Rosencrantz and Guildenstern Are Dead (1967). Samuel
        French.
        An existential comedy featuring two student acquaintances of
Hamlet and what went on behind the scenes of Shakespeare's play.
Actually, the two don't know. They don't even know why they were
in Elsinore at the time (they were "sent for"). As it turns out they
have a hard time remembering which one is Rosencrantz and which
one Guildenstern. The Players come and go, Hamlet comes through
reading words, people are killed, and the two anti-agents find that
their only exit is death.
        14 men, 2 women, 12 extras, 6 musicians; unit set. Royal-
        ty: $50-35.

_____. Travesties (1975). Samuel French.
        Travesties is an intellectual literary fantasy, made partly
out of characters and techniques from Oscar Wilde and partly out of
an obscure historical fact: James Joyce, Lenin, and Dadaist artist
Tristan Tzara all lived in Zurich during World War I, as did minor
British consular official Henry Carr. Of course when the author puts
these things together he ends up letting Henry Carr be the hero, ap-
pearing in the play as an old man in one scene and a contemporary
of revolutionaries in the next. One interesting technique in the play
is the "time slip," when the story jumps off the track and has to be
started again at the point where it went wild.
        5 men, 3 women; 2 interiors. Royalty on application.

STOREY, David. The Changing Room (1972). Samuel French.
        Americans would call the changing room a lockerroom, which
is the setting of the play before, at halftime, and after a rugby
football game in the North of England. The players on the team are
working-class men who play this kind of blood-letting football to earn
a few dollars and put some glory in their lives. We see them arrive, joke and banter, dress out, come in injured from a brutal first

half, and finally enter victorious after the game, clean up, and leave.

     22 men; 1 interior. Royalty: $50-35.

_____ . The Contractor (1970). Samuel French.
     There is no dramatic incident in this play. In the first act a tent is being assembled on Mr. Ewbank's lawn, in the second act it is being decorated, in the third it is taken down. In between, a wedding takes place (Ewbank's daughter), and we are introduced to Ewbank's family, parents, and the men who work for him (he is "the contractor" who owns the tent company). His workmen are social outcasts whom no one else will hire, and though they may quit him, he never fires anybody.
     9 men, 3 women; 1 interior. Royalty: $50-25.

_____ . Home (1971). Samuel French.
     The setting is a bare terrace, peopled by mental patients who think they are in a private hotel, or on an island, or who know exactly where they are. There is no real plot, only dialogue--some of which makes sense and some which doesn't. The events are confined to one day on the terrace, where we learn compassion, sympathy, and respect for the people institutionalized there.
     3 men, 2 women; exterior set. Royalty: $50-35.

_____ . In Celebration (1973). Dramatic Publishing Company.
     Three sons, educated up the social ladder from the working class existence of their British parents, return home to celebrate their parents' wedding anniversary. One son is wild and cruel; one is successful and smug; the youngest is self-pitying. Layers of fears and hatreds, guilts and atonements are revealed within the family setting.
     5 men, 2 women; 1 interior. Royalty: $50.

STOWE, Mrs. Harriet Beecher. Uncle Tom's Cabin (1853). Version by George L. Aiken, French in the 1850's; also in MOSS-2; Aiken version revised by A. E. Thomas, Appleton, 1934; CERC.
     Introduces Eliza crossing the ice, Topsy (who just growed), and the faithful slave Uncle Tom with his loyalty to the St. Clare family, his love for little Eva, and his death under Simon Legree.
     French editions: 6 acts; 15 men, 6 women; simple interiors and exteriors. Thomas' version: 26 men, 10 women, extras; 23 scenes in 3 acts, with 9 interiors & 7 exteriors. Costumes of the period. No royalty.

STREETER, Edward. Mr. Hobbs' Vacation. See entry under Leslie, F. Andrew.

STRINDBERG, August. Comrades (1888). Tr. by Oland, Luce, 1913; in TUCG, in TUCM; tr. by Samuel, Lond., Hendersons, 1914.
     A gifted artist, Axel, prostitutes his art to earn money for his wife Berta, also an artist. When both send pictures to a salon,

he attaches his number to hers to insure it a place.   When this is
rejected, she humiliates him by having it returned during a party.
Learning it was her picture, she tries to propitiate him, but he
drives her out into the streets.   The play rather shows Strindberg's
anti-feministic attitude and cynicism toward women.
       4 acts; 4 men, 8 women; 1 interior.

_____.   The Father (1887).   Tr. by Erichsen, Lond., Duck-
   worth, & Luce, 1907; DIC; TRE-1, 2, & 3; in TREA-2; tr. by
   Oland in his Plays, v. 2, Luce, 1912; tr. by Locock, Lond.,
   Cape, 1931; tr. by Locock & others in Lucky Peter's Travels,
   Anglo-Swedish Literary Foundation, 1931.
       The wife definitely plots to drive her husband insane, and the
mental struggle is so great that she succeeds.   The situation and
atmosphere are well developed and show strikingly his animus against
women.
       3 acts; 5 men, 3 women; 1 interior.

_____.   Swanwhite (1902).   Tr. by Bjorkman in his Plays, ser.
   3, Scribner, & Lond., Duckworth, 1913; tr. by Oland in his
   Plays, v. 3, Luce, 1914.
       A fantastic trifle about Swanwhite and her Prince, based on
the magical power of love which breaks all spells and makes good
triumph over evil.   Has a poetic mystical atmosphere.
       2 acts; 10 men, 7 women; 1 interior; fanciful costumes.

STRONG, Austin.   Seventh Heaven (1922).   Samuel French.
       Chico, a sewer cleaner in Paris, is courageous because he
has faith in himself.   He is able to help all who come in contact
with him.   He rescues Diane, who is rather adrift in Paris, and
proclaims her his wife just as he must leave for the First World
War.   Diane waits four years for his return, but on Armistice Day
gets word that she believes he is dead.   But he returns, and she
is restored to her lover and her religion.
       3 acts; 11 men, 4 women; 1 interior, 1 exterior; French and
   military costumes.   Royalty: $25.

_____.   Three Wise Fools (1918).   Samuel French.
       A splendid trio--doctor, judge, and financier--live in a self-
made rut, when into their machine-like lives bursts Sidney Fairchild,
a young girl, daughter of the woman they all three had loved in
earlier years.   At first they are annoyed, but they adopt her as a
ward.   Changes take place which quite upset their routine, but make
them more human.
       3 acts; 11 men, 2 women; 1 interior.   Royalty: $25.

STRONG, Phil.   State Fair.   See entry under McMahon, Luella.

STUART, Jesse.   The Thread That Runs So True.   See entry under
   Lawrence, Reginald.

STURGES, Preston.   Strictly Dishonorable (1929).   Samuel French.
       In the days of the speak-easy, Isabelle gets interested in an

opera singer, Gus di Ravo. To escape arrest she must spend the
night somewhere, and Gus takes her to his apartment, assuring her
that his intentions are strictly dishonorable. But he retires to
another room while she sleeps on the sofa. In the morning he is
romantic again, announces his love for Isabelle and his intention to
marry her.
  3 acts; 7 men, 1 woman; 2 interiors. Royalty: $25-20.

SUDERMANN, Hermann. Honor (1889). Tr. by Baukhage. French,
    1915.
  Presents situations in which various aspects of satisfying
honor are shown, from patching up sick honor with money to fighting
a duel. Robert Heinecke, of humble parents returns from India after
10 years, where he managed things for the Mühlingk firm, and so
successfully that he became a protégé of Count Trast, a coffee king.
Robert finds his proletariat home in sad condition and his sister Alma seduced by Kurt, the merchant's son. Mühlingk gives 40,000
marks to her father to satisfy her honor, expels them from their
home, and fires Robert. He makes his final report and pays back
the money (lent by his friend Trast), and as he leaves, the merchant's daughter, Leonore, who has loved him since childhood, though
forbidden by her father to show it, leaves her family to go with him
to a new position with Trast.
  4 acts; 11 men, 6 women; 2 interiors.

_____. John the Baptist (1893). Tr. by Marshall in FRA v. 17;
    in Poet Lore, v. 11, 1899; Lane, 1909; abridged in Pierce &
    Matthews, v. 2.
  Presents scenes in the life of John, the forerunner of Jesus.
John has believed in an eye for an eye but is impressed by the new
doctrine of love and forgiveness of enemies. He makes an enemy
of Herodias because of reproof for her evil doings. Salome, the
sensuous young girl would entice him. Herod would spare him.
  5 acts; 29 men, 8 women, 2 children, extras; 3 interiors,
    4 exteriors; costumes of the period.

_____. The Joy of Living (1902). Tr. by Wharton. Scribner,
    1902.
  Countess Beata, wife of Michael, has intrigued for 15 years
with Richard. When she finds that the two men have become friends,
she ends the love affair. After Richard has been elected to the
Reichstag his opponent Meixner brings up this affair as a scandal.
Richard sets his affairs in order to do away with himself and makes
a speech on the sanctity of the home. Meixner is so impressed he
returns the compromising letters. Then Beata gives a luncheon to
the two men, asks who dares to live, and drinks to the joy of living;
she falls dead of the poison.
  5 acts; 14 men, 3 women; 2 interiors; costumes of the
    period (1899).

_____. Magda (1893). Tr. by Winslow. Bost., Lamson, 1895;
    French, 1895; in WATI; in WATL-2.
  As a young girl Magda has left home to avoid a marriage

which her father desired. She returns as a successful singer, but
her free attitude, which has resulted in an illegitimate child, continues to cause trouble. Her claim of a right to develop her own
individuality brings about a well-devined struggle between the old and
the new, the conservative and the radical, the conventional idea of
home, parental authority, moral standards and the modern idea of
the rights of children and personal freedom.
    4 acts; 6 men, 8 women; 1 interior.

_____. The Vale of Content (1896). Tr. by Leonard in DIC.
    Elizabeth has married the headmaster of the school; she
meets again a former lover, von Roecknitz, who urges her to go
away with him. She confides in her husband and goes back to happiness in the corner. Treats the eternal triangle with good sense and
subtle psychology, showing that happiness and content come rather
from duties faithfully performed.
    3 acts; 6 men, 6 women; 1 interior, 1 exterior.

SUTRO, Alfred. The Fascinating Mr. Vanderveldt (1906). French,
    1906.
    Clarice, a young widow, is told by her domineering mother
that she must marry again and some one with money. She is told
to choose between an elderly judge and a musician. Meantime she
is wooed by Mr. Vanderveldt, who has a bad reputation with women.
He plans an episode of a stranded car in an isolated community, but
she outwits him with a spark-plug and finds Col. Rayner more to
her liking.
    4 acts; 8 men, 8 women, 1 lad of 15; 3 interiors, 1 exterior.

_____. The Two Virtues (1914). Lond., Duckworth, Brentano,
    & French, 1914.
    Deftly characterizes four women, two of whom, Isabel and
Lady Milligan, represent Chastity, while the other two, Freda and
Alice, represent Charity. The charity pair oppose the love of
Freda and Jeffrey and cause them to part, but cannot keep them
separated.
    4 acts; 3 men, 5 women; 2 interiors.

_____. The Walls of Jericho (1904). French, 1906; MAP.
    Fighting Jack Frobisher, having made his pile in Queens-
land, returns to England, and with his money is welcomed into the
smart set. He marries Alethea, daughter of the Marquis of Steven-
ton, an autocratic aristocrat, but is losing his grip in the fast London society. Urged on by Hankey Bannister, his old pal in Australia, Jack resolves to assert his strength and raise his voice in protest to make the walls come tumbling down. When he does, in
tense scenes with the Marquis and Alethea, he reestablishes himself
as Fighting Jack.
    4 acts; 13 men, 8 women, extras; 4 interiors.

SYNGE, John Millington. Deirdre of the Sorrows (1910). N.Y.,
    J. Quinn, 1911; in his Works, Mansel, & Luce, 1912; in his
    Plays, Lond., Allen, 1924 & 1932; in Theatre Arts for Aug.
    1950.

Develops poetically the ancient Irish legend. Though pledged
to Conchubor, the elderly King of Ulster, Deirdre marries young
Naise and lives for seven idyllic years in the forest with him and
the sons of Uena. The king tricks them into returning and traitor-
ously slays the men. Deirdre kills herself in sorrow and remorse.
   3 acts; 6 men, 3 women, extras; 2 interiors, 1 exterior;
   costumes of the period.

_____. The Playboy of the Western World (1907). Dublin,
   Maunsel, 1909, Luce, 1911; in his Works, Maunsel, 1910 &
Luce 1912, v. 2; in his Plays Lond., Allen, 1924 & 1932;
Random House, 1935; French carries; CEW; CLS; DUR; FIG;
HAU. Act. ed., Samuel French.
   Develops a strange imaginative Irish character, Christy Ma-
hon, who deceives himself and others into thinking he is a hero because he has killed, as he thinks, his domineering old father.
When his resurrected father appears, and he tries to kill him
again, Christy loses his glamor as hero, even with Pegeen. He
and his father escape together. The lilt and cadence of the diction,
of which Synge was a master, are its supreme excellence.
   3 acts; 7 men, 5 women, extras; 1 interior. French royalty: $25-20.

_____. The Well of the Saints (1905). Lond., Bullen, 1905; in
   his Works, Dublin, Maunsel, 1910 & Luce, 1912; in his Plays,
Lond., Allen, 1924 & 1932.
   A blind old couple are beautifully happy because every one
has told them how beautiful they are. The Saint restores their sight
and they see their ugliness. In course of time they lose their sight
again, but when the Saint gives them the chance to restore it, the
husband dashes the holy water from the Saint's hands, and they per-
sist in their blindness.
   3 acts; 4 men, 3 women; 2 interiors.

SZOGYI, Alex. A Country Scandal. See entry under Chekhov, Anton P.

TABER, Richard. Is Zat So? See entry under Gleason, James.

TABORI, George. Brecht on Brecht. See entry under Brecht,
   Bertolt.

_____. The Emperor's Clothes (1953). Samuel French.
   An idealistic young boy who worships his father creates serious problems for the man in this tragicomedy set in Budapest.
The father, an outspoken liberal, has been dismissed from his job
as a teacher because he refused to compromise his principles. To
support his family he takes a job as a proofreader of trashy fiction,
but this pays so poorly he cannot afford to buy a Christmas tree
for his family. The son, thinking he can raise money, starts a
secret society and charges dues for membership. Although he gets
the money for the tree, the totalitarian regime learns of the society
and arrests the father as the head of the organization. Faced with

inquisition and imprisonment the man compromises himself, but this destroys the idealistic respect of his son. So, in spite of the tortures he must face, the father retracts his earlier confession and redeems himself as a hero in the eyes of his son.

    12 men, 3 women; 1 interior. Royalty: $50-25.

TAGGART, Tom. Deadwood Dick (or, A Game of Gold) (1953). Samuel French.

    A blood-and-thunder western melodrama based on the most exciting situations, colorful characters, and amusing dialogue from Edward L. Wheeler's dime novels of Deadwood Dick, published in the 1870's. Daughters are long-lost, gold mines are stolen, heroines are kidnapped, and escapes are hairbreadthed.

    7 men, 7 women, extras; 1 interior. Royalty: $25-20.

_____, with James Reach. Dear Phoebe (1956). Based on characters created by Alex Gottlieb. Samuel French.

    This comedy recounts the adventures of a former college professor who becomes a lovelorn columnist, "Aunt Phoebe Goodheart." The young professor, Bill Hastings, soon falls in love with the pretty female sports editor, Mickey Riley. Then the complications develop rapidly. "Aunt Phoebe" receives a letter from a brassy French floozy with a Bronx accent, Rochelle Mignonne, indicating that she has evidence which will implicate night club owner Big Joe Moroni in a sports-fix scandal. Bill dresses up as Aunt Phoebe and along with Mickey goes to question Rochelle, only to find her just murdered. Exciting and funny situations follow before virtue and true love finally triumph--and the case is solved before the morning deadline.

    6 men, 7 women; 1 interior. Royalty: $35-25.

TAMAYO y BAUS, Manuel. A New Drama (1867). Tr. by Fitzgerald & Guild, Hispanic Society Pubn. #90, 1915.

    Depicts Shakespeare and his company rehearsing and presenting a new play. In technique a well-nigh perfect example of a play within a play. The lines of the new drama fit the situation of jealousy and envy among the actors of the company, Yorick the comedian and Walton the tragedian with Edmund, Yorick's foster-son, contending for the affections of Yorick's wife Alice.

    3 acts; 7 men, 1 woman, extras; 3 interiors; costumes of 1605 in England.

TARKINGTON, Booth. Clarence (1919). Samuel French.

    Clarence, whose last name is uncertain, but who "has been in the army," enters the Wheeler household in a rather vague capacity, which develops into that of a solvent for the perplexities of the whole family.

    4 acts; 5 men, 5 women; 2 interiors. Royalty: $25-20.

_____. The Intimate Strangers (1921). French, 1924; COH.

    Pits the adult charm and humor of Aunt Isabel against the rambunctious youth of her niece Florence, to the perplexity of the male.

3 acts; 4 men, 4 women; 2 interiors.

_____ and H. L. Wilson. The Man from Home (1907). Harper,
1908; revised form, French, 1934; CERC; abridged in Mantle &
Sherwood 1899-1909.

The shrewd Indiana lawyer, Daniel Pike, outwits the fortune
hunters in the Italian resort who have victimized his wards by pseu-
do-aristocratic snobbishness.

4 acts; 11 men, 3 women, extras; 1 interior, 2 exteriors.
French royalty: $25-20.

_____. Seventeen (1918). Samuel French.
Willie Baxter woos Lolo the baby-talk lady, steals his father's
best suit, and has many difficulties, some caused by his little sister Jane, some by the Negro servant Genesis, and others by Lolo's
worthy swains.

4 acts; 8 men, 6 women; 2 interiors, 1 exterior (can be
played with 1 interior). Royalty: $25-20.

TAYLOR, Renee, with Joseph Bologna. Lovers and Other Strangers
(1968). Samuel French.

A set of four comedies on the general subject of the superiority of women. In the first, a young man who sets out to seduce a
young woman has the tables turned on him. In the second, a married couple can't figure out whose turn it is to initiate sex. Next
comes a nervous fiancé to his girl's apartment at four in the morning, trying to get out of the wedding. By the time he leaves she is
dealing with the important matters like renting his wedding suit. In
the last "playlet" a married couple of 30 years confess their failures
and their fights in order to save their son's marriage.

5 men, 5 women; 4 interiors. Royalty: $50-25.

TAYLOR, Samuel. The Happy Time (1950). Dramatists Play Service.

Depicts the Bonnard family in their French-Canadian home.
Their uninhibited behavior has its effect on the adolescent Bibi. The
charming girl Mignonette is brought in to help and thrills Bibi with
young love. He steals her nightgowns; Uncle Desmonde is accused
of the theft though he had retained only her gloves. When Uncle
Desmonde and Mignonette become engaged, and Sally takes the braces
off her teeth, Bibi finds he is thrilled by her.

3 acts; 8 men, 4 women; 2 interiors. Royalty: $50-25.

_____. The Pleasure of His Company (1958). Dramatists Play
Service.

This successful comedy has drawn much critical praise for
its wit as well as its sound philosophy. The story concerns an international playboy who returns to his wife's home to give away their
daughter in marriage. Since he hasn't seen her since she was a
little girl, he is surprised and pleased to find she has grown into a
a beautiful young woman. He turns on all his playboy charms, and
despite the efforts of the mother and the fiancé, completely capti-
vates the girl. The impasse is finally resolved, however, when the

girl decides she still wants to marry. But first she wants to take
a trip abroad with her father, solving the problem happily for all
involved.
> 5 men, 2 women; 1 interior. Royalty: $50-25.

_____ . Sabrina Fair (1953). Dramatists Play Service.
Interesting characters and a surprising finish make this an
entertaining romantic comedy. Sabrina is the daughter of the family
chauffeur for the Larabee family, who are very wealthy and impec-
cably genteel. After working in Paris for five years, Sabrina, an
extremely intelligent and attractive girl, returns home to see if she
still loves the oldest Larabee son, Linus, a cynical tycoon who has
taken over control of the family fortune. Sabrina discovers she
does love Linus, but his brother pays the most attention to her.
Mr. Larabee forgets his only passion--attending funerals--when Sabrina's father reveals that he too is a millionaire and consents to
Linus' marrying Sabrina. A rich Frenchman who is in love with
Sabrina, a wise-cracking magazine editor, and the exaggeratedly
narrow-minded Mrs. Larabee all add to the comic situations in the
play.
> 7 men, 7 women; 1 exterior. Royalty: $50-25.

TEICHMANN, Howard, with George S. Kaufman. The Solid Gold
   Cadillac (1953). Dramatists Play Service.
The President of General Products has accepted a governmental position, and his successor must be elected along with other
new corporation officers. Things go smoothly at the annual stock
holders' meeting until a little old lady who owns ten shares of stock
begins asking questions--like what does the chairman of the board do
to earn $170,000 a year. To shut her up, the corporation gives the
lady a $150 a week job, which, the officers are frightened to learn,
she takes seriously. She writes chatty letters to other minority
stockholders and discovers that the corporation has forced into bankruptcy one of their own subsidiary firms. When she approaches the
former president with the mess that the new board of directors has
caused, the president quits his government job and tries to regain
control of his company. A power fight results, and the bad guys
are about to win. Then the proxies from the small shareholders
start pouring in and the company is saved.
> 26 men (doubling possible); 10 women (extras); exterior and
> interior sets. Royalty: $50-25.

TENNYSON, Alfred Tennyson, 1st Baron. Becket (pub. 1884; prod.
   1893). In his Poetical Works, Houghton; in his Works, Macmillan, 1893; MOSO; SMK; abridged in Pierce & Matthews, v. 1.
Becket irritates King Henry II before his appointment as
Archbishop of Canterbury because he does not deem himself worthy
of the honor. After his appointment he enrages the king by his utter
devotion to the Church, refusing any compromise with the State, for
while he signs the Customs, he will not seal. To rid himself of
"this pestilent priest, " the king causes his murder in his cathedral.
A second theme concerns Henry's romantic and domestic life, pic-
turing his morganatic wife Rosamund in her secret bower, but

tracked there by his jealous neglected wife, Eleanor of Aquitaine.
Becket arrives in time to save Rosamund from dagger and poison.
Prolog & 5 acts; 22 men, 1 boy, 3 women, extras; 8 in-
teriors; costumes of the period.

_____. The Foresters, Robin Hood and Maid Marian (1892).
Macmillan, 1892; in his Works, Macmillan, 1893, v. 6; also
Macmillan, 1908, v. 9.
Maid Marian with her sick father takes refuge in Sherwood
Forest where Robin Hood heads his band of outlaws. She is made
their queen. There also comes King Richard Coeur de Lion, who
settles matters with his brother John and the Sheriff.
4 acts; 12 men, 3 women, extras; 1 interior, 5 exteriors;
costumes of the period.

TERENCE (Publius Terentius Afer). The Brothers (Adelphi, 160
B. C.). Tr. by Sergeaunt in Loeb Library; by Riley in Bohn's,
tr. by Colman, Harper, 1859; tr. by Perry, Oxford, 1929; in
DUC; TREA-1.
The two brothers represent two schools of thought as to the
way to bring up boys. Demea, a married man with two sons, living
in the country, is very strict with his son Ctesipho and believes he
is a proper youth. Micio, a bachelor, living in the city, is mild
and kind to the other son, Aeschinus, his nephew, whom he has
adopted. Ctesipho, however, is a real profligate and hypocritical;
he abducts a girl, for which the kindhearted Aeschinus takes the
blame. When Demea learns of this, he seeks out Micio, and decides
to become more kind and considerate. Micio is persuaded to marry
his neighbor Sostrata.
5 acts; 10 men, 4 women; 1 exterior (a street before the 2
houses of Micio and Sostrata).

_____. Phormio (161 B. C.). Tr. by Sergeaunt in Loeb Libra-
ry; tr. by Riley in Bohn's; tr. by Perry, Oxford, 1929; tr. by
Clark, French; tr. by Morgan in CLF-1; CLS; DUC; MAU.
Old Chremes had secretly married the wealthy Nausistrata in
Lemnos and is the father of a son, Phaedria, and a daughter,
Phanium, who comes to Athens as a slave girl and of course without
money. His brother Demipho has a son Antipho and they wish him
to marry a music-girl, but he hasn't the money. Phormio, the bene-
volent intriguer, now steps in and schemes to get the money, and by
his success, both Antipho and Phaedria can marry. When Chremes
tries to get some money back from Phormio, a secret affair of his
is brought to light. The scheming parasite, Phormio, is typical of
the Roman comedies, providing much of the humor of the plays.
5 acts; 11 men, 2 women; 1 exterior (a street before 3
houses).

THOMA, Ludwig. Moral (1908). Tr. by Recht, Knopf, 1916; DID.
Some worthy dignitaries of a small town, leading citizens and
officers in the Society for the suppression of vice, are aghast at
realizing that all their names are recorded in the account books of
a bawd lately arrested. They are in a panic for fear they will be

exposed. The list is stolen by the president. The police official
berates the zeal of his subordinates. The lady is paid off and the
affair smoothed over.
   3 acts; 9 men, 7 women, extras; 2 interiors.

THOMAS, A. E. Uncle Tom's Cabin. See entry under Stowe, Harriet B.

THOMAS, Augustus. Arizona (1899). Russell, 1899; Dramatic
   Publishing Company, 1915.
   Vivid scenes are enacted at the Canby ranch and Col. Bon-
ham's army post, where the dashing villain, Capt. Hodgman, creates
predicaments for honest Lt. Denton, who is accused of betraying the
Colonel's wife Estrella, of the theft of the jewels, and later of shooting Hodgman.
   4 acts; 11 men, 5 women; 2 interiors, 1 exterior; some
   military costumes of the period.

_____. As a Man Thinks (1911). Duffield, 1911; BAK; abridged
   in Pierce & Matthews, v. 1.
   The Jewish physician, Dr. Seelig, advises the Christian editor Clayton that life's assurance depends on "as a man thinks." He
may have a foolish wife, but he must have confidence that if he forgives it will be forgiven unto him.
   4 acts; 9 men, 4 women; 3 interiors.

_____. The Copperhead (1917). French, 1922; COH.
   Like Cooper's Spy, Milt Shanks heroically performs his mis-
understood mission in the Civil war and endures revilings for 40
years, confessing only when his granddaughter would suffer. Then
he is honored.
   4 acts; 9 men, 6 women; 1 interior, 1 exterior (1 interior
   possible with a 40-year change).

_____. The Witching Hour (1907). French, 1916; DIC; MOSJ;
   MOSL; QUIK; QUIL; abridged in Mantle & Sherwood 1899-1909;
   abridged in Pierce & Matthews, v. 1.
   Based on mental telepathy and thought transference, the hypnotic power attained by Jack Brookfield is doubtless false to reality,
but can be believed in dramatically. The mellow second act gives
a charming atmosphere. Has several exciting moments and good
comedy.
   4 acts; 11 men, 3 women; 2 interiors.

THOMAS, Brandon. Charley's Aunt (1892). Samuel French.
   Two Oxford undergraduates, Jack Chesney and Charles Wyke-
ham, must have a proper chaperone when entertaining their sweethearts, Kitty and Amy; so when Charley's aunt, Donna Lucia d'Alva-
dorez (from Brazil "where the nuts come from") cannot arrive for
the luncheon and tête-à-tête in their room, they induce Lord Babber-
ley to impersonate her. He has a merry time with the girls, and,
as the very wealthy aunt, he is much sought after by Jack's father
and the solicitor. The situation is further complicated when the real

aunt shows up.
    3 acts; 6 men, 4 women; 2 interiors, 1 exterior.   Royalty:
$25.

THOMAS, Caitlin. Dylan. See entry under Michaels, Sidney.

THOMAS, Dylan. Dylan. See entry under Michaels, Sidney.

_____. Under Milk Wood (1953). Samuel French.
    The lives and souls of the inhabitants of a provincial Welsh
fishing village are explored in this earthy drama. The conflicts and
problems of a series of characters are revealed through the eyes of
the dramatist (The Onlooker). There is a sea captain who dreams
of the dead, a draper who makes promises of love to his wife,
children playing kissing games, and a lunatic who eats out of his
dog's dish while his 66 clocks tick away the time.
    17 men, 17 women; area staging. Royalty: $50-25.

THOMAS, Robert. Catch Me If You Can. See entry under Wein-
    stock, Jack.

THOMPSON, Denman and George W. Ryer. The Old Homestead
    (1886). Baker, 1927 (revised from original text); CERC.
    Small-town lad goes to the big city. His father, the lovable
old farmer, Joshua Whitcomb, worries about him there, but the boy
makes good and returns in time to pay off the mortgage on the old
homestead.
    4 acts; 9 men, 7 women (reduced by doubling from 19 men,
12 women), extras; 2 interiors, 2 exteriors.

THURBER, James, with Elliott Nugent. The Male Animal. (1940).
    Samuel French.
    Starts with the mild announcement by Tommy Turner, a young
teacher of English, that he will read Vanzetti's last letter to his
class as a model of prose. This inflames the editor of the college
paper and Tommy may be fired as a "Red." His life is further
complicated by the return for the 10-year reunion of Joe Ferguson,
the great football hero and former suitor to Tommy's wife. He even
tells Ellen to go with Joe. But she finally realizes that Tommy is
a pretty good male animal and sticks to him.
    3 acts; 8 men, 5 women; 1 interior. Royalty: $50-25.

_____. A Thurber Carnival (Revue) (1960). Samuel French.
    A delightful revue of Thurber sketches. Includes "The Night
the Bed Fell," the fable of the unicorn in the garden, "Gentlemen
Shoppers," "The Secret Life of Walter Mitty," "File and Forget,"
and many scenes out of Thurber cartoons. No musical talent needed
to produce this revue.
    5 men, 4 women, extras (if desired). Periaktoe and travel-
lers. Royalty: $50-25.

TILLER, Ted. Count Dracula (1972). Samuel French.
    Mina is the latest victim of Count Dracula, who can trans-

form himself into a bat, materialize from fog, dissolve in mist.
The beautiful young woman is the ward of Dr. Seward, who runs an
insane asylum. Mina's fiancé arrives from London, worried over
her trance-like state and anxious for Professor Van Helsing
(specialist in rare diseases) to cure her. On the other side are
Dr. Seward's demented sister and a schizophrenic inmate in league
with the vampire.

    7 men, 2 women; 1 interior (and one inset). Royalty: $50-
25.

TOBIN, John. The Honeymoon (1804). Dramatic Pub. Co., &
    French, carried; in N.Y. Drama, v. 4 #40, 1878; in Inchbald,
    v. 25; BAT v. 16.

    Pretending that he is a peasant, the Duke Aranza conducts
his bride to a cottage in the country. Proud Juliana, after a struggle, submits to a month's trial, during which she is tamed less
roughly than Shakespeare's Katherina. On the other hand, the
woman-hating Rolando is won by Zamora, who has followed him as
his page Eugenio.

    5 acts; 10 men, 4 women, extras; 5 interiors, 3 exteriors;
costumes of the period.

TOLKEIN, J. R. R. The Hobbit. See entry under Gray, Patricia.

TOLLER, Ernst. The Blind Goddess (1932). Tr. by Crankshaw,
    Lond., Lane, 1934; in his Seven Plays, Lane, 1935; adapted by
    Denis Johnston as Blind Man's Buff, Random House, 1939.

    A doctor is accused of poisoning his wife because of his love
for his secretary. In the trial scene he admits so much that he is
convicted. Later evidence is found which proves it was suicide.
He is released, but has no prospect ahead. Justice, which imprisons the innocent as well as the guilty, damages for life.

    5 acts; 22 men, 10 women, extras; 6 interiors, 1 exterior.
The Johnston adaptation has 3 acts; 11 men, 2 women, 1 girl,
extras; 4 interiors.

       . The Machine-Wreckers (1922). Tr. by Dukes, Lond.,
    Benn, & Knopf, 1923; in his Seven Plays, Lane, 1935; MOSH.

    Jimmy Corbett, leader of revolting weavers, is slain by the
thoughtless mob which refuses to see that nothing can be accomplished by the destruction of machinery. The play is based on the
revolt of the English Chartists in Nottingham in 1811; the prolog
includes Lord Byron's speech in defense of the rioters, 1812.

    Prolog & 5 acts; 20 men, 2 women, children & extras; 7 in-
teriors, 4 exteriors; costumes of the period.

       . Man and the Masses (1921). Tr. by Untermeyer, Dou-
    bleday, 1924; WATI; BATL-4; tr. by Mendel in his Seven Plays,
    Lane, 1935.

    Sonia tries in vain to convert the raging masses to the prin-
ciple of peaceful humanitarianism. She wants to free the slaves in
coal mines and factories; her revolt is too successful, for they want
to war against the State. When the rebellion is crushed she is made

the scape-goat and sentenced to execution. The play is based on
the social revolution of 1873.
    7 scenes, 6 men, 3 women, extras; 5 interiors, 2 exteriors.

_____. No More Peace (1937). Tr. by Crankshaw, Farrar,
    1937; CALM.
    On Mt. Olympus Napoleon and St. Francis are arguing whether
mankind really wants peace. They look down at the imaginary State
of Dunkelstein where a peace festival is interrupted by a telegram
from Napoleon that war has been declared. The behavior of the
people is brilliantly satirized; even Socrates fails to restore peace
by reason. Peace comes only when they learn that the war was a
trick of the Olympians.
    2 acts; 14 men, 3 women, extras; 3 interiors.

_____. Pastor Hall (1938). Tr. by Spender & Hunt, Random
    House, 1939.
    A German clergyman, Pastor Hall, defies the Nazi storm-
troopers, and because of letters found among his papers, he is sent
to a concentration camp. When threatened with 25 lashes, he escapes; he will return to his pulpit and will doubtless be re-arrested.
Shows how the Nazis got their way through family threatenings.
    3 acts; 14 men, 3 women, extras; 2 interiors, 1 exterior.

TOLSTOI, Graf Lev N. The Fruits of Enlightenment (1891). Tr.
    anon., Luce, 1911; tr. by Maude as Fruits of Culture, Con-
    stable, 1905; same in his Plays, Oxford, 1923; tr. by Dole in
    his Works, v. 16, Scribner, 1902; same in his Dramatic Works,
    Crowell, 1923.
    In the midst of the idle rich, a group of starving peasants
ask for payment of land agreed to be sold. A peasant girl, pretending to have the powers of a medium, helps her fellows to purchase
land from a proprietor who had hitherto refused to sell it. Depicts
the so-called cultured classes, who, despite pretended enlightenment
and happiness, are underneath really unhappy and gullible.
    4 acts; 22 men, 11 women; 3 interiors; Russian costumes.

_____. The Living Corpse (1900). Tr. by Evarts, Phila.,
    Brown Bros., 1912; tr. by Wright as The Man Who Was Dead,
    Dodd, 1912; tr. anon. as Redemption, N.Y., 1919; tr. by
    Maude in his Plays, Oxford, 1923; tr. by Dole in his Dramatic
    Works, Crowell, 1923; CHA.
    Fedya, unhappy at home, leaves Lisa his wife and is believed
to be drowned; Lisa marries again. Fedya sinks into social depths
but kills himself rather than to have Lisa arrested for bigamy.
    6 acts; 19 men, 8 women; 10 interiors.

_____. The Power of Darkness (1886). Tr. by Dole in his
    Works, v. 16, Scribner, 1902; same in his Dramatic Works,
    Crowell, 1923; tr. by Maude in his Plays, Constable, 1905;
    same Oxford, 1923; & in his Plays, v. 17, Oxford, 1937; DIK-
    1; NOY; TRE-3; TREA-2.
    A peasant farmhand, Nikita, has wronged an orphan girl,

Marina, has caused a wife to murder her husband so as to marry
him, and has taken his wife's young step-daughter as his mistress.
When she gives birth to a child, Nikita, urged on by his evil-spirited
mother, kills the baby by crushing it with a board in the barn.
Haunted by the baby's cries, he takes to drink and tries to kill himself; an old soldier succeeds in giving Nikita courage to give himself
up to justice. His God-fearing father assures him that God will forgive him.
　　5 acts; 13 men, 7 women, 1 girl; 2 interiors, 3 exteriors.

TOTHEROH, Dan. Moor Born (1934). Samuel French.
　　Presents three years in the lives of the Brontë family at
Haworth parsonage in bleak Yorkshire. The three sisters discover
they have a common talent--to write; but their dissolute brother
Bramwell has none of their native genius. While sacrificing for
him, they proceed for each to write a novel. They are published
under their pseudonym of Bell: Anne, the gentle, wrote Agnes
Grey; Charlotte the practical, as Currer Bell, wrote Jane Eyre;
Emily, the passionate, wrote Wuthering Heights.
　　5 scenes; 3 men, 5 women; 1 interior; costumes of 1840.
　　Royalty: $25-20.

TOWNLEY, James. High Life Below Stairs (1759). BAT v. 16;
　　BRI v. 2; MOR; OXB v. 15.
　　Servants are feasting and making merry at his expense while
Lovel, the master, is away, on a pretended trip into the country.
He returns, armed with pistols, feigning to be drunk, calls forth
the ringleaders, and discharges them. He replaces them with
honest servants.
　　2 acts; 5 men, 3 women, extras; 1 interior; costumes of the
period.

TRAVERS, Robert. Anatomy of a Murder. See entry under Winer,
　　Elihu.

TREADWELL, Sophie. Hope for a Harvest (1941). French, 1942;
　　abridged in Mantle 1941/42.
　　Immigrants have taken most of the land of Elliott Martin, a
peach-grower in California; he is making his living at a filling station. His cousin, Carlotta, returns from fallen France and rouses
him to improve the once-fertile land. His daughter is matched with
an Italian boy, Victor de Lucchi, and the future has hope.
　　3 acts; 5 men, 5 women; 2 interiors.

TRZCINSKI, Edmund. Stalag 17. See entry under Bevan, Donald.

TULLY, R. W. The Rose of the Rancho. See entry under Belasco,
　　David.

TURGENEV, Ivan S. A Month in the Country (1850). Tr. by Man-
　　dell in his Plays, Macmillan, 1924; tr. & adapted by Williams,
　　Lond., Heinemann, 1943; NOY; FAMK; tr. by Noyes, TREA-1;
　　tr. by Garnett in his Three Famous Plays, Scribner, 1952;

adapted by Williams, French.

Natalia is bored in an isolated community. Mikhail, a friend
of her husband, comes to visit but his platonic friendship does not
suffice. Aleksei, a young tutor, is engaged to teach her son, and
the lonely woman falls in love with him. Because of jealousy of her
ward, Vera, she confesses her love to Aleksei, which frightens him
away. Mikhail also leaves, and she is left to her routine existence.

5 acts; 7 men, 5 women, 1 boy; 2 interiors, 1 exterior;
Russian costumes of the period. French royalty: $35-25.

TUTTLE, Day. $E=MC^2$. See entry under Davis, Hallie Flanagan.

TYLER, Royall. The Contrast (1787). Dunlap Society, 1887; HAL;
MOSS-1; QUIK; QUIL.

First play by an American on an American subject to be produced on the American stage. Introduces Jonathan, an agreeable
Yankee rustic of sturdy New England stock who unwittingly attends
a theatre. Maria, the unwilling fiancée of Dimple, a scheming
English fop, meets her ideal in Col. Manly, who has native worth
but is lacking a social grace. Her father discovers the true qualities of the two suitors and sees the wisdom of her choice.

5 acts; 5 men, 4 women, extras; 3 interiors, 1 exterior;
costumes of the period.

UDALL, Nicholas. Ralph Roister Doister (1553). ADA; BAS; BAT;
BOA; GAY; MAT; MIO v. 2; PAR; SCW.

Ralph is a confident braggart, and believes he can win the
lady by writing his love, but Merrygreek changes the punctuation
which alters the sense. Ralph is out of luck with Dame Custance,
who is won by Gawin Goodluck.

5 acts; 9 men, 4 women; simple scenery; costumes of the
period.

USTINOV, Peter. The Love of Four Colonels (1953). Dramatists
Play Service.

Four colonels, representing the United States, England,
France, and Russia, are arguing around the conference table in the
four-power zone of Germany following World War II. The conference
is getting nowhere, and when the four are invited to a nearby castle
by a man called Wicked Fairy, they decide to go. There they are
joined by The Good Fairy, and they meet The Sleeping Beauty.
Each colonel sees Sleeping Beauty as his own national ideal, and
each gets a chance (unsuccessful) to waken and claim her.

6 men, 2 women; stylized sets, interiors and exteriors.
Royalty: $50-25.

_____. Photo Finish (1962). Dramatists Play Service.

Sam, a rather important author, is eighty years old. For
sixty of these years he has been married to, and has fought with,
his wife Stella. One night he receives a strange visitor who turns
out to be Sam at age sixty. Next comes Sam at age forty and Sam
at twenty. Old Sam tries to keep the others from making what he
realizes were mistakes in his life: marrying Stella at twenty, not

leaving her at forty, becoming involved with another woman at sixty.
He is unsuccessful. Finally the Victorian version of Sam appears.
    6 men, 5 women; 1 interior. Royalty: $50-25.

_____. Romanoff and Juliet (1956). Dramatists Play Service.
    The president of a small country (it has a standing army of
two soldiers) is being courted by both the communist and free world
countries because it lies right between the East and the West. The
Russians send an ambassador (Romanoff) who has a son. The United
States sends a diplomat who has a daughter (Juliet). While the two
governmental representatives alternately bribe and threaten the president of the strategic country, young Romanoff and Juliet quietly fall
in love. National rivalries are forgotten in the midst of the excitement of a wedding.
    9 men, 4 women; unit set. Royalty: $50-25.

VAJDA, Ernö. Fata Morgana (1915). Tr. by Burrell & Moeller,
    Doubleday, 1924; French, 1931.
    A Budapest coquette, Mathilde, wife of Gabriel, arrives to
spend the night and go to a ball with relatives. But the telegram
not having been delivered, there is no one home except Georg, an
18-year-old student, who immediately falls in love with her. She
leads him on and even goes to him for the night. Next morning all
return, with them her husband. Georg protests that she is engaged
to him; she appeals to him, and he gallantly tells Gabriel that he
imagined things. His mirage has vanished, and, disillusioned, he
goes back to his studies.
    3 acts; 7 men, 8 women; 1 interior.

VALE, Martin. The Two Mrs. Carrolls (1935). Samuel French.
    The handsome painter, Geoffrey Carroll, is married happily
to his second wife, Sally, until he meets Cecily. Then he thinks
to get rid of Sally by slow poison, even as he had tried to get rid
of Harriet, the first Mrs. Carroll. In the nick of time Harriet
hears of the affair and warns Sally. Geoffrey tries to strangle
Sally; failing in this he commits suicide.
    3 acts; 3 men, 5 women; 2 interiors. Royalty: $50-25.

VALENCY, Maurice. The Enchanted. See entry under Giraudoux,
    Jean.

_____. The Madwoman of Chaillot. See entry under Giraudoux,
    Jean.

_____. Ondine. See entry under Giraudoux, Jean.

_____. The Visit. See entry under Duerrenmatt, Friedrich.

van DRUTEN, John. Bell, Book, and Candle (1950). Dramatists
    Play Service.
    Even in modern Manhattan we find a modern enchanting sor-
ceress, Gillian Holroyd. Through her familiar, a cat named Pye-
wacket, she quickly but naturally brings things to pass, such as the

arrival of the lodger upstairs, Shepherd Henderson, and the author, Sidney Redlich. She shares this witching power with her brother Nicky and her Aunt Queenie. She wins the love of Shep until he learns he was hexed. When she tries to lure him back, she finds she has lost her power, for witches can't fall in love. He finds her different, quite human in fact, and realizes he loves her. She gives up witchcraft for love.

    3 men, 2 women; 1 interior. Royalty: $50-25.

_____, with Leslie Morris. The Damask Cheek (1942). Samuel French.

    A demure English girl in her 30's, Rhoda, comes to visit her snobbish aunt in New York. She falls in love with Jimmie, who is already engaged to a superficially glamorous actress, Calla. She doesn't love Jimmie any too much; Rhoda buys her off, and Jimmie discovers the feminine graces and resources of Rhoda.

    3 men, 6 women; 1 interior. Royalty: $35-25.

_____. The Distaff Side (1933). Samuel French.

    Presents the problems of the women in an English middle-class family: the mother, querulous Mrs. Venables; her three daughters: Nellie, dully living her married life in the provinces; Liz, socially rebellious, divorced, and living on the continent; Evie, a womanly widow, who has had a happy life, doing for others; and Evie's daughter, Alex, unconventional, with present-day sex freedom, and wooed by two suitors who represent very different things

    5 men, 8 women; 2 interiors. Royalty: $35-25.

_____. The Druid Circle (1947). Dramatists Play Service.

    The passionate young love of Tom Ellis and Megan, students in a small university near the border of Wales, is dangerously threatened by the coldness of old Professor White and his domineering elderly colleagues of the Druid Circle who sit in judgment. Their affairs are discussed also by the gossiping women of the small community. The young people are defended by Maddox and his wife Brenda.

    5 men, 6 women; 3 interiors (can be played with 2). Royalty: $50-25.

_____. I Am a Camera (1951). Dramatists Play Service.

    Drama Critics' Award, 1951/52. A character study of a giddy English girl in Berlin in 1930, a night-club singer who is quite amoral. Young Isherwood reports their devoted relationship as they drift along, acting as a camera which sees all. He also reports the love story of a young Jewish couple who are victims of savage Nazi persecution.

    7 scenes in 3 acts; 3 men, 4 women; 1 interior. Royalty: $50-25.

_____. I Remember Mama (1944). Dramatists Play Service.

    (There are two versions of this play: one for high schools and another for college and community groups.) A heartwarming study of American family life with a Norwegian background. Pre-

sents several episodes showing Mama, with the help of her husband
and Uncle Chris, bringing up children in a modest San Francisco
home.   Mama is a sweet and capable manager, gets her children
educated, starts one of them as a writer.
   2 acts; 9 men (including boys), 13 women (including girls);
   1 unit set, showing interior and exterior.   Royalty: high
   school version, $25; college version, $35-25.

_____. Old Acquaintance (1940).   Samuel French.
   A serious novelist, Katharine, and a popular novelist, Mildred, are great friends.   Katharine becomes interested in Rudd, 10
years younger, but he falls for Deirdre, Mildred's daughter.   The
two women discuss the situation in scintillating fashion, and to the
astonishment of all it cements their friendship further; it strains
but does not break it.
   3 acts; 2 men, 5 women; 2 interiors.   Royalty: $35-25.

_____. There's Always Juliet (1931).   Samuel French.
   Leonora, an Englishwoman, and Dwight, an American, meet
at a tea party in England and are attracted to each other.   As she
is trying to learn his identity, he calls.   As they begin to understand
each other, he is recalled to America.   He proposes, she hesitates,
and reluctantly they part.   But he gets three more days of grace before he sails, during which she accepts him.
   3 acts; 2 men, 2 women; 1 interior.   Royalty: $35-25.

_____. The Voice of the Turtle (1943).   Dramatists Play Ser-
vice.
   Sally is living in Olive's apartment and is left to entertain
Olive's attractive boy friend, Sgt. Bill Page, when Olive goes to
meet another flame.   Sally and Bill get interested in each other
during the three days of his leave; they fall in love, and agree to
marry.   A gay, amoral play which seems to make immorality
attractive, as each of the three is sophisticated and has had many
past affairs which have exceeded rigid social conventions.
   3 acts; 1 man, 2 women; 1 interior.   Royalty: $50-25.

_____. Young Woodley (1925).   Samuel French.
   An upright and sensitive young student believes himself so
in love and so attracted to Laura, the wife of the school's headmaster, that he thinks he has done something dreadful and is
ashamed of it.   Laura, with maturer understanding, helps him find
a proper perspective of true love.
   3 acts; 7 men, 2 women; 2 interiors.   Royalty: $25.

VANE, Sutton.   Outward Bound (1923).   Samuel French.
   To the various passengers on a Stygian steamship, who have
been fearful at facing the unknown Examiner, it is implied that
death does not release from struggle nor punish for weakness but
starts them anew in their fight for ultimate contentment.   They are
all allotted their proper places.   The two suicides (called "half-
ways") are enabled to return to life again.
   3 acts; 6 men, 3 women; 1 interior.   Royalty: $25-20.

van ITALLIE, Jean-Claude.   America Hurrah (1967).   Dramatists
     Play Service.
     A single bill comprised of three one-acts ("Interview," "TV,"
"Motel") comprising a satirical, stylized, comic, and absurdist view
of modern life.   The first topic is an employment interview, where
the four masked interviewers try to destroy the self-respect of a
scrubwoman, a house painter, a banker, and a lady's maid.   The
second topic is television, and we watch three normal workers moni-
toring a television program in progress.   Last, three actors in doll
masks perform to an off-stage voice as a motel landlady mouths
platitudes and a tough couple wrecks everything in sight.
     4 men, 4 women to 8 men, 8 women, 3 either sex; stylized
     interiors.   Royalty: $50-25.

_____.   Interview.   See America Hurrah.

_____.   Motel.   See America Hurrah.

_____.   TV.   See America Hurrah.

_____.   The Serpent (1969).   Dramatists Play Service.
     This play, the author says, "is a ceremony reflecting the
minds and lives of the people performing it."   Therefore the words
and movements in the text are a skeleton on which the actors will
"put their own flesh."   Mostly the play is a celebration of love,
using the story of The Book of Genesis as it relates to modern experience.
     Approximately 16 performers with a minimum of 7 men, 7
     women; open stage.   Royalty: $50-25.

VARESI, Gilda and Dolly Byrne.   Enter Madame (1920).   Putnam,
     1921; Longmans, 1924; abridged in Mantle 1920/21.
     Contrasts the artistic and the scientific minds in marriage.
A temperamental prima-donna, spoiled, petted, stormy, alternating
tantrums and tenderness, has differences with her more prosaic
husband.   He wearies of trotting from place to place with all her
entourage (including the dog), but she wins him back.
     3 acts; 5 men, 5 women; 1 interior possible.

VEGA CARPIO, Lope Félix de.   The Gardener's Dog (1618).   Tr.
     by Underhill in his Four Plays, Scribner, 1936; tr. by Cham-
     bers as The Dog in the Manger in BAT v. 6.
     Diana, Countess of Belflor, sought by many in marriage,
falls in love with Teodoro, her secretary, but he has already pledged
himself to Marcella.   Diana will not marry him nor let him marry
Marcella; she is a dog in the manger, the gardener's dog who will
not eat himself nor let others eat.   Two suitors, a Count and a
Marquis, wish to do away with Teodoro and hire a lackey, Tristan,
to kill him; but Tristan arranges for him to be found as the long-
lost son of a Count Lodovico, and through this honor Teodoro gets
Diana.
     3 acts; 14 men, 4 women, extras; many scenes, interior
     and exterior; costumes of the period.

_____. The King, the Greatest Alcalde (1635). Tr. by Underhill in Poet Lore, v. 29, 1918; also in his Four Plays, Scribner, 1936; CLF-2.

Don Tello blesses the betrothal of his shepherd Sancho to Elvira, daughter of the farmer Nuño, but when he sees the beauty of the girl, he carries her off and tries to persuade her to become his mistress. Sancho appeals to the King, who comes in person, after Don Tello had disregarded his order. He has Don Tello acknowledge Elvira as wife, so she might inherit, then he has him beheaded and his property given to Sancho and Elvira.

3 acts; 11 men, 4 women, extras; 9 interiors, 5 exteriors; costumes of the period.

_____. The Sheep Well (1619). Tr. by Underhill in his Four Plays, Scribner, 1936; KRE; TREA-1.

The peasants in the village of Fuente Ovejuna unite to resist oppression by the military. The local Commander has seized and aims to seduce Laurencia, married to a peasant Frondoso. No longer acting like sheep, the peasants attack the palace and the Commander is killed. They all agree that they will say the entire populace did it. The judge can find no one in the village of 300 who will confess otherwise than that Fuente Ovejuna did it, even under torture, though they know that Estaban gave the actual stroke.

3 acts; 20 men, 4 women, extras; various exterior scenes; costumes of the period (1476).

_____. The Star of Seville (ca. 1615). Tr. by Hayden in MAU; also in Clark, W. S.

The King orders a Spanish knight, Don Sancho, to kill his friend, the brother of Stella, his fiancée. He does as ordered, and the King tries to protect him; Don Sancho escapes the death penalty only when the King has made full confession, for even he must bow to justice. Even though they are betrothed with the King's blessing, Don Sancho and Stella mutually agree they must abandon their prospective marriage through chivalric sentiments of honor and gallantry, but especially because, though exonerated, he has killed her brother.

3 acts; 12 men, 3 women, extras; 4 interiors, 2 exteriors; costumes of the Middle Ages.

VEILLER, Bayard. The Thirteenth Chair (1916). Samuel French.

During a seance Edward Wales is stabbed to death but with no dagger in evidence. The medium's daughter is suspected but cleared when her mother uses her mindreading power to discover the real murderer.

3 acts; 10 men, 7 women; 1 interior. Royalty: $25-20.

_____. The Trial of Mary Dugan (1927). Samuel French.

Entire action takes place in the courtroom. With the evidence all against her, her younger brother, Jimmy, a fledgling lawyer, arrives from California, takes over the case, and defends her passionately. He also learns for the first time the sacrifices she has made to pay for his education. He proves the murderer was lefthanded and shows him up.

3 acts; 20 men, 7 women, extras; 1 interior. Royalty: $25-20.

_____. Within the Law (1912). French, 1917; CARC.
    Mary Turner is sent to prison for three years for a theft in Gilder's Emporium which she did not commit. On her release she vows to get even; she operates a blackmailing scheme but always within the law, being supervised by a clever lawyer. After trapping the merchant's son, Dick Gilder, into marriage, she feels her cup of vengeance is about full. Then she becomes involved in a murder at the Gilder house and finds she loves Dick.
    4 acts; 15 men, 5 women; 4 interiors.

VERNE, Jules. Around the World in 80 Days. See entry under Dawes, Rodney.

VERNER, Gerals. Toward Zero. See entry under Christie, Agatha.

VERNEUIL, Louis. Affairs of State (1950). Samuel French.
    On a background of Washington political intrigue a love story is developed. A young Senator, George Henderson, is persuaded to take Irene Elliott as wife in name only, to offset his affection for Constance, wife of Philip Russell, a former Secretary of State. Irene, a mousy schoolteacher, in love with George from the start, blossoms into a charming hostess, as he falls in love with his hired wife, while Philip gets to keep Constance.
    3 acts; 4 men, 2 women; 1 interior. Royalty: $50-25.

VIDAL, Gore. The Best Man (1960). Dramatists Play Service.
    Deals with the fight for the presidential nomination. William Russell, ex-Secretary of State, is a scholar and a man of high principles. Joseph Cantwell is an intense, ruthless politician without moral scruples. Cantwell gets possession of some papers revealing that his rival once suffered a mental crackup. He threatens to release the information if Russell does not throw his support to him. Russell then uncovers evidence which suggests that Cantwell was once homosexual. Arthur Hockstrader, an ex-President who supports Russell, tries unsuccessfully to persuade his man to use the dirt he has uncovered. Finally, at the convention, Russell ruins Cantwell by withdrawing from the race and supporting another candidate.
    14 men, 6 women; interiors. Royalty: $50-25.

_____. Visit to a Small Planet (1957). Dramatists Play Service.
    A visitor from another planet decides to start a war for his own amusement in a very average town. The visitor has intended to arrive in time for the Civil War but arrives in 1957. He tries to make the best of it, though, and is quite impressed by such things as hydrogen bombs. In fact, he's enchanted by all the new playthings the 20th century has invented for war-making, and he sees no reason why they can't be put to use for his own amusement. It takes the combined efforts of the entire cast--an average general, an average boy and girl in love, an average TV newscaster, and an

above average Siamese cat--to persuade him to abandon his war.
8 men, 2 women; 1 interior. Royalty: $50-25.

VIERTEL, Peter and Irwin Shaw. The Survivors (1948). Dramatists Play Service.

Young Steve Decker, a Union soldier just out of four years
in a Confederate prison, returns to Missouri to take part in the feud
between the Deckers and the Camerons. His plan is to kill the hard-
bitten ranchman, Tom Cameron; but first he wants to know the truth
of the case against the Camerons. Thus arguments on both sides
are presented, concluding with the futility of killing as a means of
settlement.
3 acts; 13 men, 2 women, extras; 2 sets; costumes of 1865.
Royalty: $35-25.

VILDRAC, Charles. Michel Auclair (1922). Tr. & adapted by
Sidney Howard in LEV 1932; carried by French.

Michel returns after a year and finds his old sweetheart
Suzanne has married a stupid dishonest soldier, Blondeau. Michel
studies his rival's character and goes about to make him a husband
worthy of the girl.
3 acts; 5 men, 2 women; 1 interior, 1 exterior.

_____. The Steamship Tenacity (1920). Tr. by Newberry in
Poet Lore, v. 32, 1921; DIE; tr. by Sidney Howard in TUCG;
TUCM.

Two ex-soldiers, Bastien and Ségard, are on their way to
Canada but are delayed at the French seaport while the steamship
is being repaired. Both fall in love with Thérèse, the pretty waitress at the café, but Bastien the realist runs off with her, leaving
Ségard the dreamer to sail alone. Old Hidoux represents the voice
of experience.
3 acts; 5 men, 2 women, extras; 1 interior.

VINCENT, Allen. Letters to Lucerne. See entry under Rotter,
Fritz.

VOLLMER, Lula. The Hill Between (1939). Longmans, 1939.

A mountain boy, Brent, has become a successful doctor in
the city and married Anna, a society girl. They come back to
visit the mountain folk, among whom he realizes there is great
need for medical aid. Anna doesn't fit in with the mountain people
and wants to go back to the city at once; she also wishes to take
with her his sister Ellen, although she is in love with and engaged
to Lars, a wholesome mountain boy. When the time comes to
leave, Brent decides his place is in the mountains, and he lets
Anna go back to the city.
3 acts; 4 men, 3 women, plus 6 men and 5 women at the
dance, also extras; 1 interior; mountain costumes.

_____. Moonshine and Honeysuckle (1933). Samuel French.

Features a feud in the Kentucky mountains between the Be-
vinses and the Gaddises, the origin of which is forgotten. Clem

Betts strives to bring harmony by marrying off Annie Bevins to Buck Gaddis. "Cracker" Gaddis, a little shrew, wants to keep the feud alive, and Peg Leg (Paw) Gaddis rides his mule into the church to break up the wedding. But after his trial for disturbing the peace, the feud is finally ended.

   3 acts; 8 men, 5 women; 1 exterior; mountain costumes.
   Royalty: $10.

_____. Sun-Up (1923). Brentano, 1924; also Longmans; QUIL; TUCD; TUCM; abridged in Mantle 1923/24.

   The widow Cagle in the mountains of North Carolina has been ever opposed to that dread abstraction--the law. She believes "the law" killed her husband and took away her boy Rufe to fight that feud war in France--about 40 miles east of Asheville! As she is ready to shoot the son of the revenuer who killed her husband, the spirit of Rufe whispers love and less hate; she has a change of heart and resolves to live in peace.

   3 acts; 7 men, 2 women; 1 interior; mountain costumes.

VOLTAIRE. Mérope (1743). Tr. by Fleming in his Dramatic Works, Paris, Dumont, 1901.

   Mérope welcomes back to Messenia her son Aegytus. He returns unknown, but his identity is revealed by his father's armor and is confirmed by old Narbas, who rescued him as an infant and has brought him up for 15 years as father and son. Aegytus slays Polyphontes who has usurped the crown after killing his father and hoping to marry Mérope to confirm the accession. Written by Voltaire as a play from which the ordinary love interest is excluded; emotion is created through Mérope's love for her son.

   5 acts; 5 men, 2 women, extras; exterior scenes; Greek costumes.

_____. Zaïre (1732). Tr. as Zara in Inchbald v. 7; tr. by Fleming in his Dramatic Works, Paris, Dumont, 1901-03.

   Zaïre, captive since birth in Palestine, wins the love of Osman, Sultan of Jerusalem, and though a Christian by birth, has been brought up as a Moslem. Nérestan, a French gentleman, who had escaped two years before from the Moslem prison to obtain ransom money, returns and is granted the release of all but Zaïre and the aged Lusignan. At Zaïre's request Osman also releases him from 20 years' captivity. He proves to be the father of both Zaïre and Nérestan, and begs her to become a Christian. She is torn between her love for Osman and her desire to be baptized as a Christian. In trying to leave the seraglio, she is wrongfully stabbed by Osman who thinks she is going to a lover, but on learning the truth, stabs himself.

   5 acts; 7 men, 2 women, extras; 1 interior; costumes of the period and place.

VONNEGUT, Kurt, Jr. Happy Birthday, Wanda June (1970). Samuel French.

   A woman with a little boy is about to be declared a widow (her husband, a famous big game hunter and adventurer, disappeared

in the Amazon jungle years ago). She and her son and her two
suitors (a doctor and a vacuum cleaner salesman) are celebrating
her "late" husband's birthday with a cake decorated for a Wanda
June when her husband unexpectedly shows up after all this time
with his friend, a bush pilot. He is an awful person, it turns out,
who is unsuccessful in getting his son to shoot him and unsuccessful at shooting himself. A wild and funny story in the Vonnegut
manner.
     5 men, 2 women, 2 children; 1 interior, scrim. Royalty:
$50-35.

_____. Welcome to the Monkey House (1970). Adapted by
    Christopher Sergel. Dramatic Publishing Company.
     Scenes from Vonnegut's collection of short stories, beginning
with a young man who searches for identity and companionship by
acting in amateur theatricals and ending with a high school music
teacher's attempt to salvage a rebellious male student.
     Variable cast of 10 to 24; 2 sets. Royalty: $35.

WALKER, Joseph A. The River Niger (1973). Samuel French.
     John Williams, a mid-fifties poet/house painter, and his
family live in Harlem. John is proud of his son Jeff, who is
scheduled to return from service as an Air Force lieutenant, even
though his best friend Dudley is unimpressed by any black man serving in the "white man's air force." When Jeff gets home, it turns
out that he is too anti-establishment to suit his father and not
enough to suit his militant black friends. At the end of the play
the hero is John, whose hard drinking and poetic composition have
left him the kind of strength to assume the penalties of a younger
generation's clash with the white man's law.
     Black cast of 9 men, 4 women; 1 interior. Royalty: $50-
35.

WALKER, Peter. Mirth and Mayhem (1974). Performance Pub-
    lishing.
     A group of girls decides to spend the night in a house where
three murders have been committed, to prove that they are as brave
as boys. They expect their boyfriends to try to scare them as a
joke, but they finally come to believe that the people who show up
are for real. Actually, the strangers are television actors rehearsing a program on the sinister history of the house. The two groups
totally misunderstand each other, and everything gets worse when a
real murder takes place.
     5 men, 15 women; representational set. Royalty: $35.

_____. Tom Jones. See entry under Fielding, Henry.

WALLACH, Ira. The Absence of a Cello (1965). Dramatists Play
    Service.
     A physicist is so broke that he is willing to seek a job with
a big corporation at a salary of $60,000. When the scientist be-
comes aware of corporation standards of conformity, he stores away
the rolled-up trousers he wears, hides the books on medieval history

his wife writes, and conceals the cello he plays with pick-up
quartets.   Even friends and relatives are brought in to reinforce
the conservative image.   But the man from personnel sees through
the pose, and suggests that any man who alters himself to please a
corporation is in no position to blame a corporation for its demands
on employees.   More fun follows.
    3 men, 4 women; 1 interior.   Royalty: $50-25.

WALPOLE, Hugh.   <u>Kind Lady</u>.   See entry under Chodorov, Edward.

WALTER, Eugene.   <u>The Easiest Way</u> (1908).   Dillingham, 1911;
    Houghton, 1921; <u>DID</u>; MOSS-3; abridged in Mantle & Sherwood
    1909-1919.
    An actress, Laura, after a life of struggle, meets a man she
really loves, a newspaper reporter.   But she is the mistress of a
wealthy man who can give her ease; she hasn't the strength to take
the hard narrow path that would lead to happiness.   In the end she
loses both men.
    4 acts; 3 men, 3 women; 2 interiors, 1 exterior.

WARD, Douglas Turner.   <u>Happy Ending and Day of Absence</u> (1965).
    Dramatists Play Service.
    Two short plays with an all black cast, part of a single bill
which had a long run off-Broadway.   In "Happy Ending," sisters
Ellie and Vi sit in the kitchen of a Harlem tenement bemoaning the
end of their jobs.   One is maid and the other laundress for the
wealthy (white) Harrisons, but since Mr. H. discovered his wife in
adultery it appears that the marriage and home will break up, along
with the black women's jobs.   A nephew chides the two for caring,
but Ellie explains to him all the fringe benefits (household graft) that
go along with their employment.   By the end of the play the Harrisons have got together again and have called Ellie to come babysit
for them.   In "Day of Absence," described by the author as "a Re-
verse Minstrel Show," the black cast makes up a whiteface and
plays the residents of a Southern town in which all the blacks have
strangely disappeared.   A crisis is clearly at hand.   White infants
scream when they are cared for by their own parents, policemen
have no one to club, the Klansmen no one to intimidate.   The mayor
of the town pleads with the Governor the President, the NAACP to
send him some black citizens.
    "Happy Ending": 2 men, 2 women; 1 interior.   Royalty:
    $25-15.   "Day of Absence": 8 men, 6 women (many roles
    doubled); unit set.   Royalty: $25-15.

WARREN, Robert Penn.   <u>All the King's Men</u> (1948).   Dramatists
    Play Service.
    Mr. Warren's disclaimer notwithstanding, the play treats the
story of Huey Long, Governor of Louisiana.   Willie Stark is the
name of the political figure in the play who rises from a simple
country boy to absolute dictator of the state.   Though his methods
are corrupt, Stark is able to accomplish things for the people which
remain only unattainable ideals for more honest politicians.
    14 men, 4 women; extras; open stage with minimum props.
    Royalty: $35-25.

WASSERMAN, Dale. <u>One Flew Over the Cuckoo's Nest</u> (1963).
Based on Ken Kesey's novel. Samuel French.

A devil-may-care character makes the mistake of arranging
to spend time in a mental institution instead of a prison. He runs
into a head nurse who runs the hospital with an iron hand and who
hates him for interfering with the way she handles her "boys." A
power struggle develops, and the new inmate is given electro-shock
treatments for his first offense, and finally a frontal lobotomy. To
keep him from living the rest of his life as a vegetable, the other
inmates smother him.

17 men, 5 women; 1 interior and inset. Royalty: $50-25.

WATKINS, Maurine. <u>Chicago</u> (1926). Knopf, 1927; abridged in
Mantle 1926/27.

Roxie Hart shoots Casely and is of course arrested. Such a
story is a set-up for Jake the reporter and Bill Flynn the lawyer.
Coached by Flynn, Roxie so works on the jury that she is found
"not guilty."

3 acts; 18 men, 8 women; 4 interiors.

WEBSTER, John. <u>The Duchess of Malfi</u> (ca. 1617). In his <u>Com-
plete Works</u>, v. 2, Houghton, 1928; (earlier edns., 1830, 1857);
in Mermaid ser., Scribner, 1888; in Belles Lettres ser.,
Heath, 1904; in Ebony ser., Dodd, 1930; in Temple classics,
Dutton, 1937; BAS; DUN; HARC v. 7; HOW; MAT; NEI; OLH;
OLI v. 2; SCH; SCI; TAU; THA; TRE-1 & 2; TREA-1; WHE.

The widowed Duchess secretly marries her steward Antonio,
thus giving offense to her brothers. In revenge, the brothers kill
her and her children; the betrayer, de Bosola, kills the brothers
and Antonio. In the end, all are wiped out: a total of 10 slain,
one poisoned, and one going mad.

5 acts; 12 men, 3 women, extras; 7 interiors, 2 exteriors;
costumes of the period.

WEDEKIND, Frank. <u>Such Is Life</u> (1903). Tr. by Ziegler, Phila.,
Brown, 1912 & 1916; in DIE; in TUCG.

King Nicolo and his daughter, Alma, are thrust out of the
kingdom of Perugia when the citizens revolt and place a Master
Butcher on the throne. He becomes a tailor and Alma a stenographer. For lese majestie he is arrested; after release they join
a circus where he gives a take-off of a king before his supplanter
who appoints him (unrecognized) as the Court Fool. He dies as
such, trying to prove that Alma is a princess.

5 acts; 24 men, 2 women, extras; 4 interiors, 4 exteriors;
costumes.

WEINSTOCK, Jack and Willie Gilbert. <u>Catch Me If You Can</u> (1965).
Based on the play by Robert Thomas. Samuel French.

A whodunit that takes place at a mountain lodge, where an
advertising man has just brought his new bride for a honeymoon.
Immediately she disappears. A young woman arrives who claims
she's his new wife (though he denies it) and a priest who backs up
her story. After a delicatessen owner arrives there are two murders at the isolated lodge. A mystery-comedy with some startling

twists.
    5 men, 2 women; 1 interior. Royalty: $50-25.

WEISS, Peter. The Investigation (1966). Dramatic Publishing Com-
    pany.
    Deals with the Frankfurt trial of the atrocities of Auschwitz.
The house lights are kept on during the play, contributing to the
sense of participation, and the stage is bare except for some chairs
and tables. Through the course of the play testimony is heard from
the accused and from the witnesses for the prosecution. A powerful
and intense play.
    28 men, 2 women; bare stage. Royalty: $50.

_____ . The Persecution and Assassination of Jean Paul Marat
    as Performed by the Inmates of the Asylum of Charenton Under
    the Direction of the Marquis de Sade (Marat/Sade) (1965). Eng-
    lish version by Geoffrey Skelton. Verse adaptation by Adrian
    Mitchell. Dramatic Publishing Company.
    The basic action of the play is a play put on by the inmates
of the Charenton Asylum for the benefit of the Director of the institution and his two lady friends. The Marquis de Sade (who actually
was an inmate there and was known to have staged plays during his
confinement) stages a wild drama dealing with events leading up to
the slaying of Marat by Charlotte Corday. The inmate-actors, in
grubby dress, have their own anguish to express besides that inherent in their play.
    9 men, 3 women, bits and extras; 1 set. Royalty: $75-50.

WEITZENKORN, Louis. Five-Star Final (1930). French, 1931;
    abridged in Mantle 1930/31.
    In this strong attack on yellow journalism, the tabloid paper
plays up to Nancy Voorhees murder of 20 years ago in order to boost
its circulation. When this is published, Nancy and her husband
poison themselves, and Jenny, their daughter, accuses Hinchcliffe,
the owner of the paper, of murder. Philip, her fiancé, stands by
her. Randall, the managing editor, has to carry it through, but he
denounces Hinchcliffe as he leaves the paper.
    3 acts in 19 scenes; 16 men, 10 women; various interiors.

WELLER, Michael. Moonchildren (1971). Samuel French.
    The setting is a student apartment in a university town in-
habited by five college senior men and three coeds. What they have
in common is the senselessness of their lives, their inability to
commit to any purpose, and their mockery of the plastic up-tight
establishment and straight world. They take on policemen, landla-
dies, and salesmen with the same kind of witty boredom that they
bring to the anti-war movement and other causes they think they
feel deeply about.
    12 men, 3 women; 1 interior. Royalty: $50-35.

WELLES, Orson. Moby Dick-Rehearsed (1965). Based on Herman
    Melville's novel. Samuel French.
    In this melodrama, Welles manages to accommodate the story

to the stage with an ingenious contrivance. First he presents a Shakespearean company rehearsing King Lear. Then they decide to try a new play entitled "Moby Dick." With rehearsal platforms as the deck, and a ladder serving as mast, the company proceeds to enact the epic saga of Captain Ahab and the Pequod.
>   12 men, 2 women; stage props. Royalty: $35-25.

WELTY, Eudora. The Ponder Heart. See entry under Fields, Joseph.

WERFEL, Franz. Jacobowsky and the Colonel (1944). Adapted by S. N. Behrman. Dramatists Play Service.
>   The little Jewish refugee, Jacobowsky, who has survived by his wits, is contrasted with the Polish Colonel, who maintains his feudalistic attitude. They want to escape from France ahead of the invading Germans. Finally the Colonel realizes that Jacobowsky has precisely those admirable qualities necessary for survival. Marianne is a symbol of the spirit of oppressed France; she will await the Colonel's return.
>   3 acts; 23 men (some as extras), 5 women; 2 interiors, 4 exteriors. Royalty: $50-25.

_____. Juarez and Maximillian (1924). Tr. by Langner, Simon & Schuster for Theatre Guild, 1926.
>   Presents incidents in the Mexican career of Emperor Maximillian. After he signed a decree that all revolutionaries be shot, his popularity waned rapidly; his troops were defeated by the troops of Juarez, led by Diaz; he was taken and shot. Maximillian was the victim of his own blind idealism and failure to understand the Mexicans. The influence of Juarez is felt throughout the play though he never appears.
>   3 acts & epilog in 13 scenes; 26 men, 1 boy of 3, 3 women, extras; 8 interiors, 3 exteriors.

_____. Paul Among the Jews (1926). Tr. by Levertoff, Lond., Diocesan House, 1928; Lond., Grey Walls Press, 1943.
>   Paul returns to Jerusalem as a Christian and visits his old teacher, Gamaliel, also Barnabas, Peter, and James. He believes that orthodox Judaism has been transcended by the new faith and gospel of love; that the Jews by their fanaticism have given the Romans a pretext for denying their liberties. Peter takes one attitude, Paul another.
>   6 scenes; 18 men, 1 woman, extras; 5 interiors, 1 exterior.

_____. The Song of Bernadette. See entry under Kerr, Jean.

WESKER, Arnold. Chips with Everything (1962). Samuel French.
>   A patrician youth with all the qualifications for officers school has no desire for leadership in this drama about the training of Air Force recruits. These military novices are first exposed to drill-master Corporal Hill whose opening words are, "I am not a happy man." Then the wing commander informs the group that they are not really at peace. But the recruits survive the officers and

such adventures as a boisterous, rebellious Christmas party, and finally arrive at their graduation as the play comes to a close.
23 men; various settings. Royalty: $50-25.

WETZEL, Donald. <u>All Summer Long.</u> See entry under Anderson, Robert.

WEXLEY, John. <u>The Last Mile</u> (1930). Samuel French.
A thrilling presentation of a jailbreak, depicting the actions and psychology of several men in the death-cell in an Oklahoma prison. Killer Mears engineers the break, but when he realizes he is licked, he walks out into machine gun fire.
3 acts; 16 men, 0 women; 1 interior. Royalty: $50-25.

_____. <u>They Shall Not Die</u> (1934). Samuel French.
Negro boys and two white girls are taken off a freight train and thrown into jail. The girls are bribed by the sheriff to charge the colored boys with rape, and the boys are beaten into confessing. Later Lucy admits she has given false testimony. In the final court room scene, despite the excellent brief by the defense lawyer, it is evident the trial is a complete frame-up motivated by race prejudice, with little hope for the boys.
52 men, 5 women; 5 interiors. Royalty: $25.

WHARTON, Edith. <u>Ethan Frome.</u> See entry under Davis, Owen.

_____. <u>The Old Maid</u> (1935). Adapted by Zoë Akins. Samuel French.
Pulitzer prize play for 1935. Charlotte, the real mother, never reveals her secret that the child who regards her as a hard-hearted old maid is her illegitimate daughter. Her yearning mother-love strikes a tragic note when her sister wins the girl's affection.
5 men, 9 women; 3 interiors. Royalty: $25-20.

WHEELER, Edward L. <u>Deadwood Dick.</u> See entry under Taggart, Tom.

WHITE, George. <u>Royal Gambit.</u> See entry under Gressieker, Hermann.

WHITMAN, Walt. See Paul Shyre's <u>A Whitman Portrait.</u>

WIBBERLEY, Leonard. <u>The Mouse That Roared</u> (1963). Dramatic Publishing Company.
Duchess Gloriana, the pretty 22-year-old ruler of a tiny nation in the Alps, learns that her country is near bankruptcy. To get funds she decides to declare war on the U.S., reasoning that though her country would certainly lose, the U.S. would pour in aid, relief, and rehabilitation on the vanquished. But the U.S. State Department considers Gloriana's "Declaration" a prank, and she orders her army to invade so that they can surrender and reap the rewards. In a completely unexpected development, however, the invasion succeeds and her army wins! The unfolding of this surprising

turn of events should provide a very entertaining play.
20 or more characters; 1 interior. Royalty: $50-35.

_____. 1776 and All That (1973). Dramatic Publishing Company.
A 4th of July costume party at the White House is unexpectedly joined by George Washington, Benjamin Franklin, Thomas Jefferson, and King George III---all residents of Heaven. They are still
arguing about the old issues (democracy vs. the divine right of
kings), but they are soon involved in the new ones (human rights, the
future of America, etc.) with those who currently run the government.
9 men, 8 women, extras; several playing areas. Royalty:
$35.

WIED, Gustav Johannes. 2 X 2 = 5 (1906). Tr. by Boyd & Koppel
in LEG.
A liberal champion of truth and freedom accepts a position
with a good salary on a newspaper whose policy he had formerly
disapproved; he does so for the sake of his wife and children.
Others in the play change readily, as when a radical concedes to
convention. Thus all are inclined to adapt the truth to suit themselves.
4 acts; 11 men, 7 women; 3 interiors.

WIERS-JENSSEN, Hans. The Witch (1910). Tr. by Masefield,
Little Brown, 1917; Brentano, 1926.
Anne Petersdotter at 17 marries the palace chaplain, the elderly (55) Absolon. For love of Anne he had spared her mother,
accused of being a witch. Martin, his son, returns from study
abroad and falls in love with his young step-mother, and she with
him. She tries her hypnotic power which she believes she has inherited from her mother and succeeds in willing the death of Absolon. Accused of sorcery, she is asked to prove her innocence by
touching the corpse. In doing so she loses her reason and confesses
she tried to bewitch both husband and stepson.
4 acts; 9 men, 5 women; extras; 2 interiors, 1 exterior;
costumes of 16th century, Norway.

WILBRANDT, Adolf. The Master of Palmyra (1889). Tr. by Stork
in FRA v. 16; tr. by Olive in Poet Lore, v. 13, 1902.
Apelles, the Master, returns as conqueror and is greeted by
Pausanius, the Care-releaser. Apelles asks to live forever. He
has four episodes with women in his long life: Zoe, Phoebe, Per-
sida, and Zenobia. At the end of each experience, Pausanius appears and asks if he still wishes to live forever. In the epilog,
Apelles sees in Zenobia, who is a humble benefactress of the poor,
a reincarnation of Zoe and Phoebe, and he is content to die.
Prolog, 3 acts & epilog; 13 men, 6 women, extras; 1 interior, 3 exteriors; costumes of the period (4th century
A.D.).

WILDE, Oscar. An Ideal Husband (1895). In the various editions
of his Works: French carried.

Robert Chilton, now an Under-Secretary and famous for his probity, sold a state secret 18 years before. This appears in an incriminating letter held by the adventurous Mrs. Cheveley. She forces him to favor a project which he had formerly opposed; but since his wife is so disappointed, he advises Mrs. Cheveley that he cannot keep his promise. Though his dishonesty in the matter is revealed, the affair is cleared up and he is offered a Cabinet post.
    4 acts; 9 men, 6 women; 3 interiors.

_____. The Importance of Being Earnest (1895). In every edition of his Collected Works; acting editions carried by Baker & French; in ASH; CAR; CEU; MOSO; SMR; STE; TRE-1, 2, & 3; TREA-3; TUCD; TUCM; WHI; abridged in Pierce & Matthews v. 1.
    As an alibi for week-end holidays Jack Worthing invents a younger brother Earnest who frequently demands attention. His friend Algy introduces himself as Earnest to Jack's ward, Cecily, but confusion reigns when Jack proposes to Gwendolyn (Algy's cousin) as Earnest, for she feels she is fated to marry an Earnest. Jack and Algy decide to be rechristened, since both girls seem to be engaged to Earnest. Jack turns out to be Algy's long lost brother, left as a baby in a handbag in Victoria station, and he is actually named Earnest.
    3 acts; 5 men, 4 women; 2 interiors, 1 exterior. No royalty.

_____. Lady Windermere's Fan (1892). In every edition of his Collected Works; acting editions carried by Baker and French; DIC; HUD; LIE; MAT; MOO; RUB; SMO; TAU; abridged in Pierce & Matthews v. 1.
    Young Lady Windermere quarrels with her husband for his attentions to a Mrs. Erlynne, unaware that she is her mother, whom she supposed deceased, and that he is only trying to help the lady. Leaving a note that she is leaving to elope with her lover, she goes to Lord Darlington's apartments. Mrs. Erlynne, finding the note follows her there and persuades her to escape unnoticed. When the men come and find Lady Windermere's fan, Mrs. Erlynne emerges as if from an assignation and takes the blame for having brought along the fan by mistake. She thus saves her daughter's reputation at the cost of her own.
    4 acts; 7 men, 6 women; 3 interiors. No royalty.

_____. A Woman of No Importance (1893). In most of his Collected Works; COT.
    When Gerald Arbuthnot, a clerk, is offered the position of secretary to Lord Illingworth, his mother is unwilling to reveal to him that Lord Illingworth is his father who never married her because she was a woman of no importance. But when Lord Illingworth insults Gerald's fiancée Hester and Gerald attempts to kill him, she confesses that he is his father. Illingworth now offers to marry her, but she dismisses him as a man of no importance.
    4 acts; 8 men, 7 women; 3 interiors, 1 exterior.

WILDENBRUCH, Ernst von. King Henry (1896). Tr. by Wernaer
   in Drama v. 5, 1915; FRA v. 17.
   Henry is the conqueror of the Saxons and King of Germany,
but he wishes to be crowned Emperor by the Pope. The Pope refuses. When Henry writes a deposing letter, the Pope excommuni-
cates him. His wife Bertha persuades him to be a penitent, and he
is one for three days at Canossa. Later he wins over Pope Gregory
and is to be crowned Emperor by the succeeding Pope.
   Prolog & 4 acts; many men, 3 women, some children, extras; 6 interiors, 1 exterior; costumes of the period (about
   1075).

WILDER, Thornton. Lucrece. See entry under Obey, Andre.

_____. The Matchmaker (1954). Samuel French.
   Set in 1880 New York, this farce humorously depicts the attempts of a rich old Yonkers merchant to find a suitable mate. To
this end he employs a matchmaker, a woman who involves him in a
series of madcap escapades resulting in chaos for his business and
the lives of all around him. The merchant soon finds he loves his
matchmaker and the two become engaged, but not before the wily
lady has forced him to give up his blustery, domineering ways.
   9 men, 7 women; 4 interiors. Royalty: $50-25.

_____. Our Town (1938). Samuel French.
   Pulitzer prize play 1938. Saga of a small New England
town, depicting life, love, and death. George Gibbs and Emily
Webb fall in love and marry. Emily, after her death, returns for
her 12th birthday, but finds the living are unseeing and troubled,
not realizing their possibilities.
   3 acts; 17 men, 7 women, extras; 1 bare stage. Royalty:
   $25-20.

_____. The Skin of Our Teeth (1942). Samuel French.
   Pulitzer prize play 1943. Playful spoofing with a serious un-
dertone. Presents a satiric story of the extraordinary adventures
of the Antrobus family (i. e. Man) down through the ages from the
Ice Age. They have survived a thousand calamities by the skin of
their teeth and are practically indestructible while Man has his
family and his books. Introduces many outstanding events in the
history of man, such as the discovery of the wheel and the invention
of the alphabet. Man has learned much and is still learning.
   3 acts; 5 men, 5 women, many extras; 1 interior; 1 exterior.
   Royalty: $50-25.

WILLIAMS, Emlyn. The Corn Is Green (1938). Dramatists Play
   Service.
   A school-teacher, Miss Moffat, goes to a Welsh mining town,
starts a school for the underprivileged miners, and there discovers
a genius in a young tough collier, Morgan Evans. She coaches him
through to win a scholarship at Oxford.
   3 acts; 10 men, 5 women, extras; 1 interior. Royalty: $35-25.

_____. A Murder Has Been Arranged (1928). Samuel French.
        Sir Charles Jasper stands to inherit two million pounds on
his fortieth birthday. When that day arrives he gives a party to
celebrate his new wealth. The gaiety is momentarily interrupted by
the arrival of Maurice, a nephew who will receive the fortune if
Sir Charles dies. Maurice induces his uncle to drink poison and
write a suicide note. In the climax to this melodrama, however,
the remaining guests trap Maurice into confessing the murder.
        4 men, 5 women; 1 interior. Royalty: $25-20.

_____. Night Must Fall (1935). Samuel French.
        Danny is a bell-hop in a resort hotel, and yet a dashing
young assassin. The murder of a guest in the hotel is traced to
him by Olivia, who nevertheless is fascinated by him when her aunt,
old Mrs. Bramson, adds him to the household servants. Danny is
powerless in the grip of his homicidal instincts and plots to murder
Mrs. Bramson for her money. The police take him away to be
hanged, leaving Olivia relieved but desolate.
        3 acts; 4 men, 5 women; 1 interior. Royalty: $25-20.

_____. Someone Waiting (1953). Dramatists Play Service.
        A student has failed his law exams. Part of the reason is
that he hates his adopted father, but mostly the boy is upset because
his best friend has just been executed for murdering a servant girl
in their apartment. The new tutor for the student turns out to be
the father of the executed friend, and has taken the position to ad-
minister justice to the real murderer. After many misdirections,
the murder is solved.
        4 men, 5 women; 1 interior. Royalty: $35-25.

WILLIAMS, Herschel. Janie. See entry under Bentham, Josephine.

WILLIAMS, Hugh and Margaret Williams. The Irregular Verb To
    Love (1961). Samuel French.
        Hedda Rankin returns home from prison to find that nothing
has gone right during her absence. Her husband, a zoo official,
has been unfaithful; her daughter will not marry the man she loves;
and her son has just returned from abroad with a Greek girl who
speaks no English. Hedda sets out to straighten out everyone's affairs, and takes credit for doing so. But it is her husband who
makes things right again.
        4 men, 5 women; 1 interior. Royalty: $50-25.

WILLIAMS, Jesse Lynch. Why Marry? (1917). Scribner, 1918;
    CORF; QUI; abridged in Mantle & Sherwood 1909-1919.
        1st Pulitzer prize play, 1918. Skillfully depicts within the
circle of one family the various kinds of marriages, from the girl
brought up to be married to the one who doesn't want to be married. Centers around the problem of Helen and whether to go to
Paris with Dr. Ernest Hamilton with or without marriage. Deftly
defines the ancient and necessary institution. Originally pub. 1914
as "And so they were married."
        3 acts; 7 men, 3 women; 1 interior.

WILLIAMS, Tennessee. <u>Camino Real</u> (1953). Dramatists Play
  Service.
     A fantasy set in a walled community. The only character
who has access to the outside is Don Quixote, the "victim of romantic folly. " Other people shut in include Camille, Casanova, and Kilroy, a former boxer, always a patsy, whose heart has been corrupted. Finally Kilroy becomes fit to be the companion of Don
Quixote, and they leave together.
     26 men (doubling possible); 10 women; extras; exterior, in-
teriors. Royalty: $50-25.

_____. <u>Cat on a Hot Tin Roof</u> (1955). Dramatists Play Service.
     All of the characters in the play are as insecure and desper-
ate as the proverbial "cat" of the title. Big Daddy is dying of can-
cer, and everyone is greedy for his wealth. Brick is tortured by
the notion that he is a latent homosexual, and he refuses to sleep in
the same bed with his wife, Maggie, who finds her own desires unfulfilled. Sins of the past, greed for the future, and an unwilling-
ness to face the truths of the present motivate Big Daddy's family.
     8 men, 5 women, 4 children; 1 interior. Royalty: $50-25.

_____. <u>The Glass Menagerie</u> (1945). Dramatists Play Service.
     The fragile cripple, Laura, is so repressed that she has
lost contact with reality and finds refuge in the enjoyment of her
glass figures. To her mother's regret she has no "gentlemen cal-
lers. " For Mother Amanda lives in the past, reminiscing of her
youth. She is much excited when son Tom brings Jim home to dinner, until it turns out that Jim is already engaged to be married.
Tom leaves home as his father did, but he can't lose the memory
of Laura.
     2 men, 2 women; 1 interior. Royalty: $50-25.

_____. <u>The Milk Train Doesn't Stop Here Anymore</u> (1962).
  Dramatists Play Service.
     Mrs. Goforth has lived a full and lecherous life. Now, in
one of her villas on the southern coast of Italy, she dictates her
memoirs to secretaries and tape recorders with the absurd notion
that they will provide an important social commentary. Chris
Flanders, a young poet, arrives at the villa. His enemies call
him "the angel of death" because of his presence at the deaths of
so many elderly women. Mrs. Goforth sees in Chris the opportunity
to have one last sexual fling before death, and she tries to buy him.
Only near the end does she realize he is not for sale--he merely
wishes to soothe her at the time of death.
     5 men, 4 women; unit set. Royalty: $50-25.

_____. <u>The Night of the Iguana</u> (1959). Dramatists Play Ser-
  vice.
     Maxine, a nymphomanical widow, runs a cheap resort hotel
in Mexico. For her comfort, she keeps two young native houseboys.
The chief visitors to the hotel are the Rev. T. Lawrence Shannon,
defrocked as a result of his sexual activities; Miss Hannah Jelkes,
a forty-year-old virgin who does quick portraits for a fee; and her

aged grandfather, who recites poems. The chief conflict among the
characters is between Shannon and Hannah, who clash immediately
but who finally assist one another. Throughout the play the message comes across that life must be endured, and that one must
find a way--any way--to survive.
        8 men, 6 women; 1 exterior. Royalty: $50-25.

_____. Orpheus Descending (1957). Dramatists Play Service.
        Transfers the Orpheus legend to a small Southern town. Val
Xavier, a wandering guitar player, is given a job in the Tarrance
Mercantile Store. The storekeeper is an invalid, and soon Val becomes the lover of the storekeeper's wife, Lady. The townspeople
are outraged over the alliance, especially the sheriff, who orders
Val to leave town. Later he organizes a lynch mob to take care of
him. When Val embraces Lady in a goodbye scene, her husband
appears and shoots her. Val runs away but is killed by the townspeople.
        10 men, 9 women; 1 interior. Royalty: $50-25.

_____. Period of Adjustment (1960). Dramatists Play Service.
        Tennessee Williams' only comedy, a delightful one involving
"periods of adjustment" for two married couples. One couple,
Ralph Bates and his wife, have just broken up after five years of
marriage. Another couple, George Haverstick and his bride of a
day, turns up at Ralph's house on Christmas Eve. Ralph and
George, it seems, were war buddies. The problem with Ralph and
his wife is that they have in-law trouble. The problem with George,
the groom, is that he has the shakes and cannot go through with his
wedding night responsibilities. At the end, both couples are reconciled.
        4 men, 5 women; 1 interior. Royalty: $50-25.

_____. Small Craft Warnings (1972). Dramatists Play Service.
        The setting is "Monk's Place," a seedy bar on the coast of
Southern California. A storm is approaching, and small craft
warnings have been posted, leading the aging physician who has lost
his license to practice to remark to bar owner Monk: "You're running a place of refuge for vulnerable human vessels." Which is
true. Each of the social rejects tells his/her story of the emptiness
of existence.
        7 men, 2 women; 1 interior. Royalty: $50-25.

_____. A Streetcar Named Desire (1947). Dramatists Play Ser-
        vice.
        Blanche DuBois comes to visit her sister Stella and her
brother-in-law Stanley Kowalski, something of a brute. Blanche
plays the southern lady, but Stanley discovers that she has driven
to suicide her homosexual husband, has lost her teaching job for an
affair with a teenage boy, and has been virtually thrown out of town
for promiscuity. Her pretense enrages Stanley, and while Stella is
having his child he rapes Blanche, who is committed to a mental
institution.
        6 men, 6 women; 1 interior-exterior set. Royalty: $50-25.

_____. Suddenly Last Summer (1958). Dramatists Play Service.
The long one-act play treats the sensual and corrupt life of
poet Sebastian Venable, who does not appear on stage. We find out
about Sebastian's shocking death from his cousin, Catherine Holly,
who witnessed it. The rest of the old New Orleans family, especially Mrs. Venable, is anxious to have Catherine deny the death story.
Sebastian's mother is so anxious, in fact, that she has had the girl
placed in a mental institution and will even order a frontal lobotomy
performed to silence her. Catherine's mother and brother, greedy
for Mrs. Venable's wealth, beg and threaten Catherine to please
their rich relation.
2 men, 5 women; 1 exterior. Royalty: $35-25.

_____. Summer and Smoke (1948). Dramatists Play Service.
A prim, restrained, somewhat puritanical Southern girl, Alma Winemiller, falls in love with a lecherous unpuritanical young
doctor next door, John Buchanan. They are drawn to each other,
yet repelled by the truths of propriety, which however are as unsub-
stantial as smoke. The doctor has thrown away his talents in dalliance, but straightens up when he has to carry on his father's practice and finally realizes that her ideals are basically right. But now
he has given his love to another, leaving Alma frustrated and disillusioned.
8 men, 6 women; 1 unit set. Royalty: $50-25.

_____. Sweet Bird of Youth (1958). Dramatists Play Service.
Chance Wayne, an actor, has become the kept man of Princess Kosmonopolis, a has-been movie actress who is addicted to
liquor, drugs, and young men. Though she is using Chance, he is
using her too--he lures her to his southern home town so that he
can see the girl he loved and left behind, Heavenly Finley. Chance
discovers that before he left town he transmitted a disease to Heavenly, which her father corrected by having her sterilized. He feels
the guilt for having ruined her young life and does not resist when
her brothers arrive to castrate him.
15 men, 7 women; interiors. Royalty: $50-25.

_____, with Donald Windham. You Touched Me! (1945). Samuel
French.
As a lad of 12, Hadrian had been adopted by Capt. Cornelius
Rockley. At 15 he left for Canada; at 20 he returns to find everything the same, only more unattractive. He is now a Flight Lieutenant in the Canadian Air Force. He was always in love with the
timid and repressed Matilda, who has been domineered over by her
prudish Aunt Emmie. The Captain drowns his sorrows in drink but
assists Hadrian in overcoming the sensitiveness of Matilda and
finally blesses their engagement.
4 men, 3 women; 1 interior. Royalty: $50-25.

WILMURT, Arthur. Noah. See entry under Obey, Andre.

WILSON, H. L. The Man from Home. See entry under Tarkington,
Booth.

WILSON, Lanford. The Hot L Baltimore (1973). Dramatists Play
    Service.
    The action takes place in the lobby of a rundown hotel with
an "e" missing from its marquee. The residents meet and interact
with one another during the course of a day--the young and the old,
the defiant and the resigned, each character emerging clearly through
the overlapping conversations which humorously go on.
    10 men, 7 women; 1 interior. Royalty: $50.

_____. The Rimers of Eldritch (1967). Dramatists Play Service.
    Eldritch is a Middle Western town that operates out of catch-
word morality and maintains a capability for the vicious. The citizens of the town are on stage throughout the play, speaking from
platforms. Framed around a mystery (a man has been murdered but
we don't know who it was, who killed him, or why), the play highlights invididual townspeople and relationships--ugly and beautiful:
a middleaged woman who has fallen in love with a young man who
works for her, a coarse woman mistreating her senile mother, a
tender relationship between a young man and a crippled girl.
    7 men, 10 women; platform staging. Royalty: $50-25.

_____. Serenading Louie (1976). Dramatists Play Service.
    A single setting represents the homes of two couples in this
play, "as though such residences are so alike and furnished so
similarly as to make scene changes redundant." Carl and Mary
are one couple (he is a businessman and former college quarter-
back; she is having an affair with his accountant). Gabby and Alex
are their longtime friends (she is always in control; he is infatuated
with a 17-year-old flower child). What is going on in marriages
mostly has to do with loneliness, which is communicated to the
characters on stage and directly to the audience as well. The end
of the play, a murder-suicide, is especially powerful.
    2 men, 2 women; 1 interior. Royalty: $50-25.

WINDHAM, Donald. You Touched Me! See entry under Williams,
    Tennessee.

WINER, Elihu. Anatomy of a Murder (1964). Adapted from Rob-
    ert Travers' novel. Samuel French.
    This play depicts the attempts of a former district attorney
to establish himself as a defense lawyer after his re-election bid
had failed. Paul Biegler is the lawyer, and his first case is a
sensational one. He takes on the defense of an Army lieutenant accused of murdering a bartender who had allegedly raped his wife.
Biegler soon finds that he has more than just legal problems. He
develops an intense dislike for his client, but is constantly dis-
tracted by his client's seductive wife. This becomes a case with
political overtones, too, as the State Attorney General's office gets
involved to try to insure that the newly elected district attorney
wins this case. Using every legal device and dramatic courtroom
revelation possible, however, Biegler wins his case.
    16 men, 2 women; 4 interiors, 2 insets. Royalty: $50-
    25.

WINTER, Keith. The Shining Hour (1934). Samuel French.
    This story, which runs the gamut of human emotions, centers around the Linden family, who inhabit an English countryside estate. Henry Linden, after being absent for several years, brings Mariella, his bride, home to live. She is different from Henry's people in that she is only half English and cannot understand fully the feelings of the true English. She falls in love with David, her brother-in-law, but complicates matters by thinking so highly of David's wife that she has trouble betraying her. A climax follows that tends to wreck the whole household.
    3 men, 3 women; 1 interior. Royalty: $25-20.

WOLFE, Thomas. Look Homeward Angel. See entry under Frings, Ketti.

WOLFE, Winifred. Ask Any Girl. See entry under Sergel, Christopher.

_____. If a Man Answers. See entry under Rogers, David.

WOLFSON, Victor. Excursion (1937). Dramatists Play Service.
    After 30 years on the route from Manhattan to Coney Island, Captain Obadiah Rich's excursion ship "Happiness" is to be turned into a garbage scow. The Captain and his brother Jonathan plan on the final return trip to head for a magic isle south of Trinidad where his passengers may begin life anew. But the fog holds them back and the Coast Guard makes them return, so they must go back to their unromantic dull jobs.
    3 acts; 18 men, 10 women; 1 interior in 2 parts: the ship's cabin and the ship's deck. Royalty: $25.

WOOD, Mrs. Henry. East Lynne (1861). In N.Y. Drama, v. 4 #46, 1878; Penn Pub. Co., 1894; carried by French; CERC.
    Isabel is happy with her husband, Archibald Carlyle, until Sir Francis Levison plants suspicion in her mind that he is untrue to her while he is meeting Barbara Hare to help her brother. Isabel leaves with the villainous Sir Francis; they go to France where he deserts her. Meantime Archibald thinks she is dead and marries Barbara. He also proves her brother innocent of the murder, which is fixed on Sir Francis. Isabel comes back to East Lynne, disguised as an old governess, Madame Vine. On her death-bed she is recognized by Archibald and forgiven.
    5 acts; 7 men, 7 women, 1 boy; varied interior and exterior sets; costumes of the period. Royalty: $0-2.50.

WOOLL, Edward. Libel! (1934). Samuel French.
    Sir Mark Loddon brings libel suit against a London newspaper which says he is neither a baronet nor a Loddon. He resembles Frank Wembly, a Canadian. Both escaped from a German prison camp; suffering shell-shock, Mark remembers nothing of his life before the First World War. His wife comes to doubt him too, believing he is Wembley. His trench coat is produced at the trial; from the lining he produces her photograph and other docu-

ments; thus he is proved to be Sir Mark.
    3 acts; 20 men, 4 women; 1 interior (court room).   Royalty:
$25-20.

WOOLLCOTT, Alexander and George S. Kaufman.   The Dark Tower
    (1933).   Samuel French.
    The leading actors, Jessica Wells and her brother Damon,
are ready to produce "The Dark Tower" when her supposedly dead
husband, Stanley, appears.   He has always had a vicious hypnotic
influence over her, and she again goes into a decline.   Stanley is
willing to be bought off, and proposes an arrangement with a Mr.
Sarnoff.   At the meeting Stanley is stabbed to death and Sarnoff dis-
appears--but he reappears privately, for he is her brother Damon
disguised, and he has saved his sister.
    3 acts; 9 men, 5 women; 2 interiors.   Royalty: $50.

WOUK, Herman.   The Caine Mutiny Court-Martial (1954).   Samuel
    French.
    This World War II sea story was described by the New York
Times as a version superior to the novel "in the artfulness of its
craftsmanship."   The court-martial arises from a young lieutenant's
relieving his captain of command during a typhoon on the grounds
that he was psychopathic.   Naval tradition clearly forbids any such
usurpation of power, but in the intriguing courtroom scenes the de-
fenses of the captain finally collapse.   With his disintegration of
sanity evident to them, the court clears the lieutenant.
    19 men (6 non-speaking); curtained set, desks and chairs.
Royalty: $50-25.

_____.   The Traitor (1949).   Samuel French.
    An idealistic young scientist, Allen Carr, believes that the
safety of the world lies in all nations (especially U.S.A. & Russia)
having the atom bomb.   So he altruistically turns over bomb secrets
to a Russian spy.   Realizing his mistake in thus betraying his
country, he redeems himself by leading the chief spy into a trap.
    15 men, 3 women; 1 interior.   Royalty: $50-25.

WRIGHT, Anna Perrott Rose.   Room for One More.   See entry un-
    der Davidson, William.

YAFFE, James.   Dear Me, The Sky Is Falling.   See entry under
    Spigelgass, Leonard.

YORDAN, Philip.   Anna Lucasta (1944).   Dramatists Play Service.
    Anna has erred and is driven from her home in Pennsylvania
by her father; she goes to New York, where she associates with
Danny.   Meanwhile Papa Lucasta gets a letter from his old friend in
Alabama that he is sending his son Rudolf north with $800 to find a
wife, perhaps his daughter.   So Anna is brought back and finds that
Rudolf suits her; they are married.   But Danny follows her and persuades her to go back to New York with him; she goes, but Rudolf
follows and wins her back again.
    3 acts; 9 men, 5 women; 2 interiors.   Royalty: $50-25.

ZAMACOIS, Miguel. The Jesters (1907). Tr. by Raphael in rhymed
hexameters, Brentano, 1908.

Two wealthy noblemen, to decide a bet and win a wife, assume
the characters of jesters, René as Chicot, and Robert as Narcissus.
In this guise they woo Solange, the daughter of the impoverished
noble, Baron de Mautpré. René gives the impecunious baron a
chest of gold which he says was dug up on his grounds, and by art-
ful talk, despite a false hump, is successful.

4 acts; 13 men, 2 women; 2 interiors, 2 exteriors; costumes
and settings of the 16th century.

ZANGWILL, Israel. The Melting Pot (1908). Macmillan, 1908;
revised edition, Macmillan, & Lond., Heinemann, 1914.

Represents America as the crucible in which immigrants from
all nations are to be fused into the perfect human type; America as-
similates the alien. Bases the situations on the love of a Jew for a
Christian. Strong in ideals and patriotism.

4 acts; 5 men, 4 women; 2 interiors, 1 exterior.

ZEYER, Julius. Diarmuid and Grainne (ca. 1886). Tr. by Noyes
& Mezirka in Poet Lore, v. 44, 1938.

The young daughter of the King of Erin, Grainne, is given in
marriage by her father to Finn, King of the Fennians. He has
power of healing in his hand. But Brainne loves Diarmuid, and together they flee to Midac's castle. Midac has sworn vengeance on
the murderer of his father, who, he believes, is Finn; but Diarmuid
confesses it was his father; whereupon Midac stabs him. When Finn
comes he refuses to heal him and he dies. When Grianne returns
she stabs herself. Finn's son and grandson desert him and he is
left alone in his old age. One of the legends of Erin.

4 acts; 7 men, 1 woman, extras; 2 interiors, 2 exteriors;
costumes of the period (3rd century in Ireland).

ZINDEL, Paul. And Miss Reardon Drinks a Little (1971). Dramatists Play Service.

The three Reardon sisters have been brought up in a home
with a domineering mother and an absent father. The mother has
died, one sister is married and on her own, one is drinking too
much, and one is on the brink of madness. The married sister arrives for dinner to argue for committing her "sick" sister to an institution. Resentments which have been dormant for many years
begin to crop up, and the unexpected arrival of a neighborhood
couple only makes things worse.

2 men, 5 women; 1 interior. Royalty: $50-35.

_____. The Effect of Gamma Rays on Man-in-the-Moon Mari-
golds (1970). Dramatists Play Service.

Even a dung heap can occasionally produce a beautiful flower,
which is what happens in this play. The flower is Tillie, who undertakes a gamma ray experiment for her school science project.
The dung heap is her home, run with an iron hand and an acid
tongue by her mother Beatrice, who can only hurt when she needs
to love and ridicule when she needs to encourage and praise. She

is even harder, in fact, on her other daughter Ruth, who is prettier than Tillie but subject to convulsions as a way of coping.
    No men, 5 women; 1 interior. Royalty: $50-35.

_____. The Secret Affairs of Mildred Wild (1972). Dramatists
    Play Service.
    Mildred Wild lives in Greenwich Village in quarters behind the candy store which she operates with her husband. Her place is filled with movie magazines and memorabilia, a tribute to the 3000 movies she has seen and the fantasy life she has created to escape reality. When the outside world intrudes on her through her husband, her sister-in-law, landlord, butcher, or man in charge of tearing down her building she plays a movie scene on the world.
    4 men, 5 women; 1 interior. Royalty: $50-35.

ZOLA, Emile. Therese. See entry under Job, Thomas.

ZWEIG, Stefan. Jeremiah (1917). Tr. by Paul, Seltzer, 1922;
    Viking Pr., 1939.
    Depicts scenes in the life of the prophet, from his poignant realization that he has been chosen to interpret the Lord to his people, through his fruitless attempts during the siege and capture of Jerusalem.
    9 scenes; 10 men, 2 women, extras; 3 interiors, 3 exteriors; costumes of the period.

CAST INDEX

1 Character

Krapp's Last Tape   34

2 Characters

Dumb Waiter   245
Fourposter   138
Green Julia   1
Happy Days   34
I'm Herbert   11
Jesse and the Bandit Queen   107
Next   210
Owl and the Pussycat   203
Same Time, Next Year   299
Sea Horse   222
Sleuth   281
Staircase   91
Two for the Seesaw   117
Zoo Story   5

3 Characters

Aspern Papers   257
Boesman and Lena   110
Dutchman   165
I'll Be Home for Christmas   11
Luv   276
Maids   115
Old Ladies   2
Old Times   246
Pardon   187
Phoenix Too Frequent   109
Private Ear and the Public Eye
   282
Rattle of a Simple Man   91
Rivalry   71
Slow Dance on the Killing
   Ground   136
Star-Spangled Girl   298
Subject Was Roses   120
Voice of the Turtle   325

White Liars   282
World of Carl Sandburg   271

4 Characters

Adaptation   210
Any Wednesday   257
Butterflies Are Free   116
Collection   245
Deathwatch   115
Emperor Jones   230
Endgame   33
Footsteps of Doves   11
Glass Menagerie   341
Happy Ending   332
Killing of Sister George   204
Knack   161
Knock Knock   98
Last of the Red Hot Lovers   297
Marriage-Go-Round   305
Mollusc   80
Moon for the Misbegotten   231
Moon Is Blue   145
No Exit   274
Noel Coward in Two Keys   73
On Approval   194
Price   213
Seascape   4
Second Man   37
Serenading Louie   344
Shock of Recognition   11
Springtime for Henry   191
There's Always Juliet   325
Wager   210
Whitman Portrait   296
Who's Afraid of Virginia Woolf?
   4

5 Characters

Angel Street (Gaslight)   134
Balcony   142

349

6 Characters

7 Characters

8 Characters

9 Characters

10 Characters

11 Characters

12 Characters

13 Characters

Anastasia 46
Andre 90
Another Part of the Forest 143
As a Man Thinks 317
Balcony (Genet) 115
Butter-and-Egg Man 168
Canticle for Leibowitz 110
Captain Brassbound's Conversion
  288
Concert 25
Conscious Lovers 304
Dear Phoebe 313
Death and Life of Larry Benson
  266
Death and Life of Sneaky Fitch
  267
Death of a Salesman 212
Death Takes a Holiday 60
Devil's Disciple 288
Distaff Side 324
Famous Mrs. Fair 104
Fashion 223
Fifth Season 257
Gentle People 291
Gentleman from Athens 184
Giboyer's Son 21
Henrietta 150
Henry IV 246
Hole in the Head 277
If a Man Answers 264
Imaginary Invalid 218
Iron Cross 259
Is Life Worth Living? 263
Jane Eyre 54
January Thaw 265
Kiss the Boys Good-Bye 48
Ladies and Hussers 107
Lady Frederick 209
Lady Windermere's Fan 338
Last of the DeMullins 135
Learned Ladies 218
Letters to Lucerne 269
Light Up the Sky 137
Male Animal 318
Mary Broome 221
Member of the Wedding 197
Mid-Channel 243
Millie Goes a Miss 226
Mr. Barry's Etchings 55
Month in the Country 321
Othello 285

Philadelphia, Here I Come 108
Philaster: or, Love Lies
  Bleeding 33
Phormio 316
Poor Bitos 15
Poverty Is No Crime 236
Private Enterprise 95
Ralph Roister Doister 322
Rebel Women 24
Ring Round the Moon 16
River Niger 331
Romanoff and Juliet 323
School for Slavery 44
Sea Gull 63
Seven Keys to Baldpate 68
Small War on Murray Hill 294
Spring Dance 30
Tenth Man 62
They Knew What They Wanted
  152
Thieves' Carnival 16
Three Wise Fools 309
Tragedy of Nan 207
Traveller without Luggage 17
Warren Hastings 99
What Happened to Jones 53
Wheeler Dealers 189
White Steed 59
Will Shakespeare 79
Wolves 265

14 Characters

Alien Corn 151
All the Way Home 223
Amen Corner 25
Anna Lucasta 346
Arsenic and Old Lace 175
Beyond Our Power 44
Blacks 115
Blind Goddess 319
Blockhead 110
Le Bourgeois Gentilhomme 217
Brothers (Terence) 316
Case of Libel 85
Case of Rebellious Susan 163
Cassilis Engagement 134
Cave Dwellers 272
Children's Hour 143
Chinese Lantern 150
Christopher Blake 137
Cradle Song 206
Dark Tower 346

16 Characters

17 Characters

18 Characters

20 Characters

19 Characters

21 Characters

22 Characters

All Women

INDEX OF SELECTED SUBJECTS

THE BLACK EXPERIENCE

MYSTERY (AND DETECTIVE)

NEWSPAPER

OLD FASHIONED MELODRAMA

PRISON

RELIGIOUS

SCHOOL AND COLLEGE LIFE

TEENAGER

WAR

PRIZE PLAYS

LONG RUNNING PLAYS ON THE NEW YORK STAGE

The following non-musical plays have had runs of 500 or more continuous performances in a Broadway or Off-Broadway (OB) theater.

Number of Performances	Play
3,224	Life with Father
3,182	Tobacco Road
2,327	Abie's Irish Rose
1,775	Harvey
1,642	Born Yesterday
1,572	Mary, Mary
1,557	The Voice of the Turtle
1,530	Barefoot in the Park
1,444	Arsenic and Old Lace
1,408 (OB)	The Blacks
1,295	Angel Street
1,291	Lightnin'
1,234	Cactus Flower
1,222	Sleuth
1,157	Mister Roberts
1,141	The Seven-Year Itch
1,128	Butterflies Are Free
1,097	Plaza Suite
1,027	The Teahouse of the August Moon
1,025 (OB)	One Flew over the Cuckoo's Nest
1,007	Never Too Late
1,000 (OB)	The Boys in the Band
982	Any Wednesday
964	The Odd Couple
957	Anna Lucasta
956	Kiss and Tell
943 (OB)	The Hot L Baltimore
924	The Moon Is Blue
901	Luv
867	The Bat
864	My Sister Eileen
860	Song of Norway
855	A Streetcar Named Desire
844	That Championship Season
837	You Can't Take It with You
835	Three Men on a Horse

832	The Subject Was Roses
819 (OB)	The Effect of Gamma Rays on Man-in-the-Moon Marigolds
806	Inherit the Wind
796	No Time for Sergeants
789	The Ladder
780	Forty Carats
780	The Prisoner of Second Avenue
780 (OB)	A View from the Bridge
765	State of the Union
760	The First Year
755	You Know I Can't Hear You When the Water's Running
750	Two for the Seesaw
742	Death of a Salesman
739	The Man Who Came to Dinner
725 (OB)	The Pocket Watch
722	Claudia
722 (OB)	The Connection
720	The Gold Diggers
717	The Diary of Anne Frank
714	I Remember Mama
712	Tea and Sympathy
710	Junior Miss
707 (OB)	Adaptation/Next
706	Last of the Red Hot Lovers
704	Seventh Heaven
700	The Miracle Worker
694	Cat on a Hot Tin Roof
692	Peg o' My Heart
692 (OB)	Scuba Duba
691	The Children's Hour
687	Dead End
686	The Lion and the Mouse
686	White Cargo
685 (OB)	The Knack
683	Dear Ruth
680	East Is West
677	Come Blow Your Horn
672 (OB)	The Balcony
671	The Doughgirls
670	The Impossible Years
669	Boy Meets Girl
667	Beyond the Fringe
664	Who's Afraid of Virginia Woolf?
657	Blithe Spirit
657	A Trip to Chinatown
657	The Women
654	The Fifth Season
648	Rain
645	Witness for the Prosecution
642	Janie
640	The Green Pastures

639		Auntie Mame
637		A Man for All Seasons
634	(OB)	America Hurrah
632		The Fourposter
623		The Tenth Man
618		Is Zat So?
615		Anniversary Waltz
614		The Happy Time
613		Separate Rooms
610		Affairs of State
607	(OB)	Hogan's Goat
603		Broadway
603		Adonis
601		Street Scene
600		Kiki
600	(OB)	The Trojan Women
598		Don't Drink the Water
596		A Cociety Circus
585		The Two Mrs. Carrolls
582	(OB)	Krapp's Last Tape & The Zoo Story
581		Detective Story
578	(OB)	The Dumb Waiter and The Collection
577		Brother Rat
571	(OB)	The Crucible
571		The Show-Off
565	(OB)	The Iceman Cometh
564		Happy Birthday
564		Look Homeward, Angel
561		The Glass Menagerie
557		Strictly Dishonorable
556		A Majority of One
556		Great White Hope
556		Toys in the Attic
556		Sunrise at Campobello
545	(OB)	The Hostage
541		Within the Law
540		The Music Master
538		The Sunshine Boys
538		What a Life
530		A Raisin in the Sun
529	(OB)	Six Characters in Search of an Author
526		The Solid Gold Cadillac
522		The Boomerang
521		Rosalinda
520		The Best Man
517		Victoria Regina
509	(OB)	The Dirtiest Show in Town
508		The World of Suzie Wong
504	(OB)	Happy Ending & Day of Absence
501		The Member of the Wedding

POPULAR PLAYS FOR HIGH SCHOOL PRODUCTION, 1974-1975*

The following are the most frequently produced full-length plays (all categories) by Thespian affiliated schools during the 1974-1974 school year. This list was tabulated from schools which submitted Annual Reports of their dramatic seasons. What follows is neither a Thespian recommended playlist nor a comprehensive account of the national secondary school theater.

Title	Number of Productions	Title	Number of Productions
You're a Good Man, Charlie Brown	56	The Sound of Music	26
Our Town	42	Barefoot in the Park	24
You Can't Take It with You	42	The Matchmaker	24
Harvey	41	The Diary of Anne Frank	23
Story Theatre	41	Fiddler on the Roof	23
Arsenic and Old Lace	39	The Boyfriend	22
The Effect of Gamma Rays on Man-in-the-Moon Marigolds	35	Cheaper by the Dozen	22
Bye Bye Birdie	33	The Mouse That Roared	22
The Man Who Came to Dinner	33	My Fair Lady	22
M*A*S*H	33	Thurber Carnival	22
The Music Man	33	Brigadoon	21
The Miracle Worker	32	The Curious Savage	21
Up the Down Staircase	31	Don't Drink the Water	21
Godspell	30	No, No Nanette	21
A Midsummer Night's Dream	30	Once Upon a Mattress	20
South Pacific	29	West Side Story	20
The Fantastics	28	Blithe Spirit	19
Lil' Abner	28	Flowers for Algernon	19
The Wizard of Oz	28	Winnie the Pooh	19
The Crucible	27	Annie Get Your Gun	18
Oklahoma	27	Anything Goes	18
Guys and Dolls	26	Carousel	17
		Plaza Suite	17
		Teahouse of the August Moon	17
		Dark of the Moon	16
		Spoon River Anthology	16
		Cinderella	15

*Reprinted by permission of Dramatics Magazine.

385

Title	Number of Productions	Title	Number of Productions
The Importance of Being Earnest	15	Me, Junie Moon	12
The King and I	15	Alice in Wonderland	11
The Imaginary Invalid	14	Charley's Aunt	11
The Odd Couple	14	Dirty Work at the Crossroads	11
Bad Seed	13	The Glass Menagerie	11
Hello Dolly!	13	My Three Angels	11
Inherit the Wind	13	David and Lisa	10
Mame	13	Dracula	10
Star Spangled Girl	13	George Washington Slept Here	10
Ten Little Indians	13	The Haunting of Hill House	10
Camelot	12		
I Remember Mama	12	How to Succeed in Business	10
The Mousetrap	12	The Pajama Game	10
The Night of January 16th	12	Romeo and Juliet	10
Oliver	12	Rumpelstiltskin	10
See How They Run	12	Tom Jones	10
Tell Me That You Love			

FREQUENTLY PRODUCED PLAYS
(HIGH SCHOOL THEATER)

The following list is a cumulation of major productions of full-length plays by reporting National Thespian Society Schools from the 1957-1958 through the 1974-1975 seasons. This list is not a Thespian-recommended play-list, nor does it represent statistics of the entire secondary school theater. Only plays with 100 or more productions have been included. (It should be noted that plays with less than ten productions in any single season were not reported in the annual lists and therefore are not reflected in this cumulation.)

Play	Number of seasons with 10 or more productions	Total Productions
Our Town	18	1234
You Can't Take It with You	18	1029
Curious Savage	18	904
Arsenic and Old Lace	18	878
Diary of Anne Frank	17	773
The Mouse That Roared	13	722
Harvey	18	692
The Night of January 16th	18	689

Play	Number of seasons with 10 or more productions	Total Productions
The Miracle Worker	13	573
The Man Who Came to Dinner	18	568
Oklahoma!	15	565
Our Hearts Were Young and Gay	15	476
Bye Bye Birdie	13	466
The Music Man	13	466
Teahouse of the August Moon	18	446
The Crucible	15	445
The Wizard of Oz	16	417
Brigadoon	15	406
South Pacific	15	402
Cheaper by the Dozen	18	393
Blithe Spirit	18	381
Up the Down Staircase	6	366
Charley's Aunt	18	356
Annie, Get Your Gun	17	347
Time Out for Ginger	11	344
The Sound of Music	11	338
The Importance of Being Earnest	15	308
The Glass Menagerie	17	306
My Fair Lady	11	304
Ask Any Girl	10	303
Li'l Abner	14	297
You're a Good Man, Charlie Brown	4	288
Carousel	15	270
I Remember Mama	14	258
The Skin of Our Teeth	12	255
Inherit the Wind	14	234
Ten Little Indians	17	232
The King and I	13	231
Guys and Dolls	10	224
David and Lisa	8	221
Camelot	11	217
Alice in Wonderland	12	215
Onions in the Stew	10	214
Antigone	14	207
My Three Angels	12	204
A Midsummer Night's Dream	12	201
The Boy Friend	14	200
The Matchmaker	9	198
Spoon River Anthology	10	197
Meet Me in St. Louis	11	194
Winnie-the-Poo	11	194
George Washington Slept Here	14	190
Madwoman of Chaillot	11	182
Oliver	9	182
Fiddler on the Roof	5	182
Barefoot in the Park	8	180

Play	Number of seasons with 10 or more productions	Total Productions
Flowers for Algernon	6	178
Pygmalion	10	174
Cinderella	12	172
Dino	8	172
A Thurber Carnival	9	171
Mrs. McThing	10	170
Hello, Dolly	6	167
Finian's Rainbow	12	160
See How They Run	11	155
The Odd Couple	7	152
Pillow Talk	7	151
The Fantasticks	9	147
Tom Jones	8	142
Dark of the Moon	8	139
Once Upon a Mattress	8	139
Don't Drink the Water	6	136
The Imaginary Invalid	9	131
Hansel and Gretel	9	125
1984	8	125
Life with Father	10	124
January Thaw	9	121
Stage Door	8	118
Carnival	8	115
The Little Dog Laughed	6	109
Little Women	8	107
Bull in a China Shop	6	106
The Remarkable Incident at Carson Corners	7	104
Bad Seed	7	101

MOST POPULAR PLAYS FOR AMATEUR GROUPS

(Recommended by the Publishers)

PLAYS RECOMMENDED FOR "ALL GROUPS"

(By the Publishers)

ADDRESSES OF PLAY PUBLISHERS REPRESENTED

Dramatic Publishing Company
86 East Randolph Street
Chicago, Illinois 60601

Dramatists Play Service
440 Park Avenue South
New York, New York 10016

Performance Publishing
978 North McLean Blvd.
Elgin, Illinois 60120

Pioneer Drama Service
2172 South Colorado Blvd.
Denver, Colorado 80222

Samuel French, Inc.
25 West 45th Street
New York, New York 10036

ABBREVIATIONS USED FOR CITING COLLECTIONS

Note: These are Francis K. W. Drury's abbreviations used in his 1953 original edition of Guide to Best Plays. I have retained these citations for plays not handled by a major play publisher, plays which represent most of the Classical and National Drama entries included in this volume. The reader is advised, however, that these abbreviations to collections are not comprehensive. See John H. Ottemiller's Index to Plays in Collections, Sixth Edition (Metuchen, N.J.: The Scarecrow Press, 1976) for the latest word.

ADA Adams, J. Q., ed. Chief pre-Shakespearean Dramas. Houghton, 1924.

AND Anderson, G. K. & Walton, E. L., eds. This generation. Scott, Foresman, 1939.

ASH Ashton, J. W., ed. Types of English drama. Macmillan, 1940.

BAK Baker, G. P., ed. Modern American plays. Harcourt, 1920.

BAS Baskervil, Heltzel, & Nethercot, eds. Elizabethan and Stuart plays. Holt, 1934.

BAT Bates, Alfred, ed. The drama. 22v. London, Athenian society, 1903-04.

BEL Bell, John. British theatre. 36v. Lond., 1791-1802.

BEN Bentley, Eric, ed. The play. Prentice-Hall, 1951.

BES Mantle, Burns, ed. The best plays of [the year], 1919-1947. 28v. Dodd, 1920- (Continued by John Chapman, and others, to the present).

BLO Bloomfield, M. W. & Elliot, R. C., eds. Ten plays. Rinehart, 1951.

BOA Boas, F. S., ed. Five pre-Shakespearian comedies (Early Tudor period). Oxford, 1934.

BRI British drama. 2v. Lond., 1824-25; reprinted in Phila., T. Davis, 1850.

CALM Campbell, Van Gundy, & Shrodes, eds. Patterns for living. Macmillan, 1940.

CAP Canfield, Curtis, ed. Plays of the Irish renaissance, 1880-1930. N.Y., Washburn, 1929.

CAR Carpenter, Bruce, comp. A book of dramas. Prentice-Hall, 1929.

CARC Cartmell, Van H. & Cerf, B. A., eds. Famous plays of crime and detection. Blakiston, 1946.

CER Cerf, B. A., ed. Pocket book of modern American

plays.   Pocket Books, 1942.

CERC   Cerf, B. A. & Cartmell, Van H., comps.   S. R. O.
       (Standing Room Only); the most successful plays in the
       history of the American stage.   Doubleday, 1944, 1946.

CET   Cerf, B. A. & Cartmell, Van H., eds.   Sixteen famous
       American plays.   Garden City, 1941; Modern Library,
       1942.

CEU   Cerf, B. A. & Cartmell, Van H., comps.   Sixteen fa-
       mous British plays.   Garden City, 1942; Modern Library,
       1943.

CEW   Cerf, B. A. & Cartmell, Van H., eds.   Sixteen famous
       European plays.   Garden City, 1943.

CHA   Chandler, F. H. & Cordell, R. A., eds.   Twentieth
       century plays.   Nelson, 1934.

CHAP   Chandler, F. W. & Cordell, R. A., eds.   Twentieth
       century plays, American.   Revised Nelson, 1939.

CHAR   Chandler, F. W. & Cordell, R. A., eds.   Twentieth
       century plays, British.   Rev. & enl.   Nelson, 1941.
       Chapman, John, Best plays, continues Mantle (BES).

CLA   Clark, B. H. & Davenport, W. H., eds.   Nine modern
       American plays.   Appleton, 1951.

CLDM   Clark, B. H., ed.   Masterpieces of modern Spanish
       drama.   Duffield, 1917; later Appleton-Century.

CLF   Clark, B. H., ed.   World drama.   2v.   Appleton, 1933.

CLS   Clark, Wm. Smith, II.   Chief patterns of world drama,
       Aeschylus to Anderson.   Houghton, 1946.

COD   Coffman, G. R., ed.   A book of modern plays.   Scott,
       Foresman, 1925.

COF   Coffman, G. R., ed.   Five significant English plays.
       Nelson, 1930.

COH   Cohen, Helen L., ed.   Longer plays by modern authors
       (American).   Harcourt, 1922.

COJ   Cohen, Helen L., ed.   Milestones of the drama.   Har-
       court, 1940.

CORE   Cordell, Kathryn Coe & W. H., eds.   The Pulitzer prize
       plays.   Various new eds.   Random House, 1935- .

COT   Cordell, R. A., ed.   Representative modern plays,
       British and American.   Nelson, 1929.

CRI   (The) Critics' prize plays.   World Pub. Co., 1945.

DIB   Dibdin, T. J.   The London theatre.   12v.   London.,
       1814-25.

DIC   Dickinson, T. H., ed.   Chief contemporary dramatists,
       [ser. 1].   Houghton, 1915.

DID   Dickinson, T. H., ed.   Chief contemporary dramatists,
       ser. 2.   Houghton, 1921.

DIE   Dickinson, T. H., ed.   Chief contemporary dramatists,
       ser. 3.   Houghton, 1930.

DIG   Dickinson, T. H. & Crawford, J. R., eds.   Contempora-
       ry plays: England & America.   Houghton, 1925.

DIK   Dickinson, T. H., ed.   Continental plays.   2v.   Hough-
       ton, 1935.

DOB   Dobrée, Bonamy, ed.   Five restoration tragedies.   Ox-
       ford, 1928.

DUC   Duckworth, G. E., ed. The complete Roman drama.
         2v. Random House, 1942.
DUN   Dunn, Esther C., ed. Eight famous Elizabethan plays.
         Modern Library, 1932.
DUR   Durham, W. H. & Dodds, J. W., eds. British and
         American plays, 1939-1945. Oxford, 1947.
FAMA   Famous plays of 1931. Lond., Gollancz, 1932.
FAMB   Famous plays of 1932. Lond., Gollancz, 1932
FAMC   Famous plays of 1932-33. Lond., Gollancz, 1933.
FAMD   Famous plays of 1933. Lond., Gollancz, 1934.
FAME   Famous plays of 1933-34. Lond., Gollancz, 1934.
FAMF   Famous plays of 1934. Lond., Gollancz, 1934
AMG   Famous plays of 1934-35. Lond., Gollancz, 1935.
FAMH   Famous plays of 1935. Lond., Gollancz, 1935.
FAMI   Famous plays of 1935-36. Lond., Gollancz, 1936.
FAMJ   Famous plays of 1936. Lond., Gollancz, 1936.
FAMK   Famous plays of 1937. Lond., Gollancz, 1937.
FAML   Famous plays of 1938-39. Lond., Gollancz, 1939.
FAO   Famous plays of today. Lond., Gollancz, 1929.
FIG   Five great modern Irish plays. Modern Library, 1941.
FIP   Five plays of 1937. Lond., Hamilton, 1937.
FIR   Five plays of 1940. Lond., Hamilton, 1940.
FIT   Fitts, Dudley, ed. Greek plays in modern translation.
         Dial Press, 1947.
FOUP   Four plays of 1936. Lond., Hamilton, 1936.
FRA   Francke, Kuno, ed. The German classics of the 19th
         and 20th centuries. 20v. German Pubn Society, 1913-14.
FUL   Fullington, J. F-J. & others, eds. The new college
         omnibus. Harcourt, 1938.
FULT   Fulton, A. R., ed. Drama and theatre, illustrated by 7
         modern plays. Holt, 1946.
GAS   Gassner, John, ed. Twenty best plays of the modern
         American theatre [ser. 1]. Crown Pubs., 1939.
GAS-2   Gassner, John, ed. Best plays of the modern American
         theatre, 2nd series. Crown Pubs., 1947.
GAS-3   Gassner, John, ed. Best American plays, 3rd ser.,
         1945-1951. Crown Pubs., 1952.
GASE   Gassner, John, ed. Twenty-five best plays of the modern
         American theatre; early series. Crown Pubs., 1949.
GAY   Gayley, C. M. & Thaler, Alwin, eds. Representative
         English comedies. 4v. Macmillan, 1903-36.
GOSA   Gosse, E. W., ed. Restoration plays from Dryden to
         Farquhar. (Everyman's Library) Dent, & Dutton, 1932.
GOW   Gow, J. R. & Hanlon, Helen T., eds. Five Broadway
         plays. Harper, 1948.
GREN   Grene, David, tr. Three Greek tragedies in translation.
         Univ. of Chicago Pr., 1942.
HAL   Halline, Allan G., ed. American plays. Amer. Book
         Co., 1935.
HAM   Hamilton, Edith, tr. Three Greek plays. Norton, 1937.
HAN   Hampden, John, comp. Eighteenth century plays. (Ev-
         eryman's library) Dent, & Dutton, 1928.
HARC   Harvard classics. 50v. Collier, 1909-10.

HAT   Hatcher, H. H., ed. Modern American dramas. Har-
        court, 1941.
HATS   Hatcher, H. H., ed. Modern dramas, shorter edition.
        Harcourt, 1944.
HAU   Hatcher, H. H., ed. Modern British dramas. Har-
        court, 1941.
HAV   Hatcher, H. H., ed. Modern continental dramas. Har-
        court, 1941.
HIL   Hildreth, W. H. & Dumble, W. R., eds. Five contem-
        porary American plays. Harper, 1939.
HOW   Howard, Edwin J., ed. Ten Elizabethan plays. Nelson,
        1931.
HUD   Hubbell, J. B. & Beaty, J. C., eds. An introduction to
        drama. Macmillan, 1927; revised ed., 1932.
INCH   Inchbald, Mrs. Elizabeth S., ed. The British theatre.
        25v. London, 1808.
KAT   Katzin, Winifred, comp. Eight European plays. Bren-
        tano, 1927.
KRE   Kreymborg, Alfred, ed. Poetic drama. Modern Age
        Books, 1941.
LAW   Law, F. H., ed. Modern plays, short and long. Cen-
        tury, 1924.
LEG   LeGallienne, Eva, ed. Eva LeGallienne's Civic repertory
        plays. Norton, 1928.
LEV   Leverton, Garrett, ed. Plays for the college theatre.
        French, 1932.
LIE   Lieder, P. A. & others, eds. British drama. Hough-
        ton, 1929.
LOC   Locke, A. L. & Montgomery, G., eds. Plays of Negro
        life. Harper, 1927.
        Mantle, Best plays. see BES
MAP   Marriott, J. W., ed. Great modern British plays.
        Harrap, 1929.
MAT   Matthews, Brander & Lieder, P. R., eds. Chief Brit-
        ish dramatists. Houghton, 1924.
MAU   Matthews, Brander, ed. Chief European dramatists,
        500 B.C. to 1879 A.D. Houghton, 1916.
MCD   McDermott, J. F., ed. Modern plays. Harcourt, 1932.
MCI   McIlwraith, A. K., ed. Five Elizabethan comedies.
        Oxford, 1934.
MCJ   McIlwraith, A. K., ed. Five Elizabethan tragedies.
        Oxford, 1938.
MCM   MacMillan, W. D. & Jones, H. M., eds. Plays of
        the Restoration and 18th century. Holt, 1931, & 1938.
MIL   Millett, F. B. & Bentley, G. E., eds. The play's the
        thing. Appleton-Century, 1936.
MIO   Minor Elizabethan drama. (Everyman's library) Dent,
        & Dutton, 2v. 1939.
MOD   Modern plays. (Everyman's library) Dent, & Dutton,
        1937.
MOO   Moore, J. R., ed. Representative English drama.
        Ginn, 1929.
MOR   Morgan, A. E., comp. English plays, 1660-1820.

PR 1245 .M3

PN 6112 .M4

PR 1263 .M25

PN 6112 .M52

Harper, 1935.

MOS	Sayler, O. M., ed. Moscow art theatre series of Russian plays [ser. 1]. Brentano, 1923.
MOSA	Sayler, O. M., ed. Moscow art theatre series of Russian plays [ser. 2]. Brentano, 1923.
MOSE	Moses, M. J., ed. British plays from the Restoration to 1820. 2v. Little, Brown, 1929.
MOSH	Moses, M. J., ed. Dramas of modernism and their forerunners. Little, Brown, 1931; rev. by O. J. Campbell, 1941.
MOSJ	Moses, M. J., ed. Representative American dramas, national and local. Little, Brown, 1925.
MOSL	Moses, M. J., ed. Representative American dramas, national and local. Revised by J. W. Krutch. Little, Brown, 1941.
MOSO	Moses, M. J., ed. Representative British dramas, Victorian and modern. Little, Brown, 1918; rev. ed., 1931.
MOSQ	Moses, M. J., ed. Representative continental dramas, revolutionary and transitional. Little, Brown, 1924.
MOSS-1	Moses, M. J., ed. Representative plays by American dramatists; v. 1; 1767-1819. Dutton, 1918.
MOSS-2	Moses, M. J., ed. Representative plays by American dramatists; v. 2; 1815-1858. Dutton, 1925.
MOSS-3	Moses, M. J., ed. Representative plays by American dramatists; v. 3; 1856-1911. Dutton, 1921.
MYB	My best play; an anthology of plays chosen by their own authors. Lond., Faber & Faber, 1934.
NAG	Nagelberg, M. M., ed. Drama in our time. Harcourt, 1948.
NEI	Neilson, W. A., ed. Chief Elizabethan dramatists. Houghton, 1911.
NET	Nettleton, G. H. & Case, A. E., eds. British dramatists from Dryden to Sheridan. Houghton, 1939.
NOY	Noyes, G. R., ed. & tr. Masterpieces of the Russian drama. Appleton, 1933.
OAT	Oates, W. J. & O'Neill, E. G., Jr., eds. The complete Greek drama; all the extant tragedies. 2v. Random House, 1938.
OLH	Oliphant, E. H. C., ed. Elizabethan dramatists other than Shakespeare. Prentice-Hall, 1931.
OLI	Oliphant, E. H. C., ed. Shakespeare and his fellow dramatists. 2v. Prentice-Hall, 1929.
OXB	Oxberry, W., ed. The new English drama. 21v. London, 1818-25.
PAR	Parks, E. W. & Beatty, R. C., eds. The English drama; an anthology, 900-1642. Norton, 1935.
PEN	Pence, R. V., ed. Dramas by present-day writers. Scribner, 1927.
Pierce & Matthews -1	Pierce, J. A. & Matthews, Brander, eds. Masterpieces of modern drama: English and American. [v. 1]. Doubleday, 1915.

Pierce & Matthews -2	Pierce, J. A. & Matthews, Brander, eds. Master-pieces of modern drama: Foreign [v.2]. Doubleday, 1915.
PLAD	Plays of a half-decade. Gollancz, 1933.
PLAP	Plays of to-day. 3v. London, Sidgwick & Jackson, 1925-30.
QUI	Quinn, A. H., ed. Contemporary American plays. Scribner, 1923.
QUIK	Quinn, A. H., ed. Representative American plays. Century, rev. ed., 1921.
QUIL	Quinn, A. H., ed. Representative American plays, 1767-1935. Century Co. Ed. 3, 1925; Ed. 5, 1930; Ed. 6, 1938.
RUB	Rubinstein, H. F., ed. Great English plays. Harper, 1928.
RYL	Rylands, G. H. W., ed. Elizabethan tragedy; six representative plays (excluding Shakespeare). London, Bell, 1933.
SCA-1, 2, 3	Scandinavian plays of the 20th century. (American-Scandinavian Foundation) Princeton Univ. Press, 1944.
SCH	Schelling, F. E., ed. Typical Elizabethan plays, by contemporaries and immediate successors of Shakespeare. Harper, 1926.
SCI	Schelling, F. E. & Black, W. W., eds. Typical Elizabethan plays. Rev. ed. Harper, 1931.
SCW	Schweikert, H. C., ed. Early English plays. Harcourt, 1928.
SIXD	Six plays. London, Gollancz, 1931.
SIXH	Six plays. London, Heinemann, 1934.
SIXL	Six plays of 1939. London, Heinemann, 1939.
SIXP	Six plays of today. London, Heinemann, 1939.
SMI	Smith, R. M., ed. Types of domestic tragedy. Prentice-Hall, 1928.
SMK	Smith, R. M., ed. Types of historical drama. Prentice-Hall, 1928.
SML	Smith, R. M., ed. Types of philosophic drama. Prentice-Hall, 1928.
SMN	Smith, R. M., ed. Types of romantic drama. Prentice-Hall, 1928.
SMO	Smith, R. M., ed. Types of social comedy. Prentice-Hall, 1928.
SMP	Smith, R. M., ed. Types of world tragedy. Prentice-Hall, 1928.
SMR	Smith, R. M., ed. Types of farce-comedy. Prentice-Hall, 1928.
SPE	Spencer, Hazelton, ed. Elizabethan plays. Little, Brown, 1933.
STA	Stauffer, Ruth M., comp. The progress of drama through the centuries. Macmillan, 1927.
STE	Steeves, H. R., ed. Plays from the modern theatre. Heath, 1931.
STM	Stevens, D. H., ed. Types of English drama, 1660-1780. Ginn, 1923.
TAU	Tatlock, J. S. P. & Martin, R. G., eds. Representative English plays, from the miracle plays to Pinero. Ed.

	2 rev. & enl. Appleton-Century, 1938.
TAY	Taylor, W. D., ed. Eighteenth-century comedy. Oxford, 1929.
TEN	Cooper, Lane, ed. Ten Greek plays. Oxford, 1929.
THA	Thayer, W. R., ed. The best Elizabethan plays. Ginn, 1890.
THF	Theatre Guild anthology. Random House, 1936.
THH	Theatre omnibus: six outstanding recent successes. London, Hamilton, 1938.
THO	Thomas, Russell, ed. Plays and the theatre. Little, Brown, 1937.
THR	Clark, B. H., ed. Three modern plays from the French. Holt, 1914.
TRE	Mantle, Burns & Gassner, J., eds. A treasury of the theatre. 2v. Simon & Schuster, 1935.
TRE-2 (2v.)	Mantle, Burns & others, eds. A treasury of the theatre, rev...for colleges by Buck, Gassner, & Alberson. Simon & Schuster, 1940 2v. (v.1 from Ibsen to Odets; v.2 from Aeschylus to Hebbel)
TRE-3	Gassner, John, ed. A treasury of the theatre [ser. 3]. Dryden press, 1950. (From Ibsen's Ghosts to Miller's Death of a Salesman)
TREA-1	Gassner, John, ed. A treasury of the theatre [v.1]. Simon & Schuster, 1951. (From Aeschylus' Agamemnon to Turgenev's A Month in the Country)
TREA-2	Gassner, John, ed. A treasury of the theatre [v.2]. Simon & Schuster, 1951. (From Ibsen to Sartre)
TREA-3	Gassner, John, ed. A treasury of the theatre [v. 3]. Simon & Schuster, 1951. (From Wilde to Miller)
TUCD	Tucker, S. M., ed. Modern American and British plays. Harper, 1931.
TUCG	Tucker, S. M., ed. Modern continental plays. Harper, 1929.
TUCJ	Tucker, S. M., ed. Modern plays. Macmillan, 1932.
TUCM	Tucker, S. M., ed. Twenty-five modern plays. Harper, 1931; revised ed., 1948.
TUQ	Tupper, F. & Tupper, J. W., eds. Representative English dramas from Dryden to Sheridan. Oxford 1914; rev. ed., 1934.
TUR	Turrell, C. A., ed. Contemporary Spanish dramatists. Badger, 1919.
TWE	Twelve famous plays of the Restoration and eighteenth century. Modern library, 1933.
UHL	Uhler, J. E., ed. The best eighteenth-century comedies. Crofts, 1930.
WATC	Watson, E. B. & Pressey, W. B., comps. Contemporary drama: American plays. 2v. Scribner, 1931 (v.1), 1938 (v.2).
WATF	Watson, E. B. & Pressey, W. B., comps. Contemporary drama: English and Irish plays. 2v. Scribner, 1931.
WATI	Watson, E. B. & Pressey, W. B., comps. Contemporary drama: European, English, Irish and American

	plays. Scribner, 1941.
WATL	Watson, E. B. & Pressey, W. B., comps. Contemporary drama: European plays. 4v. Scribner, 1931-34.
WATO	Watson, E. B. & Pressey, W. B., comps. Contemporary drama: nine plays, American, English, European. Scribner, 1941.
WATR	Watson, E. B. & Pressey, W. B., eds. Five modern plays. Scribner, 1933.
WHE	Wheeler, C. B., ed. Six plays by contemporaries of Shakespeare. (World's classics) Oxford, 1928.
WHI	Whitman, C. H., ed. Representative modern dramas. Macmillan, 1936.
WHK	Whitman, C. H., ed. Seven contemporary plays. Houghton, 1931.
WOR	World's great plays; a collection of seven. World Pub. Co., 1944.

INDEX OF TITLES